100 Years *of* Madness

The Illinois High School Association Boys' Basketball Tournament

100 YEARS OF MADNESS

IHSA

The Illinois High School Association
Boys' Basketball Tournament

Scott
JOHNSON

Curt
HERRON

Pat
HESTON

Jeff
LAMPE

Bob
LEAVITT

Foreword by Jim Flynn

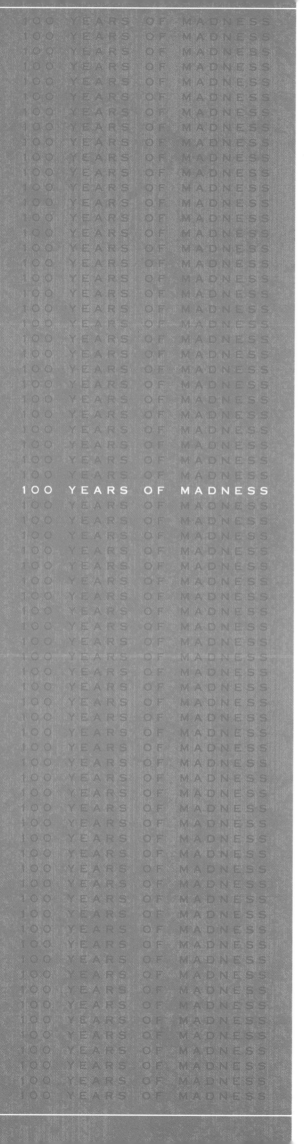

Dedication

To all the great players and coaches of
"America's Original March Madness,"
whose lives wrote the stories
we merely relate.

Copyright © 2006 Illinois High School Association

All rights reserved.

No part of this book may be reproduced, stored in a retrieval system, or transmitted
in any form, by any means, including mechanical, electronic, photocopying, recording,
or otherwise, without prior written permission of the
Illinois High School Association, P.O. Box 2715, Bloomington, IL, 61702-2715.

First printing, November, 2006.

Library of Congress Cataloging-in-Publication Data

Johnson, Scott (1956-); Herron, Curtis W. (1964-);
Heston, Patrick C. (1950-   ); Lampe, Jeffrey D. (1967-);
and Leavitt, Robert Payson (1944-).
**100 Years of Madness: The Illinois High School Association
Boys' Basketball Tournament**
Scott Johnson, Curt Herron, Pat Heston, Jeff Lampe, & Bob Leavitt
1st ed. p. cm.

ISBN 0-9601166-6-4 (softcover)
ISBN 0-9601166-7-2 (hardcover)
1. Basketball—Tournaments—Illinois—History. I. Title

Graphic design by Kathy Casper of IHSA.

Portions of this book were previously published in
Classical Madness: A Celebration of Class A and AA Boys Basketball in Illinois
(Bloomington: IHSA, 1996)

For ordering information, visit the IHSA Web site at www.ihsa.org
Telephone orders: 309-663-6377

Printed by

Peoria, Ill.

Table of Contents

100 YEARS OF MADNESS

Foreword

by Jim Flynn

The gym lights gleam like a beacon beam
And a million motors hum
In a good will flight on a Friday night;
For basketball beckons "Come!"
A sharp-shooting mite is king tonight.
The Madness of March is running.
The winged feet fly, the ball sails high
And field goal hunters are gunning.

— H.V. Porter, "Basketball Ides of March"

It all started for me — this love affair with March Madness — at Silas Willard Grade School in Galesburg, in the early Fifties, with John Thiel's running and gunning Silver Streaks the talk of the town.

Radio station WGIL broadcast the games both home and away. It still does today.

Back then, when the Silver Streaks played in the State Tournament in the morning or afternoon of a school day, if your grades were high and your work was done, you would be excused to listen to the game on the radio in the janitor's room.

Any boy in the fifth and sixth grades could sign up for the citywide basketball program. There were two leagues — the Animal and the Bird. Games were played on Saturday in the basement court of Steele Gym. At the end of the season the Animal League all-stars played the Bird League all-stars during halftime of a Galesburg High home game on the varsity court upstairs in Steele Gym. If you played in that game, chances were you had a future in basketball as a Silver Streak. I played point guard on the Bird League all-star team in sixth grade, but I never got to wear the jersey with the lightning bolt across its front.

One of the worst moments in my life was on the day Coach Thiel came to our house before the start of my freshman year. He told me to go cross-town to Corpus Christi High School because I'd never make the Galesburg team.

I still follow the exploits of Galesburg's Silver Streaks, more than 60 years of absolutely wonderful memories. During my lifetime Galesburg High School has played in the IHSA Boys' State Final Basketball Tournament 13 times.

On the other hand, from 1963 through the state tournaments of 2004, I had the opportunity to be involved personally in every boys' state tournament — 55 of them. For two years I was a student assistant in the University of Illinois Sports Information Office, which was responsible for administering the press operation at the state tournament. Then I covered the tournament as a reporter for the *Moline Dispatch* and *Springfield Journal-Register* before serving as Assistant Sports Information Director at Illinois. At the 1972 Class AA tournament Harry Fitzhugh asked me to interview for a position on the IHSA administrative staff. I got the job. The rest, as they say, is history.

The Boys' State Basketball Tournament is 100 years old. Much has happened on the court and off it during these 100 years, particularly the last 50.

The tournament went from a Sweet Sixteen to an Elite Eight. It went from a three-day marathon to a weekend-only affair. It grew from a single-class extravaganza to Class A and Class AA. It was played in historic Huff Gym, in Assembly Hall, and now at the Peoria Civic Center. Every year since 1952 the games have been televised to fans throughout the state. The progress of each game now is posted on the IHSA Web site as it happens.

With the advent of the three-point field goal came the shooting competition during the state series which leads to the finale in the Three-Point Showdown. Each weekend 64 shooters compete in the three-point competition and 64 slam dunkers battle to be King of the Hill. That gives 256 additional boys from across the state a chance to come to the state tournament and be part of the big show.

Galesburg coach John Thiel and one of his most successful Silver Streak teams — the 1966 state runner-up.

Fans attending the games today have the interactive March Madness Experience to enjoy when the games are not being played — or when their team is not on the Carver Arena court. Grade school teams play exhibition games on the courts in the March Madness Experience, and the Illinois Basketball Coaches Association conducts a free clinic for boys and girls on Saturday of the Class AA weekend. For many years the March Madness Grade School Field Trip brought nearly 5,000 grade school students to the Civic Center on the Wednesday between the Class A and Class AA state tournaments. And Access the

Experience for students with disabilities is held between the two tournaments and attracts more than 500 young people and their able-bodied helpers.

The authors of this book have captured the tantalizing essence of the IHSA Boys' State Final Basketball Tournament. There is no other like it in the nation. March Madness is an IHSA thing, always has been and always will be. Enjoy yourself as you wander through these pages. Take time to remember your own personal March Madness moments, because:

It's called March Madness. It may be the most contagious ailment in Illinois since the common cold. It strikes everywhere — from Chicago to Cairo, from Galena to Paris — sometime during the third month of the year. It is accompanied by tears — of joy and sorrow — and a distinct increase in the heartbeat. It is not fatal, yet everyone who catches it is infected for life.

A CENTURY OF MEMORIES

100

IHSA

Celebrating 100 years of
IHSA Boys Basketball Tournaments

Learning to Fly 1908–1929

Broken noses and betting scandals.

Cantankerous coaches and preposterous pairings.

A player with an artificial leg.

Who says high school basketball needs slam dunks and three-pointers to be entertaining?

Fast action in the Men's Gym Annex, 1920s.

FROM YMCA NOVELTY TO
POPULAR
PASTIME
IN TWO DECADES

PEORIA '08

HINSDALE '09

BLOOMINGTON '10-'16

ROCKFORD '11-'19

BATAVIA '12

GALESBURG '13

HILLSBORO '14

FREEPORT '15 '26

SPRINGFIELD '17

CENTRALIA '18-'22

MT. VERNON '20

MARION '21

VILLA GROVE '23

ELGIN '24-'25

MT. CARMEL '27

CANTON '28

JOHNSTON CITY '29

Basketball in its infancy was low-scoring, its plays lacking in strategy, its players frequently unskilled — but it was never boring.

Spectators shoehorned themselves into the narrow state tournament seats, wondering what could possibly happen next.

The fleeting images from this period reveal a sport full of spirit and rapidly working its way into the hearts of fans across Illinois.

Scott Johnson recalls the first era of the IHSA basketball tournament, when anything could happen on the basketball court — and often did.

1908 double-cross
When Rockford backed out, Peoria jumped in

If you **love** controversy and intrigue, if you *crave* a story of revenge and miscalculation, look no further than the Illinois high school basketball tournament — the tournament of 1908, that is.

by Scott Johnson

Before the first ticket was sold or the first leather-laced jump ball was tossed in the air, coaches and players found themselves locked in a heated off-court battle that threatened the viability of the new event. Angry words were exchanged and schools withdrew from the competition. And yet, because that was pretty much standard procedure in the early days of sport, the story has been buried in newspaper accounts for almost 100 years.

The missing team

Historians have hinted something was amiss with the teams selected to play in the 1908 tournament, the only state tourney field to be filled by invitation. They wondered why Rockford, an undefeated powerhouse and claimant to the previous year's mythical state title, was nowhere to be found, and assumed Rockford was somehow overlooked.

In fact, Rockford was one of the first teams invited, and if the squad had competed it may well have beaten Peoria for the state title. To understand why Rockford did not accept the invitation and a chance to win the first IHSAA-sanctioned state championship, it's important to understand interscholastic competition in the early 1900s.

Rockford had won the "state championship" of the 1906-07 season by defeating Washington, the reigning champ of the northern part of the state. In those days, the basketball "championship" was passed around in much the same way a boxing title is today. A hopeful team would send a challenge to the current champion, and the champion would set the terms for the confrontation, usually a game on its own court. The team's captain, not the coach, fielded these challenges, presented them to the team, and handled the scheduling chores.

Under the challenge system, Rockford was still considered to be the state champion when the 1907-08 season got under way. Only a couple of teams even came close to taking away their title. Mostly, the northern boys rang up huge wins over such teams as Genoa (89-11), DeKalb (88-13), and Elgin (94-13).

Around the beginning of February 1908, it became apparent the only team in the state with a realistic chance of stopping the Rockford juggernaut was the undefeated squad from Peoria, which issued a formal challenge for the title. William Forrest,

Peoria's reward for winning the 1908 state championship was a satin banner decorated with bronze reflectors and gold fringe.

Celebrating 100 years of IHSA Boys Basketball Tournaments

one of the stars of Peoria's squad, had played for the Rockford team the year before. Whatever ill feelings this transfer of allegiance may have caused are not recorded, but clearly the Rockford players did not appreciate the particulars of Peoria's offer.

Rockford had already booked a home game with Washington for March 28 and, unwilling to arrange for two central Illinois teams to travel north, extended a not-so-friendly suggestion to Peoria to "go out and get a reputation" by beating Washington first. The winner of the Peoria-Washington match could then come to Rockford to compete for the state title.

This proposition was received coolly by the Peoria team and local newspapers. Peorians were insulted because their team was clearly better than Washington, which had already lost twice to Wheaton. Furthermore, Peoria and Washington were archrivals who agreed on almost nothing: Peoria refused to play on Washington's court, and vice versa. There would be no "playoff game." Instead, Peoria offered to meet Rockford in a home-and-home series, or alternatively, one game on a neutral court in Ottawa.

A new tournament

About this time, near the end of February, the IHSAA announced its plans for the inaugural state tournament at Oak Park. Rockford, Peoria, and Washington were all invited by the tournament selection committee. The dates — March 28 and 29 — were a problem, because Washington was already scheduled to play in Rockford on the 28th. The site was also a problem. Rockford and Oak Park were bickering over a fight that had occurred after a football game the previous fall, and although the tournament would be held at the "neutral" Oak Park YMCA, it was being supervised by the athletic director of Oak Park High School, Lewis Omer. Peoria and Washington accepted their invitations. Rockford put its invitation on hold.

Meanwhile, the battle between Rockford and Peoria continued in telegrams and newspaper columns. Rockford refused to budge from its position that Washington and Peoria should play off for the right to challenge the state champion.

In the middle of March, chinks started to appear in the armor of the two great teams. First, the Peorians lost to their cross-town rivals from Spalding, a team they'd beaten easily earlier in the season. Rockford partisans chuckled with glee. A week later, Rockford hit the road to play Mt. Carroll, a strong team

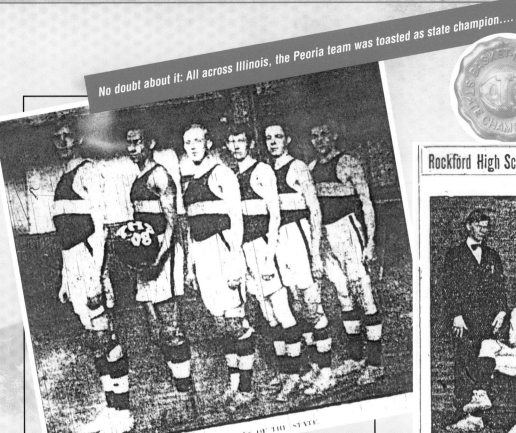

THE CHAMPIONS OF THE STATE

Rockford High School Basketball Team; Champions of the State, 1907-1908

that had piled up 117 points against an Iowa five the previous weekend. When the game ended in a tie, Rockford left the floor in protest, arguing that the Mt. Carroll scorer converted two of the home team's free throws into field goals. Although the referee later backed up Rockford's claim, Peoria newspapers spared no ink in detailing how the cowardly Rockford team had refused to play off a tie.

The double-cross

By this time, Rockford had formally declined its invitation to play in the state tournament because it already had a commitment to play Washington for the "state title" on March 28. But Washington was entered in the tournament at Oak Park, and as luck would have it, scheduled to play Peoria in the opening round.

Rockford realized it had been double-crossed. After shunning the official state tournament because of its squabble with Oak Park, and now lacking a rival for its own "state championship" game, Rockford was about to finish its season out of the limelight. So the team decided to hold Washington to its contract, which may have included a sizable penalty for failing to appear. Washington was forced to withdraw from the state tournament and travel to Rockford instead. On Friday, March 28, Rockford beat the downstate team 57-21 for the last unsanctioned "state championship."

That same night, at the tournament in Oak Park, Peoria received a first-round win over Washington by default. Peoria sailed to the first IHSAA state title the next day with wins over Wheaton, Hinsdale, and Rock Island. Watching

the final game from the stands, perhaps with his head in his hands, was Coach Donald Kays of Rockford.

After the tournament, the Rockford team softened its stance. Now apparently satisfied with Peoria's reputation, Rockford was willing to meet the downstate school on that neutral court in Ottawa to settle the title question once and for all. But Peoria, owner of the official state championship banner, wisely chose to disband its basketball team and prepare for the baseball season instead.

Where the great Rockford "state champion" team might have earned an honored place in Illinois history, it now merits only a footnote. Oddly, recognition also proved hard to come by for the real state champion. For many years, printed tournament records mistakenly listed Washington instead of Peoria as the first school to win the crown.

For the unusual tournament of 1908, it took almost a century to set the record straight.

Clippings from the Chicago Tribune herald a new era of high school sport.

STATE TITLE WON BY PEORIA

Distillery City Basketball Players Defeat Rock Island.

FINAL PLAYED LAST NIGHT.

Illinois High School Championship Settled in Oak Park Gym.

Peoria High school, winner of the middle section tourney, last night won the Illinois state high school basketball championship, defeating the Rock Island five, winner in the northern section, 48 to 29, at the Oak Park Y. M. C. A. gymnasium.

In the semi-finals played in the afternoon these schools eliminated the two Chicago institutions, Peoria defeating Hinsdale, 32 to 24, and Rock Island winning from Oak Park, 36 to 28.

The final match was brilliantly contested during the first half, when Peoria scored 20 to 15 by the boys from the arsenal town. In second period the players from the distillery city worked with machinelike precision, and placed the result beyond doubt before half of the period had expired.

In the previous games, Conway, the left forward, was a host in himself, his dodging and accurate throwing the Rock Island guards. He threw field baskets, and at that was handicapped by a sprained ankle sustained in the ___ Lineup:

[48].

Right forward	Rock Island [29].
Left forward	Voss
Center	Lutt
Left guard	Brenner
Right guard	Young
	Streckfus

Prefzger, Conway, 11; Forrest, 7; Wor-g, 6; Brenner, 4. Free throws—Lutt, 7; ___. Points awarded—Rock Island, 2

ak Park, 41; Hinsdale, 27.

___ther night game to decide third place ___ in a victory for Oak Park over Hins-___ to 27. Lineup:
___rk [41].

Right forward	Hinsdale [27].
Left forward	Curtis
Center	Clark

SCHOOL FIVES START PLAY

State Championship in Basketball Begins at Oak Park.

ROCK ISLAND BOY IS STAR.

Voss Handicapped by Artificial Leg; Scores Ten Goals.

High school basketball teams, champions of six divisions of the State High School Athletic association, clashed yesterday at the Oak Park Y. M. C. A. in the preliminary rounds for the state championship. Peoria High proved the sensation of the evening,

1908

PEORIA
State Champions of 1908

FRONT ROW (left to right):
Frank Worley, Lynch Conway,
Bill Forrest. SECOND ROW:
Frank Trefzger, Jim Luke,
Coach Les Straesser, Charles
Drysdale, Linton Turner.

**Lewis Omer, Oak Park
athletic director and
founder of the IHSA boys'
basketball tournament.**

It took a lot of convincing before the Illinois High School Athletic Association finally gave in to Lewis Omer.

As athletic director at Oak Park, Omer had a vision of a winner-take-all tournament where high school teams from all over Illinois would determine a real state basketball champion, with no more bogus claims from pretenders in far-flung regions of the state.

The IHSAA wanted to be sure such a meet could be run fairly and economically. Omer pledged his pocketbook to the effort and enlisted Harvey Woodruff of the *Chicago Tribune* and Fred Hayner of the *Chicago Daily News* to research the contenders. He invited about two dozen teams, with Oak Park considered the local favorite, while Peoria, Rockford, Rock Island, and Washington provided strong challenges from downstate.

As the winter snows slowly melted away, so did Omer's tournament field. Rockford declined its invitation on the grounds it already owned the state championship. By the time the tournament was at hand, the field had dwindled to just 14 teams. Three of those withdrew at the last moment, throwing the tournament schedule into disarray.

On Friday, March 28, 1908, at precisely 2 o'clock, Omer's tournament tipped off, with Geneva playing Mt. Carroll at the high school gym and Hinsdale facing Riverside-Brookfield at the YMCA.

Gate receipts from the first day proved that the IHSAA's fears that the tournament might not pay for itself were

unfounded. The bleachers and gallery were full for every session, and the Oak Park paper reported that "swarms of high school girls were present to encourage their heroes." Many fans shouted themselves hoarse.

The time-honored practice of second-guessing the tournament administration got its start on opening day. Who exactly had invited this team from Riverside-Brookfield? The squad must have shown some spark to the Chicago writers, but its performance in the state final was strictly second-rate as Hinsdale administered a 60-9 shellacking. The 51-point margin of victory in the first game

of the first tournament still ranks as the largest ever.

The rest of the meet was full of surprises. One player, Andy Voss of Rock Island, scored 20 points in a quarterfinal game despite being hobbled by an artificial leg.

The sensation of the tournament was Peoria forward Lynch Conway. In the final game, Peoria led Rock Island only 20-15 before Conway caught fire in the second half. Despite playing on a sprained ankle suffered in the semifinal, Conway tossed in 22 points as Peoria scored an impressive 48-29 triumph. Conway's mark of 11 field goals in the title game lasted until 1950.

State Final Tournament Scores

First Round
Hinsdale (Twp.) 60, Riverside (R.-Brookfield) 9
Mt. Carroll 47, Geneva 20
Rock Island 31, Evanston (Twp.) 23
Oak Park (O.P.-River Forest) 58, St. Charles 27

Quarterfinals
Peoria 41, Wheaton 26
Hinsdale (Twp.) 34, Mt. Carroll 29
Rock Island 50, LaSalle (L.-Peru) 9
Oak Park (O.P. River Forest) (bye)

Semifinals
Peoria 32, Hinsdale 24
Rock Island 36, Oak Park (O.P.-River Forest) 28

Finals
Oak Park (O.P.-River Forest) 41, Hinsdale (Twp.) 27 (third place)
Peoria 48, Rock Island 29 (title)

Scoring Leaders

Player, School	G	FG	FT	Pts
Mitchell, Oak Park (O.P.-River Forest)	3	18	29	65
Richard Liitt, Rock Island	4	15	32	62
Frank Trefzger, Peoria	3	4	41	49
Goodwin Clark, Hinsdale (Twp.)	4	21	4	46
Lynch Conway, Peoria	3	20	0	40

All-Tournament First Team

Player, School	Ht.	Yr.
Howard Blodgett, Hinsdale (Twp.)		
Lynch Conway, Peoria		Sr.
William Forrest, Peoria		
Richard Liitt, Rock Island		So.
Frank Worley, Peoria		

Championship Game Box Score

Oak Park YMCA, March 28, 1908

PEORIA (48)
Coach Les Straesser

Player	FG-A	FT-A	Pts	PF
Lynch Conway	11	0	22	
Charles Drysdale	0	0	0	
William Forrest	7	0	14	
Frank Trefzger	1	8	10	
Frank Worley	1	0	2	
TOTAL	20	8	48	

ROCK ISLAND (29)
Coach W.E. Brown

Player	FG-A	FT-A	Pts	PF
Dan Brennan	4	0	8	
Richard Liitt	0	7	7	
John Streckfus	0	0	0	
Andy Voss	0	0	0	
Walter Young	6	0	12	
AWARDED			2	
TOTAL	10	7	29	

Peoria	20	28	—	48
Rock Island	15	14	—	29

Officials: Horton, Barlow.

Impressed with Lewis Omer's efforts in 1908, the IHSAA made the state tournament an annual event. The Association chose the Bloomington YMCA as the next tournament site after receiving many requests from downstate schools to choose a more centrally located city.

An invitational format had been necessary for the trial run in 1908. But in the tournament's second installment, the state association gave all its member schools a chance to participate.

Involving everyone meant setting up preliminary tournaments in four districts of the state, from which both the champion and runner-up would advance. The state final also included a consolation bracket — "a complicated arrangement that takes a man with an algebraic head to solve and comprehend," according to one news report — in which first-round losers could eventually achieve second place.

At the new central Illinois location, the favorite was Washington, led by a big center named Forrest Moyer. Located just 30 miles from the tournament site, Washington brought nearly 500 rooters by car and train and established an early record for noise.

The action really started to heat up when the semifinal round losers, Rock Island and Bloomington, locked horns in a consolation match. In the first half, Rock Island's Walter Young broke his nose when he ran into George Hinshaw of Bloomington. Later in the game, Richard Liitt of Rock Island and Fred Dolan of Bloomington scuffled and were ejected from the game. Both teams finished the battle with just four players on the floor.

In the championship game, the boys from Hinsdale, fourth-place finishers in 1908, slowly pulled away from Washington. The northern team managed only four baskets, none in the first half, but rallied behind Fred Cortis's seven free throws to earn an 18-13 decision. With an enrollment of only 100 students, Hinsdale was the smallest school to win the state championship until Hebron triumphed in 1952 with 98.

Dejected but apparently still full of energy, Washington was then sent off to play the final game of the tournament against Mt. Carroll to determine second place. Mt. Carroll had already played four games, coming all the way through the consolation bracket, and had nothing left for the nightcap. Washington won easily, 64-13, in the tournament's second 51-point rout in as many years.

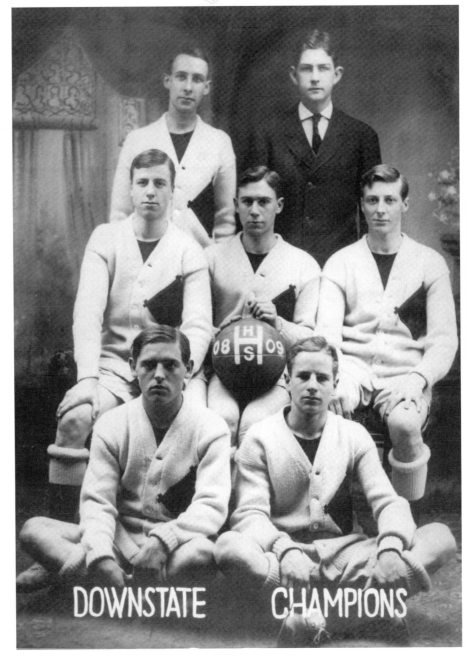

DOWNSTATE CHAMPIONS

HINSDALE (TWP.)
State Champions of 1909

FRONT ROW (left to right): Fred Bahlmann, Woodbury Melcher. SECOND ROW: Fred Cortis, Gilbert Keith, Preston Davidson. THIRD ROW: Frank Dana, Coach Arthur Collins.

1909

State Final Tournament Scores

Quarterfinals
Bloomington 30, Centralia 19
Hinsdale (Twp.) 56, Mt. Carroll 7
Washington 42, Joliet (Twp.) 25
Rock Island 42, Mt. Vernon 11

Semifinals
Hinsdale (Twp.) 21, Bloomington 14

Consolation Round
Mt. Carroll 44, Centralia 17
Joliet (Twp.) 28, Mt. Vernon 25

Semifinals
Washington 20, Rock Island 12

Consolation Round
Mt. Carroll 33, Joliet (Twp.) 32
Rock Island 33, Bloomington 21
Mt. Carroll 26, Rock Island 9

Finals
Hinsdale (Twp.) 18, Washington 13 (title)

Consolation Round
Washington 64, Mt. Carroll 13 (for second and third place)

Scoring Leaders

Player, School	G	FG	FT	Pts
Richard Liitt, Rock Island	4	14	21	49
Lyons, Joliet (Twp.)	3	10	26	46
Kline, Mt. Carroll	4	18	8	44
Harold Hufford, Bloomington	3	7	23	37
Preston Davidson, Hinsdale (Twp.)	3	17	0	34

All-Tournament First Team

Player, School	Ht.	Yr.
Melburn Evans, Mt. Vernon		
Gilbert Keith, Hinsdale (Twp.)		
Richard Liitt, Rock Island		Jr.
Meinhardt Ryf, Washington		
Sidney Steenburgh, Rock Island		

Championship Game Box Score

Bloomington YMCA, March 20, 1909

HINSDALE (TWP.) (18)
Coach Arthur Collins

Player	FG-A	FT-A	Pts	PF
Fred Bahlmann	0	0	0	
Fred Cortis	0	7	7	
Frank Dana	0	0	0	
Preston Davidson	3	0	6	
Gilbert Keith	1	3	5	
TOTAL	4	10	18	

WASHINGTON (13)
Coach Charles Wright

Player	FG-A	FT-A	Pts	PF
Cullom Long	0	0	0	
Forrest Moyer	3	0	6	
Roy Risser	1	0	2	
Meinhardt Ryf	0	3	3	
Steele Zinser	1	0	2	
TOTAL	5	3	13	

Hinsdale (Twp.)	5	13	—	18
Washington	6	7	—	13

Officials: Mitchell, Robinson.

Celebrating 100 years of IHSA Boys Basketball Tournaments

1910

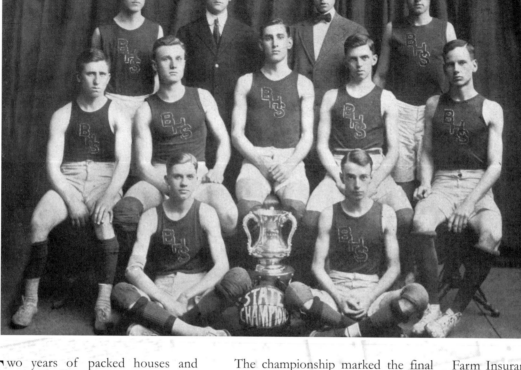

BLOOMINGTON
State Champions of 1910

FRONT ROW (left to right):
Byron Darst, Harold Hufford.
SECOND ROW: Laurence Twomey,
Fred Wollrab, Walter Sutherland,
Adlai Rust, Lewis Kessler.
THIRD ROW: Eugene Hamill,
Faculty Mgr. W.F. Schilling, Coach
Thomas O'Neil, Bruce Jarrett.

Two years of packed houses and exciting play suggested the state basketball tournament would be successful for many years to come. Under the all-comers format, so many schools wanted to get into the act that the IHSAA was forced to increase the number of districts from four to six for the 1910 tournament. That resulted in an awkward series of byes in both the quarterfinal and consolation rounds of the state finals.

Early dynasties were already in evidence at the 1910 finals, which were held at the Bloomington YMCA. Four of the schools advancing to the state finals — Bloomington, Hinsdale, Mt. Vernon, and Rock Island — were repeaters from the previous year.

The semifinal game between Rock Island and Hinsdale was the hardest-fought battle of the tournament. It featured a match-up between two of the earliest high school stars, Richard Liitt of Rock Island and Gilbert Keith of Hinsdale, fearsome centers, each playing in his third state tournament. Keith won the individual scoring battle 17-11, but Liitt and Rock Island won the game 37-27, and the right to play in the championship game.

The other finalist was Bloomington, a 52-10 winner over Mt. Sterling. Bloomington was familiar with the surroundings but, unlike Hinsdale, handicapped by having to play three games in two days.

The championship marked the final tourney appearance of Liitt. With 15 points in the title game, the Rock Island star finished his tournament career with 154, a record that stood until 1950. In 11 games he made 70 free throws, still a record as of 2007 (one player could shoot all the free throws for a team until 1924).

Despite Liitt's best efforts, Bloomington won the contest 32-25 behind Harold Hufford's 14 points. Teammates Harold Sutherland, Fred Wollrab, and Adlai Rust, the future CEO of State Farm Insurance, were named to the all-tournament squad chosen by the officials.

Bedlam reigned in Bloomington after the game. According to the *Pantagraph*, "Staid business men and middle-aged married women became for the moment as wild with enthusiasm as the chollie boys of the high school. Hats were thrown in the air and horns tooted a babel of noise. Then the uproarious mob surged upon the street and continued for an hour in the freer air its jubilation."

Some things never change.

Celebrating 100 years of IHSA Boys Basketball Tournaments

State Final Tournament Scores				
Quarterfinals				
Bloomington 36, Nokomis 17				
Rock Island 27, Mt. Vernon 24				
Semifinals				
Bloomington 52, Mt. Sterling 10				
Rock Island 37, Hinsdale (Twp.) 27				
Consolation Round				
Mt. Vernon (bye) (Nokomis chose not to continue)				
Hinsdale (Twp.) 44, Mt. Sterling 22				
Finals				
Hinsdale (Twp.) 26, Mt. Vernon 21 (third place)				
Bloomington 32, Rock Island 25 (title)				

Scoring Leaders				
Player, School	**G**	**FG**	**FT**	**Pts**
Richard Liitt, Rock Island	3	13	17	43
Harold Hufford, Bloomington	3	11	14	38
Melburn Evans, Mt. Vernon	2	10	15	35
Fred Wollrab, Bloomington	3	17	0	34
Preston Davidson, Hinsdale (Twp.)	3	14	4	32

All-Tournament First Team		
Player, School	**Ht.**	**Yr.**
Harold Hufford, Bloomington	6-2	Sr.
Richard Liitt, Rock Island		Sr.
Adlai Rust, Bloomington	6-1	Sr.
John Streckfus, Rock Island		
Fred Wollrab, Bloomington	6-2	Sr.

Championship Game Box Score				
Bloomington YMCA, March 12, 1910				
BLOOMINGTON (32)				
Coach Tom O'Neill				
Player	**FG-A**	**FT-A**	**Pts**	**PF**
Byron Darst	1	0	2	
Harold Hufford	4	6	14	
Adlai Rust	3	0	6	
Walter Sutherland	0	0	0	
Fred Wollrab	4	0	8	
AWARDED			2	
TOTAL	12	6	32	
ROCK ISLAND (25)				
Coach F.W. Gray				
Player	**FG-A**	**FT-A**	**Pts**	**PF**
Harry Behneman	2	0	4	
Richard Liitt	4	7	15	
James McManus	1	0	2	
Sidney Steenburgh	0	0	0	
John Streckfus	2	0	4	
TOTAL	9	7	25	
Bloomington	19	13	—	32
Rock Island	10	15	—	25

Officials: G.O. Langstead, George DeKruif.

The 1911 tourney, played at the new gymnasium at Bradley Polytechnic Institute in Peoria, almost ground to a halt in a battle over balls.

Two games into the meet, it was discovered that a ball manufactured by Reach had been used when a Spalding ball was explicitly called for. A closer examination of the problem showed the rule book published by Spalding demanded a Spalding ball, while the Reach rule book would settle for nothing but a Reach. The officials wisely ruled all balls were created equal and the tournament resumed.

On the court, Rockford, making its first appearance in the state tournament, was finally able to make up for refusing to play in the 1908 inaugural. Led by a pair of clever forwards named Frank Johnson and Frank Thomas, the northern squad dominated the tournament like few teams have since.

By reputation, Jacksonville and Washington were good matches for Rockford, but that was merely an illusion. "The red and black" made quick work of a slow Jacksonville team in the first quarterfinal game. In the other quarterfinal, Washington looked bad and felt worse. A few days before the tournament, two of Washington's best players were stricken by the mumps, prompting a request from the school to postpone the tournament, which was denied. The result was a 42-21 loss to Paris.

In the finals, Rockford was matched with Mt. Carroll, a high-scoring quintet making its third state-tourney appearance in four years. In the previous round, Mt. Carroll and Paris had combined for 88 points, a tournament record that stood until 1939. But in the championship game it was Rockford that put on a scoring exhibition. Johnson scored 20 points and Thomas added 18 as Rockford surged to a 60-15 victory.

Local spectators, not inclined to root for their great rival from the north, were won over by the spectacular shooting. "When the Rockford boys hit the forty point total the Peoria fans called loudly for fifty," wrote one newspaper, "but the Rockford team was not content to stop at that mark."

The 45-point margin remains the largest in championship game history.

State Final Tournament Scores

Quarterfinals
Rockford 39, Jacksonville 23
Paris 42, Washington 21

Semifinals
Rockford 44, Granite City 30
Mt. Carroll 58, Paris 30

Finals
Granite City 44, Paris 35 (third place)
Rockford 60, Mt. Carroll 15 (title)

Scoring Leaders

Player, School	G	FG	FT	Pts
Arbuckle, Paris	3	26	7	59
Frank Thomas, Rockford	3	20	11	51
Frank Johnson, Rockford	3	23	0	46
Walter Smith, Mt. Carroll	2	13	8	34
Schellenberger, Paris	3	15	0	30

All-Tournament First Team

Player, School	Ht.	Yr.
Frank Johnson, Rockford		
Walter Smith, Mt. Carroll		
Casson Squire, Rockford		
Frank Thomas, Rockford		
Roger Welsh, Rockford		

Championship Game Box Score

Bradley Gym, Peoria, March 11, 1911

ROCKFORD (60)
Coach Ralph Vennum

Player	FG-A	FT-A	Pts	PF
Roy Collentine	2	0	4	
Frank Johnson	10	0	20	
Casson Squire	4	0	8	
Frank Thomas	7	4	18	
Roger Welsh	5	0	10	
TOTAL	28	4	60	

MT. CARROLL (15)
Coach unknown

Player	FG-A	FT-A	Pts	PF
Dwight Bennett	1	0	2	
Ralph Eskelson	0	0	0	
Lloyd Fox	1	0	2	
Harry Ross	0	0	0	
Walter Smith	2	7	11	
TOTAL	4	7	15	

Officials: Bruce Rutherford, Earl Bridges.

ROCKFORD
State Champions of 1911

FRONT ROW (left to right): Roy Collentine. SECOND ROW: Frank Thomas, Frank Johnson, Casson Squire. THIRD ROW: Roger Welsh, Coach Ralph Vennum.

1911

BATAVIA
State Champions of 1912

FRONT ROW (left to right):
Dwight Emigh, Parks Bailey,
Raymond McDermott,
Charles Barr. SECOND ROW:
Horace Bone, Walter Trantow,
Hanson. THIRD ROW:
Coach K.C. Merrick.

1912

The Decatur YMCA was the site of the 1912 tournament, a six-team affair filled with spine-tingling games from start to finish. All in all, spectators saw nine games decided by an average of less than five points — the most closely contested tournament in the first 99 years of state tournament play.

Tinkering with the format yet again, the IHSAA introduced an unusual twist: instead of awarding byes to two quarterfinalists, all six teams played in the quarterfinal round. The three losers then had the chance to play through a consolation bracket and reenter the tournament as a semifinalist.

One team, Galesburg, was lucky just to be in the six-team field. Eliminated by Mt. Carroll in the district championship, Galesburg received new life when the northern team withdrew from state competition after its best player quit.

In one consolation-bracket game, Hillsboro beat Canton in the tournament's first overtime, won in the last seconds on a long, backwards, over-the-head shot by Lynn Denton. "It is as impossible in the execution as in the description," wrote the *Decatur Herald*.

There's a reason tournaments don't have play-back consolation brackets anymore, and perhaps this is it. Decatur, having defeated Galesburg in the quarterfinals 27-26, waited patiently for the losers' bracket to produce its semifinal opponent, which turned out to be Galesburg, the team it had just beaten. Decatur succumbed to the inevitable and lost 36-23, while the twice-resurrected Galesburg team advanced to the championship game against Batavia.

Aided by the strong free throw shooting of its captain, Raymond McDermott, Batavia held off Galesburg's comeback bid in the title game 28-25. McDermott sank eight of ten free throw attempts to ensure the victory. After the postgame celebration, the Batavia team traveled to the University of Illinois, where players spent the night at the fraternity houses of Batavia alumni.

By way of trivia, Batavia was the first consolidated school to win the state championship. Prior to 1910 there were two high school districts in Batavia, East and West, one on each side of the Fox River. The combined school enjoyed immediate success on the basketball floor and was an athletic power for many years thereafter.

State Final Tournament Scores

Quarterfinals
Batavia 32, Canton 23
Granite City 39, Hillsboro 27
Decatur 27, Galesburg 26

Consolation Round
Hillsboro 32, Canton 31 (OT)
Galesburg 33, Hillsboro 27

Semifinals
Batavia 29, Granite City 26
Galesburg 36, Decatur 23

Finals
Granite City 38, Decatur 31 (third place)
Batavia 28, Galesburg 25 (title)

Scoring Leaders

Player, School	G	FG	FT	Pts
Walter Frame, Hillsboro	3	11	20	42
Raymond McDermott, Batavia	3	15	8	38
Herbert Pihl, Galesburg	4	13	8	34
Harry Branding, Granite City	3	16	0	32
Ernest Robertson, Granite City	3	14	3	31

All-Tournament First Team

Player, School	Ht.	Yr.
Harry Branding, Granite City		
Oscar Dammann, Hillsboro		
Eric Erickson, Galesburg	5-9	Jr.
Arthur Harry, Decatur		
Raymond McDermott, Batavia	6-1	Sr.
Ernest Robertson, Granite City		

Championship Game Box Score

Decatur YMCA, March 9, 1912

BATAVIA (28)
Coach K.C. Merrick

Player	FG-A	FT-A	Pts	PF
Charles Barr	0	0	0	0
Horace Bone	0	0	0	2
Dwight Emigh	1	0	2	4
Raymond McDermott	2	8	12	2
Parks Bailey	2	0	4	3
Walter Trantow	5	0	10	1
TOTAL	10	8	28	12

GALESBURG (25)
Coach T.W. Callihan

Player	FG-A	FT-A	Pts	PF
Gordon Bridge	2	1	5	1
Eric Erickson	3	0	6	3
John Halladay	0	0	0	1
Lawrence Ingersol	0	0	0	0
Fred Phillips	0	0	0	4
Herbert Pihl	4	4	12	0
AWARDED			2	
TOTAL	9	5	25	9

Batavia	14	14	—	28
Galesburg	11	14	—	25

Officials: Rufus Gilbert, Ted Rose.

Galesburg 37
Peoria Manual 36

GALESBURG
State Champions of 1913

*FRONT ROW (left to right):
Lawerence Ingersol, Herbert Pihl,
Belford Van Pelt. SECOND ROW:
Mgr. Rose, Greer, Eric Erickson,
Byron Scott, Coach Harry Hayes.*

State Final Tournament Scores

Quarterfinals
Galesburg 39, Mt. Vernon 33
Winnetka (New Trier) 33, Hillsboro 19
Peoria (Manual) 47, Abingdon 20

Semifinals
Galesburg 37, Winnetka (New Trier) 30
Hillsboro chosen by lot to enter semifinals
Peoria (Manual) 29, Hillsboro 24

Finals
Winnetka (New Trier) chose not to play third-place game
Galesburg 37, Peoria (Manual) 36 (title)

Scoring Leaders

Player, School	G	FG	FT	Pts
Lester DeTrempe, Peoria (Manual)	3	28	5	61
Herbert Pihl, Galesburg	3	16	23	55
Herbert Kincaid, Winnetka (New Trier)	2	11	12	34
Lynn Denton, Hillsboro	2	5	14	24
Belford Van Pelt, Galesburg	3	9	0	18
William Angelsea, Peoria (Manual)	3	8	2	18

All-Tournament First Team

Player, School	Ht.	Yr.
William Angelsea, Peoria (Manual)		
Lester DeTrempe, Peoria (Manual)		
Eric Erickson, Galesburg	5-9	Sr.
Wilbur Kortkamp, Hillsboro		
Herbert Pihl, Galesburg		

Championship Game Box Score

Bradley Gym, Peoria, March 8, 1913

GALESBURG (37)
Coach Harry Hayes

Player	FG-A	FT-A	Pts	PF
Eric Erickson	1	0	2	
Lawrence Ingersol	3	0	6	
Herbert Pihl	6	9-13	21	
Byron Scott	0	0	0	
Belford Van Pelt	4	0	8	
TOTAL	14	9	37	

PEORIA (MANUAL) (36)
Coach Charles Mason

Player	FG-A	FT-A	Pts	PF
William Angelsea	3	1	7	
Lester DeTrempe	8	1	17	
Rodney Doering	3	0	6	
Dan Ewell	1	1	3	
Gus Keupper	1	0	2	
Ralph Werner	0	1	1	
TOTAL	16	4	36	

Galesburg	18	19	—	37
Peoria (Manual)	15	21	—	36

Officials: Musselman, Davis.

Still shy a few credits on its degree in bracketology, the IHSAA returned its basketball tournament to the Bradley Institute gymnasium with yet another awkward six-team arrangement, though thankfully without the confusion of a consolation bracket. The solution to the problem was hardly an improvement: this time, one of the quarterfinal losers was drawn at random to continue as a semifinalist, a method almost certain to generate hard feelings.

Unlike the tournament's first visit in 1911, hometown Peoria fans had a local team to cheer for. Manual had suffered only one loss, a mid-season setback to the tournament favorite, Galesburg, the 1912 runner-up. The brackets seemed to indicate a rematch was in the offing.

Galesburg survived a close call with Mt. Vernon in the first game of the meet. In another quarterfinal, an Abingdon player stole an inbounds pass and scored a basket — for Manual. It was the first time in tournament history, but not the last, that a player scored a goal for the wrong team. Manual didn't need the help and won easily. Hillsboro turned out to be the lucky quarterfinal loser, but organizers were smart enough not to pair Hillsboro with the team it had just lost to.

The semifinals played out as expected, and Manual and Galesburg prepared for a title battle. But when the time came for the third-place game, fans were surprised to see three different teams on the floor. New Trier, a semifinal loser, had already headed home, "their best forward too sick to play and the entire team in bad shape," according to the *Peoria Star*. Fans were instead treated to an exhibition game staged by players from Hillsboro, Abingdon, and Mt. Vernon.

A crowd of about 1,000, the largest ever to witness a title game, got its money's worth and more. With their team leading 18-15 at halftime, Galesburg rooters "put on a parade around the gym and carried out the lock-step in great style."

The lead alternated throughout the second half as Herbert Pihl of Galesburg and Lester DeTrempe of Manual reached double figures. The game came down to the last few seconds with Galesburg leading 37-36.

When DeTrempe launched a shot that "circled the hoop and hung on the edge for several moments, absolute silence awaited the final drop of the ball."

It fell outside the ring, and the Galesburg team returned home with a magnificent loving cup, serenaded by peals from the high school bell.

*Celebrating 100 years of
IHSA Boys Basketball Tournaments*

For the first time, the tournament was uncomplicated by byes, consolation brackets, or qualifying runners-up. The eight district winners that took the floor at the Decatur YMCA played off in a no-nonsense, single-elimination competition — the first Elite Eight, if you will, though it would not be so called for many years. So perfect was the format, so devoid of controversy and confusion, it lasted only two years.

Other elements of the modern tournament were already in evidence. Newspaper prognostications were plentiful and usually wrong. For instance, Evanston Academy and University High of Normal won their quarterfinal games handily and on that basis were picked to meet in the title game. They both lost in the semifinals. The upset of tournament favorite Centralia by Freeport in the quarterfinals also incited more than a little hand-wringing among the scribes.

There were also reports of the emotion that sometimes sweeps away fans of the modern version of March Madness. During a timeout late in the game against Freeport, a girl from Centralia crossed the court to ask how much time was left. When informed it was against the rules to tell her or anyone else, she returned to her seat, crying. After the quarterfinal loss, according to one report, "the disappointed delegation of Centralia rooters tore their hair, wept, and gave other manifestations of intense grief."

The championship game pitted an up-and-coming squad from Freeport against Hillsboro, playing in its third straight state final tournament. Hillsboro's team was much taller, controlling the flow of the game and the center jumps, and won easily 42-19. Forward Eugene Seymour scored 20 points in the title game and 54 in the tournament to lead all scorers.

After six northern champions, Hillsboro brought the tournament trophy to the southern half of the state for the first time. Before the team left on its trip to Decatur, the superintendent of the Hillsboro schools had told the boys if they won the state title they could have anything upon their return. Naturally, they asked for a day off school and so on Monday they were treated to a parade around the streets of their hometown.

State Final Tournament Scores

Quarterfinals
Evanston (E. Academy) 49, Galesburg 23
Hillsboro 43, Granite City 40
Normal (University) 29, Peoria (Manual) 27
Freeport 33, Centralia 30

Semifinals
Hillsboro 37, Evanston (E. Academy) 31
Freeport 32, Normal (University) 20

Finals
Normal (University) 31, Evanston (E. Academy) 23 (third place)
Hillsboro 42, Freeport 19 (title)

Scoring Leaders

Player, School	G	FG	FT	Pts
Eugene Seymour, Hillsboro	3	16	22	54
Dick Gambrill, Evanston (E. Academy)	3	6	24	36
Leo Koehler, Freeport	3	17	0	34
Ken Cram, Evanston (E. Academy)	3	14	0	28
Ira Henemeyer, Hillsboro	3	14	0	28

All-Tournament First Team

Player, School	Ht.	Yr.
Rodney Doering, Peoria (Manual)		
John Felmley, Normal (University)		
Dick Gambrill, Evanston (E. Academy)		
Chester Guthrie, Hillsboro		
Leo Koehler, Freeport	5-8	Jr.

Championship Game Box Score

Decatur YMCA, March 14, 1914

HILLSBORO (42)
Coach D.O. Kime

Player	FG-A	FT-A	Pts	PF
Edward Elledge	1	0	2	
Chester Guthrie	4	0	8	
Ira Henemeyer	5	0	10	
Wilbur Kortkamp	1	0	2	
Brenton Marland	0	0	0	
Eugene Seymour	8	4	20	
TOTAL	19	4	42	

FREEPORT (19)
Coach Dan Daugherty

Player	FG-A	FT-A	Pts	PF
John Bonn/Barnds	0	0	0	
Torrey Foy	1	3	5	
Julius Guhl	0	0	0	
John Hart	1	0	2	
Oscar Hill	4	0	8	
Leo Koehler	2	0	4	
Chester Langenstine	0	0	0	
Russell Mullinix	0	0	0	
TOTAL	8	3	19	

Hillsboro	17	25	—	42
Freeport	16	3	—	19

Officials: Ralph Tenney, Clarence Howell.

1914

HILLSBORO
State Champions of 1914

FRONT ROW (left to right): Ira Henemeyer, Edward Elledge, Brenton Marland. SECOND ROW: Wilbur Kortkamp, Chester Guthrie, Eugene Seymour, Coach D.O. Kime.

FREEPORT
State Champions of 1915

FRONT ROW (left to right): Russell Mullinix, Paul Gilbert, Herbert Biersach. SECOND ROW: Torrey Foy, Oscar Hill, Leo Koehler, Mgr. Julius Guhl. THIRD ROW: Coach D.B. Daugherty, Chester Langenstein, Glenn "Pat" Holmes.

State Final Tournament Scores

Quarterfinals

Springfield 21, Rock Island 19 (OT)
Shelbyville 30, Naperville 20
Carbondale (University) 22, Decatur 21
Freeport 41, Granite City 20

Semifinals

Springfield 27, Shelbyville 10
Freeport 38, Carbondale (University) 14

Finals

Shelbyville 33, Carbondale (University) 8 (third place)
Freeport 27, Springfield 11 (title)

Scoring Leaders

Player, School	G	FG	FT	Pts
Torrey Foy, Freeport	3	9	21	39
C. Klauser, Shelbyville	3	12	10	34
Leo Koehler, Freeport	3	15	1	31
Oscar Hill, Freeport	3	13	0	26
C. Cox, Shelbyville	3	12	0	24

All-Tournament First Team

Player, School	Ht.	Yr.
Torrey Foy, Freeport	5-8	Sr.
Oscar Hill, Freeport	5-7	Sr.
Leo Koehler, Freeport	5-8	Sr.
Chester Langenstine, Freeport	6-0	Sr.
Edward Sternaman, Springfield	5-5	Sr.

Championship Game Box Score

Millikin Gym, Decatur, March 13, 1915

FREEPORT (27)
Coach Dan Daugherty

Player	FG-A	FT-A	Pts	PF
Torrey Foy	2	12	16	
Oscar Hill	3	0	6	
Glenn Holmes	0	0	0	
Leo Koehler	2	0	4	
Chester Langenstine	0	0	0	
AWARDED				1
TOTAL	7	12	27	

SPRINGFIELD (11)
Coach Arthur Nevins

Player	FG-A	FT-A	Pts	PF
Walter Bowles	0	0	0	
Art Dawson	1	6	8	
Jerome Dunne	0	0	0	
Harry Eielson	1	0	2	
Isaac Sawyer	0	0	0	
Fred Smith	0	0	0	
Edward Sternaman	0	0	0	
Clifford Turnbull	0	0	0	
Raymond Wilson	0	0	0	
AWARDED				1
TOTAL	2	6	11	

Freeport	11	16	—	27
Springfield	6	5	—	11

Officials: W.H. Gunn, C.P. Shipley.

The peripatetic IHSAA boys basket-ball tournament moved for the fifth year in a row, this time to the new gymnasium at Millikin University in Decatur. There the tournament would find a home of sorts, staying put for three years, the longest run at any venue prior to the move to Champaign-Urbana in 1919.

Freeport, the previous year's runner-up, proved to be one of the most dominant champions of all time. The swift squad swept through the field with wins of 41-20 over Granite City in the quarterfinals, 38-14 over Carbondale in the semis, and 27-11 over Springfield in the championship game.

"Freeport displayed more basketball in a few minutes," wrote the *Decatur Herald*, "than all the other teams showed together." Freeport's starters rested in the second half of the first two contests while the second string finished up the chores.

One measure of Freeport's dominance is the fact that four of its starters — forwards Oscar Hill and Leo Koehler, center Chester Langenstine, and guard Torrey Foy — were named to the five-man all-tournament team. Unlike Hillsboro the year before, Freeport won with speed and not height. Langenstine was the only six-footer on the club, and just barely. Koehler, who was hailed by one newspaper as "by far the best forward in the state among high school players," was only 5-foot-8.

Ironically it was the fifth starter, Glenn "Pat" Holmes, who now rates special mention in the IHSA basketball record book. When Freeport claimed its second state championship in 1926, Holmes became the first man to play for and coach a state champion.

Glenn "Pat" Holmes, Freeport's fifth starter, became the first man to play for and coach a state champion when he led Freeport to a title in 1926.

Although there is no written record of the event, the 1915 championship may have been the first attended by an Illinois governor. Springfield sophomore Jerome Dunne, whose basket in overtime won the quarterfinal contest against Rock Island, was the youngest son of Governor Edward Dunne.

1915

1916

BLOOMINGTON
State Champions of 1916

FRONT ROW (left to right):
Norton Richardson, Russell Strange.
SECOND ROW: Clarence Bean,
Delmar Gottschalk, Verne Greiner,
Layard Mace, Mevis Jennings.
THIRD ROW: Francis McMurray,
Theodore Bean, George Morrison,
Coach Earl McClure.

As the number of schools participating in the basketball tournament continued to grow, the IHSAA increased the number of district tournaments around the state to 11, reverting to a state final full of unwieldy byes.

More unsettling was an eligibility controversy that threatened to stop the tournament in its tracks. Four district champions — Arthur, DuQuoin, Springfield, and Robinson — were accused of using ineligible players, precipitating a day-long meeting of the IHSAA Board of Control.

When the dust settled, Springfield lost one starter, while Arthur was ousted from the tournament entirely and replaced by Shelbyville. Shortly after the *Arthur Graphic Clarion* compared the IHSAA Board to the Kaiser of Germany, the animosity escalated even further when one of the ineligible players attacked a Shelbyville official riding the train to the state final in Decatur.

The incident left a cloud over the tournament, as the three schools that were allowed to continue play all ended up winning trophies. Northern schools, used to having their way in the tournament, were completely shut out of the semifinal round and quite unhappy at the turn of events. After his team was upset by Bloomington in the quarterfinal round, the coach from Joliet mentioned that the northern delegation might secede

because of the poor treatment the schools had received from the floor officials.

Luckily, the champion was free of taint and a popular favorite. Bloomington became the first school to win two state championships, achieving the feat in a span of just seven years. The victors made their mark with defense, holding three opponents to a total of 41 points. Bloomington's offensive output in the title game against Robinson was at the

time the smallest ever by a state champion, but it was more than enough for a 25-17 victory. Though they finished well down the standings in the scoring derby, juniors Layard Mace and George Morrison were named to the all-tournament team, presaging a possible Bloomington repeat in the 1917 tourney.

The total attendance for the tournament's five sessions was 3,794, a record. More than 1,150 packed into the Millikin gym for the championship game.

State Final Tournament Scores

First Round
Moline 34, Canton 33 (OT)
DuQuoin 40, Shelbyville 25
Joliet (Twp.) 43, Granite City 22

Quarterfinals
Robinson 24, Aurora (East) 19
Springfield 18, Rockford 11
Bloomington 16, Joliet (Twp.) 11
DuQuoin 30, Moline 15

Semifinals
Robinson 14, DuQuoin 13
Bloomington 19, Springfield 13

Finals
DuQuoin 33, Springfield 13 (third place)
Bloomington 25, Robinson 17 (title)

Scoring Leaders

Player, School	G	FG	FT	Pts
Ray Harrell, DuQuoin	4	16	26	58
Benton Springer, Robinson	3	17	7	41
Calkins, Joliet (Twp.)	2	12	7	31
Layard Mace, Bloomington	3	11	3	25
C. Wedirquist, Moline	2	4	16	24

All-Tournament First Team

Player, School	Ht.	Yr.
Jacobs, Joliet (Twp.)	5-9	Jr.
Layard Mace, Bloomington	5-10	Jr.
George Morrison, Bloomington	5-8	Jr.
Benton Springer, Robinson	6-3	Sr.
Don Willi, DuQuoin	5-7	Sr.

Championship Game Box Score

Millikin Gym, Decatur, March 11, 1916

BLOOMINGTON (25)
Coach Earl McClure

Player	FG-A	FT-A	Pts	PF
Theodore Bean	3	0	6	4
Delmar Gottschalk	0	0	0	
Vern Greiner	3	3	9	
Mevis Jennings	1	0	2	
Layard Mace	4	0	8	
Francis McMurray	0	0	0	
George Morrison	0	0	0	
TOTAL	11	3	25	

ROBINSON (17)
Coach William Livingston

Player	FG-A	FT-A	Pts	PF
Douglas Dewey	0	1	1	
Eddie Kirk	0	0	0	
Paul Norris	0	0	0	
Benton Springer	5	3	13	
Chalon Titsworth	1	1	3	
TOTAL	6	5	17	

Bloomington	13	12	—	25
Robinson	6	11	—	17

Officials: C.E. Howell, William Duerr.

SPRINGFIELD
State Champions of 1917

FRONT ROW (left to right):
Vernon Edwards, Nelson Jones,
Ben Clouser, Harry Eielson,
Jerome Dunne, Max Poscover,
Sternaman. SECOND ROW: Asst.
Coach A.S. Nevins, George
Teasley, Blanbelt, Mayor H.S.
Betty, Portridge, Paoli, Coach
Roy Wentz.

State Final Tournament Scores

First Round
DuQuoin 24, Harvey (Thornton) 23
Bloomington 18, Decatur 12
Lawrenceville 31, Centralia 23
Peoria (Manual) 27, Aurora (East) 19

Quarterfinals
Springfield 34, Rock Island 23
Bloomington 15, DuQuoin 10
Peoria (Manual) 20, Lawrenceville 9
Belvidere 24, Sullivan 16

Semifinals
Springfield 14, Bloomington 9
Belvidere 16, Peoria (Manual) 6

Finals
Bloomington 20, Peoria (Manual) 9 (third place)
Springfield 32, Belvidere 11 (title)

Scoring Leaders

Player, School	G	FG	FT	Pts
Layard Mace, Bloomington	4	8	16	32
Myron Silvius, Belvidere	3	13	0	26
Eugene "Buck" Wilson, Peoria (Manual)	4	12	0	24
Max Poscover, Springfield	3	10	3	23
Harry Eielson, Springfield	3	10	0	20
Ben Lear, Belvidere	3	6	8	20
Corliss Easterday, Lawrenceville	2	10	0	20
Jerome Dunne, Springfield	3	10	0	20

All-Tournament First Team

Player, School	Ht.	Yr.
Harry Eielson, Springfield	6-2	Sr.
Frank Engelke, Peoria (Manual)		Sr.
Layard Mace, Bloomington	5-10	Sr.
George Morrison, Bloomington	5-8	Sr.
Eugene "Buck" Wilson, Peoria (Manual)		Sr.

Championship Game Box Score

Millikin Gym, Decatur, March 10, 1917

SPRINGFIELD (32)
Coach Roy Wentz

Player	FG-A	FT-A	Pts	PF
Ben Clouser	3	4-6	10	
Jerome Dunne	4	0-0	8	
Vernon Edwards	0	0-1	0	
Harry Eielson	4	0-0	8	
Nelson Jones	0	0-0	0	
Harry Lock	0	0-0	0	
Max Poscover	3	0-1	6	
George Teasley	0	0-0	0	
TOTAL	14	4-8	32	

BELVIDERE (11)
Coach Joseph Swanson

Player	FG-A	FT-A	Pts	PF
Herbert Comstock	0	0-0	0	
Harold Gilroy	0	3-4	3	
Allie Jukes	0	0-0	0	
Ben Lear	1	2-2	4	
Myron Silvius	2	0-0	4	
Stan Wells	0	0-0	0	
TOTAL	3	5-6	11	

Springfield	6	26 —	32
Belvidere	5	6 —	11

Officials: C.P. Shipley, Charles Lantz.

> *Tournament officials told the coaches to play the third-place game or forget about trophies — and their schools' expense checks.*

In an unfortunate reprise of the 1916 tournament, off-the-court events shared the limelight with the championship basketball being played at Decatur's Millikin Gymnasium.

Another eligibility dispute embroiled the IHSAA Board of Control, which tossed out Mt. Olive at the 11th hour and ordered up a district title playoff between Sullivan and Taylorville immediately before the first state tournament game.

Meanwhile, the reigning champions from Bloomington almost missed the chance to defend their title because of a smallpox outbreak at the high school. The basketball team was ordered to stay home — the only time in tournament history that avoiding class for a week earned a team the right to play in the tournament.

Reports that two Springfield students were found drunk and dazed under the bleachers and that gamblers had taken up to $2,000 in bets on the games did not lighten matters.

Finally, when Bloomington lost its semifinal game to Springfield and Coach E.W. McClure tried to engineer a deal with Peoria Manual coach Charles Mason to abandon the third-place game, IHSAA officials had had enough. They told the coaches to play the game or forget about trophies — and their schools' expense checks.

After all that turmoil, Springfield's 32-11 championship-game victory over Belvidere was almost an anticlimax. Culminating a three-year run in which the school finished second, fourth, and first, Springfield led only 6-5 at halftime but pulled away in the final 20 minutes. Throughout the tournament, Springfield got balanced scoring from its big four of Harry Eielson, Ben Clouser, Max Poscover, and Jerome Dunne.

Falling inconspicuously in the first round was the team from Centralia, in its first state tournament appearance under Coach Arthur L. Trout. The basketball world would soon hear more from Trout and his Orphans.

From the Y to the U
Looking for a place to call home

Basketball was *invented* at the YMCA Training School in **1891** and migrated slowly to high schools, which were not built with athletic competition in mind. When the IHSA tournament first went looking for places to play, the most suitable sites were **YMCA** *buildings*.

The inaugural state tournament was held in 1908 at the Oak Park YMCA. The building, now used for luxury apartments, still stands on North Scoville Avenue near downtown Oak Park.

★ OAK PARK YMCA ★

by Scott Johnson

At Oak Park (1908), Bloomington (1909 and 1910), and Decatur (1912 and 1914), YMCAs provided decent-sized courts and room for perhaps a few hundred crowded spectators. Two universities — Bradley in Peoria (1911 and 1913) and Millikin in Decatur — also hosted the state tournament during the early period, perhaps with the idea of boosting their athletic programs. Millikin provided a measure of consistency, hosting three consecutive tournaments from 1915 to 1917.

As was typical at the time, the floor in all of these gymnasiums was circled by an elevated running track that doubled as a balcony for spectators, making shots from the corners impossible.

In 1918, the finals moved to the brand-new Springfield High School, the only time the state finals were contested at a high school except for a single game played at Oak Park-River Forest in 1908.

Unlike the previous venues, the Springfield gym was built for an audience. It featured retractable bleachers on one side of the court and a glassed-in viewing area above one of the baskets — the only skybox in tournament history. Though it was not saddled with a running-track balcony, the gymnasium still had its quirks: five steel posts just inches from one sideline and a spiral staircase, descending to a locker room, that cut off one corner of the court.

Continued growth demanded a permanent home. In 1919, the finals moved to the Men's Gym Annex at the University of Illinois, where the college team played. The building, later renamed Kenney Gym, was the tournament's first real spectator arena, with bleachers and a spacious balcony on all four sides of the court. In just seven years, increasing interest in sporting events made the Annex obsolete, and the IHSA tournament began its long love affair with Huff Gym.

Celebrating 100 years of IHSA Boys Basketball Tournaments

The Bloomington YMCA, located at the southeast corner of East and Washington streets, hosted the tournament in 1909 and 1910.

★ BLOOMINGTON YMCA ★

The Bradley Gymnasium, home to the state finals in 1911 and 1913, is now the Hartmann Center for the Performing Arts.

★ BRADLEY GYMNASIUM ★

★ DECATUR YMCA ★

In 1912 and 1914, the IHSA state finals were held at the Decatur YMCA, on the southeast corner of Church and Prairie streets. The interior view shows the running track and a blinding glare from the polished hardwood floor.

★ MILLIKIN GYMNASIUM ★

The state finals moved to the brand-new Millikin University Gymnasium in 1915 for a three-year stay. A manual scoreboard is visible above and to the right of the backboard in the interior view.

★ SPRINGFIELD H.S. ★

Springfield High School became the only high school facility to host the IHSA tournament in 1918. Its gymnasium featured full bleachers along one side of the court and steel pillars, padded with mats, to make things interesting.

The finals played in six buildings — seven if you include the single game at Oak Park and River Forest High — but never stayed in any place long enough to get comfortable until 1919, when the Big U beckoned . . .

★ MEN'S GYM ANNEX ★

The Men's Gym Annex of the University of Illinois was the tournament's first permanent home, hosting the finals from 1919 to 1925. Now known as Kenney Gym, it's an odd relic in the middle of a modern engineering campus, used by college recreation programs and University High School teams.

illinois high school association

Celebrating 100 years of
IHSA Boys Basketball Tournaments

CENTRALIA, *State Champions of 1918*

FRONT ROW (left to right): Henry Hurd, Harold Hartley, Wade Storer. SECOND ROW: Coach Arthur Trout, Telle Lederman, Stanley Thomas, Charles "Jumbo" Maddox, Harry Blakeley, T.W. Clarida.

1918

University High of Normal. Down 13-6 at halftime, U-High rallied to tie the score at 24. The teams fought through one five-minute extra period, then another and another before U-High finally clinched a 30-26 victory.

Centralia emerged from the day's events the clear favorite but needed an overtime of its own and a last-second tip-in by Charles "Jumbo" Maddox (all 6-foot-3 of him) to eliminate Shelbyville in the semifinals. Then in the title game, Coach Arthur Trout's charges proved too tall, too brawny, and and too accurate for the upstarts from U-High. The final score of 35-29 served warning of Trout's future as a coaching legend.

"Much credit must be given to the Centralia coach, A. L. Trout," wrote the *State Journal Register*, "who had four inexperienced men to develop at the first of the season, Maddox being the only old player on his bench. His work of turning out a championship team in a season's time is remarkable."

Continuing its search for a permanent site, the IHSAA boys basketball tournament took a chance on the brand-new Springfield High School gymnasium, which offered seating for 1,500 spectators. As home of the defending state champions, it also promised a partisan, hometown crowd. The 1918 tournament marked the only time state final games were played at a high school, except for one game in the inaugural tournament.

A funny thing happened on the way to the state final, however: Springfield lost in district play to Clinton, setting up a wide-open, 13-team tournament that was spread over three days for the first time.

With the invention of the electronic scoreboard still years away, the manual system suffered a tough test in the first round when New Trier was erroneously awarded a one-point victory over Elgin. The losers immediately protested that one of their field goals had not been recorded. A hot argument at the scorer's table ensued before the result was reversed and Elgin was given a 26-25 win.

The quarterfinal round, held on Friday, offered an indication of the final result. While Centralia rolled over Elgin,

the other three games were all very close. In one contest, Shelbyville edged DuQuoin by a single point; in another, Canton was forced into overtime by Jerseyville. Most exciting of all was the clash between Lawrenceville and

State Final Tournament Scores

First Round

DuQuoin 21, Rockford 18
Elgin 26, Winnetka (New Trier) 25
Centralia 32, Galesburg 30
Normal (University) 28, Champaign 18
Lawrenceville 23, Clinton 18

Quarterfinals

Shelbyville 18, DuQuoin 17
Centralia 37, Elgin 15
Normal (University) 30, Lawrenceville 26 (3 OT)
Canton 35, Jerseyville (Jersey) 27 (OT)

Semifinals

Centralia 25, Shelbyville 23 (OT)
Normal (University) 20, Canton 19

Finals

Canton 20, Shelbyville 19 (third place)
Centralia 35, Normal (University) 29 (title)

Scoring Leaders

Player, School	G	FG	FT	Pts
Clyde Murphy, Canton	3	14	10	38
Bane Pierce, Normal (University)	4	17	3	37
Henry Capen, Normal (University)	4	17	0	34
Harold Hartley, Centralia	4	5	23	33
Charles "Jumbo" Maddox, Centralia	4	16	0	32

All-Tournament First Team

Player, School	Ht.	Yr.
Harry Blakeley, Centralia	6-1	Sr.
Alvin Hoffman, Normal (University)		
Charles "Jumbo" Maddox, Centralia	6-3	Sr.
Bane Pierce, Normal (University)		
H.D. Waggoner, Lawrenceville	5-9	Sr.

Championship Game Box Score

Springfield High School, March 16, 1918

CENTRALIA (35)
Coach Arthur Trout

Player	FG-A	FT-A	Pts	PF
Harry Blakeley	6	0	12	1
Harold Hartley	0	3	3	1
Henry Hurd	3	0	6	0
Telle Lederman	3	0	6	0
Charles "Jumbo" Maddox	4	0	8	1
Wade Storer	0	0	0	0
TOTAL	16	3	35	3

NORMAL (UNIVERSITY) (29)
Coach Francis James

Player	FG-A	FT-A	Pts	PF
Arthur Buck	0	1	1	1
Henry Capen	5	0	10	0
Alvin Hoffman	0	0	0	2
Bane Pierce	3	0	6	0
Clarence Westhoff	6	0	12	1
TOTAL	14	1	29	4

Centralia	9	8	10	8 —	35
Normal (University)	10	6	4	9 —	29

Officials: unknown.

ROCKFORD
State Champions of 1919

FRONT ROW (left to right): Ralph Baker, Hugh Powell, Joel Carlson, Rex Enright, Harry Englund. BACK ROW: Coach Frank Winters.

1919 University of Illinois

In 1919 the IHSAA finally found a permanent home for its basketball tournament at the University of Illinois. Why it took so long to arrange this marriage is a mystery. The University already sponsored the state high school track and field meet (since 1893), the tennis tournament (since 1912), and the golf tournament (since 1916). It was obvious the state basketball tournament belonged in Champaign-Urbana as well.

Perhaps it was simple shortsightedness on someone's part. But when the University of Chicago started a national tournament for high school teams, the U of I quickly overcame its bureaucratic obstacles. Realizing their Western Conference foe now had the jump on the top basketball talent, officials at the state's flagship university pushed hard to host the IHSAA event, offering use of the new Men's Gym Annex in Urbana, lodging for the teams in various fraternity houses, and $900 to boot.

As with many of the early tournaments, local fans were able to root for a hometown favorite. Champaign won its first-round game over Alton, but in the quarterfinals ran into a big roadblock named Max Poscover. Now a senior, the Springfield forward was the dominant force in the tournament. Poscover scored 14 points in Springfield's 18-9 quarterfinal win over Champaign and for the tournament led all scorers with 58 points in four games.

In the other bracket, Rockford rolled forward, crushing its early-round opponents. Springfield and Rockford both won close semifinal games to set up a first: a championship clash between former state champions. The northern school couldn't stop Poscover, who made 18 points, but limited his teammates to just two in a 39-20 win. Harry Englund (16 points) and Rex Enright (14 points) starred for Rockford.

The *Daily Illini* reported "the event which has just passed, if it becomes a University of Illinois institution, will become as big a thing in Illini sport annals as the annual Interscholastic [the high school track, tennis, and golf meets]. The officials of the Athletic association are making every effort to have the games here permanently and the chances for such an event seem all in Illinois' favor."

With crowds of 3,000 or more for every session, the tournament netted over $2,500, a tremendous sum at the time. Little more convincing was required. The tournament would not go looking for a new home for almost eight decades.

1919

State Final Tournament Scores

First Round

Champaign 23, Alton 19
Springfield 30, Morris 15
Shelbyville 28, Atwood 26 (OT)
Herrin 18, Rock Island 14
Rockford 31, Flora 10

Quarterfinals

Peoria 50, Barry 15
Springfield 18, Champaign 9
Herrin 16, Shelbyville 15
Rockford 37, Dundee 10

Semifinals

Springfield 20, Peoria 18
Rockford 19, Herrin 14

Finals

Peoria 24, Herrin 10 (third place)
Rockford 39, Springfield 20 (title)

Scoring Leaders

Player, School	G	FG	FT	Pts
Max Poscover, Springfield	4	19	20	58
Rex Enright, Rockford	4	21	1	43
Harry Englund, Rockford	4	19	1	39
Glen "Frenchy" Haussler, Peoria	3	14	6	34
Johnnie Zinzer, Peoria	3	14	0	28

All Tournament First Team

Player, School	Ht.	Yr.
Joel Carlson, Rockford		
Harry Englund, Rockford		
Glen "Frenchy" Haussler, Peoria	5-11	Jr.
Max Poscover, Springfield	6-0	Sr.
Hugh Powell, Rockford		

Championship Game Box Score

Men's Gym Annex, Urbana, March 15, 1919

ROCKFORD (39)
Coach Frank Winters

Player	FG-A	FT-A	Pts	PF
Joel Carlson	1	0	2	2
Harry Englund	8	0	16	1
Rex Enright	7	0	14	1
Hugh Powell	0	0	0	0
Leslie Sodergren	2	3	7	1
TOTAL	18	3	39	5

SPRINGFIELD (20)
Coach Martin Shale

Player	FG-A	FT-A	Pts	PF
Tom Greenan	1	0	2	2
Harry Hodde	0	0	0	2
Ira Johnson	0	0	0	2
Lyle Marland	0	0	0	1
Max Poscover	6	6	18	3
TOTAL	7	6	20	10

Rockford	8	11	11	9	—	39
Springfield	5	1	10	4	—	20

Officials: Charles Lantz, Fred "Brick" Young.

1920

MT. VERNON
State Champions of 1920

LEFT: Coach Floyd Stables.
FRONT ROW (left to right):
Milton Forsyth, Russell Miller,
James Johnson. SECOND ROW:
Roy Miller, Chester Staley.
THIRD ROW: Harris, Thomas
Wells, Harel Ester.

I n its second year at the University of Illinois, the tournament welcomed 16 district champions, but no sportswriter's pen wrote odes to the "Sweet Sixteen." That designation was still years away.

The increase in the number of districts allowed a radical shift in the balance of power. Of the four district winners from southern Illinois, three — Olney, Mt. Vernon, and Marion — raced through the first two rounds and into the semifinals. The lone semifinal representative from north of the National Road (U.S. 40) was Canton, a western Illinois school.

Starring for Olney was the tournament's first great scoring machine, Leland Stilwell. At 6-foot-4, Stilwell was among the tallest players to have played the high school game in Illinois, and he used his height to every advantage. Stilwell scored 34 points in his first-round test, 10 more than the entire Champaign team. In the quarterfinal he logged 17, nearly outscoring Galesburg. Canton allowed Stilwell, somewhat hampered by a leg injury, 16 points in the semifinal but knocked Olney out of the tournament by shutting down his teammates. Olney finished fourth, with Stilwell scoring 81 of his team's 114 points. Shortly afterward Stilwell became the University of Illinois' first high-profile recruit credited to the state tourna-

ment. His single-game high of 34 points stood as a record for 30 years.

Mt. Vernon won the all-southern skirmish in the other semifinal with a 15-13 victory over Marion.

The championship game introduced Illinois basketball fans to a pair of future

dynasties. Canton would wear out the road to Champaign in the 1920s, while Mt. Vernon would go on to win four state titles over the course of the next four decades.

In this meeting, Mt. Vernon held on for an 18-14 win behind the slick play of forwards Russell Miller and Roy Miller (who were not related). As the final gun sounded, the team was carried off the court on the shoulders of the hometown rooters.

State Final Tournament Scores

First Round
Canton 16, Peoria (Manual) 14 (2 OT)
Joliet (Twp.) 40, Streator (Twp.) 25
Olney 43, Champaign 24
Galesburg 25, Shelbyville 23
Marion 23, Decatur 17
Rockford 45, Centralia 41
Bloomington 35, Jerseyville (Jersey) 29
Mt. Vernon 25, Elgin 13

Quarterfinals
Canton 35, Joliet (Twp.) 19
Olney 33, Galesburg 22
Marion 22, Rockford 20
Mt. Vernon 25, Bloomington 24

Semifinals
Canton 37, Olney 18
Mt. Vernon 15, Marion 13

Finals
Marion 29, Olney 20 (third place)
Mt. Vernon 18, Canton 14 (title)

Scoring Leaders

Player, School	G	FG	FT	Pts
Leland Stilwell, Olney	4	25	31	81
Clyde Campbell, Canton	4	25	0	50
Russell Miller, Mt. Vernon	4	13	23	49
Valentine, Marion	4	15	1	31
Roy Miller, Mt. Vernon	4	15	0	30

All-Tournament First Team

Player, School	Ht.	Yr.
Claude Berry, Canton	5-8	Sr.
Claudius Cummins, Centralia	6-2	Jr.
Russell Miller, Mt. Vernon		
Tophill Simon, Canton	6-1	Fr.
Leland Stilwell, Olney	6-4	Sr.

Championship Game Box Score

Men's Gym Annex, Urbana, March 20, 1920

MT. VERNON (18)
Coach Floyd Stables

Player	FG-A	FT-A	Pts	PF
Milton Forsyth	1	0	2	0
Jimmy Johnson	0	0	0	1
Roy Miller	2	0	4	0
Russell Miller	4	4	12	0
Chester Staley	0	0	0	1
TOTAL	7	4	18	2

CANTON (14)
Coach R.A. Deffenbaugh

Player	FG-A	FT-A	Pts	PF
Claude Berry	0	4	4	2
Clyde Campbell	2	0	4	0
Hubert Davalt	0	0	0	0
Fred Johnson	0	0	0	0
Marlon Negley	2	0	4	2
Roger Perkins	1	0	2	0
Tophill Simon	0	0	0	1
TOTAL	5	4	14	5

Mt. Vernon	9	2	2	5	—	18
Canton	5	2	4	3	—	14

Officials: Charles Lantz, Fred "Brick" Young.

MARION, State Champions of 1921

FRONT ROW (left to right): John Slater, Owen Stotlar, Raymond Biggs, Norman Belford, William Wallace.
SECOND ROW: Coach Edwin Schreiber, Willis Stone, Ray Robinson, Luke Johnson.

State Final Tournament Scores

Preliminary Round

Batavia 27, Mt. Carmel 22
Collinsville 21, Fairbury 15
Flora 24, Moline 22
Galesburg 29, Charleston 7
Marion 15, Elgin 14 (OT)

First Round

Streator (Twp.) 42, Trenton 14
Rockford 45, Pittsfield 13
Batavia 31, Peoria 26
Collinsville 19, Flora 17
Marion 19, Galesburg 15 (2 OT)
Macomb 38, Springfield 19
Winnetka (New Trier) 34, Decatur 31
Champaign 37, Mt. Vernon 27

Quarterfinals

Rockford 29, Streator (Twp.) 28
Batavia 24, Collinsville 9
Marion 25, Macomb 15
Winnetka (New Trier) 29, Champaign 28

Semifinals

Rockford 32, Batavia 21
Marion 26, Winnetka (New Trier) 24 (OT)

Finals

Winnetka (New Trier) 33, Batavia 28 (third place)
Marion 24, Rockford 23 (title)

Scoring Leaders

Player, School	G	FG	FT	Pts
John Mauer, Batavia	4	16	26	58
Norman Belford, Marion	5	16	23	55
Ralph Baker, Rockford	4	15	12	42
Warren Kasch, Rockford	4	16	3	35
Russ Daugherity, Streator (Twp.)	2	12	7	31

All-Tournament First Team

Player, School	Ht.	Yr.
Ralph Baker, Rockford		Jr.
Norman Belford, Marion	6-0	Jr.
Raymond Biggs, Marion	6-0	Sr.
Wesley Carlson, Rockford		
Russ Daugherity, Streator (Twp.)	6-0	Sr.
Curtis Parker, Winnetka (New Trier)	5-11	Sr.
Albert Rand, Winnetka (New Trier)	5-9	Sr.

Championship Game Box Score

Men's Gym Annex, Urbana, March 19, 1921

MARION (24)
Coach Edwin Schreiber

Player	FG-A	FT-A	Pts	PF
Norman Belford	2	5	9	1
Raymond Biggs	0	0	0	0
Luke Johnson	1	0	2	0
Ray Robinson	1	0	2	1
John Slater	1	1	3	0
Willis Stone	1	0	2	0
Owen Stotlar	0	0	0	3
William Wallace	3	0	6	0
TOTAL	9	6	24	5

ROCKFORD (23)
Coach E.U. McDonald

Player	FG-A	FT-A	Pts	PF
Ralph Baker	7	1	15	2
Wesley Carlson	1	0	2	1
George Fridley	0	0	0	0
Warren Kasch	2	0	4	1
Thomas Ledger	1	0	2	2
Carl Miltmore	0	0	0	0
Edward Pelgen	0	0	0	1
TOTAL	11	1	23	7

Marion	4	7	4	9	—	24
Rockford	8	10	4	1	—	23

Officials: Fred "Brick" Young, Howard Millard.

If bigger is better, the 1921 tournament was the ultimate, the pinnacle, the be-all and end-all. If it had a theme, it would have been "21 in '21," as the champions of 21 district tournaments battled it out in the largest state tournament ever staged.

The field included small schools — Trenton (enrollment 53) and Fairbury (enrollment 140) were the tiniest — mid-sized schools like Marion and Streator, and just about every large school on the map: Elgin, Champaign, Decatur, Galesburg, Moline, New Trier, Peoria, Rockford, and Springfield.

The plethora of teams required a preliminary round conducted on Thursday before the "first round" even got under way.

The fans loved it.

It was non-stop basketball for three days, Illinois-style, that at its end pitted perennial favorite Rockford against a battle-weary squad from Marion. In its first three games at state, Rockford was tested only once, a one-point quarterfinal win over Streator.

Meanwhile, to reach the championship Marion had to struggle through four games, three of them overtime affairs. In the opener, Marion needed an extra period to nudge Elgin 15-14, then required two overtimes to gain a 19-15 decision over Galesburg. After a breather against Macomb in the quarterfinals, Marion went into overtime once again in the semis, beating New Trier 26-24. The consensus was the southern Illinois team would be too tuckered out to take down the venerable squad from the north.

For three quarters those predictions were right on the money as Rockford and its star Ralph Baker controlled the flow of the game. Then the underdog awoke. With Marion trailing 22-15, Norman Belford ignited a rally with two baskets, and William Wallace capped it with a

pretty shot to take the lead. For the last two and a half minutes, Marion held the ball under the Rockford basket, "an exhibition of stalling that has never been equaled in the tournament," according to the *Champaign News-Gazette*. Marion's 24-23 triumph brought the championship to southern Illinois for the third time in four years.

While the 21-team field was a popular and financial success, the logistics of running such a large tournament stretched the university to its fullest. Even as play got under way, urgent calls were made to fraternities to handle the influx of players and their rooters.

A smaller state tournament was needed. But how could it be achieved?

Tournament reform was right around the corner.

1921

Charles W. Whitten, who ran the IHSAA from 1922 to 1942.

In his annual report, Will C. Robb, the outgoing vice president of the IHSAA Board of Control, wrote that "the basketball tournaments might very well become a source of appreciable income for the association treasury." True enough for the tournament as a whole, but the state final itself simply could not continue to expand haphazardly.

To solve the problem, the Association turned to its new vice president, Charles W. Whitten, principal of DeKalb High School, and asked him to restructure the tournament. Whitten's plan called for three levels: district tournaments,

reduction of teams (and games) from 21 to four.

In terms of school enrollment, bigger was not necessarily better during the early years of the tournament, as 1922 showed. In the semifinals, undefeated Atwood, enrollment 123, outscored Peoria 5-0 in the fourth quarter to sneak into the championship game. Atwood's opponent was Arthur Trout's Centralia team, enrollment 483, and an easy winner over Rockford (with 2,225 students) in the other semifinal contest.

Centralia had fallen four times during the season, twice to the defending cham-

CENTRALIA
State Champions of 1922

FRONT ROW (left to right): Vernon Drenckpohl, Fred Holland. SECOND ROW: Lloyd Keller, Marc Hughes, Wiley Cox, Leonard Parker, Harry Lender. THIRD ROW: Clarence "Bud" Saul, John Lichtenfeld, Clarence Barr, L.N. Hanna, T.W. Clarida, Coach Arthur Trout.

State Final Tournament Scores
Semifinals
Centralia 31, Rockford 23
Atwood 17, Peoria 15
Finals
Rockford 45, Peoria 26 (third place)
Centralia 24, Atwood 16 (title)

Scoring Leaders

Player, School	G	FG	FT	Pts
Ralph Baker, Rockford	2	7	14	28
Marc Hughes, Centralia	2	4	13	21
Angelsea, Peoria	2	6	6	18
Claude Ware, Atwood	2	4	7	15
Harold Gleichman, Rockford	2	7	0	14
Stevens, Rockford	2	7	0	14
Harry Lender, Centralia	2	7	0	14

All-Tournament First Team

Player, School	Ht.	Yr.
Ralph Baker, Rockford		Sr.
Wiley Cox, Centralia	5-9	Sr.
Leonard Parker, Centralia	6-2	Sr.
Wayne Reeder, Atwood	6-1	Sr.
Claude Ware, Atwood	6-0	Sr.

Championship Game Box Score
Men's Gym Annex, Urbana, March 18, 1922

CENTRALIA (24)
Coach Arthur Trout

Player	FG-A	FT-A	Pts	PF
Clarence Barr	0	0	0	0
Wiley Cox	6	0	12	2
Marc Hughes	0	6	6	2
Lloyd Keller	1	0	2	0
Harry Lender	2	0	4	2
John Lichtenfeld	0	0	0	0
Leonard Parker	0	0	0	1
TOTAL	9	6	24	7

ATWOOD (16)
Coach Lawrence Hamilton

Player	FG-A	FT-A	Pts	PF
Hugh Harshbarger	3	0	6	1
Laverne Manaugh	1	0	2	1
Stoughton Reeder	1	0	2	0
Wayne Reeder	1	0	2	1
Claude Ware	1	2	4	2
TOTAL	7	2	16	5

Centralia	5	7	7	5	—	24
Atwood	5	7	2	2	—	16

Officials: Fred "Brick" Young, M.W. Driggs.

1922

sectional tournaments of seven or eight teams each, and a four-team state final.

A total of 429 teams entered the state tournament in 1922, with the new sectionals creating a frenzy at Aurora, Decatur, Peoria, and Mt. Vernon. In the sectional championship games, Rockford defeated New Trier, Atwood downed Bloomington, Peoria defeated Watseka, and Centralia beat Marion.

But in contrast to the well-received sectionals, the state final was considered a dud. The *Champaign Daily Gazette* moaned that "the state finals did not furnish the brand of basketball that was expected." That reaction was inevitable, given the

pions from Marion. But in the title game, they displayed the skill and brains required to win a grueling tournament. Falling behind late in the game, Atwood was content to stand under the basket and wait out a stall. The *Gazette* gave credit to Trout, noting that had the Atwood boys "been coached, they might have displayed a better brand of ball."

Blessed with a tournament that had become, if anything, too successful, IHSAA board members finally had the means to take themselves out of the loop. In July 1922, they hired Whitten as the Association's first full-time executive.

VILLA GROVE
State Champions of 1923

Coach Curtis Pulliam.
Team members included:
Wayne Hulse, William Barmore, Kenneth
Reynolds, Ernest Combs, Harold Sanders.

All but lost in the annals of tournament history is a David-and-Goliath story nearly matching Hebron's historic triumph in 1952.

The sectional title games, representing the final eight teams in the tournament, showed an interesting mix of large and small schools. In the most closely watched contest, Rockford traveled to Joliet's new field house and beat the local team 15-10. In other games, Villa Grove defeated Mt. Pulaski at Decatur, Canton upset Peoria Manual at Peoria, and Greenville downed Marion at Centralia.

Undefeated in 1923, Rockford was all but conceded the title. The *News-Gazette* reported that "Rockford has come to basketball tournaments here for five years, each year heralded as unbeatable. Just what will happen no one dares say."

The other three teams apparently offered little competition. Neither Greenville (four losses) nor Canton (five) seemed to be of championship caliber; only little Villa Grove, with a 21-2 record, appeared to have a prayer against the perennial favorite. Rockford's student body of 2,349 was more than 12 times that of Villa Grove. But one of Villa Grove's 185 students was William Barmore, and in the championship game, he put on a basket-shooting clinic.

In a tight game that neither team led by more than four points, the 125-pound forward found his range late in the game, shooting mostly underhanded shots. The *News-Gazette* delivered this report:

"With but eight minutes to play, the overworked, seemingly dead-tired lightweights looked hopelessly beaten. But a change of pass tactics gave the ball to Barmore just outside the free throw line.

Four times on this play the light-haired boy swished them through the net, and added a single count by the foul route, and the final gun brought the whole town on the floor to carry Barmore and the rest of the newly crowned state champs triumphantly from the court."

Barmore finished with 22 points in the 32-29 victory, tying Lynch Conway's title-game record from 1908.

Villa Grove High School is still in business but has never returned to the state final tournament, leaving it with a perfect record: one appearance, one state championship.

1923

State Final Tournament Scores
Semifinals
Rockford 36, Greenville 23
Villa Grove 38, Canton 23
Finals
Canton 12, Greenville 10 (third place)
Villa Grove 32, Rockford 29 (title)

Scoring Leaders

Player, School	G	FG	FT	Pts
Louis Behr, Rockford	2	12	7	31
William Barmore, Villa Grove	2	12	7	31
Kenneth Reynolds, Villa Grove	2	12	0	24
Harold Gleichman, Rockford	2	11	0	22
Oliver Mettler, Canton	2	4	11	19

All-Tournament First Team

Player, School	Ht.	Yr.
William Barmore, Villa Grove	5-6	Sr.
Louis Behr, Rockford		
Ernest Combs, Villa Grove	5-10	Sr.
Harold Gleichman, Rockford		
Clifford Nelson, Rockford		
Kenneth Reynolds, Villa Grove	5-10	Sr.

Championship Game Box Score
Men's Gym Annex, Urbana, March 17, 1923

VILLA GROVE (32)
Coach Curtis Pulliam

Player	FG-A	FT-A	Pts	PF
William Barmore	8	6-12	22	1
Ernest Combs	0	0-0	0	3
Wayne Hulse	1	0-0	2	1
Kenneth Reynolds	4	0-0	8	1
Harold Sanders	0	0-0	0	0
TOTAL	13	6-12	32	6

ROCKFORD (29)
Coach E.U. McDonald

Player	FG-A	FT-A	Pts	PF
Louis Behr	4	5-11	13	1
Harold Gleichman	7	0-0	14	0
Ralph Johnson	0	0-0	0	0
Fred Kulberg	0	0-0	0	3
Clifford Nelson	0	0-0	0	0
Robert Reitsch	0	0-0	0	2
Anthony Roskie	1	0-0	2	1
TOTAL	12	5-11	29	7

Villa Grove	9	6	7	10	—	32
Rockford	8	6	7	8	—	29

Officials: Fred "Brick" Young, Sam Barry.

ELGIN
State Champions of 1924

FRONT ROW (left to right): Ted Stern, Bates Stone, Doug Mills, Herb Hill, Haywood Biggers.
SECOND ROW: Coach Mark Wilson, Elmer Johnson, Andy Solyom, Louis "Soup" Semeny, Harry Lange, Fred Lehman, Faculty Mgr. E.C. Waggoner.

1924

The state championship returned to the northern part of the state for the first time in five years, but not without a coaching curiosity.

Play started with thirty-five district tournaments. The winners funneled into the four sectionals, where none of the championship games was particularly close. At Joliet, Elgin defeated Batavia; at Peoria, Canton beat Bloomington. Further south at Decatur, Athens was a winner over Morrisonville, and at Benton, West Frankfort downed Centralia.

Of the coaches leading teams into the state tournament, two were fast on their way to becoming legends. Canton's mentor, Mark Peterman, already had 1923's third-place finish to his credit, with even greater tournament success ahead. Athens was headed by H. V. Porter, a Renaissance man in every sense of the word: future administrator for the IHSAA and the National Federation of State High School Associations, father of March Madness, and future inductee in the Naismith Memorial Basketball Hall of Fame. Elgin, on the other hand, was headed by Mark Wilson, who had coached only seven varsity basketball games in his career.

At the start of the season, Elgin had hired Otto Vogel, a 24-year-old outfielder with the Chicago Cubs, to direct the squad. When spring training beckoned, Vogel shipped out for California. Wilson, Elgin's football coach, took over the 13-1 squad and marched them directly to the state finals. Meanwhile, out in Los Angeles, Vogel broke his wrist and was already out of action by the time his former team took the court in the Men's Gym Annex.

In the semifinals, Athens slipped past West Frankfort and Elgin edged Canton to set up the championship affair.

Weight was considered just as important as height in those days, but the "heavyweight" Elgin team surprised the experts by also displaying speedy floor work, a clever offense, and a tight "five-man defense." Louis "Soup" Semeny starred in the title game, scoring 12 points as Elgin kept Athens at bay throughout.

Elgin went on to finish sixth in the National Basketball Tournament at the University of Chicago after losing in the first round to the eventual champion. At the end of the run, Wilson went back to football and Elgin started looking for another new basketball coach.

State Final Tournament Scores
Semifinals
Elgin 16, Canton 14
Athens 26, West Frankfort (Frankfort) 19
Finals
Canton 30, West Frankfort (Frankfort) 6 (third place)
Elgin 28, Athens 17 (title)

Scoring Leaders

Player, School	G	FG	FT	Pts
Oliver Mettler, Canton	2	8	2	18
Bruce Perkins, Athens	2	6	4	16
Louis "Soup" Semeny, Elgin	2	6	3	15
Sherman Deutch, Canton	2	4	4	12
John Zalenas, Athens	2	4	3	11
Henry Winterbauer, Athens	2	4	3	11
Harry Lange, Elgin	2	3	5	11

All-Tournament First Team

Player, School	Ht.	Yr.
John Bokoski, Athens	5-10	Sr.
Sherman Deutch, Canton	5-10	Sr.
Herbert Hill, Elgin	5-9	Jr.
Harry Lange, Elgin	6-1	Sr.
Louis "Soup" Semeny, Elgin	5-10	Sr.

Championship Game Box Score
Men's Gym Annex, Urbana, March 22, 1924

ELGIN (28)
Coach Mark Wilson

Player	FG-A	FT-A	Pts	PF
Herbert Hill	1	1-2	3	2
Harry Lange	3	3-5	9	2
Fred Lehman	0	0-0	0	0
Doug Mills	1	4-5	6	1
Louis "Soup" Semeny	4	2-2	10	2
Andrew Solyom	0	0-0	0	4
TOTAL	9	10-14	28	11

ATHENS (17)
Coach H.V. Porter

Player	FG-A	FT-A	Pts	PF
John Bokoski	0	0-2	0	2
Herman Hibbs	1	1-1	3	0
Bruce Perkins	3	0-0	6	0
Edward Winterbauer	0	0-0	0	0
Henry Winterbauer	2	2-5	6	2
John Zalenas	0	2-2	2	1
TOTAL	6	5-10	17	5

Elgin	9	8	4	7	—	28
Athens	1	6	5	5	—	17

Officials: Fred "Brick" Young, Art Swedberg

Elgin's Maroons were the first team to win back-to-back state titles.

The results of the preliminary rounds of the 1925 tournament were just crazy enough to force the IHSAA to think about restructuring once again.

There were 37 district tournaments in 1925, meaning the four sectionals contained either nine or ten teams, requiring all kinds of byes and play-in games. And, oh, those sectional finals!

At Peoria, 3,000 people watched as Canton made two shots in the final minutes to defeat Peoria High 15-14. At Joliet, another 3,000 saw the defending state champs from Elgin beat Freeport 10-9. In southern Illinois, Marion upended Mt. Vernon 18-17 on Centralia's floor. And at Springfield, in the only sectional final not decided by one point, Champaign beat Athens 22-20 — in overtime.

Wouldn't they have made great quarterfinal games at Champaign-Urbana?

Another reason to expand: the University of Illinois would soon have a new arena with much more room for spectators. The New Gymnasium (Huff Gym) was under construction on the south edge of campus, making the 1925 state tournament the last to be played in the Men's Gym Annex.

Elgin, now coached by Cliff Adams, made sure it was a memorable one. No defending champion had ever advanced to the state title game, but the northerners quickly erased that barrier by downing Canton in the second semifinal. Champaign, making its fifth state tournament appearance, advanced with a win over Marion.

Elgin's team featured three starters from the previous season

— Doug Mills, Herbert Hill, and Andy Solyom — and the squad seemed to know its way around the Gym Annex floor very well, despite Champaign's hometown advantage. Mills and Chapman Wells scored with regularity and Solyom controlled the center jump nearly every time. Elgin led the entire game, becoming the first school to win back-to-back state titles.

Winning two in a row was hailed as a near-miracle at the time. It would be another 25 years before the feat was duplicated by Mt. Vernon.

In 1937, Mills coached Joliet into the state finals before moving to the University of Illinois, where he coached the famed "Whiz Kids" team of the 1940s and later served as athletic director.

State Final Tournament Scores

Semifinals

Champaign 23, Marion 15
Elgin 31, Canton 15

Finals

Canton 33, Marion 17 (third place)
Elgin 25, Champaign 17 (title)

Scoring Leaders

Player, School	G	FG	FT	Pts
Doug Mills, Elgin	2	10	2	22
Frank McCallister, Champaign	2	7	2	16
Gale Allen, Canton	2	5	5	15
Hurem Derment, Champaign	2	4	3	11
Gerald Slavik, Elgin	2	5	1	11

All-Tournament First Team

Player, School	Ht.	Yr.
Don Gamble, Champaign	5-11	Sr.
Herbert Hill, Elgin	5-9	Sr.
Frank McCallister, Champaign	6-1	Sr.
Doug Mills, Elgin	6-0	Sr.
Andrew Solyom, Elgin	5-11	Sr.

Championship Game Box Score

Men's Gym Annex, Urbana, March 21, 1925

ELGIN (25)
Coach Cliff Adams

Player	FG-A	FT-A	Pts	PF
Herbert Hill	1	2	4	0
Doug Mills	3	1	7	1
Gerald Slavik	2	1	5	0
Andrew Solyom	1	0	2	2
Chapman Wells	3	1	7	1
TOTAL	10	5	25	4

CHAMPAIGN (17)
Coach Les Moyer

Player	FG-A	FT-A	Pts	PF
Hurem Derment	1	2	4	1
Raymond Fisher	0	0	0	0
Don Gamble	1	0	2	3
Fred Hyland	1	3	5	0
William Johnson	0	0	0	0
Frank McCallister	2	2	6	0
TOTAL	5	7	17	4

Elgin	5	8	6	6	—	25
Champaign	4	1	8	4	—	17

Officials: Fred "Brick" Young, Art Swedberg.

1925

ELGIN
State Champions of 1925

FRONT ROW (left to right): Doug Mills, Andy Solyom, Herb Hill, Jerry Slavik, Carl Ackemann. SECOND ROW: Coach Cliff Adams, Oswald Hill, Chapman Wells, Roy Flora, Haywood Biggers, Faculty Mgr. E.O. Waggoner.

FREEPORT
State Champions of 1926

LEFT TO RIGHT:
Harold Shippee, Quinter Bere,
Herbert Keith, Howard
Broughton, Harold Neidigh,
Ralph Johnston,
Maurice McClanathan,
Ralph Ruthe, Herbert
Stimpert, Charles Stone,
Coach Glenn "Pat" Holmes.

1926

The 1926 tournament was full of milestones. For the first time, the University of Illinois' "New Gym," capacity 7,000, hosted the four sectional winners. Canton notched its fourth consecutive appearance in the state semifinals, a record. Athens was back for another run at the championship. And Freeport coach Pat Holmes was about to make history.

None of that was enough to keep sportswriters focused on the game. Instead, most of the scuttlebutt focused on expansion of the state final.

Afraid the University of Chicago's huge national high school basketball tournament was stealing the limelight, and jealous of Indiana's 16-team tourney, the *News-Gazette* demanded, "We want more than four teams in the state finals next year, and we don't mean maybe."

Standing resolutely against any change was IHSAA executive Charles W. Whitten. "What Indiana school officials and newspapers try to make their basketball state finals," he said, "is just what Illinois school officials are not trying to do, and that is to make the final championship battles a *spectacle*. Illinois school officials have often discussed the 16-team system, but will never adopt it under any circumstances."

Whitten was a powerful force in high school athletics, as stern and stubborn as they come, but even he lost a few battles.

In sectional play, Freeport defeated Elgin, the two-time defending state champion, before finishing off Joliet. Flora beat Christopher, Athens defeated Nokomis, and Canton downed Tremont in other sectional finals.

The state championship matched Canton, in its second title-game appearance, against Freeport.

Holmes, the Freeport coach, had played on the school's 1915 title squad, and with a win would become the first person to celebrate a state championship as both player and coach. The game was close for three quarters, but in the final frame Herbert Stimpert

cut loose with four field goals to cement the Freeport victory. While the Pretzels won for the second time, Canton settled for its second runner-up trophy. Stimpert finished with a game-high 15 points for Freeport.

Once again victory was credited to speed and height. But just as it appeared the giants of the north had developed a lock on the state championship, with three straight titles won by Northern Illinois Conference teams, the worm turned yet again.

State Final Tournament Scores
Semifinals

Canton 20, Flora 18
Freeport 21, Athens 15

Finals

Flora 23, Athens 14 (third place)
Freeport 24, Canton 13 (title)

Scoring Leaders

Player, School	G	FG	FT	Pts
Phil Mann, Flora	2	8	2	18
Herbert Stimpert, Freeport	2	7	3	17
Herbert Keith, Freeport	2	8	1	17
Elmer Knowles, Flora	2	4	5	13
Dick Morgan, Canton	2	5	2	12

All-Tournament First Team

Player, School	Ht.	Yr.
Herbert Keith, Freeport	5-8	Sr.
Maurice McClanahan, Freeport	5-10	Sr.
Dick Morgan, Canton	5-9	Sr.
Herbert Stimpert, Freeport	6-1	Sr.
Jim Wells, Athens	6-0	Sr.

Championship Game Box Score
Huff Gym, Champaign, March 20, 1926

FREEPORT (24)
Coach Glenn "Pat" Holmes

Player	FG-A	FT-A	Pts	PF
Howard Broughton	0	0-0	0	1
Herbert Keith	3	0-4	6	2
Maurice McClanahan	1	1-2	3	2
Ralph Ruthe	0	0-0	0	1
Herbert Stimpert	6	3-4	15	2
TOTAL	10	4-10	24	8

CANTON (13)
Coach Mark Peterman

Player	FG-A	FT-A	Pts	PF
Russell Cardosi	0	0-0	0	2
Nathan Deutch	1	1-2	3	1
Eddie Lane	2	1-2	5	2
Dick Morgan	1	1-3	3	0
Dave Vance	0	2-2	2	0
TOTAL	4	5-9	13	5

Freeport	7	2	5	10	—	24
Canton	4	6	2	1	—	13

Officials: Fred "Brick" Young, Art Swedberg.

Charles W. Whitten may have been dead-set against turning the state final into a spectacle, but something had to give somewhere. With 11 teams from the Chicago Public League participating for the first time, and 48 district tournaments spread across the state, expansion of some sort was inevitable.

The IHSAA solved the immediate problem by increasing the number of sectionals — and the number of state finalists — from four to eight. The "big tournament" proponents didn't get their wish, but the stone wall of resistance to a 16-team format was crumbling.

The first eight-team final since 1915 included two new entries — East St. Louis and Mt. Olive — and six schools that had made it to state before: Athens, Champaign, Mt. Carmel, Peoria, Rockford, and St. Charles.

The two northern teams suffered resounding defeats in the quarterfinals, leaving the field wide open for another region to claim basketball superiority. East St. Louis, Peoria, and Champaign were all easy winners, but it was Mt. Carmel (enrollment 416), and a pair of cousins, Elbert and Robert Kamp, who drew raves for their play against Athens.

The southeastern Illinois school continued to impress in the semifinal against Champaign as the Kamps, both 6-foot juniors, continued to dominate, totaling 21 points. Peoria, seeking to repeat its 1908 championship, walloped East St. Louis in the other semifinal.

Unintimidated by history, Mt. Carmel came out swinging against Peoria and took a 13-7 first-quarter lead. The scoring slowed after that point, but Peoria could not recover. The Kamps combined for 13 points, but Mt. Carmel's George Eaton led all scorers with 11. After the gun sounded, a huge throng carried off the players on their shoulders, snake-dancing to the beat of an American Legion drum corps.

In the end, the title bout was "a triumph for the Indiana style of basketball offensive," according to the *Urbana Courier.* "Break-and-run, shoot-and-shoot-again, long passes and a fast-breaking offense of heavy artillery and accurate aim — that was the machinery of Mt. Carmel's attack, which emanated from competition with the strong Indiana teams of the Wabash Valley."

MT. CARMEL, *State Champions of 1927*

FRONT ROW (left to right): Coach Cliff Garrett, Robert Kamp, George Eaton, Frank Henneberger, Elbert "Babe" Kamp, Alfred Elzey. SECOND ROW: Crawford, George Crum, Everett Hawkins, Davidson, Wise.

1927

State Final Tournament Scores

Quarterfinals
East St. Louis 26, Rockford 12
Peoria 42, St. Charles 15
Champaign 34, Mt. Olive 21
Mt. Carmel 35, Athens 19

Semifinals
Peoria 33, East St. Louis 11
Mt. Carmel 35, Champaign 24

Finals
East St. Louis 25, Champaign 20 (third place)
Mt. Carmel 24, Peoria 18 (title)

Scoring Leaders

Player, School	G	FG	FT	Pts
Elbert "Babe" Kamp, Mt. Carmel	3	15	6	36
George Soper, Peoria	3	16	2	34
George Eaton, Mt. Carmel	3	11	7	29
James Greene, Peoria	3	12	5	29
Verne Carson, Champaign	3	10	6	26

All-Tournament First Team

Player, School	Ht.	Yr.
Verne Carson, Champaign	6-2	Sr.
John Gimming, Peoria		Jr.
Elbert "Babe" Kamp, Mt. Carmel	6-0	Jr.
Robert Kamp, Mt. Carmel	6-0	Jr.
George Soper, Peoria		So.

Championship Game Box Score

Huff Gym, Champaign, March 26, 1927

MT. CARMEL (24)
Coach Cliff Garrett

Player	FG-A	FT-A	Pts	PF
George Crum	0	0-0	0	0
George Eaton	4	3-5	11	0
Alfred Elzey	0	0-0	0	1
Frank Henneberger	0	0-0	0	3
Elbert "Babe" Kamp	4	0-0	8	1
Robert Kamp	2	1-1	5	4
TOTAL	10	4-6	24	9

PEORIA (18)
Coach Salen Herke

Player	FG-A	FT-A	Pts	PF
John Gimming	0	0-1	0	2
James Greene	2	3-5	7	1
George Soper	3	2-5	8	1
Lorenz Tower	0	0-1	0	0
Arthur Verner	1	1-3	3	1
TOTAL	6	6-15	18	5

Mt. Carmel	13	4	4	3	—	24
Peoria	7	4	6	1	—	18

Officials: Fred "Brick" Young, Leo Johnson.

1928

CANTON
State Champions of 1928

FRONT ROW (left to right):
Chester Eddy, Charles Coleman,
Russell Cardosi, Fred Schnell,
Frank Mace. SECOND ROW:
Harry Maxwell, Edgar Brons,
Joe Moore, Al Pschirrer,
Fred Carmack, Coach Mark
Peterman.

1928

After finishing third, third, third, and second in four straight tourneys from 1923 to 1926, Mark Peterman brought another Canton squad to Champaign in 1928 with only one goal in mind — the state championship — and an unpopular way to achieve it: the "slow-break."

The slow-break was Peterman's special contribution to basketball strategy, born of necessity in 1926 when his team came up short, so to speak. Modern fans would call Peterman's invention "the four corners," or less charitably, "stalling." In 1928 it was a revelation. Dazzled by Peterman's success, many coaches adopted the new offense, depressing scoring totals for years to come.

According to a *News-Gazette* report on one Canton game, "the ball was dribbled back away from the center of the court. It was apparently tossed about aimlessly. The opponents would wonder what it was all about and seem at a loss. Then the ball would suddenly be whipped to a player standing unmolested under the hoop, or an opposing player would neglect to cover a Canton player, who would slowly and coolly take a pot shot at the basket."

With 786 students, Canton was the largest school in the eight-team tournament field. Three others, Griggsville (130 students), Witt (105), and tiny Hutsonville (90), remain prime examples of the

brief period in tournament history when even the smallest schools, for reasons that have never been fully understood, somehow managed to hold their own with the big boys.

Canton came out stalling in the quarterfinals and connected on 10 of 19 field goal attempts in an easy 23-11 decision over Benton. Also winning was West Aurora, making its first state tournament appearance, along with two of the Little Davids, Witt and Griggsville.

The Canton-Witt semifinal was touted as "the irresistible force meeting the immovable object." In this case, Canton's methodical play overcame the speedy attack of Witt, but by a mere 19-17 count.

The title game was best summed up by the *News-Gazette*'s headline: "West High of Aurora Bewildered by Sleepy System of Peterman." With a final score of 18-9, the 1928 championship game will undoubtedly remain the lowest-scoring of all time (although the 2006 Class AA title game gave it an unexpected challenge, if adjusted for score inflation).

Reflecting popular sentiment, University of Illinois coach Craig Ruby remarked that "the Canton system of basketball is the best way to win" but was so uninteresting it ought to be outlawed.

Canton finished second in the national tournament, losing to Ashland, Kentucky 15-10.

State Final Tournament Scores

Quarterfinals
Witt 33, Streator (Twp.) 31 (OT)
Canton 23, Benton 11
Aurora (West) 28, Rochelle 14
Griggsville 22, Hutsonville 21

Semifinals
Canton 19, Witt 17
Aurora (West) 31, Griggsville 24

Finals
Witt 40, Griggsville 26 (third place)
Canton 18, Aurora (West) 9 (title)

Scoring Leaders

Player, School	G	FG	FT	Pts
Clarence Anderson, Aurora (West)	3	9	9	27
James Beadle, Griggsville	3	10	4	24
Alois Hanisko, Witt	3	10	3	23
Harry Brown, Griggsville	3	11	1	23
George Chervinko, Witt	3	8	5	21

All-Tournament First Team

Player, School	Ht.	Yr.
William Barnes, Aurora (West)	6-2	Sr.
Harry Brown, Griggsville	6-4	So.
Russell Cardosi, Canton	5-10	Sr.
George Chervinko, Witt	5-8	Sr.
Charles Coleman, Canton	5-10	Jr.
William Connell, Streator (Twp.)	5-11	Jr.
Virgil Dixon, Streator (Twp.)	6-2	Sr.
Chester Eddy, Canton	5-9	So.

Championship Game Box Score
Huff Gym, Champaign, March 24, 1928

CANTON (18)
Coach Mark Peterman

Player	FG-A	FT-A	Pts	PF
Russell Cardosi	0	1-2	1	0
Fred Carmack	0	0-0	0	0
Charles Coleman	3	1-1	7	2
Chester Eddy	3	2-2	8	0
Frank Mace	0	2-3	2	3
Frederick Schnell	0	0-1	0	4
TOTAL	6	6-9	18	9

AURORA (WEST) (9)
Coach Ralph Fletcher

Player	FG-A	FT-A	Pts	PF
Elmer Alexander	0	0-0	0	1
Clarence Anderson	3	3-7	9	3
William Barnes	0	0-1	0	0
Phillip Hazlett	0	0-1	0	0
Ray Vorreis	0	0-0	0	0
Arthur Whitson	0	0-0	0	1
TOTAL	3	3-9	9	5

Canton	2	6	2	8	—	18
Aurora (West)	3	0	3	3	—	9

Officials: Fred "Brick" Young, Lyle Clarno.

Johnston City 30
Champaign 2-1

Canton did not qualify for the 1929 state finals, but the spirit of Mark Peterman pervaded Huff Gym.

While some teams still preferred the fast game, others seemed to have honed the slow-break to perfection. Case in point: Johnston City.

Coach La Rue Van Meter denied that his team played "the Canton game," but it was surely some variant thereof. In the southern squad's quarterfinal game against Lincoln, time practically stood still for 16 minutes. The resulting 2-1 halftime score was the lowest in tournament history.

Johnston City won the contest 14-9, prompting this comment from the *News-Gazette*: "While we are quite willing to admit that Johnston City has some basketball team, a truly great one, we do NOT like their style of play. The people want 'forward march,' not 'backward march.' "

In another quarterfinal game, Coach Adolph Rupp, soon to become a legend at the University of Kentucky, guided Freeport past Wheaton. Champaign's win over Mt. Carmel and Peoria's victory over Witt rounded out the first day's action.

In the semifinals, Champaign had an easy time with Freeport, and Johnston City pulled out a come-from-behind, 19-15 victory over Peoria.

Just as in 1925, the hometown crowd was rooting fiercely for a Maroon championship. Champaign forced Johnston City to speed up its game somewhat, pulling to within 19-18 at the end of three quarters. But Johnston City proved too fast, too accurate, and too cagey for Champaign, closing out the game in easy fashion 30-21.

The previous year Van Meter, who attended Bloomington High School in 1916 but did not make its championship squad, had to dismiss his seniors and turn to a group of juniors and sophomores. Players like Hubert Pearce, Tony Blazine, and Ralph Davison turned the mining community of Johnston City from a football town into a basketball hotbed practically overnight.

Meanwhile, the 1929 tournament marked the end of an era on the court. It was the last of 12 straight state meets officiated by Fred "Brick" Young, sports editor of the *Bloomington Pantagraph*.

JOHNSTON CITY, State Champions of 1929

FRONT ROW (left to right): Hubert Pearce, Ralph Davison, Hubert Groves, Tony Blazine, Albert Feduris. SECOND ROW: William Polikaitis, Stanley Sudosky, Dwight Hafeli, Charles Hafeli, Marshall Ellis, Coach LaRue Van Meter. THIRD ROW: Asst. Coach L.A. Alderman, John Podlesnik, Raymond Hobbs, Clyde Jobe, Ira Clark, Carl Williams, Cecil Fletcher.

State Final Tournament Scores

Quarterfinals
Champaign 43, Mt. Carmel 30
Freeport 30, Wheaton 28
Peoria 27, Witt 18
Johnston City 14, Lincoln 9

Semifinals
Champaign 40, Freeport 24
Johnston City 19, Peoria 15

Finals
Freeport 27, Peoria 15 (third place)
Johnston City 30, Champaign 21 (title)

Scoring Leaders

Player, School	G	FG	FT	Pts
Albert Hall, Champaign	3	10	6	26
Don Brewer, Freeport	3	10	6	26
George Soper, Peoria	3	8	9	25
William Hagerman, Champaign	3	9	5	23
Danny Sullivan, Freeport	3	9	3	21

All-Tournament First Team

Player, School	Ht.	Yr.
Roger Cox, Champaign	6-3	Sr.
Ralph Davison, Johnston City	5-10	Jr.
Albert Feduris, Johnston City	6-0	So.
William Hagerman, Champaign	6-2	Sr.
George Soper, Peoria		Sr.

Championship Game Box Score

Huff Gym, Champaign, March 23, 1929

JOHNSTON CITY (30)
Coach LaRue Van Meter

Player	FG-A	FT-A	Pts	PF
Tony Blazine	3	1-2	7	1
Ralph Davison	2	4-5	8	1
Albert Feduris	1	0-1	2	2
Hubert Groves	1	0-0	2	1
Dwight Hafeli	0	1-1	1	0
Hubert Pearce	5	0-1	10	3
TOTAL	12	6-10	30	8

CHAMPAIGN (21)
Coach Les Moyer

Player	FG-A	FT-A	Pts	PF
Fred Armstrong	0	0-0	0	0
Roger Cox	0	0-0	0	1
Emerson Dexter	1	0-0	2	3
Roy Goudie	0	1-3	1	1
William Hagerman	2	2-3	6	1
Albert Hall	4	2-3	10	1
Archie McDonald	1	0-1	2	0
TOTAL	8	5-10	21	7

Johnston City	10	4	5	11	—	30
Champaign	10	3	5	3	—	21

Officials: Fred "Brick" Young, Carl Johnson.

TEAMS

Selected by Scott Johnson

Rockford, 1911

Frank Thomas and Frank Johnson starred as Rockford tossed aside three state tournament opponents like matchsticks, wrapping up with a 45-point win over Mt. Carroll in the title game. Four of the five starters were named to the all-tournament team and Rockford finished 19-1.

Freeport, 1915

Freeport (18-2) doubled the score — at least — on every opponent in the state finals and won the title game over Springfield going away, 27-11. As with Rockford of 1911, four of the five starting players were named to the all-tournament team. The fifth, Pat Holmes, later coached Freeport to a state title.

Rockford, 1919

Another powerhouse from Rockford with another one-two scoring punch in Rex Enright and Harry Englund. Rolled over Springfield 39-20 in the title game to wrap up the season with a sparkling 23-1 mark.

Elgin, 1924

The first of Elgin's back-to-back champions featured unstoppable stars Louis "Soup" Semeny and Doug Mills. With only one loss against Illinois teams, Elgin went on to the national tournament and finished sixth with a final record of 25-3. Mills returned in 1925 to lead a second band of state champs.

Canton, 1928

Mark Peterman's slow-break strategy reached its perfection in 1928. Canton lost six regular-season games but waited out a state championship, then took second in the national tournament of champions at the University of Chicago, finishing at 37-7.

COACHES

Arthur Trout
Centralia

The first coach to win two state titles was one of the first permanent faculty coaches and easily the most successful of the bunch. Won 809 games in his 37-year career and was the first to win three state championships (1918, 1922, 1942).

Mark Peterman
Canton

Peterman's slow-break strategy was so successful (and so widely imitated) that the rule book was changed to thwart it. Still the only coach to win titles at two different schools (Canton 1928, Springfield 1935) and the only coach to bring home seven state-tournament trophies.

Salen Herke
Peoria

Herke directed seven teams to state from 1919 to 1935, winning four trophies topped by a runner-up finish in 1927. Retired from coaching in 1943 with 409 wins.

Les Moyer
Champaign

Moyer's early Champaign teams set the stage for later triumphs by Harry Combes. Won second twice with his Maroons, in 1925 and 1929, sandwiching in a third place in 1927. In all, Moyer-led squads made six appearances from 1925 to 1938.

H. V. Porter
Athens

In his abbreviated coaching career, H.V. Porter took Cinderella Athens (enrollment around 160) to the ball three times, earning second in 1924 and fourth in 1926. Moved into IHSA job in 1928 and on to the Naismith Memorial Basketball Hall of Fame in 1960.

PLAYERS

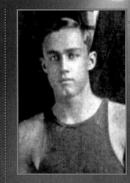

Lynch Conway, *Peoria, 1908*
Peoria's star forward exploded for 22 points in the first state championship game, a record that stood for 42 years. Went on to a stellar career at Bradley Polytechnic Institute and was later as an athletic official.

Richard Liitt, *Rock Island, 1908-09-10*
Liitt was the only player of the era to be named to three all-tournament teams. His tournament career point total, 154, was not exceeded until 1950. His tournament career free-throw total, 70, remains the record 97 years later.

Herbert Pihl, *Galesburg, 1912-13*
Pihl was the scoring star of Galesburg's champions. Tallied 38 points in a second place finish in 1912 and 55 more the next year, including 21 in a title-game triumph over Peoria Manual.

Leo Koehler, *Freeport, 1914-15*
A two-time all-tournament selection, Koehler guided Freeport from a runner-up finish in 1914 to the state title in 1915. Finished third in scoring both years, behind players who shot all of their team's free throws. Koehler made only one.

Layard Mace, *Bloomington, 1916-17*
Mace was an all-tourney pick two years running. Bloomington won the title in 1916 and finished third in 1917, when Mace led all scorers with 32 points.

Max "Hippo" Poscover, *Springfield, 1917-19*
Poscover helped Springfield to a state title in 1917 as a sophomore, then easily led the 1919 field in scoring (58 points in four games) as Springfield finished second. Went on to a Hall of Fame career at Davis and Elkins College in Elkins, West Virginia.

Leland Stilwell, *Olney, 1920*
The tournament's first superstar scorer, wowed crowds in 1920 with astounding 34-point game against Champaign. Starred at the University of Illinois and later served as the team doctor.

Ralph "Moon" Baker, *Rockford, 1919-20-21-22*
Played on four state tournament teams, winning first, second, and third, and scored 117 points in 11 games. A star football player at Northwestern University and member of the College Football Hall of Fame.

Doug Mills, *Elgin, 1924-25*
Star of the low-scoring "final-four" era, Mills played in only four tournament games (scoring 32 points), but won two state titles. Later coach of Joliet and the University of Illinois "Whiz Kids."

George Soper, *Peoria, 1927-29*
Never played for a champion (Peoria's best during his career was second in 1927), but he managed to score 59 points in six tourney games in low-scoring era. Named to the all-tourney team as a sophomore and again as a senior.

Sixteen is Sweet   1930–1950

When the court was silent and the bleachers empty, filling the gigantic gymnasium seemed an impossible task.

Huff offered a permanent home for the IHSA tournament, in a building designed specifically for basketball, but mostly it offered room to grow.

Nature abhors a vacuum. So when the seats in the upper reaches sat vacant for a couple of years, the inclination to add teams to the tournament field proved irresistible.

Huff Gym before the doors opened for the Sweet Sixteen, 1934.

A PAGEANT OF
BASKETBALL
UNSURPASSED IN THE WORLD

MANUAL (Peoria) '30

DECATUR '31-'36-'45

MORTON (Cicero) '32-'41

THORNTON '33

QUINCY '34

SPRINGFIELD '35

JOLIET '37

DUNDEE '38

ROCKFORD '39

GRANITE CITY '40

CENTRALIA '42

PARIS '43-'47

TAYLORVILLE '44

CHAMPAIGN '46

PINCKNEYVILLE '48

MT. VERNON '49-'50

The tournament ballooned from four teams to eight, and from eight teams to what many still consider the perfect expression of basketball bliss: the Sweet Sixteen.

Despite a Depression and a World War — or perhaps because of them — fans flocked to Champaign-Urbana to witness the passion and pageantry of high school's most spectacular sporting event.

Simply put, Huff was hoops heaven.

Curt Herron examines the tournament during an era of unbridled popularity, when there was no place in the world you would rather be on a cold night in March.

1930

The 1930 tournament may have lacked familiar faces, but it certainly didn't lack heart-pounding competition.

The early rounds featured a trio of slow-break spectaculars, including Georgetown's 1-0 victory over Homer at Westville, the lowest-scoring game in tournament history. Illiopolis needed six overtimes to nip Clinton 9-8 at Decatur, setting a tourney mark for longest game. In the sectionals, Peoria Manual needed three overtimes to pull out a 12-11 win over Canton.

Of the eight state finalists, Atwood was the most recent returnee, having qualified in 1922, while Beardstown, Carbondale and Waterman were all newcomers to the competition.

The quarterfinals were decided by a total of just eight points, the most competitive quarterfinal round in state history.

The nail-biting started when Bloomington nipped Abingdon 20-19 in the first game and then Olney won by the widest margin in a 21-18 victory over Carbondale.

The third quarterfinal went to Beardstown 29-27 over Waterman, but not before a state-finals-record four overtimes. Waterman, with only 85 students, put up a 15-10 lead after three quarters, but Beardstown tied the game at 17 at the end of regulation. Ernie Eveland's Waterman squad owned leads in each of the first three overtimes before Beardstown scored the first six points in the final period to wrap up the marathon.

In the last quarterfinal, Peoria Manual outlasted Atwood with an 18-16 victory.

The action wasn't quite as dramatic in the semifinals, as Bloomington defeated Olney by 10 points while Manual gained a 31-25 win over Beardstown.

In the title game, Bloomington aimed to become the first school to capture three state titles. Manual hoped to follow in the footsteps of Peoria High, which won the first state tournament in 1908.

Manual was directed by Telfer Mead, who had coached in Illinois prior to serving in World War I. After that, he became a college coach in Utah and Nebraska before returning to take the reins at Manual in December 1929.

Like Mead, Bloomington's Gene Harrison was making his first and only appearance as a coach at the state tournament. Bloomington's hopes were boosted by the presence of three starters who had played for a sectional-qualifying team at Danvers, a three-year school, in 1929: Don Argo, Clark Buescher and Gerald Cooke.

By contrast, Manual used a mostly junior lineup that made quick work of the title game. Manual took a 8-3 lead after one quarter and never trailed, though Bloomington managed to pull to within 25-20 early in the final period. Manual's 38-25 championship was its last until 1994.

State Final Tournament Scores

Quarterfinals

Bloomington 20, Abingdon 19
Olney 21, Carbondale 18
Beardstown 29, Waterman 27 (4 OT)
Peoria (Manual) 18, Atwood 16

Semifinals

Bloomington 33, Olney 23
Peoria (Manual) 31, Beardstown 25

Finals

Olney 27, Beardstown 18 (third place)
Peoria (Manual) 38, Bloomington 25 (title)

Scoring Leaders

Player, School	G	FG	FT	Pts
Charles Wolgemuth, Peoria (Manual)	3	13	3	29
Robert Clauss, Peoria (Manual)	3	13	1	27
Gerald Cooke, Bloomington	3	9	5	23
Clyde Peter Martin, Beardstown	3	8	6	22
Frank "Mike" Myers, Beardstown	2	10	1	21
Don Argo, Bloomington	3	8	5	21
Willis Venters, Beardstown	3	9	3	21

All-Tournament First Team

Player, School	Ht.	Yr.
Wilbur Auspurger, Bloomington	5-11	Jr.
Robert Clauss, Peoria (Manual)	5-8	Jr.
Gerald Cooke, Bloomington	6-0	Sr.
Neve Harms, Peoria (Manual)	6-2	Sr.
Clyde Peter Martin, Beardstown	6-4	Sr.

Championship Game Box Score

Huff Gym, Champaign, March 22, 1930

PEORIA (MANUAL) (38)
Coach Telfer Mead

Player	FG-A	FT-A	Pts	PF
Harvey Benson	0	3-3	3	2
Robert Clauss	5	0-0	10	2
Neve Harms	2	4-10	8	1
Ben Schwartz	1	0-0	2	3
Kenny Shoup	1	0-0	2	0
Charles Wolgemuth	6	1-3	13	2
TOTAL	15	8-16	38	10

BLOOMINGTON (25)
Coach Eugene Harrison

Player	FG-A	FT-A	Pts	PF
Don Argo	4	4-4	12	2
Wilbur Auspurger	1	1-4	3	1
Clark Buescher	0	1-1	1	4
Gerald Cooke	4	1-2	9	1
Jay Hallett	0	0-3	0	2
Woodruff Johnson	0	0-0	0	0
TOTAL	9	7-14	25	10

Peoria (Manual)	8	10	7	13	—	38
Bloomington	3	7	6	9	—	25

Officials: Art Cox, A.C. Serfling.

There was a new force to be reckoned with at the 1931 state tournament.

Decatur, which had won only one game in five previous trips to the state finals, made its first appearance under the direction of a new coach, Gay Kintner, who was destined to become a legend. All told, Kintner and his Reds would make 11 trips to the state finals and play for championships four times, winning three titles.

But as the 1931 state finals began, the focus was squarely on other teams, and with good reason.

Defending champion Peoria Manual was back with a new coach, Paul Holliday, and five players who had played in the 1930 state final game. In addition, 1929 champion Johnston City made the field. LaRue Van Meter was still calling the shots in Johnston City, but with only three players who had seen action in the 1929 finals.

Two schools reached state for the first time: local favorite Rantoul and the first qualifier from the Chicago Public School League, Harrison Tech. Prior to 1931, the cards were stacked against Chicago teams. Not all city schools belonged to the IHSAA, and the Public League used complicated rules concerning age and eligibility, right down to how many football players could be on a basketball team.

Decatur pulled off one of the biggest upsets in sectional play, knocking off Mark Peterman's Springfield team 16-14 to avenge a pair of earlier defeats. Johnston City rallied past Benton in the sectional semifinals at Carbondale and then beat Simpson in overtime in the finals. With an enrollment of just 29 students, Simpson was the smallest school ever to make the final 16 of the state tournament.

In the state semifinals, Decatur earned its first title-game appearance with a 27-20 win over Harrison.

Galesburg nipped Johnston City 28-27 in the other semifinal to secure its first trip to the championship game since 1913. A pair of reserves helped Galesburg pull out the dramatic victory. Joe Burford hit the tying bucket with 30 seconds left, and Edward Belden hit a free throw after time had expired.

The third-place game featured an interesting sibling rivalry. Tony Blazine, who had also played in the 1929 finals, was a senior at Johnston City while his brother Carl was a freshman on the Harrison Tech squad. Harrison rallied from a 16-1 deficit to beat Johnston City 28-26 in overtime. Although Carl won this Battle of the Blazines, Tony went on to a long pro football career with the Chicago Cardinals and New York Giants.

The finale started well for Galesburg, which held a 16-8 halftime advantage. But Decatur outscored the Streaks 12-2 in the third quarter, then scored the first eight points of the final period to claim a 30-26 victory. Ray Rex scored 12 points to lead the Reds while Culver "Coke" Mills paced Galesburg with 11 points.

With just 29 students, Simpson was the smallest school to reach the round of 16.

State Final Tournament Scores

Quarterfinals

Chicago (Harrison) 44, Mt. Vernon 33
Decatur 24, Collinsville 23
Galesburg 30, Peoria (Manual) 22
Johnston City 23, Rantoul 14

Semifinals

Decatur 27, Chicago (Harrison) 20
Galesburg 28, Johnston City 27

Finals

Chicago (Harrison) 28, Johnston City 26 (OT) (third place)
Decatur 30, Galesburg 26 (title)

Scoring Leaders

Player, School	G	FG	FT	Pts
Eddie Odron, Chicago (Harrison)	3	14	11	39
Ray Rex, Decatur	3	11	8	30
Culver Mills, Galesburg	3	10	9	29
Raymond Hobbs, Johnston City	3	9	5	23
Bruce Tyler, Mt. Vernon	1	11	1	23

All-Tournament First Team

Player, School	Ht.	Yr.
Robert Anderson, Galesburg	5-8	Sr.
Howard Ashely, Galesburg	5-9	Sr.
Tony Blazine, Johnston City	6-0	Sr.
Robert Gauen, Collinsville	6-4	Sr.
Paul Hill, Decatur		
Culver Mills, Galesburg	5-11	Sr.
Eddie Odron, Chicago (Harrison)		
Ray Rex, Decatur		Sr.
Al Schroeder, Decatur		
John Stuckey, Decatur		

Championship Game Box Score

Huff Gym, Champaign, March 21, 1931

DECATUR (30)
Coach Gay Kintner

Player	FG-A	FT-A	Pts	PF
Duane Garver	0	0-0	0	0
Eugene Heger	0	0-0	0	0
Paul Hill	2	3-6	7	0
Dwight Martin	0	0-0	0	4
Ray Rex	5	2-2	12	4
Al Schroeder	2	2-4	6	2
John Stuckey	0	5-5	5	1
TOTAL	9	12-17	30	11

GALESBURG (26)
Coach Gerald Phillips

Player	FG-A	FT-A	Pts	PF
Robert Anderson	2	1-4	5	1
Howard Ashely	1	0-0	2	3
Harold Henderson	0	4-4	4	2
Culver Mills	4	3-4	11	4
Paul Mitchell	0	2-3	2	4
Don Robinson	1	0-0	2	0
TOTAL	8	10-15	26	14

Decatur	2	6	12	10	— 30
Galesburg	6	10	2	8	— 26

Officials: Arthur Bergstrom, Milton Forsyth.

DECATUR, State Champions of 1931

FRONT ROW (left to right): Alfred Schroeder, Raymond Rex, John Stuckey, Paul Hill, Dwight Martin, Duane Garver.
SECOND ROW: Wayne Schroeder, Eugene Heger, Martin McDaniel, George Keller, Mgr. Russell Shafer, Coach Gay Kintner.

Morton won the national tournament in 1927 but had never before been to the state finals.

As the 1932 state tournament kicked off, no Cook County school had ever won a state title or, for that matter, played in the championship game. But Morton of Cicero was about to change all that, advancing to state five times in the next 14 years, with Coach Norm Ziebell leading the way the first four.

Although Morton had never before qualified for state, it had already earned fame by capturing the National Interscholastic Tournament at the University of Chicago in 1927. But after a third-place finish in the Suburban League in 1932, Morton didn't figure to challenge the likes of perennial power Canton or southern threats such as Lawrenceville and Benton.

Among other finalists, Hillsboro reached state for the first time since 1914 by beating Monticello, which starred future Champaign coach Harry Combes.

The first quarterfinal match-up at Huff Gym featured a tactical battle between Canton and its former coach, Mark Peterman, now in charge at Springfield. The game was close for three quarters before Canton claimed a 19-12 slowdown win.

In other quarterfinal action, Lawrenceville earned a shot at a state trophy by defeating Rantoul 31-21, and tourney-newcomer Kewanee edged Benton 12-11, setting a state-finals record for the fewest points by a winning team. Morton

had few troubles in a 29-12 win over Hillsboro.

Canton advanced to the championship game for the third time in seven years when it defeated Lawrenceville 24-20 in one semifinal. In the second game, Morton earned a berth in the finals with a 28-20 win over Kewanee.

Even though Peterman was no longer in charge, Canton still had plenty of history on its side in the championship game. For the eighth time in 15 seasons, the Plowboys were assured of a top-three finish. And against Morton, Archie Chadd's team appeared to be in a good

position to claim another first-place trophy after taking a 13-11 halftime lead. But Morton went on a 13-1 tear in the final quarter to post a 30-16 win. The three points scored by Canton in the second half constitute a title-game record for offensive futility.

Leading the way for Morton in the championship game was Erwin Eral, who scored nine points, while tourney scoring leader and all-tournament pick Irwin Kopecky added eight. Jim Vopicka, who would later coach two Morton teams to the state finals, also was all-tournament for the winners.

State Final Tournament Scores

Quarterfinals

Canton 19, Springfield 12
Lawrenceville 31, Rantoul 21
Kewanee 12, Benton 11
Cicero (Morton) 29, Hillsboro 12

Semifinals

Canton 24, Lawrenceville 20
Cicero (Morton) 28, Kewanee 20

Finals

Lawrenceville 27, Kewanee 19 (third place)
Cicero (Morton) 30, Canton 16 (title)

Scoring Leaders

Player, School	G	FG	FT	Pts
Irwin Kopecky, Cicero (Morton)	3	11	7	29
Paul Weger, Lawrenceville	3	11	6	28
James Vopicka, Cicero (Morton)	3	9	4	22
Elmer Mettler, Canton	3	9	3	21
Chalmer Price, Kewanee	3	7	6	20

All-Tournament First Team

Player, School	Ht.	Yr.
Irwin Kopecky, Cicero (Morton)	6-1	Sr.
Elmer Mettler, Canton		
Francis Vandermeer, Canton		
James Vopicka, Cicero (Morton)	6-1	Sr.
Paul Weger, Lawrenceville	5-11	Sr.

Championship Game Box Score

Huff Gym, Champaign, March 26, 1932

CICERO (MORTON) (30)
Coach Norm Ziebell

Player	FG-A	FT-A	Pts	PF
Stanley Cech	0	0	0	0
William Dostal	0	0	0	0
Erwin Eral	4	1	9	0
Charles Fendrych	1	0	2	1
Charles Hermanek	0	0	0	0
William Kokes	2	2	6	1
Irwin Kopecky	2	4	8	0
James Vopicka	2	1	5	1
TOTAL	11	8-10	30	3

CANTON (16)
Coach Archie Chadd

Player	FG-A	FT-A	Pts	PF
William Davis	0	0	0	0
Rolla McMullen	0	2	2	0
Elmer Mettler	3	1	7	2
Virgil Pilcher	0	0	0	0
Grady Stanfel	1	1	3	1
Melvin Taylor	0	1	1	1
Francis Vandermeer	1	1	3	2
TOTAL	5	6-7	16	6

Cicero (Morton)	6	5	6	13	—	30
Canton	4	9	2	1	—	16

Officials: Harlow Sutherland, R.L. Ashley.

CICERO (MORTON)
State Champions of 1932

FRONT ROW (left to right): Erwin Eral, William Kokes, Irwin Kopecky, James Vopicka, Charles Fendrych, Charles Hermanek. SECOND ROW: Coach Norm Ziebell, Mgr. Jania, William Dostal, Sirovy, Lang, Stanley Cech, Kayse, Mgr. Fencl, Trainer Hynd.

After suffering through the plodding slow-break style employed by Canton and the many copycat teams from other parts of the state, basketball fans were hoping for a change.

That's just what coach Jack Lipe and Thornton Township of Harvey brought to the state finals in 1933. By all accounts, the Flying Clouds played the most exciting brand of basketball the state of Illinois had ever seen. Lipe, a member of Decatur's 1921 state-final squad, employed a high-scoring, fast-break attack led by an athlete who would soon be hailed as one of the greatest in state history.

Lou Boudreau, the future National Baseball Hall of Fame shortstop, player-manager, and Chicago Cubs broadcaster, was the star of a program that made state history by advancing to three straight state championship games.

Thornton had not been a factor in prior state tournaments, having lost its only previous game in 1917. But after rallying to defeat Sycamore 23-19 in the finals at the rugged Joliet Sectional, the Flying Clouds rated as a tournament favorite.

Three teams that participated in the 1932 tournament, Canton, Benton and Springfield, were also back in the field and highly regarded.

Meanwhile, Mahomet, with only 109 students, earned its first state trip by rallying late to stun Streator 29-23 in the sectional finals at Normal. Gillespie and the Chicago Public League champ, Lake View, also made their first appearances.

Another state qualifier, Benton, was the first team since Rockford in 1923 to reach the state tournament without any defeats. Hubert Tabor's Rangers owned a 34-0 mark.

The closest quarterfinal contest was the final one, between Benton and 1932 runner-up Canton. The teams played to an 18-18 tie through regulation and scored three points apiece in the first overtime before Benton pulled out a 23-21 victory in the second extra period.

In the semifinals, Mark Peterman advanced a team to the title game for the third time in eight years when Springfield held Gillespie scoreless in the third period to capture a 17-14 win. Thornton handed Benton its first loss of the season in the other semifinal, 28-19.

The 1933 state championship game pitted one of the tournament's greatest players, Boudreau, against one of its greatest coaches, Peterman. Thornton hoped to play a fast game, while Springfield wanted to use the slow-break. Which style would control the game?

That question was answered quickly as the halftime score showed Springfield with a 6-4 advantage. Thornton scored the only two points of the third period to force a 6-6 tie going into the final eight minutes. But despite being forced into a slowdown game, the Flying Clouds took control in the final stanza, building a 14-9 lead. Springfield closed to within one in the late going.

Springfield's Leroy Halberg attempted a short shot in the final seconds, but Thornton's Darwin Hutchins knocked it away to preserve the victory at 14-13. The final score tied the standard for fewest points by both squads in a title game and also set a mark for the fewest points by a winning team.

Tom Nisbet, who later coached three Thornton teams to state, led the winners with nine points.

HARVEY (THORNTON)
State Champions of 1933

FRONT ROW (left to right): Ted Sliwinski, Tom Nisbet, Lou Boudreau, Miles Klein, Darwin Hutchins, Howard McMorris. SECOND ROW: Mgr. Frank Cuspak, John Vogler, Kenneth Hellman, Raymond Jenkins, Gordon McComb, Coach Jack Lipe.

1933

State Final Tournament Scores

Quarterfinals

Springfield 30, Hutsonville 15
Gillespie 25, Chicago (Lake View) 23
Harvey (Thornton) 39, Mahomet 28
Benton 23, Canton 21 (2 OT)

Semifinals

Springfield 17, Gillespie 14
Harvey (Thornton) 28, Benton 19

Finals

Benton 36, Gillespie 18 (third place)
Harvey (Thornton) 14, Springfield 13 (title)

Scoring Leaders

Player, School	G	FG	FT	Pts
Wilbur Henry, Benton	3	9	17	35
Lou Boudreau, Harvey (Thornton)	3	12	3	27
Ralph Fellin, Gillespie	3	8	4	20
Leroy Halberg, Springfield	3	9	2	20
Darwin Hutchins, Harvey (Thornton)	3	7	5	19

All-Tournament First Team

Player, School	Ht.	Yr.
Lou Boudreau, Harvey (Thornton)	5-10	So.
Chuck Frazee, Springfield	5-9	Sr.
Leroy Halberg, Springfield	6-3	Sr.
Wilbur Henry, Benton	6-2	Sr.
Darwin Hutchins, Harvey (Thornton)	6-1	Jr.

Championship Game Box Score

Huff Gym, Champaign, March 25, 1933

HARVEY (THORNTON) (14)
Coach Jack Lipe

Player	FG-A	FT-A	Pts	PF
Lou Boudreau	1	0	2	4
Darwin Hutchins	1	1	3	0
Miles Klein	0	0	0	0
Howard McMorris	0	0	0	0
Tom Nisbet	1	7	9	0
Ted Sliwinski	0	0	0	1
TOTAL	3	8-9	14	5

SPRINGFIELD (13)
Coach Mark Peterman

Player	FG-A	FT-A	Pts	PF
Robert Cook	0	0	0	3
Chuck Frazee	2	0	4	0
Bob Good	0	0	0	0
Leroy Halberg	2	1	5	3
William Martin	0	1	1	1
Pete Urbanckas	0	0	0	0
Charles Warren	1	1	3	2
TOTAL	5	3	13	9

Harvey (Thornton)	2	2	2	8	—	14
Springfield	3	3	0	7	—	13

Officials: Harlow Sutherland, R.L. Ashley.

Huff happiness
Old gym still full of tourney memories

For **37 years**, longer than any other venue, George Huff Gymnasium in **Champaign** served as home to the finals of the **IHSA** boys' basketball tournament.

by Pat Heston

Constructed in 1925 at a cost of $772,000, the facility was brand-new when it opened its doors to the 19-year-old tournament in March of 1926. Later named after longtime U of I athletic director George Huff, the gym's capacity fluctuated from 6,925 to 7,903, selling out annually.

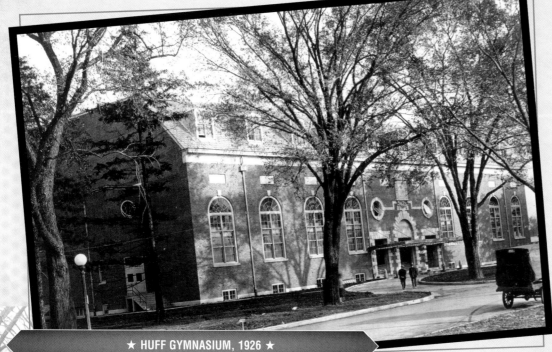

★ HUFF GYMNASIUM, 1926 ★

Freeport's Pretzels were the first team to win a state championship at Huff, coming from behind in the second half to clobber Canton 24-13. They would add their next title on the 25th anniversary of the tournament's move into the facility, belting Moline 71-51 behind 24 points from McKinley Davis.

Huff Gym showcased scores of the finest players Illinois has ever seen. Dwight Eddleman played there, as did Lou Boudreau, Andy Philip, Ted Beach, Max Hooper, Bruce Brothers, Ted Caiazza, and "Sweet" Charlie Brown. Each etched his name deeply and forever into the history of that grand old hall.

Huff Gym was home to the first undefeated team (1944 Taylorville) and the first "district" team (1952 Hebron) to win it all. The title game's first overtime and Coach Vergil Fletcher's first tournament win both came at Huff Gym. It launched careers, birthed legends, and fulfilled dreams.

Huff Gym also dashed its share of dreams. Centralia's unbeatable "Wonder Five" fell by a point when Dwight Eddleman's game-winning shot was disallowed because a referee mistook a hash mark for the out-of-bounds line. Jim Brown and his DuSable Panthers, shouldering the hopes of a city, lost a heartbreaker at Huff, forever immortalized in a classic photo of Paxton Lumpkin clutching a towel to his face and weeping.

Huff Gym was synonymous with history in the making.

The first all-black squad to reach the state finals (1936 New Phillips) and the first all-black squad to win the state tournament (1958 Marshall) did so at Huff. A pair of regional tournament losers, given new life in the sectionals, reversed course and won state titles, adding to the gym's mystique.

Jerry Kuemmerle once scored 49 points in a tournament game and Ted Caiazza averaged more than 30 through four games — both on Huff hardwood. Eddleman and Andy Phillip each nearly single-handedly led astonishing fourth-quarter surges that turned certain defeat into at-the-horn victory. Nine times teams carried spotless records into the final game. Five won out; the others stumbled in heart-rending finishes.

Lodging in Champaign-Urbana was at a premium in the Huff era. High school boys slept on bunk beds set up in the West Great Hall of Memorial Stadium.

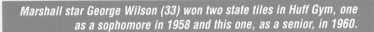

Marshall star George Wilson (33) won two state titles in Huff Gym, one as a sophomore in 1958 and this one, as a senior, in 1960.

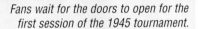

Fans wait for the doors to open for the first session of the 1945 tournament.

A CENTURY OF MEMORIES
2007
IHSA
100
Celebrating 100 years of
IHSA Boys Basketball Tournaments

During the golden age of Illinois high school basketball, Huff Gym was center stage.

Despite its wooden seats and obstructed views, Huff was a great place to experience the state tournament. With an ambiance both cozy and carnival-like, it was unsurpassed as a state-final venue. Unforgettable to fans who witnessed the spectacle first-hand was a pair of behemoth baskets, like great living beasts, rolled into place on each baseline.

On one wall, looming over the floor, hung a large map of Illinois with 16 lights — one for each of the surviving teams. A red bulb represented each school, remaining lit as long as the team remained alive. When two teams played, their respective lights blinked. Afterwards, the loser's light went out, while the winner's became a steady glow. It went on like that until only one light remained: the state champion.

The lone light burning on the last Saturday night, March 24, 1962, was that of Stephen Decatur High School, a 49-48 winner over Chicago Carver in one of the most thrilling final games in history. Soon, even that bulb grew dark as the tournament found a sparkling new home across town.

Yet for those who remember it, Huff Gym, the state tournament's most beloved icon, continues to burn brightly in their hearts.

The student section of Huff Gymnasium in 1948.

QUINCY
State Champions of 1934

FRONT ROW (left to right): John Bingaman, Robert Reeves, Bill Rineberg, Harry Hall, Perry Barclift. SECOND ROW: John Zimmerman, Joe Martin, Howard Roan, Everett Turner, Abe Razien, George Evans. THIRD ROW: Coach Sam Storby, Mgr. Junior Roan, Mgr. Lawrence Hanson, Mgr. Jess Nickerson, Asst. Coach Fred Barnes.

1934

The 1934 state tournament sported a new look — the "Sweet Sixteen" — that coaches and fans had demanded for years.

The format would be used for 22 tournaments, through the 1955 state finals, and remains the standard for determining state-tournament records.

To achieve its goal of having 16 state finalists, the IHSAA boosted the number of sectionals to 16. District runners-up were allowed to advance automatically, preserving the eight-team sectional field that was also the preference of coaches and fans.

With all the changes set in place for the 1934 tournament, it was appropriate that the champion was a school that was new to the field but would become a fixture for years to come. The school that fit that bill was Quincy, which had not previously qualified for the state finals but went on to set records for appearances, games, and wins.

Quincy wasn't the only Sweet Sixteen debutant. For the first time ever, two Chicago Public League schools, Lane Tech and Marshall, qualified. Local favorite Urbana also made its first appearance, while little Equality advanced for the only time in its history.

The title-game combatants from the year before, Thornton and Springfield, earned trips to Huff Gym, as did four district runner-up squads, Champaign, Lawrenceville, Marion, and Marshall. Champaign had lost to intercity rival Urbana in the district finals, but the teams

advanced to the state meet through different sectionals.

The closest games at the state meet came on the first day of action, including Urbana's 33-30 upset of Peoria and Equality's 21-20 triumph over Marion. Later in the session, Lane pulled out a 13-11 victory over Springfield on a basket by Ted Annell in sudden-death, triple overtime.

There wasn't a whole lot of drama in the semifinals as both Quincy and Thornton picked up easy victories on

their way to the championship game. Quincy jumped to a 16-1 lead after one period and captured a 39-18 triumph over Moline while Thornton grabbed a 22-5 halftime lead in its 30-20 victory over Equality.

The third-place game featured an interesting match-up of coaches who later became familiar faces at the state finals. Dolph Stanley, who headed Equality, took nine teams to state from a record five schools, including champion Taylorville in 1944. Moline's George Senneff led his Maroons to state in six of the next seven years for a total of eight trips overall. Equality won the battle 38-26, paced by Bill Barringer, who scored 17 points.

For the state championship, Jack Lipe's once-beaten Thornton squad was a big favorite over Selmer "Sam" Storby's twice-beaten Quincy team.

Quincy owned a slim 16-15 halftime lead but outscored Thornton 12-2 in the third period on the way to a 39-27 upset. Perry Barclift, who tied Bill Hart for tourney scoring honors and also was an all-tournament selection, tossed in a game-high 22 points, while Harry Hall chipped in with 12 points for the winners.

Tom Nisbet, who later played pro basketball, led Thornton with nine points, and Lou Boudreau added eight.

State Final Tournament Scores

First Round

Charleston 36, Freeport 14
Quincy 31, Centralia 23
Moline 26, Lawrenceville 21
Urbana 33, Peoria 30
Equality 21, Marion 20
Chicago (Marshall) 37, Champaign 17
Chicago (Lane) 13, Springfield 11 (3 OT)
Harvey (Thornton) 42, Streator (Twp.) 21

Quarterfinals

Quincy 29, Charleston 20
Moline 25, Urbana 20
Equality 33, Chicago (Marshall) 17
Harvey (Thornton) 40, Chicago (Lane) 18

Semifinals

Quincy 39, Moline 18
Harvey (Thornton) 30, Equality 20

Finals

Equality 38, Moline 26 (third place)
Quincy 39, Harvey (Thornton) 27 (title)

Scoring Leaders

Player, School	G	FG	FT	Pts
Bill Hart, Moline	4	17	9	43
Perry Barclift, Quincy	4	19	5	43
W.R. Barringer, Equality	4	15	11	41
Kenneth Hellman, Harvey (Thornton)	4	17	6	40
Bill Rineberg, Quincy	4	15	4	34

All-Tournament First Team

Player, School	Ht.	Yr.
Perry Barclift, Quincy		Sr.
Lou Boudreau, Harvey (Thornton)	5-10	Jr.
Bill Hart, Moline		Sr.
Darwin Hutchins, Harvey (Thornton)	6-1	Sr.
Tom Nisbet, Harvey (Thornton)	5-9	Sr.

Championship Game Box Score

Huff Gym, Champaign, March 24, 1934

QUINCY (39)
Coach Selmer "Sam" Storby

Player	FG-A	FT-A	Pts	PF
Perry Barclift	11-23	0-2	22	2
John Bingaman	2-8	0-1	4	0
George Evans	0-0	0-0	0	0
Harry Hall	6-17	0-1	12	0
Joe Martin	0-1	0-0	0	0
Bobby Reeves	0-1	0-2	0	3
Bill Rineberg	0-6	0-0	0	4
Howard Roan	0-2	0-0	0	0
Everett Turner	0-0	0-0	0	0
John Zimmerman	0-0	1-1	1	0
TOTAL	19-58	1-7	39	9

HARVEY (THORNTON) (27)
Coach Jack Lipe

Player	FG-A	FT-A	Pts	PF
Lou Boudreau	4-10	0-2	8	1
Kenneth Hellman	1-4	1-5	3	0
Darwin Hutchins	0-5	0-0	0	2
Gordon McComb	3-7	1-4	7	4
Howard McMorris	0-0	0-0	0	0
Tom Nisbet	4-14	1-2	9	0
TOTAL	12-40	3-13	27	7

Quincy	6	10	12	11	— 39
Harvey (Thornton)	8	7	2	10	— 27

Officials: R.L. Ashley, Wendell Williams.

Along with great coaches and athletes, history came into play in the 1935 state finals.

Thornton of Harvey was attempting to notch a record third-straight trip to the championship game. Quincy was hoping to become the first back-to-back winner since the Elgin teams a decade earlier. Rockford was seeking a record third championship. And Springfield's Mark Peterman, who had already won a state title at Canton in 1928, was trying to cement his legacy by becoming the first coach to win a state championship at two schools.

At the district level, a series of mismatches between large and small schools,

State Final Tournament Scores

First Round

Moline 34, Joliet (Twp.) 15
Quincy 27, Rockford 24
Springfield 26, Mt. Carmel 21
Champaign 25, Highland Park (Deerfield-Shields) 21
Harvey (Thornton) 43, Marion 30
Peoria 40, Danville 22
Hillsboro 45, Pinckneyville 24
Pekin 39, Galesburg 31

Quarterfinals

Moline 31, Quincy 30
Springfield 28, Champaign 16
Harvey (Thornton) 45, Peoria 28
Pekin 37, Hillsboro 19

Semifinals

Springfield 23, Moline 20
Harvey (Thornton) 35, Pekin 20

Finals

Pekin 22, Moline 16 (third place)
Springfield 24, Harvey (Thornton) 19 (title)

Scoring Leaders

Player, School	G	FG	FT	Pts
Herb Scheffler, Springfield	4	18	11	47
Kenneth Hellman, Harvey (Thornton)	4	21	4	46
Robert Grant, Pekin	4	14	9	37
Gordon McComb, Harvey (Thornton)	4	14	6	34
Chester Marshall, Pekin	4	11	7	29

All-Tournament First Team

Player, School	Ht.	Yr.
Lou Boudreau, Harvey (Thornton)	5-10	Sr.
Kenneth Hellman, Harvey (Thornton)	6-4	
Chester Marshall, Pekin	6-1	Sr.
Gordon McComb, Harvey (Thornton)	6-3	
Herb Scheffler, Springfield	6-4	Sr.

Championship Game Box Score

Huff Gym, Champaign, March 23, 1935

SPRINGFIELD (24)
Coach Mark Peterman

Player	FG-A	FT-A	Pts	PF
Emerson Dailey	0	0	0	1
Parry Feaman	4	1	9	0
Paul Nunes	1	0	2	0
Whitey "Junior" Sapp	0	0	0	2
Herb Scheffler	6	1	13	1
TOTAL	11	2-6	24	4

HARVEY (THORNTON) (19)
Coach Jack Lipe

Player	FG-A	FT-A	Pts	PF
Edward Beinor	0	1	1	2
Lou Boudreau	5	0	10	1
Kenneth Hellman	1	0	2	1
Gordon McComb	1	1	3	1
Howard McMorris	0	1	1	1
William Shumpes	1	0	2	0
TOTAL	8	3-6	19	6

Springfield	2	8	6	8	— 24
Harvey (Thornton)	0	10	3	6	— 19

Officials: John Robb, J.B. Travnicek.

exemplified by Joliet's 136-5 romp over tiny Mokena, doomed the traditional district-sectional format. In this, the final year of the setup, 62 district champions and 62 runners-up qualified for sectional play, as did four teams from the Chicago Public League.

There was little drama in the sectional finals as most favorites rolled along. In the closest contest, once-beaten Danville needed to go overtime before claiming a 16-14 win over Oblong. Joliet, coached by Doug Mills, a standout on Elgin's two state championship teams, upset West Aurora 23-19 in the Joliet sectional finals.

The Big Twelve Conference recorded one of the most successful showings by any league, advancing five schools to the Sweet Sixteen: Champaign, Danville, Pekin, Peoria, and Springfield. Seven squads that competed at the state tournament in 1934 returned, while Danville, Deerfield-Shields of Highland Park, Pekin, and Pinckneyville all advanced to the state meet for the first time.

Quincy's hopes of another title were dashed in the quarterfinals when the Blue Devils fell 31-30 to Moline. Meanwhile, Springfield outscored Champaign 17-6 in the second half to claim a 28-16 victory.

In the semifinal between Springfield and Moline, the score was tied at 17 with four minutes to go before Springfield eked out a 23-20 victory. Thornton had a much easier time, jumping to a 29-16 lead after three periods as it rolled over Pekin by a 35-20 count.

The championship game was the classic that most expected, featuring Jack Lipe's Flying Clouds, who had played in the last two state championship games, against Peterman and his Solons, hoping to avenge their 1933 title-game defeat by Thornton.

Once again Thornton was led by Lou Boudreau, who was making his third straight appearance in a state championship game, along with teammate Howard McMorris.

Before a crowd estimated at 7,500, Springfield controlled the pace, taking a 2-0 lead after one period. Thornton pressed on, forcing a 10-10 tie at halftime. With four minutes left and Springfield holding on to a 20-19 advantage, Herb Scheffler and Perry Feaman scored critical baskets. The late surge helped Springfield to a 24-19 victory and earned Peterman a new niche in the record book.

Scheffler, who later coached and officiated in the state finals, led the winners with 13 points. In his final high school game, Boudreau paced Thornton with 10.

SPRINGFIELD
State Champions of 1935

FRONT ROW (left to right): Duane Fultz, Herb Scheffler, Robert Miller, Whitney Sapp, Joy Roof, Coach Mark Peterman. SECOND ROW: Robert Farris, Perry Feaman, Paul Nunes, Emerson Dailey, Quentin Engle.

An early image from the Sweet Sixteen: Springfield vs. Champaign in the quarterfinals.

1935

DECATUR
State Champions of 1936

FRONT ROW (left to right):
Ken Park, Harold Baker,
Paul Weingand, Dale Minick,
Eddie Reynolds. SECOND ROW:
Coach Gay Kintner,
Wendell Bauman, Dean Butt,
Robert Fisher, Victor Walters,
William Dearth.

Regional tournaments were held for the first time in 1936.

1936

To reduce the number of mismatches between large schools and small ones, the IHSAA implemented a drastic change for the 1936 tournament.

A new stage — the regional — was inserted after the district. In the revised format, district tournaments were reserved for weaker teams and served merely to narrow the field for the main event. Each of the 61 districts produced a winner, runner-up, and sometimes a third-place team that moved on to regional tournaments.

The field was full of top-flight coaches, three of them with new teams. Ernie Eveland, who had coached Waterman to state in 1930, brought Paris to the finals for the first time since 1911. Dolph Stanley followed up on his success at Equality by leading Mt. Pulaski to a state berth. Selmer "Sam" Storby, who had coached the 1934 Quincy champions, returned with Proviso in that school's inaugural appearance. Arthur Trout and Gay Kintner, two other coaches with state-title credentials, were also in attendance.

Besides Proviso, six other schools made their first state appearance at the 1936 tourney: Fulton, Hull, Mt. Pulaski, Vandalia, Zeigler, and New Phillips from Chicago's South Side.

While Proviso was viewed as a real threat to win the championship, Trout's Centralia squad and Kintner's Decatur team were long shots, both having lost at least 10 games. In fact, Decatur headed into the playoffs on a five-game losing streak and had to rally late to edge Athens 20-19 in the sectional opener. Danville, the Big Twelve champion, entered the state finals with a 20-0 record and was viewed by most as the team to beat.

Danville's hopes were nearly dashed in its first game at state, however, when overtime was necessary to beat Centralia 28-26. Dick Jones made a bucket just before the end of regulation play and then hit two free throws in a sudden-death period to win.

Proviso was eliminated by Johnston City after being outscored 12-1 in the final quarter in a 24-18 loss.

In the quarterfinals, Danville had to rally from a 21-14 deficit to force overtime before picking up a 31-29 win over Moline. Johnston City withstood a late challenge by Vandalia for a 30-26 decision, and Decatur hung on for a 30-27 victory over Hull, the smallest school in the field with just 94 students.

Danville gained its first slot in the title game with a 36-33 win over Mt. Pulaski in the semifinals. In the other contest, Decatur needed a last-second driving lay-up by Dale Minick to earn a 20-19 victory.

The title game featured a pair of Big Twelve squads that had not met during the season. Ned Whitesell's Danville team was attempting to become the first unbeaten champion while Decatur was hoping it could make history as the champion with the most losses.

Danville appeared on its way to completing a perfect season, grabbing a 15-12 halftime lead. But Decatur moved ahead 19-18 with a period to go and pulled off the 26-22 upset, giving an unlikely second state title to Kintner.

State Final Tournament Scores

First Round

Fulton 25, Paris 19
Mt. Pulaski 22, Joliet (Twp.) 16
Danville 28, Centralia 26 (OT)
Moline 32, Aurora (West) 19
Johnston City 24, Maywood (Proviso) 18
Vandalia 40, Zeigler 36
Decatur 17, Peoria (Manual) 13
Hull 35, Chicago (New Phillips) 23

Quarterfinals

Mt. Pulaski 32, Fulton 18
Danville 31, Moline 29 (OT)
Johnston City 30, Vandalia 26
Decatur 30, Hull 27

Semifinals

Danville 36, Mt. Pulaski 33
Decatur 20, Johnston City 19

Finals

Johnston City 32, Mt. Pulaski 20 (third place)
Decatur 26, Danville 22 (title)

Scoring Leaders

Player, School	G	FG	FT	Pts
Clyde Rodden, Johnston City	4	19	4	42
Daraid Staley, Mt. Pulaski	4	10	13	33
Dick Jones, Danville	4	13	6	32
Carl Brevi, Johnston City	4	13	4	30
Harry Martin, Mt. Pulaski	4	9	9	27
Dale Minick, Decatur	4	11	5	27
Orval Spurlin, Vandalia	2	7	13	27

All-Tournament First Team

Player, School	Ht.	Yr.
Jim "Floss" Anders, Moline	6-3	Sr.
Dick Jones, Danville	6-1	
Dale Minick, Decatur		
Ken Park, Decatur	5-9	Jr.
Daraid Staley, Mt. Pulaski	6-2	Jr.

Championship Game Box Score

Huff Gym, Champaign, March 21, 1936

DECATUR (26)
Coach Gay Kintner

Player	FG-A	FT-A	Pts	PF
Harold Baker	0	3-4	3	1
William Dearth	0	0-1	0	1
Dale Minick	2	2-2	6	1
Ken Park	2	2-4	6	2
Eddie Reynolds	0	1-2	1	3
Paul Weingand	4	2-2	10	2
TOTAL	8	10-15	26	10

DANVILLE (22)
Coach Ned Whitesell

Player	FG-A	FT-A	Pts	PF
Dick Jones	2	3-4	7	2
Herman Owens	1	0-2	2	3
Jack Owens	1	2-3	4	1
Jean Tuggle	2	1-2	5	1
Bob Williams	2	0-2	4	4
TOTAL	8	6-13	22	11

Decatur	3	9	7	7	—	26
Danville	6	9	3	4	—	22

Officials: J.B. Travnicek, John Hall.

With two all-tournament players back from its 1936 state champion, it was a good bet Gay Kintner's Decatur squad would make another title run in 1937.

Kintner was attempting to surpass Mark Peterman and Arthur Trout and become the first coach to win three titles, while Moline's George Senneff brought his fourth straight squad to state, tying Peterman for that record. But just like the previous year, Decatur stumbled down the stretch and entered the state tournament with 11 losses.

That seemed to leave the door open for squads such as Joliet, Moline, and Vandalia, which also had key players back from teams that qualified in 1936.

While Dundee entered the state finals with an impressive 37-1 record, LaSalle-Peru carried a modest 12-12 mark in its first state appearance since 1908.

Four schools were new to the Sweet Sixteen: Oblong, Rushville, Woodstock, and Wells of Chicago, which earned the first automatic berth given to the Chicago Public League champion.

Among the favorites, Moline had the closest call in the first round at Huff Gym with a 24-23 victory over a heartbroken Dundee squad.

In the quarterfinals, Pekin needed a late basket from Tom Maloney to pull out a 27-26 victory over Woodstock. The last game of the evening turned out to be one of the most unusual in tournament history. Decatur took advantage of 19 missed shots by Moline to grab a 3-0 halftime lead, leaving Moline with an embarrassing record — fewest points in a half — that is guaranteed to stand forever. The Reds went on to win 14-11.

Joliet earned its first appearance in a state championship game by edging Collinsville 28-26 in the first semifinal

contest. In the other, Decatur beat Pekin 23-15 to earn a second straight title berth.

Decatur was trying to become the first repeat champion since the Elgin teams of 1924 and 1925. Returning only two regulars (Dale Minick and Ken Park) from the 1936 squad, Decatur squared off against a Joliet team making its third consecutive state trip. Joliet, coached by Herm Walser, had four players (Benny Macuk, Willard Aschenbrenner, Mike Savich, and Charles Winston) who had seen action in the previous two state appearances.

That experience proved to be an advantage as the Steelmen shot out to a 9-3 lead after one quarter and never trailed. The final count was 40-20. Joliet's 20-point margin of victory was the largest since 1917, when Springfield claimed a 32-11 win over Belvidere. Macuk scored 16 points to lead the winners and wrap up tourney scoring honors with 59 points.

In an unusual awards-stand mix-up, Joliet received the second-place trophy and Decatur got the title trophy. The teams were on their way home when notified of the mistake.

JOLIET (TWP.)
State Champions of 1937

FRONT ROW (left to right): George Macuk, Louis Ginnetti, William Moore, Frank Wardley, Harold Starr. SECOND ROW: Willard Aschenbrenner, Benjamin Macuk, Michael Savich, Charles Winston, LeRoy Hagen.

State Final Tournament Scores
First Round

Vandalia 28, Zeigler 26
Joliet (Twp.) 31, Athens 24
Chicago (Wells) 23, Galesburg 20
Collinsville 34, Carbondale 23
Woodstock 37, Oblong 31
Pekin 25, Rushville 24
Moline 24, Dundee 23
Decatur 21, LaSalle (L.-Peru) 10

Quarterfinals

Joliet (Twp.) 43, Vandalia 19
Collinsville 20, Chicago (Wells) 18
Pekin 27, Woodstock 26
Decatur 14, Moline 11

Semifinals

Joliet (Twp.) 28, Collinsville 26
Decatur 23, Pekin 15

Finals

Collinsville 31, Pekin 18 (third place)
Joliet (Twp.) 40, Decatur 20 (title)

Scoring Leaders

Player, School	G	FG	FT	Pts
Benny Macuk, Joliet (Twp.)	4	28	3	59
Walter "Hoot" Evers, Collinsville	4	11	10	32
Eddie Evers, Collinsville	4	13	4	30
Dale Minick, Decatur	4	13	3	29
Melvin Richter, Collinsville	4	14	0	28

All-Tournament First Team

Player, School	Ht.	Yr.
Benny Macuk, Joliet (Twp.)	5-7	Sr.
Ken Park, Decatur	5-9	Sr.
Melvin Richter, Collinsville		
Mike Savich, Joliet (Twp.)	5-11	
Charles Winston, Joliet (Twp.)	6-1	Sr.

Championship Game Box Score
Huff Gym, Champaign, March 20, 1937

JOLIET (TWP.) (40)
Coach Herman Walser

Player	FG-A	FT-A	Pts	PF
Willard Aschenbrenner	1-8	3-4	5	2
Louis Ginetti	1-1	0-0	2	1
Leroy Hagan	3-9	0-0	6	2
Benny Macuk	7-28	2-4	16	0
George Macuk	0-0	0-0	0	0
Bill Moore	0-0	0-2	0	2
Mike Savich	3-15	1-3	7	2
Harold Starr	0-1	1-2	1	0
Frank Wardley	0-0	0-0	0	0
Charles Winston	1-8	1-1	3	1
TOTAL	16-70	8-16	40	10

DECATUR (20)
Coach Gay Kintner

Player	FG-A	FT-A	Pts	PF
Bob Campbell	0-1	0-0	0	1
Lee Cook	1-4	1-3	3	1
Elzea Kirby	0-1	0-1	0	0
Dale Minick	3-14	0-3	6	3
Ken Park	2-20	1-1	5	2
Ham Schlene	0-2	1-2	1	0
Joe Shellabarger	0-0	0-0	0	0
George Smith	1-4	1-2	3	4
William White	1-6	0-0	2	1
Pete Williams	0-2	0-0	0	0
TOTAL	8-54	4-12	20	12

Joliet (Twp.)	9	4	9	18	—	40
Decatur	3	5	5	7	—	20

Officials: John Hall, Ernest Lieberson.

1937

Celebrating 100 years of IHSA Boys Basketball Tournaments

The small-town magic of the Sweet Sixteen made its first appearance in the 1938 state tournament.

The tourney featured two schools of fewer than 100 students, including one that played for the championship. It was an unexpected turn of events, considering that small schools had been relegated to preliminary district tournaments two years earlier.

Reed-Custer of Braidwood, with an enrollment of 96, won its district and then avenged its only two losses of the year by beating Coal City in the regional finals. Reed-Custer then beat Streator 38-23 in the Pontiac Sectional finals to reach Champaign.

Milton, a Pike County school of just 66 students, was the smallest school ever to play at Huff Gym. Only 27 boys attended the school, and of the 21 who were eligible, 15 were on the team. Like Reed-Custer, Milton started at the district level. It lost to Pittsfield 38-28 in the regional finals but reversed that defeat with a 30-28 win in the sectional championship.

Three other schools also took part in their first state tournament: Harrisburg, Chicago's Von Steuben, and Glenbard of Glen Ellyn.

Dundee, the pre-tournament favorite, entered the meet with a 30-game winning streak, thanks to a 45-36 victory over Coal City in the Joliet Sectional finals.

Sweet Sixteen play began with Von Steuben overcoming an early 15-0 deficit to claim a 32-31 win over Granite City. Milton's hopes for state success were doomed when center Donald Parks contracted measles. The underdogs wound up dropping a 36-25 decision to Harrisburg.

In the quarterfinals, Von Steuben continued to surprise as Bernard Weksler scored a late bucket to give his team a 29-27 win over Johnston City. Bill Hocking tossed in 15 points to lead Reed-Custer to a 35-30 victory over Galesburg in the next game. Paris prevailed when Lyle Willan got a rebound basket in the second overtime to give his team a 24-22 win over Carbondale. In the last quarterfinal, Dundee used 17 points from Don Blanken to win 38-26 over Harrisburg.

Although the match-ups were enticing, neither semifinal was close. Reed-Custer beat Von Steuben 38-24 in the first; in the second, Dundee defeated Paris 51-36, with Blanken's 24 points again leading the way.

The title game matched a coaching legend, Dundee's Eugene DeLacey, who won 675 games in a career that lasted until 1959, and Louis Bottino, who did double-duty as principal at the tiny school in Braidwood. Only two smaller schools had ever reached the championship game prior to Reed-Custer's run: Washington (78 students in 1909) and Mt. Carroll (83 in 1911).

The dark horse squad from Will County looked pretty good for a half as the teams played to a 17-17 draw. But Dundee outscored Reed-Custer 7-4 in the third quarter and 12-8 in the final period to pull out a 36-29 victory, its 34th in a row.

All-tourney pick and tourney scoring leader Blanken paced the Cardunals with 15 points while Chris Hansen had 10 points.

State Final Tournament Scores

First Round

Johnston City 32, Champaign 26
Chicago (Von Steuben) 32, Granite City 31
Galesburg 23, Rock Island 21
Braidwood (Reed-Custer) 27, Glen Ellyn (Glenbard) 19
Carbondale 36, Rockford 30
Paris 33, Decatur 20
Harrisburg 36, Milton 25
Dundee 36, Pekin 29

Quarterfinals

Chicago (Von Steuben) 29, Johnston City 27
Braidwood (Reed-Custer) 35, Galesburg 30
Paris 24, Carbondale 22 (2 OT)
Dundee 38, Harrisburg 26

Semifinals

Braidwood (Reed-Custer) 38, Chicago (Von Steuben) 24
Dundee 51, Paris 36

Finals

Paris 30, Chicago (Von Steuben) 20 (third place)
Dundee 36, Braidwood (Reed-Custer) 29 (title)

Scoring Leaders

Player, School	G	FG	FT	Pts
Don Blanken, Dundee	4	28	9	65
Bill Hocking, Braidwood (Reed-Custer)	4	24	7	55
Bernard Weksler, Chicago (Von Steuben)	4	22	5	49
Chris Hansen, Dundee	4	13	8	34
Arthur Melahn, Dundee	4	13	7	33

All-Tournament First Team

Player, School	Ht.	Yr.
Don Blanken, Dundee	6-2	Sr.
Scott Gill, Carbondale	5-8	Sr.
Bill Hocking, Braidwood (Reed-Custer)	6-0	Sr.
Henry Lutz, Carbondale	5-11	Sr.
Arthur Melahn, Dundee	6-3	Sr.

Championship Game Box Score

Huff Gym, Champaign, March 19, 1938

DUNDEE (36)
Coach Eugene DeLacey

Player	FG-A	FT-A	Pts	PF
Donald Adams	1-5	1-4	3	1
Don Blanken	7-23	1-1	15	1
Chris Hansen	3-19	4-5	10	2
Arthur Melahn	1-5	0-0	2	2
John Schumacher	3-6	0-0	6	0
TOTAL	15-58	6-10	36	6

BRAIDWOOD (REED-CUSTER) (29)
Coach Louis Bottino

Player	FG-A	FT-A	Pts	PF
Frank Bohac	0-1	1-1	1	0
Lawrence Crichton	3-8	0-0	6	1
Bill Hocking	6-21	1-2	13	0
Robert Patterson	0-4	0-1	0	3
Stan Simpson	0-12	1-2	1	2
Edwin Viglia	4-15	0-1	8	3
TOTAL	13-61	3-7	29	9

Dundee	9	8	7	12	— 36
Braidwood (Reed-Custer)	10	7	4	8	— 29

Officials: Ernest Lieberson, Ron Gibbs.

The 1939 state tournament featured something old and something new.

Rockford, which hadn't won any games at the state meet since placing second in 1923, was seeking to become the first school to capture three championships.

Meanwhile, two individuals who played huge roles in the golden era of the state tournament — Champaign's first-year coach Harry Combes and Centralia freshman Dwight "Dike" Eddleman — made their debuts.

The Champaign Maroons would play in the tournament seven times during Combes' nine years at the helm, winning five trophies and playing for three straight titles. Eddleman would establish himself as Illinois' greatest scorer while leading Centralia to three trophies in four seasons.

Champaign earned its berth by beating Urbana 38-33 in the Champaign Sectional, avenging a regional-title loss to its twin-city rival. Five schools came to the state final for the first time: Wood River, Bradley, Dwight, Roodhouse, and Peoria Woodruff, a regional runner-up.

Also making its debut, high on the wall at one end of the court, was a large map of Illinois with a light for each of the 16 teams. Devised by university employee Bill Pfisterer, the map would provide many lasting memories during the tournament's run in Huff Gym.

In a pair of opening-round thrillers, Arthur Trout's Centralia squad outscored Bradley 17-9 in the fourth quarter to pull out a 37-31 victory, while Woodruff used an 18-6 fourth-quarter edge to claim a 45-39 win over Gillespie.

The quarterfinals featured Eddleman scoring 24 points in a 41-35 victory over Champaign and Paris' Ralph Hooker notching 22 points to lead the Tigers past Woodruff, 51-42.

Rockford gained a spot in the championship with a 43-27 over Wood River in the semifinals. Bob Wallin paced the Rabs with 11 points. In the other semifinal, Paris claimed a 39-30 victory to earn its first title trip. Henson scored 22 points for the Tigers, while Eddleman was held to five.

The title game, pitting Jim Laude's 22-2 Rockford squad against Ernie Eveland's 37-2 Paris team, was touted as a real offensive battle, and it turned out to be just that. Rockford jumped to a 32-19

State Final Tournament Scores

First Round
Wood River (East Alton-W.R.) 34, Moline 22
Cicero (Morton) 42, Chicago (Lane) 37
Rockford 50, Canton 24
Zeigler 21, Roodhouse 11
Champaign 41, Dwight 30
Centralia 37, Bradley (B.-Bourbonnais) 31
Paris 25, Flora 22
Peoria (Woodruff) 45, Gillespie 39

Quarterfinals
Wood River (East Alton-W.R.) 33, Cicero (Morton) 19
Rockford 47, Zeigler 34
Centralia 41, Champaign 35
Paris 51, Peoria (Woodruff) 42

Semifinals
Rockford 43, Wood River (East Alton-W.R.) 27
Paris 39, Centralia 30

Finals
Wood River (East Alton-W.R.) 34, Centralia 28 (third place)
Rockford 53, Paris 44 (title)

Scoring Leaders

Player, School	G	FG	FT	Pts
Floyd Henson, Paris	4	26	10	62
Stanley Stasica, Rockford	4	23	15	61
Ralph Hooker, Paris	4	22	12	56
Bob Wallin, Rockford	4	15	14	44
Dwight "Dike" Eddleman, Centralia	4	16	9	41

All-Tournament First Team

Player, School	Ht.	Yr.
Floyd Henson, Paris	6-1	Sr.
Kenneth Polivka, Cicero (Morton)	5-11	Sr.
Eugene Speck, Rockford	6-0	Jr.
Stanley Stasica, Rockford	5-10	Sr.
Bob Wallin, Rockford	6-4	Jr.

Championship Game Box Score
Huff Gym, Champaign, March 18, 1939

ROCKFORD (53)
Coach James Laude

Player	FG-A	FT-A	Pts	PF
Frank Alonzo	2-11	2-3	6	2
Harlan Anderson	0-0	0-0	0	0
Norman Anderson	4-16	2-3	10	1
Paul McDaniels	0-0	0-0	0	0
Eugene Speck	4-12	2-2	10	2
Stanley Stasica	6-19	2-3	14	1
Bob Wallin	4-14	5-7	13	1
TOTAL	20-72	13-18	53	7

PARIS (44)
Coach Ernie Eveland

Player	FG-A	FT-A	Pts	PF
Harold Anderson	2-6	1-1	5	1
Thomas Burton	0-5	1-1	1	2
Robert Calimese	2-3	1-2	5	3
Floyd Henson	7-31	1-1	15	1
Ralph Hooker	6-27	3-3	15	2
Lawrence Humerickhouse	1-3	1-1	3	3
TOTAL	18-75	8-9	44	12

Rockford	11	21	13	8	—	53
Paris	9	10	14	11	—	44

Officials: Ron Gibbs, A.C. Daugherty.

> **The lighted map of Illinois made its first appearance on the wall of Huff Gym in 1939.**

ROCKFORD, State Champions of 1939

FRONT ROW (left to right): Robert Wallin, Eugene Speck, Stanley Stasica, Frank Alonzo, Norman Anderson.
SECOND ROW: Harlan Anderson, George Champion, Keith Mulford, Coach Jim Laude, Albert Volsch, Paul McDaniels.

halftime lead and went on to defeat the Tigers 53-44 in the highest-scoring championship game to that time. Rockford's 193 points in four games broke another tournament record.

All-tournament selection Stanley Stasica led the Rabs with 14 points, while Wallin added 13.

While Paris would return to the title game three more times in the next eight years, winning twice, Rockford High's glory days were over. By 1941, the school was no more, its enrollment split between new East and West High Schools that would establish their own state tournament traditions.

Celebrating 100 years of IHSA Boys Basketball Tournaments

Second-chance champs
Losing wasn't the end of the world

One of the most *popular* attractions of the Illinois High School Association's **basketball** tournament has been its win-or-go-home *format*.

by Curt Herron

But for several years in the 1930s and 1940s, the tournament featured an odd double-elimination structure that allowed teams to lose during the postseason and still challenge for a state championship.

Two teams — Granite City in 1940 and Morton of Cicero in 1941 — lost regional championship games, but proceeded to make the most of their second chance by capturing a state title.

It was a time of trial and error in the state tournament, triggered by the rising popularity of the sport, the shortage of acceptable facilities, and the growing pressure to increase the state final field from 8 to 16 teams.

The curious format opened the door for many unusual scenarios before the tournament shifted back to single-elimination in 1943. Teams avenged defeats from earlier in the tournament, pairs of teams from the same regional ended up at state, and a few teams even managed to lose three times during one postseason.

Eliminating byes

The first experiment with allowing losing teams to advance occurred in 1930 when the IHSAA (as it was known until 1940) could not find enough large gymnasiums to hold the proper number of district tournaments. Desperate, the association tried a plan so unpopular it lasted just one year.

With 64 slots in the sectionals and only 56 district winners, eight teams were needed to complete the field. The lucky squads were chosen at random from the losers of the district finals, with the fourth team in alphabetical order in each group advancing to the sectional.

Of the eight teams that gained new life, only two managed to win a game. One was Elgin, which lost to Dundee in the district finals but then defeated the Cardunals in the sectional opener, the only time in state tournament history that teams have met in consecutive games.

During the next three years, the state association was usually able to get around the problem of advancing district losers by simply increasing the number of districts.

There were two exceptions, however, and both benefited teams from southern Illinois. In 1931 and 1933, one team from the southern part of the state was drawn at random to fill out a sectional field. In the first instance, Pinckneyville dropped its opening contest, but two years later, Herrin managed to collect a sectional win before suffering its second tourney defeat.

The Sweet Sixteen

In 1934, coaches and fans finally got their wish when the number of teams advancing to Champaign doubled from 8 to 16 teams. The number of sectional tournaments also increased to 16. To preserve the popular eight-team format at the sectional level, runners-up from the district tournaments were allowed to advance automatically.

A total of nine teams that lost in the district finals advanced to sectional championship games, and three of those (Champaign, Lawrenceville, and Marion) moved on to the first edition of the Sweet Sixteen. In the sectional finals, Lawrenceville beat Eldorado and Marion defeated Zeigler in showdowns between squads that had been beaten in district finals.

In another twist, Champaign lost to rival Urbana in the district finals. But when the teams were assigned to different sectionals, both managed to advance to state, becoming the first pair of teams to pull off that feat.

A year later, seven squads that fell in the district finals advanced to sectional title games. One was Deerfield-Shields of Highland Park, which fell to New Trier in the district finals but then avenged that defeat in the sectional finals.

Regionals

The 1936 state tournament signaled one of the biggest changes in the meet's long history: the introduction of regional tournaments between the district and sectional levels. Regional runners-up advanced automatically to the sectional stage. At the district level, runners-up and occasionally even a third-place team were allowed to advance to the regionals to fill out the field.

Ten squads that lost in regional finals managed to make their way to sectional championships in 1936. Three of those (Johnston City, Moline, and Zeigler) advanced to the finals in Champaign.

For the first time, teams that already had lost during the tournament — Johnston City and Moline — managed to win a game in the state finals. While Moline's hopes were dashed in the quarterfinals, Johnston City took third place to complete its historic tournament run.

In a good example of how bizarre the tournament had become, the 1936 sectionals featured a squad that had not even made the finals of its district meet. After finishing third in district play, Hampshire took second in its regional and yet continued to advance. Hampshire's loss in the sectional opener was its third — and final — defeat of the postseason series.

In 1937, 10 regional runners-up advanced to sectional finals, and four moved on to state. For the first time, teams that had met in a regional final, winner Dundee and loser Woodstock, qualified for the Sweet Sixteen. The other two regional title-game losers who moved on were Carbondale and Zeigler, who both avenged regional title defeats in sectional finals. Carbondale turned the tables on Anna-Jonesboro while Zeigler got the better of DuQuoin in the second postseason meeting.

A new high of 11 squads that had lost in the regional finals advanced to sectional title games in 1938, but only three would eventually move on to Champaign.

Milton, a Cinderella district entrant with only 66 students, avenged a regional final loss to Pittsfield by defeating that squad in the sectional finals. But Milton and the two other already-beaten teams, Glenbard and Granite City, all came up short in their only games in Champaign.

Coal City also made history in 1938 by becoming only the second school to lose to both the eventual state champion and runner-up in the same tournament. Coal City lost to rival Braidwood Reed-Custer in the regional finals and was eliminated in the sectional finals by eventual state champion Dundee. (The other case occurred in 1909, when Mt. Carroll lost to both Hinsdale and Washington in an unusual state-finals setup.)

Runners-up make mark at state

While only eight regional runners-up advanced to sectional title games in 1939, half managed to advance to the Sweet Sixteen, setting a record that would last just one year. Champaign, Morton of Cicero, and Peoria Woodruff all won their first games in the competition before falling in the quarterfinals. Woodruff's win over Gillespie was the first battle between regional runners-up to take place at the state finals. The three first-round winners among regional runners-up set another record that would last for only one year.

Two other schools, Indianola and Nebo, tied Hampshire's record with three losses in the postseason, dropping one game apiece in district, regional and sectional play.

State champs!

The 1940 state meet was the most significant of the double-elimination era for several reasons.

Start with the record 13 teams that lost in the regional finals but worked their way back into sectional championship games. Of those, seven won, meaning nearly half of the Sweet Sixteen field already had a tournament loss on the books by the time they reached Champaign.

Three of those teams reached the semifinals. And most importantly, two made it to the championship game, setting up the first state-title game involving one, let alone two, regional runners-up.

Leading the way in the historic tournament was eventual champion Granite City, which lost to rival Wood River in the regional finals but reversed the decision in the sectional title game. Herrin also lost in the regional finals but bounced back to advance to state.

In the historic championship contest, Granite City captured a 24-22 victory and its only state title.

Four-team finals

The sixteen-team field at the one-year-only "quarterfinal tournaments" of 1941 consisted of 15 sectional winners plus Freeport, a sectional runner-up. Freeport earned its spot when the Chicago Public League refused to send its champion, Manley, because of a bylaw dispute. The names of the three sectional losers feeding into the Elgin Quarterfinal were put in a hat, and Freeport was drawn at random to fill Manley's spot. Freeport thus became the only team to lose a sectional game and participate in the state finals.

While only four teams advanced to Huff Gym in the experimental state finals, two regional runners-up managed to crack that small group and go on to play for the state title. Morton of Cicero had lost to Proviso, while Urbana had fallen to Homer in regional competition.

Both Morton and Urbana pulled out exciting semifinal victories to guarantee a second state-title match-up of regional runners-up. The state championship game followed the same pattern as the semifinals as Morton rallied to pull out a 32-31 victory over Urbana, becoming the second regional runner-up in as many years to win a state title.

End of the era

The 1942 tournament was the end of the road for the double-elimination tournament. There weren't many success stories in the experiment's final chapter.

Homer became the third and final team to lose in the district finals and then come back and win a regional title. Milton (1940) and Reed-Custer (1941) had accomplished the same feat during the previous two years. In addition, Melvin and Palestine became the last teams to lose three times during the same postseason.

Defending state champion Morton returned to the Sweet Sixteen after losing again in the regional finals. It bounced back from its loss to York to defeat the same squad for the sectional championship.

Of the seven regional losers who advanced to sectional championship games, only two, Morton and Olney, managed to win. That tied the 1935 mark for the fewest regional runners-up in a Sweet Sixteen field. The seven sectional finalists also equaled the low-water mark for those teams, also set in 1935.

In 1943, the IHSA adopted the format that existed until the advent of two classes in 1972. District winners fed into regionals and then four regional champions advanced through pre-arranged sectionals into the Sweet Sixteen. The days of advancing through the state tournament after suffering a defeat had come to an end.

Celebrating 100 years of
IHSA Boys Basketball Tournaments

GRANITE CITY
State Champions of 1940

FRONT ROW (sitting, left to right): Danny Eftimoff, Andy Phillip, Evon Parsaghian, Andy Rapoff, Edward "Ebbie" Mueller.
SECOND ROW: Coach Byron Bozarth, George Gages, Mgr. Harold Brown, Everett Daniels, Ed Hoff, Sam Mouradian, Andy Hagopian.

1940

The 1940 Sweet Sixteen field was a curious mix. In addition to the runners-up, a record seven teams made their first appearances in the state finals: Bloom of Chicago Heights, Casey, Crane Tech of Chicago, Hebron, Lewistown, Salem, and Taylorville, the third school led to state by Dolph Stanley.

First-round action got under way at Huff Gym with Paris holding on for a 36-35 overtime decision over Taylorville. Paris led by 15 points at halftime. Lewistown scored a comeback win over sentimental favorite Hebron, enrollment 101, using a 13-6 edge in the fourth quarter to pull out a 31-30 victory.

All kinds of records fell near the end of the round. Dundee's 72-47 victory over Rushville set marks for the most points by a winning team, a losing team, and of course, both teams.

In the semifinals, Herrin knocked off Champaign 21-17 to move to its first state-title game. Dallas Lillich led the Tigers with 14 points.

Moline led Granite City by seven points with five minutes to go in the other semifinal, but the Warriors rallied to claim a 41-38 victory, with Phillip scoring 16 points.

The championship match-up assured the southern part of the state its first title since Johnston City in 1929. There wouldn't be another all-south title battle until 1957, when Herrin upset Collinsville.

It was an unlikely meeting, considering neither squad had won a regional title. While Granite City entered with five losses, Russell Emery's Tigers had been beaten seven times. The game may not have looked like a classic on paper, but it ended with a dramatic finish.

Herrin took a 16-8 lead just before halftime, but as it had done throughout the tournament, Granite City fought back in the second half, holding Herrin scoreless in the third period to pull close at 16-15.

With the score knotted at 22 and 12 seconds on the clock, Evon Parsaghian hit a basket to give Granite City the victory. Phillip added another 15 points for Granite City while Fred Campbell had 13 for Herrin.

Phillip went on to star for the Whiz Kids at the University of Illinois and later enjoyed a 12-year pro career with four different teams. He was enshrined in the Naismith Memorial Basketball Hall of Fame in 1961.

By modern rules, Granite City couldn't have won the title.

Byron Bozarth's Happy Warriors became the first school in history to win a state championship after losing a game in the state series — in this instance, a regional title.

Granite City wasn't alone in that regard. Six other members of the Sweet Sixteen lost in the regional finals and two, like Granite City, were trophy winners: second-place Herrin and fourth-place Champaign. Two teams that reached the quarterfinals, Dundee and Salem, were also regional runners-up.

All of these teams had the good fortune to lose in the only round in which losing was allowed. What the other teams didn't have was Andy Phillip, one of the greatest Illinois basketball players of all time.

State Final Tournament Scores
First Round
Champaign 44, Chicago (Crane) 25
Salem 55, Beardstown 29
Herrin 30, Chicago Heights (Bloom Twp.) 25
Paris 36, Taylorville 35 (OT)
Moline 28, Casey 23
Lewistown 31, Hebron 30
Dundee 72, Rushville 47
Granite City 45, Streator (Twp.) 31
Quarterfinals
Champaign 34, Salem 30
Herrin 29, Paris 22
Moline 49, Lewistown 32
Granite City 35, Dundee 30
Semifinals
Herrin 21, Champaign 17
Granite City 41, Moline 38
Finals
Moline 51, Champaign 33 (third place)
Granite City 24, Herrin 22 (title)

Scoring Leaders

Player, School	G	FG	FT	Pts
Andy Phillip, Granite City	4	19	15	53
Dallas Lillich, Herrin	4	14	16	44
Fred Campbell, Herrin	4	16	9	41
Bob Johnson, Moline	4	15	6	36
Ken Menke, Dundee	2	15	3	33
Dave Brasmer, Moline	4	15	3	33

All-Tournament First Team

Player, School	Ht.	Yr.
Fred Campbell, Herrin	6-0	Sr.
George Gages, Granite City		
Dallas Lillich, Herrin		
Ken Menke, Dundee	6-2	Sr.
Andy Phillip, Granite City	6-1	Sr.

Championship Game Box Score
Huff Gym, Champaign, March 16, 1940

GRANITE CITY (24)
Coach Byron Bozarth

Player	FG-A	FT-A	Pts	PF
Everett Daniels	0-0	0-0	0	0
Dan Eftimoff	0-8	0-1	0	3
George Gages	2-13	0-1	4	0
Andy Hagopian	0-2	0-1	0	0
Edward Hoff	0-0	0-0	0	0
Edward "Ebbie" Mueller	0-1	0-1	0	0
Evon Parsaghian	2-9	1-2	5	2
Andy Phillip	6-23	3-4	15	3
TOTAL	10-56	4-10	24	8

HERRIN (22)
Coach Russell Emery

Player	FG-A	FT-A	Pts	PF
Fred Campbell	6-20	1-2	13	1
Leon Davis	0-3	0-1	0	2
Dallas Lillich	3-14	1-2	7	2
Junior Newlin	0-2	0-1	0	1
Edward Parsons	1-2	0-2	2	3
TOTAL	10-41	2-8	22	9

Granite City	5	6	4	9 —	24
Herrin	10	6	0	6 —	22

Officials: Ralph Elliott, Stuart LeGault.

Shunning the Sweet Sixteen format for a bit of radical experimentation, the IHSA pared down the field by sending the 16 sectional winners to four "quarterfinal sites." The winners at Centralia, Elgin, Pekin, and Springfield advanced to Huff Gym under this one-time-only tournament structure.

In another oddity, Freeport, which lost to East Rockford in the sectional final, earned a spot in the final 16 when the Chicago Public League, in the midst of a dispute over the new IHSA constitution, refused to send its champion.

As the quarterfinal tournaments began, Arthur Trout's 41-1 Centralia squad, the "Wonder Five," was an overwhelming favorite. Centralia had won 40 straight and was averaging over 50 points a game, thanks in large part to Dwight "Dike" Eddleman. Both the team's and Eddleman's season point totals were state records.

Centralia won its own quarterfinal tournament easily. In the first game, Eddleman tossed in 24 points in a 45-24 win over Paris, and then the Orphans romped to a 54-20 title game romp over Carbondale.

At the Elgin tourney, Morton of Cicero used 15 points from Chet Strumillo to advance to the state semifinals with a 39-25 victory.

In the closest of the quarterfinal title games, Canton nipped Sterling 29-28 at Pekin by holding off a late rally.

Urbana moved on to the state semifinals with a 50-30 win over Pittsfield at Springfield. Fred Green led the Tigers with 26 points.

Although only four games were played in Champaign in 1941, the tournament was one of the most exciting ever. All but the third-place game were decided by a single point, and one went into overtime.

In the first semifinal, Morton stunned Centralia by taking a 19-8 halftime lead. The Orphans staged a furious rally but came up short, 30-29, in one of the greatest upsets in state tournament history. Joseph Demkovich led a balanced Morton attack with nine points while Eddleman scored 15 in a losing effort for Centralia, whose record winning streak came to an end at 42 games.

The next game was just as wild as Urbana forced Canton into overtime with a 12-4 fourth-quarter edge and went on to claim a 39-38 win, advancing to a state title game for the only time in its history. Green led the Tigers with 22 points.

In the championship, Norm Ziebell and his 22-4 Morton squad hoped to duplicate their title effort from nine years earlier, while Lew Stephens' 22-10 Urbana squad pushed for a spot in history as a rare 10-loss champion.

As in 1940, both finalists were regional runners-up, assuring a second straight state champion with a tournament loss en route to the title game.

Urbana overcame a 16-15 halftime deficit to move in front 28-24 with eight minutes to go. Green, who had 14 points, fouled out soon after, providing an opening for Morton. Ziebell's team went on a 7-3 spree to pull out a 32-31 win.

Strumillo led Morton with eight points. Green finished with a scoring record of 87 points, edging Eddleman by six points.

State Final Tournament Scores

Quarterfinal Tournaments

At Centralia
Carbondale 27, Mattoon 25
Centralia 45, Paris 24
Centralia 54, Carbondale 20 (title)
No third-place game was played.

At Elgin
Waterman 27, Freeport 12
Cicero (Morton) 46, Rockford (East) 32
Freeport 29, Rockford (East) 27 (third place)
Cicero (Morton) 39, Waterman 25 (title)

At Pekin
Canton 40, Streator (Twp.) 22
Sterling 50, Athens 21
Athens 46, Streator (Twp.) 35 (third place)
Canton 29, Sterling 28 (title)

At Springfield [Armory]
Urbana 44, Collinsville 36
Pittsfield 29, Springfield (Feitshans) 19
Collinsville 44, Springfield (Feitshans) 28 (third place)
Urbana 50, Pittsfield 30 (title)

Semifinals
Cicero (Morton) 30, Centralia 29
Urbana 39, Canton 38 (OT)

Finals
Centralia 67, Canton 37 (third place)
Cicero (Morton) 32, Urbana 31 (title)

Scoring Leaders

Player, School	G	FG	FT	Pts
Fred Green, Urbana	4	40	7	87
Dwight "Dike" Eddleman, Centralia	4	36	9	81
Bob Conner, Canton	4	18	5	41
Chester Strumillo, Cicero (Morton)	4	17	7	41
Jack Klosterman, Centralia	4	16	8	40
Ray Leitner, Cicero (Morton)	4	15	10	40

All-Tournament First Team

Player, School	Ht.	Yr.
Dwight "Dike" Eddleman, Centralia	6-2	Jr.
Fred Green, Urbana	6-6	Sr.
Robert Michael, Centralia	5-10	Sr.
Ed Pschirrer, Canton	5-9	Sr.
Chester Strumillo, Cicero (Morton)	5-11	Sr.

Championship Game Box Score

Huff Gym, Champaign, March 22, 1941

CICERO (MORTON) (32)
Coach Norm Ziebell

Player	FG-A	FT-A	Pts	PF
Joseph Demkovich	2-6	3-5	7	1
Robert Hoffman	2-6	1-3	5	1
Arnold Laver	1-5	2-3	4	2
Ray Leitner	2-7	3-6	7	3
Fred Ploegman	0-4	1-1	1	0
Chester Strumillo	3-16	2-4	8	0
Charles Tourek	0-0	0-0	0	0
TOTAL	10-44	12-22	32	7

URBANA (31)
Coach Lew Stephens

Player	FG-A	FT-A	Pts	PF
Walt Franklin	1-10	0-2	2	2
Bob Gibson	1-11	2-2	4	4
Fred Green	6-13	2-4	14	4
Leal Nelson	4-7	1-1	9	1
Clyde Rusk	1-4	0-0	2	1
Nelson Walden	0-1	0-0	0	0
George Widing	0-0	0-0	0	0
TOTAL	13-46	5-9	31	12

Cicero (Morton)	7	9	8	8	32
Urbana	9	6	13	3	— 31

Officials: Edward Marfell, M.S. Vaughn.

CICERO (MORTON)
State Champions of 1941

FRONT ROW (left to right): Mgr. Robert Yonko, Charles Cuda, Fred Ploegman, Chet Strumillo, Ray Leitner, Robert Hoffman, Robert Soucek.
SECOND ROW: Trainer Ben Shack, Frank Hulka, Edward Vosyka, Joe Demokovich, Arnold Laver, Joe Grove, Joe Novotny, Charles Tourek, Coach Norm Ziebell.

1942

CENTRALIA
State Champions of 1942

FRONT ROW (left to right): Bernard Schifferdecker, Bob Wham, Fred Pearson, Dwight Eddleman, Farrell Robinson, Jim Seyler. SECOND ROW: Bill Davies, Farrell Benefiel, Coach Arthur Trout, Asst. Coach Harry Lutz, Mgr. Harry Fortney, Jim Edgar, Virgil Krutsinger.

Arthur Trout brought a Centralia team to state in 1942 for the third time in four years, still smarting from the shocking upset loss to Morton of Cicero in the 1941 tournament.

But Centralia was no favorite this time. While senior superstar Dwight "Dike" Eddleman still led the way for Trout's squad, the other returning players had scored a total of four points during the previous year's trip to Champaign.

Centralia almost didn't make it back to state at all, as the Orphans had to rally past rival Mt. Vernon 43-42 in the Centralia Sectional final. Farrell Robinson stole the ball and made a three-point play in the final seconds to avenge a pair of regular-season losses to the Rams.

Defending champion Morton of Cicero also returned, but like Centralia, had graduated most of its best players. Morton lost in the regional finals to York, but reversed that decision for the sectional title.

With Centralia and Morton losing favor, the door was wide open for Ernie Eveland's unbeaten Paris squad, which had rolled to 36 straight victories.

The *Champaign News-Gazette* proclaimed the tournament field the greatest in history since the champion of every major conference but one was on hand and every team had a winning record.

Four new squads joined the Sweet Sixteen field in 1942: Chicago's Lindblom, Dixon, Normal Community, and Cathedral of Springfield.

Two state records were set in the first round. Decatur's Eddie Root broke the

modern-day scoring mark (since 1924, when players were required to shoot their own free throws) when he made 25 in the Reds' 53-37 win over Dixon. Two games later, Eddleman broke that short-lived record when he scored 26 to lead the Orphans to a 42-28 victory over West Frankfort.

In the semifinals, Paris claimed a 28-21 win over Morton. Nate Middleton led Paris with 13 points. Centralia advanced to the title game for the first time in 20

years when it rallied to win 45-42 over Freeport, behind 19 points from Eddleman.

All indications pointed to Paris wrapping up a perfect 40-0 season in the state championship match with 33-6 Centralia. The Tigers had beaten the Orphans 47-36 during the season.

Paris fulfilled those expectations as it broke away in the third quarter to grab a 25-16 lead and built its advantage to 30-17 with just over six minutes remaining in the contest. With Robinson out with fouls, a Centralia comeback seemed unlikely at best.

But down the stretch, Centralia staged perhaps the greatest come-from-behind win in state history, outscoring Paris 18-3 to claim a stunning 35-33 victory. Jim Seyler scored eight of his nine points during the run, while Eddleman added six, including two game-tying free throws with 55 seconds remaining and the game-winning bucket with 15 seconds left. As a result, Centralia joined Rockford as Illinois' only three-time state champion.

Tourney scoring leader and all-tourney pick Eddleman scored 16 points in the title game. The Centralia superstar finished his career with a staggering 2,702 points, a 17.3 average in 156 games. Widely proclaimed as the state's best schoolboy athlete, he would go on to become a three-sport star at the University of Illinois and an Olympic high-jumper.

State Final Tournament Scores

First Round
Paris 64, Urbana 40
Streator (Twp.) 45, Normal (Community) 34
Decatur 53, Dixon 37
Cicero (Morton) 47, Springfield (Cathedral) 32
Centralia 42, West Frankfort (Frankfort) 28
Wood River (East Alton-W.R.) 35, Chicago (Lindblom) 19
Freeport 42, Moline 24
Olney 47, Quincy 40

Quarterfinals
Paris 43, Streator (Twp.) 32
Cicero (Morton) 49, Decatur 45
Centralia 31, Wood River (East Alton-W.R.) 29
Freeport 29, Olney 24

Semifinals
Paris 28, Cicero (Morton) 21
Centralia 45, Freeport 42

Finals
Freeport 31, Cicero (Morton) 30 (third place)
Centralia 35, Paris 33 (title)

Scoring Leaders

Player, School	G	FG	FT	Pts
Dwight "Dike" Eddleman, Centralia	4	30	12	72
Gerry Dirksen, Freeport	4	23	13	59
Nate Middleton, Paris	4	24	4	52
Joe Malecek, Cicero (Morton)	4	19	7	45
Dave Humerickhouse, Paris	4	13	19	45

All-Tournament First Team

Player, School	Ht.	Yr.
Gerry Dirksen, Freeport	6-2	Sr.
Earl Dodd, Wood River (East Alton-W.R.)	6-5	Sr.
Dwight "Dike" Eddleman, Centralia	6-2	Sr.
Nate Middleton, Paris	5-9	Sr.
Charles Tourek, Cicero (Morton)	6-2	Sr.

Championship Game Box Score

Huff Gym, Champaign, March 21, 1942

CENTRALIA (35)
Coach Arthur Trout

Player	FG-A	FT-A	Pts	PF
Dwight "Dike" Eddleman	6	4-6	16	1
Fred Pearson	2	2-3	6	1
Farrell Robinson	0	2-3	2	4
Bernard Schifferdecker	1	0-0	2	2
Jim Seyler	3	3-5	9	1
Robert Wham	0	0-1	0	0
TOTAL	12	11-18	35	9

PARIS (33)
Coach Ernie Eveland

Player	FG-A	FT-A	Pts	PF
Warren Collier	3	0-1	6	1
Dick Foley	3	0-1	6	2
Gene Hancock	0	0-0	0	0
Dave Humerickhouse	1	3-4	5	2
Nate Middleton	5	0-2	10	4
Max Norman	1	4-5	6	4
Paul Pederson	0	0-0	0	0
TOTAL	13	7-13	33	13

Centralia	4	10	2	19	—	35
Paris	8	6	11	8	—	33

Officials: Carl Johnson, B.C. Beck.

After watching the 1942 state title slip away in heartbreaking fashion, Ernie Eveland's Paris squad was determined not to let the same thing happen again. The Tigers entered the 1943 state tournament as one of the favorites, ranking just behind Moline, their eventual opponent in the championship game.

Taylorville had finished the season atop the first wire-service state rankings compiled by United Press International, but fell one game short of a trip to state in a 39-36 loss to Decatur in the final of the Decatur Sectional.

In an important change, the IHSA finally abolished the rule that allowed regional runners-up to advance to the sectional, thereby reducing the field at each sectional tournament from eight teams to four.

Three schools earned their first state tournament appearance in 1943: Anna-Jonesboro, West Rockford, and Chicago's Kelvyn Park.

In the opening round, Salem outscored Canton 21-8 in the final quarter to claim a 49-47 victory, thanks in part to 25 points from Roy Gatewood. Champaign rallied in the final period to nip Quincy 33-32, and Paris set a state tourney scoring mark with a 74-40 victory over Joliet.

West Frankfort led Moline 33-29 in one of the top quarterfinal games, but the Maroons went on to pull out a 39-37 win behind 15 points from Frank DeMeyer. There was more drama in the next game as Salem needed overtime to pull out a 49-46 upset of Champaign.

Moline earned its first title game appearance when it claimed a 45-39 semifinal win over Elgin. Cal Anders led the winners with 14 points.

In the second semi, Paris gained a repeat trip to the finals when it bounced back from a 26-22 halftime deficit to beat Salem 53-50. Gordon Taylor paced the Tigers with 16 points, while Gatewood scored 22 points for Salem.

Gatewood finished with a state-finals scoring record of 96 points after notching 29 in Salem's 69-58 third-place victory over Elgin.

Several other records were set in the consolation game, including the total of 127 points, which broke the mark of 119 set by Dundee and Rushville in 1940. Elgin's 58 points also set a tournament record for a losing effort.

The state championship game pitted teams that had been ranked second and third at the end of the regular season. Roger Potter's 24-3 Moline squad was the favorite, perhaps due to its 37-34 regular-season victory over 35-2 Paris. While the Tigers had fallen in state title games twice in the previous four years, the championship game was new territory for the Maroons.

When the title game tipped off at Huff Gym, Paris proved too tough for Moline. The Tigers forged a 21-16 halftime lead and went on to claim a 46-37 victory to capture their first state championship. In the process, Paris set a record by scoring 218 points in four games.

Taylor scored 12 points, while Delbert Glover added 10 points for the Tigers.

State Final Tournament Scores

First Round

Elgin 60, Rockford (West) 56
Wood River (East Alton-W.R.) 55, Pekin 49
Moline 45, Anna (A.-Jonesboro) 30
West Frankfort (Frankfort) 55, Decatur 39
Salem 49, Canton 47
Champaign 33, Quincy 32
Paris 74, Joliet (Twp.) 40
Chicago (Kelvyn Park) 45, Kewanee 30

Quarterfinals

Elgin 44, Wood River (East Alton-W.R.) 40
Moline 39, West Frankfort (Frankfort) 37
Salem 49, Champaign 46 (OT)
Paris 45, Chicago (Kelvyn Park) 34

Semifinals

Moline 45, Elgin 39
Paris 53, Salem 50

Finals

Salem 69, Elgin 58 (third place)
Paris 46, Moline 37 (title)

Scoring Leaders

Player, School	G	FG	FT	Pts
Roy Gatewood, Salem	4	37	22	96
Bob Morton, Elgin	4	25	10	60
Gordon Taylor, Paris	4	25	4	54
Bob Menke, Elgin	4	19	13	51
Frank DeMeyer, Moline	4	20	10	50

All-Tournament First Team

Player, School	Ht.	Yr.
Cal Anders, Moline	6-0	Sr.
Frank DeMeyer, Moline	6-0	Sr.
Dick Foley, Paris	5-11	Sr.
Roy Gatewood, Salem	6-3	Sr.
Bill Hall, Moline	6-2	Sr.
Dave Humerickhouse, Paris	6-2	Sr.
John McCrudden, Rockford (West)	6-2	Sr.

Championship Game Box Score

Huff Gym, Champaign, March 20, 1943

PARIS (46)
Coach Ernie Eveland

Player	FG-A	FT-A	Pts	PF
Dick Foley	3-7	2-3	8	3
Delbert Glover	5-13	0-0	10	3
Dave Humerickhouse	0-13	1-2	1	2
Max Norman	1-6	5-5	7	4
Paul Pedersen	3-8	2-4	8	0
Gordon Taylor	6-12	0-0	12	0
TOTAL	18-59	10-14	46	12

MOLINE (37)
Coach Roger Potter

Player	FG-A	FT-A	Pts	PF
Cal Anders	3-15	2-5	8	0
Porter Bennett	0-5	0-0	0	3
Frank DeMeyer	5-13	2-4	12	4
Jim Grafton	2-5	1-1	5	4
Bill Hall	2-12	1-1	5	1
Harold Heiland	0-1	0-0	0	0
Eli Markovich	0-0	0-0	0	0
Jim Schell	0-0	0-0	0	0
LeRoy Skantz	1-4	0-1	2	0
Albert Van Landuy	2-7	1-3	5	1
TOTAL	15-62	7-15	37	13

Paris	8	13	14	11	—	46
Moline	6	10	10	11	—	37

Officials: Carl Johnson, Greg Shoaff.

PARIS
State Champions of 1943

FRONT ROW (left to right): Bob Cochran, John Cychol, Chester Dahlgren, Lyle "Nick" Swinford, Don Blair.
SECOND ROW: Paul Pedersen, Gordon Taylor, Dick Foley, Del Glover, Max Norman, Dave Humerickhouse, Coach Ernie Eveland.

1943

Taylorville finished the regular season atop the United Press International rankings, the first high school basketball poll taken in Illinois.

For 36 years, no team had been able to accomplish the ultimate goal. But in 1944, one team finally rose above the rest to become the first unbeaten state champion in Illinois history.

Taylorville's Tornadoes, top-ranked at the end of the 1943 regular season only to suffer an upset in the sectional final, entered tournament play as the team to beat. Dolph Stanley's squad owned a 41-0 record as the Sweet Sixteen converged on Huff Gym, thanks largely to the play of its two all-staters, Johnny Orr and Ron Bontemps.

Two other top-five squads failed to earn a trip to Champaign. One of those was Pinckneyville, upset by West Frankfort 38-36 in double overtime in the Centralia Sectional semifinals. Unbeaten Robinson fell to defending state champion Paris 33-32 in the Paris Sectional finals as Ernie Eveland's Tigers earned a record seventh straight state appearance.

Ten teams returned from the 1943 field. The only newcomers were Kankakee, Marseilles, and Chicago's South Shore.

In opening-round games, Anna-Jonesboro's Carroll Belcher broke the modern-day scoring record of 29 points by notching 33 to help his team to a 55-34 win over Marseilles.

West Rockford crushed Kankakee 71-22 as Dale Bowers equaled the Kays' point total, Taylorville rolled past East St. Louis 52-34 as Orr tossed in 17 points, and Kewanee knocked out defending champion Paris 36-34 with 12 points from Frank Nosalik.

South Shore earned its spot in the final four when it outscored West Rockford 12-2 in the final quarter to capture a 39-33 quarterfinal victory. All-stater Paul Schnackenberg paced the Tars with 19 points.

In the next contest, Canton led Champaign 26-19 at halftime, but the Maroons used a 20-2 advantage in the third quarter to claim a 57-42 win. Jesse Clements led Champaign with 16 points.

Finally, Taylorville won 51-30 over Kewanee as Orr scored 20 points. In doing so, the Tornadoes became the first team to win 43 straight games in one season, breaking the mark of 42 set by the 1941 Centralia team.

The semifinals opened in exciting fashion as Elgin overcame a 31-19 halftime deficit to pull out a 48-47 victory over South Shore. Jack Burmaster, who later coached Evanston to the 1968 title and served as a tournament broadcaster, led the Maroons with 12 points.

In the second semifinal, Harry Combes' Champaign team gave Taylorville its best battle of the season, but fell short for the fourth time as the Tornadoes prevailed 40-36. Don Janssen scored 11 points to lead the way for Taylorville, which tied Dundee's state record of 44 consecutive victories, set across two seasons from 1938 to 1939.

Taylorville entered the finals as a heavy favorite over John Krafft's 21-3 Elgin team. Elgin led 10-8 after one quarter, but Taylorville moved ahead 24-19 by halftime. After Burmaster fouled out in the fourth quarter, the Tornadoes broke the game open with a 19-4 outburst to win 56-33.

Taylorville was paced by its two all-tournament selections, Bontemps (18 points) and Orr (17).

Stanley moved up to a coaching position at Beloit College before returning to the high school game at Rockford Auburn. Orr went on to a notable career as a college coach at the University of Michigan and Iowa State.

State Final Tournament Scores

First Round

Anna (A.-Jonesboro) 55, Marseilles 34
Elgin 39, Pekin 38
Rockford (West) 71, Kankakee 22
Chicago (South Shore) 62, Quincy 38
Canton 47, West Frankfort (Frankfort) 39
Champaign 44, Mt. Carmel 32
Taylorville 52, East St. Louis 34
Kewanee 36, Paris 34

Quarterfinals

Elgin 65, Anna (A.-Jonesboro) 38
Chicago (South Shore) 39, Rockford (West) 33
Champaign 57, Canton 42
Taylorville 51, Kewanee 30

Semifinals

Elgin 48, Chicago (South Shore) 47
Taylorville 40, Champaign 36

Finals

Chicago (South Shore) 52, Champaign 34 (third place)
Taylorville 56, Elgin 33 (title)

Scoring Leaders

Player, School	G	FG	FT	Pts
Paul Schnackenberg, Chicago (S. Shore)	4	25	16	66
Johnny Orr, Taylorville	4	28	8	64
Dan Trahey, Chicago (South Shore)	4	21	19	61
Ronald Bontemps, Taylorville	4	20	9	49
Jim Rager, Elgin	4	20	6	46

All-Tournament First Team

Player, School	Ht.	Yr.
Ronald Bontemps, Taylorville	6-3	Sr.
Jack Burmaster, Elgin	6-2	Sr.
Jesse Clements, Champaign	6-1	Jr.
Johnny Orr, Taylorville	6-2	Sr.
Paul Schnackenberg, Chicago (South Shore)	5-11	Sr.

Championship Game Box Score

Huff Gym, Champaign, March 18, 1944

TAYLORVILLE (56)
Coach Dolph Stanley

Player	FG-A	FT-A	Pts	PF
Schultte Bishop	2-8	1-2	5	4
Ronald Bontemps	8-20	2-3	18	1
Dale Brown	0-1	0-0	0	0
Dean Duncan	0-1	1-1	1	1
Don Janssen	1-5	0-1	2	2
Dave Jones	3-9	2-4	8	4
Joe McAdam	0-0	1-1	1	0
Johnny Orr	7-19	3-5	17	2
Charles Reister	2-6	0-1	4	1
Jack Richards	0-0	0-0	0	0
TOTAL	23-69	10-18	56	15

ELGIN (33)
Coach John Krafft

Player	FG-A	FT-A	Pts	PF
Jack Burmaster	1-4	1-1	3	5
Bill Goedert	0-2	0-0	0	1
Howard Kugath	2-7	1-1	5	1
Bill Myers	0-1	1-1	1	1
Tom Parker	0-1	0-1	0	1
Karl Plath	2-15	2-8	6	4
Jim Rager	1-14	2-2	4	2
Sam Sauceda	4-15	6-7	14	2
TOTAL	10-59	13-21	33	17

Taylorville	8	16	13	19	—	56
Elgin	10	9	10	4	—	33

Officials: Carl Johnson, R.C. Kaegel.

TAYLORVILLE, State Champions of 1944

FRONT ROW (left to right): Schultte Bishop, Johnny Orr, Ron Bontemps, Dave Jones, Dean Duncan.
SECOND ROW: Coach Dolph Stanley, Charles Reister, Jack Richards, Dale Brown, Don Janssen, Joe McAdam.

HISTORIC CHAMPIONSHIP

Taylorville battles Elgin in the 1944 title game. With its victory, Taylorville earned a place in history as the state's first undefeated basketball champion.

Taylorville team members greet adoring fans in their hometown gym after returning from a victorious weekend in Champaign.

Coach Dolph Stanley and his players gather for a celebration in the Taylorville High School gymnasium.

East St. Louis and Taylorville mix it up in 1944 quarterfinal action. That's Johnny Orr of Taylorville (43) stretching for the loose ball.

1944

More than a game
High school basketball's victory over segregation

When it's **played** the way it's supposed to be played, basketball happens in the air; flying, floating, elevated above the floor, levitating the way oppressed people of this earth *imagine* themselves in their *dreams*.

— John Edgar Wideman

by Pat Heston

If you know nothing about East St. Louis Lincoln and the Tigers' run to their first state championship, know this: When the squad hoisted the trophy the night of March 20, 1982, they were not alone. Alongside stood the ghosts of a bygone era.

Joining the celebration were unseen athletes such as Leonard Tucker, Marvin Winkler, Luther Farrell, Lee Arthur Morris, Eugene Lewis, "Peck" Price, and "Tater" Chandler. Nearby were coaches like Joe Russell, Ernie Page, John T. Caldwell, and C. K. Cole — all of them unable to step onto a state-finals floor because their skin was black.

Staking a claim to the Tigers' trophy were neighboring Brooklyn Lovejoy and 13 other schools once barred from state tournament play: the members of the former Southern Illinois Conference of Colored High Schools (SICCHS).

There have been more exciting title games than Lincoln's 56-50 victory over Chicago Mendel Catholic, but few were more significant.

A league of their own

African-American players and teams had already etched their names into state-finals lore. Peoria's Lynch Conway, the tournament's first great black athlete, scored 22 points in the 1908 championship game. Chicago New Phillips sent the first all-black squad to state in 1936.

Meanwhile, relegated to a league of their own, was the SICCHS — 15 schools located in three geographic pockets essentially south and west of a line running from St. Louis through Benton to Paducah, Kentucky.

Near St. Louis in the Metro-East counties of Madison and St. Clair were five schools: Brooklyn Lovejoy, Edwardsville Lincoln, East St. Louis Lincoln, Madison Dunbar, and Venice Lincoln.

The second cluster of schools was four in number, squeezed into a small square in the middle of "Egypt," the 17 southernmost counties of Illinois: DuQuoin Lincoln, Colp, Murphysboro Douglass, and Carbondale Attucks.

The Deep South or Ohio River schools were located near Kentucky in the two southern tips of the state. Using modern markers, four of them — Cairo Sumner, Mound City Lovejoy, Mounds Douglass, and Sandusky Young — were near Interstate 57, and two others — Brookport Lincoln and Metropolis Dunbar — were near Interstate 24.

Sadly, the three areas represented lingering bastions of segregation in Illinois prep basketball — a fact impossible to appreciate without realizing how much southern Illinois shared with the American South in both geography and tradition.

Illinois is one of the longest of the United States when measured north to south. Cairo, for example, is significantly further south than Richmond, Virginia, the capitol of the Confederacy. In fact, a full two-thirds of all battles in the Civil War occurred on soil further north than Cairo.

In a sentence, racial segregation was a resolute mindset in the southern third of the state. As a result, some of the finest coaches, players, and teams the state has ever seen were unjustly isolated from the rest of Illinois.

The late Joe Russell of Bradley University, former coach at Mounds Douglass High School, remembered those days with a combination of pain and pleasure.

"To be ostracized like we were hurt very much," he said. "But, my, what a time it was! Some of the greatest players ever to step onto a court, some of the greatest coaches ever to mold young lives, some of the greatest teams ever to play in Illinois were going head-to-head off basketball's beaten path. Few people ever saw them. Few ever knew."

Celebrating 100 years of IHSA Boys Basketball Tournaments

★ CARBONDALE ATTUCKS '42 ★

finals. From 1942 to 1945, this "Colored Conference championship game" played at the state tournament, wedged between Friday's quarterfinal sessions.

In the first such meeting, John C. Clark's Carbondale Attucks squad nipped Cairo Sumner 30-28 in the most exciting of the short series of title games.

Changes made prior to the 1943 playoffs guaranteed that the schools meeting for the championship in Champaign would not be from the same geographic area. The next three title games featured one team from the Deep South and a second from the Metro-East.

In 1943, Carbondale Attucks advanced from the Cairo District and met the winner from the East St. Louis District, Madison Dunbar. Attucks seized a quick lead and held it to the end, defeating Dunbar 53-41. Both teams displayed a smooth passing attack and, according to some sportswriters, made shots "bordering on the miraculous."

Dunbar returned to the championship game in 1944, meeting newcomer Mounds Douglass. Gene Cross of Douglass, one of the premier players in the state and one day to be one of the great coaches in SICCHS history, scored eight of his game-high 19 points to spark the second quarter surge that put his team up 23-20 at the half. Dunbar stayed within striking distance until late in the

Former Madison Dunbar mentor George Smith agreed, "The teams, the players, the coaches were unforgettable, just like the days themselves. We were segregated, isolated, off the radar of the rest of the state, even the rest of southern Illinois, but we were playing a game that others only dreamed of playing."

Walk into one of the south's band-box gyms at the height of segregation for a game between two all-black schools and you were time-warped into the future — end-to-end action, between-the-legs dribbles, behind-the-back passes and above-the-rim shots.

One-time Madison Dunbar coach, the late Ernie Page, Sr., reflected on the experience shortly after his 91st birthday. "Fans outside of southern Illinois, and even the majority of fans from southern Illinois, never knew what they missed. Hundreds, thousands of fans from the south had no idea what incredible talent was showcasing itself nightly under their very noses."

Organized around 1919 and segregated from their neighbors as well as other IHSAA members, conference schools were forced to maintain a low profile. The first barrier fell in 1929 when the IHSAA (as it was known until 1940) allowed the SICCHS schools to join the association. Membership did not include all the privileges, however. The IHSAA supplied trophies for the conference's annual postseason tournament, but little more in the way of assistance.

But more than a decade after admitting the SICCHS schools, the state association took the first small steps toward making them equal partners. Starting in 1942, the IHSA organized two district basketball tournaments for the conference, with the winners meeting at Huff Gym during the state

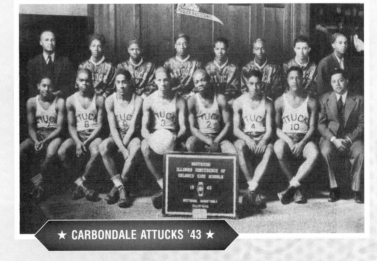

★ CARBONDALE ATTUCKS '43 ★

game, eventually falling short 49-34.

The 1945 finale again featured the Mounds and Madison entries, the third straight title game appearance for Coach Ernie Page's Dunbar five. Marvin Winkler had a great second half for Dunbar, scoring a team best 13 points for the game, but 15 each from Len Tucker and Bobby Harris keyed a second half explosion that vaulted Douglass to the 44-29 victory.

It was the last Colored Conference championship ever played.

Partial integration

The evolution of integration in southern Illinois required many difficult decades, but the process would have been even longer and more grueling had it not been for high school basketball. In truth, it was the game of basketball, possibly more than any other single factor, that helped break segregation's stranglehold in southern Illinois.

continued on next page

★ MOUNDS DOUGLASS '44 ★

FRONT ROW (left to right): Otis Forrest, Bobby Harris, Clarence Harrell, Gene Cross, Leonard Tucker. SECOND ROW: Coach J.E. Price, Robert Parker, Ulysses Watkins, Eddie Moore. THIRD ROW: Everette Scurlock, Devon Cross, Manager William Atkinson.

FRONT ROW (left to right): Everett Scurlock, Robert Parker, Leonard Tucker, Bobby Harris, James Ellis. SECOND ROW: Manager William Atkinson, Ulysses Watkins, Charles McGee, James Morris, Devon Cross, Coach J.E. Price. THIRD ROW: Manager C.W. Dixon, James Bailey, Frank Nesbitt, John Henry Ringold.

★ MOUNDS DOUGLASS '45 ★

In addition to slow but steady advances by the IHSA, some schools on the northern fringes of the southern third of the state began to strike blows for integration. Two all-white schools were the most courageous in the quest to eradicate segregation from high school basketball in the region.

On Christmas Eve 1945, Livingston High School hosted an all-black squad from Madison Dunbar in the first integrated basketball game played in the southern third of the state. During Christmas week one year later, Gillespie High School became the first all-white team from southern Illinois to play a basketball game on the court of an all-black school as its team traveled to Madison Dunbar.

Not to be overlooked was the courageous contribution of Dunbar, which stepped beyond convention and across age-old cultural lines to play all-white schools.

Such events were exceptions to the unwritten rule of segregation that held sway in the area, but they were cracks in a dam which would soon break, forever altering the landscape of the state.

In 1946, the IHSA Board of Directors voted to allow SICCHS schools into the state tournament. Winners from all-black district tournaments advanced to regional tournaments as close as a host school would accept them. That usually meant somewhere near the northern fringe of what was called "Egypt." Mounds Douglass, refused by two regional tournaments, finally gained acceptance at Benton, where Floyd Smith, president of the IHSA, was principal.

On February 28, in the regional semifinals, Douglass upset second-ranked West Frankfort 55-51, sending shock waves throughout the state. "W. Frankfort Defeated By Colored Team," screamed the *Belleville News-Democrat* headline in disbelief. The celebration was short-lived. The next night, Johnston City buried Douglass 59-38.

Douglass and Carbondale Attucks dominated the Deep South district from 1946 to 1953, although Cairo Sumner won the honors once, in 1948. Meanwhile, in the Metro-East, Madison Dunbar and East St. Louis Lincoln took turns winning district championships.

The winners, however, had trouble competing with larger schools in regional action. It was 1949 before a SICCHS school finally won a regional tournament. East St. Louis Lincoln accomplished the feat, but lost to Brownstown's Bombers in the sectional semifinals.

Madison Dunbar followed suit the next season, losing a first-round sectional game to Collinsville.

In 1952, Carbondale Attucks met No. 2 Centralia in the sectional final at West Frankfort, taking the Orphans to the wire before surrendering a late lead and losing 71-64.

Finally, following the 1952-53 season, basketball segregation officially vanished from the south as Illinois completely integrated its district tournaments.

Finally, following the 1952-53 season, basketball segregation officially vanished from the south as Illinois completely integrated its district tournaments.

The arrival of integration

In 1954, Mounds Douglass won the first integrated district tournament in southern Illinois, at Anna-Jonesboro, then claimed the regional title at Wolf Lake, before heading to Harrisburg for arguably the toughest sectional in the state

Sparked by 6-foot-8 All-American center Archie Dees, Mt. Carmel drilled Douglass 97-68. The next night, Mt. Vernon nipped Mt. Carmel 70-69 on two Al Avant free throws after time expired. Mt. Vernon captured the 1954 state title, upsetting unbeaten Chicago DuSable.

Three years later, East St. Louis Lincoln became the first SICCHS school to crack the AP statewide poll, crafting a 28-0 record and climbing to No. 11 in the rankings. However, that Tigers team, fueled by a standout player named Bennie Lewis, slipped in the regional final against crosstown rival East St. Louis Senior.

In addition to Mounds Douglass, only three other SICCHS teams won regional tournaments after 1953. East St. Louis Lincoln finally broke through in 1958, and both Douglass and Carbondale Attucks duplicated the feat in 1960.

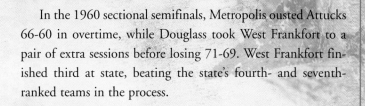

In the 1960 sectional semifinals, Metropolis ousted Attucks 66-60 in overtime, while Douglass took West Frankfort to a pair of extra sessions before losing 71-69. West Frankfort finished third at state, beating the state's fourth- and seventh-ranked teams in the process.

Breakthrough

East St. Louis Lincoln became the first former SICCHS school to win a sectional tournament, reaching the 1980 Carbondale Super-Sectional only to take it on the chin against Effingham and 7-foot-2 Uwe Blab, 74-58.

Despite the setback, Lincoln's players, including sophomores Tyrone Jackson and Todd Porter, refused to let the long-cherished dream die. They were determined to reach Champaign and, in the process, to make history.

Two years later, Jackson, Porter, and their teammates did exactly that.

In 1982, Lincoln went a near-perfect 29-1, beating Mendel to capture the school's first state title. It was also the first state championship by a former SICCHS school, the culmination of a generations-long dream. By decade's end, the Tigers would add three more championships, in 1987, 1988, and 1989.

Lincoln merged with East St. Louis Senior following the 1999 season, leaving only Brooklyn Lovejoy as a surviving SICCHS school. The rest eventually consolidated with other schools. To this day, Lincoln has the highest tournament winning percentage (.800) of any school with at least five tournament visits.

When Bennie Lewis coached his alma mater to its first state title in 1982, it was a win, not simply for Lincoln and East St. Louis, but for schools from DuQuoin south to the Ohio River and from Edwardsville southwest to the Mississippi. It was a win for players like Bobby Harris, Oris Hill, Robert "Honey" Jackson, Eugene Lowery, William Jenkins and Floyd "Dunbar Slim" Johnson; a win for coaches like John Algee, "Big Tree" and "Little Tree" Harris, Gene Cross, John C. Clark, and Charles "Fess" Smith.

It was a win for so much more than a school.

It was a win for basketball itself.

East St. Louis Lincoln players celebrate the school's first state title after beating Chicago Mendel in the 1982 Class AA finals. Lincoln closed in 1999, leaving Brooklyn Lovejoy as the only SICCHS member school still operating.

DECATUR
State Champions of 1945

FRONT ROW (left to right):
Ralph Rutherford, Bob Doster,
George Riley, Bob Neuendorf,
John Malerich, Tom Krigbaum.
SECOND ROW: Coach Gay Kintner,
Bob Kurek, Bob Stauber,
Jim Arnold, Bob Hoyt.

Dick Kelly of Champaign cuts past
George Riley of Decatur in the 1945
title game.

1945

Big Twelve rivals Champaign and Decatur finished the regular season as the state's two top-ranked teams and appeared to be on a collision course for the 1945 state championship.

Gay Kintner's Reds defeated Paris 46-36 in the Mattoon sectional final in one of the most anticipated pre-state clashes.

Decatur's win halted the record seven-year streak of sectional titles and Sweet Sixteen appearances by Ernie Eveland's Tigers.

There was a relatively new look to the 1945 tournament, with only four squads back from the previous season. The only new entrants to the tournament were district winner Somonauk, with only 88 students, and Chicago Public League champion Senn.

Top-ranked Champaign's hopes were nearly derailed in the first round by Morton of Cicero, but the Maroons overcame a 45-33 deficit with five minutes to go to claim a 47-46 win. The game featured a coaching match-up of Champaign's Harry Combes and Morton's Jim Vopicka, college roommates and teammates at the University of Illinois.

Galesburg had to rally past West Frankfort in the final quarter to claim a 45-42 win before second-ranked Decatur showed off its offensive firepower, setting a record for points as it rolled past Collinsville 77-45. Decatur received a record 34 points and 16 field goals from

Bob Doster, who tied the all-time tourney point mark set by Olney's Leland Stilwell in 1920.

In the first quarterfinal game, Champaign demonstrated that it could score points, too, crushing Somonauk 77-28 to tie Decatur's record from the night before.

That set the stage for one of the tournament's classic games, with Decatur and Galesburg ringing up points at a pace never seen before. In the final seconds, Decatur's Ralph Rutherford stole the ball and converted a three-point play to force a 66-66 tie. The Reds finally pulled out a 73-72 victory when Doster hit a short shot with two seconds remaining in overtime. The 145 points obliterated the previous record of 127 points set by Salem and Elgin two seasons before. George Riley of Decatur tossed in 30 points to lead all scorers.

The semifinals didn't feature as much drama as Champaign rolled past Quincy

50-32, thanks to 16 points from Ted Beach, and Decatur advanced with a 62-46 win over Moline as Doster scored 27.

On paper, the championship game figured to be another classic between Champaign and Decatur. The Reds had won the first meeting 52-50 and the Maroons had answered with a 44-42 victory. But Champaign was able to use only eight players in the final due to illness and injury. The IHSA sought to help the Maroons by loosening tourney rules to allow some replacements, but Champaign athletic director Les Moyer refused the offer, saying he didn't want to set a bad precedent.

Ahead 26-19 at halftime, Decatur held its lead and went on to claim a 62-54 victory. Doster outscored Riley 18-16 to edge his teammate 96-93 for scoring honors and tie the tournament mark set by Salem's Roy Gatewood in 1943. Jesse Clements paced the Maroons with 19.

Kintner won his third title, equaling Centralia's Arthur Trout, and Decatur joined Rockford and Centralia as the only three-time state champs. The Reds, the highest-scoring team in history to that time, poured in a record 274 points in the tournament.

State Final Tournament Scores

First Round
Somonauk 44, Carbondale 35
Champaign 47, Cicero (Morton) 46
Quincy 46, Springfield 38
Peoria 38, Flora 36
Galesburg 45, West Frankfort (Frankfort) 42
Decatur 77, Collinsville 45
Elgin 44, Rockford (East) 39
Moline 35, Chicago (Senn) 32

Quarterfinals
Champaign 77, Somonauk 28
Quincy 54, Peoria 46
Decatur 73, Galesburg 72 (OT)
Moline 41, Elgin 39

Semifinals
Champaign 50, Quincy 32
Decatur 62, Moline 46

Finals
Quincy 49, Moline 47 (third place)
Decatur 62, Champaign 54 (title)

Scoring Leaders

Player, School	G	FG	FT	Pts
Bob Doster, Decatur	4	41	14	96
George Riley, Decatur	4	40	13	93
Dwight Humphrey, Moline	4	25	13	63
Ted Beach, Champaign	4	26	10	62
Dick Heitholt, Quincy	4	22	16	60

All-Tournament First Team

Player, School	Ht.	Yr.
Jesse Clements, Champaign	6-1	Sr.
Bob Doster, Decatur	6-1	Sr.
Dwight Humphrey, Moline	5-8	Sr.
Ray McClure, Galesburg	5-11	Sr.
George Riley, Decatur	6-7	Sr.

Championship Game Box Score

Huff Gym, Champaign, March 17, 1945

DECATUR (62)
Coach Gay Kintner

Player	FG-A	FT-A	Pts	PF
James Arnold	0-0	0-0	0	0
Bob Doster	6-16	6-9	18	3
Bob Hoyt	0-0	0-1	0	0
Tom Krigbaum	0-3	2-5	2	4
Robert Kurek	0-1	0-0	0	0
John Malerich	5-17	4-6	14	1
Bob Neuendorf	0-4	1-1	1	1
George Riley	8-23	0-1	16	5
Ralph Rutherford	5-10	1-2	11	3
Bob Stauber	0-0	0-0	0	0
TOTAL	24-74	14-25	62	17

CHAMPAIGN (54)
Coach Harry Combes

Player	FG-A	FT-A	Pts	PF
Ted Beach	5-14	3-3	13	1
Jesse Clements	9-19	1-1	19	2
Jim Cottrell	0-1	0-0	0	2
Pete Fletcher	1-1	1-2	3	1
Earl Harrison	1-5	1-1	3	4
Dick Kelly	2-6	4-6	8	3
Fred Major	0-0	2-3	2	2
Dick Paterson	3-12	0-0	6	5
TOTAL	21-58	12-16	54	20

Decatur	14	12	17	19	—	62
Champaign	9	10	16	19	—	54

Officials: Ernest Driggers, Edward Murphy.

Earl Harrison of Champaign struggles
for a loose ball in the 1946 title game against
Centralia. Champaign won the game, 54-48.

1946

After coming up a bit short of winning a state championship in 1945, Harry Combes' 1946 Champaign team entered the Sweet Sixteen 34-1 and top-ranked, with a lineup that featured several key returnees.

One of Champaign's biggest threats figured to be West Frankfort, which was ranked second heading into the postseason and had beaten the Maroons 56-44. But the Redbirds, who had been southern Illinois' representative at state for four straight years, fell in a historic upset to Mounds Douglass, 55-51, in the regional semifinals.

Surprises were common leading up to the state finals as half of the state's top 10 teams failed to earn a trip to Champaign. Host Centralia knocked off rival Mt. Vernon, and Dundee defeated Waukegan in top-10 sectional showdowns. Meanwhile, Robinson advanced to state for the first time in 30 years when it upset Paris in the Robinson Sectional final.

There were four newcomers to the Sweet Sixteen: Calumet City's Thornton Fractional, Chicago's Tilden Tech, Pana, and Pontiac.

The highlight of the first round at Huff Gym was Centralia, making its record-tying 10th tournament appearance under Arthur Trout, outscoring Kewanee 20-4 in the final period to claim a 50-36 decision.

In the quarterfinals, Dundee jumped out to a 14-5 lead after one quarter and made it stand, knocking off defending state champion Decatur 55-48 behind 17 points from Charles Grover. Champaign earned its way back into the semifinals the same way, claiming an 18-7 advantage after one period and holding on to defeat Marion 55-43. Ted Beach led the way for the Maroons with 15 points.

As the action moved into the semis, Centralia scored the only point in overtime to claim a 45-44 victory over Dundee. The Cardunals trailed 24-11 at halftime but nearly rallied to win. Centralia's Arnold Gluck hit three free throws during the final minute of regulation play to force a tie and then hit the game-winner a minute into the overtime.

Champaign took the other semifinal with a 53-47 victory over Jim Laude's East Rockford team. Beach paced the Maroons with 24 points while the Rabs received 23 points from tourney scoring leader Louis Proctor.

The championship game featured two teams with some of the richest state tournament history. Making a record 16th state appearance, the Maroons were still aiming for their first title, while Trout was hoping to become the first coach, and Centralia the first school, to capture four state championships.

Champaign entered the contest with a 26-game winning streak. The Orphans were 29-9 on the season, with one of their losses, a 46-36 setback, coming against the Maroons. Although Centralia had a tall team and Trout's famous kiss shot was a dangerous weapon, Champaign was favored by most observers.

After a close first quarter, Champaign gained a 23-13 halftime advantage. Although Centralia rallied to get to within 40-36 in the fourth quarter, Champaign went on to claim a 54-48 victory for its first state championship. The Maroons were paced by Beach, who led all scorers with 22 points, and Jim Cottrell, who added 14 points.

State Final Tournament Scores

First Round
Decatur 59, Pana 41
Dundee 56, Quincy 49
Centralia 50, Kewanee 36
Robinson 47, Pontiac 44
Rockford (East) 74, Chicago (Tilden) 53
Collinsville 50, Springfield (Cathedral) 28
Marion 42, Calumet City (Thornton Fractional) 38 (OT)
Champaign 49, Galesburg 40

Quarterfinals
Dundee 55, Decatur 48
Centralia 63, Robinson 50
Rockford (East) 43, Collinsville 37
Champaign 55, Marion 43

Semifinals
Centralia 45, Dundee 44 (OT)
Champaign 53, Rockford (East) 47

Finals
Dundee 59, Rockford (East) 53 (third place)
Champaign 54, Centralia 48 (title)

Scoring Leaders

Player, School	G	FG	FT	Pts
Louis Proctor, Rockford (East)	4	31	24	86
Charles Grover, Dundee	4	29	16	74
Ted Beach, Champaign	4	30	11	71
Colin Anderson, Centralia	4	23	13	59
Bill Erickson, Rockford (East)	4	23	9	55

All-Tournament First Team

Player, School	Ht.	Yr.
Colin Anderson, Centralia	6-3	Sr.
Ted Beach, Champaign	6-2	Jr.
Jim Cottrell, Champaign	5-11	Sr.
Benton Odum, Marion	6-1	Sr.
Louis Proctor, Rockford (East)	6-4	Sr.

Championship Game Box Score

Huff Gym, Champaign, March 16, 1946

CHAMPAIGN (54)
Coach Harry Combes

Player	FG-A	FT-A	Pts	PF
Ted Beach	9-15	4-4	22	1
Jim Cottrell	6-11	2-2	14	5
Rodney Fletcher	3-6	0-1	6	3
Earl Harrison	3-10	0-1	6	2
Bill Johnston	0-0	0-0	0	0
Fred Major	0-5	1-1	1	1
John McDermott	2-3	1-4	5	1
TOTAL	23-50	8-13	54	13

CENTRALIA (48)
Coach Arthur Trout

Player	FG-A	FT-A	Pts	PF
Colin Anderson	7-24	0-1	14	1
Ken McBride	2-14	2-3	6	4
Charles Oland	3-11	1-1	7	1
Harold Rush	4-11	7-7	15	2
Don Schnake	3-7	0-1	6	1
TOTAL	19-67	10-13	48	11

Champaign	7	16	13	18	—	54
Centralia	8	5	11	24	—	48

Officials: Williams Downes, Walter Johnson.

CHAMPAIGN
State Champions of 1946

FRONT ROW (left to right):
Ted Beach, Jim Cottrell,
Earl Harrison, Fred Major,
Rodney Fletcher.
SECOND ROW: Asst. Coach
Harold Jester, Kirby Knox,
Bobby Clark, John McDermott,
Dick Petry, Bill Johnston,
Coach Harry Combes.

1947

As the 1947 state tournament approached, Champaign had high hopes it could stage a repeat performance of its state title, but there were plenty of other dangerous squads in the state.

The big postseason showdowns started right away when top-ranked Dundee and second-ranked Elgin met at Woodstock, the only time the state's top two teams have met in a regional tournament. The rankings proved correct as the Cardunals were victorious, 37-26.

Ernie Eveland's fourth-ranked Paris team advanced to the sectional final for a record 12th straight time and then earned a trip to state with a 36-34 victory over Mattoon at Charleston. In another sectional final, Kewanee avenged both its regular season losses when it defeated Rock Island 58-47 in a showdown of top-10 squads at Moline.

Murphysboro was the only new face in the Sweet Sixteen field.

The tournament proved to be a historic finale for a coaching legend. Mark Peterman, who had directed the great Canton teams of the 1920s and continued his success at Springfield in the 1930s, became the first coach to bring 11 teams to state when he led his Senators back to Champaign for the last time. Unfortunately, Springfield met No. 1 Dundee in the opening round and fell by a 69-47 count.

In the quarterfinals, Pekin held off Collinsville 42-41 as Charles Busby scored 15 points for the winners, including the game-winner with four seconds

PARIS
State Champions of 1947

FRONT ROW (left to right): Don Glover, Dow Morris, Duane "Bucky" Eveland, Bob Owens, Glen Vietor, John Wilson, Coach Ernie Eveland.
SECOND ROW: Mgr. Floyd Garrett, Max Wilson, Fred Blair, Ronnie Beeson, Ronnie Cummins, Dick Henson.

left. Champaign knocked off Dundee 47-45 when Ray Walters hit a bucket with two seconds left.

Paris advanced to the semifinals with a 49-37 win over South Shore as John Wilson had 14 for the Tigers. In the last quarterfinal game, Pinckneyville assured itself its first state trophy, crushing Kewanee 47-26 behind 15 points from Robert Johnson.

Champaign earned a berth in the title game with a convincing win over Pekin, 73-53, in the first semifinal contest. Ted

Beach scored 20 points, as did teammate Fred Major, Jr.

In the other semifinal, Paris grabbed a 46-39 lead after three quarters and went on to claim a 57-50 victory over Pinckneyville, advancing to the title game for the fourth time in nine years. Robert Owens paced the Tigers with 20 points.

The championship featured what were likely the top two programs in the state during the 1940s. Eveland's Paris team was in the title game for the third time in six years, while Harry Combes's Champaign team was playing in its third straight championship contest, tying the record set by Thornton from 1933 to 1935.

The title game appeared evenly matched, with Paris at 39-2 and the defending state champs at 33-3. But the Tigers owned an easy 57-39 victory over the Maroons during the regular season, and the championship turned into a similar romp as Paris led 47-33 with a quarter to go. The final score of 58-37 gave Paris its second state championship in five seasons.

Owens led Paris with 22 points, while teammate Glen Vietor chipped in with 14. Champaign was paced by Rod Fletcher and Beach, who scored 11 apiece.

State Final Tournament Scores

First Round
Collinsville 48, Flora 37
Pekin 54, Marseilles 47
Dundee 69, Springfield 47
Champaign 52, Murphysboro 39
Paris 70, Beardstown 33
Chicago (South Shore) 43, Galesburg 37
Kewanee 56, Rockford (East) 53
Pinckneyville 45, Aurora (East) 34

Quarterfinals
Pekin 42, Collinsville 41
Champaign 47, Dundee 45
Paris 49, Chicago (South Shore) 37
Pinckneyville 47, Kewanee 26

Semifinals
Champaign 73, Pekin 53
Paris 57, Pinckneyville 50

Finals
Pinckneyville 47, Pekin 42 (third place)
Paris 58, Champaign 37 (title)

Scoring Leaders

Player, School	G	FG	FT	Pts
Robert Owens, Paris	4	29	14	72
Ted Beach, Champaign	4	30	5	65
Bert Van Horn, Pekin	4	15	19	49
Frank Gladson, Pinckneyville	4	17	12	46
Glen Vietor, Paris	4	20	5	45
Charles Busby, Pekin	4	16	13	45

All-Tournament First Team

Player, School	Ht.	Yr.
Ted Beach, Champaign	6-2	Sr.
Jake Fendley, Chicago (South Shore)	6-1	Sr.
Frank Gladson, Pinckneyville	5-10	Jr.
Charles Grover, Dundee	6-1	Sr.
Robert Owens, Paris	6-2	Sr.

Championship Game Box Score
Huff Gym, Champaign, March 22, 1947

PARIS (58)
Coach Ernie Eveland

Player	FG-A	FT-A	Pts	PF
Don Glover	2-6	3-3	7	1
Richard Henson	1-2	1-1	3	0
Dow Morris	1-4	2-3	4	3
Robert Owens	9-18	4-4	22	4
Glen Vietor	6-16	2-3	14	2
John Wilson	3-6	2-3	8	2
TOTAL	22-52	14-17	58	12

CHAMPAIGN (37)
Coach Harry Combes

Player	FG-A	FT-A	Pts	PF
Ted Beach	5-20	1-1	11	0
Bernard Bryant	0-2	0-0	0	0
Bobby Clark	0-1	0-2	0	1
Rodney Fletcher	4-19	3-7	11	4
Fred Major	2-6	1-1	5	1
John McDermott	2-2	0-0	4	3
Dick Petry	0-2	0-1	0	3
Ray Walters	1-8	4-4	6	2
Wayne Wells	0-3	0-0	0	1
Kenneth Wilk	0-1	0-0	0	0
TOTAL	14-64	9-16	37	15

Paris	10	17	20	11	—	58
Champaign	7	13	13	4	—	37

Officials: Sam Gillespie, Ted Search Sr..

High School Champs

With top-five teams Dundee and Salem losing in the regional finals of the 1948 tournament, and Ernie Eveland's Paris squad falling one step short of a 13th straight sectional final appearance, the door was open for some new contenders.

Top-ranked Pekin and second-ranked Collinsville were both 27-1, while sixth-ranked Pinckneyville brought a 29-1 record to the Sweet Sixteen.

The only two other returnees to the state tournament were Champaign, a humble 13-14 under new coach Harold Jester, and Jim Laude's East Rockford team, which wasn't ranked despite a 23-3 record.

Of these five returning squads, Merrill "Duster" Thomas's Pinckneyville team had the hardest time securing its spot. In the sectional title game, the Panthers needed to overcome a 30-27 deficit going into the fourth quarter to win 40-39 against Centralia.

In notable opening-round games at Huff Gym, Pekin held off a late charge by LaSalle-Peru to win 50-46, and East Rockford had to go overtime to claim a 54-53 victory over Champaign and Rodney Fletcher, who scored 22 points. Virgil "Cuss" Wilson's 21-10 Marion squad pulled off one of the biggest tourney shockers in years with a 65-60 upset over Collinsville.

Pinckneyville kicked off the quarterfinal round with an easy 58-36 victory over Springfield Cathedral. The winners were led by 17 points from Tom Millikin. East Rockford overcame a 49-46 deficit with two minutes to go to nip Marshall 51-49 as Peter Anderson led the E-Rabs with 20 points.

In the first semifinal, Pinckneyville used slowdown tactics to perfection as it upset Pekin 36-31. Ahead just 27-23 after three quarters, the Panthers opened the fourth quarter with eight straight points to take control. David Davis led the winners with 12 points.

East Rockford grabbed a 51-39 lead early in the fourth quarter and then watched the lead slip to just four points before recovering to defeat LaGrange Lyons 61-54 in the other semifinal. Frank Calacurcio scored 16 points for East, and Sherman Norton had the same total for the Lions, who were hampered by an injury to star Jim Hoffman.

Fans hoping for a thrilling championship game were disappointed as Pinckneyville shot out to an 18-6 lead after one quarter and increased it to 35-19 at halftime. The final was 65-39, as Pinckneyville won its first state title.

Two-time all-tournament selections Frank Gladson and Robert Johnson led the winners with 21 points each. Millikin, who scored eight for Pinckneyville in the title game, would later coach Proviso East's 1969 squad to the state championship.

With an enrollment of 430, Pinckneyville was the smallest school since Johnston City (412 in 1929) to capture the state crown. The 26-point title triumph was the second-largest in history, behind Rockford's 60-15 romp over Mt. Carroll in 1911. Pinckneyville's 65 points were also the most in a title game.

After the state tournament, Thomas confided to the *Champaign News-Gazette* that he thought that sectional win over Centralia was the real state championship.

PINCKNEYVILLE, State Champions of 1948

FRONT ROW (left to right): Percy Clippard, Tom Millikin, Bob Johnson, Dave Davis, Frank Gladson. SECOND ROW: Bill Nesbitt, Mgr. Dick Luke, Dick Craig, Bill Williams, Bill McCrary, Charles Gruner, Coach Merrill "Duster" Thomas.

State Final Tournament Scores

First Round

Springfield (Cathedral) 57, Harvey (Thornton) 50
Pinckneyville 45, Moline 35
Pekin 50, LaSalle (L.-Peru) 46
Marion 65, Collinsville 60
LaGrange (Lyons) 61, Hillsboro 44
Canton 41, Quincy 37
Rockford (East) 54, Champaign 53 (OT)
Chicago (Marshall) 54, Robinson 49

Quarterfinals

Pinckneyville 58, Springfield (Cathedral) 36
Pekin 53, Marion 45
LaGrange (Lyons) 45, Canton 41
Rockford (East) 51, Chicago (Marshall) 49

Semifinals

Pinckneyville 36, Pekin 31
Rockford (East) 61, LaGrange (Lyons) 54

Finals

Pekin 45, LaGrange (Lyons) 38 (third place)
Pinckneyville 65, Rockford (East) 39 (title)

Scoring Leaders

Player, School	G	FG	FT	Pts
Peter Anderson, Rockford (East)	4	24	10	58
Robert Johnson, Pinckneyville	4	17	20	54
Sherman Norton, LaGrange (Lyons)	4	22	7	51
Irv Bemoras, Chicago (Marshall)	2	17	15	49
Frank Gladson, Pinckneyville	4	17	13	47

All-Tournament First Team

Player, School	Ht	Yr.
Irv Bemoras, Chicago (Marshall)	6-3	Sr.
Charles Busby, Pekin	6-2	Sr.
Rodney Fletcher, Champaign	6-3	Sr.
Frank Gladson, Pinckneyville	5-10	Sr.
Sam Miranda, Collinsville	5-10	Sr.

Championship Game Box Score

Huff Gym, Champaign, March 20, 1948

PINCKNEYVILLE (65)
Coach Merrill "Duster" Thomas

Player	FG-A	FT-A	Pts	PF
Percy Clippard	1-5	3-7	5	3
Richard Craig	0-0	0-0	0	0
David Davis	3-15	3-4	9	0
Frank Gladson	8-21	5-6	21	1
Charles Gruner	0-0	0-0	0	0
Robert Johnson	7-20	7-9	21	3
Richard Luke	0-1	1-1	1	1
William McCrary	0-0	0-0	0	0
Tom Millikin	4-13	0-2	8	3
William Williams	0-0	0-0	0	0
TOTAL	23-75	19-29	65	11

ROCKFORD (EAST) (39)
Coach James Laude

Player	FG-A	FT-A	Pts	PF
Peter Anderson	4-10	3-4	11	3
Frank Calacurcio	2-6	0-2	4	4
Donald Harris	0-2	0-0	0	0
Walter Johnson	2-4	3-4	7	5
Eugene Lenz	0-0	0-0	0	3
Harold Samorian	1-7	0-0	2	0
George Sheatz	0-1	2-2	2	0
Gordon Stang	0-1	0-0	0	0
Eugene Tarabilda	3-11	0-0	6	2
William Weaver	3-9	1-2	7	3
TOTAL	15-51	9-14	39	20

Pinckneyville	18	17	16	14	—	65
Rockford (East)	6	13	10	10	—	39

Officials: Ted Search Sr., William Carlin.

1949

As in 1948, the final regular-season poll was a poor predictor of the 1949 state tournament field.

Only two teams ranked among the state's top 10 made it all the way to the Sweet Sixteen. Top-ranked Elgin earned a trip, as did fourth-ranked Mt. Vernon, a school that had not played at Huff Gym since 1931.

The Sweet Sixteen

Sectional Champions

The rest fell hard. Despite setting a state record by averaging nearly 67 points a game, second-ranked Danville lost 38-32 to the last remaining district school, Potomac, in the semifinals of the Champaign Sectional. Third-ranked and undefeated Teutopolis was halted convincingly by Effingham in regional play, while fifth-ranked Kankakee was upset 51-46 by host Joliet in the sectional semifinals.

Mt. Vernon didn't face much opposition on its road to Champaign, except for one game that was a throwback to the 1920s. In the regional final, the Rams had to overcome stalling tactics by Fairfield to claim a 12-7 victory.

Champaign, playing in a state-record 13th consecutive sectional title game, defeated Potomac 35-31. That earned the Maroons a record-tying seventh straight state tournament appearance.

Jim "Red" Lewis brought his fifth straight Pekin team to the state tournament. He led the program there in both 1943 and 1944, didn't coach the next two years during military service, then brought them back again each year from 1947 to 1949.

Gay Kintner's Decatur team tipped the Sweet Sixteen off in style, shooting a sizzling 56 percent from the floor and setting a single-game points record in crushing Pittsfield 82-48. The best game of the day was West Aurora's 45-42 upset over Elgin. West's John Biever tossed in 26 points, while the Maroons received 20 points from Bob Survant.

As action moved to the quarterfinals, Mt. Vernon used a 34-point record-tying outburst by Max Hooper to notch a 71-51 win over Decatur. In the next contest, Biever scored 20 to lead West Aurora to a 34-33 victory over Tilden Tech, led by 12 points from future NBA great Johnny Kerr.

In the first semifinal game, Mt. Vernon jumped to a 23-17 halftime lead and went on to claim a 37-31 victory over West Aurora. Hooper and Walt Moore scored 12 points apiece for the Rams.

Hillsboro grabbed a 30-22 halftime advantage in the other semifinal, finishing with a 50-43 victory over Nashville. Leroy Ott tossed in 20 points for Hillsboro, which advanced to the title game for the first time since its championship in 1914.

Although Stanley Changnon of Mt. Vernon was a coaching veteran of more than 20 years and Hillsboro's Fred Ewald was in just his first season, the state championship turned into a real dogfight.

Hillsboro led 20-19 at halftime, but Mt. Vernon pulled back in front 32-31 with a quarter to go. Thanks to three quick buckets from Hooper to open the fourth period, the Rams built a seven-point lead. Hillsboro came no closer than six points after that as Mt. Vernon captured a 45-39 victory.

Hooper took tourney scoring honors over Biever with 81 points by tossing in a game-high 21, while Richard Sturgeon and Ott had 11 points each for Hillsboro.

MT. VERNON
State Champions of 1949

FRONT ROW (left to right): Eddie King, John Riley, Max Hooper, Walter Moore, Bob Lee. SECOND ROW: Mgr. Bob Musick, Bob Wood, Sam Kirk, Wiley Mays, Coach Stan Changnon, Jim Wilson, Bob Brown.

State Final Tournament Scores

First Round

Decatur 82, Pittsfield 48
Mt. Vernon 54, Johnston City 52
Chicago (Tilden) 68, Oneida (ROVA) 41
Aurora (West) 45, Elgin 42
Moline 64, Rockford (West) 38
Nashville 43, Ottawa (Twp.) 39
Pekin 60, Robinson 52
Hillsboro 45, Champaign 44 (OT)

Quarterfinals

Mt. Vernon 71, Decatur 51
Aurora (West) 34, Chicago (Tilden) 33
Nashville 33, Moline 31
Hillsboro 45, Pekin 39

Semifinals

Mt. Vernon 37, Aurora (West) 31
Hillsboro 50, Nashville 43

Finals

Aurora (West) 49, Nashville 39 (third place)
Mt. Vernon 45, Hillsboro 39 (title)

Scoring Leaders

Player, School	G	FG	FT	Pts
Max Hooper, Mt. Vernon	4	31	19	81
John Biever, Aurora (West)	4	30	12	72
Leroy Ott, Hillsboro	4	24	10	58
Robert Kimpling, Nashville	4	16	13	45
Richard Sturgeon, Hillsboro	4	15	13	43

All-Tournament First Team

Player, School	Ht.	Yr.
John Biever, Aurora (West)	6-2	Jr.
Alan Brandt, Nashville	5-11	Jr.
Max Hooper, Mt. Vernon	6-5	Jr.
Walt Moore, Mt. Vernon	6-2	So.
Leroy Ott, Hillsboro	5-11	Sr.

Championship Game Box Score

Huff Gym, Champaign, March 19, 1949

MT. VERNON (45)
Coach Stan Changnon

Player	FG-A	FT-A	Pts	PF
Max Hooper	9-23	3-6	21	1
Eddie King	2-2	1-2	5	3
Bobby Lee	1-7	0-0	2	4
Wiley Mays	3-6	3-6	9	3
Walt Moore	2-13	3-6	7	0
John Riley	0-1	1-1	1	1
TOTAL	17-52	11-21	45	12

HILLSBORO (39)
Coach Fred Ewald

Player	FG-A	FT-A	Pts	PF
Charles Boston	1-9	1-1	3	3
George Demas	1-2	0-2	2	5
William Helfer	1-1	0-0	2	2
Leroy Ott	5-16	1-2	11	5
Richard Sturgeon	4-14	3-5	11	4
Roscoe Sydnor	0-1	0-0	0	1
Stanley Wallace	3-12	4-5	10	4
TOTAL	15-55	9-15	39	24

Mt. Vernon	12	7	13	13	—	45
Hillsboro	12	8	11	8	—	39

Officials: Gordon Kickels, Robert Young.

With all-stater Max Hooper, Walt Moore, and a number of other top players returning from the 1949 state championship squad, Mt. Vernon hoped to duplicate Elgin's feat of winning back-to-back titles.

After rolling to a 24-0 record in the regular season, Stanley Changnon's Rams were the team to beat while 21-1 Danville drew the No. 2 ranking. Those squads ended up on a collision course for top honors in the 1950 tournament.

Mt. Vernon's biggest obstacle prior to Champaign was a meeting with rival Centralia in the sectional semifinals at Centralia. The Rams claimed a 44-37 victory over the Orphans as Hooper tossed in 26 points.

Third-ranked Morton of Cicero and fourth-ranked West Aurora were the favorites from the Chicago area, but Morton fell to Elgin at Waukegan, while West Aurora was upset by host Bradley in sectional play.

The 1950 tourney field featured only four squads that had competed the previous year: Mt. Vernon, Elgin, Johnston City, and Chicago's Tilden Tech. Two newcomers, Monmouth and Peoria's Spalding, also took part.

In the quarterfinals at Huff Gym, Elgin shot out to a 34-20 halftime lead as it defeated Tilden 59-50 behind 15 points from Willard Schuldt. Mt. Vernon then turned in a record scoring effort in crushing Freeport 86-61. Hooper led the way for the Rams with 20 points, but Moore, Eddie King, John Riley, and Bobby Brown each added 15 or 16 points.

Collinsville captured a 54-46 victory as Chuck Kraak led the way with 22 points. And in the last quarterfinal contest, Danville outscored Bradley 18-11 in the final quarter to notch a 59-52 victory. Gene Loerscher paced the winners with 20 points.

Mt. Vernon had a close call in the semifinals, defeating Elgin 57-49 after

building a 32-17 halftime advantage. As usual, Hooper starred for the Rams with 26 points, while Schuldt again paced the Maroons with a 15-point performance.

Vergil Fletcher's Collinsville team looked like it would secure an all-southern title game after cruising to a 39-29 halftime lead over Danville in the other semifinal. But Danville rallied, outscoring the Kahoks 21-13 in the final quarter to pull out a 62-60 victory. Ron Rigoni scored 19 points and William Spangler added 17 for Lawrence Newtson's Danville squad, which advanced to the finals for the first time since 1936.

For the second time in six years, the championship game matched No. 1 (32-0 Mt. Vernon) against No. 2 (29-1 Danville), but the contest did not live up to the hype. Mt. Vernon took a 40-33 halftime lead, then outscored Danville 25-11 in the third quarter, rolling to a historic 85-61 victory.

Hooper concluded his career by setting tournament marks of 36 points in a game and 104 in a tournament. Fellow all-tourney picks Moore and Riley added 17 and 15 in the title contest.

Mt. Vernon's 85 points in the final easily surpassed the mark of 65 points set just two years earlier by Pinckneyville, and remained the state record until 1972 when Thornridge put 104 on the board in the title game. The Rams scored a record 293 points in the tournament.

MT. VERNON
State Champions of 1950

FRONT ROW (left to right): Bob Brown, John Riley, Max Hooper, Walter Moore, Eddie King.
BACK ROW: Coach Stan Changnon, James McMain, Mose Stokes, Charles Owens, Jim Stokes, Bob Wood.

Mt. Vernon was the second school to win back-to-back state championships.

State Final Tournament Scores

First Round
Chicago (Tilden) 46, Sterling 35
Elgin 75, Lawrenceville 40
Freeport 69, Paris 56
Mt. Vernon 65, Peoria (Spalding) 48
Quincy 62, Taylorville 42
Collinsville 69, Kewanee 52
Danville 69, Monmouth 49
Bradley (B.-Bourbonnais) 67, Johnston City 55

Quarterfinals
Elgin 59, Chicago (Tilden) 50
Mt. Vernon 86, Freeport 61
Collinsville 54, Quincy 46
Danville 59, Bradley (B.-Bourbonnais) 52

Semifinals
Mt. Vernon 57, Elgin 49
Danville 62, Collinsville 60

Finals
Elgin 81, Collinsville 65 (third place)
Mt. Vernon 85, Danville 61 (title)

Scoring Leaders

Player, School	G	FG	FT	Pts
Max Hooper, Mt. Vernon	4	46	12	104
Chuck Kraak, Collinsville	4	38	18	94
Willard Schuldt, Elgin	4	24	21	69
Bob Wright, Danville	4	25	15	65
Gene Loerscher, Danville	4	22	12	56
William Spangler, Danville	4	27	2	56

All-Tournament First Team

Player, School	Ht.	Yr.
Max Hooper, Mt. Vernon	6-5	Sr.
Chuck Kraak, Collinsville	6-4	Sr.
Walt Moore, Mt. Vernon	6-2	Jr.
John Riley, Mt. Vernon	6-3	Jr.
Bob Wright, Danville	5-11	Sr.

Championship Game Box Score

Huff Gym, Champaign, March 18, 1950

MT. VERNON (85)
Coach Stan Changnon

Player	FG-A	FT-A	Pts	PF
Bobby Brown	4-13	1-1	9	1
Max Hooper	16-28	4-5	36	1
Eddie King	4-11	0-4	8	1
James McMain	0-0	0-0	0	1
Walt Moore	8-13	1-3	17	2
Charles Owens	0-0	0-0	0	0
John Riley	7-14	1-1	15	5
Jim Stokes	0-0	0-0	0	0
Mose Stokes	0-0	0-0	0	1
Bobby Dean Wood	0-1	0-0	0	0
TOTAL	39-80	7-14	85	12

DANVILLE (61)
Coach Lawrence Newtson

Player	FG-A	FT-A	Pts	PF
Walter Jackowski	0-0	0-0	0	0
Gene Loerscher	6-10	2-4	14	2
Gene Michaelson	0-0	0-0	0	1
Robert Pacot	0-0	0-1	0	0
William Quam	0-1	0-1	0	1
Ron Rigoni	2-12	2-4	6	3
Sammy Sams	4-11	0-1	8	2
William Spangler	11-20	0-0	22	0
Pete Werner	0-1	0-0	0	0
Bob Wright	5-15	1-6	11	4
TOTAL	28-70	5-17	61	13

Mt. Vernon	18	22	25	20	— 85
Danville	17	16	11	17	— 61

Officials: Harold Inman, Lynn Gibbs.

TEAMS

Selected by Curt Herron

Thornton, 1933

The most famous team of the 1930s, not necessarily due to its dominance, but because of the way that it changed the game. Coach Jack Lipe went with a new fast-break strategy, powered by Dar Hutchins and future Baseball Hall of Famer Lou Boudreau. The Flying Clouds wrapped up a 24-3 season by rallying past slow-down masters Springfield in the finals.

Taylorville, 1944

Accomplished what no other team had managed to achieve in 36 previous attempts, an unbeaten state championship. Dolph Stanley's team arrived in Champaign having won all 41 of its games. Paced by John Orr and Ron Bontemps. Taylorville got past Champaign in the semifinals by four points for its fourth victory of the year over the Maroons, then rolled past Elgin 56-33 in the championship game.

Decatur, 1945

Rewrote the record book by defeating Champaign 62-54 in the title game. Gay Kintner's 37-2 Runnin' Reds scored 274 points in the tournament to break the old standard by 56 points. Decatur also set new records for points in a game (77). After rolling past Collinsville, Decatur nipped Galesburg 73-72 in overtime before beating Moline in the semifinals. All-tournament picks Bob Doster (96 points) and George Riley (93 points) led the way.

Paris, 1947

Won its four tournament games by an average of 19.25 points, the largest winning margin for any champ since Freeport in 1915, in claiming the school's second state championship in five years. Ernie Eveland's squad rolled past defending state champion Champaign 58-37 in the state title game. Tournament scoring leader Robert Owens was the lone all-tourney pick for the 40-2 state champs.

Mt. Vernon, 1950

Duplicated Taylorville's achievement to become the second undefeated state champion. Stanley Changnon's Rams broke Decatur's 1945 tournament scoring record with 293 points. Mt. Vernon capped its 33-0 season and repeated as champion by crushing Danville 85-61 in the title game. Max Hooper scored a tournament-record 104 points while Walt Moore and John Riley were the Rams' other all-tourney picks.

COACHES

Gay Kintner
Decatur
Led the Reds to state championships in 1931, 1936, and 1945, becoming the second coach to win three titles. His squads posted a 19-8 record (70 percent) in 10 tournament trips from 1931 to 1951. Took back-to-back 11-loss teams to the title game, beating unbeaten Danville with the first group in 1936.

Norm Ziebell
Cicero Morton & Moline
Led Morton to state championships in 1932 and 1941 and claimed a second-place showing with Moline in 1951. His 1941 Morton squad stunned Centralia's heavily favored "Wonder Five" in the semifinals. Despite losing in the regional finals in 1941 and 1942, Ziebell's teams won a trophy both years.

Dolph Stanley
Equality, Mt. Pulaski, & Taylorville
Became the first coach to lead three different schools to final-four finishes. The highlight was leading Taylorville, the first unbeaten state champion, to a 45-0 season in 1944. Led Equality to third place in 1934 and Mt. Pulaski to fourth place in 1936.

Ernie Eveland
Waterman & Paris
Directed Paris to state titles in 1943 and 1947 while just missing out on another one in 1942. Eveland set a state record, which still stands, by bringing teams to the state tournament seven straight years (1938-44). Overall, his squads went 18-8 (69 percent) in 10 state tournament appearances during a 20-year span.

Harry Combes
Champaign
Coached only nine seasons before moving to the University of Illinois in 1947, but led the Maroons to seven state tournament appearances during his tenure. Combes was just the second coach to lead three straight teams to championship games. His 1946 squad won the state title; runner-up in 1945 and 1947.

PLAYERS

Lou Boudreau, *Thornton, 1933-34-35*
Played in three straight state championship games, winning the title with the first team in 1933. Was the second player to be named to three all-tournament teams. The future Baseball Hall of Famer scored 76 points in 11 games for one of the state's most popular teams.

Ken Park, *Decatur, 1936-37*
This floor general helped get the Reds to back-to-back state title games in 1936 and 1937, earning all-tournament honors both years. Despite double-digit losses, the 1936 team finished first and the 1937 squad took second. Pat Harmon of the *News-Gazette* wrote in his 1937 all-state story, "Park was Decatur. Park is Decatur. Enough said."

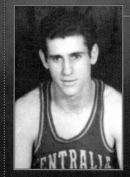

Dike Eddleman, *Centralia, 1939-41-42*
Led the Orphans to state trophies in each of his three appearances, including the state championship in his senior season of 1942. Eddleman was all-tournament in both 1941 and 1942 and won the tourney scoring title in 1942 with 72 points, second in 1941 with 81.

Andy Phillip, *Granite City, 1940*
Scored a tournament-high 53 points to lead the Happy Warriors to their only state championship in 1940. The all-tournament selection had 15 of his team's 24 points in the title win over Herrin. Phillip is enshrined in the Naismith Basketball Hall of Fame.

Roy Gatewood, *Salem, 1943*
Broke the tournament scoring record with 96 points to help his team to a third-place finish in 1943. Scored 20 or more points in each of his four games, capping things with a modern-era scoring record of 29 points in the third-place contest against Elgin.

Johnny Orr, *Taylorville, 1944*
Along with teammate and fellow all-tournament selection Ron Bontemps, helped the 1944 Tornadoes to become the first unbeaten champions in state history. Scored 64 points in four games for a 16.0 average, but missed winning the tournament scoring honors by two points. Scored 20 points in a quarterfinal win over Kewanee.

Bob Doster, *Decatur, 1943-45*
Helped lead the Runnin' Reds to a tournament-record 274 points as they captured the 1945 state title. Made the all-tournament team after tying the tournament scoring mark of 96 points. Also tied or set marks for points in a game (34) and field goals (16) in win over Collinsville.

Ted Beach, *Champaign, 1945-46-47*
Helped Champaign to the state championship game three years in a row from 1945 to 1947. Ranked among the top four scorers in each of the three tournaments he played in. Finished with a total of 198 points for his state tourney career, a record at the time.

Walt Moore, *Mt. Vernon, 1949-50*
Earned all-tournament honors as a sophomore while helping the Rams to the 1949 title and duplicated that honor as a member of the unbeaten 1950 champions. Moore scored 82 points, averaging 10.3 points per game. Saved his best for last, scoring 17 in the 1950 title-game victory over Danville.

Max Hooper, *Mt. Vernon, 1949-50*
Led the Rams to back-to-back state championships in 1949 and 1950 by scoring 185 points in eight games, good for a 23.1 average. Was the scoring leader in 1949, when he scored 81 points, and in 1950, when he set a new record with 104 points. Set a state record by scoring 36 points in the 1950 championship game.

A Golden Age   1951–1971

You can forgive the fans in 1955 for feeling frozen in time, because for them, things were pretty much as they had always been.

Illinois had crowned a single state champion for 48 years. Huff Gym had hosted the tournament for 30. The Sweet Sixteen was 22 and still going strong.

But the winds of change were blowing.

The years that followed marked the rise of the modern game of basketball, of acrobatic players and modern strategies, of slam dunks and full-court presses.

Timeout in Huff Gym during the final Sweet Sixteen, 1955.

THE LARGEST AND BEST-LOVED BASKETBALL TOURNAMENT IN THE COUNTRY

FREEPORT '51

HEBRON '52

LYONS '53-'70

MT. VERNON '54

WEST ROCKFORD '55-'56

HERRIN '57

MARSHALL (Chicago) '58-'60

SPRINGFIELD '59

COLLINSVILLE '61-'65

DECATUR '62

CARVER '63

PEKIN '64-'67

THORNTON '66

EVANSTON '68

PROVISO EAST '69

THORNRIDGE '71

They marked the rise of dominant city and suburban schools to the virtual exclusion of small towns and even smaller Cinderellas.

They also marked the end of three tournament traditions.

In a span of a few seasons, the Sweet Sixteen was gone, if not entirely forgotten; venerable Huff Gym had given way to its space-age neighbor, Assembly Hall; and Illinois was preparing to crown two state champions, a move that left the high school basketball world in upheaval.

Pat Heston reviews the Golden Era, the final years of one-class basketball, as the tournament struggled with the changing realities of interscholastic competition.

71

FREEPORT
State Champions of 1951

FRONT ROW (left to right):
Tom Williams, Ben Dorsey, Gene Schmitt,
Coach Harry Kinert, McKinley "Deacon"
Davis, Harlan Fritz. SECOND ROW: Roger
Meads, Eugene Ingold, Asst. Coach Joe
Spudich, Jim Hill, Bill Spahn, Carl Cain.

1951

Conspicuously absent from the 44th state tournament was top-ranked and undefeated Morton of Cicero, victims of a 47-46 upset at the hands of Hinsdale in a regional final. That opened the door for Freeport's Pretzels, 27-2 on the season and tabbed second in statewide polls.

Coach Harry Kinert fashioned a potent but balanced offensive machine with a defensive penchant for shutting down an opponent's top scorer. Powered by the all-state tandem of McKinley "Deacon" Davis and Ben Dorsey, the favorites hoped to join Rockford, Centralia, Decatur, and Mt. Vernon as the only three-time state champions.

Making their ninth tournament trip, but first since finishing third in 1942, the Pretzels owned five trophies, garnered under four different coaches, including titles in both 1915 and 1926. Title number three appeared to be in the proverbial cards.

Fifteen other squads had visions of stopping the Freeport Express. Among teams ranked in the season-ending poll, Quincy (No. 6), Marion (8), Lincoln (11) and Danville (14) remained in play. Two district survivors were also alive: Odell St. Paul, with only 72 students, was 31-2; Macomb Western, 110 students strong, was 28-2. Both Little Davids lost in the opening round.

One team that did not lose the first day was Decatur. The Reds upended Danville 68-58, handing veteran coach Gay Kintner his 500th career victory. Making his 10th state tournament visit, Kintner had four trophies and a trio of titles to his credit.

Freeport edged Edwardsville 67-64 in first-round action as all five starters scored between 11 and 17 points. From then on, no opponent seriously challenged the Pretzels, as the favorites bested Marion and all-state sensation John Kent 65-51, then blew past Decatur 88-60 in the semifinals.

Filling in the championship bracket was Moline, reaching the finale for the second time in eight years. Coach Norm Ziebell's unheralded Maroons were eight-time losers but flaunted a quality all-state player in Bob Van Vooren. Still, it was not enough to stop the Freeport juggernaut as four Pretzels scored in double digits, paced by 24 points from Davis. The favorites won decisively 71-51, capturing their first state crown in a quarter of a century.

Earlier, Quincy nipped Decatur 60-58 for consolation honors. The Reds' fourth-place finish gave coach Kintner his last tournament trophy. Quincy's all-state center Bruce Brothers poured in 14 points, setting the stage for Quincy's run at the 1952 state title.

State Final Tournament Scores

First Round
Marion 70, Macomb (Western) 65
Freeport 67, Edwardsville 64
Peoria (Woodruff) 76, Odell (St. Paul) 62
Decatur 68, Danville 58
Moline 59, Pinckneyville 55
Robinson 60, Chicago (Parker) 46
Lincoln 54, Oak Park (O.P.-River Forest) 41
Quincy 58, Hinsdale (Twp.) 46

Quarterfinals
Freeport 65, Marion 51
Decatur 73, Peoria (Woodruff) 50
Moline 59, Robinson 44
Quincy 65, Lincoln 63

Semifinals
Freeport 88, Decatur 60
Moline 64, Quincy 63 (OT)

Finals
Quincy 60, Decatur 58 (third place)
Freeport 71, Moline 51 (title)

Scoring Leaders

Player, School	G	FG	FT	Pts
Ken Norman, Decatur	4	31	17	79
McKinley "Deacon" Davis, Freeport	4	31	11	73
Bruce Brothers, Quincy	4	24	25	73
Bill Heitholt, Quincy	4	27	12	66
Karl Meurlot, Decatur	4	27	12	66

All-Tournament First Team

Player, School	Ht.	Yr.
Bruce Brothers, Quincy	6-5	Jr.
McKinley "Deacon" Davis, Freeport	6-2	Sr.
Ben Dorsey, Freeport	5-11	Sr.
John Kent, Marion	6-1	Sr.
Bob Van Vooren, Moline	6-0	Sr.

Championship Game Box Score

Huff Gym, Champaign, March 17, 1951

FREEPORT (71)
Coach Harry Kinert

Player	FG-A	FT-A	Pts	PF
Carl Cain	0-0	0-0	0	0
McKinley "Deacon" Davis	10-21	4-5	24	4
Ben Dorsey	6-16	1-1	13	0
Harlan Fritz	5-16	0-0	10	3
James Hill	0-1	0-0	0	0
Eugene Ingold	0-2	0-0	0	1
Roger Meads	0-0	1-1	1	0
Gene Schmitt	2-7	3-4	7	1
William Spahn	0-0	0-0	0	0
Tom Williams	6-14	4-6	16	5
TOTAL	29-77	13-17	71	14

MOLINE (51)
Coach Norm Ziebell

Player	FG-A	FT-A	Pts	PF
Bob Anders	2-7	2-2	6	2
Don Carothers	5-14	0-0	10	1
Austin Duke	1-7	0-1	2	5
Mark Engdahl	1-3	1-5	3	1
George Hoke	4-10	1-4	9	2
Ray Pearson	1-7	0-0	2	0
William Seaberg	2-7	0-0	4	0
Ted Simpson	1-3	1-2	3	0
Bob Van Vooren	5-15	2-2	12	2
TOTAL	22-73	7-16	51	13

Freeport	22	20	10	19	—	71
Moline	15	13	15	8	—	51

Officials: L.J. Hackett, Burdell Smith.

U sually lost in the shuffle of the 1952 state tournament, the silver anniversary of the opening of Huff Gym, is the fact that eventual champion Hebron was the favorite, ranked No. 1 in the state most of the season.

Nevertheless, many prognosticators felt that winning 11 straight postseason games, the last four at Champaign against quality large schools, was too arduous a task for a "district team" like Hebron. With just 98 students, Hebron had to fight through a preliminary tournament just to reach the regional round. Only one district team, Braidwood in 1938, had ever reached the title game.

Still, with only one loss in 32 games and a lineup boasting a trio of all-state players — Paul Judson (6-foot-3), Phil Judson (6-2) and Bill Schulz (6-10) — Hebron's Green Giants were the cream of the Sweet Sixteen crop.

Not to be outdone, Quincy's Blue Devils had the most formidable front line in the state, led by 6-5 all-state center Bruce Brothers, and including 6-4

Charles Fast and 6-2 Jack Gower. Guards Phil Harvey and Dick Thompson rounded out a deep squad for Coach George Latham.

The sleeper of the field, and potential spoiler, was 29-3 Mt. Vernon, ranked eighth and on a roll. True to form, the Rams, who had not lost a first-round tournament game since 1931 and who had never lost to a southern Illinois team in state finals play, squeaked past Kankakee and Pinckneyville to win their

record-tying tenth consecutive tournament game and place themselves on the verge of their third title in four years.

It took powerful Quincy to stop that streak, 54-51 in the semifinals. Coupled with Hebron's 64-56 triumph over Rock Island, it set up a championship-game clash that had fans — the vast majority of whom were rooting for Hebron — on the edge of their seats.

Quincy grabbed a 16-14 first-quarter edge. Hebron shaved a point off that lead in each of the next two stanzas, knotting the score at 48 after three frames.

Starting the fourth quarter with a 7-2 spurt, Hebron seized a sudden 55-50 lead. Then, with 4:30 remaining, Bruce Brothers fouled out. Don Wilbrandt's free throw gave the Green Giants a six-point lead.

No one told Quincy that the game was over, however. Fast and Gower keyed a six-point run, forcing a 58-58 tie at the end of regulation. For the first time, the championship game went to overtime.

Hebron put it away early in the extra session, outscoring Quincy 6-1 to pocket an unforgettable 64-59 win.

The IHSA eliminated district tournaments in 1972 when the state went to dual-class tournaments, leaving Hebron's place in history forever secure.

1952

State Final Tournament Scores

First Round
Mt. Vernon 57, Kankakee 56 (OT)
Pinckneyville 56, Chicago (Roosevelt) 44
Taylorville 82, Peoria (Manual) 64
Quincy 74, Freeport 68
Hebron (Alden-H.) 55, Champaign 46
Lawrenceville 63, Madison 61
Jacksonville 57, Ottawa (Twp.) 47
Rock Island 56, Harvey (Thornton) 35

Quarterfinals
Mt. Vernon 55, Pinckneyville 51
Quincy 69, Taylorville 64
Hebron (Alden-H.) 65, Lawrenceville 55
Rock Island 61, Jacksonville 49

Semifinals
Quincy 54, Mt. Vernon 51
Hebron (Alden-H.) 64, Rock Island 56

Finals
Mt. Vernon 71, Rock Island 70 (third place)
Hebron (Alden-H.) 64, Quincy 59 (OT) (title)

Scoring Leaders

Player, School	G	FG	FT	Pts
Bruce Brothers, Quincy	4	34	23	91
Gerald Hansen, Rock Island	4	34	6	74
Bill Schulz, Hebron (Alden-H.)	4	29	7	65
Paul Judson, Hebron (Alden-H.)	4	21	17	59
Merrell Clark, Rock Island	4	22	13	57

All-Tournament First Team

Player, School	Ht.	Yr.
Bruce Brothers, Quincy	6-5	Sr.
Carl Cain, Freeport	6-2	Sr.
Gerald Hansen, Rock Island	6-4	Sr.
Paul Judson, Hebron (Alden-H.)	6-3	Sr.
Bill Ridley, Taylorville	5-7	Sr.

Championship Game Box Score
Huff Gym, Champaign, March 22, 1952

HEBRON (ALDEN-H.) (64)
Coach Russ Ahearn

Player	FG-A	FT-A	Pts	PF
Paul Judson	6-12	1-4	13	3
Phil Judson	3-8	6-7	12	3
Bill Schulz	12-16	0-1	24	2
Ken Spooner	2-7	1-1	5	3
Don Wilbrandt	3-16	4-7	10	4
TOTAL	26-59	12-20	64	15

QUINCY (59)
Coach George Latham

Player	FG-A	FT-A	Pts	PF
Bruce Brothers	8-12	4-6	20	5
Charley Fast	3-10	4-5	10	4
Jack Gower	5-10	1-2	11	2
Phillip Harvey	2-12	4-4	8	2
Tom Payne	1-5	0-0	2	1
Richard Thompson	2-14	4-4	8	0
TOTAL	21-63	17-21	59	14

Hebron (Alden-H.)	14	20	14	10	6 —	64
Quincy	16	19	13	10	1 —	59

Officials: Clyde McQueen, Russell Shields.

Cinderella stories
Small schools enchanted fans young and old

For its first **64 years**, the IHSA boys' state **basketball** tournament was a single-class spectacle with schools of every size vying for the same *championship* trophy.

by Pat Heston

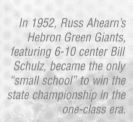
In 1952, Russ Ahearn's Hebron Green Giants, featuring 6-10 center Bill Schulz, became the only "small school" to win the state championship in the one-class era.

In 1931, for example, tiny schools such as Cornland and Emden, each with an enrollment of 10 students, were in the same mix with mammoth Chicago Schurz and its 8,814 students.

The early state tournaments featured many small schools (such as Riverside-Brookfield's 48 in 1908) and many enrollment mismatches. The only true Cinderella, however, emerged in 1923 when Villa Grove, enrollment 185, stunned prohibitive favorite Rockford, nearly 13 times larger.

Haves and have-nots

In 1931, an abrupt and unexplained shift occurred. That year the average enrollment of the eight finalists soared from 506 (in 1930) to 1,531. For the next 40 years, until Illinois adopted two-class basketball following the 1971 tournament, state finalists on average boasted nearly 1,400 students, dipping below 1,000 only eight times, with a low of 868.

As a rule, larger schools dominated their much smaller opponents in the early rounds of the postseason. By the mid-1930s, things were completely out of hand.

Thornton, a school of nearly 2,000 students, mauled Monee 85-2 in 1933 first-round action. In 1936, Thornton dismantled tiny Manhattan 117-8. Similarly, Joliet, with an enrollment of 3,500, overwhelmed Mokena 136-5. Routs proved to be the rule, rather than the exception, when teams of disproportionate enrollments met.

In 1936, the state association, in an effort to level the playing field, established a preliminary tournament — the district — where the smallest schools in a geographic area could play each other before advancing a champion to the regional round. It was a survival-of-the-fittest scenario with only the strongest of the Davids advancing to meet Goliath. The system remained in place until Illinois went to a multiple-class format in 1972.

curtain raiser before being battered by the state's top-ranked team. Champaign, with an enrollment eight times that of Somonauk's 88, blew past the Little Davids 77-28.

Odell St. Paul, with a head count of 72, failed to get past Peoria Woodruff in the opening round of 1951. One year later, Bobby Page-fueled Madison just missed a first-night victory, nipped by Lawrenceville 63-61.

Bowen, with 90 students — the last school of fewer than 100 to make it to state in a one-class format — rode high into the 1954 finals only to meet 28-0 Chicago DuSable, the talk of the tournament. DuSable launched a state-finals record 110 shots in blasting Bowen 87-64.

In 1961, Danville Schlarman, with 293 students — easily the smallest school in the finals field — upended highly favored Clinton 76-75 in the Decatur Super-Sectional, when all-state scoring ace Bryan Williams hit a court-length toss at the buzzer. The celebration, however, was short-lived as Schlarman advanced to a date with defending champion Chicago Marshall, which ended in a 61-36 Schlarman loss.

Geneva in 1963 had big Bob Johansen, a 6-5 all-state stand-out, leading the way, and the largest enrollment (522) of any district team to reach the finals. The Vikings edged Bloom 60-52 in the Hinsdale Super-Sectional, but fell to eventual state champion Chicago Carver 57-50 in the Friday night finale.

continued on next page

During the 34-year lifetime of this plan, 10 district teams reached the state finals, providing a series of memorable Cinderella moments.

In 1938, the third year of the new format, a pair of district teams reached Champaign's Huff Gym. Milton, with only 66 students, lost a Sweet Sixteen match to Harrisburg 36-25, but Braidwood Reed-Custer raced past a trio of tournament foes to tangle with top-rated Dundee for the state title. With only 96 students, Braidwood was the smallest school to reach the title game in a one-class system. But Braidwood faded down the stretch, losing to the favored Cardunals 36-29.

Limited success

Most other Cinderella squads met with less success once they reached the "Sweet Sixteen" ball.

Hebron, with an enrollment of 101, fell to Lewistown 31-30 in the first round of the 1940 tournament. In 1945, Somonauk's Bobcats beat Carbondale in the tournament's

ABOVE:
Fans engulf the Hebron motorcade as the Green Giants arrive winning the 1952 state title.

RIGHT:
Braidwood's 1938 team, coached by Louis Bottino, reached the championship game before falling to Dundee.

★ BRAIDWOOD ★

The Cobden Appleknockers arrive in Champaign for the 1964 state tournament. Coached by Dick Ruggles, Cobden was the third and last "district school" to play in the state title game.

Others made the final dance

The only Cinderella team for whom midnight did not strike was Hebron's Green Giants in 1952.

Coached by Russ Ahearn and powered by the all-state trio of Bill Schulz (6-10) and the Judson twins, Paul and Phil, Hebron climaxed a sensational 35-1 campaign with an unforgettable 64-59 overtime win against Bruce Brothers-led Quincy, a school more than 10 times its size. Hebron was the smallest school (98 students) ever to win a single-class title, and the Green Giants' victory — the only championship by a "district school" — remains, perhaps, the most memorable accomplishment in a century of state tournament play.

Cobden's Appleknockers attempted to duplicate the amazing feat a dozen years later.

Unranked and standing 32-2 on the year, Dick Ruggles' tall and lanky lads made it all the way to the 1964 title tilt against favored Pekin. The overwhelming choice of the 16,128 crammed into Champaign's Assembly Hall, Cobden fell behind 31-24 after 16 minutes, due largely to Pekin's phenomenal 68 percent shooting from the field, and never gained the lead. Pekin shattered Cobden's season and every district team's dream, 50-45.

The beloved Appleknockers were the last district team to reach the state finals, but other small schools earned the affection of state tournament fans in the years that followed.

The carriage awaits

Nine years after Cobden, in a tournament where the average enrollment of the other six finalists was 2,367, Okawville (250 students) and Effingham St. Anthony (280) tried on the magical glass slippers. Midnight struck for both teams on Friday, March 20, 1970, but not before one last remarkable dance.

After edging unranked Mt. Vernon 66-64 in the Carbondale Super-Sectional, Okawville could not handle Joliet Central and hot-shooting sophomore sensation Roger Powell, dropping a 56-43 decision to the Steelmen.

St. Anthony, however, came much closer to the magic, flirting with a place in roundball history.

It started with an 85-79 double-overtime upset of fourth-ranked Collinsville in the Charleston Super-Sectional. That sent the Bulldogs to Friday's first quarterfinal game against LaGrange Lyons. Not only was Lyons a huge school — more than 5,000 students — but the team was a spotless 28-0 and ranked No. 1 in the state.

The Cinderella Bulldogs fell behind early and big, but a second-half surge put St. Anthony in front with just 1:12 remaining. The favorites tied the game with less than a minute left, and then regained the lead only 13 seconds from the horn, hanging on for a spine-tingling 89-88 decision.

The game marked the last hurrah of the true Cinderella in Illinois high school basketball.

The magic now remains only in memory. Soon, perhaps, even that will fade. In time, we may forget them all — those dreamlike Cinderellas from a century's worth of tournaments that once lived that impossible but magnificent dream.

Atwood in 1922, Witt in 1929, Waterman in 1930, Equality in 1934, Hull in 1936, Roodhouse in 1939, Shawneetown in 1955 — all of them fading photos of the way it used to be.

So — people on the verge of the next 100 years — this is the way we were in Illinois during the first century of basketball. It was a marvelous, magical time, a time when Cinderella danced as long as the night allowed. And once — only once, to be sure, but what a once it was — Cinderella danced the whole night through.

Equality, which finished fourth with just 154 students in 1934, was the first of five schools coached to state by Dolph Stanley.

★ EQUALITY ★

The clock approaches midnight for Cinderella in 1970. Okawville (enrollment 250) was the last "small school" eliminated from the state finals before the advent of Class A.

When top-ranked, 26-0 Kankakee met third-ranked, 23-0 LaGrange Lyons in the semifinals of the Joliet Sectional, many insisted the 1953 state championship was decided right there.

Never in modern tournament history had two unbeaten teams faced off in the postseason.

Coached by Earl Jones and fueled by Dick Rapp and state scoring champion Harv Schmidt, Kankakee hoped to improve on the previous year's Sweet Sixteen appearance.

All-state pivot man Ted Caiazza, 6-foot-7, anchored LaGrange, capably supported by forwards Joel and Leon McRae and guards Chuck Sedgwick and Nate Smith. At the helm was Greg Sloan in his 10th and final season at the school.

In a game that lived up to its billing, LaGrange upset the Kays 83-74 behind Caiazza's 31 points, 18 more from Sedgwick and 16 from Joel McRae. Schmidt, a 6-6 center who would later play and coach at the University of Illinois, finished his dazzling career with a 37-point performance.

LaGrange opened play in Huff Gym against up-and-coming Chicago DuSable. All-state guard Paxton Lumpkin poured through 29 points for the Panthers, but Caiazza and Company were too much. Joel McRae scored 23, brother Leon chipped in 14, Smith added 11, while Caiazza netted a game-high 31. The favorites won handily 85-68.

Against Decatur St. Teresa the next day, Caiazza scored all of his team's 21 first-quarter points, fueling a 75-43 romp. He finished with 38 points — a tournament record.

Next up for the favorites was second-ranked Pinckneyville. Caiazza cashed in 27 points, leading LaGrange to a surprisingly easy 78-65 win.

The final obstacle for LaGrange was Dawson Hawkins' Peoria Central Lions, 29-3 and powered by 6-5 all-state center Hiles Stout, averaging 27 points through three tournament games.

Stout hit his average in the finale, but Caiazza countered with 25 and Joel McRae netted a dozen as LaGrange claimed a 72-60 triumph and the

school's first state title. LaGrange was the tournament's third undefeated champion, following Taylorville and Mt. Vernon.

Stout finished with 108 points, the best four-game total by a player who did not lead the field in scoring. Caiazza ended up on top, scorching the Huff Gym nets for 121 points, shattering Max Hooper's record total of 104 from 1950. In the process, LaGrange set a four-game scoring record of 310 points, destined to stand for only 364 days.

LaGRANGE (LYONS), State Champions of 1953

FRONT ROW (left to right): Leon McRae, Joel McRae, Ted Caiazza, Robert Caffey, Dick Williams, Harold Caffey. SECOND ROW: Steve Heeter, John Pendexter, Ron DeSantis, Russ Blake, Wayne Kennedy, J. Groeser, Coach Greg Sloan. THIRD ROW: Nate Smith, Phil Brooks, Charles Sedgwick, Joe Lawlor, Willard Johnson, Mgr. Jim O'Donnell.

State Final Tournament Scores

First Round
LaGrange (Lyons) 85, Chicago (DuSable) 68
Decatur (St. Teresa) 54, Canton 52
Pinckneyville 48, DeKalb 42
Jacksonville 57, Hillsboro 52 (OT)
West Frankfort (Frankfort) 67, Elgin 64
Peoria 81, Highland 53
Ottawa (Twp.) 80, Rock Island 66
Danville (Schlarman) 73, Lawrenceville 65

Quarterfinals
LaGrange (Lyons) 75, Decatur (St. Teresa) 43
Pinckneyville 58, Jacksonville 57
Peoria 70, West Frankfort (Frankfort) 68
Danville (Schlarman) 56, Ottawa (Twp.) 43

Semifinals
LaGrange (Lyons) 78, Pinckneyville 65
Peoria 66, Danville (Schlarman) 58

Finals
Pinckneyville 71, Danville (Schlarman) 42 (third place)
LaGrange (Lyons) 72, Peoria 60 (title)

Scoring Leaders

Player, School	G	FG	FT	Pts
Ted Caiazza, LaGrange (Lyons)	4	50	21	121
Hiles Stout, Peoria	4	40	28	108
Tony Davis, Danville (Schlarman)	4	35	19	89
Joel McRae, LaGrange (Lyons)	4	27	11	65
Ron Pursell, Pinckneyville	4	23	19	65

All-Tournament First Team

Player, School	Ht.	Yr.
Ted Caiazza, LaGrange (Lyons)	6-7	Jr.
Tony Davis, Danville (Schlarman)	6-8	Sr.
Paxton Lumpkin, Chicago (DuSable)	6-0	Jr.
Joel McRae, LaGrange (Lyons)	6-4	Sr.
Hiles Stout, Peoria	6-4	Sr.

Championship Game Box Score

Huff Gym, Champaign, March 21, 1953

LAGRANGE (LYONS) (72)
Coach Greg Sloan

Player	FG-A	FT-A	Pts	PF
Bob Caffey	4-10	2-4	10	4
Ted Caiazza	11-23	3-6	25	2
Willard Johnson	0-0	0-0	0	0
Joe Lawlor	0-0	7-8	7	4
Dave McKeig	0-0	0-0	0	0
Joel McRae	4-10	4-5	12	3
Leon McRae	3-6	0-0	6	4
Chuck Sedgwick	3-10	2-2	8	5
Nate Smith	1-9	2-2	4	3
TOTAL	26-68	20-27	72	25

PEORIA (60)
Coach Dawson "Dawdy" Hawkins

Player	FG-A	FT-A	Pts	PF
Jim Ashby	0-3	1-1	1	0
Hal Douglas	5-10	6-9	16	4
Jerry Green	0-1	1-4	1	3
Leon Hurst	0-0	0-0	0	0
Dave Lancaster	0-1	1-1	1	1
Jerry Lewis	1-2	3-3	5	5
Nick Panos	0-2	0-0	0	0
Hiles Stout	10-25	7-9	27	2
Al Swanson	3-7	1-2	7	1
Chet Ziegler	0-2	2-6	2	2
TOTAL	19-53	22-35	60	18

LaGrange (Lyons)	20	22	13	17	—	72
Peoria	17	18	10	15	—	60

Officials: Art Bouxsein, Frank Falzone.

1953 state champs

1954 CHAMPS

Al Avant of Mt. Vernon grabs a rebound during the 1954 championship game against DuSable.

MT. VERNON, *State Champions of 1954*

FRONT ROW (left to right): Al Avant, Don Richards, Larry Whitlock, Fred Deichman, Goff Thompson.
SECOND ROW: Coach Harold Hutchins, Kim Driggers, Gale Fruend, George Mendenall, Jerry Clark, Gene Brookman.

The talk of the 1954 tournament was Coach Jim Brown's DuSable Panthers, standing 28-0 on the season and sporting a threesome of all-state players: Paxton Lumpkin, Shellie McMillon, and "Sweet" Charlie Brown. Armed with a ferocious full-court press and a spectacular three-lane fast-break, DuSable turned 95 shots per game into an 82.8 scoring average. Lumpkin, McMillon, and Brown accounted for 71 of those points.

Mid-season graduation robbed the Panthers of two starters, Bobby Jackson and Curley Johnson. Taking their place, but not filling their shoes, were McKinley Cowsen and the Dennis brothers, Karl and Brian. With Jackson and Johnson in the lineup, it is doubtful DuSable could have been touched. Even minus the gifted duo, the Windy City five were simply awesome.

With Lumpkin averaging 21 points, Brown 23, and McMillon 24, the Panthers roared past three outmanned opponents. They blasted Bowen, a tiny school from western Illinois, 87-64 — a game in which DuSable launched 110 shots — before disposing of Quincy 80-66 and Edwardsville 89-73.

Mt. Vernon, with its 15th straight regional title in hand, arrived at Champaign on the strength of a one-point sectional win over highly regarded Mt. Carmel and all-American center Archie

Dees. The Rams won the game on two free throws after time had expired. Playing in its third title game in six years, Mt. Vernon had won 14 of its last 15 games at state.

The Rams had not lost a title game in three previous tries, while the Panthers had not won a tournament game in two previous trips to Champaign.

The North-South showdown for the championship was a classic.

In one of the most controversial games in tournament history, DuSable claimed a 20-18 first quarter lead, increased it to 35-29 at the 2:13 mark of the second, then watched it slowly slip away as foul totals mounted.

The Panthers drew even at 70 late in the fourth frame, but fouls and turnovers kept them off the

board down the stretch. Before it was over, three DuSable players had fouled out — Lumpkin and Brown in the last 11 seconds. Behind 23 points from all-state guard Al Avant and 25 more from unheralded Don Richards, Mt. Vernon shocked previously unbeaten Du Sable 76-70. The memorable upset made Mt. Vernon the state's first four-time titleist.

State Final Tournament Scores

First Round
Mt. Vernon 61, Danville 54
Moline 70, Rockford (East) 53
Harvey (Thornton) 83, Toledo (Cumberland) 59
Pinckneyville 43, Springfield 37
Quincy 64, Princeton 60
Chicago (DuSable) 87, Bowen 64
Barrington 57, Litchfield 38
Edwardsville 60, Peoria 54

Quarterfinals
Mt. Vernon 73, Moline 59
Pinckneyville 61, Harvey (Thornton) 47
Chicago (DuSable) 80, Quincy 66
Edwardsville 59, Barrington 57 (OT)

Semifinals
Mt. Vernon 70, Pinckneyville 44
Chicago (DuSable) 89, Edwardsville 73

Finals
Pinckneyville 54, Edwardsville 42 (third place)
Mt. Vernon 76, Chicago (DuSable) 70 (title)

Scoring Leaders

Player, School	G	FG	FT	Pts
Shellie McMillon, Chicago (DuSable)	4	41	13	95
Charlie Brown, Chicago (DuSable)	4	40	13	93
Al Avant, Mt. Vernon	4	28	27	83
Bob Gregor, Edwardsville	4	30	19	79
Paxton Lumpkin, Chicago (DuSable)	4	33	10	76

All-Tournament First Team

Player, School	Ht	Yr
Charlie Brown, Chicago (DuSable)	6-2	Sr.
Bob Gregor, Edwardsville	6-3	Sr.
Paxton Lumpkin, Chicago (DuSable)	6-0	Sr.
Don Ohl, Edwardsville	6-2	Sr.
Gene Pursell, Pinckneyville	6-5	Sr.

Championship Game Box Score

Huff Gym, Champaign, March 20, 1954

MT. VERNON (76)
Coach Harold Hutchins

Player	FG-A	FT-A	Pts	PF
Al Avant	9-22	5-6	23	2
Jerry Clark	1-4	1-1	3	3
Fred Deichman	1-4	1-2	3	1
Don Richards	9-19	7-8	25	2
Goff Thompson	3-8	5-7	11	2
Larry Whitlock	5-11	1-1	11	2
TOTAL	28-68	20-25	76	12

CHICAGO (DUSABLE) (70)
Coach Jim Brown

Player	FG-A	FT-A	Pts	PF
Charlie Brown	11-20	1-1	23	5
McKinley Cowsen	3-7	1-1	7	1
Brian Dennis	0-1	1-1	1	0
Karl Dennis	1-4	0-0	2	5
Eugene Howard	0-0	0-0	0	0
Paxton Lumpkin	5-21	3-5	13	5
Shellie McMillon	10-15	4-9	24	3
Sterling Webb	0-0	0-0	0	0
TOTAL	30-68	10-17	70	19

Mt. Vernon	18	17	22	19	—	76
Chicago (DuSable)	20	15	22	13	—	70

Officials: John Fraser, Joe Przada.

Mt. Vernon was the first school to win four state championships.

1955

The 1955 tournament marked the end of an era in IHSA basketball. The Sweet Sixteen, beloved by coaches and fans but the bane of every principal's existence, played one last time in Huff Gym before giving way to the more compact Elite Eight.

At the same time, two state tournament legends — Ernie Eveland of Paris and Gay Kintner of Decatur — coached their final tournament games. Paris was upset 77-66 by Galesburg, while Decatur lost a narrow 58-54 decision to top-ranked West Rockford.

West's Warriors were an imposing 6-foot-7, 6-7, and 6-5 across the front. More than merely big, Nolden Gentry, John Wessels and Fred Boshela were as talented as any trio in the state. Guards Rex Parker and Rod Coffman were quality backcourt partners for Coach Alex Saudargas's smooth-as-silk quintet.

West was not invincible, however, as second-ranked, 26-2 Moline had proved early in the season, handing the Warriors their only defeat. Moline missed its chance for a Saturday night rematch when it was surprised by Princeton and all-state center Joe Ruklick 60-58 in first-round action. Ruklick eventually finished the tournament with 104 points, a record 32 points ahead of his nearest competitor.

In the semifinals, Saudargas met Pinckneyville's Merrill "Duster" Thomas, a Deep South legend who had coached one championship squad (1948) and three others that finished third (1947, 1953, 1954). West thwarted Thomas's "slow-break" strategy, claiming its first title-game berth, 54-46.

In the second semifinal game, Elgin's Maroons took on sentimental favorite Princeton. The Tigers had shattered the 32-game unbeaten streak and the Cinderella hopes of Shawneetown in the quarterfinals, despite 20 points from crowd favorite Garrison Newsome. Elgin pulled away late for a 71-66 win, reaching the finale for the fourth time.

Elgin raced to a 24-10 first quarter advantage and held a comfortable 40-27 lead at the half. West Rockford roared back in the third frame, outscoring the Maroons 20-8 and pulling within one at 48-47.

Elgin widened the gap, stretching the lead to six, 57-51, with 2:19 to play. What followed may be the most miraculous second in IHSA state tournament history.

Gentry buried a 15-footer and was fouled after the shot, hitting both ends of a one-and-one to inch West to within a pair at 57-55. Elgin's inbounds pass sailed toward half-court where Gary Siegmeier ran to meet it. So did the defender, West's Rex Parker. Parker's momentum carried him into Siegmeier, but the officials whistled Siegmeier for the foul. Parker's two free throws made it 57-all. There was still 2:18 to play. Six points in one second!

The Maroons never recovered as West Rockford claimed the championship 61-59 on Gentry's tip-in with seconds to go.

State Final Tournament Scores

First Round
Princeton 60, Moline 58
Shawneetown 61, Park Forest (Rich) 56
Elgin 63, Georgetown 40
Galesburg 77, Paris 66
Rockford (West) 58, Decatur 54
Lincoln 54, Peoria (Spalding) 52
Quincy 70, Chicago (Marshall) 59
Pinckneyville 66, Alton 60

Quarterfinals
Princeton 66, Shawneetown 48
Elgin 66, Galesburg 60 (OT)
Rockford (West) 75, Lincoln 65
Pinckneyville 53, Quincy 51

Semifinals
Elgin 71, Princeton 66
Rockford (West) 54, Pinckneyville 46

Finals
Pinckneyville 58, Princeton 53 (third place)
Rockford (West) 61, Elgin 59 (title)

Scoring Leaders

Player, School	G	FG	FT	Pts
Joe Ruklick, Princeton	4	35	34	104
Gary Smith, Elgin	4	29	14	72
Tom Aley, Elgin	4	26	16	68
Nolden Gentry, Rockford (West)	4	26	12	64
Jim Lazenby, Pinckneyville	4	11	37	59

All-Tournament First Team

Player, School	Ht.	Yr.
Dave Cadwallader, Lincoln	6-4	Jr.
Nolden Gentry, Rockford (West)	6-7	Jr.
Jim Lazenby, Pinckneyville	6-0	Sr.
Garrison Newsom, Shawneetown	5-10	Sr.
Joe Ruklick, Princeton	6-8	Sr.

Championship Game Box Score
Huff Gym, Champaign, March 19, 1955

ROCKFORD (WEST) (61)
Coach Alex Saudargas

Player	FG-A	FT-A	Pts	PF
Fred Boshela	5-11	7-12	17	3
Rod Coffman	6-9	3-4	15	4
Nolden Gentry	4-13	6-8	14	3
Don Grabow	0-1	2-2	2	0
Rex Parker	2-8	5-6	9	4
Bobby Washington	0-0	0-0	0	0
John Wessels	2-13	0-0	4	2
TOTAL	19-55	23-32	61	16

ELGIN (59)
Coach Bill Chesbrough

Player	FG-A	FT-A	Pts	PF
Tom Aley	5-10	3-4	13	2
Paul Hudgens	5-12	6-7	16	3
Earl Lamp	0-1	2-3	2	1
Charles Rachow	1-1	1-2	3	4
Gary Siegmeier	1-4	5-6	7	5
Gary Smith	6-15	6-7	18	3
TOTAL	18-43	23-29	59	18

Rockford (West)	10	17	20	14	—	61
Elgin	24	16	8	11	—	59

Officials: Tom Kouzmanoff, Jim Paterson.

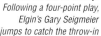

A new tournament brought with it a new format. Gone were the days of Sweet Sixteen finalists advancing to Huff Gym in Champaign. Beginning in 1956, the IHSA assigned sectional tournament survivors to eight venues spread around the state for "super-sectional" games with the winners advancing to the quarterfinals.

As the 1956 tournament commenced, defending champion West Rockford had dreams of joining Elgin (1924-25) and Mt. Vernon (1949-50) as the state's only back-to-back champions. However, third-ranked Galesburg, under the direction of first-year coach John Thiel, nearly dashed those dreams at the Moline Super-Sectional.

The Streaks sprinted to a 24-13 first quarter lead, but West cut the chasm to 29-23 by halftime and moved in front 46-41 after three. A 16-11 Galesburg surge in the fourth quarter tied the score at 57. The Warriors won it 66-64, scoring the only points of the second overtime.

Galesburg won everything but the game. The Streaks outshot West from the

time lead. Riding its patented one-two punch of Govoner Vaughn and Mannie Jackson, Edwardsville slowly chipped away at the lead, pulling within a point midway through the fourth quarter. After a timeout, the Tigers stationed themselves under the wrong basket and prepared to inbound the ball.

The St. Anthony players took the bait, rushing to the far end of the court and positioning themselves between their opponents and what was, in fact, their own basket. Vaughn broke toward the near basket — the Edwardsville basket — where he took the inbounds pass and eased in an uncontested lay-up. The Tigers, with a one-point lead, never again trailed, riding the momentum to a 73-68 win.

As the basketball gods would have it, the two first-round escape artists made it all the way to the championship game, where they hooked up in yet another down-to-the-wire finish.

Vaughn and Jackson continued to have hot hands, netting 28 and 21 points respec-

West Rockford and West Frankfort tussle in quarterfinal action at Huff Gym.

State Final Tournament Scores

Super-Sectionals

At Springfield [Armory]—Quincy 52, Springfield (Lanphier) 48
At Salem—Edwardsville 73, Effingham (St. Anthony) 68
At Peoria [Bradley]—Peoria 66, LaSalle (L.-Peru) 58
At Hinsdale (Twp.)—Oak Park (O.P.-River Forest) 62, Chicago Heights (Bloom) 57
At Moline—Rockford (West) 66, Galesburg 64 (2 OT)
At West Frankfort (Frankfort)—West Frankfort (Frankfort) 45, Pinckneyville 42
At Evanston [NU]—Chicago (Dunbar) 88, Winnetka (New Trier) 56
At Decatur—Rantoul 79, Taylorville 74

Quarterfinals

Edwardsville 68, Quincy 44
Oak Park (O.P.-River Forest) 63, Peoria 48
Rockford (West) 82, West Frankfort (Frankfort) 70
Chicago (Dunbar) 73, Rantoul 58

Semifinals

Edwardsville 88, Oak Park (O.P.-River Forest) 61
Rockford (West) 61, Chicago (Dunbar) 48

Finals

Chicago (Dunbar) 73, Oak Park (O.P.-River Forest) 56 (third place)
Rockford (West) 67, Edwardsville 65 (title)

Scoring Leaders

Player, School	G	FG	FT	Pts
John Wessels, Rockford (West)	4	42	23	107
Mannie Jackson, Edwardsville	4	40	14	94
Govoner Vaughn, Edwardsville	4	39	14	92
Mel Davis, Chicago (Dunbar)	4	40	10	90
Alphra Saunders, Chicago (Dunbar)	4	28	17	73

All-Tournament First Team

Player, School	Ht.	Yr.
Nolden Gentry, Rockford (West)	6-7	Sr.
Mannie Jackson, Edwardsville	6-2	Sr.
Don Slaughter, Rockford (West)	6-3	Sr.
Govoner Vaughn, Edwardsville	6-3	Sr.
John Wessels, Rockford (West)	6-7	Sr.

Championship Game Box Score

Huff Gym, Champaign, March 17, 1956

ROCKFORD (WEST) (67)
Coach Alex Saudargas

Player	FG-A	FT-A	Pts	PF
Tom Blake	0-1	0-0	0	0
Nolden Gentry	5-10	7-8	17	2
Don Slaughter	1-6	2-2	4	1
Bobby Washington	6-12	5-6	17	2
John Wessels	11-24	7-10	29	2
TOTAL	23-53	21-26	67	8

EDWARDSVILLE (65)
Coach Joe Lucco

Player	FG-A	FT-A	Pts	PF
James Chandler	0-1	2-3	2	3
Mannie Jackson	10-21	1-3	21	2
Gordon Mallory	0-0	0-0	0	0
Harold Patton	2-5	0-1	4	5
Richard Pulliam	1-2	0-0	2	0
Kenneth Shaw	3-5	2-2	8	2
Govoner Vaughn	13-19	2-5	28	2
TOTAL	29-53	7-14	65	14

Rockford (West)	18	15	21	13	—	67
Edwardsville	14	18	16	17	—	65

Officials: James McCoskey, Claude Rhodes.

ROCKFORD (WEST), State Champions of 1956

FRONT ROW (left to right): John Wessels, Nolden Gentry, Bobby Washington, Tom Blake, Don Slaughter.
SECOND ROW: Coach Alex Saudargas, Roger Peacock, Craig Peeples, Jay Heath, Chad Coffman, Jack Flynn.

field as well as from the line, and had the game's high scorer in Mike Owens with 29 points.

In another super-sectional nail-biter, fifth-ranked Edwardsville edged 29-1 Effingham St. Anthony with one of the most memorable bits of chicanery in the annals of tournament play. The Cinderella Bulldogs sprinted to a stunning 38-19 half-

tively. For West Rockford, John Wessels, the tournament's leading scorer, had a game-high 29, with Nolden Gentry and Bobby Washington chipping in 17 apiece. West took a 54-48 lead into the fourth quarter and hung on for a tense 67-65 triumph — a second consecutive championship, won for the second straight year by only two points.

If *Rip Van Winkle* had fallen into his famous sleep following the 1908 boys' state *basketball tournament* and awakened 50 years later for the 1957 finals, he would hardly have recognized the game of *basketball.*

by Pat Heston

Fifty years earlier, the transition from baskets with bottoms to bare rims was relatively recent. Open nets, essentially mesh sacks with the bottom cut out, became standard on rims in 1906. Backboards were barely a decade old, as was the rule that only five players per team could be on the court at any one time.

Three consecutive violations by one team resulted in an automatic point for the opponent. Dribbling, only recently allowed, was discouraged as "showboating," and the person dribbling the ball could not shoot.

There was a center jump following every basket. There was no center line and no rule requiring a team to advance to their half of the floor within 10 seconds. A four-corner offense meant literally that — a man in each corner of the floor and another at center court. There was no three-second lane to be concerned about and one designated player shot all of his team's free throws.

They played the game with a lopsided ball, which varied in shape, size and material, had laces, and was nearly impossible to control. No official rulebook for the high school game existed. They measured time in halves with quarters not making an appearance for another 10 years.

Shots from beyond 15 feet were unthinkable, free throws were tossed with two hands from the knees or below with an underhand shot, and passing was the ultimate weapon in a team's arsenal, as players without the ball positioned themselves to get as close to the basket as possible. It was common for teams to make 30, 40 or, sometimes, even 50 passes before securing and taking a high-percentage shot.

It was a sleepy-time game everywhere, even in Illinois.

The first real inklings of an awakening occurred in 1933 when a group of run-and-gun sophomores from Thornton High School in Harvey, buoyed by a brand new rule which cre-

ated a centerline and 10 second time limit, used full-court pressure defense and offensive fast-breaks, not as an occasional tactic, but as part and parcel of the game. Other up-tempo teams soon followed: Dundee in 1938, the first team to benefit from the disbanded center jump after every basket, Centralia in 1941 and Taylorville in 1944.

In 1945, the statewide press christened Decatur's fabulous five the "Runnin' Reds" by virtue of the team's fast, freewheeling style, which resulted in tournament records for most points in one game (77), most points in the title game (62) and most points in four games (274). Within a decade, the DuSable Panthers were launching nearly 100 shots per game and averaging more than 80 points an outing.

By the time the tournament was celebrating its golden anniversary in 1957, the wide-awake game was here to stay. Collinsville and Elgin, the state's top-ranked teams, averaged 75 and 73 points per game respectively, cruising into the state finals without a loss on their ledgers. It was generally felt that offense won championships, that such high-octane assaults could overwhelm any defensive challenge — a belief reinforced through four of the most amazing months in Illinois prep basketball history.

The 1956-57 season had seen some outstanding offensive accomplishments. Three players — Art Hicks of Chicago St. Elizabeth, Charles Vaughn of Tamms, and Ron Zagar of DePue — scaled the 1,000-point barrier. All-American standouts Terry Bethel of Collinsville, Chuck Brandt of Elgin, and John Tidwell of Herrin also scored points in bunches. Offense was the name of the game.

As a result, fans expected Collinsville and Elgin, potent offensive machines, to lock horns in the state championship game.

Herrin's Tigers, however, changed everything, and in the process, 1957 changed everything. Defense became pivotal, a vital part of every serious title quest to follow.

Herrin's 1957 team was a small squad, with 6-foot-4 John Tidwell the tallest starter, but the Tigers were smooth and smart on offense and unflinching on defense. Coach Earl Lee used an intricate system of screens and picks that depended on getting an opponent's big men in foul trouble, and the team's nose-to-nose defensive pressure dictated the game's tempo.

Against 27-0 Elgin in the quarterfinals, Herrin led 34-30 at the half. Early in the third quarter, Brandt, the Maroons' 6-7 pivot man, picked up his third foul and the Herrin defense kept the Elgin offense out of sync. Opening a nine-point lead near the end of the period, the Tigers stunned the previously perfect Maroons 66-60.

Against prohibitive favorite Collinsville (34-0) in the state title game, Herrin faced a pair of formidable obstacles: Bethel, a lanky 6-7, and front line partner Thom Jackson, a husky 6-5. Together, the duo averaged 50 points and 25 rebounds per game.

To counteract Collinsville's size, Herrin opened in a zone. It was a mistake. The favorites raced to a quick 8-2 advantage. Lee called a time out, switching the Tigers back to their patented man-to-man pressure. It worked like a charm.

Not five minutes into the game, Bethel picked up his third foul. The Collinsville lead was 14-10 at the first stop, but with Bethel sitting out the entire second quarter, Herrin moved in front 22-20 at intermission. Bethel was back to start the second half, but the Tigers' defense still ran the show. The score was 32-all with a quarter to play.

As the fourth quarter wore on, the Kahoks' turnovers continued to mount under the Tigers' relentless pressure. For the night, Collinsville had twice as many turnovers as Herrin.

With four minutes left, Tigers' point guard Richard Box streaked down court and found backcourt partner Willie Williams on the wing. Jackson moved over to defend, but Williams slid to the left, drove the baseline, and lifted a high-arching shot toward the hoop. The ball sailed over Jackson's extended arms

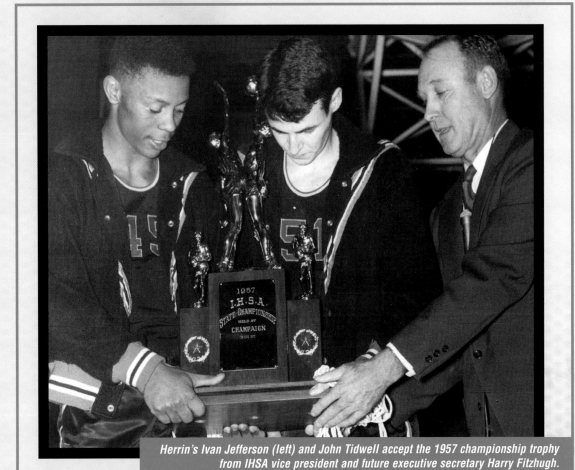

Herrin's Ivan Jefferson (left) and John Tidwell accept the 1957 championship trophy from IHSA vice president and future executive secretary Harry Fitzhugh.

and drew nothing but nylon for a 38-36 Herrin lead. The Tigers' defense took it from there, holding Collinsville to its lowest point production of the year, sealing the historic 45-42 upset win.

The 1957 championship game stands midway between Oak Park and Peoria, 50 tournaments removed from Lewis Omer's inaugural invitational in that suburb west of Chicago and the 2007 finals at Carver Arena.

It was a golden anniversary in more ways than one, forever changing the basketball mindset of the Prairie State. Before Herrin, defense was optional; after Herrin, defense was essential.

Beginning the next year, Chicago Marshall used a pressure cooker, in-your-face defense to

win two titles in three years. Within four years, Vergil Fletcher implemented his ball-press defense that put Collinsville at the top of the basketball world and helped the Kahoks win first place trophies in 1961 and 1965. Defense won championships for Carver in 1963, Pekin in 1964, Thornton in 1966, Evanston in 1968, Proviso East in 1969, and the beat goes on.

Every great offensive powerhouse in the tournament's last half-century — whether 1958 Marshall, 1961 Collinsville or 1972 Thornridge; whether 1981 Quincy, 1985 Providence St. Mel or 1993 King — won state with a voracious defense and owes a debt to the 1957 Herrin Tigers. To be sure, those subsequent defenses were stronger and swifter, more sophisticated and more intense; but, nonetheless, all were Herrin-like and all were the key to unlocking remarkable state championships.

A lot has changed in the 50 years since the Tigers' surprising march to the state title. Basketball is a radically different game today than it was then, played much more on the run and above the rim. No longer a simple game in shadowy black-and-white, it is a diverse game of flamboyant slam-dunks and rainbow three-pointers. It is all-out full throttle, all-out full court and all-out full color.

One thing is certain: Illinois no longer plays a sleepy-time game. The state awoke from that dull habit decades prior to Herrin's title run.

On one weekend in March of 1957, however, Herrin sounded yet another wake-up call. Before then, offense won games; afterwards, defense won championships. It was a watershed weekend, a lesson learned, a legacy bequeathed.

HERRIN, *State Champions of 1957*

FRONT ROW (left to right): Willie Williams, Bart Lindsey, John Hendricks, Richard Box, Jerry Miller. SECOND ROW: Asst. Coach Bob Hutchinson, Steve Heard, Ivan Jefferson, John Tidwell, Kenneth Finney, Jim Gualdoni, Coach Earl Lee.

1957

The 1957 tournament had everything a basketball fan could love.

There were two overtime thrillers, seven games decided by three points or less, and four quarterfinal games won by an average of four points each. Topping it all off was a photo-finish of a finale that toppled the state's No. 1 team.

Three *Parade* all-Americans reached the quarterfinals — centers Chuck Brandt of Elgin, John Tidwell of Herrin, and Terry Bethel of Collinsville.

A pair of unbeaten teams — Collinsville (31-0) and Elgin (26-0) — were ranked one-two in the season ending poll and headed for what seemed an almost certain championship clash.

Waiting in the wings, under the radar of tournament prognosticators, was 27-2 Herrin, sectional conqueror of fourth-ranked but favored Pinckneyville, a program with six straight visits to Champaign and a squad that coach Merrill "Duster" Thomas called the best he ever coached. Herrin blew out Pinckneyville, handing Thomas the worst postseason drubbing of his illustrious career. That game proved a sign of things to come.

In a terrific quarterfinal clash, Earl Lee's third-ranked Herrin Tigers broke a 58-58 tie with under three minutes to play and held on to stun previously perfect Elgin 66-60. In another same-day nerve-wracker,

Galesburg's Streaks took prohibitive favorite Collinsville to the wire before the Kahoks narrowly prevailed, 61-59.

Both Collinsville and Herrin won semifinal bouts, setting up the last championship game between squads from southern Illinois until the 1972 Class A finals.

Behind Bethel's 10 points and five rebounds, Collinsville claimed a 14-10 first quarter advantage, but the all-American pivot man spent the entire second quarter on the bench with three fouls. Sparked by 5-foot-8 Richard Box, Herrin whittled away at the lead, finally moving ahead 22-20 only seconds before the halftime horn.

Bethel returned for the third period, but the Kahoks managed only a two-point edge, forcing a 32-32 tie with eight minutes remaining. Halfway through the final quarter, Herrin's Willie Williams darted past Thom Jackson, drove the baseline and lifted a high-archer toward the hoop. The ball sailed over Jackson's extended arms and drew nothing but nylon, lifting the Tigers into a 38-36 lead they would never relinquish.

Holding Collinsville to its lowest point total of the season, Herrin shocked Vergil Fletcher's Kahoks with a masterful 45-42 victory, becoming the first team to oust two unbeatens in state finals play. Not counting Class A tournaments, the win was the last state title for a Deep South school through 2006.

State Final Tournament Scores

Super-Sectionals

At Decatur—Champaign 57, Maroa (M.-Forsyth) 56
At Peoria [Bradley]—Ottawa (Twp.) 58, Pekin 56 (2 OT)
At Moline—Galesburg 60, Freeport 47
At Salem—Collinsville 76, Charleston 57
At West Frankfort (Frankfort)—Herrin 57, Mt. Vernon 44
At Hinsdale (Twp.)—Elgin 53, Chicago Heights (Bloom) 52
At Evanston [NU]—Evanston (Twp.) 67, Chicago (Crane) 60
At Springfield [Armory]—Quincy (Notre Dame) 65, Springfield 53

Quarterfinals

Ottawa (Twp.) 54, Champaign 51
Collinsville 61, Galesburg 59
Herrin 66, Elgin 60
Quincy (Notre Dame) 70, Evanston (Twp.) 63

Semifinals

Collinsville 69, Ottawa (Twp.) 61
Herrin 68, Quincy (Notre Dame) 47

Finals

Ottawa (Twp.) 65, Quincy (Notre Dame) 64 (OT) (third place)
Herrin 45, Collinsville 42 (title)

Scoring Leaders

Player, School	G	FG	FT	Pts
Terry Bethel, Collinsville	4	35	43	113
Roger Trimpe, Quincy (Notre Dame)	4	23	25	71
Francis Clements, Ottawa (Twp.)	4	21	28	70
John Tidwell, Herrin	4	27	14	68
Bill Kurz, Quincy (Notre Dame)	4	23	20	66

All-Tournament First Team

Player, School	Ht.	Yr.
Terry Bethel, Collinsville	6-7	Sr.
Francis Clements, Ottawa (Twp.)	5-11	Jr.
Gary Kane, Elgin	6-4	Sr.
John Tidwell, Herrin	6-4	Sr.
Dave Tremaine, Evanston (Twp.)	6-1	Sr.

Championship Game Box Score

Huff Gym, Champaign, March 23, 1957

HERRIN (45)
Coach Earl Lee

Player	FG-A	FT-A	Pts	PF
Richard Box	6-11	5-7	17	1
Jim Gualdoni	3-7	4-10	10	2
Ivan Jefferson	2-8	4-7	8	5
Jerry Miller	0-0	0-0	0	0
John Tidwell	2-5	2-5	6	2
Willie Williams	2-6	0-0	4	0
TOTAL	15-37	15-29	45	10

COLLINSVILLE (42)
Coach Vergil Fletcher

Player	FG-A	FT-A	Pts	PF
Bart Basola	1-2	0-0	2	1
Terry Bethel	7-16	4-5	18	5
Tom Jackson	5-14	2-3	12	2
Jim Soehlke	2-2	2-2	6	1
Bob Vetter	1-1	0-0	2	0
Ernie Wilhoit	1-9	0-2	2	3
Tracy Wilhoit	0-3	0-2	0	5
TOTAL	17-47	8-14	42	17

Herrin	10	12	10	13	—	45
Collinsville	14	6	12	10	—	42

Officials: William Cox, Dwight Wilkey.

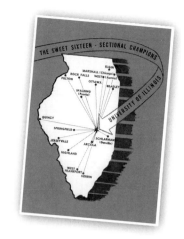

THE SWEET SIXTEEN - SECTIONAL CHAMPIONS
UNIVERSITY OF ILLINOIS

1958

The stories within the story made the 1958 tournament special.

The first was the exceptional play of Chicago Marshall sophomore sensation George Wilson, a 6-foot-6 defensive wizard and inside scoring threat. Against Elgin in the Evanston Super-Sectional, Wilson held the Maroons' 6-11 George Clark scoreless on only four shots in a 63-43 romp. Wilson also led the state tournament with an average of 21.5 points per game.

The second was the phenomenal scoring of Rock Falls, coached by Dick Haselton. The Rockets annihilated Ashton 142-36 in regional play, then smacked Danville Schlarman, 101-76 in Friday's state quarterfinals. It marked the first time a team had reached the century mark in Sweet Sixteen competition.

Story number three came out of that quarterfinal game when Schlarman guard Jerry Kuemmerle scored a

State Final Tournament Scores

Super-Sectionals

At Decatur—Danville (Schlarman) 75, Arcola 57
At Moline—Rock Falls 74, Fulton 62
At Salem—Highland 49, Jerseyville (Jersey) 46 (OT)
At Peoria [Bradley]—Peoria (Spalding) 49, Ottawa (Twp.) 44
At Springfield [Armory]—Springfield 46, Quincy 37
At Aurora (East)—Aurora (West) 57, Bradley (B.-Bourbonnais) 54
At Evanston [NU]—Chicago (Marshall) 63, Elgin 43
At West Frankfort (Frankfort)—Herrin 76, West Frankfort (Frankfort) 75

Quarterfinals

Rock Falls 101, Danville (Schlarman) 76
Peoria (Spalding) 58, Highland 49
Aurora (West) 59, Springfield 48
Chicago (Marshall) 72, Herrin 59

Semifinals

Rock Falls 66, Peoria (Spalding) 59
Chicago (Marshall) 74, Aurora (West) 62

Finals

Peoria (Spalding) 59, Aurora (West) 53 (third place)
Chicago (Marshall) 70, Rock Falls 64 (title)

Scoring Leaders

Player, School	G	FG	FT	Pts
George Wilson, Chicago (Marshall)	4	31	24	86
Ken Siebel, Rock Falls	4	25	31	81
Bill Small, Aurora (West)	4	30	20	80
Jerry Kuemmerle, Danville (Schlarman)	2	28	20	76
Dave McGann, Peoria (Spalding)	4	24	19	67

All-Tournament First Team

Player, School	Ht.	Yr.
Gary Kolb, Rock Falls	5-10	Sr.
Jerry Kuemmerle, Danville (Schlarman)	6-0	Sr.
Dave McGann, Peoria (Spalding)	5-10	Sr.
Ken Siebel, Rock Falls	6-4	Jr.
George Wilson, Chicago (Marshall)	6-6	So.

Championship Game Box Score

Huff Gym, Champaign, March 22, 1958

CHICAGO (MARSHALL) (70)
Coach Isadore "Spin" Salario

Player	FG-A	FT-A	Pts	PF
Paul Brown	0-0	0-0	0	1
Tyrone Johnson	0-2	0-0	0	3
Bobby Jones	9-20	0-2	18	3
Jimmy Jones	0-0	0-0	0	1
Steve Thomas	9-17	8-10	26	1
M.C. Thompson	6-14	5-7	17	3
George Wilson	4-10	1-6	9	4
TOTAL	28-63	14-25	70	16

ROCK FALLS (64)
Coach Dick Haselton

Player	FG-A	FT-A	Pts	PF
Jim Cain	5-13	0-1	10	4
Paul Gallentine	7-13	2-3	16	4
Gary Kolb	2-9	4-4	8	1
Doug Martin	0-2	3-4	3	4
Ken Siebel	6-18	8-11	20	4
Frank Simester	2-8	3-4	7	2
TOTAL	22-63	20-27	64	19

Chicago (Marshall)	17	15	20	18	—	70
Rock Falls	20	18	15	11	—	64

Officials: Robert Young, Edward Bronson.

tournament-record 49 points, 22 of them in the fourth quarter. Overshadowed by Kuemmerle's performance was Rock Falls' complete domination of the contest. The Rockets led 30-19 after a quarter, 61-38 at the half, 84-47 after three, and placed five men in double figures, including Kenny Siebel, whose 33 points were game-high when he left after three quarters.

The fourth story centered on Marshall, undefeated in 27 games and vying for the Windy City's first state championship. Coach Isadore "Spin" Salario had fashioned a fabulous five, built around Wilson with a solid supporting cast of Steve Thomas, M. C. Thompson, Bobby Jones and Tyrone Johnson.

The final story was the appearance of two top-ranked teams in the title game: Rock Falls, ranked No. 1 all season long, and Marshall, ranked first in the postseason poll after prognosticators tossed Chicago teams into the mix. Those two teams entered

the championship clash with a combined won-lost record of 63-1.

Marshall had assumed the favorite's role following an impressive showing against third-ranked Herrin in the quarterfinals. The 28-3 Tigers, defending state champs, survived No. 4 West Frankfort 76-75 in a super-sectional thriller on the Redbirds' own court. Against Marshall three nights later, Herrin kept losing ground, finally failing in its quest for a repeat title, 72-59.

In the title match, Rock Falls grabbed the early lead, built it to nine points with less than 6:00 left in the third quarter, and carried a 53-52 edge into the stretch run. But with Thomas powering his way to 26 points and Jones and Thompson combining for 35 more, Marshall took control late and captured an exciting 70-64 win — the Commandos' 31st win in an unblemished season.

The first state champions from the city of Chicago, the Marshall team returned to a heroes' welcome in the Loop.

CHICAGO (MARSHALL)
State Champions of 1958

*FRONT ROW (left to right):
Coach Isadore "Spin" Salario,
Mgr. Alvin Harvey, Bobby Jones,
Tyrone Johnson, George Wilson,
Steve Thomas, M.C. Thompson,
Mgr. Charles Bowen.
SECOND ROW: Isaac Patterson,
Morris Matthews, Lonnie Elliott,
Bob Smith, Jerome Faulkner,
Ben Stevenson, Ron Banks,
Paul Brown, Jim Jones, Gordon
Lemons, Asst. Coach Will Gaines.*

*Celebrating 100 years of
IHSA Boys Basketball Tournaments*

1959

Springfield had a remarkable knack in the tournament's early years for making the most of its state visits. In its first nine tries, the school claimed six trophies, including two for first and three for second. But it had been five visits and nearly 25 years since the Senators had earned tourney hardwood. That all changed in 1959.

The top four teams in the AP poll reached the quarterfinals of the tournament but, as fate would have it, were paired against one another in quarterfinal games. That prevented a first: a final day of teams ranked one through four. As it turned out, No. 3 Springfield (30-1) battled No. 4 Peoria Central (20-2) in the second afternoon game, and second-ranked Herrin (30-1) tangled with top-ranked Galesburg (27-1) to bring down the curtain.

Springfield's Senators had to fight from behind in the second half against "Dawdy" Hawkins' pesky Peoria team,

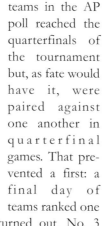

Springfield's Lynn Neff pulls a rebound away from Jim Konrad of West Aurora in the 1959 championship game.

but did so successfully, earning a 60-53 win behind 20 points from 6-foot-7 all-state center Tom Cole. That night, five double-digit scorers sparked Galesburg to a come-from-behind 73-69 victory over Herrin. The Streaks, down 41-37 at the half, used a 17-7 spurt in the third quarter to steal a lead that Herrin would never get back.

The initial semifinal game ran true to form when Coach Ray Page's Springfield crew pounded 11th-ranked Waukegan 64-40 as Cole scored 23 points and teammate George Mathis added 22. Waukegan had upset defending champion Chicago Marshall 63-62 at the Evanston Super-Sectional as the losers missed 15 of 25 free throws.

Fourteenth-ranked West Aurora, coming off a solid fourth-place finish one year earlier and powered by all-state playmaker Bill Small, splintered the title dreams of favored Galesburg in easier-than-expected fashion, 74-61.

Those wins brought about a sequel to the 1958 quarterfinals. In that one, West won handily over Springfield 59-48. This go-around, results were expected to be different. They were.

Playing a nearly flawless final game, Springfield held a thin three-point margin at the first horn but crafted a comfortable 28-19 cushion over the middle two periods, effectively putting the game out of reach. Cole scored 26 points and Mathis 19 as Springfield cruised home to its third state title 60-52.

Meanwhile, West Aurora, proud possessors of three previous trophies, once more fell short of a state crown — a frustration that would last another 41 years.

Small did his part, however, scoring 18 points in the championship to finish with a tournament-best 103 over four games.

State Final Tournament Scores

Super-Sectionals
At Salem—Madison 83, Centralia 69
At Evanston [NU]—Waukegan 63, Chicago (Marshall) 62
At Springfield [Armory]—Springfield 73, Macomb 39
At Peoria [Bradley]—Peoria 70, Ottawa (Twp.) 47
At Hinsdale (Twp.)—Aurora (West) 71, Harvey (Thornton) 58
At Decatur—Rantoul 66, Taylorville 61
At West Frankfort (Frankfort)—Herrin 62, Benton 50
At Moline—Galesburg 65, Rockford (West) 49

Quarterfinals
Waukegan 62, Madison 50
Springfield 60, Peoria 53
Aurora (West) 71, Rantoul 62
Galesburg 73, Herrin 69

Semifinals
Springfield 64, Waukegan 40
Aurora (West) 74, Galesburg 61

Finals
Galesburg 78, Waukegan 66 (third place)
Springfield 60, Aurora (West) 52 (title)

Scoring Leaders

Player, School	G	FG	FT	Pts
Bill Small, Aurora (West)	4	40	23	103
Tom Cole, Springfield	4	35	20	90
Dick Nixon, Waukegan	4	28	20	76
Dave Cox, Galesburg	4	24	19	67
Lawrence "Bumpy" Nixon, Galesburg	4	24	18	66
George Mathis, Springfield	4	21	24	66

All-Tournament First Team

Player, School	Ht.	Yr.
Tom Cole, Springfield	6-7	Sr.
Ken Doughty, Herrin	6-0	Sr.
Richard Nichols, Galesburg	6-1	Sr.
Dick Nixon, Waukegan	5-10	Sr.
Bill Small, Aurora (West)	6-2	Sr.

Championship Game Box Score

Huff Gym, Champaign, March 21, 1959

SPRINGFIELD (60)
Coach Ray Page

Player	FG-A	FT-A	Pts	PF
Tom Cole	11-21	4-7	26	2
George Mathis	7-15	5-5	19	5
Lynn Neff	1-4	1-1	3	1
Lee Pelham	1-1	0-0	2	0
Charles Shauger	3-10	4-6	10	4
Jim Wieties	0-1	0-1	0	4
TOTAL	23-52	14-20	60	16

AURORA (WEST) (52)
Coach Dick Dorsey

Player	FG-A	FT-A	Pts	PF
Jim Cronin	1-1	1-2	3	0
Jim Konrad	3-7	0-0	6	2
Ed Pottieger	1-4	2-3	4	1
John Schwenk	3-8	7-11	13	3
Larry Secor	1-4	2-2	4	5
Bill Small	7-18	4-7	18	5
Tom Young	2-4	0-0	4	0
TOTAL	18-46	16-25	52	16

Springfield	17	14	14	15	—	60
Aurora (West)	14	10	9	19	—	52

Officials: Alvin Gebhardt, Wayne Nohren.

SPRINGFIELD, *State Champions of 1959*

FRONT ROW (left to right): Mgr. Dan Britton, Ed Greenberg, Tom Frick, Bob Plohr, Lee Pelham, Bob Ferris. SECOND ROW: Coach Ray Page, Jim Wieties, George Mathis, Tom Cole, Charles Shauger, Lynn Neff, Asst. Coach John Sowinski, Asst. Coach Alby Plain.

Coach Isadore "Spin" Salario and his Marshall players celebrate the school's second state championship.

In 1960, Chicago Marshall returned to Champaign — with a vengeance. State champs in 1958, first-round upset victims in 1959, the Commandos were 27-2 with a trio of returning starters: all-American center George Wilson (6-foot-8), front-line partner Ed Franklin and Ken Moses. Charlie Jones and sparkplug Eddie Jakes, along with sixth man Jim Pitts, filled out the most physically intimidating squad in the 53-year history of the state finals.

Thirteenth-ranked Elgin was first to fall on Marshall's relentless march to the title game, losing 71-55 at Evanston. Monmouth was next, losing by 20 in quarterfinal action. Only seventh-ranked Stephen Decatur stayed relatively close to the Commandos, falling 74-62 in Saturday's first semifinal.

Meanwhile, a pair of small schools toppled much larger opponents to fight for the right to face Marshall in the finale.

Unranked West Frankfort, winners of back-to-back double-overtime games just to reach Champaign, surprised fourth-ranked Galesburg 66-63 in Friday's last quarterfinal. Led by tournament scoring leader Dave Pike, the Redbirds entered the semifinals with a lackluster 23-9 record, but on a roll.

Even smaller Bridgeport (385 students), 30-1 on the season and ranked 11th, filled in the lower bracket. Coached by Ray Estes, the Bulldogs marched to the drumbeat of speedy Bernie Gray and one of the finest sophomores in the state, 6-foot-2 Steve Cunningham.

With Granite City clearing top-ranked Pinckneyville and second-ranked Collinsville from the postseason path, Bridgeport captured its first regional title since 1936 and nabbed its first sectional crown in school history.

Bridgeport raced past Greenville 85-73 at Olney before besting No. 3 Ottawa 61-55 in its quarterfinal contest. Against West Frankfort the next afternoon, the Bulldogs' top-to-bottom balance was the difference as Bridgeport eased to a 74-60 victory.

Both Marshall and Bridgeport benefited from some early giant-killing as four ranked teams stumbled in the super-sectionals and three more fell in quarterfinal action. That left only two survivors from the AP poll standing on Saturday morning.

In the final match-up, Marshall overpowered the much smaller Bulldogs. Bridgeport had no chance. Hounded by the Commandos' size and speed, the Bulldogs shot only 32 percent, and their defense was unable to stop the favorite's inside-outside punch.

The Chicagoans stormed out of the starting gate, roaring to a 28-18 lead after eight minutes. The score was 44-30 at the half and an insurmountable 63-39 after three quarters.

All five Marshall starters scored at least 11 points, paced by Jakes, who had a game-best 18, as the Commandos won in a walk, 79-55, annexing their second title in three years.

State Final Tournament Scores

Super-Sectionals

At Evanston [NU]—Chicago (Marshall) 71, Elgin 55
At Springfield [Armory]—Monmouth 49, Springfield 48
At Aurora (East)—Maywood (Proviso East) 65, Kankakee 62
At Decatur—Decatur (Stephen Decatur) 52, Danville (Schlarman) 46
At Peoria [Bradley]—Ottawa (Twp.) 78, Pekin 66
At Olney (East Richland)—Bridgeport 85, Greenville 73
At Rock Island—Galesburg 77, DeKalb 71 (OT)
At East St. Louis—West Frankfort (Frankfort) 64, Granite City 62 (2 OT)

Quarterfinals

Chicago (Marshall) 55, Monmouth 35
Decatur (Stephen Decatur) 53, Maywood (Proviso East) 52 (OT)
Bridgeport 61, Ottawa (Twp.) 55
West Frankfort (Frankfort) 66, Galesburg 63

Semifinals

Chicago (Marshall) 74, Decatur (Stephen Decatur) 62
Bridgeport 74, West Frankfort (Frankfort) 60

Finals

West Frankfort (Frankfort) 75, Decatur (Stephen Decatur) 53 (third place)
Chicago (Marshall) 79, Bridgeport 55 (title)

Scoring Leaders

Player, School	G	FG	FT	Pts
Dave Pike, West Frankfort (Frankfort)	4	34	21	89
Eddie Jakes, Chicago (Marshall)	4	36	13	85
Steve Cunningham, Bridgeport	4	29	18	76
Tom Sidney, Decatur (Stephen Decatur)	4	29	16	74
Bernie Gray, Bridgeport	4	27	12	66

All-Tournament First Team

Player, School	Ht.	Yr.
Steve Cunningham, Bridgeport	6-2	So.
Eddie Jakes, Chicago (Marshall)	5-11	Jr.
John Love, Ottawa (Twp.)	6-4	Sr.
Tom Sidney, Decatur (Stephen Decatur)	5-10	Jr.
George Wilson, Chicago (Marshall)	6-8	Sr.

Championship Game Box Score

Huff Gym, Champaign, March 19, 1960

CHICAGO (MARSHALL) (79)
Coach Isadore "Spin" Salario

Player	FG-A	FT-A	Pts	PF
Lenwood Flint	0-0	0-0	0	0
Ed Franklin	5-10	1-2	11	1
James Giglio	2-2	0-0	4	3
Donald Jackson	1-2	0-0	2	1
Eddie Jakes	8-13	2-3	18	2
Charlie Jones	6-9	0-1	12	2
Ronald Knight	0-1	0-0	0	1
Ken Moses	7-16	1-1	15	1
Jim Pitts	0-1	0-2	0	0
George Wilson	5-9	7-8	17	1
TOTAL	34-63	11-17	79	12

BRIDGEPORT (55)
Coach Ray Estes

Player	FG-A	FT-A	Pts	PF
Jim Brown	1-7	0-0	2	4
Steve Cunningham	6-23	1-2	13	1
Bernie Gray	7-17	2-5	16	3
Clifton Joiner	0-2	0-1	0	0
Dennis Magee	5-13	1-1	11	2
Richard Martin	5-12	0-0	10	3
Dennis Oney	0-0	0-0	0	0
Mike Shuppert	0-1	3-5	3	0
TOTAL	24-75	7-14	55	13

Chicago (Marshall)	28	16	19	16	—	79
Bridgeport	18	12	9	16	—	55

Officials: Robert Young, Frank Falzone.

CHICAGO (MARSHALL), State Champions of 1960

FRONT ROW (left to right): Coach Isadore "Spin" Salario, George Wilson, Ken Moses, Eddie Jakes, Charley Jones, Ed Franklin, Athletic Director Bosco Levine. SECOND ROW: James Pitts, Donald Jackson, Wayne Stingley, Donald King, James Giglio, Lenwood Flint, Ronald Knight, Lavele Swanagain.

COLLINSVILLE
State Champions of 1961

FRONT ROW (left to right):
Robert Meadows,
Ron Mottin, Fred Riddle,
Coach Vergil Fletcher, Marc
Fletcher, Bogie Redmon,
Bob Basola, Bob Simpson.
SECOND ROW:
Asst. Coach Bill Hellyer,
Than Byrkit, Ronnie
Matikitis, Joe Brennan,
Harry Hildreth, Asst. Coach
Bert Weber.

A record 11 ranked teams remained in the hunt as the Sweet Sixteen prepared for the run at the 1961 state title. Amazingly, seven teams reached the quarterfinal round and four fought through to the semifinals.

Combined, those 11 tournament teams had won 280 games against only 25 losses (92%), an average record of 25-2. The upper bracket was especially lethal, boasting four ranked teams with a total of only four losses.

Best of the bunch were Vergil Fletcher's undefeated Collinsville Kahoks, led by 6-foot-6 all-American center Bogie Redmon, 6-3 all-state forward Fred Riddle, and a trio of Bobs — Basola, Meadows and Simpson. Fletcher had his all-winning Kahoks in a similar position four years earlier when Collinsville was ambushed by Herrin 45-42 in the championship game.

This time, the scene was the Salem Super-Sectional. Lying in wait was archrival Centralia, second-ranked and 29-1. With the final seconds slipping away, an errant Russell Coleman pass — a rare turnover in a well-played game — proved to be the difference. Collinsville cashed in on a fast-break lay-up and free throw to guarantee the 66-64 victory.

Tenth-ranked Clinton (28-2) was not as fortunate, unable to dodge Danville

Schlarman in the Decatur Super-Sectional. In an end-to-end, back-and-forth masterpiece, Clinton scored with only seconds remaining to reclaim the lead 75-74. All-American scoring ace Bryan Williams received the inbounds pass under the Clinton basket, whirled and heaved a court-length toss. The shot hit bulls-eye at the buzzer, giving Williams his 39th and 40th points of the game and Schlarman a dramatic 76-75 victory.

With the first-round close call out of the way, Collinsville went about the business of establishing itself as one of the greatest teams in Illinois high school basketball history. In perhaps the most dominant state finals performance on record, the Kahoks crushed, in succession, the state's third-, eighth- and twelfth-ranked teams by an average score of 77-46, shooting on average 56 percent from the field.

In the finale against Thornton, Collinsville broke open a 14-all game with a 43-18 tear through the second and third quarters, energized by 60 percent shooting from the field. The Kahok defense held Thornton all-state team leader Leon Clark without a point until the 1:21 mark of the fourth quarter.

The 84-50 rout was spearheaded by Redman, who rifled in 31 points and Riddle who added 24. The win capped a magnificent 32-0 season for the Kahoks.

State Final Tournament Scores

Super-Sectionals

At West Frankfort (Frankfort)—Benton 65, Belleville (Twp.) 59
At Peoria [Bradley]—Peoria (Manual) 61, Ottawa (Twp.) 45
At Salem—Collinsville 66, Centralia 64
At Rock Island—Rockford (East) 60, Moline 53
At Evanston [NU]—Chicago (Marshall) 56, Waukegan 55
At Decatur—Danville (Schlarman) 76, Clinton 75
At Springfield [Armory]—Springfield 58, Monmouth 48
At Hinsdale (Twp.)—Harvey (Thornton) 48, Cicero (Morton) 36

Quarterfinals

Peoria (Manual) 54, Benton 51 (OT)
Collinsville 71, Rockford (East) 48
Chicago (Marshall) 61, Danville (Schlarman) 36
Harvey (Thornton) 54, Springfield 52

Semifinals

Collinsville 76, Peoria (Manual) 39
Harvey (Thornton) 49, Chicago (Marshall) 47

Finals

Chicago (Marshall) 73, Peoria (Manual) 58 (third place)
Collinsville 84, Harvey (Thornton) 50 (title)

Scoring Leaders

Player, School	G	FG	FT	Pts
Bogie Redmon, Collinsville	4	39	14	92
Fred Riddle, Collinsville	4	25	26	76
Jim Pitts, Chicago (Marshall)	4	25	8	58
John Craley, Peoria (Manual)	4	24	10	58
Leon Clark, Harvey (Thornton)	4	22	9	53
Bryan Williams, Danville (Schlarman)	2	24	5	53

All-Tournament First Team

Player, School	Ht.	Yr.
Larry Bauer, Springfield	6-8	Sr.
Bob Caress, Harvey (Thornton)	6-1	Sr.
Leon Clark, Harvey (Thornton)	6-7	Jr.
Jim Pitts, Chicago (Marshall)	6-8	Jr.
Bogie Redmon, Collinsville	6-7	Sr.
Fred Riddle, Collinsville	6-3	Sr.

Springfield's Tom Frick (40) meets Leon Clark of Thornton during quarterfinal action in Huff Gymnasium.

Championship Game Box Score

Huff Gym, Champaign, March 18, 1961

COLLINSVILLE (84)
Coach Vergil Fletcher

Player	FG-A	FT-A	Pts	PF	Rb	As	St	Bl
Bob Basola	4-10	4-5	12	2				
Joe Brennan	0-1	0-0	0	0				
Than Brykit	0-0	2-4	2	0				
Harry Hildreth	1-1	0-0	2	0				
Ronnie Matikitis	0-0	0-0	0	0				
Bob Meadows	2-3	0-0	4	4				
Ronnie Mottin	0-1	0-0	0	1				
Bogie Redmon	12-17	7-12	31	2				
Fred Riddle	8-11	8-9	24	3				
Bob Simpson	3-6	3-3	9	4				
TOTAL	30-50	24-33	84	16				

HARVEY (THORNTON) (50)
Coach Bill Purden

Player	FG-A	FT-A	Pts	PF	Rb	As	St	Bl
Renault Banks	4-8	1-2	9	4				
Bob Caress	3-7	2-2	8	2				
Leon Clark	2-6	1-1	5	3				
Jack Dabon	4-8	3-3	11	4				
Al Dehnert	0-1	3-3	3	1				
Wilfred Henry	1-4	1-3	3	3				
Marvin Keeling	0-0	0-0	0	2				
Fred Lindsay	1-3	3-4	5	0				
John McKibben	1-3	2-2	4	1				
Reuben Poindexter	0-0	2-2	2	1				
TOTAL	16-40	18-22	50	21				

Collinsville	14	23	20	27	—	84
Harvey (Thornton)	14	9	9	18	—	50

Officials: Ernest Reynolds, Herb Scheffler.

It was an improbable finale, but one of the best.

The Runnin' Reds of Stephen Decatur, coached by John Schneiter, were coming off a 12-12 season and a surprise regional title in 1961. Ranked near the bottom of the statewide poll at the start of the 1962 postseason, the Reds were 27-4 and leaned heavily on 6-foot-3 all-state senior Ken Barnes.

Chicago Carver, which had not even fielded a basketball team until 1956, was unranked at 25-4. Still, they were poised for a run at the title, with an attack featuring 6-5 all-American guard Cazzie Russell and 6-6 junior center Joe Allen, one of the most intimidating players in the state.

Both teams nearly lost in the opening round. Decatur withstood a furious fourth-quarter rally to hold off upstart Urbana 41-40, while Carver overcame a Chicago St. Patrick defense that held Russell to only eight points, hanging on for a 48-42 win.

Carver next upset top-ranked Centralia, 56-50, as Russell and Allen scored 22 and 16 points respectively,

while the Challengers' defense limited the Orphans to 29 percent shooting.

Decatur opened evening action with a 61-56 edging of ninth-ranked Rock Island. The five-point margin of victory

was the Reds' largest in four tournament games.

Decatur struggled again in the semifinals, playing just well enough to nip Quincy, 47-44. Carver had an easier time against little McLeansboro, running past the Foxes 54-41, as Russell poured in 25 points.

Carver opened the championship game with an 11-2 stretch. The referee disallowed another Carver basket when he blew his whistle in response to a time-out request from the Chicago team's bench. Soon after, Allen tumbled to the floor with a knee injury and left the game, never to return. But Carver still led 20-10 after one period.

With Allen out, the Reds moved more freely on offense while Carver lost its inside game. Decatur still trailed, but only 27-25, at the half, and seized the lead, 39-34, after three quarters. Carver rallied at the close, tying the game. Then, with less than a minute to play, the Challengers' Bruce Raickett, who earlier had taken a blow to the head, passed the ball directly to Decatur's Jerry Hill. The Reds waited for the final shot. Barnes was fouled with six seconds to play, his free throw providing the winning margin.

Despite Russell's game-high totals of 24 points and 15 rebounds, Carver fell agonizingly short of the coveted crown. Decatur captured its fourth state title in thrilling fashion, 49-48.

DECATUR (STEPHEN DECATUR)
State Champions of 1962

FRONT ROW (left to right): Gary Stewart, Prentis Jones, James "Bulldog" Johnson, Ken Barnes. SECOND ROW: Asst. Coach Jack Kenny, Dave Hayes, Lee Endsley, Jack Sunderlik, Bruce Gray, Jim Hallihan, Jerry Hill, Coach John Schneiter.

1962

State Final Tournament Scores

Super-Sectionals

At Eldorad—McLeansboro 53, Marion 52
At Aurora (East —Elmhurst (York) 84, Harvey (Thornton) 63
At East St. Louis—Centralia 78, Belleville (Twp.) 66
At Evanston [NU]—Chicago (Carver) 48, Chicago (St. Patrick) 42
At Rock Island—Rock Island 64, Rockford (Auburn) 44
At Decatur—Decatur (Stephen Decatur) 41, Urbana 40
At Quincy—Quincy 72, Springfield 53
At Peoria [Bradley]—Washington 58, Pontiac 57

Quarterfinals

McLeansboro 84, Elmhurst (York) 68
Chicago (Carver) 56, Centralia 50
Decatur (Stephen Decatur) 61, Rock Island 56
Quincy 45, Washington 37

Semifinals

Chicago (Carver) 54, McLeansboro 41
Decatur (Stephen Decatur) 47, Quincy 44

Finals

Quincy 85, McLeansboro 45 (third place)
Decatur (Stephen Decatur) 49, Chicago (Carver) 48 (title)

Scoring Leaders

Player, School	G	FG	FT	Pts
Jim Burns, McLeansboro	4	31	23	85
Cazzie Russell, Chicago (Carver)	4	34	11	79
Ken Barnes, Decatur (Stephen Decatur)	4	24	9	57
Jim Johnson, Decatur (Stephen Decatur)	4	19	15	53
Fred Grimmett, Quincy	4	15	21	51
Joe Allen, Chicago (Carver)	4	23	5	51

All-Tournament First Team

Player, School	Ht.	Yr.
Joe Allen, Chicago (Carver)	6-6	Jr.
Ken Barnes, Decatur (Stephen Decatur)	6-3	Sr.
Jim Burns, McLeansboro	6-3	Jr.
Fred Grimmett, Quincy	5-8	Jr.
Cazzie Russell, Chicago (Carver)	6-5	Sr.
Ron Teague, Rock Island	5-10	Sr.

Championship Game Box Score

Huff Gym, Champaign, March 24, 1962

DECATUR (STEPHEN DECATUR) (49)
Coach John Schneiter

Player	FG-A	FT-A	Pts	PF	Rb	As	St	Bl
Ken Barnes	3-11	4-6	10	1				
Jim Hallihan	2-5	0-0	4	1				
Jerry Hill	3-11	1-1	7	3				
Jim Johnson	7-11	3-3	17	2				
Prentis Jones	5-13	1-3	11	2				
TOTAL	20-51	9-13	49	9				

CHICAGO (CARVER) (48)
Coach Larry Hawkins

Player	FG-A	FT-A	Pts	PF	Rb	As	St	Bl
Joe Allen	2-6	0-0	4	1				
Bob Cifax	0-1	0-0	0	0				
Harold Dade	1-2	0-1	2	0				
Gerry Jones	3-6	0-0	6	2				
Curtis Kirk	2-4	1-2	5	2				
Joe McEwen	0-0	0-0	0	1				
Marlbert Pradd	2-3	0-0	4	0				
Bruce Raickett	1-4	1-3	3	2				
Cazzie Russell	11-24	2-4	24	3				
TOTAL	22-50	4-10	48	11				

Decatur (Stephen Decatur)	10	15	14	10	—	49
Chicago (Carver)	20	7	7	14	—	48

Officials: Alvin Gebhardt, Joseph Starcevic.

Huff Gym, with its sell-out crowds of 6,925, gave way after 37 years to the spacious and sparkling-new Assembly Hall, where a record 16,310 fans watched Saturday's semifinals.

No. 1 Centralia (31-1) and a trio of unranked teams started the day in a quest for the state title. It was a memorable Saturday — one of the most spine-tingling final days in tournament history.

In the first semifinal, Centralia overcame a seven-point Springfield Lanphier lead in the second half to escape with a 50-46 win. Ron Johnson, a 5-foot-10 all-state senior, scored 21 points for the winners.

Peoria Central held a tenuous 19-17 halftime lead, but was dead-even with Chicago Carver after three quarters — and after four, when 6-6 center Joe Allen made a lay-up to force an extra session. Carver won in overtime 40-37.

What followed was a timeless North-South showdown.

Carver's 15-12 first quarter lead grew to 21-14 before a Centralia surge closed the gap. The score was 30-26 at the half, 43-39 after three quarters, and 47-41 when the Orphans rallied.

Don Duncan's two field goals made it 47-45. Johnson's jumper and free throws inched Centralia to the front, 49-47, not three minutes from the finish.

Ken Maxey's four free throws, the last with 2:10 remaining, gave Carver a 51-49 lead. Rich Zgol's free throw trimmed the margin to one, and when Herb Williams hit a jumper just 30 seconds from the horn, Centralia recaptured the lead, 52-51.

Twelve seconds later, Allen's pass into the paint was batted away, picked up by Centralia's Williams, who dribbled twice and then handed the ball to Duncan, who called an ill-advised timeout. Carver coach Larry Hawkins inserted sophomore Anthony Smedley, a defensive specialist.

Duncan inbounded the ball to Williams, who was promptly double-teamed. In a controversial no-call, Williams was thumped from behind and knocked forward, forcing him to dribble to avoid traveling. When he attempted a quick pass, Smedley batted the ball and then swiped it, pivoted once, dribbled to the baseline, and launched a hurried 18-footer — only his third shot of the tournament. The shot went in and Carver was back in front 53-52.

As the horn sounded, Robert Cifax partially blocked a desperation jumper by Centralia's Cliff Berger, giving the city of Chicago its third state title in six years.

56th ILLINOIS STATE CHAMPIONSHIP

IHSA

HIGH SCHOOL BASKETBALL TOURNAMENT

MARCH 22-23, 1963 ASSEMBLY HALL UNIVERSITY OF ILLINOIS

25¢ OFFICIAL PROGRAM

1963

CHICAGO (CARVER)
State Champions of 1963

FRONT ROW (left to right): Kenneth Maxey, Ricardo Armstrong, Robert Cifax, Elree Cox, Carter Gilmer, Anthony Smedley, Mgr. Tyrone Parker.
SECOND ROW: Coach Larry Hawkins, Fred Hickman, William Hornsby, Gerry Jones, Edward Kendall, Curtis Kirk, Adolph Lawerence, Asst. Coach Horace Howard.
THIRD ROW: Joseph Allen, Peter Norfleet, Michele Page, Leslie Patmon, Charles Glenn.

The 1963 tournament was the first to be played at Assembly Hall on the campus of the University of Illinois.

State Final Tournament Scores

Super-Sectionals
At Salem—Centralia 69, Collinsville 48
At West Frankfort (Frankfort)—Metropolis 53, Herrin 52
At Quincy—Springfield (Lanphier) 91, Galesburg 67
At Moline—Rockford (Auburn) 62, Aledo 51 (forfeited)
At Peoria [Bradley]—Peoria 35, Braidwood (Reed-Custer) 34
At Decatur—Decatur (Stephen Decatur) 93, Watseka 73
At Evanston [NU]—Chicago (Carver) 54, Waukegan 41
At Hinsdale (Twp.)—Geneva 60, Chicago Heights (Bloom) 52

Quarterfinals
Centralia 74, Metropolis 45
Springfield (Lanphier) 58, Rockford (Auburn) 56
Peoria 60, Decatur (Stephen Decatur) 45
Chicago (Carver) 57, Geneva 50

Semifinals
Centralia 50, Springfield (Lanphier) 46
Chicago (Carver) 40, Peoria 37 (OT)

Finals
Springfield (Lanphier) 60, Peoria 47 (third place)
Chicago (Carver) 53, Centralia 52 (title)

Scoring Leaders

Player, School	G	FG	FT	Pts
Craig Alexander, Peoria	4	25	36	86
Ron Johnson, Centralia	4	37	5	79
Mike Rodgerson, Springfield (Lanphier)	4	24	22	70
Calvin Pettit, Springfield (Lanphier)	4	24	21	69
Joe Allen, Chicago (Carver)	4	27	13	67

All-Tournament First Team

Player, School	Ht.	Yr.
Craig Alexander, Peoria	6-5	Sr.
Don Duncan, Centralia	5-10	Sr.
Bob Johansen, Geneva	6-5	Sr.
Ron Johnson, Centralia	5-10	Sr.
Calvin Pettit, Springfield (Lanphier)	6-4	Jr.
Herb Williams, Centralia	6-3	Sr.

Championship Game Box Score

Assembly Hall, Champaign, March 23, 1963

CHICAGO (CARVER) (53)
Coach Larry Hawkins

Player	FG-A	FT-A	Pts	PF	Rb	As	St	Bl
Joe Allen	8-12	2-4	18	2	17			
Bob Cifax	4-15	2-2	10	1	8			
Charles Glenn	1-4	1-1	3	1	1			
Gerry Jones	0-0	0-0	0	1	4			
Curtis Kirk	1-6	0-1	2	3	3			
Ken Maxey	7-13	4-6	18	3	5			
Michele Page	0-0	0-0	0	0	0			
Anthony Smedley	1-1	0-0	2	0	0			
TOTAL	22-51	9-14	53	11	38			

CENTRALIA (52)
Coach Bob Jones

Player	FG-A	FT-A	Pts	PF	Rb	As	St	Bl
Cliff Berger	2-12	2-2	6	2	8			
Don Duncan	5-11	2-2	12	3	4			
Carl "Skip" Heinrichsmeyer	4-9	0-1	8	3	2			
Ron Johnson	8-20	2-4	18	0	4			
Merritt Pulley	0-0	0-0	0	1	0			
Herb Williams	1-2	3-5	5	1	8			
Rich Zgol	1-2	1-2	3	0	2			
TOTAL	21-56	10-16	52	10	28			

Chicago (Carver)	15	15	13	10	— 53
Centralia	12	14	13	13	— 52

Officials: Tony Sacco, Tony Tortorello.

Carver's Curtis Kirk skies over Carl Heinrichsmeyer of Centralia in the title game.

A Centralia cheerleader reacts as Anthony Smedley's shot flies toward the basket. At least three photographers missed a chance to capture the most famous field goal in tourney history.

1963

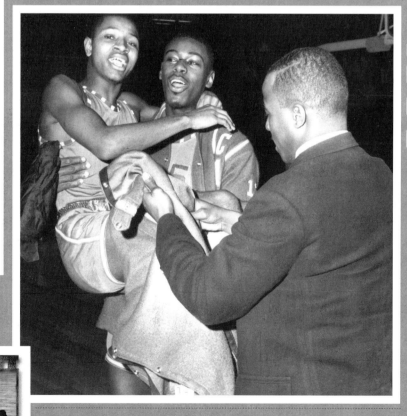

Smedley (in warm-up) responds to the call from Coach Larry Hawkins, surrounds Centralia's Herb Williams, lets fly from the corner, receives a hero's welcome back to the bench.

Carver's Anthony Smedley is cradled by a teammate after making the game-winning shot.

1964

PEKIN

State Champions of 1964

LEFT TO RIGHT: Trainer Jimmie "Doc" Lee, Asst. Coach Duncan Reid, Mgr. Richard Pitsek, Mike Gilliam, Ron Ahten, Tom Waskowski, Dave Golden, Steve Noriuel, Toney Buzeck, Jim Sommer, Amel Massa, Jim Couch, Fred Quade, Dan McDonald, Rick Venturi, Ron Rhoades, Mgr. Terry Vogel, Asst. Coach Joe Venturi, Coach Dawson Hawkins.

A string of super-sectional surprises and narrow escapes set the tone for the 1964 state tournament.

Pinckneyville fought Cobden's Appleknockers through three overtimes before falling 66-64. Ten-time loser Rock Island Alleman nipped Rockford Auburn 57-56. Glenbard East edged Bradley-Bourbonnais by five, and eighth-ranked Pekin beat Streator after trailing 12-3 at the first stop.

Two other teams, both powerhouses, fell right off the bat. No. 3 Chicago Crane (23-1) blew a sizeable fourth quarter lead and lost to Evanston 55-53 in double overtime. Unbeaten Collinsville, ranked No. 1 and energized by 6-foot-5 all-American center Rodger Bohnenstiehl, stumbled before second-ranked Centralia 55-50. The Orphans were on a four-year run where they were ranked either first or second and had an average annual record of 30-2. The upset put Centralia on the doorstep of its fourth state title, but the surprises were just beginning.

The beat went on at Champaign. Unranked Cobden trailed 44-40 entering the fourth quarter, but kicked it up a notch to upset seventh-ranked Galesburg 60-57. That night, a last-second basket by Alleman's all-state junior Steve Spanich sank prohibitive favorite Centralia 57-56 in an overtime stunner.

Pekin and No. 4 Stephen Decatur were the only ranked teams left on Saturday. Alleman was attempting to become the first private school to win a state title, and Cobden was vying for only the second title by a district team, Hebron having turned the trick in 1952.

Pekin's 69-36 trouncing of Alleman ended private-school hopes, but the possibility of a district champion remained very much alive as Cobden outlasted Decatur 44-38. Cobden was aided by an amazing six points in five seconds, consisting of a made free throw, a rebound basket off a missed free throw, a foul, another rebound basket off a missed free throw, another foul, and yet a final free throw. Had Cobden been more successful from the line, Decatur might have won.

The Appleknockers were the obvious crowd favorite Saturday night. Dick Ruggles' tall, lanky squad of Ken Flick, Chuck and Jim Neal, and the Smith boys — Bob, Jim and Ken — had become household names after only two games in Champaign. The magical season, however, came to an abrupt end against Pekin.

Pekin's 68 percent shooting in the first half gave Dawson Hawkins' boys a lead they would never surrender. Fueled by a game-high 18 points from Dave Golden and 12 more from Jim Couch, Pekin dashed Cobden's Cinderella dreams 50-45.

State Final Tournament Scores

Super-Sectionals

At Evanston [NU]—Evanston (Twp.) 55, Chicago (Crane) 53 (2 OT)
At Normal [ISU]—Decatur (Stephen Decatur) 53, Arcola 37
At West Frankfort (Frankfort)—Cobden 68, Pinckneyville 66 (3 OT)
At Springfield [Armory]—Galesburg 79, Springfield (Lanphier) 66
At Salem—Centralia 55, Collinsville 50
At Rock Island—Rock Island (Alleman) 57, Rockford (Auburn) 56
At Peoria [Bradley]—Pekin 61, Streator (Twp.) 46
At Aurora (East)—Lombard (Glenbard East) 42, Bradley (B.-Bourbonnais) 37

Quarterfinals

Decatur (Stephen Decatur) 73, Evanston (Twp.) 59
Cobden 60, Galesburg 57
Rock Island (Alleman) 57, Centralia 56 (OT)
Pekin 84, Lombard (Glenbard East) 43

Semifinals

Cobden 44, Decatur (Stephen Decatur) 38
Pekin 69, Rock Island (Alleman) 36

Finals

Decatur (Stephen Decatur) 73, Rock Island (Alleman) 54 (third place)
Pekin 50, Cobden 45 (title)

Scoring Leaders

Player, School	G	FG	FT	Pts
Jack Sunderlik, Decatur (Stephen Decatur)	4	32	19	83
Dave Golden, Pekin	4	22	24	68
Kenny Flick, Cobden	4	23	16	62
John McGonigle, Rock Island (Alleman)	4	26	6	58
Jim Sommer, Pekin	4	19	20	58

All-Tournament First Team

Player, School	Ht.	Yr.
Cliff Berger, Centralia	6-8	Sr.
Kenny Flick, Cobden	6-5	Sr.
Dave Golden, Pekin	6-0	Jr.
Ron Rhoades, Pekin	5-8	Jr.
Jim Sommer, Pekin	6-3	Sr.
Steve Spanich, Rock Island (Alleman)	6-2	Jr.
Jack Sunderlik, Decatur (Stephen Decatur)	6-1	Sr.

Championship Game Box Score

Assembly Hall, Champaign, March 21, 1964

PEKIN (50)
Coach Dawson "Dawdy" Hawkins

Player	FG-A	FT-A	Pts	PF	Rb	As	St	Bl
Toney Buzick	0-0	0-0	0	0	0	1		
Jim Couch	4-10	4-4	12	0	2			
Dave Golden	6-10	6-6	18	5	4			
Amel Massa	0-4	2-3	2	2	6			
Ron Rhoades	4-7	1-3	9	3	2			
Jim Sommer	3-9	3-3	9	2	8			
Rick Venturi	0-0	0-0	0	0	0			
TOTAL	17-40	16-19	50	12	23			

COBDEN (45)
Coach Dick Ruggles

Player	FG-A	FT-A	Pts	PF	Rb	As	St	Bl
Rodney Clutts	0-3	0-0	0	1	0			
Darrell Crimmins	0-0	0-0	0	0	0			
Kenny Flick	2-6	0-0	4	0	5			
Roger Garner	0-0	0-0	0	0	0			
Chuck Neal	3-7	1-3	7	4	8			
Jim Neal	4-7	1-3	9	3	5			
Bob Smith	0-2	0-2	0	4	1			
Jim Smith	4-8	0-1	8	2	2			
Ken Smith	8-15	1-1	17	3	5			
Roy Witthoff	0-0	0-0	0	1	1			
TOTAL	21-48	3-10	45	18	27			

Pekin	15	16	5	14	— 50
Cobden	8	16	7	14	— 45

Officials: Joseph Starcevic, Robert Brodbeck.

If you believed the pollsters, the South had little chance of claiming the 1965 state title.

Perennial power Centralia, after four straight trips to state and 120 wins in 129 games, was noticeably absent. Collinsville was on hand, but this was a rebuilding year for Coach Vergil Fletcher, who returned only one regular, stocky guard Jack Darlington, from the previous year's 28-1 team.

Fletcher, however, did hold a pair of wild cards in his hand. One was a dead-eye

State Final Tournament Scores

Super-Sectionals

At Evanston [NU]—Chicago (Marshall) 69, Winnetka (New Trier) 52 (forfeited)
At Moline—Moline 64, Freeport 47
At Peoria [Bradley]—Lockport (Central) 67, Pekin 61
At Olney (East Richland)—Collinsville 82, Lawrenceville 58
At Normal [ISU]—Decatur (Stephen Decatur) 54, Danville 52
At Macomb [WIU]—Quincy 56, Jacksonville 52
At Aurora (East)—Harvey (Thornton) 64, Franklin Park (East Leyden) 57
At Carbondale [SIU]—Marion 65, Mt. Vernon 57

Quarterfinals

Chicago (Marshall) 75, Moline 72 (forfeited)
Collinsville 70, Lockport (Central) 45
Quincy 71, Decatur (Stephen Decatur) 62
Harvey (Thornton) 64, Marion 60

Semifinals

Collinsville 76, Chicago (Marshall) 64
Quincy 64, Harvey (Thornton) 59

Finals

Chicago (Marshall) 66, Harvey (Thornton) 59 (forfeited) (third place)
Collinsville 55, Quincy 52 (title)

Scoring Leaders

Player, School	G	FG	FT	Pts
Dennis Pace, Collinsville	4	44	24	112
Rich Bradshaw, Chicago (Marshall)	4	40	18	98
Harry Hall, Harvey (Thornton)	4	27	28	82
Gary Thompson, Quincy	4	27	18	72
Steve Kuberski, Moline	2	24	16	64
Charles Conway, Chicago (Marshall)	4	26	12	64

All-Tournament First Team

Player, School	Ht.	Yr.
Rich Bradshaw, Chicago (Marshall)	6-3	Jr.
Charles Conway, Chicago (Marshall)	6-0	Jr.
Jack Darlington, Collinsville	6-0	Sr.
Bill Ford, Lockport (Central)	6-5	Jr.
Harry Hall, Harvey (Thornton)	6-2	Sr.
Steve Kuberski, Moline	6-6	Sr.
Dennis Pace, Collinsville	6-5	Sr.
Gary Rottman, Quincy	6-3	Sr.
Dave Scholz, Decatur (Stephen Decatur)	6-6	Sr.
Gary Thompson, Quincy	5-9	Sr.

Championship Game Box Score
Assembly Hall, Champaign, March 20, 1965

COLLINSVILLE (55)
Coach Vergil Fletcher

Player	FG-A	FT-A	Pts	PF	Rb	As	St	Bl
Don Birger	4-9	3-4	11	3	7			
Jack Darlington	7-12	3-3	17	2	5			
Steve Gauen	0-3	4-4	4	3	0			
Dennis Pace	5-13	5-7	15	4	10			
Harry Parker	4-10	0-0	8	2	2			
TOTAL	20-47	15-18	55	14	24			

QUINCY (52)
Coach Sherrill Hanks

Player	FG-A	FT-A	Pts	PF	Rb	As	St	Bl
John Buch	2-3	1-2	5	1	7			
Kurt Genteman	4-10	1-2	9	3	2			
Jim Jenkins	0-1	0-0	0	1	1			
Bob McMahan	6-7	4-4	16	2	7			
Tim Miles	0-0	0-0	0	0	0			
Gary Rottman	0-2	1-2	1	0	2			
Harry Shair	0-1	2-3	2	1	4			
Marv Sprague	3-11	0-1	6	3	2			
Gary Thompson	4-7	5-8	13	1	3			
TOTAL	19-42	14-22	52	12	28			

Collinsville	10	14	17	14	—	55
Quincy	11	9	14	18	—	52

Officials: Thomas Frangella, Augie Jacobs.

shooter, a 6-foot-5 senior center named Dennis Pace, who played significantly taller than his size. Another was, in the coach's own words, "The best pressing team I've ever had."

Despite Fletcher's sales pitch, pollsters were unconvinced. Judging that the real talent and power lay elsewhere, prognosticators tabbed Harvey Thornton the state's best team. Sparked by 6-2 all-state standout Harry Hall, the Wildcats were 26-1. Pekin (28-1) was No. 2 and returned three starters from the 1964 championship team, including all-American team leader Dave Golden. Twice-beaten Stephen Decatur and once-beaten Freeport were ranked third and fourth respectively.

Upsets started in the super-sectionals, when Moline shocked Freeport with a resounding 64-47 win behind 30 points from all-state center Steve Kuberski. The same night, Lockport Central derailed Pekin's repeat express 67-61, shooting 59 per cent from the floor.

The upset magic was gone by Friday. Moline got 34 points from Kuberski but lost to Chicago Marshall 75-72. Meanwhile, the Porters fell apart under the full-court pressure of Collinsville's fabled ball-press, losing convincingly 70-45.

Quincy dropped Decatur from the field 71-62, and Thornton

squeaked by Marion 64-60 to fill in the final-day bracket.

Collinsville opened semifinal play with a 76-64 win over Marshall as all-state center Dennis Pace scored 29 points, complementing 41- and 27-point performances in the first two rounds.

Coach Sherrill Hanks' 13th-ranked Blue Devils followed by upending Thornton 64-59. Gary Rottman paced Quincy with 24 points on 8-of-11 shooting from the field and a perfect 8-of-8 from the line.

Surprise finalists Quincy and Collinsville hooked up in a barnburner of a game.

The Kahoks slowly built a lead through the middle frames, carrying a 41-34 advantage into the fourth quarter. Fueled by all-state guard Gary Thompson, unheralded Bob McMahan and 6-8 center John Buch, the Blue Devils narrowed the gap but could never close it. Behind Darlington (17 points) and Pace (15), Collinsville claimed its second title in five years, clipping Quincy 55-52.

Pace netted a tournament best 112 points for the four games — at the time the third best total ever, trailing only LaGrange's Ted Caiazza (121 points in 1953) and Collinsville's Terry Bethel (113 in 1957).

COLLINSVILLE
State Champions of 1965

FRONT ROW (left to right): Bruce Evans, Mike Vincent, Dennis Arnold, Keith Ziesel, Mike Belobraydic.
SECOND ROW: Asst. Coach Frank Pitol, Harry Parker, Donald Birger, Dennis Pace, Jack Darlington, Steve Gauen, Coach Vergil Fletcher.

1965

Scenes from a Telecast: Ed McMahon interviews coaches' wives; Marilyn Van Derbur (Miss America 1958) chats with girlfriends; Dad considers ordering a two-line Illinois Bell telephone for Sis; Vince Lloyd and Jack Drees hold down the fort in Tournament Central.

At the heart of the word *"dynasty"* is the idea of rule maintained over a prolonged period. In terms of the IHSA boys' state basketball tournament, a dynasty requires tournament trips and trophies over *significant* time.

by Pat Heston

By that standard, only a handful of teams in Illinois' single class era, the 64-year stretch from 1908 to 1971, can truly be classified as dynasties.

Here are those that led the pack for at least 10 consecutive years.

ROCKFORD (17 years, 1906-07 through 1922-23)

If consensus counts, Rockford was the best prep team in America in both 1907 and 1908. The northern team ran off a state-record 27 straight wins, including a 155-2 shellacking of the Army's Third Regiment team.

After turning down an invitation to the state's first playoff in 1908, Rockford dominated the early years of the tournament, making eight trips to state, collecting five trophies (1911-19-21-22-23), and winning a pair of convincing championships (1911 and 1919). Five times Rockford was the consensus pick as the state's top team. Three times the school was the prohibitive favorite to win the tournament.

In 1911, Rockford fashioned a nearly unbeatable team, humiliating an overmatched Mt. Carroll squad 60-15 in the championship game. That 45-point margin is still the largest in final game history. Then, in 1919, Rockford slapped Springfield 39-20 to complete a 23-1 season.

Marion shocked Rockford 24-23 in the 1921 finale, outscoring the heavily favored team 9-1 in the fourth quarter. Two years later, Villa Grove's 32-29 championship win stunned Rockford and the state in the first title game upset of truly epic proportions.

STATE CHAMPIONS 1928 ★ 2ND PL. NATIONALS

"Opie" ESHELMAN — al PSCHIRRER — Harry MAXWELL — Claude McMULLIN — Vernon PHILLIPS — Joe MOORE — Ray SMITH — Morrow SCHNELL

Chester EDDY — Fred SCHNELL — Edgar BRONS — Russell CARDOSI — Frank MACE — Charles COLEMAN — Junior CARMACK — COACH Mark PETERMAN

★ CANTON ★

CANTON (15 years, 1917-18 through 1931-32)

Canton's third-place finish in the 1918 state tournament, under Coach C. B. Smith, launched perhaps the most dominant run in boys' state basketball history. From 1918 to 1932, the Ploughboys made eight trips to state, winning a trophy each time — a feat never again duplicated.

R. A. Deffenbaugh was the coach in 1920 when Canton completed a 23-4 season with an 18-14 title game loss to Mt. Vernon. Deffenbaugh handed the reigns to Mark Peterman and the Canton program soared to new heights.

Peterman crafted a 13-7 season in 1921, a rebuilding year, then had a 23-game winner the following campaign. Beginning in 1923, the

Paris fans engulf the victorious 1943 team on the floor of Huff Gymnasium.

Dow Morris gets a boost from a pair of schoolmates after Paris beat Champaign for the 1947 state championship.

coach led four straight teams to the semifinals, five in the next six years, with an annual average of 27 wins. Canton finished third three times (1923-24-25) and second once (1926), losing to the eventual state champion each time.

In 1928, Canton doubled the score on West Aurora in the championship game, claiming an 18-9 triumph. Four years later, Archie Chadd coached Canton to yet another trophy, losing the finale to Morton of Cicero.

PARIS (12 years, 1935-36 through 1946-47)

Ernie Eveland won 779 high school basketball games, nearly half of them in a 12-year stretch (1936-47) at Paris.

After a quarterfinal appearance in 1936, Paris strung together six straight seasons of at least 31 wins (1938-43), finishing third once (1938), second twice (1939-42), and first once (1943). Eveland's Tigers were 39-0 in 1942 and considered the finest team in the tournament's 35-year history, but dropped a stunning 35-33 title-game decision to Centralia, when Dike Eddleman led the Orphans to what many consider the greatest comeback in state championship annals.

Five years later, Eveland was back with a 40-game winner and this time there was no final-game upset. Behind a title-game record tying 22 points from 6-2 senior Robert Owens, the Tigers trounced defending champion Champaign 58-37.

As part of the Eveland mystique, Paris traveled to the state tournament seven straight seasons from 1938 to 1944. Only two other teams, Champaign and Rockford Boylan, and only one other coach, Boylan's Steve Goers, have turned the trick. The Tigers' average record through the seven-year stretch was 33-4.

CHAMPAIGN (12 years, 1937-38 through 1948-49)

Champaign made 10 tournament visits in 12 years from 1938 to 1949, including the last seven in succession. Seven of those trips came during the nine-year tenure of Coach Harry Combes.

Combes and Champaign came tantalizingly close to matching Elgin's record of back-to-back state championships, yet only won a single title.

In 1944, the Maroons met Dolph Stanley's Taylorville Tornadoes for the fourth time on the year. Taylorville, the odds on favorite, was 43-0 heading into its semifinal showdown. The Maroons missed by a whisker, falling 40-36. The Tornadoes went on to rout Elgin 56-33 for the title.

continued on next page

Champaign's Rod Fletcher battles Kenneth McBride of Centralia for a rebound in the 1946 championship game.

IHSA executive secretary Al Willis presents the 1946 first-place trophy to Champaign captain Jim Cottrell and coach Harry Combes.

Champaign returned in 1945 as the state's top ranked team, but lost the championship game to second-ranked Decatur 62-54. One year later, the Maroons won it all, clipping Centralia 54-48 in Coach Arthur Trout's fourth and final title game appearance. In 1947, Champaign lost the finale to Paris. From 1943 to 1947, statewide polls ranked the Maroons fifth or better.

Harold Jester replaced Combes to start the 1947-48 season and promptly took two more teams to state.

COLLINSVILLE (11 years, 1956-57 through 1966-67)

The Collinsville Kahoks' average record from 1957 to 1967 was 26-3. Coach Vergil Fletcher guided six of his record 14 teams to state during that time, including a trio of teams with unblemished records.

The 1957 Kahoks were 34-0 before getting derailed by Herrin 45-42 in the championship game. Four years later, Collinsville roared through a 32-0 campaign, establishing itself as one of the greatest teams in Illinois roundball history. Fletcher's 1964 edition was 28-0 and ranked number one before being ambushed by second-ranked Centralia 55-50 in the Salem Super-Sectional.

The Kahoks reached the title game three times in 11 years, winning two championships (1961 and 1965). Only once in that span were the Kahoks unranked in season-ending polls. Five times they finished ranked first or second.

Collinsville won 80 percent of its state finals games in Champaign, and when the Kahoks did lose, it was not by much. Their average margin of defeat at Champaign was 4.5 points. Fletcher won 12 of his record 21 tournament games during the Kahoks' 11-year run.

PINCKNEYVILLE (10 years, 1946-47 through 1955-56)

Merrill "Duster" Thomas coached at Pinckneyville for 19 years (1939-47). During the first eight seasons, his teams compiled average records of 20-9 while capturing three regional titles. But over his last 11 years, Pinckneyville won nine regional tournaments, eight sectionals, five state trophies, and turned in an average record of 27-5.

The Panthers were third-place finishers in 1947 and, one year later, reigned as state champions, razing East Rockford 65-39 in the finale.

Thomas missed state each of the next two seasons, but when his Panthers returned in 1951, it was the first of six straight visits. Three of those teams finished third in successive seasons (1953-54-55), losing to the eventual state champion each time, and ended the tournament with identical 33-3 marks.

In all, five of Thomas' Pinckneyville teams won at least 31 games and five others won at least 26.

The tournament streak ended in Thomas' final season at the helm when his Panthers, ranked fourth, fell to third-ranked Herrin in the sectional tournament championship. Herrin went on to win the state title.

The Best of the Best

Looking at the entire 64-year history of single class basketball in Illinois, the schools that dominated tournament play will probably surprise those who have only known two-class basketball.

An analysis of tournament appearances, state-finals winning percentage, and final-four finishes yields the following top-10 list:

1. Decatur
2. Champaign (Central)
3. Springfield
4. Galesburg
5. Centralia
6. Canton
7. Mt. Vernon
8. Rockford
9. Freeport
10. Paris

Particularly striking about the list is that four of the schools — Champaign Central, Canton, Paris and Rockford — have never been to state in the two-class system. Paris last appeared in 1971, Champaign Central in 1969, Canton in 1953 and Rockford in 1939, 68 years ago, a year before closing its doors for good. Only two of the schools, Galesburg, second in 1998AA and Centralia, third in 2002AA, have won trophies in the past 38 years (through 2006).

However, the schools represented on the list were so dominant from 1908 to 1971 that they must be considered dynasties in a larger sense. Seven of those schools remain in the top 20 all-time after 99 years of state tournament action. Programs still in the top 20 are Decatur (No. 5), Galesburg (6), Centralia (7), Champaign Central (9), Springfield (11), Mt. Vernon (14) and Canton (17).

If nothing else, the figures reveal how dominant and unforgettable the early, single-class dynasties of the state tournament really were.

ABOVE: Collinsville's Bogie Redmon returns to Earth in the Kahoks' 1961 quarterfinal win over East Rockford.

RIGHT: 1965 Kahok players cheer after capturing the sectional championship.

HARVEY (THORNTON)
State Champions of 1966

FRONT ROW (left to right): Estes Ross, Rich Rateree, Garland Mays, Leonard Solomon.
SECOND ROW: Asst. Coach Tom Hanrahan, LaMarr Thomas, Bob Landowski, Hershel Lewis, Paul Gilliam, Jim Ard, Larry Tanter, Garry Carter, Kevin Roberson, Coach Bob Anderson.

I f the 1966 tournament had unfolded as promised, unbeaten Benton would have met Harvey Thornton in a rematch of powerhouses. The squads had met in the championship game of the Centralia Holiday Tournament in December of 1965 with Benton walking away a 70-63 winner.

Led by the all-state duo of Jim Adkins and Rich Yunkus, Benton's Rangers were 30-0. Thornton was 26-2 with a tough-as-nails all-state combo in 6-foot-7 Jim Ard and 6-1 LaMarr Thomas.

Fourth-ranked Belleville, sparked by scoring sensation Joe Wiley, a 6-3 all-state center, and No. 6 Galesburg, powered by all-state guard Dale Kelley, provided stiff challenges for the top teams.

But the impressive roll call did not stop there. Nine former state champions and eight ranked teams reached the super-sectional round, with a combined history of 53 tournament trophies, 32 title game appearances, and 18 championships.

No favorites stumbled in first round play, but Belleville came close, slipping by Lawrenceville 92-88 in double overtime.

Friday's quarterfinals opened with back-to-back bangs.

Belleville defeated Joliet Central 74-72 as Wiley scored 27, and Galesburg tripped Benton 73-71 behind Kelley's 37 points, his final two coming on a last-sec-

ond 30-footer. Also winning were Thornton, 59-44 over New Trier, and Decatur, 57-44 over West Rockford.

Saturday brought another cardiac special when Belleville met Galesburg. Wiley scored 32, but it was not enough. Kelley's 37 iced the Streaks' 65-64 win. That set up a dual run at the four-game individual scoring record of 121 points held by LaGrange's Ted Caiazza. After three games, Kelley had 105 points, Wiley 97.

With Ard ringing up 25 points and three other Wildcats reaching double digits, Thornton blasted Decatur 67-45 in the second game, cruising to the school's fifth title game, the second in five years.

Wiley eclipsed Caiazza's mark late in the third-place game, scoring 31 points, 128 for the tournament.

Kelley needed only 23 points to equal the new total, but it was not to be. Thornton exploded out of the gate, thundering to an insurmountable 47-25 halftime lead. The Wildcats' vigorous defense stifled Kelley, who managed only a dozen points, hitting just three shots in 13 attempts from the field. Still, the 5-11 guard finished with 117 points, the most ever by a player who did not lead the field in scoring.

Rich Rateree scored 24 for the winners, while Thomas, Ard and Paul Gilliam combined for 40 more as Thornton slammed the Streaks 74-60 — win number 30 in 32 tries.

Galesburg's Dale Kelley is surrounded by Thornton's LaMarr Thomas (31) and Jim Ard (35) in the 1966 title game.

State Final Tournament Scores

Super-Sectionals

At East St. Louis—Belleville (Twp.) 92, Lawrenceville 88 (2 OT)
At Peoria [Bradley]—Joliet (Central) 63, Pekin 50
At Macomb [WIU]—Galesburg 69, Springfield 65
At Carbondale [SIU]—Benton 46, Centralia 43
At Hinsdale (Twp.)—Harvey (Thornton) 61, Wheaton (Central) 57
At Evanston [NU]—Winnetka (New Trier) 78, Chicago (Marshall) 60
At Rock Island—Rockford (West) 54, Rock Island 51
At Normal [ISU]—Decatur (Stephen Decatur) 68, Urbana 56

Quarterfinals

Belleville (Twp.) 74, Joliet (Central) 72
Galesburg 73, Benton 71
Harvey (Thornton) 59, Winnetka (New Trier) 44
Decatur (Stephen Decatur) 57, Rockford (West) 44

Semifinals

Galesburg 65, Belleville (Twp.) 64
Harvey (Thornton) 67, Decatur (Stephen Decatur) 45

Finals

Belleville (Twp.) 84, Decatur (Stephen Decatur) 57 (third place)
Harvey (Thornton) 74, Galesburg 60 (title)

Scoring Leaders

Player, School	G	FG	FT	Pts
Joe Wiley, Belleville (Twp.)	4	45	38	128
Dale Kelley, Galesburg	4	36	45	117
Jim Ard, Harvey (Thornton)	4	27	13	67
Rich Rateree, Harvey (Thornton)	4	25	10	60
Bill Snellings, Belleville (Twp.)	4	23	13	59

All-Tournament First Team

Player, School	Ht.	Yr.
Jim Ard, Harvey (Thornton)	6-7	Sr.
Albert Crusoe, Joliet (Central)	5-9	Sr.
Dale Kelley, Galesburg	5-11	Sr.
Lamarr Thomas, Harvey (Thornton)	6-1	Sr.
Joe Wiley, Belleville (Twp.)	6-3	Sr.

Championship Game Box Score

Assembly Hall, Champaign, March 19, 1966

HARVEY (THORNTON) (74)
Coach Bob Anderson

Player	FG-A	FT-A	Pts	PF	Rb	As	St	Bl
Jim Ard	6-7	1-2	13	5	10			
Paul Gilliam	4-13	3-6	11	1	6			
Bob Landowski	1-5	4-5	6	5	9			
Hershel Lewis	0-0	0-0	0	0	0			
Garland Mays	1-3	1-2	3	0	1			
Rich Rateree	10-15	4-5	24	3	2			
Estes Ross	0-2	1-2	1	1	1			
Leonard Solomon	0-0	0-0	0	0	0			
Larry Tanter	0-0	0-0	0	0	0			
Lamarr Thomas	6-14	4-5	16	4	4			
TOTAL	28-59	18-27	74	19	33			

GALESBURG (60)
Coach John Thiel

Player	FG-A	FT-A	Pts	PF	Rb	As	St	Bl
Terry Childers	1-2	0-0	2	0	2			
Mike Drasites	2-2	3-5	7	4	10			
Lugene Finley	0-0	0-0	0	0	0			
Bob Jasperson	2-7	1-2	5	5	3			
Dale Kelley	3-13	6-8	12	1	7			
Bruce LaViolette	4-7	3-3	11	4	3			
Leon Luckett	0-0	0-0	0	0	0			
Steve Marshall	0-1	0-0	0	0	0			
Roland McDougald	3-9	4-4	10	1	1			
Barry Swanson	5-6	3-5	13	3	5			
TOTAL	20-47	20-27	60	18	31			

Harvey (Thornton)	20	27	13	14	—	74
Galesburg	12	13	18	17	—	60

Officials: Tom Alexander, Jean DesMarteau.

Carbondale's Early Lester and
Terry Wallace celebrate an overtime win over West Rockford in
the 1967 semfinals.

State Final Tournament Scores

Super-Sectionals
At Peoria [Bradley]—Pekin 77, Toluca 64
At Aurora (East)—Elmhurst (York) 72, Chicago (Harlan) 70
At Macomb [WIU]—Springfield 70, Quincy 68 (2 OT)
At Normal [ISU]—Champaign (Central) 36, Decatur (Stephen Decatur) 35
At Evanston [NU]—Flossmoor (Homewood-F.) 69, North Chicago 65 (OT)
At Moline—Rockford (West) 62, Moline 61
At Carbondale [SIU]—Carbondale 59, Benton 53
At Charleston [EIU]—Collinsville 59, Effingham 48

Quarterfinals
Pekin 94, Elmhurst (York) 70
Springfield 64, Champaign (Central) 61
Rockford (West) 79, Flossmoor (Homewood-F.) 60
Carbondale 53, Collinsville 47

Semifinals
Pekin 77, Springfield 61
Carbondale 67, Rockford (West) 66 (OT)

Finals
Springfield 81, Rockford (West) 65 (third place)
Pekin 75, Carbondale 59 (title)

Scoring Leaders

Player, School	G	FG	FT	Pts
Dave Robisch, Springfield	4	57	38	152
Fred Miller, Pekin	4	44	15	103
Cal Glover, Rockford (West)	4	34	4	72
Barry Moran, Pekin	4	26	16	68
James Sallis, Rockford (West)	4	23	18	64

All-Tournament First Team

Player, School	Ht.	Yr.
L.C. Brasfield, Carbondale	6-3	Sr.
Cal Glover, Rockford (West)	6-2	Sr.
Fred Miller, Pekin	6-4	Sr.
Barry Moran, Pekin	6-5	Jr.
Tom Parker, Collinsville	6-5	Jr.
Dave Robisch, Springfield	6-9	Sr.

Championship Game Box Score
Assembly Hall, Champaign, March 18, 1967

PEKIN (75)
Coach Dawson "Dawdy" Hawkins

Player	FG-A	FT-A	Pts	PF	Rb	As	St	Bl
Mark Freidinger	6-12	1-2	13	1	2			
Rich Hawkins	0-0	0-0	0	1	0			
Doug Jones	3-9	0-2	6	1	2			
Steve Kingdon	0-0	0-0	0	1	0			
Scott Lange	1-4	0-0	2	1	2			
Dave Martin	0-5	0-0	0	1	4			
Fred Miller	16-20	4-7	36	2	7			
Barry Moran	4-9	3-4	11	3	9			
John Venturi	0-0	0-0	0	0	0			
Tom Vucich	2-3	3-4	7	0	1			
TOTAL	32-62	11-19	75	11	27			

CARBONDALE (59)
Coach John Cherry

Player	FG-A	FT-A	Pts	PF	Rb	As	St	Bl
L.C. Brasfield	8-12	3-3	19	2	7			
Bob Crane	0-0	0-0	0	0	0			
Phil Gilbert	3-8	0-0	6	3	1			
Billy "Early" Laster	5-6	0-3	10	5	2			
Ken Lewis	3-4	1-1	7	0	0			
Geoff Partlow	0-0	0-0	0	0	0			
Billy Perkins	7-10	0-1	14	4	11			
Chuck Taylor	1-1	1-3	3	0	1			
Terry Wallace	0-3	0-0	0	2	1			
Dave Walls	0-0	0-0	0	0	1			
TOTAL	27-44	5-11	59	16	24			

Pekin	16	18	21	20	—	75
Carbondale	17	6	17	19	—	59

Officials: Tom Alexander, Paul Blakeman.

Pekin had 6-4 all-state center Fred Miller manning the paint, 6-5 Barry Moran providing the muscle, and playmaker Mark Freidinger running the floor. Springfield had Robisch, who worked his way to 41 points and 18 boards, but Pekin shut down the remaining Springfield starters and won handily, 77-61.

It took an extra stanza to settle the next game, won by Carbondale 67-66 over West Rockford, as all five Terrier starters scored in double figures. West had the lead in the fourth quarter but was thwarted by the defensive muscle of Carbondale, which finally caught the Warriors at 59-59 to force overtime.

That night, Robisch powered in 39 points, setting a four-game scoring record of 152, an average of 38 per game. He also finished with 77 rebounds, still the four-game standard.

In the finale, Pekin's Fred Miller was unstoppable, matching a championship-game record with 36 points on 16 field goals, shooting 80 percent from the field. Dawdy Hawkins' boys claimed the title, 75-59.

PEKIN
State Champions of 1967

FRONT ROW (left to right): Trainer Jimmie "Doc" Lee, Jerry Norman, Tom Vucich, Mark Freidinger, Dick Marshall, John Venturi, Rich Hawkins.
SECOND ROW: Coach Dawson "Dawdy" Hawkins, Mgr. Clark Joesting, Dave Martin, Doug Jones, Ken Higham, Kim Seeber, Mgr. Randy Brienan.
THIRD ROW: Asst. Coach Bob Ortegal, Asst. Coach Joe Venturi, Fred Miller, Steve Kingdon, Scott Lange, Barry Moran, Mgr. Barry Soffietti.

The state's top four ranked teams, and five of the top seven, finished the 1966-67 regular season without a loss. But the regional and sectional rounds were not kind to Waukegan, Lawrenceville, and Danville Schlarman. All were upset, leaving only two unbeaten squads still standing when the super-sectional round commenced.

Rich Herrin's unbeaten Benton Rangers were once again the top team in statewide polls. All-American center Rich Yunkus, 6-foot-7, teamed with 6-8 post partner Greg Fustin, Bill Lowery, Danny Johnson, and Jerry Hoover to fuel Benton, 30-0 heading into the super-sectional.

West Rockford was also undefeated. The third-ranked, 26-0 Warriors, coached by Alex Saudargas, were two-time state champs (1955-56), led this time around by all-state selection Jim Sallis and 6-2 Cal Glover.

The media tabbed southern powers Carbondale (26-2) and Collinsville (27-2) as viable title contenders, while labeling mid-state entries Springfield (27-2) and Pekin (27-2) as dark horses.

South Seven foes Benton and Carbondale met for the third time in the SIU Super-Sectional. The Rangers had easily won the first two; this time Carbondale prevailed. L. C. Brasfield's 17 points all but canceled Yunkus's 18 and the Terriers rallied late for a 59-53 upset victory.

At Macomb, Springfield used every bit of what it had, including 47 points and 20 rebounds from 6-9 all-American pivot man Dave Robisch, to turn back Quincy 70-68 in double overtime. Robisch's 19 field goals established a new tournament record. Rockford and Champaign both claimed one-point wins, while Homewood-Flossmoor nipped North Chicago in overtime.

All of the favored teams won quarterfinal games — though Springfield and Carbondale did so narrowly — setting the table for a memorable final day.

1968

EVANSTON (TWP.)
State Champions of 1968

FRONT ROW (left to right):
Alvin Keith, Mike Hart,
Odell Johnson, Orestes Arrieta,
Alton Hill, Bill Battinus.
SECOND ROW:
Asst. Coach Steve Power,
Ron Cooper, Farrell Jones,
Bob Lackey, Walt Perrin,
Coach Jack Burmaster.

Evanston coach Jack Burmaster had already crossed paths with Rockford Auburn coach Dolph Stanley. The two first met in the state championship game of 1944 when Burmaster played for Elgin and Stanley coached Taylorville. Burmaster tallied three points in that game, but Stanley and Taylorville won the title 56-33 to complete an unparalleled 45-0 season. If Evanston and Auburn could sweep through their respective brackets, the two men would meet for the title once more, this time with both as coaches.

Burmaster brought his third Evanston team to state, but had never advanced beyond the quarterfinal round. Stanley, by contrast, had coached a record three different schools to the trophy round. Auburn was the fourth school Stanley had brought to state — also a record — but the Knights had yet to play on the tournament's final day.

Coach Walter Moore of Carbondale also had state championship experience as a player, teaming with Max Hooper to lead Mt. Vernon to consecutive titles in 1949 and 1950. Moore replaced John Cherry, who had guided the Terriers to a runner-up finish in 1967. In so doing, Moore became the first African-American coach at an integrated high school in southern Illinois.

Two teams had perfect records heading into the Sweet Sixteen. Danville Schlarman was unbeaten for the second straight year, 30-0 and ranked eighth, but fell to 14th-ranked LaSalle-Peru 77-68 at Normal. Effingham's Hearts were also 30-0 and ranked No. 1 in the state, but could not handle fifth-ranked Galesburg

as the Streaks won in overwhelming fashion, 85-52, in the quarterfinal finale.

From the opening tip, though, Evanston looked every bit the state champion. The Wildkits upended second-ranked Lockport Central 70-58 behind 40 combined points by 6-foot-6 Farrell Jones and 6-4 Bob Lackey. Peoria Central fell next 70-48, and Chicago Public League champion Crane came up short 70-54 in the semifinals.

After swamping Effingham, Galesburg's Silver Streaks fought for their lives on Saturday afternoon to hold off

determined DeKalb 63-60. The win gave Coach John Thiel's team a 27-2 record and a title game date with 29-1 Evanston.

It was déjà vu all over again in the finale. Eerily reminiscent of 1966, Galesburg fell behind early and big. It was 42-25 by halftime and Evanston won going away 70-51. Red-hot Ron Cooper broke loose for an uncharacteristic 21 points and eight rebounds in the blowout.

In a numerical oddity, the Wildkits scored exactly 70 points in each of the four tournament games.

State Final Tournament Scores
Super-Sectionals
At Carbondale [SIU]—Carbondale 68, Mt. Vernon 66
At Hinsdale (Central)—Chicago (Crane) 73, LaGrange (Lyons) 61
At Evanston [NU]—Evanston (Twp.) 70, Lockport (Central) 58
At Peoria [Bradley]—Peoria 83, Springfield (Lanphier) 72
At Normal [ISU]—LaSalle (L.-Peru) 77, Danville (Schlarman) 68
At DeKalb [NIU]—DeKalb 73, Rockford (Auburn) 53
At Macomb [WIU]—Galesburg 61, Quincy 60 (OT)
At Charleston [EIU]—Effingham 54, Belleville (West) 49 (OT)

Quarterfinals
Chicago (Crane) 64, Carbondale 63 (OT)
Evanston (Twp.) 70, Peoria 48
DeKalb 82, LaSalle (L.-Peru) 77
Galesburg 85, Effingham 52

Semifinals
Evanston (Twp.) 70, Chicago (Crane) 54
Galesburg 63, DeKalb 60

Finals
Chicago (Crane) 82, DeKalb 62 (third place)
Evanston (Twp.) 70, Galesburg 51 (title)

Scoring Leaders

Player, School	G	FG	FT	Pts
Jerome Freeman, Chicago (Crane)	4	37	13	87
Bob Lackey, Evanston (Twp.)	4	31	18	80
Ruben Triplett, Galesburg	4	31	10	72
Mark Voreis, DeKalb	4	26	15	67
Ron Shoger, DeKalb	4	25	9	59

All-Tournament First Team

Player, School	Ht.	Yr.
Jerome Freeman, Chicago (Crane)	5-10	Sr.
Farrel Jones, Evanston (Twp.)	6-6	Sr.
Bob Lackey, Evanston (Twp.)	6-4	Sr.
Les Taylor, Carbondale	6-4	Jr.
Ruben Triplett, Galesburg	6-6	Jr.

Championship Game Box Score
Assembly Hall, Champaign, March 23, 1968

EVANSTON (TWP.) (70)
Coach Jack Burmaster

Player	FG-A	FT-A	Pts	PF	Rb	As	St	Bl
Orestes Arrieta	1-1	0-0	2	0	1			
Bill Battinus	5-12	1-2	11	2	6			
Ron Cooper	5-8	11-14	21	1	8			
Mike Hart	0-0	0-1	0	0	1			
Alton Hill	0-1	0-0	0	0	1			
Odell Johnson	0-0	0-0	0	0	0			
Farrel Jones	5-13	0-0	10	1	7			
Alvin Keith	0-1	1-2	1	1	1			
Bob Lackey	6-13	3-4	15	5	8			
Walt Perrin	4-13	2-6	10	3	3			
TOTAL	26-62	18-29	70	13	36			

GALESBURG (51)
Coach John Thiel

Player	FG-A	FT-A	Pts	PF	Rb	As	St	Bl
Mike Doyle	0-1	0-0	0	0	0			
Lugene Finley	0-3	0-0	0	0	4			
Leon Luckett	4-9	0-0	8	1	5			
Roland McDougald	0-1	0-1	0	2	1			
Fred Mims	6-10	1-3	13	1	6			
Steve Olson	2-7	2-4	6	1	3			
Jim Reinebach	3-5	1-2	7	4	2			
Zack Thiel	1-1	0-0	2	1	0			
Ruben Triplett	3-11	4-4	10	5	9			
Dave Wood	2-6	1-2	5	2	2			
TOTAL	21-54	9-16	51	17	32			

Evanston (Twp.)	18	24	15	13	— 70
Galesburg	16	9	14	12	— 51

Officials: Ernest Reynolds, Fred Gibson.

State Final Tournament Scores

Super-Sectionals

At Carbondale [SIU]—Mt. Vernon 71, Carbondale 63
At DeKalb [NIU]—Aurora (East) 67, Dixon 50
At Peoria [Bradley]—Peoria (Spalding) 47, Lincoln 41
At Charleston [EIU]—Belleville (East) 47, Mattoon 45
At Macomb [WIU]—Galesburg 77, Quincy 64
At Normal [ISU]—Champaign (Central) 55, Normal (Community) 53 (3 OT)
At Evanston [NU]—Waukegan 63, Harvey (Thornton) 61
At Hinsdale (Central)—Maywood (Proviso East) 47, Chicago (Hirsch) 46

Quarterfinals

Aurora (East) 52, Mt. Vernon 46
Peoria (Spalding) 80, Belleville (East) 61
Champaign (Central) 62, Galesburg 57
Maywood (Proviso East) 52, Waukegan 44

Semifinals

Peoria (Spalding) 66, Aurora (East) 53
Maywood (Proviso East) 37, Champaign (Central) 36

Finals

Champaign (Central) 56, Aurora (East) 49 (third place)
Maywood (Proviso East) 58, Peoria (Spalding) 51 (title)

Scoring Leaders

Player, School	G	FG	FT	Pts
Clyde Turner, Champaign (Central)	4	38	15	91
Alvin O'Neal, Peoria (Spalding)	4	33	20	86
Tom Kivisto, Aurora (East)	4	29	18	76
Algie Neal, Aurora (East)	4	32	5	69
Jim Brewer, Maywood (Proviso East)	4	18	20	56

All-Tournament First Team

Player, School	Ht.	Yr.
Jim Brewer, Maywood (Proviso East)	6-6	Sr.
Tom Kivisto, Aurora (East)	6-3	Jr.
Algie Neal, Aurora (East)	6-1	Sr.
Alvin O'Neal, Peoria (Spalding)	6-5	Sr.
Ruben Triplett, Galesburg	6-6	Sr.
Clyde Turner, Champaign (Central)	6-6	Sr.

Championship Game Box Score

Assembly Hall, Champaign, March 22, 1969

MAYWOOD (PROVISO EAST) (58)
Coach Tom Millikin

Player	FG-A	FT-A	Pts	PF	Rb	As	St	Bl
William Allen	3-9	10-12	16	3	4			
Pete Bouzeos	3-5	0-0	6	3	7			
Jim Brewer	5-9	7-10	17	3	9			
Ira Carswell	1-3	0-2	2	1	3			
John Munchoff	0-1	0-0	0	0	0			
Keith Rash	0-0	0-0	0	0	0			
Harv Roberts	2-7	1-2	5	2	8			
Ralph Sykes	0-1	0-0	0	0	1			
Walt Williams	5-10	2-4	12	3	7			
TOTAL	19-45	20-30	58	15	39			

PEORIA (SPALDING) (51)
Coach Ron Patterson

Player	FG-A	FT-A	Pts	PF	Rb	As	St	Bl
Lamonia Barksdale	4-15	3-4	11	0	11			
Art Jenkins	0-6	0-0	0	3	0			
Rich Lavin	1-1	0-0	2	0	0			
Marty McGann	1-2	0-0	2	1	2			
Jim Moore	2-3	0-2	4	4	1			
Alvin O'Neal	4-13	3-3	11	2	9			
Rick Schaidle	0-0	0-0	0	4	0			
Steve Schrader	2-3	0-1	4	0	1			
Charles Thorell	3-7	7-8	13	4	2			
Ken Wolbeck	2-6	0-0	4	3	9			
TOTAL	19-56	13-18	51	21	35			

Maywood (Proviso East)	9	19	12	18	— 58
Peoria (Spalding)	4	11	14	22	— 51

Officials: Jean DesMarteau, Glen Van Proyen.

MAYWOOD (PROVISO EAST)
State Champions of 1969

FRONT ROW (left to right): Walt Williams, Harvey Roberts, Jim Brewer, Pete Bouzeos, Bill Allen. SECOND ROW: Howard Godfrey, John Munchoff, Ralph Sykes, Ira Carswell, Keith Rash. THIRD ROW: Asst. Coach William Ebenezer, Steve Glos, Ted Pelikan, Ernest Lewis, Kirk Shearburn, Coach Tom Millikin.

Eight years after a top-ranked team last won a state championship, the Pirates of Proviso East hoped to put an end to the drought. The task would not be easy. Eight other ranked teams made it to the super-sectional round, including No. 2 Galesburg, which had put the only blemish on the Pirates' slate.

If Proviso East could win it all, Coach Tom Millikin would join Freeport's Glenn "Pat" Holmes as the only men to play on and later coach state championship teams. Holmes did both at Freeport. Millikin was a member of "Duster" Thomas's 1948 title team at Pinckneyville.

Millikin had a premier post player in 6-foot-6 all-American selection Jim Brewer and an exceptional supporting cast. Top to bottom, they were the best team in the state. As it turned out, they were also lucky, as state champions must be.

In the super-sectional the Pirates escaped Chicago Hirsch 47-46, fighting back from a double-digit deficit in the fourth quarter. Three nights later, at Assembly Hall, Waukegan fell 52-44, but Brewer suffered a severely sprained ankle. With the ankle treated and taped, Brewer played hurt in the semifinals.

Galesburg's anticipated rematch with Proviso East never materialized. All-state center Clyde Turner scored 27 points as Champaign Central edged Galesburg 62-57, gaining its own shot at the favorites.

It was a shot the Maroons nearly missed. Fourteenth-ranked Normal Community took No. 9 Champaign to the wire at the Normal Super-Sectional, but the Maroons came from behind in the fourth quarter and eventually won 55-53 in triple overtime.

The semifinal showdown between Champaign and Proviso East was one of the most memorable games in years.

The Pirates took a 19-16 halftime lead, holding the Maroons without a field goal for nearly 12 minutes, including the entire second quarter. Champaign fought back to a 30-29 third-quarter edge. That set up an intense finish.

Down 36-35, Proviso East stalled away the game's final seconds, spreading its offense for Brewer to go one-on-one against Turner. Making his move, Brewer popped a 17-foot jumper. Fouled on the attempt, his two free throws, only six seconds from the end, won it 37-36.

The head-to-head battle between Brewer and Turner was as exciting as the game itself. Brewer, who averaged 16.3 points in his three other tourney games, scored only seven points. Turner, who boasted a 27.3 average, finished with nine.

After that, The title game was almost anti-climactic.

Proviso East took command early, sweeping to a 28-15 lead at the break, and coasted to a 58-51 victory over Peoria Spalding, the first private school to reach the championship game.

1970

East Moline's Tommy Haliburton squeezes through Dave Wehrmeister and Owen Brown of Lyons Township, while teammate Bob Hunter stands by.

State Final Tournament Scores

Super-Sectionals

At Charleston [EIU]—Effingham (St. Anthony) 85, Collinsville 79 (2 OT)
At DeKalb [NIU]—LaGrange (Lyons) 60, Sterling 42
At Carbondale [SIU]—Okawville 66, Mt. Vernon 64
At Evanston [NU]—Joliet (Central) 71, Park Ridge (Maine South) 68
At Aurora (East)—Aurora (East) 68, Chicago (Harlan) 61
At Peoria [Bradley]—Peoria (Spalding) 41, Lincoln 37
At Normal [ISU]—LaSalle (L.-Peru) 81, Danville 63
At Macomb [WIU]—East Moline (United) 75, Pittsfield 54

Quarterfinals

LaGrange (Lyons) 89, Effingham (St. Anthony) 88
Joliet (Central) 56, Okawville 43
Peoria (Spalding) 73, Aurora (East) 56
East Moline (United) 68, LaSalle (L.-Peru) 66

Semifinals

LaGrange (Lyons) 63, Joliet (Central) 52
East Moline (United) 77, Peoria (Spalding) 59

Finals

Joliet (Central) 82, Peoria (Spalding) 75 (third place)
LaGrange (Lyons) 71, East Moline (United) 52 (title)

Scoring Leaders

Player, School	G	FG	FT	Pts
Roger Powell, Joliet (Central)	4	34	22	90
Marcus Washington, LaGrange (Lyons)	4	25	24	74
Owen Brown, LaGrange (Lyons)	4	34	5	73
Bob Hunter, East Moline (United)	4	27	13	67
Ken Wolbeck, Peoria (Spalding)	4	21	23	65

All-Tournament First Team

Player, School	Ht.	Yr.
Owen Brown, LaGrange (Lyons)	6-8	Jr.
Tommy Haliburton, East Moline (United)	6-4	Sr.
Gary Novak, LaSalle (L.-Peru)	6-7	Sr.
Roger Powell, Joliet (Central)	6-3	So.
Mel Samuels, East Moline (United)	5-10	Sr.
Marcus Washington, LaGrange (Lyons)	6-1	Sr.
Ken Wolbeck, Peoria (Spalding)	6-7	Sr.

Championship Game Box Score

Assembly Hall, Champaign, March 21, 1970

LAGRANGE (LYONS) (71)
Coach Ron Nikcevich

Player	FG-A	FT-A	Pts	PF	Rb	As	St	Bl
Owen Brown	11-24	2-5	24	3	24			
Alex Crist	1-1	0-0	2	0	0			
John Dethmer	1-1	0-0	2	0	0			
Steve Heinzelman	0-5	1-2	1	1	10			
Larry Lindberg	0-0	0-0	0	0	0			
Paul Makris	0-0	0-0	0	1	0			
Scott Shaw	6-10	2-2	14	1	5			
Dave Van Skike	8-14	2-2	18	2	4			
Marcus Washington	3-10	4-5	10	2	4			
Dave Wehrmeister	0-1	0-1	0	1	0			
TOTAL	30-66	11-17	71	11	47			

EAST MOLINE (UNITED) (52)
Coach Cliff Talley

Player	FG-A	FT-A	Pts	PF	Rb	As	St	Bl
Craig Davis	8-18	0-0	16	2	10			
Willie Dyer	0-2	0-0	0	0	0			
Bob Gardner	0-1	0-0	0	1	1			
Daryl Griffin	1-7	2-3	4	2	1			
Tommy Haliburton	2-10	2-3	6	4	3			
Bob Hunter	6-12	2-2	14	2	5			
Bob Officer	0-7	6-7	6	1	2			
Mel Samuels	3-6	0-1	6	1	2			
TOTAL	20-63	12-16	52	13	24			

LaGrange (Lyons)	16	14	17	24	— 71
East Moline (United)	16	12	14	10	— 52

Officials: Ted Search Jr., Richard Henley.

With Ron Nikcevich at the helm, LaGrange Lyons hoped to become the first undefeated state champion since Collinsville in 1961. Led by all-staters Owen Brown, a 6-foot-8 junior, and 6-1 senior Marcus Washington, the Lions brushed aside all 27 foes to become the pollsters' No. 1 pick.

Finishing on top would not be easy, however. Among the state's top six ranked teams, only Galesburg was missing. The obstacles waiting to trip up the Lions were many.

St. Patrick's Day upsets cleared two obstacles from Lyons' path.

In super-sectional action, Lincoln (30-0, ranked second) lost to unheralded Peoria Spalding 41-37, while unranked Effingham St. Anthony staged a second-half rally to topple fourth-ranked Collinsville 85-78 in double overtime behind Mike Wente's 33 points.

No. 5 LaSalle-Peru was the next ranked team to slip, falling 68-66 to No. 6 East Moline in the quarterfinals.

But the most extraordinary game of that round came when Lyons met St. Anthony.

The favorites seized a 2-0 lead just 20 seconds into the contest and never trailed for the next 30 minutes and 28 seconds.

At the break, Lyons seemed to be in complete control with a 50-35 advantage.

Lyons led by 17 in the third quarter before the St. Anthony found its shooting eye. A late six-point run, climaxed by Dave Brumleve's quarter-closing jumper, trimmed the lead to six, 67-61, with one period to go.

St. Anthony tied the game at 77 with 4:45 to play — the first tie since the 6:04 mark of the first quarter. Lyons regained the lead on a Steve Heinzelman jumper, but it was quickly even again. Finally, with 1:12 remaining, Wente's lay-up gave St. Anthony the lead 85-84.

Following another tie at the 33-second mark, Heinzelman sank a jumper

(0:13), Washington nailed a free throw (0:02), and Lyons led 89-86. Wente's uncontested lay-up at the horn made it 89-88.

La Grange beat Joliet Central and sensational sophomore scorer Roger Powell 63-52 in the semifinals. East Moline upended Peoria Spalding 77-59 to assure a championship game between the last two ranked teams.

Lyons held a slim 30-28 lead at the half, boosted it to 47-42 after three, and used a 24-10 fourth quarter to bury the Panthers 71-52 as Owen Brown turned in a rousing 24-point, 24-rebound performance — the latter still a title game record.

LaGRANGE (LYONS)
State Champions of 1970

FRONT ROW (left to right): Mgr. Rick Skoda, Mark Neer, Larry Lindberg, Bob Whitelaw, Jeff Hill, Scott Shaw, Marcus Washington, Paul Makris, Tom Wickham, Dan Przewoznik, Chuck Pribyl, Mgr. Al Tucek.
SECOND ROW: Mgr. Kevin Dwyer, Mgr. Jim Hilborn, Kevin Cummings, Mike Danner, Dave Wehrmeister, Steve Heinzelman, Owen Brown, Alex Christ, Greg Szatko, Dave Van Skike, Jim Dethmer, Tom Vogele, Craig Meyer, Coach Ron Nikcevich, Delton Stamp.

DOLTON (THORNRIDGE)
State Champions of 1971

FRONT ROW (left to right):
Mgr. Jeff Groger, Greg Rose, Tony Jackson,
Coach Ron Ferguson, Mike Bonczyk,
Jim Loggins, Mgr. Rick Remmert.
SECOND ROW: Gary Ferguson,
Asst. Coach Frank Nardi, Quinn Buckner,
Chuck Hogan, Mark McClain, Boyd Batts,
Al Vest, Mike Henry, Asst. Coach Al Holverson.

Thornridge was the last school to win a one-class championship and the first to win a large-school (Class AA) championship.

State Final Tournament Scores

Super-Sectionals

At Carbondale [SIU]—Benton 60, Nashville 52
At Evanston [NU]—Oak Lawn (Community) 66, Winnetka (New Trier East) 54
At Peoria [Bradley]—Springfield (Lanphier) 81, Peoria (Woodruff) 68
At DeKalb [NIU]—Rockford (Boylan) 64, Elgin (Larkin) 54
At Macomb [WIU]—Kewanee 60, Quincy (Catholic Boys) 59
At Crete (C.-Monee)—Dolton (Thornridge) 73, Chicago (Harlan) 63
At Charleston [EIU]—Paris 77, Granite City 48
At Normal [ISU]—Danville 62, Normal (University) 61

Quarterfinals

Oak Lawn (Community) 71, Benton 58
Springfield (Lanphier) 92, Rockford (Boylan) 78
Dolton (Thornridge) 63, Kewanee 58
Danville 63, Paris 61

Semifinals

Oak Lawn (Community) 69, Springfield (Lanphier) 65
Dolton (Thornridge) 57, Danville 47

Finals

Danville 77, Springfield (Lanphier) 57 (third place)
Dolton (Thornridge) 52, Oak Lawn (Community) 50 (title)

Scoring Leaders

Player, School	G	FG	FT	Pts
Jim Kopatz, Springfield (Lanphier)	4	49	13	111
C.J. Kupec, Oak Lawn (Community)	4	30	27	87
Charles Evans, Danville	4	20	39	79
Quinn Buckner, Dolton (Thornridge)	4	29	13	71
Jim Bocinsky, Oak Lawn (Community)	4	26	18	70

All-Tournament First Team

Player, School	Ht.	Yr.
Quinn Buckner, Dolton (Thornridge)	6-3	Jr.
Charles Evans, Danville	6-4	Sr.
Jim Kopatz, Springfield (Lanphier)	6-1	Jr.
C.J. Kupec, Oak Lawn (Community)	6-7	Sr.
Tommy Smith, Kewanee	6-4	Sr.
Otho Tucker, Paris	6-6	Sr.

Championship Game Box Score

Assembly Hall, Champaign, March 20, 1971

DOLTON (THORNRIDGE) (52)
Coach Ron Ferguson

Player	FG-A	FT-A	Pts	PF	Rb	As	St	Bl
Boyd Batts	3-8	0-1	6	3	4	2		
Mike Bonczyk	3-6	1-1	7	3	0	7		
Quinn Buckner	8-18	2-3	18	2	8	2		
Mike Henry	5-11	3-4	13	1	10	1		
Mike McClain	2-2	0-0	4	2	3	2		
Greg Rose	2-10	0-0	4	1	2	3		
TOTAL	23-55	6-9	52	12	27	17		

OAK LAWN (COMMUNITY) (50)
Coach Len Scaduto

Player	FG-A	FT-A	Pts	PF	Rb	As	St	Bl
Brett Arnold	2-4	0-1	4	3	10	0		
Jim Bocinsky	6-11	3-3	15	0	2	1		
Bob Carr	1-7	5-8	7	1	9	3		
Tom Dubetz	0-3	2-2	2	1	1	4		
C.J. Kupec	9-15	4-4	22	2	8	4		
TOTAL	18-40	14-18	50	7	30	12		

Dolton (Thornridge)	17	11	13	11	— 52
Oak Lawn (Community)	10	13	15	12	— 50

Officials: Harry Forrester, Patrick McGann.

The 1971 tournament marked the final year of single-class basketball in Illinois. The rationale for expansion to two classes, which had been debated for many years, was simple: smaller schools wanted a better chance of winning regional tournaments and earning a trip to the state finals.

But as if mocking the impending change, five schools that would be pigeonholed into Class A the following year advanced to the Sweet Sixteen in 1971: fourth-ranked Benton, eighth-ranked Normal University, Quincy Catholic Boys, Nashville and Kewanee. For good measure, another small school, Mounds Meridian, put the only blemish on the record of Thornridge, the state's top-ranked team.

Capping off the historic nature of the tournament was the presence of coaching legend Dolph Stanley, who brought his fifth different school to state, a tournament record that appears unapproachable.

Stanley, who had previously guided Equality, Mt. Pulaski, Taylorville, and Rockford Auburn to the Sweet Sixteen, brought Rockford Boylan to Champaign, losing to Springfield Lanphier and tournament scoring leader Jim Kopatz in a wild 92-78 quarterfinal game. The visit was the Silver Fox's ninth and final trip to state.

The Paris Tigers' dreams of following LaGrange's 1970 undefeated championship with one of their own vanished in dramatic fashion in Friday night's finale. Trailing 16th-ranked Danville 42-25 at the half, Paris charged out of the third-quarter gate. Sparked by 6-foot-6 All-State senior Otho Tucker, the Tigers drew within 51-46 with eight minutes to play. Continuing to close the gap, Paris ultimately fell a basket short, dropping a 63-61 heartbreaker, its only loss in 31 games.

In the last one-class championship game, the Thornridge Falcons — fueled by all-state guard Quinn Buckner, a 6-foot-3 junior with mercury-quick hands — met the unranked Oak Lawn Spartans, powered by all-state strongman C. J. Kupec, a 6-7 senior who owned the paint. It marked the first title game match-up between two Cook County teams, and it was a game to remember.

Thornridge closed the first quarter with an 8-1 spurt for a 17-10 advantage. The margin widened to 10 before Jim Bocinsky led a Spartan charge that shaved the lead to five, 28-23, at the half.

The Falcons led 32-25 when Kupec ignited a 9-2 run, resulting in a brief 34-34 tie. A late Thornridge rally put the lead back to five, 41-38, at quarter's end.

Kupec and Bocinsky combined for 10 points down the stretch, drawing the Spartans within 52-50 just 30 seconds from the finish. With 21 seconds left, Buckner missed a free throw. The Spartans had the last possession, but missed two shots in the final four seconds, one a lay-up, to give Thornridge the win.

1951-1971

1971

TEAMS

Selected by Pat Heston

LaGrange Lyons, 1953

Lyons rewrote the tournament record books with a dominant performance, sweeping past a quartet of state-finals foes by an average margin of 19 points, netting a record 310 points in four games. All-state center Ted Caiazza shattered the single-tournament record with 121 points as LaGrange finished 29-0.

Chicago Marshall, 1958

Isadore "Spin" Salario's Commandos were 31-0 and Chicago's first state champions. The soul of the squad was 6-foot-6 sophomore sensation George Wilson, unstoppable in the paint and one of the all-time great defensive players. Marshall defeated one of the tournament's most explosive offensive powerhouses, Rock Falls, 70-64 for the title.

Collinsville, 1961

The second Vergil Fletcher-coached team to reach the title game undefeated, the Kahoks finished 32-0, led by all-American Bogie Redmon, all-stater Fred Riddle and three Bobs — Basola, Simpson and Meadows. At Champaign, Collinsville swept by the state's third-, eighth- and twelfth-ranked teams by an average score of 77-45.

Thornton, 1966

Powered by the inside-outside punch of Jim Ard and Lamarr Thomas, the 30-2 Wildcats barely broke a sweat in coasting past three outmanned opponents at Champaign's Assembly Hall. The final challenger was sixth-ranked, 27-2 Galesburg. Thornton raced to a 47-25 half-time lead, en route to a 74-60 title game win.

Evanston, 1968

Coach Jack Burmaster's top-ranked Wildkits, 30-1, spanked second-ranked Lockport Central 70-58 in a relatively easy super-sectional win, and then blasted past a trio of classy challengers 70-48, 70-54, and 70-51 to grab the title. Bob Lackey and Farrell Jones fueled the squad that fused finesse with physical strength.

A CLOSER LOOK AT SOME OF THE OUTSTANDING TEAMS, COACHES, AND PLAYERS WHO PARTICIPATED IN STATE FINAL TOURNAMENTS FROM **1951-1971**

(listed in chronological order)

COACHES

Merrill "Duster" Thomas
Pinckneyville

In the era, Thomas could never duplicate his state title drive of 1948, but his Pinckneyville Panthers made state six straight years from 1951 to 1956, finishing third three years in succession (1953-54-55) with identical 33-3 records and losing to the eventual state champion each time.

Vergil Fletcher
Collinsville

In 32 years at Collinsville, Fletcher made a then-record 14 Sweet Sixteen appearances, including four with unbeaten squads. In the era, his teams finished second once (1957) and first twice (1961, 1965) — earlier finishing fourth (1950) and later third (1978AA) — as Fletcher coached a record 34 tournament games, winning 21.

Dawson "Dawdy" Hawkins
Peoria & Pekin

Hawkins guided eight teams to state-finals berths, four each at Peoria and Pekin, reaching three title games and winning two championships. His Pekin teams went 8-2 in Sweet Sixteen play and won convincing titles in 1964 and 1967, winning by more than 20 points per game.

Alex Saudargas
West Rockford

In two different coaching stints at West Rockford, Alex Saudargas fashioned a quartet of Sweet Sixteen teams, with an average record of better than 27-2. He claimed back-to-back state championships in 1955 and 1956, then took an undefeated squad to the semifinals in 1967.

Isadore "Spin" Salario
Marshall

Salario built Chicago Marshall into a perennial state power, taking the Commandos to state four times and claiming a pair of impressive state titles — one with a 31-0 powerhouse that was Chicago's first championship team — and narrowly missing a third.

PLAYERS

Bruce Brothers, *Quincy, 1950-51-52*
One of the best small centers the tournament has ever seen, Brothers, 6-foot-5, ended his senior season as the number three all-time scorer in state finals history with 190 points. He was the heart of a Quincy team that made three trips to Champaign, finishing third and second.

Ted Caiazza, *LaGrange Lyons, 1953*
Ted Caiazza was the most overpowering offensive presence in the state tournament's first 60 years. His 121 points in the 1953 finals obliterated the previous four-game record as the 6-7 all-American fueled a LaGrange Lyons offense that swept to an undefeated state title.

Paxton Lumpkin, *Chicago DuSable, 1953-54*
The consummate floor general, the 6-foot Lumpkin, with a genius-level basketball IQ, was a Ferrari in a De Soto world. He may have been the most exciting player of all time. Scoring 27 points and dishing out 11 assists on an average night, Lumpkin had no equal in his day.

Charlie Brown, *Chicago DuSable, 1953-54*
Brown averaged 20 points per game in two tournaments while playing alongside a pair of all-state teammates, one a first team all-America selection. His picture-perfect jump shot earned him the moniker "Sweet," which nearly always preceded his name.

Joe Ruklick, *Princeton, 1954-55*
A 6-8 first-team all-state center, Ruklick was a 16-year-old senior when he led the 1955 state finals in scoring with 104 points and his Princeton Tigers to the state semifinals. In five tournament games, Ruklick averaged 26 points per game, one of the best marks in postseason history.

Bill Small, *West Aurora, 1958-59*
The 6-2 all-state team leader of West Aurora, Small averaged 23 points per game in two tournaments, trailing at the time only Max Hooper. He powered the Blackhawks to a pair of semifinal appearances, beating Springfield in the 1958 quarterfinals, and then losing to the Senators for the 1959 title.

George Wilson, *Chicago Marshall, 1958-59-60*
The most intimidating defensive player of his era, perhaps ever, Wilson led Chicago Marshall to a pair of convincing championships. In 10 tournament games, the 6-8 all-American center averaged 17 points and six boards an outing, while shutting off the paint to opposing centers. No one ever did it better.

Cazzie Russell, *Chicago Carver, 1962*
At 6-5, he was Illinois' most dominant guard during its one-class basketball era (1908-71). A first-team all-America selection, Russell was Carver's superstar, scoring 24 points and grabbing 15 rebounds in the Challengers' state championship game loss — the final game of his illustrious high school career.

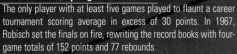
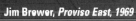
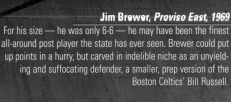

Dave Robisch, *Springfield, 1966-67*
The only player with at least five games played to flaunt a career tournament scoring average in excess of 30 points. In 1967, Robisch set the finals on fire, rewriting the record books with four-game totals of 152 points and 77 rebounds.

Jim Brewer, *Proviso East, 1969*
For his size — he was only 6-6 — he may have been the finest all-around post player the state has ever seen. Brewer could put up points in a hurry, but carved in indelible niche as an unyielding and suffocating defender, a smaller, prep version of the Boston Celtics' Bill Russell.

100 Legends

of IHSA Boys Basketball Tournament

The 100 Legends of the IHSA Boys' Basketball Tournament were announced on April 12, 2006 — just in time to tip off the centennial celebration of March Madness.

The first 82 Legends were selected by fans in an online election that ran from November 2005 through March 2006. The remaining 18 Legends were selected by a blue-ribbon committee.

The Legends chosen by the public were selected from a ballot of 281 coaches and players, broken down into seven regions of the state (the divisions of the IHSA Board of Directors) and three tournament eras.

The number of names on each ballot and the number of Legends elected from each ballot varied by era. From each Pioneer Era (1908-40) ballot, 2 of 6 nominees were elected; from the Golden Age (1941-71), 4 of 15 nominees were elected;

and from Modern Times (1972-2005), 6 of 20 nominees were elected. To be eligible for election, an individual had to have played in or coached at least one game in the state final tournament, including the super-sectional round.

The 100 Legends, or their surviving family members, were invited to attend the 2007 boys' tournament and take part in several special events at the centennial gala. In the months leading up to the state tournament, the Legends were also asked to participate in one of 25 preliminary celebrations held around the state, where they had an opportunity to autograph a commemorative Ball of Fame.

★ ★ ★ ★ ★

The 100 Legends feature an eclectic mix of talent that spans several generations. Two of the Legends, Lynch Conway and Richard Liitt, played in the first championship game in 1908. Another, Jon Scheyer, born 98 years after Conway, had not yet graduated from high school when he was named to the team.

Of the 100 Legends, 68 made the team as players, 22 qualified as coaches, and nine had state tournament experience in both roles. Two Legends, Andy Phillip and Isiah Thomas, are enshrined in the Naismith Memorial Basketball Hall of Fame. Another, Lou Boudreau, is in the Major League Baseball Hall of Fame. The team also includes one man who neither played nor coached, but had a tremendous impact on the tournament: Jim Flynn of the Illinois High School Association.

All in all, the 100 Legends represent a fascinating cross-section of the many hundreds of great players and coaches who have given their hearts and souls to the IHSA boys' basketball state tournament — America's Original March Madness — over the past 100 years.

★ ★ ★ ★ ★ ★ ★ ★ ★ ★ ★

Sergio McClain
Wayne McClain
John McDougal
Tom Michael
Fred Miller
Doug Mills
Dale Minick
Johnny Orr
Mark Pancratz
Mark Peterman
Andy Phillip
Gene Pingatore
Roger Powell
Bogie Redmon
Quentin Richardson
Dave Robisch
Chuck Rolinski
Cazzie Russell
Herb Scheffler
Jon Scheyer
Bill Schulz
Jay Shidler
Jack Sikma
Marty Simmons
Dolph Stanley
Lyndon Swanson
John Thiel
Isiah Thomas
Merrill "Duster" Thomas
Gary Tidwell
Arthur Trout
Dick Van Scyoc
Bob Van Vooren
Brian Vance
John Wessels
Frank Williams
George Wilson
Bob Zerrusen

IHSA
Illinois High School Association

1908 2007 ★ 100 LEGENDS ★
OF THE IHSA BOYS
BASKETBALL TOURNAMENT

100 Legends of IHSA Boys' Basketball Tournament

★ Joe Allen ★
Chicago Carver

Muscular center on Carver's two state tournament squads...scored 51 points in the 1962 tournament, when Stephen Decatur upset Carver in the title game...came back with 67 in 1963 as Carver outlasted Centralia...notched 18 points and grabbed 17 rebounds in the title game...made 50 of 85 field goals (59%) in eight tournament games...played college ball at Bradley University...died in 1997.

★ Dusty Bensko ★
Pleasant Plains

Star of Pleasant Plains' championship drive in 2000, when he was a junior...scored 101 points in tournament, including memorable 32-point effort in triple-overtime semifinal against Riverton...hit record 17 of 17 free throws in that game, including 12 straight in final overtime...for tournament career, finished with 119 points, 40 rebounds in 5 games...played baseball, not basketball, at University of Illinois.

★ Jeff Baker ★
Maine South

Smooth-shooting guard poured it on when it counted in the 1979 state tournament...put in 21 points in super-sectional when Maine South won on last-second shot over New Trier West...30 points and nine rebounds in semifinal win over East Moline...wrapped up with 26 points and 10 boards in championship game win over Quincy...finished tourney with 89 points (on 36-of-65 shooting) and 35 rebounds...played college ball at Texas Christian University.

★ Brad Bickett ★
Ohio (player), Bureau Valley (coach)

Two-way Legend with experience as both a player and coach...led tiny Ohio (enrollment 69) to Class A title game in 1986, smallest school to reach the championship...scored 103 points in those four games, which ended with a loss to Teutopolis...combined with 30 in 1985 super-sectional, had three straight tournament games over 30 points...played college ball at Eureka...then coached Bureau Valley to three consecutive third-place finishes in Class A in 2000, 2001, and 2002.

★ Kenny Battle ★
West Aurora

Slam-dunking forward for the 1984 West Aurora squad that finished third...tallied 86 points in four games, with a 28-point high against Champaign Centennial in quarterfinals...25 points in consolation game win over St. Joseph...went on to star at Northern Illinois University, and then on the "Flying Illini" squad that made the Final Four in 1989...played pro ball for four years and also performed with the Harlem Globetrotters.

★ Don Blanken ★
Dundee

Star of Dundee's only state champion, in 1938...team lost to Moline in first round in 1937, setting stage for championship run...scored 65 of "high-scoring" Dundee team's 161 points for tournament...high of 24 in the semifinals in 51-36 win over Paris...played his college ball at Purdue University...member of Dayton Metropolitans, early NBL team.

★ Boyd Batts ★
Thornridge

Center of the devastating Thornridge team won back-to-back titles in 1971 and 1972...scored 141 points and grabbed 98 rebounds in eight tournament games...in 1972, poured in 34 points on 15-of-20 shooting with 18 rebounds in quarterfinal win over Collinsville...topped that with 37 points (14-of-18) and 15 rebounds in title tilt against Quincy...played at University of Nevada-Las Vegas and University of Hawaii.

★ Lou Boudreau ★
Thornton

First high school basketball superstar, guided Thornton to three straight championship games..."Flying Clouds" finished first in 1933, second in 1934 and 1935...scored 76 points in 11 games, with a high of 18 in 1933 quarterfinal against Mahomet...played basketball at University of Illinois, but left school to pursue baseball career...wise choice, as he was elected to the National Baseball Hall of Fame in 1970 for his long career as a player, manager, and broadcaster...died in 2001.

★ Ted Beach ★
Champaign

Second player to participate in three state championship contests...played in 12 tournament games and set career scoring record of 198 points, which lasted until Jay Shidler of Lawrenceville edged by in 1976...finished 1946 championship run with a flourish scoring 24 in semifinal and 22 in title fray against Centralia...moved with high school coach Harry Combes to play college ball down the street at University of Illinois...member of state tournament bench crew for many years at Assembly Hall.

★ Jamie Brandon ★
Chicago King

Versatile guard-forward of the early King dynasty, played in 13 state tournament games and totaled 269 points, the all-time record...added 77 rebounds and 28 assists in Elite Eight competition...topped 30 points twice in King's run to third place in 1989...returned in 1990 to lead King to the state title, with games of 26-28-27-25 points...played college ball at Louisiana State University.

★ Jim Brewer ★
Proviso East

Six-foot-six center was instrumental in Proviso East's first state title in 1969, scoring 56 points and grabbing 40 rebounds in the four-game title drive...in championship game against Peoria Spalding, scored 17 and pulled down nine rebounds...went to University of Minnesota to play college ball and played on the ill-fated 1972 Olympic team...then embarked on a nine-year pro career.

★ Jack Burmaster ★
Elgin (player), Evanston (coach)

Star guard on 1944 Elgin squad that fell to undefeated Taylorville in title game...played college ball at University of Illinois and one year of pro ball for Sheboygan...then coached Evanston to four state tournament appearances from 1957 to 1972, including school's only state championship in 1968...later appeared as color commentator on IHSA state tournament television broadcasts...died in 2005.

★ Bruce Brothers ★
Quincy

Mainstay of the Quincy teams that finished third in 1951 and then second to Hebron in 1952...racked up 190 points in 10 tournament games, eight points shy of Ted Beach's record and good enough for 13th place on the all-time list...scored at least 20 in every game of the 1952 tourney with a high of 25 in quarterfinal against Taylorville...played college basketball at University of Illinois...died in 1986.

★ Ed Butkovich ★
Canton (player), Mt. Pulaski (coach)

Player on Canton's 1953 Sweet Sixteen team and longtime coach at Mt. Pulaski...led the Toppers to a championship in 1976 and followed up with a fourth-place finish in 1977...brought home hardware one more time with a second-place finish in 1984...played his college ball at St. Louis University and Western Illinois University...later served as assistant coach at Lincoln College...died on trip to away game in 2002.

★ Charlie Brown ★
Chicago DuSable

Forward on DuSable's high-flying state tournament squads in 1953 and 1954...scored 93 points in the 1954 tournament with games of 23, 24, 23, and 23...DuSable finished second to Mt. Vernon...played college ball at University of Seattle...drafted by Cincinnati Royals...officiated the Class AA title game in 1994, 40 years after DuSable's loss...one of only two men to play in and referee a championship (Herb Scheffler is the other).

★ Ted Caiazza ★
LaGrange Lyons

Dominating center who averaged over 30 points per game during Lyons Township's drive to the state title in 1953...started off with 31 against DuSable, added 38 versus Decatur St. Teresa, and cleaned up with 27 against Pinckneyville and 25 in the final game against Peoria, setting a new one-tournament standard, since broken...played college ball for the University of Illinois.

★ Quinn Buckner ★
Thornridge

Leader of the Thornridge squad that many still consider the best ever...team won final one-class title in 1971 and first Class AA title in 1972...scored 147 points and grabbed 63 rebounds in eight games of tournament play, capped by a 28-point performance in 1972 title game versus Quincy...went on to star at Indiana University and play in 1976 Olympics before embarking on 10-year pro career...works as broadcaster for the Indiana Pacers and CBS...inducted into the National High School Sports Hall of Fame in 1989.

★ Andy Calmes ★
Warrensburg-Latham

Forward came up big in 2003 as Warrensburg-Latham claimed its first trophy ever, a third-place finish...scored 27 points in quarterfinal battle against Cissna Park, finished tournament with 78 points and 31 rebounds...counting totals from 2002 super-sectional loss, his total output was 93 points in five games...playing college ball at Truman State University in Kirksville, Mo.

★ Chuck Buescher ★
Peoria Central

Veteran coach led Peoria High to four title-game appearances...lost close championship battles in 1983 (to Springfield Lanphier) and 1989 (triple overtime to East St. Louis Lincoln)...held on to win nail-biting back-to-back titles in 2003 and 2004 at Carver Arena in Peoria...attended Danvers and East Peoria High Schools...played college ball at Bradley University and served as assistant there after high school coaching career.

★ Cliff Cameron ★
Pleasant Plains

Guided Pleasant Plains to championships just two years apart...first squad in 2000 won every game by double digits but needed three overtimes in crucial semifinal against Riverton...2002 team won a nailbiter over Herrin in the championship game...still coaching at Plains after eight seasons...attended Virden High School...played basketball at Lincoln Land.

100 Legends of IHSA Boys' Basketball Tournament

★ Francis Clements ★
Ottawa

Five-foot-eleven junior guard was the star of Ottawa's only state placer in 1957…notched 70 points as Ottawa took third in a series of close games…Clements scored 19 in a double-overtime super-sectional win over Pekin and capped his effort with 16 points in another overtime, this time in the consolation game against Quincy Notre Dame…scored 19 in 1958 supers but Ottawa could not get past Peoria Spalding…played college ball at Valparaiso University.

★ Landon "Sonny" Cox ★
Chicago King

Fashioned three state champions at King High School in Chicago, with victories in 1986, 1990, and 1993…also picked up second place in 1987, third in 1989 and 1999 to share Class AA record of six total trophies with Bennie Lewis…grew up in Cincinnati…played baseball in college at Kentucky State University…is an accomplished jazz saxophonist.

★ Jeff Clements ★
Mt. Pulaski

Star of Mt. Pulaski's 1976 and 1977 squads that finished first and fourth respectively…as a sophomore in 1976, tallied 35 points in quarterfinal win over Eldorado and 87 for the four-game tournament…reprised his performance in 1977 with 66 points…finished his tournament career with 179 points in nine games…continued career at Illinois Wesleyan University.

★ Bruce Douglas ★
Quincy

Star of Quincy's unstoppable 1981 team, shooting 79 points and shooting 66% from the field…subbed on the second-place 1979 squad and scored 89 points in 1982 when Quincy's 64-game winning streak was broken in the semifinals by Mendel Catholic…played 12 state tournament games and scored 182 points…went on to star at University of Illinois…had a cup of coffee in the pros in 1987.

★ Harry Combes ★
Champaign

Led Champaign High to seven state tournament appearances in nine years from 1939 to 1947…captured fourth place in 1940 and 1944 before starting three years of amazing runs to the championship game…Champaign finished second in 1945, first in 1946, and second in 1947…left high school ranks to take over head coaching reins at University of Illinois from Doug Mills…coached UI for 20 years…died in 1977.

★ Walter Downing ★
Providence Catholic

Willowy center led Providence to third in 1978 and a state championship in 1979, when he was a junior…in 10 state tournament games, scored 184 points and grabbed 80 rebounds, but is best known as a shot-blocker…rejected a record 12 shots in 1978 quarterfinal against Ottawa Marquette, but this stat was not always recorded…played college ball at Marquette University.

★ Lynch Conway ★
Peoria

Star of the first state champion team and the first state championship game in 1908…scored 11 baskets in title tilt, a record that stood until 1950…also state champion in the high jump in 1907 with a leap of 5-7 3/4, placed second in the 100-yard dash in 1908…later a star at Bradley University and city engineer in Peoria…died in 1939.

★ Mike Duff ★
Eldorado

High-scoring center put on a show at the 1977 tournament, logging 36, 37, 22, and 36 points for a total of 131 as Eldorado finished third…combined with his performance in six tournament games in 1975 and 1976, he finished with 252 points and 112 field goals, both Class A records for a tournament career…died in tragic plane crash of Evansville University basketball team in December, 1977.

★ Dick Corn ★
Benton (player), Pinckneyville (coach)

Has won more Class A regional championships than anyone (23 in 31 years at Pinckneyville) but it took a while for the trophies to start coming…took his first squad to Elite Eight in 1988 and finished second to Pana…won first title in 1994 over Eureka on Ryan Bruns' last-second shot…captured another in 2001, winning title-game rematch with Pana…then finished fourth in 2006…played on Benton's 1967 Sweet Sixteen team…then to college at Monmouth.

★ Dwight "Dike" Eddleman ★
Centralia

Widely hailed as Illinois' best schoolboy athlete of the first half-century (1900-50)…set the state scoring record in his senior year with 2,702 career points…scored 194 points in 12 tournament games, with Centralia finishing fourth in 1939, third in 1941, and first in 1942…starred at Illinois and played pro for four years…three-time state high jump champion, finished second in 1948 Olympics…inducted into the National High School Sports Hall of Fame in 1983…died in 2001.

★ LaPhonso Ellis ★
East St. Louis Lincoln

Six-foot-ten star of the first two of East St. Louis Lincoln's three consecutive champions, he dominated scoring, rebounding, and blocked shot totals...held to two points in 1987 semifinal, he responded with 27 against King in title game...in 1988, he totaled 94 points, including a title game log of 26 points, 15 rebounds, and 9 blocked shots...played college ball at University of Notre Dame and had an 11-year pro career.

★ Vergil Fletcher ★
Collinsville

Coached more state tournament victories (21) and more state tournament games (34) than any man...Collinsville's first state champion in 1961 was a juggernaut that won three Elite Eight games by a combined 94 points...the 1965 team made him the seventh coach to win two state titles...Collinsville also took second in 1957, third in 1978 (Class AA), and fourth in 1950...all told his teams played in 14 state tournaments...attended Johnston City High School...inducted into the National High School Sports Hall of Fame in 1983.

★ Melvin Ely ★
Thornton

Came up big in three straight tournaments with only Peoria Manual blocking the way each time...scored 15 in the 1995 championship game as a sophomore...returned in 1996 to register 69 points on 30-of-50 shooting, falling to Manual again in the final...finished career with 57 more points in 1997 state finals...in 12 games, totaled 157 points, 79 rebounds, and 39 blocked shots...played college ball at Fresno State...then on to a pro career.

★ Jim Flynn ★
IHSA

IHSA administrator for 31 years...hired as editor, marketer and public relations spokesman...tirelessly promoted the phrase "March Madness" until it became popular beyond Illinois...the brains behind the March Madness Experience...wrote volumes about the basketball tournaments and inspired many others to do the same...retired from IHSA in 2004...grew up in Galesburg and Springfield.

★ Ernie Eveland ★
Waterman, Paris

Piled up 10 state tournament appearances from small towns, first at Waterman and later at Paris...Paris won in 1943 and 1947, and fell in 1942 title game only because of Dike Eddleman's heroics...also finished second in 1939 and third in 1938...first coach to win state titles in two sports, he led the Paris cross country team to championships in 1947, 1948, and 1949...retired from coaching in 1958...native of Lewistown...died in 1987.

★ Larry Graham ★
Madison

Second Class A coach to log two state championships, after Ron Felling...his 1977 squad ended years of frustration in Madison with a convincing win over Aurora Central Catholic in the title game...after a fourth-place finish in 1980, the 1981 squad turned the trick again with a win over Dunlap...coached his teams to six state tournament appearances...later coached at SIU-Edwardsville and Florissant Valley College...native of Indiana.

★ Ron Felling ★
Lawrenceville

Colorful coach led Lawrenceville to four state titles, becoming first coach to accomplish the feat...his 1972 squad won the inaugural Class A championship...repeated in 1974 with exciting title-game win over Ottawa Marquette...1982 and 1983 squads won 68 games in a row, a state record, and became state's only back-to-back undefeated state champions...after leaving high school coaching, worked for Bobby Knight at Indiana University...native of Indiana.

★ Bob Grant ★
Pekin

Star of Pekin's first great team, which went 29-4 under Coach Glenn "Frenchy" Haussler... scored 37 points in four games, with a high of 12 in a 37-19 quarterfinal win over Hillsboro...scored another 10 points as Pekin finished third with a 22-16 win over Moline...offered college scholarship at Illinois Wesleyan, but returned home...was the only write-in candidate to be elected to the 100 Legends...died in 1999.

★ Michael Finley ★
Proviso East

Mainstay of the first of two heralded heralded Proviso East teams of the 1990s, and one of the "Three Amigos"...led the 1991 squad with 56 points in four state tourney games...scored 14 in the title game, a 68-61 win over Peoria Manual...college career at University of Wisconsin...long pro career had reached 11 seasons by 2006.

★ Lowell Hamilton ★
Providence-St. Mel

Dominant center led Providence-St. Mel to a third-place finish in 1984 and the Class A state title in 1985...scored 165 points and grabbed 94 rebounds in 11 career state tournament games over four seasons...blocked 19 shots in three Elite Eight games in 1984, including eight against Lena-Winslow in the third-place game...starred for the University of Illinois.

100 Legends of IHSA Boys' Basketball Tournament

★ Dawson "Dawdy" Hawkins ★
Peoria Central, Pekin

Took nine teams to the Sweet Sixteen, the first four times with Peoria High…led the 1953 squad to second place, finishing with loss to Lyons Twp…struck gold at Pekin in 1964, downing Cobden in memorable state championship game…then again in 1967, with a win over Carbondale in the title match-up…also coached a state championship team at Lincoln Northeast, in his home state of Nebraska, in 1948…died in 1997.

★ Shawn Jeppson ★
Spring Valley Hall

Only player to score 50 points in a state championship game, he did it with 51 in losing, overtime effort against Warsaw in 1997…scored 116 points in 1997 tournament and returned Hall to the title game in 1998 against Nauvoo-Colusa…freak injury hampered his performance in championship game as Hall was runner-up for second straight year…totaled 182 points and 43 rebounds in 8 tournament games…played college ball at Illinois State University.

★ Bill Heisler ★
Warsaw

Plucky guard was leader of Warsaw's surprising champions in 1997…scored 114 points with 19 assists in four games…unloaded in overtime title contest against Spring Valley Hall, ringing up 36 points including six three-pointers…in four tourney games made 16 of 27 three-point attempts (59%)…played college ball at Western Illinois University.

★ Dave Johnson ★
ROVA

Six-foot-eight center put up big numbers in the 1976 Class A meet…set Class A mark of 19 free throws made in semifinal game against Lawrenceville, when he scored 33 altogether…added 28 in title game against Mt. Pulaski but ROVA fell 59-58…finished with totals of 105 points and 48 rebounds for the four-game tournament…played college ball at Drake University.

★ Max Hooper ★
Mt. Vernon

High-scoring center on Mt. Vernon's back-to-back champions, only the second team to accomplish that feat…in 1949, scored 81 points, 34 in the quarterfinal game against Decatur…followed up that feat with 104 points in the 1950 tournament, including 36 in the title game against Danville, a record that stood for 22 years…first player to lead the tournament field in scoring twice…played college ball at University of Illinois.

★ Paul Judson ★
Hebron

The guard half of Hebron's famed Judson twins, led school to unforgettable overtime victory over Quincy in 1952…scored 59 points in the tournament, with high games of 17 in the first round and quarterfinals…finished with 21 of 43 shooting from the field…played basketball at the University of Illinois and against the Harlem Globetrotters…coached Dundee girls to the state quarterfinals in 1978.

★ Walt Hoult ★
Chrisman

A sophomore on Chrisman's 1985 Class A runner-up, came back in 1987 to lead the Cardinals to a third-place finish…scored 35 and pulled down 23 rebounds in 1987 super-sectional win over Tri-City…finished tournament career with 119 points and 66 rebounds in eight games…third-place finisher in Class A high jump in 1986 and 1987…ran track and field at Millikin University.

★ Phil Judson ★
Hebron

The forward half of Hebron's famed Judson twins…school's championship in 1952 only time a "district (small) school" won the one-class tournament, which was discontinued after 1971…scored 46 points in the tournament…played basketball at the University of Illinois and against the Harlem Globetrotters….later coached at Zion-Benton.

★ Cal Hubbard ★
Normal University

Directed University High into the state finals seven times over a 10-year period from 1990 to 1999, finishing with three trophies…1992 squad was runner-up to small-school darling Findlay…1995 squad won it all in a 56-54 squeaker over Aurora Christian…then in 1997, U-High pulled out a third-place finish…finished 17th year as head coach in 2006.

★ Gordon Kerkman ★
West Aurora

Veteran coach has brought West Aurora to the state tournament 10 times, winning five trophies…broke City of Aurora's long championship drought with an upset win over Westinghouse in 2000…West also finished second in 1997, losing memorable title contest to Peoria Manual…added third-place trophies in 1980, 1984, and 2004…native of Iowa…played basketball and baseball at Coe College.

★ Gay Kintner ★

Decatur

One of the three great coaches of the early years, he followed Arthur Trout into the three-time-winner club…Decatur won it all in 1931, again in 1936, and one more time in 1945…among a total of 11 state tournament appearances, he added a second-place finish in 1937 and a fourth in 1951…was in his 32nd year as head coach in 1960 when he collapsed and died at halftime of a game at Decatur MacArthur.

★ Tom Kleinschmidt ★

Gordon Tech

Brawny forward put up big numbers in two state tournament appearances…after super-sectional loss in 1989, led Gordon Tech to the championship game in 1990, falling to King in title game…scored 34 points in 82-80 super-sectional win over Blue Island Eisenhower and 38 in semifinal win over Quincy to put Gordon into title contest…totaled 148 points in just five games…went to DePaul University for college career.

★ Jerry Kuemmerle ★

Danville Schlarman

Shortest tournament career of any Legend player (just two games), but he made the most of it…scored 27 points in 1958 super-sectional win over Arcola to set up quarterfinal match-up at Huff Gym with high-scoring Rock Falls…scored 49 points in that battle, a tournament record that lasted until 1984… he sank 17 of 29 field goal attempts and 15 of 17 from the line, but it was not enough as Rock Falls prevailed 101-76…played college ball at Christian Brothers University in Memphis.

★ C.J. Kupec ★

Oak Lawn

Six-foot-seven center who paced Oak Lawn to a second-place finish in 1971, in final single-class tournament…scored 87 points and pulled down 48 rebounds in four games…scored 28 in super-sectional against New Trier East and grabbed 17 rebounds in the semifinal win over Springfield Lanphier…played basketball at University of Michigan and then three years in the pros.

★ Jerry Leggett ★

Rich Central, Quincy

Coached at five schools but will always be remembered for his Quincy teams…second-place finish in 1979 was a prelude of things to come…1981 team went undefeated and breezed easily through tournament play…returned undefeated in 1982, losing stunner to Mendel Catholic, but retaining third place on unbelievable inbounds play…added fourth-place trophies in 1987 and 1990…finished career at Moline, where he attended high school…played college ball at Beloit…died in 1998.

★ Bennie Lewis ★

East St. Louis Lincoln, East St. Louis Senior

One of only two coaches to win four state titles (Ron Felling being the other)…guided first East St. Louis Lincoln, and then Senior, to a total of 11 Sweet Sixteen appearances…brought Lincoln its first state title in 1982…then set new standard by winning three straight state championships in 1987, 1988, and 1989, the last a triple-overtime thriller…finished third in 1990 (with Lincoln) and 2000 (with East St. Louis Senior)…born in Mississippi…played in college at Langston University in Oklahoma.

★ Marcus Liberty ★

Chicago King

Key cog in King's 1986 state championship squad, scoring 64 points…had to take matters into his own hands the next year, putting up games of 41, 23, 38, and 41 points in the state tournament stretch, but…it wasn't enough, as East St. Louis Lincoln won the title tilt 79-62…his 143-point tournament stands as Class AA record…only Class AA player to top 40 twice in the same tournament…played for University of Illinois and then four years of pro ball.

★ Richard Liitt ★

Rock Island

Unquestioned star of the first three state tournaments, still holds the tournament career record for total free throws made (70)…record has stood for incredible 96 years (Jon Scheyer finished with 69)…also held record for points in a tournament career, 154, which lasted until broken by Dike Eddleman in 1942…Rock Island finished second, fourth, and second in three-year span…high game (25) in tournament came in first contest as a sophomore (rest of team scored six)…died in 1953.

★ Kenneth "Jack" Lipe ★

Decatur (player), Thornton (coach)

Iconoclastic coach of Thornton's teams during the Lou Boudreau era…guided the school to its first championship in 1933 and followed up with second-place finishes in 1934 and 1935…later removed his team from the tournament for several years in dispute over IHSA's hosting policy…played on Decatur's state tournament team in 1921…college basketball at University of Illinois….died in 1998.

★ Shaun Livingston ★

Peoria Central

Slender guard led Peoria High to consecutive titles in 2003 and 2004 while scoring 122 points and pulling down 51 rebounds…scored last-second bucket to defeat Thornwood in the 2003 title tilt…tallied 20 and 27 in final two games of 2004 as Peoria edged Carbondale and Homewood-Flossmoor…first prep point guard to be picked in first round of NBA draft (No. 4 by L.A. Clippers).

100 Legends of IHSA Boys' Basketball Tournament

★ Paxton Lumpkin ★
Chicago DuSable

Exciting guard on DuSable's famous team, scored 29 in his Huff Gym debut in 1953 loss to eventual champion Lyons Twp...returned next season with hot shooting, dribbling and passing in determined march to championship game...31 in semifinal over Edwardsville his tournament high, on 13-for 27 shooting...scored 13 in loss to Mt. Vernon in title game...played at Indiana State and Indiana University before starring for the Harlem Globetrotters...died in 1991.

★ Tom Michael ★
Carlyle

Six-foot-eight center paced Carlyle's charge to the state title in 1989...was a one-man wrecking crew in the semifinal against Prairie Central, totaling 45 points, nine rebounds, and seven blocks in 67-62 win...followed up that evening with 28 more against Rock Island Alleman in 65-56 state championship triumph...totaled 121 for the tournament, averaging over 30 ppg...played college ball at University of Illinois and works there as an assistant coach.

★ Cuonzo Martin ★
East St. Louis Lincoln

Emerging from the shadow of LaPhonso Ellis, played on two state champions and a third-place team for East St. Louis Lincoln...rang up 68 points as a sophomore as Lincoln won its second consecutive title...added 80 more the next tournament when Lincoln became the first to win three straight...played injured his senior year but finished with 198 points (10th on all-time list) and 111 rebounds in 12 games...played college basketball at Purdue University...brief pro career...later an assistant at Purdue.

★ Fred Miller ★
Pekin

After two super-sectional losses, made the most of his final appearance in 1967...came out blazing with 25 in win over Toluca and 30 in quarterfinal game against York...saved best for last with 36-point performance in championship win over Carbondale, making 16 of 20 shots from the field...16 baskets still a title-game record... finished tourney career with 147 points in six games...played college basketball at University of Illinois.

★ Sergio McClain ★
Peoria Manual

Only two players to play in maximum 16 state-finals games and win every one, from 1994 to 1997...the last three championships won with father Wayne McClain as head coach...scored 201 points, recorded 89 rebounds in 16 games, good for eighth place on the all-time scoring list...played college basketball at University of Illinois...later coach of Peoria's ABA franchise.

★ Doug Mills ★
Elgin (player), Joliet (coach)

Star player of first high school team to win back-to-back state titles, in 1924 and 1925...totaled 32 points in four games for Elgin in low-scoring era...played college ball at University of Illinois...then coached Joliet to the state tournament in 1935...returned to the U of I as coach of the famous "Whiz Kids" and later served as athletic director...died in 1983.

★ Wayne McClain ★
Peoria Manual

After taking over for Dick Van Scyoc, was in fourth season of coaching before he lost his first tournament game...won three straight titles from 1995 to 1997 with son Sergio as his starting forward...moved up to college ranks after 2000, joining Sergio at University of Illinois as assistant coach...as high schooler, he played in state tournament for Manual on 1972 squad, finishing fourth...played college ball at Bradley University.

★ Dale Minick ★
Decatur

Stalwart of the Decatur team that won it all in 1936 and returned to the title game in 1937...in eight low-scoring state tournament games, scored a total of 56 points and exceeded double figures three times...in best game, scored 10 of team's points in 20-19 win over Johnston City in 1936 semifinal...played college basketball at Millikin University...died in 1973.

★ John McDougal ★
Salem (player), West Aurora, Rockford Lutheran (coach)

First experienced state tournament thrills as starter on Salem's third-place squad in 1943...played football and ran track at Evansville University...then embarked on long coaching career at West Aurora, where his teams finished third in 1973 and second in 1976...after a 10-year stint as head coach of Northern Illinois University, returned to high school game to direct Rockford Lutheran to fourth place in 1994...only man to coach a team to a trophy in both Class A and Class AA.

★ Johnny Orr ★
Taylorville

Hot-shooting forward on Taylorville's legendary 1944 team, first to finish the season undefeated...scored 64 points in four tournament games including 17 in title match-up against Elgin...played college ball at University of Illinois and, after a stint in the Navy, at Beloit College...after one season of pro ball, began coaching career at Milton, Wis...later coached at University of Massachusetts, University of Michigan, and Iowa State University.

★ Mark Pancratz ★
Schaumburg

Guard was star of Schaumburg's unlikely title-game win over Thornwood in 2001, scoring 21 points...also topped 20-point mark in super-sectional against Zion-Benton and quarterfinal against West Aurora...played as sophomore on Schaumburg's fourth-place finisher in 1999...total output for eight tournament games was 92 points...played college ball at University of Wisconsin at Milwaukee.

★ Bogie Redmon ★
Collinsville

Six-foot-six star of Collinsville's 1961 state title team that rolled through the season undefeated...scored 92 points in four state tournament games, capped by a 31-point, 15-rebound performance in the title game against Thornton...also put in 25 points in quarterfinal match-up with East Rockford...shot 66% for the tournament...went on to star at the University of Illinois.

★ Mark Peterman ★
Canton, Springfield

Influential coach of the early era, credited with spreading "slow-break" strategy in the 1920s and 1930s coach to win state titles at two different schools and only coach to win seven trophies...led Canton to third-place finishes in 1923, 1924, and 1925, improving to second in 1926 and first in 1928...moving to Springfield, finished second in 1934 and won another title in 1935...retired from coaching after 1947 season...died in 1968.

★ Quentin Richardson ★
Chicago Young

Six-foot-six guard-forward holds the Class AA championship game record for rebounds, pulling down 20 in Young's 1998 win over Galesburg...scored 18 points in same game...in his six-game tournament career, he scored 130 points and grabbed 69 rebounds...high was 32 in 1998 quarterfinal win over Elgin...then starred at DePaul University...later enjoyed a successful pro career.

★ Andy Phillip ★
Granite City

Following Lou Boudreau in superstar stature, hot-shooting guard led Granite City to 1940 state championship...totaled 53 points in four games as low-scoring era was in its last throes...tallied 15 of Granite City's points in 24-22 title-game win over Herrin...member of the famed "Whiz Kids" at the University of Illinois...in 1947, embarked on 11-year pro career in early NBA...inducted into the National Basketball Hall of Fame in 1961, three years after his retirement...died in 2001.

★ Dave Robisch ★
Springfield

Six-foot-nine center averaged 35 points in five state tournament games...unleashed a torrent of points in 1967...scored 47 in super-sectional against Quincy, 25 against Champaign Central, 41 in semifinal loss to Pekin, and 39 in consolation win over West Rockford...also had at least 18 rebounds in each game...his 152 points in 1967 demolished Joe Wiley's record and still ranks third...his 77 rebounds remains the state record...played college ball at Kansas...then played in the NBA and ABA for 13 years.

★ Gene Pingatore ★
St. Joseph

Longtime coach at Westchester St. Joseph, best known as mentor of Isiah Thomas, has guided the Chargers to a complete complement of trophies...championship trophy came in 1999, with 61-51 win over Gurnee Warren...finished second with Isiah in 1978, third in 1987, and fourth in 1984, all in Class AA...his teams have made 10 state final appearances.

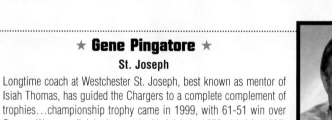

★ Chuck Rolinski ★
Toluca

"Father of two-class basketball" lobbied hard for change and finally got it in 1972... Toluca's furthest advancement in the old one-class system was a loss to eventual state champ Pekin in the 1967 super-sectional...also coached teams to the Sweet Sixteen twice in the Class A era, in 1973 and 1984...retired from coaching in 1990 after 34 years...secretary-treasurer of the Illinois Basketball Coaches Association.

★ Roger Powell ★
Joliet Central

Star of powerful Joliet Central squad that finished third in 1970...logged 90 points in four games, with a high of 26 in super-sectional victory over Maine South...tallied 25 points in semifinal loss to Lyons Twp...rebounded for 25 more in consolation match with Peoria Spalding...attended Illinois State University where he played basketball.

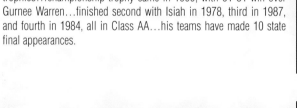

★ Cazzie Russell ★
Chicago Carver

All-everything guard for Larry Hawkins' 1962 Carver squad...led team with 79 points in 4 games...scored 22 in quarterfinal and 25 in semifinal...continued pace with 24 points in title game as Carver in one-point loss to Stephen Decatur...played his college ball at University of Michigan before embarking on a 12-year pro career...later basketball coach at Savannah (Ga.) College of Art.

100 Legends of IHSA Boys' Basketball Tournament

★ Herb Scheffler ★
Springfield

Six-foot-four center starred on the 1935 Springfield team that knocked off Thornton in the championship game…in five games of tournament action, scored 53 points, with 13 of Springfield's 24 points in the title contest…played basketball at Oklahoma, making the very first Final Four in 1939…returned to Huff Gym in 1954 as coach of the Springfield team, which lost to Pinckneyville in the first round…completed the trifecta in 1961 when he officiated the state title contest between Collinsville and Thornton…died in 2001.

★ Marty Simmons ★
Lawrenceville

Star of Lawrenceville's two undefeated state champions in 1982 and 1983…highest-scoring of many Lawrenceville shooters, with 245 points scored in a total of 10 state tournament games…also pulled down Class A record 136 rebounds…scored 43 points in 56-54 win over Providence-St. Mel in 1983 quarterfinals, including all 23 of Lawrenceville's points in the second half… played at Indiana University and University of Evansville…later the basketball coach at Southern Illinois University at Edwardsville.

★ Jon Scheyer ★
Glenbrook North

Youngest Legend graduated in 2006, but his performance was historic…in 10 tournament games he scored 236 points, fourth on all-time list…his 48 points in 2005 super-sectional win over Waukegan set a new Class AA standard…totaled 134 points in 2005 tournament as Glenbrook North won state tournament…16-for-16 performance from free throw line in quarterfinal against Brother Rice also a Class AA record…recruited to play his college basketball at Duke University.

★ Dolph Stanley ★
Equality, Mt. Pulaski, Taylorville, Rockford Auburn, Rockford Boylan

Holds "unbreakable" record of guiding five different schools into the state tournament…first hit paydirt with tiny Equality's third-place finish in 1934, then fourth with Mt. Pulaski in 1936…subsequently directed 1944 Taylorville team to state championship…after a stint at Beloit College, returned to high schools to guide Rockford Auburn and Boylan to state berths…native of Marion… played three sports at University of Illinois…died in 1990.

★ Bill Schulz ★
Hebron

Big man on the tiny Hebron team (98 students) that shocked the state by winning it all in 1952…6-10 center never played basketball until Alden consolidated with Hebron when he started eighth grade…as a junior, scored 65 points in four games in the 1952 tournament, including 24 in overtime victory over Quincy in the title game…played college ball at Northwestern University.

★ Lyndon Swanson ★
Watseka

High-scoring center helped Watseka win its only tournament hardware, a third-place trophy in 1975…scored 16 in a super-sectional loss to Lexington as a junior…next season, totaled 95 points and 55 rebounds in four state tournament games…racked up 37 points in final appearance, consolation win over Eldorado……finished second in both Class A discus and shot put in 1975…played college basketball at Texas A&M.

★ Jay Shidler ★
Lawrenceville

Remembered almost as much for his flowing mane as his incredible outside shooting…up-and-coming star as a sophomore on the 1974 state champion team…hit his stride as a senior, scoring 48 points, a Class A record for many years, in a semifinal loss to ROVA…came back in the third-place game to add 45 more and set Class A career record of 206 points, broken by Mike Duff the next year…played college basketball at University of Kentucky.

★ John Thiel ★
Galesburg

Piloted Galesburg to nine state tournament appearances over an 18-year career as head coach…took first trophy in 1959 when Galesburg finished third…Streaks made two mighty runs in the 1960s…finished second to Thornton in 1966 and second again to Evanston two years later…retired from high school coaching in 1973…drafted by both the Milwaukee Hawks (basketball) and Chicago White Sox….died in 1988.

★ Jack Sikma ★
St. Anne

Future NBA star first hit limelight at 1973 Class A state tournament, playing for St. Anne, a small town near Kankakee…made 100 points and grabbed 73 rebounds in the four games as St. Anne finished fourth…eye-popping game was a 36-point, 24-rebound, 12-block performance against Cerro Gordo in the quarterfinals…went to Illinois Wesleyan University to play ball, and graduated from there to the NBA…enjoyed 14-year career in the pros.

★ Isiah Thomas ★
St. Joseph

All-American guard on Gene Pingatore's first great team at St. Joseph…tallied 93 points and 31 rebounds in the four-game run… St. Joseph fell to Lockport in the title game, 64-47…went on to play for Bobby Knight at Indiana University…13-year NBA career ended with induction into the National Basketball Hall of Fame in 2000…later president of basketball operations and head coach of the New York Knicks.

★ Merrill "Duster" Thomas ★
Pinckneyville

Pride of Pinckneyville led small southern Illinois burg to state title and four third-place trophies in an eight-year span…initial third-place finish in 1947 proved a warm-up for spectacular 1948 team that demolished East Rockford in title game…after return trips to Huff Gym in 1951 and 1952, embarked on three-year string (1953-55) with third-place the result each time…retired from coaching in 1957…attended Illinois College but played baseball…died in 1981.

★ Gary Tidwell ★
Pana, Prairie Central

Rare two-school player who followed his stepfather and coach, Charlie Strasburger, between head coaching posts…as a sophomore in 1988, played for Pana and tallied 52 points in state-title drive…moving to Prairie Central in 1989, he added 69 points as team finished third…then as senior, added 86 more as Prairie Central finished second after overtime loss to Wesclin…finished with 207 career points, tied for fifth on all-time list…played ball in college at Olivet Nazarene University.

★ Arthur Trout ★
Centralia

Grand Old Man of high school basketball coaches, with 809 wins spanning 37 years…led Centralia to the state tournament 10 times…won state titles in 1918, 1922, and 1942, the last time with superstar Dike Eddleman…also won three other trophies, a second in 1946, third in 1941, and fourth in 1939…native of Indiana…retired from coaching in 1951…died in 1956…charter inductee into the National High School Sports Hall of Fame in 1982.

★ Dick Van Scyoc ★
Washington, Peoria Manual

Winningest boys' coach in Illinois history (826), exceeded Arthur Trout's record in his final season…also won his first state title in final game as coach, downing Carbondale in 1994 title game…previously directed Manual to second-place finish in 1991, third in 1986 and 1988, and a fourth in 1972, with his eventual successor Wayne McClain as a player…native of Eureka…attended Illinois Wesleyan and University of Illinois…had brief pro basketball career.

★ Bob Van Vooren ★
Moline

Top player on Moline's runner-up squad from 1951, Maroons' best finish to date…scored 64 points in 4 games…best effort was a 27-point performance in a 64-63 semifinal win over Quincy…followed up with 12 in title game but Moline fell to Freeport…played college ball at Marquette University.

★ Brian Vance ★
Rock Falls

Five-foot-eleven guard led Rock Falls to its state title in most dramatic fashion, sinking a last-second three-pointer to seal 45-43 win over Waterloo Gibault in the 1999 Class A finals…in five tournament games, scored 111 points and hauled in 31 rebounds…high game in that run was his first, 29 points in a loss to Farmington in the 1998 super-sectional…played college ball at Sauk Valley Community College.

★ John Wessels ★
West Rockford

Six-foot-seven center headed the West Rockford squad that became only the third to win back-to-back state championships…as a junior in 1955, scored 51 points in the four-game stretch run…came back in 1956 to pour 107 through the nets, with a 36-point effort in the quarterfinals versus West Frankfort his personal best…added 29 in the 67-65 title-game win over Edwardsville…played his college ball at University of Illinois…died in 1994.

★ Frank Williams ★
Peoria Manual

Star of two state champions, 6-3 guard known for playmaking and quick hands on defense…was bit player as freshman on Manual's 1995 champs…in starting role in 1996, scored 16 points in title-game win over Thornton…laid 20 on Thornton in 1997 semifinal that propelled Manual into title game…finished tournament career in 1998 super-sectional loss to Quincy, having scored 135 points in 10 games…played in college at University of Illinois…later enjoyed pro career.

★ George Wilson ★
Chicago Marshall

Six-foot-eight center led Marshall to two state championships, first ever for city of Chicago…as a sophomore in 1958, poured in 86 points in four games as Marshall glided to title over Rock Falls…returned with 64 points in 1960 as Marshall breezed through field…starred at University of Cincinnati and on the 1964 Olympic team…played seven years of pro ball.

★ Bob Zerrusen ★
Teutopolis

Backbone of Teutopolis' undefeated state champs in 1986…in four tournament games, 6-6 center scored 81 points on 32 of 44 field goal shooting (73%), added 44 rebounds and 10 blocked shots…key player in 75-73 super-sectional win over Venice, tallying 25 points…scored 18 (on 8-of-9 shooting) and grabbed nine rebounds in title game against Ohio…played college ball at Lakeland College.

Small Towns & Big Dreams   1972–2006

Celebrating 100 years of
IHSA Boys Basketball Tournaments

In 1970, when small-school principals were finally offered a chance to hold a basketball tournament separate from the baby-boomer-filled city and suburban powerhouses, 39 percent voted against the proposal.

Wonder how many would today?

The idea of dividing Illinois' high schools, which numbered almost 800, was the object of scorn in many corners.

View from the student section of Assembly Hall, 1981.

A NEW TOURNAMENT AND A NEW TRADITION

LAWRENCEVILLE '72-'74-'82-'83

RIDGWAY '73

VENICE '75-'87

MT. PULASKI '76

MADISON '77-'81

NASHVILLE '78

PROVIDENCE '79

LUTHER SOUTH '80

McLEANSBORO '84

PROVIDENCE-ST. MEL '85

TEUTOPOLIS '86

PANA '88

CARLYLE '89

WESCLIN '90

PITTSFIELD '91

FINDLAY '92

STAUNTON '93

PINCKNEYVILLE '94-'01

UNIVERSITY (Normal) '95

SHELBYVILLE '96

WARSAW '97

NAUVOO-COLUSA '98

ROCK FALLS '99

PLEASANT PLAINS '00-'02

HALES FRANCISCAN '03

LEO '04

SENECA '06

CLASS A

"The Goose That Laid the Golden Egg" and its impending death were matters of great concern.

That is, until the doors opened for the first Class A tournament. From Section C of Assembly Hall, a new voice was heard, from fans of six schools that had never participated in a Sweet Sixteen, let alone an Elite Eight, under the one-class system.

Naysayers became converts as Class A tournament weekend developed a tradition of small-school enthusiasm and down-home charm.

As it happens, the kids could play basketball, too.

Jeff Lampe revisits the Class A tournament, which made dreams into reality starting in 1972.

Class warfare
The fears and jeers never came

The **school** he was going to lead to the *promised* land is long gone. And the **coach** who spent most of a **lifetime** tilting at windmills would now, in his mid-70s, have trouble lifting a lance.

by Bob Leavitt

But the would-be hero of tiny Toluca became a champion on a much grander scale than he ever dreamed.

Dreams are what it has always been about for schoolboys. Chuck Rolinski became the father of the small-school state basketball tournament by finding a middle ground between dreams and reality.

Small-school players no longer awake to realize they have a snowball-in-a-sauna chance of making it to the state finals. Towns not large enough to dot some state maps now speckle the IHSA list of state champions.

Little David now has a last name other than Hebron.

Rolinski didn't set out to be Moses to the masses. He just wanted Toluca, a former coal-mining community of 1,400, to be able to see some light at the end of the state-tourney tunnel.

In 1967, Toluca (enrollment 125) had given eventual one-class state champion Pekin (enrollment 3,000) its closest Sweet Sixteen call in a 13-point super-sectional loss.

Five years later, Rolinski badgered a reluctant Illinois High School Association into a two-class playoff system. But in its 21 years of Class A existence, Toluca would never fly any higher than that one-class 1967 squad, losing small-school super-sectional games in 1973 to St. Anne and future NBA standout Jack Sikma and in 1984 to Hoopeston-East Lynn with Thad Matta, who went on to coach Ohio State University.

None of Chuck Rolinski's Toluca teams made it to the state finals, but his unrelenting push for classification opened the way for small schools to share the stage with their larger brethren.

Toluca still boasts more treasured Italian restaurants per resident than perhaps anywhere outside Italy. But Rolinski retired in 1990 with a record of 649-252. And two years later, the high school was shuttered in favor of Fieldcrest, a multi-community consolidation 10 miles down the road in Minonk.

The life-long Toluca resident still spearheads the Illinois Basketball Coaches Association, which he and former Quincy coach Sherill Hanks founded in 1971. But his real legacy is the hope held by every wide-eyed kid who presses his nose against the glass of trophy cases in towns such as Nauvoo, Findlay, Pleasant Plains, Mt. Pulaski, and Staunton.

where would the dilution of an historic state basketball tournament stop? Would there ever be an end to the erosion of glory and prestige accorded to true all-comers champions?

Indiana, one of the last one-class holdouts, didn't know where to stop, going to four classes and virtually destroying interest in the legendary tournament that had produced *Hoosiers*.

Many Illinois big schools took the view that going to two classes would not affect their programs. Some felt it should be left to the Davids to decide if they wanted to keep banging their heads against Goliaths.

Witness: Of the 183 (23 percent) principals who did not feel the need to return their ballots in the 1970 referendum, schools above the proposed cutoff of 750 showed the highest percentage of non-voters.

And late Galesburg coach John Thiel would have liked to strangle every one of them.

Thiel knew the end of the one-class state tournament could be more than a boon to small schools; it could be a boondoggle for big fish in small ponds.

Playing smaller schools, Galesburg had won 19 of 20 first-round post-season tourneys from 1920 to 1939 and 16 in a row from 1955 to 1970. But Galesburg teams have survived regional play in only 13 of the 35 Class AA tournaments from 1972 to 2006.

Meanwhile, Peoria Central, a school that had mostly gone against large-school squads in single-class regional play, put up a record run of 19 AA regional titles that finally ended in 2006.

continued on next page

ABOVE:
Galesburg's John Thiel was a vocal opponent of dividing schools into two classes.

LEFT and BELOW:
The 1952 Hebron team, shown beating Lawrenceville in the quarterfinals, was the small schools' only claim to fame ... until Lawrenceville emerged as the first Class A winner in 1972.

The end of the single-class system

The vote of IHSA member schools to adopt the two-class system for the 1972 boys state basketball tournament was 312-293, stamping the issue as the most controversial in IHSA history.

But it was never classical class warfare.

Most small schools wanted their own class. And most large schools were indifferent.

Indeed, it was left largely to the purists to argue for the status quo. And many of those resided in small school districts.

From such conservatives came perhaps the most chilling warning that once you had two classes,

With an enrollment of just 69 students, the 1986 Ohio team was the smallest school to compete in a state championship game.

"I remember a barber in Galesburg putting up a window sign asking people if they wanted two classes," Rolinski said. "The vote was 52-11 for classes. And we used that, telling people 'Who has more to lose than Galesburg?' "

A perfect plan

There were as many axes to grind as there were schools with enrollments falling in the middle third of IHSA membership.

"One of the keys to getting principals to vote for two classes was raising the enrollment cutoff from 500 to 750," Rolinski said. "That, and dropping the ideas of a playoff between A and AA champions and of allowing A schools to declare up whenever they wanted to."

The idea of denying the next Hebron its shot at the glass slipper died hard. But former East Peoria coach John Cruser put that proposal in perspective.

"If the small schools can declare up when they think they're going to be really slick," the late Cruser said, "I want to be able to declare down when I think we're going to really stink."

Certainly he would not have enjoyed exercising such an option these days, since sub-par teams don't last long in either class of state-tourney play.

"I heard a lot of Class A people say 'Bring on the big schools; we can play with them.' But that's just bar talk," Rolinski said.

"Although the line is now blurring — mostly because of the three-point shot and non-boundary small schools — it's still a different game: Small-school basketball is about team skill; big-school basketball is about individual kill."

While Harry Fitzhugh, IHSA's executive secretary, had to be dragged kicking and screaming into a two-class system, the

twin tourneys proposed by the Lithuanian coal miner's son became a gold mine of Class A ticket revenue.

"Fitzhugh and a big one-class guy from DuQuoin took me out for a steak dinner to talk me out of it, and we wound up screaming at each other right there in the restaurant," Rolinski recalled.

"I remember when WGN decided to stop telecasting state tournaments, they showed me an old memo from Harry. It read: 'Under no circumstances are you to interview Rolinski.'

"I never feared I would become known as the guy who killed a great high school basketball tournament," Rolinski said. "But in my wildest dreams I never thought it would all work out so well.

"John Thiel and I even became great friends . . . but only after he retired."

Trickle down

If folks ever wondered how much weight boys basketball carried in a state then without football playoffs, they needed only to look at how the IHSA's most wide-ranging issue was framed totally in terms of one sport.

But it didn't take a physicist to know almost all the one-class sports dominoes were lined up for the fall that would begin two years after two-class boys basketball was adopted.

If only by sheer weight of numbers, the two-class format's effect on other sports figured to be enormous — especially with the advent of interscholastic girls' athletics. And yet, potentially the strongest argument for a one-class system — individual competition — never seemed to weigh in.

While state success in team sports such as basketball can indeed be statistically linked to enrollment, such is not the case

> *"In my wildest dreams I never thought it would all work out so well."*
>
> — *Chuck Rolinski*

★ FINDLAY ★

Findlay was Illinois' smallest state champion, with an official total of just 96 students when the Falcons won the 1992 Class A title.

in more-individual sports such as golf, tennis, wrestling, and track and field (relay events notwithstanding).

In those sports, on a per-student basis, small schools garnered at least their statistical share of one-class post-season medals — if not team trophies. It is not at all rare to see a Class A track or field champ post a performance better than that of a Class AA counterpart.

Still, when it comes to individual sports as opposed to team competition, there always figure to be more Craig Virgins than Hebrons.

Look at me now

Virgin, long-distance star and favorite son of tiny Lebanon, would have stood out anywhere people could tell time. But without the small-school state basketball stage, how many folks would have caught the act of Jay Shidler, Lawrenceville's "Blond Bomber"?

"The only college that knew before the '73 state finals how good Jack Sikma could be was Wesleyan," Rolinski said of the seven-time NBA all-star. "After that, the bigs like Purdue were all over him, but he went with Wesleyan out of loyalty."

Who would know how serious they took their basketball in Mt. Pulaski, whose mighty midgets in the 1984 semifinals ran rings around Providence-St. Mel and future Mr. Basketball runner-up Lowell Hamilton, only to fall short in the title game against McLeansboro and that season's Mr. Basketball winner, Brian Sloan?

For that matter, would any small-school player ever have been voted Mr. Basketball without the exposure of the Class A finals — much less claim that honor in three of the award's first four years (1981-84)?

And who would have seen the Class A poll mocked by unranked Nauvoo-Colusa (enrollment 136) as it upended Nos. 4, 2, and 1 in 1998 Sweet Sixteen play?

Rather than dilute the quality of basketball in Illinois (as one-class proponents feared), the limelight of Class A state finals worked wonders on the skill level of small-school players. Not to mention helping college scouts discover diamonds in the dust of rural communities.

Even if it is no longer coal dust.

Findlay fans root on a once-in-a-lifetime Falcon team.

LAWRENCEVILLE
Class A State Champions of 1972

FRONT ROW (left to right): Jeff Richardson, Mgr. Bob Seber, Mark Moore. SECOND ROW: Tom Wolfe, Mike Lockhard, Walt Simmons, Bill Heidbreder, Jeff Chansler. THIRD ROW: Rick Leighty, Joe Leighty, Chuck McGaughlay, Tom Kirkwood, Mike Miller.

Twenty years after tiny Hebron captivated Illinois basketball fans, another small school earned statewide glory. This wasn't quite the Cinderella story, though, as Lawrenceville won the first Class A state championship with the largest enrollment (630 students) in the Elite Eight.

If Lawrenceville didn't exactly embody the rationale behind splitting to two classes, tiny Thomson did. Blessed with just 150 students, Thomson posted a state record for points in a season (3,006) that still stands.

And that's probably all Thomson could have accomplished if Chuck Rolinski of Toluca High School and others had not fought for two classes. Prior to 1972, Thomson had never advanced past the district level. But as a reflection of the newfound opportunities for schools with fewer than 750 students, coach Stan McCrudden's run-and-gun squad finished fourth.

Even so, the big story was Lawrenceville, which started the season 5-6 and would have ranked behind several Elite Eight qualifiers had there been an Associated Press Class A poll in 1972. Most figured Mounds Meridian — the last team to beat Class AA powerhouse Dolton Thornridge — was a heavy favorite.

But Lawrenceville, led by 6-foot-3 forward Rick Leighty, won the first of four state titles under coach Ron Felling, who said of his team, "We had a fine small-school team. The kind of team that never gets out of the one-class sectional."

Though just a sophomore, Leighty played a huge role in each of Lawrenceville's first two wins. First came a 17-point performance against Quincy Catholic Boys in the quarterfinals, a game the Indians won 57-56 thanks partly to 11-for-11 free throw shooting by reserve Tom Wolfe. Leighty's encore was even better. He racked up 31 points and 17 rebounds in a 75-68 semifinal win over Raymond Lincolnwood.

Then it was on to the historic first Class A title game, an all-south match-up against Meridian before a crowd of 11,554 at the University of Illinois' Assembly Hall.

Meridian (30-2) was determined to stop Leighty and succeeded, holding him to nine points. But Lawrenceville (25-8) benefited from the best game of senior guard Mike Lockhard's career. While his teammates struggled, Lockhard exploded for 32 points on 15-for-28 shooting to fuel a 63-57 victory.

Lockhard was particularly tenacious in the fourth quarter, during one stretch tallying 10 of his team's 12 points, including the game-winning basket that put Lawrenceville up 59-52. The only other basket during that stretch came on a jumper by Joe Leighty off a feed from Lockhard, who had averaged just 10.2 points per game.

"I guess they should give him a saliva test after tonight," Felling said.

That showdown of southern Illinois powers was a sign of things to come. In the ensuing 23 seasons, teams from the Charleston and Carbondale super-sectionals won 15 more state titles.

State Final Tournament Scores
Super-Sectionals
At Carbondale [SIU]—Mounds (Meridian) 56, DuQuoin 55
At DeKalb [NIU]—Elgin (St. Edward) 56, Shabbona 54 (OT)
At Pontiac—Streator (Woodland) 52, Palos Heights (Chicago Christian) 51 (OT)
At East Moline (United)—Thomson 84, Farmington (East) 73
At Decatur [Millikin]—Raymond (Lincolnwood) 83, Chrisman 78
At Normal [ISU]—Gibson City 69, Normal (University) 61
At Charleston [EIU]—Lawrenceville 71, Lovejoy 63
At Macomb [WIU]—Quincy (Catholic Boys) 78, Piasa (Southwestern) 66
Quarterfinals
Mounds (Meridian) 54, Elgin (St. Edward) 52
Thomson 72, Streator (Woodland) 56
Raymond (Lincolnwood) 68, Gibson City 66
Lawrenceville 57, Quincy (Catholic Boys) 56
Semifinals
Mounds (Meridian) 81, Thomson 74
Lawrenceville 75, Raymond (Lincolnwood) 68
Finals
Raymond (Lincolnwood) 90, Thomson 69 (third place)
Lawrenceville 63, Mounds (Meridian) 57 (title)

Scoring Leaders
Player, School	G	FG	FT	Pts
Don Robinson, Thomson	4	46	31	123
Dave Hobson, Raymond (Lincolnwood)	4	32	43	107
Mike Lockhard, Lawrenceville	4	37	8	82
Rick Leighty, Lawrenceville	4	25	15	65
Calvin Johnson, Mounds (Meridian)	4	24	12	60

All-Tournament First Team
Player, School	Ht.	Yr.
Dennis Graff, Gibson City	6-1	Sr.
Dave Hobson, Raymond (Lincolnwood)	6-3	Sr.
Calvin Johnson, Mounds (Meridian)	5-10	Sr.
Joe Leighty, Lawrenceville	6-4	Sr.
Dan Pieper, Quincy (Catholic Boys)	6-6	Sr.
Don Robinson, Thomson	6-0	Sr.

Championship Game Box Score
Assembly Hall, Champaign, March 11, 1972

LAWRENCEVILLE (63)
Coach Ron Felling
Player	FG-A	FT-A	Pts	PF	Rb	As	St Bl
Bill Heidbreder	2-8	2-3	6	0	2	7	
Tom Kirkwood	0-2	0-0	0	2	0	0	
Joe Leighty	2-8	2-3	6	4	4	1	
Rick Leighty	3-12	3-5	9	3	11	3	
Mike Lockhard	15-28	2-2	32	1	4	1	
Mike Miller	4-5	1-2	9	1	7	1	
Walt Simmons	0-0	0-0	0	0	0	0	
Tom Wolfe	0-1	1-2	1	5	5	0	
TEAM					10		
TOTAL	26-64	11-17	63	16	43	13	

MOUNDS (MERIDIAN) (57)
Coach Jim Byassee
Player	FG-A	FT-A	Pts	PF	Rb	As	St Bl
Curtis Bogan	4-4	6-11	14	3	10	0	
Craig Fitzgerald	2-7	2-3	6	4	9	0	
Tally Hawkins	6-10	0-3	12	3	7	4	
Jackie Howard	4-15	2-4	10	2	4	2	
Darrell Hudson	0-1	0-0	0	1	0	0	
Calvin Johnson	7-16	1-2	15	3	2	5	
Jerry Meeks	0-0	0-0	0	1	1	0	
TEAM					10		
TOTAL	23-53	11-23	57	17	43	11	

Lawrenceville	16	15	12	20	—	63
Mounds (Meridian)	15	14	10	18	—	57

Officials: Paul Brooks, Kenneth Rodermel.

SEEN AT STATE

100 YEARS OF MADNESS

100 YEARS OF MADNESS

RIDGWAY, Class A State Champions of 1973

FRONT ROW (left to right): Mike Fromm, Brent Browning, Dennis Pearce, Mike Dixon, Danny Stevens. SECOND ROW: Coach Bob Dallas, John Cross, Tony Cox, Jeff Drone, Jim Doyle, Don Wathen, Martin Duffy, Asst. Coach John Schmitt.

1973A

After one game, fans in the self-professed "Popcorn Capital of the World" were not prone to ponder a state championship. Not after Ridgway lost its season opener to Enfield, 74-69.

Hopefully nobody complained much to Coach Bob Dallas. Because over the next few months his Eagles won 32 straight, including a 54-41 decision in the title game against Maple Park Kaneland.

"I knew we had a good basketball team," Dallas said. "But when we lost our opening game to Enfield back on Nov. 1, I didn't think I'd be here with a state champion."

And yet he was, despite not boasting a player over 6-foot-3. Unranked Ridgway (32-1) made up for its lack of height with leading scorer Brent Browning (30.7 points per game in the tournament) and a strong supporting cast. That was evident in the title game, which featured Ridgway as one of the Elite Eight's smallest schools against the largest, Kaneland.

Ridgway jumped to a 34-24 halftime lead behind Browning's 18 points. The 6-2 guard did not score again, but the Eagles won anyway. Up 48-43 midway through the fourth quarter, Ridgway guard Danny Stevens scored his team's final six points — and his only six points.

Had the championship gone to overtime, the favorite would have been Kaneland (20-12), which had survived a six-overtime sectional against Elgin St. Edward.

MARCH 16-17 1973

Ridgway's quarterfinal win over Petersburg PORTA also produced an impressive performance, as Kevin Washington's 27 rebounds for the Bluejays still stands as a state record in tournament play. Browning made sure that wasn't enough to slow Ridgway, lighting up PORTA for 45 points.

This tournament was also the prep finale for St. Anne's Jack Sikma, who had a distinguished NBA career with the Seattle SuperSonics. Sikma settled for fourth despite an eye-popping 36-point, 24-rebound performance against Cerro Gordo in the quarterfinals.

The 6-8 Sikma had grown three inches from the previous season. "Nobody told us he was that tough," Cerro Gordo coach Jack Blickensderfer said after a quarterfinal loss to St. Anne. "We underestimated him from the scouting reports."

And in a touch of poetic justice, this Sweet Sixteen included Toluca and coach Chuck Rolinski, father of the two-class system. Toluca's postseason run was ended by St. Anne in the supersectionals.

Toluca was one of several teams ranked by Associated Press voters that was upset prior to the Elite Eight, the start of a trend in polling inaccuracy that would be repeated time and again.

Crowds at the tournament were up from the previous year, with 12,712 watching the final and 51,553 counted at all sessions.

State Final Tournament Scores

Super-Sectionals

At Decatur [Millikin]—Cerro Gordo 59, Morrisonville 49
At Pontiac—St. Anne 81, Toluca 62
At Carbondale [SIU]—Ridgway 57, Pinckneyville 56
At Macomb [WIU]—Petersburg (PORTA) 77, Mendon (Unity) 72
At DeKalb [NIU]—Maple Park (Kaneland) 37, Ottawa (Marquette) 35
At Rock Island—Fulton 38, Bushnell (B.-Prairie City) 37
At Normal [ISU]—Bloomington (Central Catholic) 68, Danville (Schlarman) 58
At Charleston [EIU]—Venice 71, Marshall 66

Quarterfinals

St. Anne 88, Cerro Gordo 70
Ridgway 85, Petersburg (PORTA) 79
Maple Park (Kaneland) 42, Fulton 35
Venice 55, Bloomington (Central Catholic) 53

Semifinals

Ridgway 73, St. Anne 51
Maple Park (Kaneland) 46, Venice 34

Finals

Venice 73, St. Anne 66 (third place)
Ridgway 54, Maple Park (Kaneland) 51 (title)

Scoring Leaders

Player, School	G	FG	FT	Pts
Brent Browning, Ridgway	4	45	15	105
Jack Sikma, St. Anne	4	43	14	100
Ron Henry, Venice	4	37	9	83
Mike Dixon, Ridgway	4	34	14	82
Steve Lynch, Maple Park (Kaneland)	4	33	13	79

All-Tournament First Team

Player, School	Ht.	Yr.
Brent Browning, Ridgway	6-2	Sr.
Mike Dixon, Ridgway	6-2	Sr.
Ron Henry, Venice	6-5	Jr.
Steve Lynch, Maple Park (Kaneland)	6-6	Sr.
Jack Sikma, St. Anne	6-8	Sr.
Danny Stevens, Ridgway	5-9	Jr.
Kevin Washington, Petersburg (PORTA)	6-4	Sr.

Championship Game Box Score

Assembly Hall, Champaign, March 17, 1973

RIDGWAY (54)
Coach Bob Dallas

Player	FG-A	FT-A	Pts	PF	Rb	As	St	Bl
Brent Browning	9-15	0-2	18	3	4	2		
Mike Dixon	10-19	0-0	20	0	7	1		
Jeff Drone	1-4	0-0	2	1	0	0		
Mike Fromm	1-1	0-0	2	4	0	0		
Dennis Pearce	3-8	0-1	6	4	9	0		
Danny Stevens	2-6	2-6	6	1	3	0		
TOTAL	26-53	2-6	54	13	23	3		

MAPLE PARK (KANELAND) (51)
Coach George Birket

Player	FG-A	FT-A	Pts	PF	Rb	As	St	Bl
Ron Ackerman	0-2	0-0	0	1	3	0		
Paul Johnson	1-2	0-0	2	1	1	0		
Kirk Kresse	1-5	2-2	4	1	8	1		
Steve Lynch	12-20	3-4	27	5	6	0		
Kevin Peterson	2-6	0-0	4	1	2	1		
Bill Sambrookes	4-15	6-7	14	3	14	0		
TOTAL	20-50	11-13	51	12	34	2		

Ridgway	16	18	12	8	—	54
Maple Park (Kaneland)	8	16	13	14	—	51

Officials: Paul Brooks, Donald Frits.

Celebrating 100 years of IHSA Boys Basketball

RISING TO THE OCCASION

Announcer Tom Stocker needs a boost to visit with 6-foot-8 Jack Sikma of St. Anne during the 1973 state finals.

John Lenagan of Bloomington Central Catholic penetrates the Venice defense in a quarterfinal tilt.

Bill Sambrookes of Kaneland has his hands full in the 1973 semifinals as a pair of Venice defenders move in.

1973A

1974A

LAWRENCEVILLE, *Class A State Champions of 1974*

FRONT ROW (left to right): Mgr. Mike Klein, Asst. Coach Jim Reedy, Coach Ron Felling, Asst. Coach Ken Trickett, Mgr. Wayne Pickering. SECOND ROW: Dave Hesher, Mark Joiner, Bill Heidbreder, Joe Cooper. THIRD ROW: Mike Argo, Jay Shidler, Roger Kull, Mike Myers. FOURTH ROW: Stan Dickerson, Rick Leighty, Brent Pace, Tom Wolfe.

Lawrenceville won a second title in three years thanks to a Leighty and at least two lucky bounces.

As he had two years earlier, Rick Leighty stepped up when his team needed him most. A senior who was all-tournament during Lawrenceville's first title run, Leighty was honored again after scoring 24 points and grabbing 11 rebounds in a 54-53 championship win over Ottawa Marquette.

"No one plays with the intensity of Rick," Lawrenceville coach Ron Felling said. "If he gets hurt, we'll have to roll him out in a wheelchair. We'll go as far as he'll take us."

Of Leighty's 18 second-half points, the most significant came on a pair of free throws with 3:06 left that gave Lawrenceville (30-3) a three-point lead. Following a turnover, Marquette's Nick Tabor cut the lead to one with a hoop from the corner. But after a missed free throw, a jump ball and a turnover, a long shot by Marquette's all-state guard Marty Brown skipped across the rim.

"Is there really a champion in a game like this ... except on paper?" asked Marquette coach Bob Strickland, whose 29-3 team was bidding to become the first private school to win a state basketball championship.

Prior to the thrilling finale played before a Class A record crowd of 14,552, both title contenders had to battle through grueling quarterfinals.

In Marquette's 50-47 quarterfinal win over defending champion Ridgway, 6-foot-5 senior Brown broke a 47-47 tie on a lay-up with 16 seconds remaining.

Every bit as exciting was Lawrenceville's come-from-behind quarterfinal win over Cerro Gordo, which finished the regular season ranked second — one spot ahead of the Indians. Cerro Gordo nearly made that ranking hold up.

The Broncos led 38-28 at halftime and appeared poised for victory when Homer O'Field's last-second shot spun around the rim. Instead of breaking a 62-62 tie, the ball bounced straight up, rattled around the rim again and then fell off. "I've seen a hundred shots like that go in," Cerro Gordo coach Jack Blickensderfer said.

Lawrenceville got new life and lots of Leighty, who scored 18 of his 32 points after intermission, including a long field goal to send the game into a second overtime. In that second extra period, Lawrenceville guard Bill Heidbreder, also a starter in 1972, had seven of his team's 11 points.

After the tournament, Lawrenceville retired Leighty's No. 34.

"I was not originally in favor of a Class A system and a Class A tournament," Felling said. "I thought it would dilute basketball in the state. But it has become successful. And the teams who win the tournament are just as happy as if they'd won the NCAA championship."

State Final Tournament Scores

Super-Sectionals

At Decatur [Millikin]—Cerro Gordo 75, Strasburg (Stewardson-S.) 67
At Charleston [EIU]—Lawrenceville 63, Venice 57
At Normal [ISU]—Lexington 64, Watseka 63
At Streator (Twp.)—Palos Heights (Chicago Christian) 49, Spring Valley (Hall) 40
At Macomb [WIU]—Quincy (Catholic Boys) 70, Franklin 66
At Moline—Prophetstown 77, Monmouth 60
At DeKalb [NIU]—Ottawa (Marquette) 78, South Beloit 39
At Carbondale [SIU]—Ridgway 79, Ullin (Century) 49

Quarterfinals

Lawrenceville 77, Cerro Gordo 72 (2 OT)
Palos Heights (Chicago Christian) 60, Lexington 57 (OT)
Quincy (Catholic Boys) 55, Prophetstown 44
Ottawa (Marquette) 50, Ridgway 47

Semifinals

Lawrenceville 56, Palos Heights (Chicago Christian) 43
Ottawa (Marquette) 65, Quincy (Catholic Boys) 52

Finals

Palos Heights (Chicago Christian) 71, Quincy (Catholic Boys) 62 (third place)
Lawrenceville 54, Ottawa (Marquette) 53 (title)

Scoring Leaders

Player, School	G	FG	FT	Pts
Rick Leighty, Lawrenceville	4	43	13	99
Bob Klaas, Palos Heights (Chi. Christian)	4	31	12	74
Marty Brown, Ottawa (Marquette)	4	31	8	70
Keith Renkosik, Ottawa (Marquette)	4	29	8	66
Chris Curran, Quincy (Catholic Boys)	4	26	12	64

All-Tournament First Team

Player, School	Ht.	Yr.
Marty Brown, Ottawa (Marquette)	6-5	Sr.
Chris Curran, Quincy (Catholic Boys)	6-2	Sr.
Bill Heidbreder, Lawrenceville	5-9	Sr.
Bob Klaas, Palos Heights (Chicago Christian)	6-8	Jr.
Rick Leighty, Lawrenceville	6-2	Sr.
Mark Mull, Cerro Gordo	6-3	Sr.
Jay Shidler, Lawrenceville	6-1	So.

Championship Game Box Score

Assembly Hall, Champaign, March 16, 1974

LAWRENCEVILLE (54)
Coach Ron Felling

Player	FG-A	FT-A	Pts	PF	Rb	As	St	Bl
Stanley Dickerson	1-2	0-0	2	1	6	1		
Bill Heidbreder	5-8	0-1	10	2	3	9		
Roger Kull	0-2	0-0	0	1	1	1		
Rick Leighty	10-19	4-6	24	4	11	1		
Jay Shidler	6-13	2-2	14	4	4	1		
Tim Wolfe	2-6	0-0	4	4	3	2		
TEAM					3			
TOTAL	24-50	6-9	54	16	31	15		

OTTAWA (MARQUETTE) (53)
Coach Bob Strickland

Player	FG-A	FT-A	Pts	PF	Rb	As	St	Bl
Marty Brown	6-19	1-1	13	3	4	3		
Kim Conness	2-7	0-1	4	4	8	4		
Keith Renkosik	10-17	3-9	23	2	11	1		
Jim Schaibley	0-3	0-0	0	2	8	0		
Nick Tabor	5-8	3-4	13	1	1	5		
TEAM					5			
TOTAL	23-54	7-15	53	12	37	13		

Lawrenceville	14	16	14	10	—	54
Ottawa (Marquette)	13	17	14	9	—	53

Officials: William Dickson, William England.

Jeff Wirth of Prophetstown succumbs to the
pressure defense of Quincy Catholic Boys in
a Friday quarterfinal.

ONE TICK TO GO

With the 1974 Class A state championship in the balance, Marty Brown
of Ottawa Marquette lets the ball fly. The shot missed and Lawrenceville
won its second title in three years. →

Lawrenceville Coach Ron Felling
instructs his team during a timeout
at Assembly Hall.

Cerro Gordo's Homer O'Field (left) and Lawrenceville's
Rick Leighty can't get a handle on the ball in a
double-overtime quarterfinal thriller.

1974A

Venice found the state tournament smooth sailing after a bumpy ride to Champaign.

Heart-stopping moments from Venice's season included an eight-over-time win (second-longest in state history) over Mascoutah in a mid-season tourna-ment and what many have called the most exciting shot in Charleston Super-Sectional history. That moment came courtesy of junior forward Reggie Gardner, who saved the Red Devils from sure defeat in a triple-overtime contest with Carmi.

Trailing 58-57 with six seconds remaining, Venice center Mike Henry rebounded a missed free throw and fired the ball to Gardner. As he dribbled across half-court, Gardner lost control of the ball along the sideline.

Amazingly, Gardner leaped to grab the ball before it went out of bounds, turned toward the rim and made a des-perate heave at the hoop an instant before the horn. His 35-foot shot caught noth-ing but net, sending the crowd of 5,000 into hysterics.

"I was just watching Reggie fumble the ball down the floor," Venice coach Rich Essington said. "Then I saw him throw the ball up and I thought, 'It's real-ly going in.' "

That allowed Venice to join Buda Western as one of just two members of the Associated Press' top 10 to reach the Elite Eight, as upsets were prevalent in the super-sectional round.

"It was a miracle getting here," said James Turner of Venice. "After the super, the pressure was off."

Certainly there was no pressure in the title game for second-ranked Venice (32-2, enrollment 170), which became the smallest champion since Hebron in 1952. The game was over by halftime as Venice shot to a 27-10 lead. Only a 22-point outburst in the fourth quarter by Elmhurst Timothy Christian (27-6) kept the final score of 65-46 respectable.

"We didn't belong on the floor with them," Timothy Christian coach Don Greenfield said.

Venice was hot everywhere, connect-ing on 51 percent of its shots and 19 of 21 free throws. Timothy Christian, which had won 23 of its last 24 games prior to the title contest, saw all-tournament standout Bruce VanderSchaaf finish 10 points below his 20 points-per-game season average.

Watseka rolled to third with a 74-65 win over Eldorado, getting 37 points from tournament scoring leader Lyndon Swanson.

Port Byron Riverdale provided the tournament lowlight in a 48-18 quarterfi-nal loss to Timothy Christian, scoring just six points in the second half. Riverdale's 18 points were the fewest scored in a state tournament game since Champaign lost to Herrin 21-17 in the 1940 semifinals.

VENICE
Class A State Champions of 1975

FRONT ROW (left to right): Clark Ray, Lance Austin. SECOND ROW: Jeff Corrie, Mike Logan, Mike Henry, James Crowder, James Turner, Reggie Gardner. THIRD ROW: Asst. Coach Clarence Hand, Venice Govan, Tim Walker, Algie Crawford, Larry Arnold, Ricky Salmond, Coach Rich Essington.

State Final Tournament Scores

Super-Sectionals
At Decatur [Millikin]—Morrisonville 64, Hume (Shiloh) 59
At Charleston [EIU]—Venice 59, Carmi 58 (3 OT)
At Streator (Twp.)—Buda (Western) 51, Lemont 46
At Normal [ISU]—Watseka 65, Normal (University) 59
At Carbondale [SIU]—Eldorado 58, Cairo 53
At Macomb [WIU]—Chatham (Glenwood) 54, Quincy (Catholic Boys) 51 (OT)
At East Moline (United)—Port Byron (Riverdale) 42, Bushnell (B.-Prairie City) 33
At DeKalb [NIU]—Elmhurst (Timothy Christian) 58, South Beloit 34

Quarterfinals
Venice 47, Morrisonville 41
Watseka 63, Buda (Western) 57
Eldorado 65, Chatham (Glenwood) 60
Elmhurst (Timothy Christian) 48, Port Byron (Riverdale) 18

Semifinals
Venice 57, Watseka 49
Elmhurst (Timothy Christian) 52, Eldorado 42

Finals
Watseka 74, Eldorado 65 (third place)
Venice 65, Elmhurst (Timothy Christian) 46 (title)

Scoring Leaders

Player, School	G	FG	FT	Pts
Lyndon Swanson, Watseka	4	38	19	95
Bruce Vander Schaaf, Elmhurst (Tim. Chr.)	4	29	16	74
Mike Duff, Eldorado	4	35	4	74
Reggie Gardner, Venice	4	27	9	63
Mike Henry, Venice	4	24	9	57

All-Tournament First Team

Player, School	Ht.	Yr.
Reggie Gardner, Venice	5-11	Jr.
Mike Henry, Venice	6-6	Sr.
Greg King, Eldorado	6-1	Sr.
Bob Sprowls, Buda (Western)	6-3	Sr.
Lyndon Swanson, Watseka	6-8	Sr.
Bruce Vander Schaaf, Elmhurst (Timothy Chr.)	6-4	Sr.

Championship Game Box Score

Assembly Hall, Champaign, March 15, 1975

VENICE (65)
Coach Rich Essington

Player	FG-A	FT-A	Pts	PF	Rb	As	St	Bl
Larry Arnold	0-0	0-0	0	0	1	0		
Jeff Corrie	3-10	0-0	6	2	3	9		
Algie Crawford	0-0	4-4	4	0	0	0		
James Crowder	4-8	3-4	11	3	5	3		
Reggie Gardner	4-6	5-5	13	0	8	2		
Mike Henry	6-11	0-0	12	1	3	2		
Mike Logan	0-0	2-2	2	0	0	0		
Ricky Salmond	0-0	0-0	0	0	0	0		
James Turner	6-10	5-6	17	1	6	4		
Tim Walker	0-0	0-0	0	0	0	0		
Bernie Woodrome	0-0	0-0	0	0	0	0		
TEAM					4			
TOTAL	23-45	19-21	65	7	30	20		

ELMHURST (TIMOTHY CHRISTIAN) (46)
Coach Don Greenfield

Player	FG-A	FT-A	Pts	PF	Rb	As	St	Bl
Tim Bolt	0-0	0-0	0	0	0	0		
Rich Buikema	1-1	0-0	2	0	0	0		
Jim Folgers	2-11	0-0	4	1	3	1		
Howard Hoff	4-10	0-0	8	3	6	9		
Tony Ratliff	6-10	2-2	14	4	6	0		
Doug Slinkman	0-0	0-0	0	0	0	0		
Randy Van Dahm	0-0	0-0	0	0	0	0		
Ted Vander Naald	0-0	0-0	0	0	0	0		
Bruce Vander Schaaf	5-17	0-0	10	4	7	1		
Bob Voss	0-0	0-0	0	0	0	0		
David Woldman	4-5	0-0	8	3	3	4		
Van Zeilstra	0-1	0-0	0	1	0	1		
TEAM					2			
TOTAL	22-55	2-2	46	16	27	16		

Venice	17	10	19	19	—	65
Elmhurst (Timothy Christian)	6	4	14	22	—	46

Officials: Stan Decker, Mel Klitzing.

Bruce Vander Schaaf of Timothy Christian applies pressure to a throw-in during the Trojans' 48-18 win over Port Byron Riverdale in the 1975 quarterfinals.

James Turner of Venice dribbles upcourt as Randy Van Dahm of Timothy Christian gives chase in the championship game. Turner finished with a game-high 17 points.

Venice celebrates its first Class A championship.

DEVILS' DELIGHT

Venice's Mike Henry outreaches Doug Stinkman of Timothy Christian to grab a title-game rebound.

1975A

MT. PULASKI, *Class A State Champions of 1976*

FRONT ROW (left to right): Bob Behle, Gary Helton, Danny Durchholz, Pat Przykopanski, Brad Gibbs, Scott Moore. SECOND ROW: Asst. Coach James Copper, Asst. Coach Joe Zimmerman, Gayle Cyrulik, David Welch, David Thompson, John Olson, Jeff Anderson, Jeff Clements, Coach Ed Butkovich.

"If you said Eldorado would beat us nine times in nine more games, you would probably be right."

Following his team's first upset of an unbeaten and heavily favored opponent, coach Ed Butkovich called it "a once-in-a-lifetime miracle."

Mt. Pulaski's resounding win over another unbeaten and favored squad in the semifinals dashed that idea. Maybe that's why Butkovich was almost at a loss for words after his Hilltoppers won the state title game. "In my wildest dreams I didn't foresee this," he said.

Neither did anyone else heading into the tournament, attended by a Class A record of 56,667. Mt. Pulaski (26-2) was most fans' fourth choice behind top-ranked Eldorado (31-0), No. 3 Buda Western (30-0) and traditional power No. 2 Lawrenceville (27-1) and its "Blond Bomber" Jay Shidler, who averaged 32.7 points per game.

Instead, the sweet-shooting Hilltoppers started their string of shockers with a 76-66 thumping of Eldorado in the quarterfinals. Super sophomore Jeff Clements triggered the win, scoring 35 points and sinking 13 of 20 shots.

"If you said Eldorado would beat us nine times in nine more games, you would probably be right," Butkovich said.

In the next upset, Mt. Pulaski bounced Buda. David Welch scored 20 points, David Thompson added 19 and Clements had 13 as the Hilltoppers shot 58 percent from the field. "They're all extremely fine shooters and not from just one position," Buda Western coach

Chips Giovanine said.

But Mt. Pulaski saved the best for last, nipping Oneida ROVA 59-58 in the final. Clements' baseline jumper with 42 seconds left marked his second postseason game-winner.

ROVA had two last chances at victory. Dave Johnson (28 points, 12 rebounds) missed one shot but ROVA then forced a 10-second violation. Dwight Peterson's long-range shot bounced harmlessly away, making Mt. Pulaski's first trip to state since 1936 a successful one.

So excited was Butkovich that for awhile he forgot who scored the game-winner. "I had to ask one of our players," he said.

ROVA reached the championship game by overcoming Lawrenceville and eventual Kentucky recruit Shidler, who had 48 points. That was one of three stunning performances by senior guard Shidler, who also dazzled the Assembly Hall crowds with games of 37 and 45 points. His 157 points (including 27 at the Charleston Super-Sectional) gave the "Golden Gunner" the single-tournament scoring record until 2001, when Pierre Pierce of Westmont eclipsed his mark with 159 points.

"This is Secretariat," coach Ron Felling said afterwards, his arm around Shidler. "I said I'd ride with Shide and I think I rode a pretty good stud up the line."

State Final Tournament Scores
Super-Sectionals
At Rock Island—Oneida (ROVA) 58, Port Byron (Riverdale) 52
At Normal [ISU]—Bloomington (Central Catholic) 58, Watseka 57
At DeKalb [NIU]—Aurora (Marmion Academy) 71, Winnebago 61
At Charleston [EIU]—Lawrenceville 59, Lebanon 50
At Macomb [WIU]—Havana 64, Pleasant Plains 59
At Pontiac—Buda (Western) 48, Palos Heights (Chicago Christian) 46
At Carbondale [SIU]—Eldorado 71, Cairo 56
At Decatur [Millikin]—Mt. Pulaski 67, Westville 65
Quarterfinals
Oneida (ROVA) 49, Bloomington (Central Catholic) 46
Lawrenceville 66, Aurora (Marmion Academy) 61
Buda (Western) 64, Havana 54
Mt. Pulaski 76, Eldorado 66
Semifinals
Oneida (ROVA) 77, Lawrenceville 70
Mt. Pulaski 74, Buda (Western) 56
Finals
Lawrenceville 65, Buda (Western) 57 (third place)
Mt. Pulaski 59, Oneida (ROVA) 58 (title)

Scoring Leaders

Player, School	G	FG	FT	Pts
Jay Shidler, Lawrenceville	4	63	31	157
Dave Johnson, Oneida (ROVA)	4	38	29	105
Jeff Clements, Mt. Pulaski	4	36	15	87
David Thompson, Mt. Pulaski	4	29	7	65
Ron Happach, Buda (Western)	4	25	11	61

All-Tournament First Team

Player, School	Ht.	Yr.
Jeff Clements, Mt. Pulaski	6-3	So.
Mike Duff, Eldorado	6-7	Jr.
Ron Happach, Buda (Western)	6-6	Sr.
Steve Holmes, Oneida (ROVA)	5-11	Sr.
Dave Johnson, Oneida (ROVA)	6-8	Sr.
Jay Shidler, Lawrenceville	6-1	Sr.

Championship Game Box Score
Assembly Hall, Champaign, March 13, 1976

MT. PULASKI (59)
Coach Ed Butkovich

Player	FG-A	FT-A	Pts	PF	Rb	As	St	Bl
Jeff Anderson	9-19	1-1	19	2	16	0		
Jeff Clements	9-21	0-0	18	0	4	2		
Brad Gibbs	2-6	0-0	4	0	5	4		
Scott Moore	1-4	0-0	2	1	1	0		
David Thompson	6-11	0-1	12	0	6	2		
Dave Welch	1-7	2-3	4	1	2	4		
TEAM					6			
TOTAL	28-68	3-6	59	4	40	12		

ONEIDA (ROVA) (58)
Coach Bob Meredith

Player	FG-A	FT-A	Pts	PF	Rb	As	St	Bl
John Bloss	0-2	0-0	0	1	2	0		
Randy Dooley	2-4	0-0	4	0	2	4		
Steve Holmes	0-2	0-0	0	3	2	1		
Dave Johnson	13-22	2-3	28	3	12	0		
Steve Johnson	3-3	0-0	6	1	0	0		
Dwight Peterson	4-7	0-0	8	1	4	11		
Roger Saline	6-11	0-0	12	3	2	8		
Mike Shepherd	0-1	0-0	0	1	0	0		
TEAM					4			
TOTAL	28-52	2-3	58	13	28	24		

Mt. Pulaski	14	20	11	14	—	59
Oneida (ROVA)	12	23	11	12	—	58

Officials: William England, Dave Dwyer.

1976A

TOPPERS 1976 STATE

Lawrenceville's Nathan Schnautz comes close to blocking the shot of Marmion's John Momper in a quarterfinal game.

SINGULAR SHOOTER

The lasting memory of the 1976 tournament was Lawrenceville's Jay Shidler sending a jump shot toward the basket. In three games at Assembly Hall, he tallied 37, 48, and 45 points and set a tournament scoring record.

Shidler maneuvers through traffic as Buda Western's Ron Nielsen and Dave Hartz close in. Lawrenceville won the semifinal 74-56.

ROVA's Dave Johnson goes in for two as Mt. Pulaski's Jeff Anderson defends. Johnson led all scorers in the championship game with 28.

1976A

Eldorado's Joel Clubreth struggles to control the ball after a collision with Mt. Pulaski's Brad Gibbs.

133

The Big House
Assembly Hall filled crowds with space-age awe

Affectionately dubbed "The Big House," *Champaign's* Assembly Hall was indeed *big*, bigger than any venue to host the IHSA boys' **state** basketball tournament.

Assembly Hall's unique architecture inspired photographers to give all their lenses a workout. In this shot, East Moline scores on a breakaway lay-up during the 1979 Class AA semifinal contest with Maine South.

by Pat Heston

With a seating capacity in excess of 16,000, the spacious saucer welcomed more than 2.9 million spectators during its 33-year, 57-tournament tenure.

Though lacking the old school charm and intimacy of its predecessor, Huff Gym, the magnificent mushroom was a superb home to the state finals. Gone were the obstructed views and the blinding afternoon sun that reflected off a polished hardwood floor. Assembly Hall offered a clear, panoramic view of the entire show, from the elevated playing surface to the artistically arched basket posts snapped in place at either end of the court.

The IHSA crowned the last single-class and first two-class champions at Assembly Hall. The last district team to reach the state finals (Cobden in 1964) and the first school to win three straight titles (East St. Louis Lincoln in 1987AA-88AA-89AA) played on its court. The Big House was big from the start.

Radio row was courtside and right in the action. Here, announcers from across the state provide a steady stream of commentary for fans not able to be part of the capacity crowd.

Celebrating 100 years of
IHSA Boys Basketball Tournaments

It had a classic christening in 1963 as a sell-out crowd of 16,310 witnessed a pair of down-to-the-wire semifinal skirmishes when top-ranked Centralia edged Springfield Lanphier 50-46 and unranked Chicago Carver escaped Peoria Central 40-37 in overtime. That night, in one of the greatest championship games ever played, Carver shocked Centralia 53-52 on reserve Anthony Smedley's desperation jump shot in the closing seconds.

It was an sign of things to come.

Some of the tournament's most fantastic game-ending scores occurred at Assembly Hall. Laird Smith, Vincent Jackson, Derrick Boyd, Ryan Bruns, and Kevin Jones all finished off timeless title games with near-the-buzzer baskets. Quincy's James Bailey nailed one from way out in the quarterfinals to stun prohibitive favorite Peoria Manual in 1987AA, Mike Hampton's historic shot in the 1982AA semifinals stopped Quincy's 64-game win streak, and Tim Huseman's close-in shot off a pair of dramatic passes gave Quincy the consolation title that same year.

After the 1963 championship game was in the books, other classics quickly followed. In the quarterfinals, Rock Island Alleman stunned Centralia 57-56 in overtime (1964), undefeated LaGrange Lyons nipped Effingham St. Anthony 89-88 (1970), and East Aurora outlasted Hinsdale Central 83-81 (1972AA). In the semifinals, Proviso East edged Champaign Central 37-36 (1969), Quincy raced past East Aurora 107-96 (1972AA), and Mt. Pulaski toppled Providence St. Mel 76-74 (1984A).

continued on page 137

The Assembly Hall catwalk and scoreboard loom over the court during a 1960s contest.

A production truck from WGN-TV in Chicago nestles under the edge of the saucer during an early tournament at Assembly Hall.

The sight of the Assembly Hall's mushroom dome rising above the prairie landscape made an indelible impression on every first-time visitor to the IHSA tournament.

In a trio of unforgettable finales, Chicago Mt. Carmel edged Springfield Lanphier 46-44 in double overtime (1985AA), East St. Louis Lincoln survived unbeaten Peoria Central 59-57 in three extra sessions (1989AA), and Trenton Wesclin also shot down previously perfect Prairie Central of Fairbury 83-78 in overtime (1990A).

Sixteen undefeated teams took the Assembly Hall floor for a championship game. Ten of them came out winners. Six of them did not. Two of them — Lawrenceville (33-0) and Flanagan (30-0) — went head-to-head in the 1983A finale. For three straight years (1982-84), and four times in five years (1982-86), a team with an unblemished record claimed the small school title.

Several of the consensus picks as the state's top teams in history strutted their stuff at Assembly Hall: Harvey Thornton in 1966, Evanston in 1968, LaGrange Lyons in 1970, Thornridge in 1972AA, Lockport Central in 1978AA, Quincy in 1981AA, Chicago King in 1990AA and 1993AA, and Proviso East in 1991AA and 1992AA.

So did top-drawer players such as Quinn Buckner, Joe Wiley, Isiah Thomas, Bruce Douglas, Marcus Liberty, LaPhonso Ellis, Jamie Brandon, and Sergio McClain. St. Anne's Jack Sikma scored 36 points, grabbed 24 rebounds and blocked 12 shots in a 1973A quarterfinal game. Lawrenceville's Jay Shidler scored 93 points in one day of the 1976AA tournament. Owen Brown of LaGrange Lyons netted 24 points and nabbed 24 rebounds in title game of 1970. Three years earlier, Springfield's Dave Robisch turned the finals on its ear, setting four-game records for both points (152) and rebounds (77).

From colossal upsets such as Maine South over Quincy in 1979AA to incredible coaching accomplishments such as Dolph Stanley taking his fifth different school to the state finals in 1971, whatever the event and whatever the era, Assembly Hall was always a site for the spectacular.

It may have been the only place in Illinois big enough to hold all the memories.

The view from the floor of Assembly Hall was just as impressive, and the endless sea of spectators could play tricks with a shooter's depth perception.

Just two years after Venice's state championship came Madison, located less than three miles away.

After two years of hearing about the experience from neighbors in Venice, Madison players finally got to enjoy their own state championship.

Riding hot shooting and help from an unheralded guard, Madison topped

unranked Aurora Central Catholic 71-55 in the championship.

The game was tied 26-all at halftime before Madison and Anthony King got hot. King scored nine of his 14 points in the third quarter as Madison made 12 of 16 shots to shred Central Catholic's zone-trap defense. The sixth-ranked Trojans shot 21-for-32 overall in the second half and got 18 points and 11 rebounds from Rodney Davis and 17 points from all-stater Randy Jones.

In addition to balanced scoring, Madison coach Larry Graham said his Trojans had powerful motivation.

"Venice winning the title in 1975 really helped us," Graham said. "Venice and our community are right next to one another and Venice has a sign at the edge of town that says 'Home of the 1975 State Basketball Champions.' That has been an incentive to our players."

Like that Venice team, Madison had close calls prior to the title game. In a 72-70 sectional win over unbeaten and second-ranked Lebanon, a last-second

shot by Lebanon's Harvey Thomas was disallowed even though many observers felt the shot beat the buzzer.

And Madison needed overtime in its 65-61 semifinal win over high-scoring Eldorado. The Eagles' Eddie Lane forced an extra period by knocking down two free throws in regulation. But those proved to be the last of Lane's 29 points and Eldorado could only watch as Madison, which finished 29-3, moved on behind Jones' 26 points.

Even more dramatic was the third-place game.

Trailing by 19 with 1:15 left in the third quarter, defending champion Mt. Pulaski staged a furious rally. With David Welch firing in from all over, the Hilltoppers fought to within one with 1:43 to play.

But 6-foot-7 all-stater Mike Duff (36 points, 19 rebounds) saved a stunned Eldorado squad by tipping in a missed free throw with 10 seconds left to clinch a 76-72 win.

That was revenge for Eldorado, which saw an undefeated season end at the hands of Mt. Pulaski in the 1976 quarter-finals.

Tragically, Duff died just months later when a plane carrying the University of Evansville basketball team crashed shortly after takeoff.

MADISON
Class A State Champions of 1977

FRONT ROW (left to right): Mgr. John Lake, Mgr. Rodney Williams, Mgr. Chris Branch. SECOND ROW: Asst. Coach Dave Hodges, Sylvester Collins, James Heard, Anthony King, Ken Stanley, Clayton Harris, Lloyd Williams, Randall James, DeRodney Davis, Eric Stanley, Lawerence London, Ken Boyd, Rodney Crochrell, Ron Williams, Coach Larry Graham.

State Final Tournament Scores
Super-Sectionals
At DeKalb [NIU]—Aurora (Central Catholic) 48, Maple Park (Kaneland) 42
At Streator (Twp.)—Roanoke (R.-Benson) 69, Palos Heights (Chicago Christian) 53
At Decatur [Millikin]—Mt. Pulaski 86, Monticello 59
At Normal [ISU]—Crescent City (Crescent-Iroquois) 42, Normal (University) 33
At Carbondale [SIU]—Eldorado 75, Marissa 68
At Macomb [WIU]—Pleasant Plains 71, Hamilton 60
At Charleston [EIU]—Madison 72, Robinson 48
At Moline—Morrison 54, Aledo 53
Quarterfinals
Aurora (Central Catholic) 68, Roanoke (R.-Benson) 59
Mt. Pulaski 72, Crescent City (Crescent-Iroquois) 50
Eldorado 73, Pleasant Plains 57
Madison 65, Morrison 49
Semifinals
Aurora (Central Catholic) 77, Mt. Pulaski 61
Madison 65, Eldorado 61 (OT)
Finals
Eldorado 76, Mt. Pulaski 72 (third place)
Madison 71, Aurora (Central Catholic) 55 (title)

Scoring Leaders

Player, School	G	FG	FT	Pts
Mike Duff, Eldorado	4	56	19	131
Eddie Lane, Eldorado	4	37	18	92
Randall Jones, Madison	4	41	8	90
Dave Welch, Mt. Pulaski	4	29	17	75
Jeff Clements, Mt. Pulaski	4	29	8	66

All-Tournament First Team

Player, School	Ht.	Yr.
Jeff Clements, Mt. Pulaski	6-3	Jr.
Mike Duff, Eldorado	6-7	Sr.
Randall Jones, Madison	6-5	Sr.
Eddie Lane, Eldorado	6-4	Jr.
Jack Sickles, Aurora (Central Catholic)	6-2	Sr.
Dave Welch, Mt. Pulaski	6-1	Sr.

Championship Game Box Score
Assembly Hall, Champaign, March 12, 1977
MADISON (71)
Coach Larry Graham

Player	FG-A	FT-A	Pts	PF	Rb	As	St	Bl
DeRodney Crochrell	0-0	0-0	0	0	0	0		
Rodney Davis	8-17	2-2	18	3	11	0		1
Clayton Harris	4-5	0-0	8	1	2	0		
James Heard	1-4	0-0	2	2	3	2		
Randall Jones	7-11	3-4	17	1	9	3		
Anthony King	7-14	0-0	14	3	7	6		
Anthony London	0-0	0-0	0	0	0	1		
Ron Morris	2-4	0-1	4	1	1	1		
Lloyd Williams	1-1	0-0	2	1	1	0		
Ron Williams	3-8	0-0	6	3	3	2		
TEAM					4			
TOTAL	33-64	5-7	71	15	41	16		

AURORA (CENTRAL CATHOLIC) (55)
Coach Richard Fick

Player	FG-A	FT-A	Pts	PF	Rb	As	St	Bl
Ray Bohr	0-0	0-0	0	0	0	0		
Randy Fichtel	2-8	5-7	9	1	2	2		
Joe Hartlaub	3-7	0-0	6	3	0	1		
Tom Kleckner	7-12	3-5	17	2	1	3		
Paul Perez	0-0	0-0	0	0	0	0		
Greg Peters	2-3	4-6	8	1	5	0		
Jack Sickles	4-10	0-0	8	1	2	6		
Jeff Stranckmeyer	3-7	1-2	7	4	8	0		
TEAM					7			
TOTAL	21-47	13-20	55	12	25	12		

Madison	8	18	24	21	—	71
Aurora (Central Catholic)	11	15	12	17	—	55

Officials: Wayne Bigham, Ken Hungate.

1977 A

Madison's Ron Williams avoids Tom Klechner (10) and
Randy Fichtel (24) of Aurora Central Catholic in the championship contest.

Madison players raise the IHSA trophy after winning the school's first state title. ➡

Clayton Harris unleashes a shot as time winds down in overtime against Eldorado.
Madison went on to capture a 65-61 victory and advance to the championship game.

1977A

Eldorado's Mike
Duff lays in two
points against
Pleasant Plains.
Duff held the
tournament career
scoring record
(252 points) until
it was broken by
King's Jamie
Brandon in 1990.

⬅

SCORING MACHINE

139

1978A

Nashville's "comeback kids" gave their fans plenty of thrills in 1978.

None was bigger than a 54-38 victory over Havana for the state championship. After trailing by six early in the game, second-ranked, 29-3 Nashville rallied for a convincing win. Nashville outrebounded Havana 28-17, behind 6-foot-6 twin towers John Jankowski and all-stater Roger Stieg, a junior who coach Bob Bogle once called "the franchise."

That early deficit against Havana was the least of the scares defensive-minded Nashville survived in the postseason.

First came a 12-point deficit against Cairo in the sectional final, then an eight-point margin against Metropolis in the Carbondale Super-Sectional. New Lenox Providence became the next victim when it was unable to hold a 14-point lead in the semifinals.

"We weren't used to coming from behind during the season but it seems like it was that way every time during the tournament," Bogle said. "Again, it all goes back to confidence."

The source of Nashville's confidence was its impressive defense and accurate shooting. It was no coincidence the top scorer in the tournament was Nashville's Paul Patton, with 73 points. After all, he didn't have to contend with the Hornets' pesky defense.

Consider that sharp-shooting Havana, which entered the title game 29-3 and averaging 56 percent shooting, burned Effingham St. Anthony for 63 percent in the semifinals. Tired after playing its fourth game in three days because its super-sectional was delayed by a blizzard, Havana found the hoop only 41 percent of the time against Nashville.

"I thought somebody had to play super to beat us here and that's what they did," Havana coach Bob Gregurich said. "They actually beat us at our own game. They do the things we like to do, only they did them better."

The same problem dogged Providence and 6-7 freshman center Walter Downing, who ended up third in the tournament with a 17.3 scoring average. Pitted against Nashville in the semifinals, Downing & Co. jumped to a 34-20 lead in the first half, looking nothing like the team of youngsters who'd started the season 6-5. Providence finished with a 22-9 record.

Yet Nashville steadily worked its way back into the game, and Stieg tallied seven of his team-high 24 points in the final eight minutes to help deliver the 55-52 win.

Providence shot just 40 percent in the final two quarters after hitting 61 percent in the first two.

State Final Tournament Scores
Super-Sectionals
At Charleston [EIU]—Effingham (St. Anthony) 76, Lebanon 69 (OT)
At East Moline (United)—Dakota 58, Bushnell (B.-Prairie City) 34
At Macomb [WIU]—Havana 59, Piasa (Southwestern) 47
At Decatur [Millikin]—Sullivan 69, Mt. Pulaski 59
At DeKalb [NIU]—New Lenox (Providence) 51, Marengo 47
At Pontiac—Ottawa (Marquette) 69, Chicago (Providence-St. Mel) 68
At Normal [ISU]—Mason City 60, Hoopeston (H.-East Lynn) 56
At Carbondale [SIU]—Nashville 67, Metropolis 55

Quarterfinals
Effingham (St. Anthony) 59, Dakota 57
Havana 72, Sullivan 49
New Lenox (Providence) 63, Ottawa (Marquette) 56
Nashville 69, Mason City 56

Semifinals
Havana 69, Effingham (St. Anthony) 56
Nashville 55, New Lenox (Providence) 52

Finals
New Lenox (Providence) 52, Effingham (St. Anthony) 47 (third place)
Nashville 54, Havana 38 (title)

Scoring Leaders

Player, School	G	FG	FT	Pts
Paul Patton, Nashville	4	35	3	73
Tracey Trimpe, Havana	4	26	20	72
Walter Downing, New Lenox (Providence)	4	28	13	69
Tom Grunloh, Effingham (St. Anthony)	4	28	11	67
Roger Stieg, Nashville	4	26	14	66

All-Tournament First Team

Player, School	Ht.	Yr.
Walter Downing, New Lenox (Providence)	6-8	Fr.
Tom Grunloh, Effingham (St. Anthony)	6-7	Sr.
Barney Mines, New Lenox (Providence)	6-2	Jr.
Paul Patton, Nashville	6-2	Sr.
Allen Rayhorn, Dakota	6-6	Sr.
Roger Stieg, Nashville	6-8	Jr.
Tracey Trimpe, Havana	6-4	Jr.

Championship Game Box Score
Assembly Hall, Champaign, March 11, 1978

NASHVILLE (54)
Coach Bob Bogle

Player	FG-A	FT-A	Pts	PF	Rb	As	St	Bl
MIke Borowiak	2-2	0-0	4	0	6	6		
Richard Deering	0-0	0-0	0	0	0	0		
John Jankowski	6-15	0-0	12	3	12	1		
Keith Maschoff	0-0	0-0	0	2	0	1		
Barry Morris	3-6	1-2	7	2	3	3		
Paul Patton	9-14	0-0	18	2	3	0		
Randy Ruggles	0-0	0-0	0	0	0	0		
Roger Stieg	5-9	3-3	13	3	2	4		
TEAM					2			
TOTAL	25-46	4-5	54	12	28	15		

HAVANA (38)
Coach Bob Gregurich

Player	FG-A	FT-A	Pts	PF	Rb	As	St	Bl
Derek Dierker	0-0	0-0	0	0	0	0		
Brad Gregurich	4-12	4-4	12	3	2	4		
Doug Hurst	2-4	0-0	4	1	6	0		
Roger King	3-5	0-0	6	1	4	0		
Mitch McNeil	0-0	0-0	0	0	0	0		
Kim Miller	0-0	0-1	0	0	0	0		
Terry Miller	0-0	0-0	0	0	0	0		
Dennis Morgan	0-0	0-0	0	0	0	0		
Jeff Myland	0-2	0-0	0	2	0	0		
Marc Radosevic	0-0	2-4	2	2	0	1		
Rick Sarff	0-0	0-0	0	0	0	0		
Tracey Trimpe	5-11	4-4	14	0	3	3		
TEAM					2			
TOTAL	14-34	10-13	38	9	17	8		

Nashville	8	14	12	20	—	54
Havana	12	4	12	10	—	38

Officials: Dave Dwyer, Richard Thompson.

Nashville players hoist the Class A championship trophy after their 54-38 win over Havana.

Roger Stieg and John Jankowski, a pair of 6-foot-6 juniors, posed a formidable obstacle to Nashville's opponents.

Havana's Tracey Trimpe leaps to defend against Nashville's Mike Borowiak in the title game.

DOUBLE TROUBLE

Walter Downing of Providence pivots toward the basket in a quarterfinal match-up against Ottawa Marquette.

1978A

141

NEW LENOX (PROVIDENCE), Class A State Champions of 1979

FRONT ROW (left to right): Mgr. Eddie Blackmon, Hank Shelton, Paul Druhan, Ed Loughran, Jim Robinson. SECOND ROW: Asst. Coach Jack McCarthy, Mgr. Tom Grotowsky, Trennis Curry, Tom Carruthers, Steve Cherveny, Walter Downing, Chuck Thomas, Tony Frye, Barney Mines, Coach Frank Palmasani.

CLASS A

1979A

After seven seasons of southern domination, a team north of Champaign finally left a Class A tournament as champion.

And finally, after seven years of top-ranked teams tumbling before even reaching the title game, New Lenox Providence lived up to its No. 1 ranking in the final regular season poll.

That Providence (32-1) succeeded surprised nobody who had seen 6-foot-8 sophomore Walter Downing and his teammates give eventual champ Nashville all it could handle in the semifinals one year earlier.

This time around, Providence never stumbled, riding a 30-game win streak to a state championship. The capper came as Providence handled undefeated and third-ranked Havana 46-33.

Frustrated Havana found itself down 14-2 at the end of the first quarter and never recovered. With the win, Providence became the first private school to earn a state basketball title.

"Nothing up to this point was important. We've been winning all year, but everything has been pointing to this," said Providence coach Frank Palmasani, whose lone loss on the year was to Class AA New Lenox Lincoln-Way. "I can't remember ever celebrating a win before now."

And Downing (21 points on 10-of-13 shooting, seven rebounds, four blocks)

proved to be too much for the Ducks despite the best effort of Brad Gregurich, the coach's son, who had 20 of his team's 33 points.

"Downing intimidated us," Havana coach Bob Gregurich said. "He just intimidated us."

Palmasani agreed, adding that Downing was "great offensively, but his major strength is defense. He's devastating on defense. They couldn't get anything inside off Downing, so they had to go outside."

Providence's record was 2-22 just two years earlier. "When we were going 2-22, I got down on my knees every day and said, 'Next year we get Walter Downing,'" Palmasani said. Adding Downing's inside game to Barney Mines, a top shooting guard who later starred at Bradley, left Palmasani with the core of a state champion.

Havana's output equalled the fewest points scored by a team in a state championship game since Elgin also had 33 in 1944. Offense was lacking all Saturday as Elmhurst Timothy Christian managed only 21 points in a semifinal loss to Providence, then needed two overtimes to reach 42 in a win over Riverton for third place.

Riverton's 6-8 Rich Fetter (Penn State) won the scoring duel with 24 points against Timothy Christian's 6-6 Jeff Heerdt, who had 22.

State Final Tournament Scores

Super-Sectionals

At Charleston [EIU]—Madison 98, Fairfield 82
At Macomb [WIU]—Havana 65, Pittsfield 55
At Carbondale [SIU]—Carrier Mills (C.M.-Stonefort) 50, Nashville 48
At Decatur [Millikin]—Riverton 61, Decatur (St. Teresa) 47
At DeKalb [NIU]—Elmhurst (Timothy Christian) 64, Oregon 48
At Rock Island—Brimfield 53, Lena (L.-Winslow) 52
At Normal [ISU]—Bloomington (Central Catholic) 68, Watseka 63
At Pontiac—New Lenox (Providence) 50, Kewanee (Wethersfield) 34

Quarterfinals

Havana 75, Madison 66
Riverton 67, Carrier Mills (C.M.-Stonefort) 52
Elmhurst (Timothy Christian) 74, Brimfield 43
New Lenox (Providence) 67, Bloomington (Central Catholic) 51

Semifinals

Havana 42, Riverton 35
New Lenox (Providence) 33, Elmhurst (Timothy Christian) 21

Finals

Elmhurst (Timothy Christian) 42, Riverton 40 (2 OT) (third place)
New Lenox (Providence) 46, Havana 33 (title)

Scoring Leaders

Player, School	G	FG	FT	Pts
Rich Fetter, Riverton	4	39	14	92
Jeff Heerdt, Elmhurst (Timothy Christian)	4	33	23	89
Walter Downing, New Lenox (Providence)	4	29	12	70
Brad Gregurich, Havana	4	26	6	58
Tracey Trimpe, Havana	4	24	9	57

All-Tournament First Team

Player, School	Ht.	Yr.
Walter Downing, New Lenox (Providence)	6-8	So.
Rich Fetter, Riverton	6-8	Sr.
Brad Gregurich, Havana	5-11	Sr.
Barney Mines, New Lenox (Providence)	6-2	Sr.
Tracey Trimpe, Havana	6-4	Sr.

Championship Game Box Score

Assembly Hall, Champaign, March 17, 1979

NEW LENOX (PROVIDENCE) (46)
Coach Frank Palmasani

Player	FG-A	FT-A	Pts	PF	Rb	As	St	Bl
Tom Carruthers	1-1	0-0	2	0	0	0		
Steve Cherveny	0-0	0-0	0	0	0	0		
Trennis Curry	0-4	2-2	2	3	2	2		
Walter Downing	10-13	1-3	21	4	7	1		4
Paul Druhan	0-0	0-0	0	0	0	0		
Tony Frye	0-0	1-2	1	0	1	0		
Ed Loughran	0-0	0-0	0	0	0	0		
Barney Mines	7-13	0-0	14	3	3	2		2
Jim Robinson	0-2	0-0	0	0	2	2		
Henry Shelton	0-0	0-0	0	0	0	0		
Chuck Thomas	0-0	0-0	0	2	1	0		
Baron "Tiger" Williams	2-5	2-3	6	3	5	2		3
TEAM					3			
TOTAL	20-38	6-10	46	15	24	9		

HAVANA (33)
Coach Bob Gregurich

Player	FG-A	FT-A	Pts	PF	Rb	As	St	Bl
Jim Bonnett	0-0	2-2	2	1	0	0		
Derek Dierker	0-2	0-0	0	0	0	0		
Brad Gregurich	10-21	0-0	20	2	1	0		
Darren Hartry	0-0	0-0	0	0	1	0		
Doug Hurst	0-0	0-0	0	5	5	0		
Roger King	0-3	2-3	2	3	6	2		2
Terry Miller	0-0	0-1	0	0	1	0		
Marc Radosevic	0-1	1-2	1	0	4	4		
Craig Schappaugh	0-0	0-0	0	0	1	0		
Kevin Simmering	0-0	0-0	0	0	1	0		
Alan Thompson	0-0	0-0	0	0	0	0		
Tracey Trimpe	4-7	0-1	8	0	5	2		
TEAM					3			
TOTAL	14-34	5-9	33	12	22	11		

New Lenox (Providence)	14	8	8	16	—	46
Havana	2	8	12	11	—	33

Officials: Patrick Flanagan, Ron Michaelson.

Jim Venema of Timothy Christian launches a shot over Joe Hicks of Brimfield in a quarterfinal contest.

Providence's Walter Downing celebrates after the Celtics took the Class A crown with a 46-33 victory.

DIVINE PROVIDENCE

Doug Hurst of Havana tries to avoid the long arms of Trennis Curry in the final game against Providence.

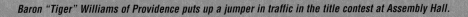

Baron "Tiger" Williams of Providence puts up a jumper in traffic in the title contest at Assembly Hall.

1979A

Downing drives home a one-handed jam in the championship game against Havana. The 6-8 sophomore was a one-man wrecking crew for Providence, scoring 21 of the team's 46 points in the title game.

Chicago Luther South's run to a state title was a "slam dunk."

Led by an athletic lineup that included future triple jump superstar Mike Conley and 6-foot-7 Pierre Cooper, fifth-ranked Luther South racked up 14 dunks in the tournament. One of those came from 5-11 point guard Conley, who went on to win a pair of Olympic medals (gold at Barcelona in 1992 and silver at Los Angeles in 1984) as well as the 1993 world championship.

"It counts the same as any basket," Cooper said. "But the stuff breaks down the other team's mind."

Along with all that rim-rattling, Luther South (27-5) also got timely free-throw shooting in its championship win over Peoria Bergan.

Both teams started their runs to the title game by winning their first regional crowns.

A Class AA participant prior to the season, Bergan (23-8) had failed to even win a regional game from 1973 to 1979 before dropping into Class A. The Trojans and Coach Rudy Keeling wasted little time making up for that, storming to the finals past better-known small-school performers.

But Bergan met its match against Luther South, which returned the Class A crown to the Chicago area after upending defending champ New Lenox Providence in the sectional final. Even so, victory required a fourth-quarter rally for the Braves, who hit 12 of 16 free throws in the final quarter and 22 of 31 overall.

"I thought we outplayed them," Keeling said, "but they made their free throws when they had to."

That included a 7-of-8 night by Dave Allen and a 7-of-11 performance by Cooper, while 6-5 Tony Martin had 21 points and four of his 10 tournament dunks.

"I never believed this team would be one to win a state tournament on free throws," Braves coach Cliff Doll said.

Yet free throws were also a key to Luther South's 59-57 semifinal win over Okawville. After Okawville pulled within 56-55 with 27 seconds left on a lay-up by surprising Greg Rennegarbe — a non-starter who led the team with 18 points — Luther South made 3-of-4 from the line down the stretch. Another key for Luther South was its 31-22 edge on the boards, which helped offset 55 percent shooting by Okawville.

"It's hard to accept that you can play well and lose," Okawville coach Dave Luechtefeld said. "Luther South just has a lot of talent — the most talent of any team we've played."

Okawville managed to head home with third place, as tournament high-scorer Gary Moeller tallied 35 points in a 77-63 win over third-ranked Madison, which had upset top-rated Lawrenceville 74-68 in overtime in the Charleston Super-Sectional.

CHICAGO (LUTHER SOUTH)
Class A State Champions of 1980

FRONT ROW (left to right): Dave Allen, Bob Gray, Pierre Cooper, Tony Martin, Freeman Jackson.
BACK ROW: Dennis Lindsey, Paul Marquardt, Ray Nutter, Mike Conley, Chris Boden, Jason Jackson.

State Final Tournament Scores

Super-Sectionals

At Decatur [Millikin]—Mt. Pulaski 50, Tuscola 43
At Carbondale [SIU]—Okawville 58, Benton 56
At Streator (Twp.)—Chicago (Luther South) 64, DePue 55
At Macomb [WIU]—Pittsfield 44, Augusta (Southeastern) 39 (2 OT)
At Moline—Peoria (Bergan) 56, Sterling (Newman Central Catholic) 55
At Normal [ISU]—Gibson City 56, Normal (University) 53
At DeKalb [NIU]—Elmhurst (Timothy Christian) 46, Franklin Grove (F. Center) 30
At Charleston [EIU]—Madison 74, Lawrenceville 68 (OT)

Quarterfinals

Okawville 55, Mt. Pulaski 53
Chicago (Luther South) 61, Pittsfield 38
Peoria (Bergan) 66, Gibson City 55
Madison 47, Elmhurst (Timothy Christian) 44

Semifinals

Chicago (Luther South) 59, Okawville 57
Peoria (Bergan) 57, Madison 51

Finals

Okawville 77, Madison 63 (third place)
Chicago (Luther South) 56, Peoria (Bergan) 51 (title)

Scoring Leaders

Player, School	G	FG	FT	Pts
Gary Moeller, Okawville	4	35	23	93
Tony Martin, Chicago (Luther South)	4	32	8	72
Scott McCabe, Peoria (Bergan)	4	30	11	71
Tom Gilles, Peoria (Bergan)	4	28	5	61
Pat Hatter, Madison	4	20	15	55

All-Tournament First Team

Player, School	Ht.	Yr.
Pierre Cooper, Chicago (Luther South)	6-8	Jr.
Tom Gilles, Peoria (Bergan)	6-1	Sr.
Tony Martin, Chicago (Luther South)	6-6	Sr.
Scott McCabe, Peoria (Bergan)	6-7	Jr.
Gary Moeller, Okawville	6-4	Sr.
Greg Rennegarbe, Okawville	5-10	So.

Championship Game Box Score

Assembly Hall, Champaign, March 15, 1980

CHICAGO (LUTHER SOUTH) (56)
Coach Cliff Doll

Player	FG-A	FT-A	Pts	PF	Rb	As	St	Bl
Dave Allen	2-3	7-8	11	2	6	3		
Mike Conley	2-4	3-5	7	2	2	3		
Pierre Cooper	2-6	7-11	11	1	4	2		
Bob Gray	2-6	2-2	6	2	7	1		
Tony Martin	9-16	3-5	21	2	6	0		
TEAM					8			
TOTAL	17-35	22-31	56	9	33	9		

PEORIA (BERGAN) (51)
Coach Rudy Keeling

Player	FG-A	FT-A	Pts	PF	Rb	As	St	Bl
Rich Amberg	1-3	0-2	2	4	4	2		
Tom Gilles	10-24	1-1	21	3	3	5		
Paul Kupfert	2-6	0-0	4	1	4	0		
Scott McCabe	7-15	2-2	16	4	11	1		
John Ruffin	0-1	0-0	0	2	1	0		
Bob Schermer	0-0	0-0	0	0	0	0		
Pat Thomas	1-5	0-0	2	2	0	4		
Casey Welch	0-0	0-0	0	3	0	1		
Steve Wittig	3-4	0-0	6	2	2	1		
TEAM					5			
TOTAL	24-58	3-5	51	21	30	14		

Chicago (Luther South)	11	13	12	20	—	56
Peoria (Bergan)	8	14	18	11	—	51

Officials: James Jones, Roger Quinlan.

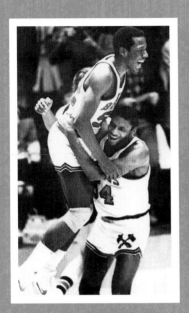

As the buzzer sounds, Tony Martin of Luther South jumps into the arms of teammate Pierre Cooper.

Tony Martin of Luther South prepares to slam against Okawville in the semifinals...

SLAM JAM

...and completes it over Peoria Bergan in the championship game.

Tony Martin and Bob Gray show off their tournament hardware. Luther South was the first Chicago team to win the Class A championship.

1980A

Mike Conley of Luther South sneaks past Peoria Bergan defenders in Luther South's 56-51 championship win. Conley later won a gold medal in the triple jump at the 1992 Olympics in Barcelona.

1981 A

State Final Tournament Scores

Super-Sectionals
At Carbondale [SIU]—Cairo 77, Pinckneyville 42
At DeKalb [NIU]—Granville (Putnam County) 66, Marengo 49
At Charleston [EIU]—Madison 80, Lawrenceville 56
At Romeoville—New Lenox (Providence Catholic) 56, Chicago
  (Luther South) 46
At Decatur [Millikin]—Pana 46, Atwood (A.-Hammond) 45
At Macomb [WIU]—Liberty 56, Pittsfield 43
At East Moline (United)—Dunlap 40, Warren 34
At Normal [ISU]—Danville (Schlarman) 53, Glasford (Illini
  Bluffs) 50

Quarterfinals
Cairo 77, Granville (Putnam County) 64
Madison 45, New Lenox (Providence Catholic) 43
Liberty 67, Pana 61
Dunlap 59, Danville (Schlarman) 50

Semifinals
Madison 70, Cairo 51
Dunlap 46, Liberty 45

Finals
Cairo 81, Liberty 54 (third place)
Madison 58, Dunlap 47 (title)

Scoring Leaders

Player, School	G	FG	FT	Pts
Anthony Webster, Cairo	4	34	10	78
Morris Hughes, Madison	4	31	11	73
Orlandus Hill, Cairo	4	35	3	73
Dion Neisen, Liberty	4	26	19	71
Lorenzo Duncan, Cairo	4	30	3	63

All-Tournament First Team

Player, School	Ht.	Yr.
Walter Downing, New Lenox (Providence Cath.)	6-8	Sr.
Lorenzo Duncan, Cairo	6-2	Sr.
Pat Hatter, Madison	6-3	Sr.
Morris Hughes, Madison	6-2	Sr.
Anthony Webster, Cairo	6-7	Sr.

Championship Game Box Score
Assembly Hall, Champaign, March 14, 1981

MADISON (58)
Coach Larry Graham

Player	FG-A	FT-A	Pts	PF	Rb	As	St	Bl
Roy Campbell	0-0	0-0	0	0	1	0	0	0
Carvel Claggett	0-0	0-1	0	2	2	3	1	0
Charles Claggett	9-15	0-0	18	3	8	0	2	0
Avery Crawford	0-1	0-0	0	1	0	0	0	0
Pat Hatter	6-16	2-2	14	1	6	4	1	1
Morris Hughes	8-14	0-1	16	4	6	1	0	0
Mark Madgett	0-0	0-0	0	0	0	0	0	1
Shannon Manson	0-0	0-0	0	0	0	0	0	0
Billy Papa	0-0	0-0	0	1	0	2	0	0
Kerwin Stanley	2-3	0-0	4	4	0	3	2	0
Dan Stern	0-0	0-0	0	0	0	0	0	0
Mark Zarr	2-5	2-5	6	1	11	0	0	1
TEAM					4			
TOTAL	27-54	4-9	58	17	38	13	6	3

DUNLAP (47)
Coach John Kimble

Player	FG-A	FT-A	Pts	PF	Rb	As	St	Bl
Linn Arbogast	2-8	0-0	4	4	0	4	1	0
Jim Beasley	0-1	0-0	0	0	0	0	0	0
Steve Berg	0-0	0-0	0	0	0	0	0	0
Karl Burchfield	1-2	2-5	4	3	4	1	0	0
Brad Burger	1-2	1-2	3	1	0	2	0	0
Dave Harlan	0-0	0-0	0	0	0	0	0	0
Mark Lowe	0-0	0-0	0	0	0	0	0	0
Scott Pierce	0-0	0-0	0	0	0	0	0	0
Frank Reinsma	0-0	0-0	0	1	1	0	0	0
Mike Reinsma	9-16	3-5	21	2	10	2	0	3
Bill Seiler	6-16	1-2	13	2	8	2	2	0
Todd Wieland	1-1	0-1	2	0	0	0	0	0
TEAM					4			
TOTAL	20-46	7-15	47	13	27	11	3	3

Madison	16	22	8	12	— 58
Dunlap	20	11	8	8	— 47

Officials: Leroy Newton, Dick Ruggles.

MADISON
Class A State Champions of 1981

*FRONT ROW (left to right):
Dan Stern, Charles Claggett,
Kerwin Stanley, Carvel Claggett,
Daryl Baker, Billy Papa.
SECOND ROW: Mgr. Chris Sharp,
Avery Crawford, Roy Campbell,
Mark Madgett, Mark Zarr,
Patrick Hatter, Morris Hughes,
Shannon Manson,
Asst. Coach David Hughes.*

This was one of several tournaments that prompted heated discussion about seeding the Elite Eight.

Had the game between top-ranked New Lenox Providence and second-ranked Madison been played Saturday night instead of Friday afternoon, it would have ranked among the best Class A title games.

The lead changed hands 10 times in the second half alone before Madison finally won, 45-43, on a lay-up by Morris Hughes. With 15 seconds left, Walter Downing had tied the game at 43 with the last of his 27 points — which included Providence's final 12.

But after a timeout, Providence was slow to set its defense. Taking advantage of the delay, Madison guard Kerwin Stanley easily dribbled through pressure and made a long bounce pass to Hughes. The 6-foot-7 all-state center scored with seven seconds left over 6-8 Downing, who had already blocked six shots. Downing was later named Illinois' first Mr. Basketball.

"We run that play every day in practice. For at least 15 minutes," Hughes said. "We were ready."

Byron Gabriel then missed a desperation shot as time expired for Providence, which had downed defending champ Luther South in the super-sectional. The only other losses for the Celtics — a team Coach Frank Palmasani said was better than his 1979 champion — were to Chicago De La Salle and the eventual unbeaten Class AA champion, Quincy, 47-42.

Not surprisingly, Providence was the toughest test of the postseason for Madison (30-2), which routed Lawrenceville in the super-sectional and won easily in a semifinal against Cairo 70-51, and in the title game against Dunlap 58-47.

Dunlap (28-5) did give the Trojans a game for three quarters. With 1:14 left in the third, Dunlap was within 40-39. Madison then took control with a 16-1 spree that included eight points from all-state guard Patrick Hatter.

"They've got enough ability to have blown us out by 30 or 40. But our kids wouldn't let it happen," said Dunlap coach John Kimble, who got 21 points from Mike Reinsma.

Dunlap reached the title game after rallying from eight down with 4:57 left in a 46-45 semifinal win over Liberty. Bill Seiler's free throws with 14 seconds left were the difference.

The title capped an impressive run for Madison, which also won the otherwise Class AA Centralia Holiday tournament and lost only to Class AA foes. The finish made the Trojans 129-20 over the past five seasons with four state berths, two titles and a fourth-place finish.

Third place went to Cairo and 6-7 all-stater Anthony Webster. In a show of class, the Pilots showed up in tuxedos to receive their medals.

AROUND THE CORNER

Billy Papa of Madison heads for the baseline while Dunlap's Linn Arbogast plays catch-up in the title game.

Madison players celebrate the school's second state title in five years with a traditional pose.

Eagles abound as Dunlap's Mike Reinsma duels Liberty's Dion Niesen (right) in a semifinal contest.

1981A

Byron Gabriel of Providence skies high to block a pass by Madison's Charles Claggett in a quarterfinal match.

An Eagle Uncle cheers on his team from the Assembly Hall seats.

LAWRENCEVILLE
Class A State Champions of 1982

FRONT ROW (left to right): Mgr. Mark Simmons, Asst. Coach George Grubbs, Coach Ron Felling, Asst. Coach Rick Herdes, Mgr. Tim Seitzinger. SECOND ROW: Darin Blair, Bill Anthony, Brian Cochran, Dave Parker, Keith Frohock, Doug Novsek, Marty Simmons, Tim Leighty, Bryan Nead, Ernie Hoh, Jeff Gher, Jeff Joines, Jay Baker.

1982A

The Lawrenceville Indians were the first Class A champions and in the first decade provided some of the most memorable small-school tournament moments. So it seemed fitting when, in 1982, Lawrenceville (34-0) became the first Class A champion to finish the season undefeated.

But perfection was not without difficulty. Top-ranked Lawrenceville battled through an Elite Eight that owned a combined record of 231-24, a .906 winning percentage that ranks as best in Class A history.

Beyond gaudy records, this tournament also provided familiar coaching faces such as Havana's Bob Gregurich and top talents with University of Illinois recruit Scott Meents of Herscher and 7-foot junior Bill Braksick of Flanagan (Illinois State).

The best action came in a pair of exciting semifinals. In the first, Lawrenceville rallied from a seven-point third-quarter deficit against Herscher. All-stater Doug Novsek hit a 20-footer with 1:48 left that pulled Lawrenceville into a 44-44 tie that lasted until the buzzer. After that, a basket by fellow all-stater Marty Simmons (16 points, 10 rebounds) and a free throw by Novsek (23 points) provided all the points the Indians needed to escape.

"This is a helluva way to make a living," Lawrenceville coach Ron Felling said. "In the overtime the first thing we had to do was catch our breath. Only in the overtime did we feel we had a chance to win."

That was true partly because Meents, who finished with 16 points and 12 rebounds, picked up his fourth and fifth fouls early in the overtime. With backup center Pat Huette already fouled out, Herscher coach Ed Sennett went deep into his bench.

"Any team that goes down to their third center is in trouble," Sennett said.

Heroics continued in the next semifinal when Jerome Birditt nailed two free throws with four seconds left as Monmouth ended Havana's 28-game win streak, 56-55.

"Last year against Quincy [Notre Dame], Jerome was in the same situation and missed," Monmouth coach Mike Mueller said. "After that game he told me, 'Coach, that will never happen again.'"

Second-ranked Monmouth was unable to muster the same performance in the title game, however. Lawrenceville raced to a 34-20 halftime lead and held on for its third championship. Simmons chalked up 21 points, 19 boards and

seven assists while Novsek chipped in with 20 points that gave him a school-record 2,183 in his career, eclipsing Jay Shidler's mark.

Herscher claimed third as Meents tallied 20 points and grabbed 12 rebounds in a 46-36 win over Havana.

"All four teams [today] were equally worthy of a title and this is undoubtedly the best four final teams I've seen [in Class A] since I've been coaching," Sennett said.

State Final Tournament Scores

Super-Sectionals
At Charleston [EIU]—Lawrenceville 67, Vandalia 61
At Carbondale [SIU]—Benton 69, Okawville 68
At New Lenox (Lincoln-Way)—Herscher 65, Chicago (Providence-St. Mel) 59
At Pontiac—Flanagan 60, Cissna Park 40
At DeKalb [NIU]—Maple Park (Kaneland) 69, Granville (Putnam County) 62
At Macomb [WIU]—Havana 44, Pittsfield 37
At Decatur [Millikin]—Stonington 56, Tolono (Unity) 54
At Rock Island—Monmouth 86, Chadwick 61

Quarterfinals
Lawrenceville 75, Benton 62
Herscher 51, Flanagan 36
Havana 72, Maple Park (Kaneland) 49
Monmouth 81, Stonington 59

Semifinals
Lawrenceville 47, Herscher 45 (OT)
Monmouth 56, Havana 55

Finals
Herscher 46, Havana 36 (third place)
Lawrenceville 67, Monmouth 53 (title)

Scoring Leaders

Player, School	G	FG	FT	Pts
Doug Novsek, Lawrenceville	4	44	6	94
Bruce Sarnes, Havana	4	40	13	93
Marty Simmons, Lawrenceville	4	32	21	85
Scott Meents, Herscher	4	37	11	85
Mike Miller, Monmouth	4	24	26	74

All-Tournament First Team

Player, School	Ht.	Yr.
Scott Meents, Herscher	6-9	Sr.
Mike Miller, Monmouth	6-5	Sr.
Doug Novsek, Lawrenceville	6-4	Sr.
Bruce Sarnes, Havana	6-5	Sr.
Marty Simmons, Lawrenceville	6-5	Jr.

Championship Game Box Score

Assembly Hall, Champaign, March 13, 1982

LAWRENCEVILLE (67)
Coach Ron Felling

Player	FG-A	FT-A	Pts	PF	Rb	As	St	Bl
Bill Anthony	0-1	0-0	0	0	0	0	0	0
Darin Blair	0-0	0-0	0	0	0	0	0	0
Brian Cochran	0-0	0-0	0	0	0	0	0	0
Keith Frohock	0-0	0-0	0	0	0	0	0	0
Jeff Gher	1-3	0-0	2	4	4	0	0	0
Ernie Hoh	4-5	5-7	13	0	1	4	2	0
Tim Leighty	5-8	1-2	11	2	6	5	1	0
Bryan Nead	0-0	0-0	0	0	0	0	0	0
Doug Novsek	10-20	0-0	20	3	1	4	0	0
Dave Parker	0-0	0-0	0	0	3	1	0	0
Marty Simmons	10-17	1-2	21	4	19	7	0	2
TEAM					3			
TOTAL	30-54	7-11	67	13	37	21	3	2

MONMOUTH (53)
Coach Mike Mueller

Player	FG-A	FT-A	Pts	PF	Rb	As	St	Bl
Jerome Birditt	7-13	2-3	16	1	9	0	0	2
Mel Blasi	3-19	0-0	6	2	0	6	0	0
Tony Deford	0-0	0-0	0	0	0	0	0	0
Fred Hayes	3-13	2-2	8	4	5	5	2	0
Jeff Johnson	0-0	0-0	0	0	0	0	0	0
John Kinney	0-1	0-0	0	0	1	0	0	0
Mark Lovdahl	0-0	0-0	0	0	0	0	0	0
Mark McCurdy	0-1	4-4	4	3	2	0	2	0
Mike Miller	7-11	5-5	19	2	5	0	1	1
Mike Murphy	0-0	0-0	0	0	0	0	0	0
Jamie Paul	0-0	0-0	0	0	1	1	0	0
Jeff Romano	0-1	0-0	0	0	0	0	0	0
TEAM					6			
TOTAL	20-59	13-14	53	13	31	11	5	3

Lawrenceville	16	18	16	17	—	67
Monmouth	10	10	16	17	—	53

Officials: Roger Quinlan, John Sullivan.

Lawrenceville's Ernie Hoh goes toe-to-toe with Monmouth's Fred Hayes during the championship game.

TITLE TIP-OFF

Lawrenceville team members proudly display the first-place trophy to their faithful fans.

Marty Simmons of Lawrenceville rises to shoot over Scott Meents of Herscher in an overtime semifinal battle.

1982A

Jubilation on the Lawrenceville sideline as the Indians notch their third Class A state championship in 11 years.

Benton's Mark Kerley arches a shot skyward in the Rangers' quarterfinal loss to Lawrenceville at Assembly Hall.

Lawrenceville's five-point win over tiny Flanagan in the title game was truly historic.

The match-up marked the first time two undefeated teams had met in any state final, as top-ranked Lawrenceville finished the season 34-0 for the second straight year while second-ranked Flanagan (enrollment 132) lost for the first time in 31 games. Lawrenceville also became the first team in 76 years of IHSA basketball history to win back-to-back titles with unbeaten records.

And Lawrenceville's 44-39 win put Ron Felling in the record books as the first coach to win four state titles. Felling stepped down after the season and two years later resurfaced on Bobby Knight's staff at Indiana. Lawrenceville's 68-game winning streak came to a halt with the opening game of the 1983-84 season.

But the streak was very much on Felling's mind following the championship.

"This win is really mind-boggling," he said. "These kids had their chances to crack. They had the pressure for 68 games."

In the title game, Marty Simmons was held 12 points under his season average but still led Lawrenceville with 20. Flanagan's 7-foot center Bill Braksick had 19 points and eight rebounds, but his mates could muster just eight field goals and four free throws.

Simmons credited teammate Ernie Hoh with helping loosen Flanagan's zone by hitting several outside shots for his 12 points.

"He just gave our team a huge lift," Simmons said. "And we were a team, if we got a lead in the fourth quarter, we were confident we could hold it because we had five guys who could take care of the ball."

As it had the year before, Lawrenceville faced its toughest game prior to the final. This time the upset-minded foe was third-ranked Chicago Providence-St. Mel in the quarterfinals. But Simmons pulled his team through with 43 points and 17 rebounds. Amazingly, he scored all 23 of his team's points in the second half, including two free throws with 13 seconds left to clinch the 56-54 win.

"You saw what a clutch player Simmons is. He's a money player," Felling said. "If he's not Mr. Basketball in Illinois there is a gross injustice. I don't see how there can be a better player in Class A or AA ... or in a lot of colleges."

Felling got no argument from St. Mel coach Tom Shields. "I don't think anybody has scored all his team's points in the second half like he did tonight," Shields said. "I can see why [Indiana coach Bobby] Knight is in love with him."

It was just part of a stunning season for Simmons, who finished with 1,087 points. Incidentally, the injustice Felling was so worried about never materialized, as Simmons was indeed named Mr. Basketball.

The flip side of Lawrenceville was Havana, where coach Bob Gregurich again reached the Elite Eight only to fall short of glory. Gregurich rang up a 236-28 record between 1976-83 with five Assembly Hall appearances and two second-place finishes but no title.

State Final Tournament Scores

Super-Sectionals

At Rockford [Metro Centre]—Tiskilwa 65, Mt. Morris 55
At Pontiac—Flanagan 87, Hoopeston (H.-East Lynn) 60
At Decatur [Millikin]—Nokomis 49, Tuscola 47 (2 OT)
At Carbondale [SIU]—McLeansboro 52, Okawville 47
At New Lenox (Lincoln-Way)—Chicago (Providence-St. Mel) 52, Palos Heights (Chicago Christian) 50
At Charleston [EIU]—Lawrenceville 62, Madison 48
At Macomb [WIU]—Havana 58, Brussels 37
At Moline—Freeport (Aquin) 72, Oneida (ROVA) 66

Quarterfinals

Flanagan 51, Tiskilwa 33
McLeansboro 62, Nokomis 36
Lawrenceville 56, Chicago (Providence-St. Mel) 54
Havana 56, Freeport (Aquin) 51

Semifinals

Flanagan 39, McLeansboro 34
Lawrenceville 54, Havana 50

Finals

McLeansboro 58, Havana 52 (third place)
Lawrenceville 44, Flanagan 39 (title)

Scoring Leaders

Player, School	G	FG	FT	Pts
Marty Simmons, Lawrenceville	4	46	36	128
Bill Braksick, Flanagan	4	35	22	92
Curt Reed, McLeansboro	4	32	8	72
Brian Sloan, McLeansboro	4	22	17	61
Mike Diemer, Freeport (Aquin)	2	22	11	55
Trevor Trimpe, Havana	4	21	13	55

All-Tournament First Team

Player, School	Ht.	Yr.
Bill Braksick, Flanagan	7-0	Sr.
Mike Diemer, Freeport (Aquin)	6-4	Sr.
Lowell Hamilton, Chicago (Providence-St. Mel)	6-7	So.
Marty Simmons, Lawrenceville	6-5	Sr.
Brian Sloan, McLeansboro	6-8	Jr.
Trevor Trimpe, Havana	6-6	Jr.

Championship Game Box Score

Assembly Hall, Champaign, March 12, 1983

LAWRENCEVILLE (44)
Coach Ron Felling

Player	FG-A	FT-A	Pts	PF	Rb	As	St	Bl
Bill Anthony	3-5	0-0	6	0	1	0	1	0
Jeff Gher	0-2	0-0	0	4	4	6	1	0
Ernie Hoh	6-14	0-0	12	0	0	5	1	0
Tim Leighty	1-6	2-4	4	2	7	2	2	1
Dave Parker	1-1	0-0	2	1	2	0	0	0
Marty Simmons	7-15	6-9	20	2	10	1	1	0
TEAM					1			
TOTAL	18-43	8-13	44	9	25	14	6	1

FLANAGAN (39)
Coach Jerry Pohl

Player	FG-A	FT-A	Pts	PF	Rb	As	St	Bl
Bill Braksick	8-13	3-4	19	2	8	0	2	4
Brian Gundy	0-1	1-3	1	4	5	5	1	0
Dan Perry	2-5	0-0	4	3	3	0	0	0
Scott Reese	2-3	2-2	6	2	3	1	0	0
Matthew Schwerin	4-15	1-1	9	2	5	5	0	0
TEAM					1			
TOTAL	16-37	7-10	39	13	25	11	3	4

Lawrenceville	6	12	12	14	—	44
Flanagan	10	8	12	9	—	39

Officials: Don Brady, Wesley Wilson.

1983A

Flanagan's Bill Bracksick, the first seven-footer in Class A tournament history, pulls down a rebound in an unprecedented title-game battle of unbeatens.

McLeansboro's Curt Reed lays in a basket in a quarterfinal match-up against Nokomis.

Flanagan's Brian Gundy receives some high-level interference from Tiskilwa's Doug Compton in a quarterfinal contest.

Lawrenceville players hoist coach Ron Felling on their shoulders to celebrate the school's fourth state championship, tying the record held by Mt. Vernon.

FOUR FOR THE BOOKS

Chris McKinney and Marty Simmons hug after Lawrenceville's victory over Flanagan in the title game.

1983A

The heyday of Class A
Eight splendid champions made believers of all

Argue all you want about the best Class A basketball team, coach, or player. When it comes to *singling* out the finest period of small-school play, there's less to **dispute.**

★ PROVIDENCE-ST. MEL ★

The Providence-St. Mel Knights, who dominated the field in 1985, are always mentioned among the strongest Class A champions.

by Jeff Lampe

The eight seasons from 1979 to 1986 stand out as the heyday of Class A.

Consider that in the tournament's first 34 years, four Class A champions finished unbeaten. All four played between 1982 and 1986.

Four Class A players have been voted Mr. Basketball in Illinois. Three were named between 1981 and 1985, a period when two other small-school hoopsters also finished as runner-up for the award.

At least four teams from that era are prominent in any discussion of the best squads in Class A history: 1985 Providence-St. Mel, 1982 Lawrenceville, 1979 Providence, and 1986 Teutopolis. Actually, anyone compiling a top 10 list of Class A champs has to at least consider McLeansboro's unbeaten 1984 team, Luther South's slam-dunking 1980 group, Madison's

underrated 1981 squad, and Lawrenceville's last titleist in 1983.

Surely you remember that team. All it did was go 34-0 to cap a state-record 68-game win streak that is arguably the single most memorable feat in Class A history.

No wonder many believe 1979-86 was the best of times for small-school hoops.

"It just seemed like there were a lot of really good teams and really good players," Lawrenceville graduate Marty Simmons said. "I can reel off a lot of names. Doug Novsek for us was a great leader. Lowell Hamilton. Havana had Trevor Trimpe. [Bill] Braksick was really good. Brian Sloan at McLeansboro."

All those all-staters and more got a chance to shine in the Elite Eight. Few shined like Simmons, though.

Prime-time players

Named Mr. Basketball as a senior in 1983, Simmons was the key to Lawrenceville's win streak and back-to-back championships in 1982 and 1983. Though he shared the scoring load in 1982 with Novsek, it's no accident Simmons was called "The Mule." Few players before or since have carried a Class A team like he did in 1983, averaging 31.9 points per game.

Most memorable was a semifinal against St. Mel when Simmons scored 43 points, including all 23 Lawrenceville scored in the second half. In fact, if not for a goal-tending call that awarded a basket to teammate Jeff Gher, Simmons would have scored the Indians' final 33 points.

Performances like that caught the fancy of fans. They also caught the eye of voters for the *Chicago Tribune*'s relatively new Mr. Basketball award. As a sign of the times, Class A players actually dominated that award in its infancy.

Walter Downing was first to be honored in 1981. Two years later Simmons outpolled Braksick. The next year Sloan won. And Hamilton nearly made it three straight small-school Mr. Basketball winners in 1985 when he finished second to Ed Horton of Springfield Lanphier.

Run through those names and you understand why college coaches paid attention to the small-school tournament in that era. All those Mr. Basketball candidates earned Division I scholarships, as did Anthony Webster of Cairo, Pierre Cooper and Tony Martin of Luther South, and Rich Fetter of Riverton.

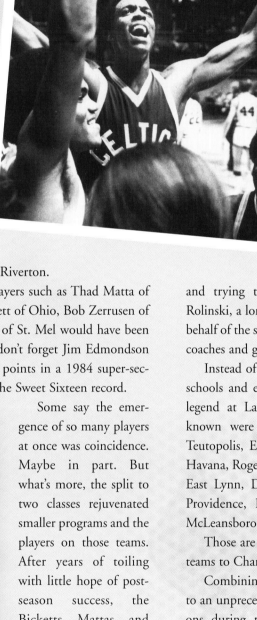

While those were the elite, players such as Thad Matta of Hoopeston-East Lynn, Brad Bickett of Ohio, Bob Zerrusen of Teutopolis, and Fernando Bunch of St. Mel would have been the stars many other years. And don't forget Jim Edmondson of Hinckley-Big Rock, whose 55 points in a 1984 super-sectional against Winnebago is still the Sweet Sixteen record.

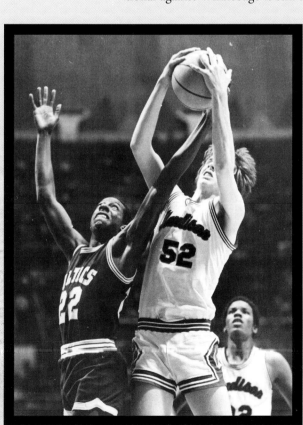

Some say the emergence of so many players at once was coincidence. Maybe in part. But what's more, the split to two classes rejuvenated smaller programs and the players on those teams. After years of toiling with little hope of post-season success, the Bicketts, Mattas, and Zerrusens could now practice last-second, game-winning shots for a state title without pretending to play for a larger school.

The impact of that mindset was not immediate in Class A. Many observers of the early tournaments commented on the uneven level of play. In those early years, Lawrenceville was dominant in part because the Indians had been competitive in single-class action.

Many other smaller schools took time to catch up. But by the end of the 1970s the top programs were in full swing.

"I think probably through the 1970s it just kind of set the stage where [Class A basketball] was catching on," Lawrenceville coach Ron Felling said. "At first I don't think they really had it together in the Chicago area and the northern part of the state."

Classy coaching

That changed as coaches saw teams such as Thomson (enrollment 150), Ridgway (202) and Venice (195) win trophies in the first two Class A tournaments. Suddenly coaches realized they didn't have to be at a big school to build a big résumé.

"Before two classes, I know a lot of the Class A coaches were getting out and trying to get into a double-A school," said Chuck Rolinski, a longtime coach at Toluca who worked tirelessly on behalf of the split. "[A second class] just inspired these kids and coaches and gave them a goal."

Instead of leaving, numerous coaches remained at Class A schools and enjoyed statewide recognition. Felling became a legend at Lawrenceville. Less legendary but certainly well known were Tom Shields at St. Mel, Ken Crawford at Teutopolis, Ed Butkovich at Mt. Pulaski, Bob Gregurich at Havana, Roger Beals at Chrisman, Randy Feller at Hoopeston-East Lynn, Dave Bennett at Pittsfield, Frank Palmasani at Providence, Bill Chumbler at Cairo, and David Lee at McLeansboro and West Frankfort.

Those are coaches whose names still resonate. All brought teams to Champaign between 1979 and 1986.

Combining talent on the floor and brains on the bench led to an unprecedented run of success. Six of eight state champions during that stretch were ranked No. 1 in the final Associated Press poll — a string that pollsters have never approached since. The two champions not ranked first were No. 2 Madison, which beat top-ranked Providence in an epic quarterfinal, and No. 5 Luther South.

Champions in those years won a combined 96 percent of their games (256-11), a total that's even more astonishing when you consider eight of the losses were to Class AA foes.

continued on next page

Epic battles

Success was not a matter of weak competition, however. Epic battles were the norm, not the exception between 1979 and 1986.

One of the most dramatic title games was in 1983, pitting 33-0 Lawrenceville and all-stater Simmons against 30-0 Flanagan and 7-foot all-stater Braksick. Lawrenceville won 44-39 to cap its 68-game win streak, but victory was no sure thing through three quarters.

Simmons admitted to being frustrated by Flanagan's match-up zone. And he credited teammate Ernie Hoh for swinging momentum to the Indians.

"What I remember about that game is Ernie Hoh," Simmons said without hesitation some 23 years later from his coaching office at Southern Illinois University-Edwardsville. "I was having a hard time getting in scoring position, but Ernie got the ball up top and stuck a jumper.

"Then he did it two more times and it was just a breath of fresh air. It was a huge lift for our team."

From there, Lawrenceville made history.

Memorable moments weren't limited to title games, as seemingly each season provided a classic clash.

In 1980, Luther South barely survived its semifinal with Okawville, which shot 55 percent but lost 59-57.

Even more dramatic was Madison's win over Providence in that 1981 quarterfinal. The lead changed hands 10 times in the second half before Madison finally won on a lay-up in the closing seconds by all-stater Morris Hughes over all-stater Downing.

Decades later, Palmasani still replays that game in his mind. "I'm not sure Madison was the best team in the state," he said. "We could have been the champ that year."

The 1982 semifinals were the closest ever, as Lawrenceville needed overtime in its 47-45 win against Herscher, and Monmouth nipped Havana 56-55.

The 1984 tourney produced what many view as Class A's most memorable upset: Mt. Pulaski's 76-74 win over St. Mel in the semis. St. Mel had won its last 10 games by an average of more than 30 points each and was considered a sure thing to meet unbeaten McLeansboro in the title game. But Butkovich's Hilltoppers built a 66-50 lead and then held on for dear life.

Sometimes battles came before the Elite Eight. On its way to the 1984 title, McLeansboro survived a 53-51 super-sectional match-up against previously unbeaten Breese Mater Dei. And in 1986 Teutopolis was down eight points with 1:54 to go before rallying past Venice at the Charleston Super-Sectional.

Changing times

No question, there were close games before 1979 and there have been close games since 1986. The same is true for talented coaches and players and successful teams. The play of Hales Franciscan in 2003 and 2005 earned favorable comparisons to those Chicago winners of old.

But many observers believe part of what made the era so special has passed. High schoolers today have more sports to choose from. They have video games, e-mail, cell phones, and other distractions the youngsters of the early 1980s never considered.

Even basketball, while still important in many communities, is no longer the all-consuming activity it once was.

"As I've watched things evolve, there's been a shift away from basketball." Crawford said. "We're in a situation where more and more kids are looking for instant gratification. In basketball you don't get instant gratification, so we're finding fewer and fewer kids willing to pay the price to be really good."

Bickett has also seen the change. A player for Ohio's Sweet Sixteen team in 1985 and runner-up in 1986, he now coaches at Bureau Valley. Under his watch, the Storm won three consecutive third-place trophies from 2000 to 2002 — becoming the first Class A team to claim a trophy in three straight seasons.

So Bickett still gets good players. But there's a difference these days.

"I just think times have changed. You don't see the same high level of basketball," Bickett said. "Back when I played, that's all we did. Our parents wanted us involved in extracurriculars, which was primarily basketball at Ohio."

"Nowadays kids have work and there's other things outside basketball. Plus there's other sports."

Bottom line?

"I just don't think the caliber of basketball is as good as what it has been," Bickett said.

Then too, Crawford laments that tournament games are no longer broadcast to a statewide or even wider audience on WGN.

"That's just one thing, but it affects kids," he said. "When we won state in 1986, I received letters from England and from Puerto Rico and people from all over the nation sent congratulatory letters. We no longer have that reach with our television coverage."

Given all that, it's doubtful we'll ever see another era like 1979-86. And for those lucky enough to have witnessed the heyday of Class A, the memories will only seem sweeter with age.

AN ERA OF WINNERS

Small school state champions from 1979 to 1986

1979 Providence (32-1)
1980 Luther South (27-5)
1981 Madison (30-2)
1982 Lawrenceville (34-0)
1983 Lawrenceville (34-0)
1984 McLeansboro (35-0)
1985 Providence-St. Mel (31-3)
1986 Teutopolis (33-0)

★ LAWRENCEVILLE ★

Lawrenceville's undefeated 1982 state championship was only the first of back-to-back perfect seasons. Marty Simmons (50) starred both seasons and finished as the tournament's all-time rebounder.

With an unbeaten championship in 1986, Teutopolis brought the string of phenomenal Class A winners to an end.

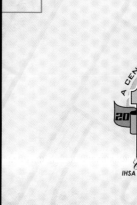

A CENTURY OF MEMORIES
20 07
IHSA
100
Celebrating 100 years of
IHSA Boys Basketball Tournaments

McLEANSBORO
Class A State Champions of 1984

FRONT ROW (left to right): Mgr. D.L. Hayter, Mark Snyder, Ernie Shelton, Tracy Sturm, Scott Cravens, Jeff Morris, Tim Biggerstaff, Jim Melton, Mgr. Tim Aydt. SECOND ROW: Coach David Lee, Heath Lasswell, Tony Rubenacker, Stacy Sturm, Brian Sloan, Bryan Cross, Jim Ingram, Brian Ingram, Asst. Coach Curt Reed, Asst. Coach Randy Smithpeters.

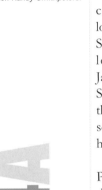

On the heels of third place the season before, unbeaten McLeansboro became the third straight top-rated team to make good on its lofty ranking.

And for the second straight year, the winning coach mounted a strong campaign to get his star named Mr. Basketball. This time McLeansboro coach David Lee lobbied for Brian Sloan, the son of long-time Utah Jazz coach Jerry Sloan. Once again the politicking paid off as the 6-foot-8 senior was tabbed for the state's top honor.

While an anticipated match-up with Providence-St. Mel never materialized thanks to Mt. Pulaski's huge upset win in the semifinals, that didn't bother Lee.

"The pressure was on us all year," Lee said. "When we were ranked No. 1 we had to go out and prove ourselves every time out."

Things didn't change any at state where the Foxes (35-0) won their three games by a total of 57 points. That included a 57-50 win over coach Ed Butkovich's Hilltoppers in the title game, during which Sloan racked up 24 points and 12 rebounds. McLeansboro trailed just once, at 10-8, and led by 10 points or more for most of the second half.

Earlier in the day, Mt. Pulaski had delivered a great performance in its still-talked-about 76-74 upset of second-ranked St. Mel — a team some expected to win the first of two straight titles.

Instead St. Mel and its five junior starters fell victim to a Hilltopper squad that ran its spread offense to perfection. Mt. Pulaski shot 63 percent from the field in the second half and 59 percent overall to make up for a 46-22 rebounding deficit.

"Those little midgets ran a ring around us," St. Mel coach Tom Shields said. "They shot so well it took us out of the game. We played every defense in our arsenal."

Leading the charge for Mt. Pulaski was senior forward Deron Powell, who was 9-for-18 from the floor for a game-high 25 points.

And Powell's five clutch free throws down the stretch staved off a rally by St. Mel.

"I don't think our kids expected Mt. Pulaski to be that good," Shields said. "Overconfidence played a part in that."

Earning an all-tournament spot was Jim Edmondson of Hinckley-Big Rock, who scored a tournament-record 55 points against Winnebago in an 80-55 super-sectional victory.

State Final Tournament Scores

Super-Sectionals
At Carbondale [SIU]—McLeansboro 53, Breese (Mater Dei) 51
At DeKalb [NIU]—Hinckley (H.-Big Rock) 80, Winnebago 65
At East Moline (United)—Lena (L.-Winslow) 65, Monmouth 53
At Macomb [WIU]—Carrollton 67, Havana 58
At Decatur [Millikin]—Mt. Pulaski 60, Chrisman 46
At Pontiac—Hoopeston (H.-East Lynn) 51, Toluca 48 (OT)
At Charleston [EIU]—Flora 62, Madison 52
At New Lenox (Lincoln-Way)—Chicago (Providence-St. Mel) 81, Kankakee (McNamara) 51

Quarterfinals
McLeansboro 64, Hinckley (H.-Big Rock) 35
Lena (L.-Winslow) 83, Carrollton 53
Mt. Pulaski 61, Hoopeston (H.-East Lynn) 54
Chicago (Providence-St. Mel) 81, Flora 48

Semifinals
McLeansboro 61, Lena (L.-Winslow) 39
Mt. Pulaski 76, Chicago (Providence-St. Mel) 74

Finals
Chicago (Providence-St. Mel) 79, Lena (L.-Winslow) 65 (third place)
McLeansboro 57, Mt. Pulaski 50 (title)

Scoring Leaders

Player, School	G	FG	FT	Pts
Brian Sloan, McLeansboro	4	30	25	85
Jim Edmondson, Hinckley (H.-Big Rock)	2	29	20	78
Deron Powell, Mt. Pulaski	4	32	13	77
Justin Yeager, Lena (L.-Winslow)	4	30	15	75
Lowell Hamilton, Chi. (Providence-St. Mel)	4	31	10	72

All-Tournament First Team

Player, School	Ht.	Yr.
Jim Edmondson, Hinckley (H.-Big Rock)	6-6	Sr.
Lowell Hamilton, Chicago (Providence-St. Mel)	6-7	Jr.
Deron Powell, Mt. Pulaski	6-1	Sr.
Brian Sloan, McLeansboro	6-8	Sr.
Tracy Sturm, McLeansboro	6-1	Sr.
Justin Yeager, Lena (L.-Winslow)	5-10	Sr.

Championship Game Box Score

Assembly Hall, Champaign, March 17, 1984

McLEANSBORO (57)
Coach David Lee

Player	FG-A	FT-A	Pts	PF	Rb	As	St	Bl
Tim Biggerstaff	0-0	0-0	0	0	0	0	0	0
Scott Cravens	2-5	4-6	8	3	4	0	1	0
Bryan Cross	3-3	4-4	10	2	3	0	0	0
Brian Ingram	0-1	0-0	0	0	0	0	0	0
Heath Lasswell	0-0	0-0	0	0	0	0	0	0
Jim Melton	0-0	0-0	0	0	0	0	0	0
Jeff Morris	2-4	1-4	5	2	1	4	3	0
Tony Rubenacker	0-0	0-0	0	0	0	0	0	0
Ernie Shelton	0-0	0-0	0	0	1	0	0	0
Brian Sloan	10-16	4-7	24	3	12	2	0	1
Stacy Sturm	0-1	2-2	2	0	2	1	0	2
Tracy Sturm	4-10	0-2	8	2	5	8	1	0
TEAM					1			
TOTAL	21-40	15-25	57	12	29	15	5	3

MT. PULASKI (50)
Coach Ed Butkovich

Player	FG-A	FT-A	Pts	PF	Rb	As	St	Bl
Darren Anderson	0-1	0-0	0	0	0	0	0	0
Doug Awe	0-0	0-0	0	0	0	0	0	0
Roger Cook	3-7	3-4	9	4	5	1	0	0
Rick Edwards	3-6	0-0	6	4	1	3	3	1
Jeff Haley	1-1	0-0	2	0	0	0	0	0
Steve Hayes	2-5	0-0	4	4	0	2	2	0
Sam Jimison	0-0	0-0	0	0	0	1	0	0
Dan McCue	0-1	0-0	0	0	3	1	0	0
Scott Olden	2-7	5-6	9	3	8	6	2	0
Brian Poole	0-0	0-0	0	0	0	0	0	0
Deron Powell	8-16	0-0	16	2	2	1	0	0
Pat Walsh	2-2	0-0	4	3	1	0	0	0
TEAM					1			
TOTAL	21-46	8-10	50	20	21	15	7	1

McLeansboro	10	17	13	17	—	57
Mt. Pulaski	10	10	8	22	—	50

Officials: Richard Carter, Jim Pownall.

McLeansboro's Brian Sloan, later named
Mr. Basketball, lays up two of his tournament-high 63 points.

POINTS GALORE

Hoopeston-East Lynn forward Bill
Sullivan looks for help as Mt.
Pulaski's Steve Hayes applies
pressure. Mt. Pulaski won the
quarterfinal contest 61-54.

Providence-St. Mel's
Terry Miles blocks a shot
by Mike Jensen of
Lena-Winslow in the
third-place game.

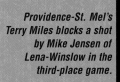

1984A

Lowell Hamilton of
Providence-St. Mel
leaps over Mt.
Pulaski's Roger
Cook to score in a
semifinal contest.
Mt. Pulaski upset
the Knights 76-74.

Scott Cravens of McLeansboro pulls down a rebound in the title game as Mt. Pulaski's Roger Cook defends.

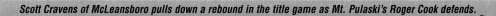

1985A

CHICAGO (PROVIDENCE-ST. MEL)
Class A State Champions of 1985

FRONT ROW (left to right):
Greg Lowery, Julian Eison,
Keith Langston, Fernando Bunch,
Keith Rice, Illya McGee,
Larry Givens. SECOND ROW:
Coach Tom Shields, Mark Smith,
Douglas Johnson, Albert Jones,
Lowell Hamilton, Steve Cox,
Terry Miles, Joe Jackson,
Asst. Coach Bill Ociepka.

This time there was no upset loss to Mt. Pulaski and no youthful letdown against Lawrenceville.

This time Chicago Providence-St. Mel lived up to the hype. Whether Lowell Hamilton & Co. also won a place in the pantheon of Class A greats was the only matter left for debate after an impressive tournament.

Coach Tom Shields certainly thought his squad was special after watching top-ranked St. Mel (31-3) roll to the title with an average victory margin of 25 points in three Elite Eight games, not to mention a 117-69 super-sectional rout of Dwight.

"I think we are the best team that has ever played on the Class A level. We have depth, overall physical talent and we're not a run-and-gun, helter-skelter outfit," Shields said. "We answered any critic we had (in the title game). It is now up to you to judge how good we are."

Even so, the title run wasn't without a scare. Ninth-ranked Hoopeston-East Lynn gave the Knights all they could handle in the semifinals, clawing to within 74-70 with 41 seconds to go and fueling thoughts of another upset.

"I think there was a little bit of déjà vu out there," said Shields, who announced before the tournament this was his final season at St. Mel. "But when I called a timeout, the feeling on the bench was one of 'Not this year.' Concerned, yes. Panicked, no."

Seconds later Fernando Bunch tallied two of his 17 points on a lay-up to spark an 8-0 run that put St. Mel back in control.

"They have five tremendous individuals," Hoopeston Coach Randy Feller said. "But the team that played well together today was us."

Hoopeston got 28 points from Kevin Root and 23 from Thad Matta, who went on to play at Southern Illinois and Butler and eventually to coach at Ohio State. Matta also came up big for Hoopeston in the third-place contest, tallying 34 points on 15-for-26 shooting.

After the semifinal scare, the title game was anticlimactic. St. Mel steamrolled Chrisman 95-63 behind 23 points from Joe Jackson and 21 points from 6-7 Hamilton. Chrisman managed just 37 percent shooting.

"Those guys are awesome," Chrisman coach Roger Beals said. "After the loss last year, I'm sure they dedicated this season to getting back here and avenging the loss to Mt. Pulaski. And they did."

Chrisman did offer a unique chapter in tournament history when Beals became perhaps the only coach to drive his team's bus to the Assembly Hall. In another oddity, Chrisman's semifinal win was aided by a scorebook error that disqualified Harvard point guard Tom King with only four personal fouls.

State Final Tournament Scores

Super-Sectionals
At Macomb [WIU]—Pittsfield 49, Warsaw 47
At Pontiac—Hoopeston (H.-East Lynn) 65, Mason City 60
At New Lenox (Lincoln-Way)—Chicago (Providence-St. Mel) 117, Dwight 69
At Rock Island—Princeville 57, Dakota 56
At Decatur [Millikin]—Chrisman 57, Mt. Pulaski 45
At Charleston [EIU]—Madison 47, Flora 45
At DeKalb [NIU]—Harvard 75, Ohio 62
At Carbondale [SIU]—Anna (A.-Jonesboro) 69, DuQuoin 68

Quarterfinals
Hoopeston (H.-East Lynn) 60, Pittsfield 58
Chicago (Providence-St. Mel) 89, Princeville 56
Chrisman 73, Madison 62
Harvard 74, Anna (A.-Jonesboro) 61

Semifinals
Chicago (Providence-St. Mel) 83, Hoopeston (H.-East Lynn) 72
Chrisman 62, Harvard 55

Finals
Hoopeston (H.-East Lynn) 84, Harvard 70 (third place)
Chicago (Providence-St. Mel) 95, Chrisman 63 (title)

Scoring Leaders

Player, School	G	FG	FT	Pts
Jamie Martin, Harvard	4	40	11	91
Steve Redman, Chrisman	4	30	28	88
Thad Matta, Hoopeston (H.-East Lynn)	4	33	20	86
Kevin Root, Hoopeston (H.-East Lynn)	4	28	15	71
Eric Schimke, Harvard	4	30	5	65

All-Tournament First Team

Player, School	Ht.	Yr.
Fernando Bunch, Chicago (Providence-St. Mel)	5-8	Sr.
Lowell Hamilton, Chicago (Providence-St. Mel)	6-7	Sr.
Jamie Martin, Harvard	6-6	Sr.
Thad Matta, Hoopeston (H.-East Lynn)	6-5	Sr.
Steve Redman, Chrisman	6-6	Sr.

Championship Game Box Score
Assembly Hall, Champaign, March 16, 1985

CHICAGO (PROVIDENCE-ST. MEL) (95)
Coach Tom Shields

Player	FG-A	FT-A	Pts	PF	Rb	As	St	Bl
Fernando Bunch	0-7	3-4	3	4	6	15	0	0
Steve Cox	1-1	0-0	2	1	3	0	0	2
Julian Eison	0-0	0-0	0	0	0	0	0	0
Lowell Hamilton	10-20	1-2	21	4	3	0	1	1
Joe Jackson	10-15	3-4	23	3	7	3	0	0
Douglas Johnson	6-9	0-0	12	2	5	0	1	1
Albert Jones	0-0	0-0	0	0	0	0	1	0
Keith Langston	2-5	0-0	4	0	1	2	1	0
Illya McGee	5-6	1-5	11	4	9	6	1	0
Terry Miles	4-6	1-4	9	0	9	0	0	2
Mark Smith	2-3	0-0	4	1	2	0	0	0
Robert Turnbow	3-4	0-0	6	0	0	1	0	0
TEAM					1			
TOTAL	43-76	9-22	95	19	46	27	5	6

CHRISMAN (63)
Coach Roger Beals

Player	FG-A	FT-A	Pts	PF	Rb	As	St	Bl
Randy DeMoss	3-4	0-0	6	3	6	2	3	0
Dale Good	0-0	0-0	0	0	0	0	0	0
Troy Hollingsworth	4-8	1-3	9	4	1	2	0	0
Walt Hoult	2-5	0-0	4	2	3	0	0	0
Greg Hunt	2-5	0-0	4	0	3	2	0	0
John Johnson	0-0	1-2	1	0	0	0	0	0
David Lawlyes	0-1	2-2	2	0	0	0	0	0
Eric Lewsader	1-3	0-2	2	5	4	1	0	0
John Morris	2-3	1-2	5	0	2	0	1	0
Wayne Pennington	1-6	2-2	4	1	3	1	0	0
Tony Randall	2-8	1-2	5	1	8	0	0	0
Steve Redman	6-19	9-9	21	2	5	1	0	0
TEAM					2			
TOTAL	23-62	17-24	63	18	37	9	4	0

Chicago (Providence-St. Mel)	30	18	16	31	—	95
Chrisman	8	23	14	18	—	63

Officials: Richard Green, Tom Roland.

CAUSE FOR CELEBRATION

← Lowell Hamilton is welcomed back to the bench by Providence-St. Mel coach Tom Shields.

Hamilton throws down one of many dunks in a high-flying tournament. The Knights scored 117, 89, 89, and 95 points in their last four contests.

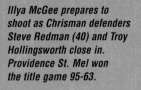

Illya McGee prepares to shoot as Chrisman defenders Steve Redman (40) and Troy Hollingsworth close in. Providence St. Mel won the title game 95-63.

Fernando Bunch of Providence-St. Mel notched a record 15 assists in the title game against Chrisman.

← Hamilton races upcourt on a fast break in a quarterfinal conquest of Princeville.

1985A

Down eight points with 1:54 remaining in the Charleston Super-Sectional, Teutopolis looked like anything but a dominant champion.

Yet somehow the Wooden Shoes rallied. First, coach Ken Crawford called for a full-court press. Then Venice turned the ball over and missed some free throws. Through it all, Teutopolis made shots.

When the game was over, when Teutopolis had come back for a 75-73 victory, the stage was finally set for an emphatic Elite Eight performance. The Wooden Shoes walked over their next three foes, winning by an average of nearly 28 points per game at Assembly Hall.

Numerically that was a more impressive showing than Providence-St. Mel posted one year earlier.

"We're unhappy we lost, but we lost to one of the best teams in the history of the state tournament," Ohio coach Lloyd Johnson said after his team was blown out in the title game 82-45. "They have everything you could want in a basketball team."

So dominant was Teutopolis (33-0), that the Shoes outrebounded opponents by an average of 42-20 per game, shot 59 percent from the floor and held opponents to 33 percent shooting. Bob Zerrusen led a balanced attack with 20.3 points and 11 rebounds per game in the Sweet Sixteen, while four others averaged at least 10 points.

"All the starters were ferocious rebounders and ferocious defenders," Crawford said. "You combine that with the fact they could all score and you get a pretty good team."

Historic, too. Two weeks later, Teutopolis became the first school to win boys' and girls' basketball titles in the same season. And the top-ranked Shoes were the last Class A team to finish unbeaten until Seneca did the same in 2006.

T-Town's closest contest was a 58-43 semifinal with third-ranked Hoopeston-East Lynn, which one year earlier gave St. Mel its toughest test. This time, Coach Randy Feller's team led at halftime, 23-19, before falling victim to relentless rebounding. Teutopolis wound up with a 43-20 edge on the boards and limited Hoopeston to 36 percent shooting.

Meanwhile, No. 13 Ohio advanced despite going scoreless in the first quarter of its 45-43 semifinal win over West Frankfort and shooting just 13 percent in the first half.

"The good Lord has to be with us," Johnson said. "It is a miracle we won this game."

With an official enrollment of just 69 students, Ohio was the smallest school ever to play in a championship game, making the Bulldogs a sentimental favorite with the crowd. But Ohio's run of miracles ended in the final, as T-Town's 37-point victory margin set a Class A championship record.

Finally, Hoopeston took third place for the second straight season by downing West Frankfort and Coach David Lee — the first Class A coach to win an Elite Eight game with two different teams. Lee also coached McLeansboro's 1984 champs.

State Final Tournament Scores

Super-Sectionals

At Normal [ISU]—Hoopeston (H.-East Lynn) 68, Roanoke (R.-Benson) 45
At Macomb [WIU]—Winchester 53, Warsaw 49
At New Lenox (Lincoln-Way)—Westmont 78, St. Anne 59
At Charleston [EIU]—Teutopolis 75, Venice 73
At DeKalb [NIU]—Ohio 74, Marengo 64
At Decatur [Millikin]—Decatur (St. Teresa) 64, Pana 58
At Moline—Kewanee 75, Annawan 52
At Carbondale [SIU]—West Frankfort (Frankfort) 60, DuQuoin 58

Quarterfinals

Hoopeston (H.-East Lynn) 51, Winchester 38
Teutopolis 76, Westmont 45
Ohio 73, Decatur (St. Teresa) 50
West Frankfort (Frankfort) 64, Kewanee 59 (OT)

Semifinals

Teutopolis 58, Hoopeston (H.-East Lynn) 43
Ohio 45, West Frankfort (Frankfort) 43

Finals

Hoopeston (H.-East Lynn) 68, West Frankfort (Frankfort) 58 (third place)
Teutopolis 82, Ohio 45 (title)

Scoring Leaders

Player, School	G	FG	FT	Pts
Brad Bickett, Ohio	4	31	41	103
Kevin Root, Hoopeston (H.-East Lynn)	4	34	20	88
Bob Zerrusen, Teutopolis	4	32	17	81
Lance Harris, Ohio	4	30	14	74
Shannon Talbot, Kewanee	2	21	14	56

All-Tournament First Team

Player, School	Ht.	Yr.
Brad Bickett, Ohio	6-2	Sr.
Lance Harris, Ohio	5-10	Sr.
Todd Kroeger, Teutopolis	6-0	Sr.
Kevin Root, Hoopeston (H.-East Lynn)	6-1	Sr.
Bob Zerrusen, Teutopolis	6-6	Sr.

Championship Game Box Score

Assembly Hall, Champaign, March 8, 1986

TEUTOPOLIS (82)
Coach Ken Crawford

Player	FG-A	FT-A	Pts	PF	Rb	As	St	Bl
Mike Donaldson	2-2	0-1	4	0	0	0	0	0
Jeff Hardiek	3-4	1-2	7	0	4	0	0	0
Rich Hartke	0-1	0-0	0	1	1	0	0	0
Theo Hemmen	4-10	2-2	10	3	8	1	1	0
Dean Hille	0-1	2-2	2	0	1	0	1	0
Todd Kroeger	5-11	2-3	12	3	2	5	5	2
Craig Pals	0-0	2-2	2	0	0	0	1	0
Dennis Ruholl	0-1	0-0	0	0	0	2	0	0
Kevin Ruholl	9-14	3-4	21	0	4	1	0	0
Tim Smith	0-0	0-0	0	0	0	0	0	0
Ted Wiessing	3-4	0-0	6	3	3	3	0	0
Bob Zerrusen	8-9	2-4	18	3	9	4	5	3
TEAM					2			
TOTAL	34-57	14-20	82	13	34	16	13	5

OHIO (45)
Coach Lloyd Johnson

Player	FG-A	FT-A	Pts	PF	Rb	As	St	Bl
Ivan Beers	0-0	0-0	0	0	0	0	0	0
Brad Bickett	6-14	2-2	14	4	4	0	3	1
Dan Doran	0-1	0-0	0	0	1	0	1	0
Dave Doran	2-4	0-0	4	2	3	1	0	0
Doug Doran	0-1	0-0	0	1	0	0	0	0
Todd Etheridge	2-2	0-0	4	0	0	0	0	0
Tim Farraher	1-5	2-2	4	4	7	0	0	1
Lance Harris	4-16	4-4	12	4	5	3	2	0
Kevin Molln	0-0	0-0	0	0	0	0	0	0
Craig O'Brien	0-0	0-2	0	1	2	0	0	0
Tim Piper	0-0	0-0	0	0	0	0	0	0
Darren Schultz	2-7	3-8	7	3	4	0	1	0
TEAM					0			
TOTAL	17-50	11-18	45	19	26	4	7	2

Teutopolis	17	18	19	28	—	82
Ohio	10	11	9	15	—	45

Officials: Jim Collins, Steve Morris.

Kevin Root of Hoopeston-East Lynn angles for a shot while Bob Zerrusen of Teutopolis does his best to prevent it in a semifinal contest won by T-Town.

Teutopolis's Kevin Ruholl outruns Brad Bickett of Ohio in a historic title-game match-up. With 69 students, Ohio was the smallest school to play in the Class A finals.

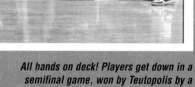

All hands on deck! Players get down in a semifinal game, won by Teutopolis by a 58-43 count over Hoopeston-East Lynn.

1986A

DOUBLE YOUR PLEASURE

Teutopolis players cheer their first school's first state championship. Two weeks later, T-Town became the first school to win boys' and girls' titles in the same year.

For much of the season, Venice all-stater Jesse Hall felt he was the object of unfair attention from referees. At 6-foot-3, blessed with quickness and breathtaking jumping ability, Hall played a physical brand of basketball better suited to the Big Ten, where he eventually played for Michigan State.

At times, Hall seemed to be playing on a different plane from his competition. In the super-sectional, one drive to the basket

Harris said. "I'm happy. I'm at a loss for words."

Understandably, Dingwerth was less pleased. "I was touching him," he said, "but you're supposed to be able to do that. I wasn't doing anything different than I was the whole game. When the whistle blew I didn't have any idea what for."

Okawville coach Dave Luechtefeld was more direct. "I'm sure [the official] realizes, along with everyone else, that he

VENICE
Class A State Champions of 1987

FRONT ROW (left to right): Coach Clinton Harris, Jr., Asst. Coach Rick Everage. SECOND ROW: Orlando Love, Dale Turner, Wilfred Wigfall, Kevin Gardner, Daryl Buie, Daryl Jackson, Jesse Hall, Johnnie Marchbanks, Vincent Harris.

stopped when his knee smacked into the forehead of a Newton player and Hall was called for charging.

Given that background, there was irony in Venice's second state title being sealed with a controversial whistle.

As the last seconds of the thrilling title game against Okawville ticked away with the score tied at 54, second-ranked Venice (29-3) had possession. But Okawville's Doug Dingwerth was whistled for a pushing foul away from the ball, sending Hall to the line.

A 60 percent free throw shooter, Hall made both freebies to finish with 19 points and seal a 56-54 title win. Okawville (29-7) had a shot at the buzzer, but Jeff Luechtefeld's 24-footer grazed the rim, one of his few misses in a 29-point, 13-for-20 shooting performance.

"I was surprised he called a foul in that situation. Usually, the only time they call it is in a shooting or rebounding situation," Venice coach Clinton

made a mistake," Dave Luechtefeld said. "You don't want to let someone win the state title on something like that."

The exciting title game marked the second straight close contest for Venice, which earlier in the day had tipped Chrisman 53-45 in the semifinals on the strength of clutch free throws by Hall and Vincent Harris. Chrisman led for much of the game before Venice finally took control at 47-45 on a basket by Daryl Jackson with 3:14 remaining. Chrisman went scoreless for the final 3:54.

Hall also had 29 points in Venice's 81-33 quarterfinal win over unbeaten Pearl City, which was coached by Ron Johnson. An insurance agent for Country Companies, Johnson had taken over the team in August when no teaching vacancies became available at the school and no other coach could be found.

State Final Tournament Scores

Super-Sectionals
At DeKalb [NIU]—Elgin (St. Edward) 63, Mendota 59
At Decatur [Millikin]—Chrisman 86, Buffalo (Tri-City) 61
At Charleston [EIU]—Venice 72, Newton 61
At East Moline (United)—Pearl City 56, Cambridge 53
At Carbondale [SIU]—Okawville 36, Carterville 34
At Normal [ISU]—Watseka 73, Clinton 60
At New Lenox (Lincoln-Way)—Ottawa (Marquette) 80, Chicago (Providence-St. Mel) 77 (OT)
At Macomb [WIU]—Beardstown 59, Auburn 58

Quarterfinals
Chrisman 69, Elgin (St. Edward) 56
Venice 81, Pearl City 33
Okawville 75, Watseka 56
Beardstown 69, Ottawa (Marquette) 61

Semifinals
Venice 53, Chrisman 45
Okawville 49, Beardstown 35

Finals
Chrisman 57, Beardstown 48 (third place)
Venice 56, Okawville 54 (title)

Scoring Leaders

Player, School	G	FG	FT	Pts
Walt Hoult, Chrisman	4	36	15	87
Jesse Hall, Venice	4	35	17	87
Jeff Luechtefeld, Okawville	4	36	6	78
Matt O'Hara, Beardstown	4	24	19	67
Doug Dingwerth, Okawville	4	25	14	64

All-Tournament First Team

Player, School	Ht.	Yr.
Doug Dingwerth, Okawville	6-2	Sr.
Jesse Hall, Venice	6-3	Sr.
Vincent Harris, Venice	5-11	Sr.
Walt Hoult, Chrisman	6-1	Sr.
Jeff Luechtefeld, Okawville	6-5	Sr.
Dennis Miller, Watseka	5-11	Jr.
Terry Morrow, Beardstown	6-5	Jr.
Matt O'Hara, Beardstown	6-7	Sr.

Championship Game Box Score

Assembly Hall, Champaign, March 14, 1987

VENICE (56)
Coach Clinton Harris

Player	FG-A	FT-A	Pts	PF	Rb	As	St	Bl
Daryl Buie	0-1	0-0	0	2	4	1	0	0
Jesse Hall	8-19	3-5	19	2	9	2	5	1
Vincent Harris	6-9	1-3	13	0	0	4	0	0
Daryl Jackson	3-4	1-2	7	0	5	1	1	1
Dale Turner	4-10	0-0	8	1	8	5	2	0
Wilfred Wigfall	4-7	1-1	9	2	5	0	0	1
TEAM					0			
TOTAL	25-50	6-11	56	7	31	13	8	3

OKAWVILLE (54)
Coach Dave Luechtefeld

Player	FG-A	FT-A	Pts	PF	Rb	As	St	Bl
Doug Dingwerth	8-20	0-0	16	5	1	5	2	0
Keith Koch	0-2	0-0	0	0	1	2	0	0
Jeff Luechtefeld	13-20	3-4	29	0	3	3	2	0
Kevin Rennegarbe	1-2	0-0	2	3	3	6	1	0
Keith Riechmann	0-2	2-2	2	0	6	3	0	0
Darren Stine	2-3	1-4	5	3	9	1	0	1
TEAM					2			
TOTAL	24-49	6-10	54	11	25	20	5	1

Venice	16	13	15	12	—	56
Okawville	17	12	12	13	—	54

Officials: Robert Richards, Richard Rokop.

1987A

Keith Reichmann of Okawville drives past
Jesse Hall of Venice in the 1987 title game.

COMING THROUGH

Hall leaps into a teammate's arms after
Venice clinched its second Class A state championship.

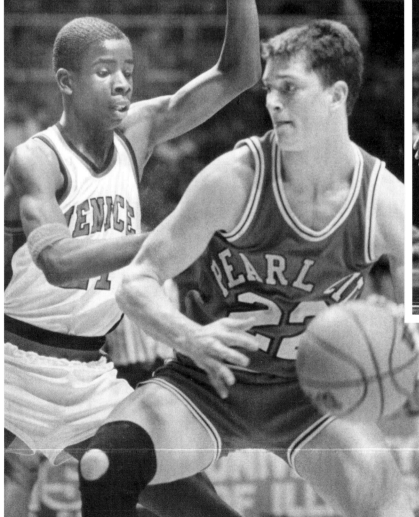

Doug Dingwerth of Okawville is a picture of concentration
in quarterfinal action as Watseka's Dennis Miller prepares to attack the lane.

Randy Asche of Pearl City contemplates a move on Venice's Wilfred
Wigfall in a quarterfinal contest. Venice cruised to an 81-33 decision.

1987A

1988 A
Pana vs. Pinckneyville

They entered the postseason ranked 13th by Associated Press pollsters. Many thought they'd lose in the super-sectional to Tuscola. Few paid much attention to Pana until the end, when coach Charlie Strasburger's squad wound up unexpected champions against favored Pinckneyville.

"I'll bet every person in this building except the Pana players, coaches, and fans thought Pinckneyville would blow us out. It feels good to bet on the old gray horse and win with a 100-to-1 shot," Strasburger said. "On the radio the other night, the announcers kept saying that Pinckneyville and Watseka were definitely the No. 1 and No. 2 teams in the state. I made a little point of reminding our boys that's the way people felt."

Evidently, the message got through. Pana (28-3) not only led for much of the title game, it also outplayed top-ranked Pinckneyville (32-3) when it mattered most. Ahead 58-57 with 1:31 remaining, Pinckneyville committed four straight turnovers. Pana never faltered as Tom Funneman scored on a three-pointer and Mark Heaton and Doug Moss added free throws to seal the 62-58 upset.

Pinckneyville had reached the title game after roaring through its first two games, routing third-ranked Watseka 83-64 in the quarterfinals and second-ranked Melrose Park Walther Lutheran in the semifinals 94-72. All-stater Barry Graskewicz led the way with 59 points in those two games but managed only 12 against Pana, which held foes to 26 percent shooting in the tournament (42-for-163).

And in the first season of three-point field goals, Pana's Funneman proved the most proficient in the Class A field. Funneman hit 10 of 25 at the Elite Eight to lead all shooters from outside the 19-foot, 9-inch arc.

In the third-place game, Walther Lutheran topped unranked St. Elmo. Brian Hill had 23 points and Andrew Amaya — who later played at Southern Illinois and in the NBA after changing his name to Ashraf Amaya — tallied 18 points and added 19 rebounds for Walther Lutheran, which just two years earlier had been 0-24.

The result was a moral victory of sorts for St. Elmo, as Walther Lutheran needed a desperation shot in regulation to force overtime. Coming into the tournament, the Eagles had not received any votes in the final regular season poll. They needed a 40-foot shot at the buzzer by Kevin Maxey to top Trenton Wesclin in the Vandalia Sectional title game.

The biggest moral victory, of course, went to underrated Pana. In the aftermath of its championship, Pana earned plenty of attention, including congratulatory calls from flying hero Chuck Yeager and Vice President George Bush, who was in Springfield campaigning for the presidential primary.

State Final Tournament Scores

Super-Sectionals
At Decatur [Millikin]—Pana 73, Tuscola 67
At Macomb [WIU]—Beardstown 55, Pittsfield 51
At DeKalb [NIU]—Forreston 81, Sandwich 63
At Charleston [EIU]—St. Elmo 54, Teutopolis 53
At Rock Island—Lena (L.-Winslow) 54, Peoria (Bergan) 50
At Lemont—Melrose Park (Walther Lutheran) 60, Kankakee (McNamara) 48
At Normal [ISU]—Watseka 76, Stanford (Olympia) 62
At Carbondale [SIU]—Pinckneyville 53, Carmi 43

Quarterfinals
Pana 63, Beardstown 34
St. Elmo 75, Forreston 67
Melrose Park (Walther Lutheran) 59, Lena (L.-Winslow) 46
Pinckneyville 83, Watseka 64

Semifinals
Pana 61, St. Elmo 51
Pinckneyville 94, Melrose Park (Walther Lutheran) 72

Finals
Melrose Park (Walther Lutheran) 71, St. Elmo 62 (OT) (third place)
Pana 62, Pinckneyville 58 (title)

Scoring Leaders

Player, School	G	FG	3P	FT	Pts
Brian Hill, Melrose Pk. (Walther Luth.)	4	39	9	16	103
Barry Graskewicz, Pinckneyville	4	34	7	8	83
Greg Feezel, St. Elmo	4	30	6	16	82
Tom Funneman, Pana	4	32	10	4	78
Andrew Amaya, Melrose Pk. (Wal. Luth.)	4	32	0	10	74

All-Tournament First Team

Player, School	Ht.	Yr.
Andrew Amaya, Melrose Park (Walther Lutheran)	6-5	Jr.
Greg Feezel, St. Elmo	6-3	Sr.
Tom Funneman, Pana	6-3	Sr.
Barry Graskewicz, Pinckneyville	6-3	Sr.
Shay Hagel, Pinckneyville	6-3	Sr.
Mark Heaton, Pana	6-1	Sr.
Brian Hill, Melrose Park (Walther Lutheran)	6-3	Sr.
Dennis Miller, Watseka	5-11	Sr.

Championship Game Box Score

Assembly Hall, Champaign, March 12, 1988

PANA (62)
Coach Charlie Strasburger

Player	FG-A	3P-A	FT-A	Pts	PF	Rb	As	St	Bl
Tom Funneman	11-18	4-7	0-0	26	2	2	2	0	2
Mark Heaton	5-9	1-1	4-10	15	4	6	4	0	0
Kevin Micek	3-4	0-0	2-3	8	4	5	1	1	0
Doug Moss	2-3	0-0	1-4	5	4	8	0	1	0
Greg Pollman	3-6	0-0	2-2	8	4	5	0	0	0
Gary Tidwell	0-8	0-4	0-0	0	2	1	2	2	0
TEAM						2			
TOTAL	24-48	5-12	9-19	62	20	29	9	4	2

PINCKNEYVILLE (58)
Coach Dick Corn

Player	FG-A	3P-A	FT-A	Pts	PF	Rb	As	St	Bl
Jimmy Bauersachs	1-5	0-0	1-4	3	2	6	0	0	0
Nathan Chapman	0-0	0-0	2-2	2	1	3	1	0	0
Aaron Epplin	2-10	0-0	7-8	11	2	5	4	4	0
Barry Graskewicz	5-15	2-5	0-0	12	4	6	2	2	1
Shay Hagel	5-6	0-0	5-8	15	5	3	4	1	0
Danny Harriss	2-9	0-0	1-2	5	2	6	0	0	0
Blake Lindner	5-9	0-0	0-0	10	1	6	0	1	1
TEAM						4			
TOTAL	20-54	2-5	16-24	58	17	39	11	8	2

Pana	16	14	13	19	—	62
Pinckneyville	17	8	19	14	—	58

Officials: Richard Preston, William Spriggs.

Celebrating 100 years of IHSA Boys Basketball

*Walther Lutheran's Brian Hill
takes a brief injury timeout as an official checks in.*

*Pinckneyville's Aaron
Epplin completes a reverse
lay-up in his team's 62-58
title-game loss to Pana.*

1988A

*Pana's team members line up to receive their
first-place medallions on the floor of Assembly Hall.*

WHOOPING IT UP

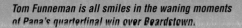

*Tom Funneman is all smiles in the waning moments
of Pana's quarterfinal win over Beardstown.*

"Anybody involved in this business believes winning is contagious."

CARLYLE
Class A State Champions of 1989

FRONT ROW (left to right): Troy Tyberendt, Scott Horner, Jason Jones, Asst. Coach Jerry Farris, Coach Brad Weathers, Steve Hoffmann, Darin Smith, Eric Nave. SECOND ROW: Eddie Huels, Mike Michael, Dean Litzenburg, Tom Michael, Jason Peters, Craig Robertson, Doug Lueking, Barclay Nothaus.

Already riding the high of a Class 2A football championship, Carlyle became the first Illinois school to win football and basketball titles in the same school year.

"Anybody involved in this business believes winning is contagious," said Carlyle coach Brad Weathers, who had three starters that also played football: Scott Horner, Eddie Huels, and Steve Hoffman. "These kids have been through a lot, so it has to help."

Even so, the key for Carlyle and its six-player rotation was 6-foot-8 all-stater Tom Michael. A University of Illinois recruit, Michael already looked at home in Assembly Hall by averaging 32.6 points per game in the tournament and shooting 76 percent from the floor (38 of 50).

That included 45 points in a 67-62 semifinal win over Prairie Central, the toughest game of the tournament for third-ranked Carlyle (32-3). Michael played the last quarter with four fouls yet still scored 14 of his team's final 21.

"I wasn't really worried about playing with four fouls because I've done it before and I know that picking up a cheap fifth foul is the worst thing to do," Michael said.

Earlier, Michael scored 25 as Carlyle won easily in the quarterfinals against a White Hall North Greene team that had upset three top-10 foes: No. 1 Piasa Southwestern in the regional final, No. 4 Jacksonville Routt in the sectional final and No. 6 Quincy Notre Dame in the super-sectional.

Michael also carried Carlyle in the final. He had 28 points in a 66-56 win over surprising Rock Island Alleman and set a Class A title-game record by shooting 83.3 percent from the field (10 of 12).

"I was just on all day," Michael said. "Everything was going pretty smoothly."

A member of the otherwise Class AA Western Big Six Conference, unranked Alleman (24-8) entered postseason play 17-7 before feasting on Class A foes. Leading the way was 6-4 center Brian Wolf, second-leading scorer in tournament play.

Alleman coasted through its first two games, including a quarterfinal win over surprising Tuscola. Down by 18 points with 7:50 to play in its super-sectional, Tuscola had somehow managed to shock No. 2 Springfield Calvary and Rennie Clemons.

Meanwhile, third-place finisher Prairie Central set the stage for a return in 1990 behind guard Gary Tidwell and coach Charlie Strasburger — both one year removed from a title at Pana.

The tournament also marked a bittersweet goodbye for Elite Eight entrant East St. Louis Assumption, which closed at the end of the school year.

State Final Tournament Scores

Super-Sectionals

At Charleston [EIU]—East St. Louis (Assumption) 73, Flora 71 (3 OT)
At Normal [ISU]—Fairbury (Prairie Central) 87, Downs (Tri-Valley) 47
At Macomb [WIU]—White Hall (North Greene) 66, Quincy (Notre Dame) 59
At Carbondale [SIU]—Carlyle 63, Norris City (N.C.-Omaha-Enfield) 58
At Lemont—Wheaton (St. Francis) 75, Aurora (A. Christian) 53
At DeKalb [NIU]—Mendota 64, Marengo 61
At Moline—Rock Island (Alleman) 54, Orion 49
At Decatur [Millikin]—Tuscola 86, Springfield (Calvary) 84

Quarterfinals

Fairbury (Prairie Central) 68, East St. Louis (Assumption) 58
Carlyle 67, White Hall (North Greene) 46
Wheaton (St. Francis) 72, Mendota 61
Rock Island (Alleman) 75, Tuscola 54

Semifinals

Carlyle 67, Fairbury (Prairie Central) 62
Rock Island (Alleman) 58, Wheaton (St. Francis) 41

Finals

Fairbury (Prairie Central) 72, Wheaton (St. Francis) 46 (third place)
Carlyle 65, Rock Island (Alleman) 56 (title)

Scoring Leaders

Player, School	G	FG	3P	FT	Pts
Tom Michael, Carlyle	4	47	0	27	121
Brian Wolf, Rock Island (Alleman)	4	23	7	24	77
Gary Tidwell, Fairbury (Prairie Central)	4	21	10	17	69
Roby Meier, Fairbury (Prairie Central)	4	27	10	3	67
Dan Lenert, Wheaton (St. Francis)	4	24	7	12	67

All-Tournament First Team

Player, School	Ht.	Yr.
Roby Meier, Fairbury (Prairie Central)	6-0	Sr.
Tom Michael, Carlyle	6-8	Sr.
Jason Peters, Carlyle	6-7	Sr.
Gary Tidwell, Fairbury (Prairie Central)	5-11	Jr.
Derek Watts, Rock Island (Alleman)	6-0	Sr.
Brian Wolf, Rock Island (Alleman)	6-4	Sr.

Championship Game Box Score

Assembly Hall, Champaign, March 11, 1989

CARLYLE (65)
Coach Brad Weathers

Player	FG-A	3P-A	FT-A	Pts	PF	Rb	As	St	Bl
Steve Hoffmann	2-5	2-4	4-7	10	0	3	4	1	0
Scott Horner	4-5	2-3	2-2	12	2	2	6	3	0
Eddie Huels	1-6	0-5	2-3	4	1	3	5	1	0
Tom Michael	10-12	0-0	8-12	28	1	7	1	0	3
Jason Peters	4-5	3-4	0-1	11	2	3	3	0	2
TEAM						0			
TOTAL	21-33	7-16	16-25	65	6	18	19	5	5

ROCK ISLAND (ALLEMAN) (56)
Coach Bob DeDoncker

Player	FG-A	3P-A	FT-A	Pts	PF	Rb	As	St	Bl
Mark Ackerman	2-5	1-3	0-0	5	5	6	2	2	0
Matt Copeland	0-0	0-0	0-0	0	0	0	0	0	0
Dave Knuckey	1-4	1-3	0-0	3	1	3	3	1	0
John Lund	0-2	0-0	0-2	0	4	2	1	0	0
Derek Watts	3-8	1-2	0-1	7	4	5	3	1	0
Brian Wolf	8-20	2-4	3-3	21	3	6	2	1	0
Matt Woods	0-3	0-0	0-0	0	0	1	0	0	0
Todd Woods	8-11	4-6	0-0	20	3	4	5	1	0
TEAM						3			
TOTAL	22-53	9-18	3-6	56	20	30	16	6	0

Carlyle	17	16	18	14	—	65
Rock Island (Alleman)	10	8	15	23	—	56

Officials: Alan Merriman, Robert Ware.

SWAN SONG

Ian Stanback of East St. Louis Assumption leaps for a ball at mid-court of a quarterfinal game against Prairie Central. Playing in its final season, Assumption was a sentimental favorite.

Prairie Central teammates Darin Bazzell and Roby Meier share a few trade secrets during a quarterfinal victory over East St. Louis Assumption.

Carlyle's Scott Horner drives the baseline for a basket as teammate Tom Michael moves in for a rebound in the title game against Rock Island Alleman.

Tom Michael of Carlyle and Daton Kupferschmid of Prairie Central tip off a semifinal match-up. Carlyle won 67-62 to reach the title game.

1989A

TRENTON (WESCLIN)
Class A State Champions of 1990

FRONT ROW (left to right): Mike Brink, Rob Wegman. SECOND ROW: Matt Fridley, Don Madenwald, Clay Macke. THIRD ROW: Coach Paul Lusk, Doug Feldt, Brent Drede, Matt Brandymeyer, Asst. Coach Jim Thompson.

There wasn't a person among the 13,518 filing out of Assembly Hall following this Class A finale who would have dared asked for a refund.

Not on a day when Trenton Wesclin (30-3) became the first Class A champ to win in overtime. Actually, fourth-ranked Wesclin needed two overtimes to down previously unbeaten and top-ranked Fairbury Prairie Central, 83-78.

"They just wouldn't be denied winning a state championship," said Wesclin coach Paul Lusk, whose team set a tournament record by shooting 51.4 percent on 3-pointers (19 of 37). "We had to play this game under some unbelievable conditions, but the kids came through it and hung in there like I knew they would."

Wesclin not only trailed most of the second half, the Warriors also played the last 2:50 of regulation and both overtimes without 6-foot-4 Paul Lusk, who took his 29 points per game to the bench after fouling out.

Still Wesclin rallied to force an extra session at 71-all on Matt Fridley's short shot with 17 seconds left. The Warriors rallied again in the first extra period, knotting the score at 76 on a lay-up by Mike Brink with 18 seconds remaining.

Prairie Central (31-1) had a good chance to win in overtime, though. With a half-second left, semifinal hero Darin Bazzell — whose last-second shot beat Norris City-Omaha-Enfield hours earlier — missed the front end of a one-and-one free-throw opportunity.

"I thought we had the game won several times," Prairie Central coach Charlie Strasburger said.

Given that reprieve, Wesclin took the lead for good on a steal and lay-up by Brent Brede and then made 5 of 6 free throws, all one-and-ones. The 6-4 Brede — who would pitch three seasons in the major leagues — scored 26 of his 36 points after halftime and grabbed 13 rebounds.

"*Hoosiers* ain't got nothing on what went on out there," said the elder Lusk, who retired from coaching after the game.

Wesclin's comeback denied Strasburger's bid to win state titles at two dfferent schools. He won in 1988 at Pana along with stepson Gary Tidwell, who led the Hawks in this title game with 26 points. Tidwell rated Prairie Central better than Pana.

Tidwell also played a major role in the Hawks' 54-52 semifinal victory, scoring 21 points against third-ranked NCOE.

Wesclin never trailed its semifinal against No. 7 Aurora Christian, which was in its second season of Illinois High School Association competition. Coach's son Paul Lusk scored 34 points and Brede added 24.

The third-place game featured two more coach's sons. Clay Gray of NCOE scored 15 to help beat Aurora Christian and 6-6 Marc Davidson, who had 20 points and 10 rebounds.

State Final Tournament Scores

Super-Sectionals
At Charleston [EIU]—Trenton (Wesclin) 72, Flora 63
At Decatur [Millikin]—Shelbyville 85, Findlay 67
At Romeoville [Lewis]—Aurora (A. Christian) 89, Kankakee (McNamara) 72
At East Moline (United)—Farmington 89, Hanover (River Ridge) 72
At Normal [ISU]—Fairbury (Prairie Central) 54, Normal (University) 49
At DeKalb [NIU]—Marengo 79, Mendota 53
At Macomb [WIU]—Pittsfield 62, Mendon (Unity) 53
At Carbondale [SIU]—Norris City (N.C.-Omaha-Enfield) 54, Waltonville 46

Quarterfinals
Trenton (Wesclin) 67, Shelbyville 52
Aurora (A. Christian) 48, Farmington 42
Fairbury (Prairie Central) 70, Marengo 51
Norris City (N.C.-Omaha-Enfield) 74, Pittsfield 50

Semifinals
Trenton (Wesclin) 83, Aurora (A. Christian) 71
Fairbury (Prairie Central) 54, Norris City (N.C.-Omaha-Enfield) 52

Finals
Norris City (N.C.-Omaha-Enfield) 48, Aurora (A. Christian) 45 (third place)
Trenton (Wesclin) 83, Fairbury (Prairie Central) 78 (2 OT) (title)

Scoring Leaders

Player, School	G	FG	3P	FT	Pts
Marc Davidson, Aurora (A. Christian)	4	38	11	21	108
Brent Brede, Trenton (Wesclin)	4	36	4	15	91
Gary Tidwell, Fairbury (Prairie Central)	4	29	8	20	86
Paul Lusk, Trenton (Wesclin)	4	27	1	29	84
Reed Jackson, Norris City (NCOE)	4	27	0	21	75

All-Tournament First Team

Player, School	Ht.	Yr.
Brent Brede, Trenton (Wesclin)	6-4	Sr.
Marc Davidson, Aurora (A. Christian)	6-6	Jr.
Reed Jackson, Norris City (NCOE)	6-5	Jr.
Paul Lusk, Trenton (Wesclin)	6-4	Sr.
Gary Tidwell, Fairbury (Prairie Central)	5-11	Sr.

Championship Game Box Score
Assembly Hall, Champaign, March 10, 1990

TRENTON (WESCLIN) (83)
Coach Paul Lusk

Player	FG-A	3P-A	FT-A	Pts	PF	Rb	As	St	Bl
Matt Brandymeyer	2-5	0-0	0-0	4	2	7	1	0	0
Brent Brede	15-24	0-2	6-6	36	2	13	1	1	1
Mike Brink	4-9	0-3	4-4	12	2	0	3	0	0
Chad Deiters	0-0	0-0	0-0	0	0	1	3	0	0
Matt Fridley	7-12	3-4	2-4	19	3	7	1	0	1
Paul Lusk	6-21	0-1	0-0	12	5	6	2	0	0
Don Madenwald	0-0	0-0	0-0	0	0	0	0	0	0
TEAM						4			
TOTAL	34-71	3-10	12-14	83	15	40	8	1	2

FAIRBURY (PRAIRIE CENTRAL) (78)
Coach Charlie Strasburger

Player	FG-A	3P-A	FT-A	Pts	PF	Rb	As	St	Bl
Kent Aberle	3-5	0-1	0-2	6	3	10	0	1	0
Darin Bazzell	8-11	0-1	1-3	17	1	0	4	0	0
Justin Cox	0-0	0-0	0-0	0	0	0	0	0	0
Mark Elliott	4-8	0-0	1-2	9	4	6	4	0	0
Daton Kupferschmid	10-20	0-0	0-1	20	3	12	2	0	3
Gary Tidwell	8-22	2-8	8-8	26	3	3	8	0	0
TEAM						2			
TOTAL	33-66	2-10	10-16	78	14	33	18	1	3

Trenton (Wesclin)	21	12	10	28	5	7	— 83
Fairbury (Prairie Central)	18	11	22	20	5	2	— 78

Officials: Richard Rokop, Terry Lipscomb.

Celebrating 100 years of IHSA Boys Basketball

Brent Brede of Trenton Wesclin lays in a sure two to help his team to a 67-52 quarterfinal win over Shelbyville.

Wesclin's Matt Fridley zooms toward the baseline in a quarterfinal contest against Shelbyville.

Fridley lets his emotions show on the awards stand.

V FOR VICTORY

Shelbyville's Matt Maton find the going tough as Wesclin's Mike Brink applies full-court pressure.

Brink uses his tongue for emphasis as he shoots over Kent Aberle of Prairie Central. Wesclin won the double-overtime title thriller 83-78.

1990A

169

PITTSFIELD
Class A State Champions of 1991

FRONT ROW (left to right) Mgr. Greg Woods, David Ballinger, Doug Wade, Josh Townley, Keith Griffeth, Jason Thompson, Rob Lemons, Ryan Nevius, Brian Feezel, Gregg Scott. SECOND ROW: Asst. Coach Steve Rylander, Jamie Sweeting, Mike Capps, Troy Taylor, Jon Borrowman, Tony Baker, David Fox, David Marable, Jason Smithers, Coach David Bennett.

State Final Tournament Scores

Super-Sectionals
At Carbondale [SIU]—McLeansboro 58, Waterloo (Gibault) 51
At Charleston [EIU]—Effingham (St. Anthony) 82, Madison 81 (OT)
At Rock Island—Orangeville 70, Dunlap 64 (OT)
At Kankakee [Olivet]—Seneca 54, Aurora (Central Catholic) 52
At Macomb [WIU]—Pittsfield 61, Augusta (Southeastern) 44
At DeKalb [NIU]—Rockford (Lutheran) 81, Spring Valley (Hall) 70
At Normal [ISU]—Stanford (Olympia) 77, Armstrong 54
At Decatur [Millikin]—Williamsville 62, Findlay 55

Quarterfinals
McLeansboro 72, Effingham (St. Anthony) 50
Seneca 54, Orangeville 44
Pittsfield 77, Rockford (Lutheran) 64
Williamsville 52, Stanford (Olympia) 50 (OT)

Semifinals
Seneca 52, McLeansboro 42
Pittsfield 42, Williamsville 25

Finals
McLeansboro 63, Williamsville 44 (third place)
Pittsfield 45, Seneca 35 (title)

Scoring Leaders

Player, School	G	FG	3P	FT	Pts
Mark Aubry, Seneca	4	35	12	23	105
Benjy Johnson, McLeansboro	4	27	0	30	84
Tony Baker, Pittsfield	4	27	3	18	75
John Patterson, Williamsville	4	19	8	16	62
Brian Hildebrand, Orangeville	2	21	0	13	55

All-Tournament First Team

Player, School	Ht.	Yr.
Mark Aubry, Seneca	6-2	Sr.
Tony Baker, Pittsfield	6-5	Sr.
Brian Hildebrand, Orangeville	6-7	Sr.
Benjy Johnson, McLeansboro	6-2	Sr.
John Patterson, Williamsville	6-0	Sr.

Championship Game Box Score

Assembly Hall, Champaign, March 9, 1991

PITTSFIELD (45)
Coach Dave Bennett

Player	FG-A	3P-A	FT-A	Pts	PF	Rb	As	St	Bl
Tony Baker	7-14	0-1	1-2	15	0	14	0	0	0
Brian Feezel	2-7	1-2	0-4	5	1	5	3	0	0
David Fox	5-12	0-0	1-4	11	1	2	3	2	1
Rob Lemons	0-0	0-0	0-0	0	0	0	0	0	0
David Marable	0-1	0-1	4-10	4	1	5	2	0	0
Greg Scott	0-0	0-0	0-0	0	0	1	0	0	0
Jamie Sweeting	3-3	0-0	2-2	8	0	6	2	0	0
Troy Taylor	0-0	0-0	0-0	0	0	0	0	0	0
Josh Townley	1-1	0-0	0-0	2	0	0	0	0	0
Doug Wade	0-0	0-0	0-0	0	0	0	0	0	0
TEAM						3			
TOTAL	18-38	1-4	8-22	45	4	35	10	2	1

SENECA (35)
Coach Doug Evans

Player	FG-A	3P-A	FT-A	Pts	PF	Rb	As	St	Bl
Jason Aubry	1-3	0-1	0-0	2	4	1	1	0	0
Mark Aubry	11-35	3-16	1-2	26	4	6	0	1	1
Darren Bedeker	0-0	0-0	0-0	0	0	0	0	0	0
Aaron Crawford	0-5	0-4	0-0	0	3	0	0	0	0
Steve Erickson	0-0	0-0	0-0	0	0	0	0	0	0
Chad Esgar	0-1	0-1	0-0	0	0	1	0	0	0
Brett Larson	2-6	0-2	0-0	4	2	11	0	1	0
Dan Matzen	1-1	0-0	1-1	3	0	0	0	0	0
David Punke	0-0	0-0	0-0	0	0	0	0	0	0
Greg Punke	0-0	0-0	0-0	0	0	0	0	0	0
Sherman Reiter	0-0	0-0	0-0	0	0	0	0	0	0
Steve Reynolds	0-0	0-0	0-0	0	1	0	0	0	0
Guy Sulzberger	0-0	0-0	0-0	0	1	0	0	0	0
Jason Vertin	0-0	0-0	0-0	0	1	3	0	0	0
TEAM						4			
TOTAL	15-51	3-24	2-3	35	16	26	1	2	1

Pittsfield		4	10	13	18	—	45
Seneca		7	9	10	9	—	35

Officials: Randy Cox, Bob Martin.

Reaching the Sweet Sixteen was nothing unusual for Dave Bennett and Pittsfield. Winning a state title was another matter.

After years of good but not-good-enough teams, Pittsfield finally earned hardware in its 12th Sweet Sixteen berth and its fourth Elite Eight appearance. Not just any trophy, either. The Saukees topped Seneca 45-35 in the first championship match-up of unranked teams since Ridgway and Maple Park Kaneland in 1973.

Perhaps it was fitting that defense-minded Pittsfield (28-6) emerged from an eight-team field that defied reason and did not record a single dunk. No. 13 Rockford Lutheran was the only ranked team in this Elite Eight, and the Saukees dusted them in the quarterfinals 77-64. In an upset-filled postseason, only three other ranked teams made the Sweet Sixteen. Pittsfield topped one, No. 14 Augusta South-

eastern, in its super-sectional.

Bennett even said that his 1990 team that lost in the quarterfinals was more talented than this edition. Naturally none of that mattered when the Saukees hoisted a first-place trophy.

"Coach has been here three times before and I know it's real important for him to get that win," said forward Tony Baker, the school's first all-stater. "Not only that win, but a state championship for the community and for what the Pittsfield program means."

The 6-foot-5 Baker was instrumental, averaging 17.6 points and 11.3 rebounds

at Assembly Hall. Like his teammates, Baker also played defense. Pittsfield held foes to 41 points and 36 percent shooting in the Elite Eight, flexing its might most obviously against semifinal foe Williamsville.

In that game the Bullets scored just 25 points, fewer than the average of prolific guard John Patterson. And Patterson had just eight against Pittsfield, though the 6-foot senior scored a game-winner in overtime against Olympia in the quarterfinals and wound up with 2,770 career points. Patterson still ranks second in free throws attempted and made in a career.

So intense were the Saukees that Seneca coach Doug Evans said he figured his team's shooting percentage must have been below zero in the final. Seneca (27-5) actually made 29 percent from the field (15 of 51). Guard Mark Aubry took 35 of those shots and made 11 for his 26 points.

Aubry also had a big role in the first two games for Seneca, which started 1-4 after winning a Class 2A football title, but then won 26 straight. The Fighting Irish guard fired in 27 of Seneca's 54 points against Orangeville and another 27 in a 52-42 semifinal win over McLeansboro.

Brian Schultz of Effingham St. Anthony bowls over the competition in a quarterfinal loss to McLeansboro at Assembly Hall.

Pittsfield's Brian Feezel drives against Williamsville's Tony Seman in a semifinal victory.

An Olympia cheerleader hopes for the best as the Spartans take on Williamsville in a quarterfinal contest.

1991 A

EYES SKYWARD

Brett Larson of Seneca takes it to the hoop against Feezel in the championship game against Pittsfield.

McLeansboro's Pete Bushur races past a defender in the Foxes' 72-50 quarterfinal victory over Effingham St. Anthony.

What's in a name?
The bittersweet saga of March Madness

Our story begins with a young man named
Henry Van Arsdale Porter, **athlete** and *scholar*,
born in Tazewell County and raised on a
farm near **Washington.**

by Scott Johnson

Act I

During his years at Illinois State Normal University, young H.V. Porter was so well-rounded it seems quaint: a varsity baseball player who sang in the glee club, played violin in the orchestra, and edited the school newspaper.

After graduation Porter started his career in education, serving as principal at four small central Illinois high schools. At each of them Porter oversaw all activities, including flourishing literary and musical groups, but despite his broad interests, he became known as a top-notch basketball coach.

At Athens High School, Porter's teams showed state championship potential. His 1924 squad finished second to Elgin and two others won trophies. In those three journeys to Champaign, he became acquainted with Charles W. Whitten, head of the IHSAA. When Whitten went looking for an assistant manager to help him run the association and edit its brand-new magazine, Porter was the natural choice.

Blessed with a quick wit and a love of words, Porter threw himself into his new project, the *Illinois High School Athlete*. The *Athlete* was an official journal, but among the more mundane announcements, Porter frequently injected epigrams, jokes, essays, and poems.

His first such effort, "The Coach's Last Words to His Players," appeared in November 1928.

By the mid-1930s Porter's poetic output had dropped off as he immersed himself in many groundbreaking projects of the National Federation of State High School Athletic Associations. Porter was a born innovator. He spearheaded the development of special rule books for high school competition (prior to that high schools used college or AAU rules), oversaw the development of the molded basketball (which finally freed players from the dreaded laces), and was instrumental in the development of the fan-shaped backboard. With such a workload, it's not surprising that his output of dactylic hexameter suffered.

Porter's muse still moved him on occasion. In March 1939, on the inside back cover of the *Illinois High School Athlete*, Porter published an unsigned essay entitled "March Madness," a paean to every basketball fanatic he had met:

When the March madness is on him, midnight jaunts of a hundred miles on successive nights make him even more alert the next day.

Basketball Ides of March

The gym lights gleam like a beacon beam
And a million motors hum
In a good will flight on a Friday night;
For basketball beckons, "Come!"
A sharp-shooting mite is king tonight.
The Madness of March is running.
The winged feet fly, the ball sails high
And field goal hunters are gunning.

The colors clash as silk suits flash
And race on a shimmering floor.
Repressions die, and partisans vie
In a goal acclaiming roar.
On Championship Trail toward a holy grail,
All fans are birds of a feather.
It's fiesta night and cares lie light
When the air is full of leather.

Since time began, the instincts of man
Prove cave and current men kin.
On tournament night the sage and the wight
Are relatives under the skin.
It's festival time, — sans reasons or rhyme
But with nation-wide appeal.
In a cyclone of hate, our ship of state
Rides high on an even keel.

With war nerves tense, the final defense
Is the courage, strength and will
In a million lives where freedom thrives
And liberty lingers still.
Now eagles fly and heroes die
Beneath some foreign arch
Let their sons tread where hate is dead
In a happy Madness of March.

—H. V. Porter.

March Madness™

H. V. Porter

Louis J. Kramp

Jim Flynn

Brent Musburger

Dave Fry

Where did Porter come up with "March Madness"? A master of doggerel, he likely coined the term himself. It's virtually certain he was the first person to use the phrase "March Madness" in print to refer to a basketball tournament.

In 1940, the year the IHSAA became the IHSA, Porter left to head the National Federation. After his departure, the association's monthly magazine (renamed the *Illinois Interscholastic*) no longer doubled as a literary review. But Porter made one last contribution, a poem named "Basketball Ides of March" that ran in the March 1942 issue. Inspired by wartime patriotism, Porter portrayed high school basketball as a pillar of democracy, closing with:

Let their sons tread where hate is dead
In a happy Madness of March.

That poem's publication easily might have been the end of the story. IHSA's magazine had a limited readership, and Porter hadn't set out to create catch phrase or a trademark. Though he headed a national sports organization, he no longer had a basketball tournament to run. For all its cleverness, "March Madness" likely would have been forgotten if not for Louis J. Kramp.

Writing out of the Associated Press office in Springfield in 1943, Kramp recalled the phrase and worked it into a pre-tournament article that ran in newspapers across the state, thus introducing "March Madness" to the general public for the first time. Four years later, from AP's Chicago bureau, Kramp wrote another article that tied together the high school basketball tournaments of all 48 states. To cap the piece, he interviewed H.V. Porter at the National Federation office — perhaps for his poetry, but probably because of his position — and left with several homespun quotes, a snippet of one of Porter's poems, and a lead that read as follows:

All across the land, the March madness
reigns supreme.

Kramp's article, reminiscent of Porter's original essay, was picked up by hundreds of newspapers across the country, many of which chose to use "March Madness" in the headline. Something clicked. End-of-the-season basketball tournaments, previously referred to in print by such clunky names as "the annual hardcourt revue" and "the short pants parade," now sported a snappy new moniker. Newspaper usage of "March Madness" was hardly restricted to Illinois. But clippings show it was most popular in the areas where basketball itself was most popular, in the Midwest and especially in Illinois.

"March Madness" made its first appearance in an IHSA state tournament souvenir program in 1951. Beyond the occasional reference, however, the IHSA made no effort to promote the term, trademark it, or use it as any kind of official name or nickname. It was enough that "March Madness" meant high school basketball. Even the *Christian Science Monitor* got the message, as a 1966 article about tournament fever attested:

For schools involved, the final stages produce
moments of undiluted ecstasy and devastation.
"March Madness," they call it in Illinois.

In the years that followed, the IHSA remained blissfully unaware of the promotional value that "March Madness" had developed without the slightest advertising. But the era when high school basketball was the only game in town, when promotion was considered unnecessary and undignified, was about to come to an end.

continued on next page

Act II

Enter now into our drama a young man who cut his teeth writing sports for the *State Journal-Register* in Springfield and the *Moline Dispatch* before joining the sports information department at the University of Illinois. Jim Flynn was unlike any previous IHSA employee — not a former principal, not a former coach or athletic director, but an honest-to-goodness newspaperman. And though he didn't share H.V. Porter's penchant for poetry, Flynn was every bit Porter's match in creativity and output.

Flynn's first order of business in September 1973 was the overhaul the *Illinois Interscholastic*, Porter's creation. Not far down the list was the unrelenting marketing and promotion of "March Madness" — the phrase itself and the tournament it referred to. For the 1974 basketball tournament programs, Flynn penned an article entitled "They Call It 'March Madness' " that ran annually for the next 16 years. He also enlisted Jim Enright, a retired sportswriter from Chicago, to write a comprehensive history of the state basketball tournament. *March Madness: The Story of High School Basketball in Illinois*, published by the IHSA in 1977, was a slam-dunk intended to prove, once and for all, that March Madness belonged to Illinois. On the dust jacket was H.V. Porter's 1942 poem.

There was only one problem. Flynn could not convince his bosses to apply for a trademark.

In retrospect it's easy to see why that would have been a good idea, but that point was not so obvious in 1977. No other group seemed likely to use the term to promote its tournament.

There were no other goods and services called "March Madness," and no apparent market for them if they did exist, and after all, didn't everybody know that March Madness meant the Illinois high school basketball tournament?

Then another former sportswriter entered the picture. Brent Musburger, who had risen from the sports desk of *Chicago's American* to become the premier sports announcer at CBS, was well acquainted with the high school tournament and "March Madness." On one fateful day, perhaps as early as 1974, he used the phrase on national television to describe the NCAA's basketball tournament.

A few years later, the publicity department at CBS realized what Jim Flynn had been saying all along — that "March Madness" had great potential as a slogan — and began using it to promote tournament telecasts. It's hard to pinpoint the date exactly. References to "March Madness" started to pop up in the *New York Times* in 1985, a sure sign that CBS's advertising had reached critical mass. It turned out that "March Madness" had name recognition through the roof, and still no one trademarked it — not the IHSA, not CBS, not the NCAA.

Not until 1991, when Dave Fry took over as executive director of the IHSA, did Jim Flynn finally get his wish. But when the trademark application was filed, Fry and Flynn found, to their dismay, that the mark had been registered in 1989 by a Chicago television production company with a talk show revolving around the NCAA tournament. The NCAA and IHSA both filed cancellation requests against the mark. In the meantime, IHSA trademarked the phrase "America's Original March Madness."

March Madness

The IHSA eventually formed a partnership with the television company, and with the rights to the trademark finally in hand, began enforcing its legal privileges against all comers, especially the NCAA. As Fry explained, IHSA's intention was never to stop the NCAA from using the term, but rather to charge a licensing fee for its use. The NCAA saw things differently, of course.

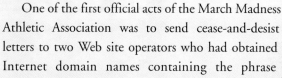

The battle was joined in 1995 when the IHSA filed suit against the NCAA's corporate partner, GTE Vantage, over a CD-ROM basketball game named "March Madness."

As Jim Flynn told George Vecsey of the *New York Times*: "I'd like to say this could be the start of a legal struggle of Olympic proportions, but I can't afford the rights fee."

In a landmark decision, U.S. Chief Judge Michael Mihm of Peoria ruled that the phrase "March Madness" had passed into the public domain and that both the NCAA and IHSA owned rights to it, making it a "dual-use" mark. Years of failing to protect the mark "assiduously" had doomed the IHSA's case.

"I feel like the last homesteader in the old western who is defending his water hold from the big guy who owns the rest of the valley," Fry lamented.

After the decision was upheld in Federal Appellate Court, the IHSA and the NCAA settled their differences. The result was the March Madness Athletic Association (MMAA), a corporation set up to control the rights to the trademark. Under the new umbrella, the NCAA owned the rights to the trademark as it applied to college basketball tournaments, while the IHSA owned the rights for all high school basketball tournaments.

Act III

With all the main players on stage, our drama now enters its third act, where the comedy of errors turns to tragedy and, in an unforeseen twist, a mysterious outsider threatens to triumph over both protagonist and antagonist.

One of the first official acts of the March Madness Athletic Association was to send cease-and-desist letters to two Web site operators who had obtained Internet domain names containing the phrase "March Madness." The IHSA had registered its version of the name, marchmadness.org, in 1996, but two variants, marchmadness.net and marchmadness.com, were registered by other entities. The owners of marchmadness.net surrendered immediately, but marchmadness.com, controlled by a Texas corporation, would not go quietly. Unable to reach a settlement, the MMAA persuaded the agency that registers domain names to put a lock on the march-madness.com site and then sued the Texas company, which immediately countersued.

The case dragged on for almost two years. Though the IHSA had little to gain from the suit, it was paying half the tab on some enormous legal fees, a mere pittance to the NCAA but a gaping money pit to the IHSA. Eventually the March Madness Athletic Association prevailed in the bench trial and subsequent appeal, providing a small measure of vindication. Ownership of the marchmadness.com domain, held in limbo for many years, was transferred to the NCAA in 2005, bringing to a close a most unusual chapter in sports history.

For its unrelenting efforts to promote and protect its trademark, the IHSA retained only marchmadness.org, "America's Original March Madness," and a portfolio of painful memories.

And what of H.V. Porter, the poet whose musings in 1939 inspired all this madness? In recognition of his many contributions to the sport, he was enshrined in the National Basketball Hall of Fame in 1960, long before "March Madness" meant much of anything outside Illinois. In the years since his death in 1975, his famous phrase has eclipsed all his practical accomplishments. Someday his plaque in Springfield, Massachusetts, will be replaced by one that properly labels him as the "Father of March Madness."

Little could he have predicted the strange chain of events his simple poem would set in motion.

Findlay vs. U-High **1992A**

FINDLAY
Class A State Champions of 1992

FRONT ROW (left to right): Cameron Lawerence, John Cruit, Tyler Bradford, Michael Beem, Jeremy Chaney, Greg Mitchell, Mgr. David Heinz. SECOND ROW: Joey Howell, Dustin Cruit, Eric Smith, Coach Michael Reynolds, Clayton Stivers, Jason Tucker, Tony Sparks, Jimmy Allen.

State Final Tournament Scores

Super-Sectionals
At Normal [ISU]—Normal (University) 56, Clifton (Central) 35
At Moline—Sherrard 55, Hanover (River Ridge) 52
At Charleston [EIU]—Fairfield 51, Freeburg 39
At Macomb [WIU]—Augusta (Southeastern) 77, Virden 50
At Carbondale [SIU]—Benton 54, Cairo 53
At Kankakee [Olivet]—Chicago (St. Martin de Porres) 71, Addison (Driscoll) 54
At Decatur [Millikin]—Findlay 62, Springfield (Calvary) 55
At DeKalb [NIU]—Elgin (St. Edward) 85, Princeton 73

Quarterfinals
Normal (University) 55, Sherrard 34
Augusta (Southeastern) 59, Fairfield 44
Benton 64, Chicago (St. Martin de Porres) 50
Findlay 74, Elgin (St. Edward) 60

Semifinals
Normal (University) 63, Augusta (Southeastern) 50
Findlay 83, Benton 74

Finals
Benton 76, Augusta (Southeastern) 69 (third place)
Findlay 61, Normal (University) 45 (title)

Scoring Leaders

Player, School	G	FG	3P	FT	Pts
JoJo Johnson, Benton	4	40	18	23	121
Jason Marlow, Augusta (Southeastern)	4	33	3	25	94
Eric Smith, Findlay	4	30	0	18	78
Clayton Stivers, Findlay	4	24	5	22	75
Chris Payne, Elgin (St. Edward)	2	19	13	12	63

All-Tournament First Team

Player, School	Ht.	Yr.
Neal Hubbard, Normal (University)	6-5	Sr.
JoJo Johnson, Benton	6-3	Sr.
Jason Marlow, Augusta (Southeastern)	6-2	Sr.
Eric Smith, Findlay	6-7	Sr.
Clayton Stivers, Findlay	6-7	Sr.

Championship Game Box Score
Assembly Hall, Champaign, March 14, 1992

FINDLAY (61)
Coach Michael Reynolds

Player	FG-A	3P-A	FT-A	Pts	PF	Rb	As	St	Bl
Jim Allen	4-7	2-5	6-7	16	1	3	5	1	0
Michael Beem	0-0	0-0	0-0	0	0	0	0	1	0
Tyler Bradford	0-0	0-0	0-0	0	0	0	0	0	0
Jeremy Chaney	0-1	0-0	0-2	0	0	0	0	0	0
Dustin Cruit	0-0	0-0	0-0	0	0	0	0	0	0
John Cruit	0-0	0-0	0-0	0	0	0	0	0	0
Joey Howell	2-6	2-2	0-0	6	3	4	1	0	0
Cameron Lawrence	0-0	0-0	0-0	0	0	0	0	0	0
Greg Mitchell	0-0	0-0	0-0	0	1	1	0	0	0
Eric Smith	7-13	0-0	2-4	16	2	8	2	0	2
Tony Sparks	1-3	0-0	0-0	2	3	4	3	0	0
Clayton Stivers	6-11	3-6	6-8	21	1	13	0	0	1
Jason Tucker	0-0	0-0	0-0	0	0	0	0	0	0
TEAM					2				
TOTAL	20-41	7-13	14-23	61	11	35	11	2	3

NORMAL (UNIVERSITY) (45)
Coach Cal Hubbard

Player	FG-A	3P-A	FT-A	Pts	PF	Rb	As	St	Bl
James Abell	0-1	0-1	0-0	0	1	3	1	0	0
Tom Feely	0-1	0-0	0-0	0	0	0	0	0	0
Bob Fitzgerald	1-9	0-5	0-0	2	4	0	1	0	0
John Handy	3-8	0-4	0-0	6	1	4	2	3	0
Neal Hubbard	3-13	2-10	2-2	10	4	6	2	2	0
Brady Knight	6-13	0-1	1-2	13	3	4	2	0	0
Dan Kotarba	1-5	0-0	0-2	2	3	7	3	0	0
Tom Maack	0-1	0-0	0-0	0	0	0	0	0	0
Jim Orsulak	0-0	0-0	0-0	0	0	0	0	0	0
Eric Strassheim	0-0	0-0	0-0	0	0	0	0	0	0
Brian Truttmann	0-0	0-0	0-2	0	0	0	0	0	0
Pete Vaughn	5-10	0-0	0-0	10	4	8	1	1	3
TEAM					1				
TOTAL	19-61	2-21	5-8	45	20	34	12	6	3

Findlay	13	12	15	21	—	61
Normal (University)	12	7	10	16	—	45

Officials: Tom Bryant, Paul Highsmith.

They were the smallest. Ever.

And finally, after three years of aching anticipation, the Findlay basketball team could also claim it was the best following a rousing 61-45 win over Normal University High in the title game.

With an enrollment of 96 students, Findlay (31-2) became the smallest school in Illinois history to win a state basketball title. The next smallest champion was Hebron, which won in 1952 with 98 students.

"That's a nice title. Some people probably think we're hicks or something with just 96 people in the school," Findlay center Eric Smith said. "But I think it really says something about us that we could band together like this and do something extraordinary."

And the ninth-ranked Falcons accomplished the extraordinary by beating opponents at their own game. Up-tempo, slowdown — Findlay did it all in its three state tourney wins.

Normal U-High came into the title game billed as the most patient team in the tournament, with solid 3-point shooters and a defense second to none. But Findlay matched Normal pass for pass, trey for trey and steal for steal and became the first team to tally more than 50 points against the Pioneers in the postseason. The Falcons also held No. 15 U-High (29-4) to 31 percent shooting.

Maybe fittingly, patience helped earn Findlay its biggest victory.

"We weren't ready for that type of slow-tempo, stalling play last year," Smith said in reference to a 1991 super-sectional upset against Williamsville. "But people have thrown all kinds of Mickey Mouse defenses at us this year and we've been able to adjust."

In the championship match, Findlay's 6-foot-7 Clayton Stivers turned in his best game of the tourney, scoring a game-high 21 points and grabbing a game-high 13 rebounds. The 6-7 Smith finished with 16 points and was awarded the tournament sportsmanship trophy, a new award.

It wasn't an easy march to first place, though, as the Falcons had to rally against Elgin St. Edward in the quarterfinals and then withstood 16th-ranked Benton and 6-3 all-state gunner JoJo Johnson in the semifinals. Johnson led the tournament with 121 points after making 31 of 84 field-goal attempts in three games.

U-High, meanwhile, used its 1-2-2 ball press to upset top-ranked and unbeaten Augusta Southeastern in the semifinals after blowing out Sherrard and slick all-state guard Eric Lawson.

Then in the third-place game, Southeastern stymied Johnson but had no answer for center Brian Holman. Holman, who racked up 22 points and 15 rebounds, had sat out Benton's semifinal game for religious reasons.

Also included in this Elite Eight field was eventual 1993 Mr. Basketball Jerry Gee and Chicago St. Martin de Porres, the first team with a sub-.500 record to reach the state final tourney since 1953.

Pete Vaughn of Normal U-High tracks down a loose ball while Findlay's Eric Smith awaits the outcome in the 1992 championship game.

Clayton Stivers scrambles for a rebound as Findlay outlasts Elgin St. Edward in quarterfinal action.

Smith parades past the championship trophy. Findlay's 61-45 win over U-High made it the smallest school to capture a state basketball title.

Bryan Brooks of Sherrard leaves no doubt about who controls the rebound in a quarterfinal loss to U-High.

SEMIFINAL SHOWDOWN

Findlay's Jim Allen looks for an outlet as Benton's Jason Tate reaches for a steal. Findlay won the semifinal in an 83-74 shootout.

1992A

1993A

STAUNTON
Class A State Champions of 1993

FRONT ROW (left to right):
Matt Popvich, Ron Hampton,
Mike Kovaly, Derek Brauer,
Brad Best. SECOND ROW:
Coach Randy Legendre,
Corey Painter, Andy Kuba,
Kevin Meyer, Brad Skertich,
Jeremy May.

When the fans settled into their seats at Assembly Hall for the 1993 Class A finale, most figured they'd already seen the state championship game.

Prevailing wisdom was that Chicago Hales Franciscan wrapped up the state title after knocking off a tough Cairo team in the semifinals. All that remained was the mundane task of thumping a slower, less-athletic Staunton team in the finals. Even some Hales Franciscan players felt that way.

Overconfidence turned out to be their downfall.

Paced by Andy Kuba's 26 points and Ron Hampton's four free throws down the stretch, unranked Staunton (27-4) upset No. 8 Hales Franciscan 66-62 to capture the first state title for the long-time "football school."

"We were the underdog coming in and we felt good about being the underdog," Staunton forward Jeremy May said. "The pressure was off so we just came in and played basketball."

While Staunton entered the game relaxed and confident, several Hales players admitted overconfidence after nipping Cairo 69-67 in the semis.

"Against Cairo, people thought that was the championship game," said Spartans guard Lonnie Brown, who paced his team with 17 points. "That game took a lot out of us."

The big man all postseason for Staunton was 6-foot-5 senior Kuba, who scored 12 in the fourth quarter, keeping Staunton in the game and winding up the second-leading scorer in the tournament.

"We dug ourselves into a lot of holes this year but always managed to get out of them," said Hales Franciscan Coach Tom Shields, who was bidding to become the first coach to win a Class A title at two schools. "This is one hole we dug too deep." Hales finished 23-11.

Kuba had come up just as big for Staunton in its toughest game prior to the championship — a 65-64 double-overtime win against Bridgeport Red Hill in the Charleston Super-Sectional. Kuba finished with 26 points and 11 rebounds in that game, tipping in his own miss with one second to go for the win. Staunton had trailed 54-48 with 20 seconds left in regulation before Kuba hit two 3-pointers to put the game into overtime.

"It was a miracle that we won the game," Kuba said.

The Cairo game in the semifinals was nearly as exciting, with Hales winning on Brown's 17-footer with 3.4 seconds left. The lead changed hands 15 times and Hales trailed for much of the second half before Brown's shot.

Cairo's 6-7 all-stater Tyrone Nesby — youngest of 14 children — was leading scorer for the tournament with 104 points, but he had just 13 against Hales in the semifinals. Nesby later starred at the University of Nevada-Las Vegas and played four seasons in the NBA.

State Final Tournament Scores

Super-Sectionals

At Carbondale [SIU]—Cairo 70, Okawville 66
At East Moline (United)—Dakota 79, Kewanee 67
At Normal [ISU]—Normal (University) 48, Fairbury (Prairie Central) 43
At Kankakee [Olivet]—Chicago (Hales Franciscan) 59, Chicago (St. Martin de Porres) 56 (OT)
At Charleston [EIU]—Staunton 65, Bridgeport (Red Hill) 64 (2 OT)
At Decatur [Millikin]—Riverton 79, Arthur 64
At DeKalb [NIU]—Mendota 69, Elgin (St. Edward) 64
At Macomb [WIU]—Hamilton 44, Pittsfield 39

Quarterfinals

Cairo 74, Dakota 54
Chicago (Hales Franciscan) 63, Normal (University) 49
Staunton 52, Riverton 43
Hamilton 75, Mendota 59

Semifinals

Chicago (Hales Franciscan) 69, Cairo 67
Staunton 52, Hamilton 42

Finals

Cairo 80, Hamilton 68 (third place)
Staunton 66, Chicago (Hales Franciscan) 62 (title)

Scoring Leaders

Player, School	G	FG	3P	FT	Pts
Tyrone Nesby, Cairo	4	42	5	15	104
Andy Kuba, Staunton	4	31	5	18	85
Lonnie Brown, Chi. (Hales Franciscan)	4	29	1	6	65
Simeon Williams, Cairo	4	23	0	18	64
Kevin Meyer, Staunton	4	25	0	12	62

All-Tournament First Team

Player, School	Ht.	Yr.
Lonnie Brown, Chicago (Hales Franciscan)	6-2	So.
Andy Kuba, Staunton	6-5	Sr.
Kurt Meister, Hamilton	6-8	Jr.
Tyrone Nesby, Cairo	6-7	Jr.
Greg Wood, Chicago (Hales Franciscan)	6-5	Jr.

Championship Game Box Score

Assembly Hall, Champaign, March 13, 1993

STAUNTON (66)
Coach Randy Legendre

Player	FG-A	3P-A	FT-A	Pts	PF	Rb	As	St	Bl
Brad Best	0-0	0-0	0-0	0	2	0	0	0	0
Ron Hampton	3-4	0-0	7-8	13	0	1	2	0	0
Andy Kuba	9-12	0-1	8-10	26	1	14	1	0	0
Jeremy May	1-4	0-1	3-5	5	2	1	1	1	0
Kevin Meyer	8-17	0-0	4-6	20	0	6	1	0	0
Brad Skertich	1-2	0-0	0-1	2	3	3	3	0	0
TEAM						3			
TOTAL	22-39	0-2	22-30	66	8	28	8	1	0

CHICAGO (HALES FRANCISCAN) (62)
Coach Tom Shields

Player	FG-A	3P-A	FT-A	Pts	PF	Rb	As	St	Bl
Shawn Baker	6-13	0-0	4-4	16	4	2	1	3	1
Lonnie Brown	8-14	0-2	1-1	17	3	2	0	2	1
Tywon Burnom	0-0	0-0	0-0	0	0	0	0	0	0
Chayim Cunningham	1-4	0-0	1-1	3	3	1	0	0	0
Sampson Essex	1-2	0-1	0-0	2	0	0	0	0	0
Keith Stanton	2-6	0-1	0-0	4	2	4	0	1	3
David Stennis	0-4	0-0	0-0	0	2	8	0	1	0
Jamar Turner	1-4	1-1	0-0	3	1	4	0	1	0
Ralph Williams	4-8	1-2	0-0	9	5	3	2	0	0
Greg Wood	4-9	0-0	0-0	8	5	5	0	0	1
TEAM						0			
TOTAL	27-64	2-7	6-6	62	25	29	3	8	6

Staunton	15	18	11	22	—	66
Chicago (Hales Franciscan)	13	17	12	20	—	62

Officials: Preston Brewer, Gene Morgan.

UPSET SPECIAL

The Staunton bench celebrates its 66-62 upset win over Hales Franciscan in the 1993 title game.

Staunton's Kevin Meyer snares a rebound as Chayim Cunningham of Hales Franciscan arrives too late in championship-game action.

Greg Wood scores on a breakaway dunk for Hales Franciscan.

Cairo's Tyrone Nesby flies out of bounds to save a loose ball in a semifinal game against Hales Franciscan.

Andy Kuba, Staunton's 6-foot-5 forward, crashes the boards in the title contest against Hales Franciscan.

1993A

1994A

Night and day. For Pinckneyville, that was the difference between this state visit and the last. The 1988 Elite Eight berth ended with top-ranked Panthers faltering down the stretch, committing four costly turnovers in the final two minutes, and losing to Pana in the title game.

But in this tournament, clutch time belonged to Pinckneyville and all-state guard Shane Hawkins. Twice in Pinckneyville's final three contests, Hawkins came through with heroics in the closing seconds of a tight game. Twice he delivered game-winning passes, the capper in a 67-65 victory over Eureka for the championship.

After a timeout with seven seconds left, Pinckneyville inbounded to Hawkins, who dribbled up the right side, drove to the middle and passed off to Ryan Bruns for a piece of Illinois history. Bruns' three-footer entered the net just as the buzzer sounded, giving No. 4 Pinckneyville (33-2) its first title since 1948.

Prior to Bruns' shot, good things had been happening for No. 6 Eureka (30-2), which clawed back from a five-point deficit with 31 seconds remaining. Matt Koeppel hit a 23-foot three-pointer to start the rally and then, following a Pinckneyville turnover and a wild scramble under the hoop, Matt Braman tied the score at 65-65.

Bruns finished with 17 points to lead Pinckneyville, while Braman's 13 points paced a group of five Eureka players in double figures.

"I'm not going to tell you it was always well played, but the way it finished should make for one of the more memorable state championships in a long time," Pinckneyville Coach Dick Corn said.

Previously, the Panthers had also battled through one of the more memorable quarterfinal games in a long time, scoring a 55-54 upset win over top-ranked and unbeaten Teutopolis.

Trailing 54-53 late in the game, Pinckneyville rushed down court with one thing in mind — getting the ball to Hawkins.

A determined Hawkins received a pass on the wing and drove hard into the lane. Drawing three T-Town defenders, he dished underneath to a wide-open Jarritt Sommer, who laid in the game-winner with 6 seconds left.

That game set the standard for what proved to be one of the most competitive quarterfinal rounds in history. Three of the four games were decided by four points or less, a reflection of this Elite Eight field's combined 231-26 record. Included in that round was Eureka's 52-50 win over Riverton on a lay-up by Braman with 7.1 seconds left — his team's lone field goal of the final quarter Eureka then stunned second-ranked Chicago St. Martin de Porres and Mr. Basketball Jerry Gee in the semifinals 58-50.

PINCKNEYVILLE
Class A State Champions of 1994

FRONT ROW (left to right): Matt Decker, Shane Hawkins, Ryan Bruns, Coach Dick Corn. SECOND ROW: Ryan Eisenhauer, Garrison Rule, Mark Radake, Brett Cleland. THIRD ROW: Jeremy Johnston, Andrew Dagner, Jarritt Somner, Kevin Kellerman, Anson Konkel, Shane McGranahan.

State Final Tournament Scores
Super-Sectionals
At Normal [ISU]—Eureka 85, Watseka 63
At Decatur [Millikin]—Riverton 55, Sullivan 52
At Rock Island—Kewanee 53, Hanover (River Ridge) 48
At Kankakee [Olivet]—Chicago (St. Martin de Porres) 64, Aurora (A. Christian) 45
At Carbondale [SIU]—Pinckneyville 53, Herrin 49
At Charleston [EIU]—Teutopolis 67, Belleville (Althoff) 53
At Macomb [WIU]—Hamilton 45, Ashland (A-C Central) 44
At DeKalb [NIU]—Rockford (Lutheran) 65, Princeton 43
Quarterfinals
Eureka 52, Riverton 50
Chicago (St. Martin de Porres) 73, Kewanee 60
Pinckneyville 55, Teutopolis 54
Rockford (Lutheran) 56, Hamilton 52
Semifinals
Eureka 58, Chicago (St. Martin de Porres) 50
Pinckneyville 80, Rockford (Lutheran) 43
Finals
Chicago (St. Martin de Porres) 63, Rockford (Lutheran) 45 (third place)
Pinckneyville 67, Eureka 65 (title)

Scoring Leaders

Player, School	G	FG	3P	FT	Pts
Eric Clark, Rockford (Lutheran)	4	36	0	19	91
Tyron Triplett, Chi. (St. Martin de Porres)	4	30	15	11	86
Shane Hawkins, Pinckneyville	4	24	9	28	85
Jerry Gee, Chicago (St. Martin de Porres)	4	33	2	10	78
Brett Cleland, Pinckneyville	4	19	3	12	53

All-Tournament First Team

Player, School	Ht.	Yr.
Eric Clark, Rockford (Lutheran)	6-8	Sr.
Jerry Gee, Chicago (St. Martin de Porres)	6-7	Sr.
Shane Hawkins, Pinckneyville	6-3	Sr.
Nathaniel Meiss, Eureka	5-11	Sr.
Tyron Triplett, Chicago (St. Martin de Porres)	6-2	So.

Championship Game Box Score
Assembly Hall, Champaign, March 12, 1994

PINCKNEYVILLE (67)
Coach Dick Corn

Player	FG-A	3P-A	FT-A	Pts	PF	Rb	As	St	Bl
Ryan Bruns	7-10	0-0	3-6	17	2	6	3	1	0
Brett Cleland	5-12	1-4	0-0	11	2	5	3	0	0
Andrew Dagner	3-7	0-0	0-0	6	4	3	0	0	0
Matt Decker	2-7	1-4	1-2	6	4	6	4	0	0
Shane Hawkins	4-12	2-6	3-4	13	0	4	3	1	0
Garrison Rule	0-0	0-0	1-2	1	1	1	0	1	0
Jarritt Sommer	6-9	0-0	1-3	13	3	3	0	1	2
TEAM						4			
TOTAL	27-57	4-14	9-17	67	16	31	14	3	2

EUREKA (65)
Coach Tim Meiss

Player	FG-A	3P-A	FT-A	Pts	PF	Rb	As	St	Bl
Brian Blunier	2-3	0-0	5-6	9	3	3	3	0	0
Matt Braman	4-9	0-0	5-5	13	4	5	1	0	2
Matt Koeppel	3-9	2-5	2-2	10	4	6	2	1	0
Jason Lane	1-1	0-0	0-0	2	0	0	1	0	0
Nathaniel Meiss	4-12	1-5	2-2	11	1	4	3	0	0
Chet Rieke	0-0	0-0	0-0	0	1	0	0	0	0
Dave Steinbeck	5-7	0-1	0-0	10	1	0	0	0	1
Bob Wettstein	4-11	0-0	2-2	10	2	8	0	0	0
TEAM						3			
TOTAL	23-52	3-11	16-17	65	16	29	10	1	3

Pinckneyville	12	16	22	17	—	67
Eureka	11	15	21	18	—	65

Officials: Don Deleu, James Sanders.

Brent Niebrugge of Teutopolis pursues a stray pass as Pinckneyville's Garrison Rule (42) stands of guard. Pinckneyville won a 55-54 squeaker to advance to the semifinals.

Jerry Gee of St. Martin de Porres, Mr. Basketball of 1994, pulls up as he meets Dave Steinbeck of Eureka in a semifinal contest.

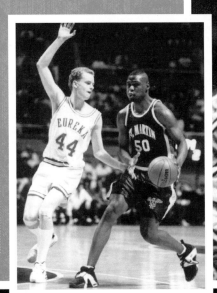

1994A

Nathanel Meiss of Eureka takes to the air to block a pass by Riverton's Beau Veihman in a quarterfinal contest.

TRAFFIC JAM

Meiss runs into traffic in the lane as Pinckneyville's Jarritt Sommer stands his ground. Pinckneyville won its second state title 67-65 on a last-second shot.

NORMAL (UNIVERSITY), Class A State Champions of 1995

FRONT ROW (left to right): Statistician Glenn Leary, Kurt Olson, Eric Schlipf, Jeremy Stanton, Jonah Batambuze, Darrin York, Matt McClintock, Student Assistant Jason Seffner, Asst. Coach Lester Hampton. SECOND ROW: Asst. Coach David Kunka, Kevin Jones, Nathan Hubbard, D.J. Hubbard, Jason Naffziger, Jason Graf, Nitai Spiro, Andy Matthews, Coach Cal Hubbard.

Christian wound up making 12 three-pointers to tie an Elite Eight record set earlier in the day by second-ranked Kinderhook West Pike, the Eagles missed their final four trey attempts.

Joe Mann led all players with 16 points while U-High's Nathan Hubbard paced his team with 15.

Aurora Christian — playing without point guard Mike Smith, who suffered a broken arm during regional play — had advanced to the title game on a last-second shot of its own, as Josh Wayne's bucket proved the difference in a 63-61 semifinal win over Rock Island Alleman.

"I was the second option, but it just happened I was the one that was open," said Wayne, who led his team with 13 rebounds and had 12 points while all-stater Mann had 19.

The third-place game, West Pike's Marty Hull fired in 24 points from all over the court to upend Alleman. The performance also gave Hull the tournament scoring title, with 100 points, and the tournament rebounding title, with 38 in four games.

No shot in Kevin Jones' basketball career had ever come more easily. Certainly none had ever meant more. And no lay-up in the history of the Normal University High boys basketball program will be replayed as frequently as Jones's with 2.6 seconds remaining in the title game.

Converting a pass from sophomore classmate Jonah Batambuze, the 6-foot-4 Jones broke a 54-54 tie with his shot, handing University High (29-3) its first state championship against top-ranked Aurora Christian (32-2).

"Never an easier shot in my life," said Jones, who also made his only other field goal attempt on the night. "But if I'd missed it I'd be dead."

The finish marked the second straight year the title came down to the final seconds and the eighth straight season a top-ranked team did not win the championship.

The key all tournament for fifth-ranked U-High was Coach Cal Hubbard's 1-2-2 ball-press defense. Hubbard brought the same defensive philosophy he'd used at Lincoln to U-High with impressive results. Just four of U-High's 1994-95 opponents topped 60 points.

"Our whole goal is to go at the heart of the other team's offense, wherever their strength is, and cut it out," Hubbard said. "If high school kids can't go to their best player or you take them out of their game, they tend to get a little nervous."

That seemed to be the case with Aurora Christian, which rushed to a 19-4 lead but was outscored 52-35 the rest of the way, including an 18-3 stretch in the final 7:12 of the title game. While Aurora

State Final Tournament Scores
Super-Sectionals
At Macomb [WIU]—Kinderhook (West Pike) 68, Carrollton 51
At Charleston [EIU]—Strasburg (Stewardson-S.) 64, Lebanon 53
At Normal [ISU]—Normal (University) 42, Mahomet (M.-Seymour) 32
At Carbondale [SIU]—Harrisburg 51, Breese (Mater Dei) 43
At Decatur [Millikin]—Shelbyville 80, Tolono (Unity) 72
At Moline—Rock Island (Alleman) 57, Orion 50
At DeKalb [NIU]—Rockford (Lutheran) 62, Yorkville 45
At Kankakee [Olivet]—Aurora (A. Christian) 65, Chicago (Tabernacle Christian) 61
Quarterfinals
Kinderhook (West Pike) 86, Strasburg (Stewardson-S.) 64
Normal (University) 59, Harrisburg 39
Rock Island (Alleman) 74, Shelbyville 66
Aurora (A. Christian) 64, Rockford (Lutheran) 44
Semifinals
Normal (University) 91, Kinderhook (West Pike) 67
Aurora (A. Christian) 63, Rock Island (Alleman) 61
Finals
Kinderhook (West Pike) 74, Rock Island (Alleman) 70 (third place)
Normal (University) 56, Aurora (A. Christian) 54 (title)

Scoring Leaders

Player, School	G	FG	3P	FT	Pts
Marty Hull, Kinderhook (West Pike)	4	40	1	19	100
Charlie Manis, Rock Island (Alleman)	4	34	0	13	81
Brian Trapkus, Rock Island (Alleman)	4	27	0	14	68
Kirk Mosley, Kinderhook (West Pike)	4	19	12	8	58
Joe Mann, Aurora (A. Christian)	4	22	6	7	57

All-Tournament First Team

Player, School	Ht.	Yr.
Nathan Hubbard, Normal (University)	6-4	Sr.
Marty Hull, Kinderhook (West Pike)	6-6	Sr.
Charlie Manis, Rock Island (Alleman)	6-7	Sr.
Joe Mann, Aurora (A. Christian)	6-3	Sr.
Kirk Mosley, Kinderhook (West Pike)	5-11	Sr.

Championship Game Box Score
Assembly Hall, Champaign, March 11, 1995
NORMAL (UNIVERSITY) (56)
Coach Cal Hubbard

Player	FG-A	3P-A	FT-A	Pts	PF	Rb	As	St	Bl
Jonah Batambuze	4-6	0-0	4-4	12	1	6	1	0	0
Jason Graf	1-2	0-0	0-0	2	3	0	1	0	0
D. J. Hubbard	2-7	1-3	0-1	5	0	2	1	1	0
Nathan Hubbard	3-10	0-2	9-10	15	2	7	2	2	0
Kevin Jones	2-2	0-0	0-0	4	3	0	2	0	0
Matt McClintock	0-0	0-0	0-0	0	0	0	0	0	0
Jason Naffziger	2-3	1-1	0-0	5	1	2	0	0	1
Kurt Olson	0-3	0-3	1-2	1	0	0	0	0	1
Eric Schlipf	0-0	0-0	0-0	0	0	0	0	0	0
Jeremy Stanton	5-7	2-3	0-0	12	1	1	2	2	0
TEAM						1			
TOTAL	19-40	4-12	14-17	56	12	22	7	7	2

AURORA (A. CHRISTIAN) (54)
Coach Don Davidson

Player	FG-A	3P-A	FT-A	Pts	PF	Rb	As	St	Bl
Julian Harrell	0-2	0-0	0-0	0	3	3	0	0	0
Joe Mann	5-13	5-11	1-2	16	4	3	2	1	0
P.J. McKinney	1-2	1-2	0-0	3	1	0	1	1	0
Brad Punke	5-12	4-10	0-0	14	0	2	6	2	0
Matt Stott	0-1	0-1	0-0	0	0	0	0	0	0
Nathan Thompson	4-11	1-6	3-5	12	2	7	0	1	2
Josh Wayne	3-4	1-1	2-2	9	5	7	2	1	0
TEAM						4			
TOTAL	18-45	12-31	6-9	54	15	26	11	6	2

Normal (University)		4	20	14	18	— 56
Aurora (A. Christian)		19	10	19	6	— 54

Officials: Bob Rowatt, Randy Rimington.

Jason Naffziger of U-High is uncontested as he shoots in the championship contest. Aurora Christian's Julian Harrell awaits the rebound.

Darrin York raises his arms in jubilation after U-High's come-from-behind 56-54 win in the 1995 title game.

U-High's Nathan Hubbard heads for the baseline in a semifinal contest against West Pike as Marty Hull does his best to stop the drive.

Governor Jim Edgar and his wife Brenda enjoy the action at the 1995 Class A tournament. Edgar was a frequent visitor during his tenure as chief executive.

STATE VISIT

Jeremy Stanton of Normal U-High works through half-court pressure in the title contest against Aurora Christian's Brad Punke.

1995A

Shelbyville 1996 State Champs

1996 A

SHELBYVILLE
Class A State Champions of 1996

FRONT ROW (left to right):
Aaron Rohdermann, Ryan
Shambo, Harlan Kennell,
Roger Jones, Kevin Herdes,
Ben Short, Jim Brix, Tim Hardy.
SECOND ROW: Coach Sean
Taylor, George Bolinger,
Mike Steers, Rich Beyers,
Todd Wilderman, Dirk Herdes,
John Evans.

Controversy having nothing to do with coaches, players, or officials surrounded the 1996 tournament — the first Elite Eight held in Peoria's Carver Arena.

The IHSA's decision to leave Champaign-Urbana after 77 years generated howls of criticism from many, including several coaches involved in this tournament. But by the time the weekend was over and fans had a chance to experience the atmosphere in downtown Peoria, many hard feelings softened.

"I can't believe how the people of Peoria have reached out," Rock Island Alleman coach Larry Schulte said. "And I was one of the doubting Thomases because I am a traditionalist and hated to leave Champaign. But I'll tell you, this is a better atmosphere."

The experience even softened Shelbyville coach Sean Taylor, who said prior to the Elite Eight he would rather have brought his top-rated team to Assembly Hall. Then again, Taylor also said he didn't care if the tournament was held at a YMCA in an obscure town.

"Wherever they hold the tournament, that's where we want to be," Taylor said.

And they were. Just barely.

Along the way to proving just how hard it is to win state, Shelbyville barely won its regional. The Rams survived that epic overtime against home team Nokomis only because 6-foot-7 Roger Jones drained a three-pointer from the corner as time expired.

And Shelbyville's stay in Peoria was nearly a short one, as the Rams came oh so close to losing a quarterfinal against fifth-ranked Mendota. Rich Beyers' short jumper with 11.9 seconds left gave Shelbyville a 53-52 lead, but Mendota's Derek Kilmartin got off a potential game-winning shot that hit the rim and bounced off as the buzzer sounded.

Maybe all those close calls explain why Shelbyville was the first team since Teutopolis in 1986 to make good on a No. 1 ranking. Taylor had other ideas.

"In the last 10 years, the sportswriters were just stupid," he said.

Whatever the case, Shelbyville (34-1) certainly looked the part of a champion through much of this season. Blessed with size in Jones and 6-9 center Beyers (Lon Kruger's first recruit at the University of Illinois) and solid guard play, the Rams' lone loss was to Springfield Calvary — a loss avenged in the sectional finals.

Shelbyville also avenged another defeat in the semifinal against third-ranked Alleman. One year earlier, Alleman had bullied Shelbyville in the quarterfinals. This time the Rams were up to the challenge in a physical 59-48 victory. The difference, according to Beyers, was defense.

"Last year we just relied on our offense. We were so offensive-oriented because we could all shoot and score," he said. "Since then we've realized you have to have a defense, too."

And this was a tournament for defense. Teams shot just 40 percent in the Elite Eight games and the final four squads made 36 percent of their field goals.

After stopping Alleman, Shelbyville's coronation in this 25th year of Class A play was more of a formality. In the title game, the Rams recorded their third win of the year over Mid-State Conference rival Breese Mater Dei 58-45. Interestingly, seventh-ranked Mater Dei could also speak to the difficulties of postseason play, since many believed the Knights had actually fielded a stronger team one year earlier, prior to a super-sectional upset.

The finale marked the first meeting between teams from the same conference in a Class A or AA title game. The last match-up of league foes in a championship was in 1955 when Rockford West ousted Elgin.

State Final Tournament Scores

Super-Sectionals
At Decatur [Millikin]—Shelbyville 77, Tuscola 44
At DeKalb [NIU]—Mendota 77, Elgin (St. Edward) 64
At Macomb [WIU]—Macomb 72, Pittsfield 59
At East Moline (United)—Rock Island (Alleman) 63, Sherrard 44
At Carbondale [SIU]—Breese (Mater Dei) 51, Golconda (Pope County) 41
At Charleston [EIU]—Lawrenceville 74, Freeburg 68 (OT)
At Kankakee [Olivet]—Chicago (Providence-St. Mel) 62, Chicago (St. Martin de Porres) 51
At Normal [ISU]—Paxton (P.-Buckley-Loda) 70, Manito (Midwest Central) 66

Quarterfinals
Shelbyville 53, Mendota 52
Rock Island (Alleman) 61, Macomb 43
Breese (Mater Dei) 73, Lawrenceville 58
Paxton (P.-Buckley-Loda) 65, Chicago (Providence-St. Mel) 64 (OT)

Semifinals
Shelbyville 59, Rock Island (Alleman) 48
Breese (Mater Dei) 55, Paxton (P.-Buckley-Loda) 51 (OT)

Finals
Rock Island (Alleman) 58, Paxton (P.-Buckley-Loda) 41 (third place)
Shelbyville 58, Breese (Mater Dei) 45 (title)

Scoring Leaders

Player, School	G	FG	3P	FT	Pts
Brian Trapkus, Rock Island (Alleman)	4	25	0	18	68
Corey Fox, Paxton (P.-Buckley-Loda)	4	23	7	10	63
Rich Beyers, Shelbyville	4	25	0	12	62
Eric Duke, Mendota	2	15	12	17	59
Patrick Voss, Rock Island (Alleman)	4	20	10	6	56

All-Tournament First Team

Player, School	Ht.	Yr.
Rich Beyers, Shelbyville	6-8	Jr.
Corey Fox, Paxton (P.-Buckley-Loda)	5-8	Jr.
Nathan Kreke, Breese (Mater Dei)	6-4	Sr.
Brian Trapkus, Rock Island (Alleman)	6-7	Sr.
Patrick Voss, Rock Island (Alleman)	5-10	Jr.

Championship Game Box Score

Carver Arena, Peoria, March 9, 1996

SHELBYVILLE (58)
Coach Sean Taylor

Player	FG-A	3P-A	FT-A	Pts	PF	Rb	As	St	Bl
Rich Beyers	6-14	0-2	3-3	15	2	11	0	1	3
Kevin Herdes	4-10	1-1	2-3	11	3	4	5	2	0
Roger Jones	2-5	0-2	3-7	7	3	9	0	1	0
Harlan Kennell	0-0	0-0	0-0	0	0	1	0	0	0
Ben Short	3-4	0-0	1-2	7	2	8	1	0	0
Mike Steers	0-5	0-5	1-3	1	2	3	3	1	0
Todd Wilderman	6-8	2-2	3-4	17	4	3	1	3	0
TEAM						1			
TOTAL	21-46	3-12	13-22	58	16	40	10	8	3

BREESE (MATER DEI) (45)
Coach Dennis Trame

Player	FG-A	3P-A	FT-A	Pts	PF	Rb	As	St	Bl
Brad Bryan	3-9	0-0	0-0	6	5	5	0	0	1
Scott Huegen	0-1	0-1	0-0	0	0	0	0	0	0
Kurt Kalmer	5-12	1-4	3-6	14	4	2	2	3	1
Nathan Kreke	2-13	1-1	0-0	5	5	3	5	0	2
Jason Miller	1-4	1-2	0-0	3	0	3	2	0	0
Troy Pingsterhaus	1-2	0-0	0-1	2	1	2	2	1	0
Bob Tebbe	0-1	0-0	0-0	0	1	0	0	0	0
Luke Woltering	1-6	0-0	5-8	7	2	6	2	0	1
Adam Zieren	3-6	2-4	0-0	8	3	5	3	1	0
TEAM						5			
TOTAL	16-54	5-12	8-15	45	21	31	16	5	5

Shelbyville	12	14	15	17	— 58
Breese (Mater Dei)	8	7	8	22	— 45

Officials: Ron Michaelson, Kent Hammond.

Breese Mater Dei's Luke Woltering cleans the glass as Shelbyville's Roger Jones tries to shake the ball loose. Shelbyville took the first state championship contested at Carver Arena with a 58-45 triumph.

Brian Trapkus of Rock Island Alleman puts back a rebound shot but finds Shelbyville center Rich Beyers's block a little close for comfort. Shelbyville won the semifinal contest.

ROUNDING THE CORNER

Dan Coyne-Logan of Rock Island Alleman prepares a play in the third-place game against the defense of Paxton-Buckley-Loda's Paul Rodeen. Alleman won 58-41.

Jerrell Dantzler of Providence-St. Mel readies a short jumper in a quarterfinal contest against Paxton-Buckley-Loda.

1996A

WARSAW
Class A State Champions of 1997

FRONT ROW (left to right): Ryan Jacquot, B. Bloyd, Matt Froman, Corey Becker, Bob Thomas, Scott Meyer. SECOND ROW: Paul Figge, Casey Shaw, Dan Buelt, Randy Crow, Bill Heisler, Chad Thompson. THIRD ROW: Coach Jeff Dahl, Bob Manley, Craig Wear, Aaron Wehner, Mark Quimby.

At breakfast the morning after the Class A title game, Shawn Jeppson looked like he had lost a heavyweight title fight.

Metaphorically, the Spring Valley Hall guard had. Despite his record-setting 51-point effort the night before, Warsaw knocked out Jeppson and his Hall teammates 92-85 in one of the more memorable Class A title games.

The defeat was the second championship-game loss of the 1996-97 school year for Hall Township. Earlier, Hall's football team had dropped the Class 3A finale to Carterville 23-20.

The loss left 6-foot-2 Jeppson almost speechless after a game in which he converted 16 of 27 field goals and 15 of 16 free throws to set an Elite Eight scoring record. Jeppson bettered Danville Schlarman gunner Jerry Kuemmerle's 49-point performance in a 1958 quarterfinal and Jay Shidler's 48-point burst in the 1976 semifinals, both of which also came in losing efforts.

Despite Jeppson's heroics, the most-talked-about shot from this title game belonged to Warsaw guard Bill Heisler, who scored 36 points.

Down 73-70 with 15 seconds left, No. 13 Warsaw called timeout and Assistant Coach Brad Froman drew up a play designed to free Heisler for a three-pointer. Point guard Dan Buelt took the inbounds pass, dished to center Craig Wear and then set a pick. Heisler took a handoff from Wear and swished his game-tying shot from the top of the key with four seconds remaining — a shot Heisler had long hoped to shoot.

"I've probably practiced that shot in the driveway 15,000 times," Heisler said. "I've got to tell you, it feels a lot better in front of 11,000 people than it does in the driveway."

From there, Warsaw (28-3) took control in overtime and made a winner out of third-year coach Jeff Dahl, who borrowed a page from Chrisman coach Roger Beals. Prior to the tournament, Dahl drove the team bus to Peoria.

Along with links to the past, this tournament provided previews of the future. Heisler (Western Illinois) and Jeppson (Illinois State) were just two of the players in this tournament who enjoyed collegiate success.

To reach the title game, 14th-ranked Hall ousted top-ranked Normal U-High and Evansville recruit Jeremy Stanton. One round earlier, U-High had topped Madison and junior guard Maurice Baker, who starred at Oklahoma State and had brief NBA stints with Portland and the Los Angeles Clippers.

This field also included Chicago St. Francis de Sales forward Sean Lampley, who starred at California and spent two years in the NBA with Miami and Golden State. In the quarterfinals, Lampley and sophomore teammate Jerell Parker (Loyola and Hartford) boosted St. Francis de Sales past Williamsfield and prolific guard Travis Lewis (Louisiana Tech), who averaged 33.1 points per game.

State Final Tournament Scores

Super-Sectionals
At DeKalb [NIU]—Spring Valley (Hall) 70, Elgin (St. Edward) 51
At Carbondale [SIU]—Nashville 60, Harrisburg 47
At Charleston [EIU]—Madison 52, Carmi (C.-White County) 38
At Normal [ISU]—Normal (University) 73, Fairbury (Prairie Central) 61
At Rock Island—Williamsfield 66, Rock Island (Alleman) 65
At Kankakee [Olivet]—Chicago (St. Francis de Sales) 69, Kankakee (McNamara) 56
At Decatur [Millikin]—Nokomis 74, Tolono (Unity) 36
At Macomb [WIU]—Warsaw 68, Pleasant Plains 66 (OT)

Quarterfinals
Spring Valley (Hall) 57, Nashville 55
Normal (University) 68, Madison 60
Chicago (St. Francis de Sales) 65, Williamsfield 53
Warsaw 64, Nokomis 51

Semifinals
Spring Valley (Hall) 68, Normal (University) 54
Warsaw 73, Chicago (St. Francis de Sales) 59

Finals
Normal (University) 60, Chicago (St. Francis de Sales) 59 (third place)
Warsaw 92, Spring Valley (Hall) 85 (OT) (title)

Scoring Leaders

Player, School	G	FG	3P	FT	Pts
Shawn Jeppson, Spring Valley (Hall)	4	37	10	32	116
Bill Heisler, Warsaw	4	37	16	24	114
Jeremy Stanton, Normal (University)	4	32	8	27	99
Craig Wear, Warsaw	4	37	0	11	85
Jerell Parker, Chi. (St. Francis de Sales)	4	28	7	5	68

All-Tournament First Team

Player, School	Ht.	Yr.
Bill Heisler, Warsaw	6-0	Sr.
Shawn Jeppson, Spring Valley (Hall)	6-2	Jr.
Travis Lewis, Williamsfield	6-0	Sr.
Jeremy Stanton, Normal (University)	6-1	Sr.
Craig Wear, Warsaw	6-6	Sr.

Championship Game Box Score
Carver Arena, Peoria, March 15, 1997

WARSAW (92)
Coach Jeff Dahl

Player	FG-A	3P-A	FT-A	Pts	PF	Rb	As	St	Bl
Dan Buelt	2-9	1-4	13-15	18	3	5	8		
Randy Crow	0-0	0-0	0-0	0	3	3	0		
Paul Figge	0-1	0-0	0-0	0	2	0	1		
Matt Froman	0-1	0-1	0-0	0	2	3	1		
Bill Heisler	9-15	6-9	12-17	36	4	2	7		
Ryan Jacquot	0-2	0-1	4-6	4	5	4	0		
Bob Manley	2-3	0-0	1-2	5	2	4	0		
Scott Meyer	0-0	0-0	0-0	0	0	0	0		
Mark Quimby	0-0	0-0	0-0	0	0	0	0		
Casey Shaw	0-0	0-0	0-0	0	0	0	0		
Bob Thomas	0-0	0-0	0-0	0	0	0	0		
Chad Thompson	0-0	0-0	0-0	0	0	0	0		
Craig Wear	14-24	0-1	1-7	29	4	13	2		
Aaron Wehner	0-0	0-0	0-0	0	0	0	0		
TEAM						2			
TOTAL	27-55	7-16	31-47	92	25	36	19		

SPRING VALLEY (HALL) (85)
Coach Eric Bryant

Player	FG-A	3P-A	FT-A	Pts	PF	Rb	As	St	Bl
Ryan Anderes	1-3	0-2	0-2	2	2	1	1		
Derek Baird	0-1	0-1	1-3	1	4	2	0		
Eric Bryant	8-17	1-2	0-0	17	5	8	3		
Adam Curran	0-1	0-0	2-4	2	4	2	0		
Denny Galetti	0-0	0-0	0-0	0	1	0	0		
Shawn Jeppson	16-27	4-8	15-16	51	4	7	2		
Craig Olson	0-0	0-0	0-0	0	0	0	0		
Chris Piontek	0-0	0-0	0-0	0	0	0	0		
Joey Reed	1-2	0-0	1-2	3	5	4	0		
David Sharp	0-0	0-0	0-0	0	0	1	1		
Nate Sobin	0-0	0-0	0-0	0	0	0	0		
Mike Spoonmore	1-6	0-1	0-0	2	5	2	0		
Nick Sterling	3-7	0-0	1-4	7	4	15	0		
Joe Strait	0-0	0-0	0-0	0	0	0	0		
Kevin Wilson	0-0	0-0	0-0	0	0	0	0		
TEAM						2			
TOTAL	30-64	5-14	20-31	85	35	44	6		

Warsaw	14	18	13	28	19	—	92
Spring Valley (Hall)	21	15	15	22	12	—	85

Officials: Gary Traub, Ray Albert Jr..

Ranked only 13th, the Warsaw Wildcats were surprise winners of the 1997 Class A title.

RECORD-SETTER

Shawn Jeppson, 6-foot-2 guard from Spring Valley Hall, pauses during the title game. Jeppson put on a historic performance, scoring 51 points in a 92-85 overtime loss to Warsaw.

Sean Lampley of St. Francis de Sales fakes as Williamsfield's Brett Tucker holds his ground in a quarterfinal battle.

Warsaw's Bill Heisler dribbles out of trouble in the championship contest against Hall. Heisler scored 36 points to lead Warsaw to a 92-85 overtime victory.

Eric Bryant of Hall isn't afraid to mix things up as he surges past U-High's Brandon Dirks. Hall won the semifinal game by a 68-54 score.

1997A

Hancock County basketball continued its mastery over Spring Valley Hall and the rest of the state in 1998.

One year after Warsaw topped Hall in the title game, unranked neighbor Nauvoo-Colusa (32-3) did the same. This time, though, the result was much more unexpected.

Hall (32-1) came into the championship top-ranked and unbeaten and had all-state guard Shawn Jeppson scoring nearly 24 points per game. Nauvoo was unranked, with a roster of unknowns.

Yet following in the tradition of previous small-school underdogs Staunton, Pana, and Mt. Pulaski, Nauvoo showed that teamwork, accurate shooting and a never-say-die attitude can take you a long way in Class A.

In Sweet Sixteen play, Nauvoo beat three undefeated teams — No. 4 Ashland A-C Central in the Macomb Super-Sectional, No. 2 Farmington in the semifinals, and No. 1 Hall for all the marbles. That was a state-tournament first.

"We were underdogs in every game in the tournament and nobody picked us to win," said Nauvoo senior David Griffiths, who led his team in scoring in two games at state. "But we knew we could beat anybody."

Some credit for that went to Warsaw, which one year earlier brought championship hardware home to Hancock County. "It made us think any school could come in here and win," Nauvoo forward Doug Siegfried said.

Nauvoo's success capped an impressive run for Hancock County, population 25,000. Though none of the seven schools in Hancock County had an enrollment of more than 246 students, their boys' and girls' basketball teams combined for 10 Elite Eight visits and nine trophies from 1992 through 1998.

Nauvoo's run was one of the grittiest. The Vikings rallied in both sectional games and in all three games at Peoria. In its quarterfinal against Chrisman, Nauvoo trailed 34-19 in the first half before eventually rallying with a 17-4 fourth-quarter surge. After three quarters against Farmington, Nauvoo was down 40-29. Then the Vikings went on a 19-7 spree and won 48-47 on a Joe Wilson free throw with one second left.

Nauvoo needed another rally in the championship, trailing Hall 32-31 after three quarters before running to a 45-39 victory. Hall suffered a bad break even prior to the game. After bumping chests with a teammate during pre-game introductions, Jeppson cut his right hand on a television camera.

"When the two players came together, the one guy's leg bumped my camera and (Jeppson's) hand came down and hit the camera lens," said cameraman Wayne Johnson of Fox Sports Chicago. "It was just one of those freak accidents."

Jeppson's two cuts required three stitches at halftime and appeared to impact the Illinois State recruit, who scored just 9 points on 4-for-10 shooting.

Farmington (33-1) finished with a school record for wins and a third-place victory over Chicago Leo and 6-foot-8 sophomore Andre Brown.

State Final Tournament Scores

Super-Sectionals
At Macomb [WIU]—Nauvoo (N.-Colusa) 59, Ashland (A-C Central) 56
At Decatur [Millikin]—Chrisman 50, Rochester 37
At Carbondale [SIU]—Nashville 51, Harrisburg 31
At Moline—Farmington 66, Rock Falls 62
At DeKalb [NIU]—Spring Valley (Hall) 70, Marengo 42
At Charleston [EIU]—Teutopolis 61, Farina (South Central) 40
At Normal [ISU]—Normal (University) 64, Armstrong 55
At Kankakee [Olivet]—Chicago (Leo) 66, Chicago (St. Francis de Sales) 55

Quarterfinals
Nauvoo (N.-Colusa) 59, Chrisman 52
Farmington 57, Nashville 54
Spring Valley (Hall) 52, Teutopolis 44
Chicago (Leo) 64, Normal (University) 59 (OT)

Semifinals
Nauvoo (N.-Colusa) 48, Farmington 47
Spring Valley (Hall) 56, Chicago (Leo) 46

Finals
Farmington 55, Chicago (Leo) 45 (third place)
Nauvoo (N.-Colusa) 45, Spring Valley (Hall) 39 (title)

Scoring Leaders

Player, School	G	FG	3P	FT	Pts
Seth Nelson, Farmington	4	23	5	20	71
Shawn Jeppson, Spring Valley (Hall)	4	27	5	7	66
Ryan Anderes, Spring Valley (Hall)	4	24	11	1	60
J.R. Jackson, Chicago (Leo)	4	21	9	8	59
David Griffiths, Nauvoo (N.-Colusa)	4	17	11	11	56

All-Tournament First Team

Player, School	Ht.	Yr.
Ryan Anderes, Spring Valley (Hall)	6-1	Sr.
David Griffiths, Nauvoo (N.-Colusa)	5-10	Sr.
Shawn Jeppson, Spring Valley (Hall)	6-2	Sr.
Seth Nelson, Farmington	6-0	Jr.
Joe Wilson, Nauvoo (N.-Colusa)	6-5	Jr.

Championship Game Box Score

Carver Arena, Peoria, March 14, 1998

NAUVOO (N.-COLUSA) (45)
Coach Reno Pinkston

Player	FG-A	3P-A	FT-A	Pts	PF	Rb	As	St	Bl
Kellen Fernetti	0-0	0-0	0-0	0	0	0	0	0	0
Paul Goetz	0-0	0-0	0-0	0	0	0	0	0	0
Brian Griffiths	0-0	0-0	0-0	0	0	0	0	0	0
David Griffiths	3-9	1-4	1-3	8	2	4	5	1	0
Kenny Haas	0-0	0-0	0-0	0	0	0	0	0	0
David Hamma	2-6	0-0	2-4	6	2	2	4	1	0
Emmett Reidner	5-11	0-0	9-10	19	2	10	3	1	0
Doug Siegfried	0-3	0-2	0-0	0	3	7	1	2	0
Marshel Stott	0-0	0-0	0-0	0	0	0	0	0	0
Patrick Weaver	0-0	0-0	0-0	0	0	0	0	0	0
Joe Wilson	4-13	4-7	0-0	12	0	3	0	1	5
TEAM						2			
TOTAL	14-42	5-13	12-17	45	9	28	13	6	5

SPRING VALLEY (HALL) (39)
Coach Eric Bryant

Player	FG-A	3P-A	FT-A	Pts	PF	Rb	As	St	Bl
Ryan Anderes	5-12	2-7	0-0	12	1	2	0	0	0
Derek Baird	0-6	0-5	0-0	0	1	6	1	0	1
Jason Burkiewicz	0-0	0-0	0-0	0	0	0	0	0	0
Adam Curran	0-0	0-0	0-0	0	2	3	0	1	0
Shawn Jeppson	4-10	1-4	0-0	9	4	4	1	1	0
Craig Olson	0-3	0-3	0-0	0	2	3	5	1	0
Tony Orlandi	0-0	0-0	0-0	0	0	0	0	0	0
Matt Peterson	0-0	0-0	0-0	0	0	0	0	0	0
Chris Piontek	0-0	0-0	0-0	0	0	0	0	0	0
Dan Prokup	0-0	0-0	0-0	0	0	1	0	0	0
Joey Reed	5-13	0-0	0-1	10	5	7	0	1	0
Jason Samolinski	0-0	0-0	0-0	0	0	0	0	0	0
Nick Sterling	4-8	0-0	0-0	8	4	10	1	1	4
Joe Strait	0-0	0-0	0-0	0	0	0	0	0	0
Kevin Wilson	0-0	0-0	0-0	0	0	0	0	0	0
TEAM						2			
TOTAL	18-52	3-19	0-1	39	19	38	8	5	5

Nauvoo (N.-Colusa)	15	5	11	14	—	45
Spring Valley (Hall)	19	7	6	7	—	39

Officials: Don Fodor, Rick Runge, Terry Elms.

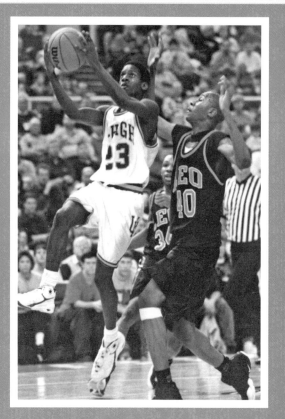

Ricky Hildreth of Normal U-High foils the defense of Leo's Jamar Thompkins in a quarterfinal match-up. Leo had the last laugh in 64-59 overtime win.

Hall's Joe Reed fins his path blocked by Emmett Reidner of Nauvoo-Colusa in the 1998 title game.

Shawn Jeppson of Spring Valley Hall pauses before crashing the Nauvoo-Colusa defense.

1998A

Reidner drives for a easy lay-in as Hall's Craig Olson can do nothing but watch.

POINTS IN THE PAINT

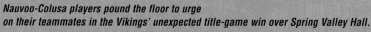

Nauvoo-Colusa players pound the floor to urge on their teammates in the Vikings' unexpected title-game win over Spring Valley Hall.

ROCK FALLS
Class A State Champions of 1999

FRONT ROW (left to right): Matt Hardy, Brian Vance, Dustin Weaver, Jorge Acosta, Kelley Westcott, Scott Hayen, Jedidiah Johnson, Mgr. Clint Smith. SECOND ROW: Asst. Coach Brad Schwarz, Matt Sartwell, Scott Vandermoon, Bryan Boerjan, Jarrod Clardie, Herb Martin, Shaun Hardy, Andrew Keaschall, Coach Thom Sigel.

1999A

Brian Vance didn't grow up dreaming about winning state in basketball. Baseball was his game. That was the reality in Rock Falls, where roundball success consisted of a runner-up finish to Chicago Marshall in 1958.

But declining enrollment and the arrival of coach Thom Sigel brought basketball to the forefront in this city of 9,500. Three years after dropping into Class A, Rock Falls found a hoops memory to replace the 1950s and set out on a record string of five straight sectional titles from 1998 to 2002.

With his prep career ticking away in the title game, Vance dribbled to the top of the key and launched one of the most dramatic game-winners in Class A history. His three-pointer with one second left capped a stunning 13-0 comeback against Waterloo Gibault and sealed a 45-43 victory for Rock Falls (30-3).

With 4:47 remaining, Gibault led 43-32 and looked poised to become the second straight unexpected, unranked champ. Even some Gibault fans were surprised to see the Hawks and 6-foot-6 John Thomas — 70 points and 40 rebounds in three games — rout No. 12 Normal U-High and No. 13 Quincy Notre Dame before the championship.

"We certainly didn't go [into the season] thinking this was the best team we've ever had," said coach Dennis Rueter, whose Hawks benefited when top-ranked Nashville fell in the regionals.

Nevertheless, Gibault (28-7) might have brought southern Illinois another title if not for Jorge Acosta. The Rock Falls sophomore, who averaged 6.5 points per game, scored 10 of his 11 points in the fourth quarter. That includ-

ed a lay-up with 32.2 seconds left to make the score 43-42.

On the next possession, Acosta knocked the ball away from Thomas. A wild scramble ensued, and Gibault's John Torisky wound up with the ball. Surprisingly, Torisky was whistled for traveling with 14.7 seconds left.

"It looks pretty shaky from my position," Rueter said. "Everything else was a foul out there. I kind of thought that would be, too. The official has to live with that call."

After a timeout, Vance swished his game-winner on a play designed for Jedidiah Johnson. Vance opted to shoot when Johnson was covered.

"I thought it was going to be short," said Vance, who had made one of eight previous shots.

In the quarterfinals, Vance had 20 points as fifth-ranked Rock Falls survived fourth-ranked Providence-St. Mel and a roster of four future college players: Stan Gaines (Minnesota and Seton Hall), Levar Seals (DePaul), Robert Harris (Illinois State) and Corey Minniefield (Loyola University Chicago).

Following the game, St. Mel coach Billy Garrett collapsed at mid-court and left on a stretcher. Garrett was later treated and released, his fainting apparently related to a blood-sugar deficiency.

State Final Tournament Scores
Super-Sectionals
At Normal [ISU]—Normal (University) 65, Lexington 42
At Carbondale [SIU]—Waterloo (Gibault) 67, Johnston City 62
At Macomb [WIU]—Quincy (Notre Dame) 55, Pittsfield 51
At Decatur [Millikin]—Riverton 78, Tolono (Unity) 63
At East Moline (United)—Rock Falls 72, Farmington 59
At Kankakee [Olivet]—Chicago (Providence-St. Mel) 58, Coal City 50
At DeKalb [NIU]—Plano 57, Forreston 54
At Charleston [EIU]—Carmi (C.-White County) 49, Hillsboro 42
Quarterfinals
Waterloo (Gibault) 67, Normal (University) 47
Quincy (Notre Dame) 59, Riverton 56
Rock Falls 47, Chicago (Providence-St. Mel) 44
Plano 40, Carmi (C.-White County) 38 (OT)
Semifinals
Waterloo (Gibault) 65, Quincy (Notre Dame) 37
Rock Falls 64, Plano 50
Finals
Quincy (Notre Dame) 69, Plano 65 (third place)
Rock Falls 45, Waterloo (Gibault) 43 (title)

Scoring Leaders

Player, School	G	FG	3P	FT	Pts
Brad Korn, Plano	4	37	2	27	103
John Thomas, Waterloo (Gibault)	4	39	0	18	96
Brian Vance, Rock Falls	4	24	11	23	82
Casey Tushaus, Quincy (Notre Dame)	4	24	12	6	66
Jason Volm, Quincy (Notre Dame)	4	16	5	20	57

All-Tournament First Team

Player, School	Ht.	Yr.
Jedidiah Johnson, Rock Falls	6-2	Sr.
Brad Korn, Plano	6-9	Sr.
Brian McNeil, Quincy (Notre Dame)	6-9	Sr.
John Thomas, Waterloo (Gibault)	6-6	Sr.
Brian Vance, Rock Falls	5-11	Sr.

Championship Game Box Score
Carver Arena, Peoria, March 13, 1999

ROCK FALLS (45)
Coach Thom Sigel

Player	FG-A	3P-A	FT-A	Pts	PF	Rb	As	St	Bl
Jorge Acosta	4-9	0-0	3-7	11	3	3	2	2	0
Bryan Boerjan	3-6	0-0	2-2	8	4	7	1	1	1
Shaun Hardy	0-0	0-0	1-2	1	0	2	0	0	0
Jedidiah Johnson	2-9	1-4	0-0	5	0	2	1	3	0
Herb Martin	2-4	0-0	2-3	6	3	5	1	2	6
Brian Vance	5-15	2-6	2-2	14	3	1	1	0	0
Kelley Wescott	0-0	0-0	0-0	0	0	0	0	0	0
TEAM						4			
TOTAL	16-43	3-10	10-16	45	13	24	6	8	7

WATERLOO (GIBAULT) (43)
Coach Dennis Rueter

Player	FG-A	3P-A	FT-A	Pts	PF	Rb	As	St	Bl
John Buchmiller	1-7	1-5	0-0	3	4	4	1	0	0
Chad Frierdich	0-0	0-0	0-0	0	0	0	0	0	0
Dan Heimos	2-4	0-0	0-0	4	2	3	0	0	0
Josh Mueth	4-5	3-3	0-0	11	1	4	2	1	0
Jeremy Nagle	3-6	0-0	2-6	8	4	8	3	0	0
John Thomas	6-15	0-0	3-4	15	3	12	1	0	3
John Torisky	1-8	0-1	0-1	2	1	4	3	2	0
TEAM						3			
TOTAL	17-45	4-9	5-11	43	15	38	10	3	3

Rock Falls	13	6	11	15	—	45
Waterloo (Gibault)	14	9	12	8	—	43

Officials: Eugene Duffy, Jerry Whitney, Larry Bruck.

Celebrating 100 years of IHSA Boys Basketball Tournaments

Gibault's John Buchmiller sets his defense while Rock Falls' Jorge Acosta dribbles between his legs in the 1999 championship game.

Acosta celebrates on the awards stand after Rock Falls' 45-43 title-game conquest of Gibault.

Josh Mueth of Waterloo Gibault lobs the ball over the outstretched arm of Quincy Notre Dame's Eric Terwelp in a semifinal contest.

VERGE OF VICTORY

Down a point with time running out in the championship game against Gibault, Brian Vance of Rock Falls (3, at far left) drills the game-winning three-pointer.

Stan Gainoo of Providence St. Mel tips a shot by Jedidiah Johnson, but Rock Falls won the quarterfinal match-up by a 47-44 score.

1999A

Traditional state tournament logic says a team playing the second semifinal is at a disadvantage later that evening. No Class A team did more to debunk that theory than seventh-ranked Pleasant Plains (34-2).

Despite battling through three overtimes in a 78-68 semifinal win over Sangamo Conference rival Riverton, Pleasant Plains had enough left to dispatch tradition-rich Teutopolis in the title game, 56-43.

The players had about two hours to rest after the semifinal.

"Oh gosh, I was worried the three overtimes would play a big part," Plains coach Cliff Cameron said. "We told the guys it's a championship game. We've got to find some extra energy. We had to suck it up and dig out and give it all we got."

Pleasant Plains did just that, outscoring second-ranked Teutopolis 23-11 in the final quarter and overcoming a 5-for-15 shooting performance by tournament high scorer Dusty Bensko.

Bensko had carried Plains in the first two games, scoring 61 points overall. In the semifinal against Riverton, the first triple-overtime game in Class A Elite Eight history, he made all 17 free throws he attempted, including 12-for-12 in the third overtime. The performance earned Bensko high praise.

"I've never coached anyone that wants to win at all costs more than Dusty Bensko," said Cameron, who was in his second season as head coach.

On the final day, Bensko played 75 of a possible 76 minutes, scored 46 points, grabbed 20 rebounds and had five steals. Even so, the championship game was more a team effort for Pleasant Plains, as Ryan Sunley and Jordan Roth scored 13 points apiece to complement Bensko's 14. Sunley also grabbed a game-high 12 rebounds as Plains outboarded the usually tenacious Teutopolis squad 42-21.

The same group of players, with Cameron as coach, had won an eighth-grade title in 1997.

"It's a little more exciting this time," said Bensko, a junior who went on to a successful baseball career at the University of Illinois.

For second-ranked Teutopolis (33-2), the loss ended what had been a memorable season. Earning comparisons to T-Town's 1986 champions, the Wooden Shoes were featured in the PBS documentary "More Than a Game."

For Bureau Valley, a five-year-old consolidation of schools in Bureau County, the tournament was the start of a streak that would see the school win three straight third-place trophies under Coach Brad Bickett. Bickett was no stranger to tournament success, having played on Ohio's runner-up squad in 1986.

PLEASANT PLAINS
Class A State Champions of 2000

FRONT ROW: Michael Cameron. SECOND ROW (left to right): Adam Suchy, Andrew Cochran, Joe Albsmeyer, Aaron Sczurko, Jeremy Pinkerton, Tyler Kastner, Bo Gum. THIRD ROW: Coach Cliff Cameron, Ryan Nelson, Josh Siterlet, Dusty Bensko, Jordan Roth, Jess Durako, Ryan Sunley, Jimmy Skeeters, Asst. Coach Dan Watson.

State Final Tournament Scores

Super-Sectionals
At Carbondale [SIU]—Nashville 58, Metropolis (Massac County) 49
At Charleston [EIU]—Teutopolis 57, Okawville 44
At DeKalb [NIU]—Manlius (Bureau Valley) 58, Aurora (A. Christian) 39
At Normal [ISU]—Fairbury (Prairie Central) 45, Mason City (Illini Central) 34
At Macomb [WIU]—Pleasant Plains 71, Pittsfield 54
At Kankakee [Olivet]—Kankakee (McNamara) 64, Westmont 53
At Decatur [Millikin]—Riverton 56, Tolono (Unity) 46
At East Moline (United)—Rock Falls 57, Rock Island (Alleman) 51

Quarterfinals
Teutopolis 48, Nashville 41 (OT)
Manlius (Bureau Valley) 69, Fairbury (Prairie Central) 65
Pleasant Plains 66, Kankakee (McNamara) 47
Riverton 52, Rock Falls 49

Semifinals
Teutopolis 60, Manlius (Bureau Valley) 42
Pleasant Plains 78, Riverton 68 (3 OT)

Finals
Manlius (Bureau Valley) 65, Riverton 62 (third place)
Pleasant Plains 56, Teutopolis 43 (title)

Scoring Leaders

Player, School	G	FG	3P	FT	Pts
Dusty Bensko, Pleasant Plains	4	30	6	35	101
Clint Cuffle, Riverton	4	36	10	13	95
Justin Yepsen, Manlius (Bureau Valley)	4	29	0	7	65
Mitch Koester, Teutopolis	4	18	8	14	58
Andrew Gobczynski, Teutopolis	4	20	0	15	55

All-Tournament First Team

Player, School	Ht.	Yr.
Dusty Bensko, Pleasant Plains	6-5	Jr.
Clint Cuffle, Riverton	6-6	Sr.
Andrew Gobczynski, Teutopolis	6-7	Sr.
Mitch Koester, Teutopolis	5-11	Sr.
Justin Yepsen, Manlius (Bureau Valley)	6-2	Sr.

Championship Game Box Score
Carver Arena, Peoria, March 11, 2000

PLEASANT PLAINS (56)
Coach Cliff Cameron

Player	FG-A	3P-A	FT-A	Pts	PF	Rb	As	St	Bl
Dusty Bensko	5-15	0-2	4-6	14	1	10	0	3	1
Jess Durako	2-5	0-0	0-0	4	4	7	0	0	1
Bo Gum	3-3	0-0	0-0	6	3	0	0	0	0
Tyler Kastner	2-7	0-1	0-0	4	2	3	4	0	0
Ryan Nelson	0-0	0-0	0-0	0	0	1	0	0	0
Jeremy Pinkerton	0-1	0-1	0-0	0	0	0	0	0	0
Jordan Roth	4-8	1-3	4-5	13	2	6	0	1	1
Aaron Sczurko	0-1	0-1	0-0	0	0	0	0	0	2
Josh Siterlet	1-1	0-0	0-0	2	0	1	0	0	0
Jimmy Skeeters	0-0	0-0	0-0	0	0	0	0	0	0
Ryan Sunley	4-7	0-0	5-5	13	4	12	2	0	3
TEAM						2			
TOTAL	21-48	1-8	13-16	56	16	42	6	4	8

TEUTOPOLIS (43)
Coach Ken Crawford

Player	FG-A	3P-A	FT-A	Pts	PF	Rb	As	St	Bl
Eric Bloemer	0-0	0-0	0-0	0	0	0	0	0	0
Andrew Gobczynski	2-7	0-0	4-4	8	3	8	1	1	2
Ted Hoene	0-0	0-0	0-0	0	0	0	0	0	0
Johnny King	3-10	1-1	4-8	11	3	2	3	4	1
Mitch Koester	6-19	2-8	2-2	16	1	2	2	2	0
Andy Mette	0-0	0-0	0-0	0	0	0	0	0	0
Aaron Niebrugge	0-1	0-0	0-0	0	0	0	0	0	0
Jeff Probst	0-0	0-0	0-0	0	0	0	0	0	0
John Repking	0-0	0-0	0-0	0	0	0	0	0	0
Nick Swingler	1-1	0-0	0-0	2	1	3	2	0	0
Todd Thoele	0-0	0-0	0-1	0	5	2	0	3	0
John Tipton	3-9	0-1	0-0	6	4	2	1	1	0
TEAM						2			
TOTAL	15-47	3-10	10-15	43	17	21	9	11	3

Pleasant Plains	10	11	12	23	— 56
Teutopolis	11	7	14	11	— 43

Officials: Dan Grimm, Dennis Held, John Fahl.

As the final buzzer of the championship game sounds, Pleasant Plains players jump for joy. Dusty Bensko (3) was the star of the semifinal win, scoring 32 points in triple overtime.

JUBILATION!

Andrew Gobczynski of Teutopolis eludes Ryan Sunley of Pleasant Plains' to attempt an acrobatic hook shot in the 2000 Class A championship.

Jordan Roth of Pleasant Plains sets up a pivot move against T-Town's Todd Thoele in the final contest.

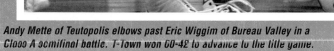

Andy Mette of Teutopolis elbows past Eric Wiggim of Bureau Valley in a Class A semifinal battle. T-Town won 60-42 to advance to the title game.

2000A

Pearls of postgame wisdom
Class A edition

Whether on the bench or at a podium,
Ron Felling stood out from his small
school ***coaching*** peers.

By Jeff Lampe

Lawrenceville coach Ron Felling shouts out an order to his squad in 1976.

Proof of Felling's coaching mastery is obvious to anyone familiar with Illinois basketball records. With his 83 percent win rate and four state titles, the Lawrenceville legend is the undisputed leader in Class A's coaching clubhouse.

Proof of Felling's verbal mastery is just as obvious to anyone who winds through microfilm copies of old newspapers. Read over 36 years of tournament coverage and you'll encounter countless folks saying "We played hard" or "It's a shame anyone had to lose this game" or "We dug a hole too deep" or "I'm proud of these kids."

Now and then, between clichés, a few folks uttered unique comments. Many came from Felling. Seldom did the Lip of Lawrenceville opt for a politically correct response.

After the Indians won it all in 1982, a reporter asked how it felt to join Decatur's Gay Kintner and Centralia's Arthur Trout as a three-time champion. Instead of rattling off a safe, "I'm honored to be considered in such lofty company," Felling offered this. "Great, except they're dead. I never knew ol' Gay or Arthur, but I can promise you I'll drink a beer to them tonight."

To some, such flippant talk was offensive. To many others, especially writers, the candor was refreshing. And while the tournament has not been the same since Felling departed, coaches and players still utter classic Class A comments.

Consider this one from Warsaw guard Bill Heisler during his team's run to the 1997 state title: "I remember watching Findlay win [in 1992] and afterward I went outside and turned the light on. I just said, 'Mom, I've got to practice.' And I was out there for two hours just dreaming about it."

Here are other memorable musings from past small-school tournaments.

Classic Class A

The Class A experience is unique. Small towns, small schools and large crowds typify the tournament that has become an institution but whose creation was controversial.

Mt. Pulaski's Ed Butkovich shares a few words during his team's run to the 1976 Class A title.

If I could come back [be reincarnated] 50 times, I'd never want to do anything but this.
1997 — Bob Anderson, Williamsfield coach, on reaching the state tournament.

Basketball in Lawrenceville is like water everywhere else: you can't live without it. You walk into our gym and you see state-title pictures the size of a Buick. It's very humbling.
1996 — Brian Stilwell, Lawrenceville coach.

It seems like when I get in a gym I jump a lot higher because I'm so used to playing in dirt and gravel. At first it's kind of hard to learn to dribble in the dirt, but I got used to it.
2004 — Felix Thurman, St. Anne senior .

Basketball is the only thing we have in Venice. Oh, once in awhile we throw a baseball team together in the spring, I guess.
1975 — James Crowder, Venice forward.

Everybody can shoot threes. Our bus driver can make 60 percent.
2004 — Gary Bowker, Pana coach, on his team's shooting prowess.

Anybody opposed to two-class basketball should go to Cissna Park, Watseka or Buda Western and they'll find out two-class basketball is the best thing that ever happened in the state of Illinois.
1975 — Keith Baldwin, Watseka coach.

We've still got a lot of non-believers, I'm sure. There's no other way playing out here in the boondocks.
1975 — Gerald "Chips" Giovanine, Buda Western coach, referring to what he felt was a lack of respect for his team due to its schedule.

Don't tell anyone about this.
1997 — Jeff Dahl, Warsaw coach, after being spotted driving the team bus to Peoria's Hotel Père Marquette.

Once basketball season starts that's all our family talks about. My grandma gets into it. My aunts, my uncles get into it. That's all anybody talks about during basketball season — how we're doing, if we won. It's the main topic of every discussion we have.
1998 — Doug Siegfried, Nauvoo-Colusa senior.

Even when I look at my team warm up, we don't look like a whole lot. We don't have a lot of guys getting over the rim and we don't have a lot of speed.
1997 — Dahl.

I was pretty relaxed during the game. But when I was in the locker room, there was a couple of them that couldn't hardly breathe, they were so nervous.
1996 — David Taylor, Macomb coach, after a quarterfinal loss to Rock Island Alleman.

I hope we have a few police officers stay behind, or somebody is going to have a field day in Nauvoo.
1998 — Reno Pinkston, Nauvoo-Colusa coach.

Religion

It's been said basketball is a religion in parts of Illinois. So it's no wonder the topics often merge at the state finals.

We say a prayer before every game, but don't ask for a win. We don't want to put God in an awkward position.
1999 — Dennis Rueter, Waterloo Gibault coach.

This has got to be a record. Didn't score in the first quarter and shot 13 percent in the first half and then win by two. The Good Lord has to be with us. They [West Frankfort] are by far the best team we've played. It is a miracle we won this game. This feels like I died and went to heaven.
1986 — Lloyd Johnson, Ohio coach, after his team overcame a 24-14 halftime deficit to down West Frankfort, 45-43, in the semifinals.

I've been asked many times what went through my mind after that last second ticked off the clock in that state title game. And I can tell you what it was: "Thank God it's over." I was so happy to win, but thank God it's over.
1986 — Ken Crawford, Teutopolis coach, on the pressure of going 33-0 and winning a championship.

continued on next page

Celebrating 100 years of IHSA Boys Basketball Tournaments

Felling's finest

After that introduction, you probably want more proof about Felling's gift for the gab. Read on.

When he acts like he's hurt I just turn my head and put my hand up so I can't see him. I'm not worried. He'd play in a wheelchair if he had to.
1974 — Felling, on all-stater Rick Leighty

We should have a string of three straight championships, but I'll take two out of three.
1974 — Felling.

He's so skinny his pajamas only have one stripe on them.
1974 — Felling, discussing Tim Wolfe, 6-2, 148-pound senior.

Someone asked me what I had for a bench then and I said, "Mahogany."
1974 — Felling, on his 1970 Lawrenceville team which he felt could have won a Class A title had there been two classes that year.

I've been at Lawrenceville for nine or ten years and all I've gotten is some "Atta-boys." My family can't eat "Atta-boys" and I can't either.
1976 — Felling, discussing his intentions to leave the school after winning the third-place game over Buda Western.

Coach Bob Gregurich of Havana contemplates his next move in a 1979 game.

The Mushroom

Before moving to Peoria's Carver Arena in 1996, the tournament was held in Champaign at the University of Illinois' Assembly Hall. That unique structure — known as "the mushroom on the prairie" — came up often.

It's like you're in the middle of a big cow pasture out there.
1972 — Stan McCrudden, Thomson coach.

The first time we were there, I didn't know how to get down to the floor. We went down to one of the ushers to see if he would let us through. He said, "No, you're going to have to go back up and go down the back stairway." I thought we were going to be late for our own game.
1972 — Felling.

There were two things responsible for our defeat. No. 1 was the Assembly Hall. No. 2 was Monmouth.
1982 — Jack Dettro, Stonington coach, after an 81-59 quarterfinal loss to Monmouth.

On winning

At least a thousand players and coaches have said winning a state title "is like a dream come true." At least ten thousand stories have used those quotes. Every now and then someone offers a fresh perspective on the experience of an Elite Eight victory.

Craig Wear was with me in the elevator at the hotel and he asked me, "How did we win this?" I told him, "Our guys have hearts 10 feet tall and 10 feet wide." And that's why we won the state championship.
1997 — Brad Froman, Warsaw assistant coach.

Our kids just stayed loose. You want to know how loose they are? Just before the award presentation, one of my players asked if he could borrow my comb so he'd look good for television.
1976 — Ed Butkovich, Mt. Pulaski coach, after defeating Oneida ROVA for first place.

Winning the state championship is all I have thought about. I would walk over to Lockport [Class AA champ] and stare at their trophy. Now we've got our own.
1979 — Walter Downing, New Lenox Providence all-stater.

If this is a dream, please don't wake me up.
2003 — Jerod Haynes, Hales Franciscan guard, after title win over Mt. Carroll.

To finally get a lead, I felt like somebody pulled an anvil off my back.
2002 — Ken Crawford, Teutopolis coach, after a 48-41 win over Nashville in the quarterfinals.

My wife, Patty, was due with our first child last Tuesday. She's been great through all this with me. This ballgame tonight was a great moment in my life but I've got my greatest moment, hopefully, coming up very soon.
1986 — Crawford, after title win over Ohio.

On losing

The harsh reality of each tournament is that only two teams end the season with a win. Needless to say, there's a fair amount of discussion about losing.

I guess that shows we're just not a team that plays well from behind.
1975 — Gordon Kinkead, Port Byron Riverdale coach, after a 48-18 loss to Elmhurst Timothy Christian in the quarterfinals.

The only difference was the championship trophy had a "1" on it and was one inch taller. One inch taller and a "1" instead of a "2" isn't much of a difference. There wasn't much difference between our ball club and Madison, either.
1981 — Todd Wieland, Dunlap player, after 58-47 loss to Madison in title game.

We just feel like the Buffalo Bills. We've been here and lost every year, but it's a thrill to be here. We wouldn't trade it for anything.
2005 — Stan Eagleson, Breese Central coach, after losing a quarterfinal game for the third straight year.

Is there any place worse in the world to have a two-game losing streak?
1993 — Cal Hubbard, Normal U-High coach, after his team lost to Hales Franciscan in the quarters 63-49. U-High had lost its previous Class A tournament game in the 1992 title game to Findlay.

I'm going to see him in my dreams the rest of my life.
1974 — Bob Strickland, Ottawa Marquette coach, after Lawrenceville's Rick Leighty led the Indians to a 54-53 win in the title game with 24 points.

You could coach for a hundred years and never prepare yourself for what happened. I can't think of anything that could be considered favorable from this game.
1994 — John McDougal, Rockford Lutheran coach, after an 80-43 loss to Pinckneyville in which his team trailed 27-5 after one quarter

I told our superintendent that if we finished second, we could claim the public school championship of the state and New Lenox could claim the parochial championship. I mean that in jest, so please print it that way.
1979 — Bob Gregurich, Havana coach, after loss to New Lenox Providence.

He said what?

Some comments defy classification but deserve repeating.

Jerry Tarkanian has his towel. I've got my water.
1998 — Pinkston, explaining his habit of sipping water through every tournament game.

Jerry Tarkanian has his towel. And I've got my rolled-up piece of paper.
2003 — Gary London, Hales Franciscan coach, on his habit of holding a rolled-up copy of his scouting report during games.

This is something you talk about for a lifetime, something they make movies about. This is something you dream about as a player and as a coach. These guys are hometown heroes.
2005 — Phil Leib, Flora coach, on the experience of reaching the Elite Eight.

There were no losers in this game. The only ones who could be losers were those who didn't buy tickets.
1982 — Mike Mueller, Monmouth coach, after a 56-55 semifinal win over Havana.

My wife picked it out and said, "Bring your lucky coat." So it doesn't matter how bad it looks. She's the boss. But back home, they give me a tough time about it.
2003 — Larry Baldwin, Cairo coach, on his unusual, electric-blue blazer.

The old-style black shoes make us look misleading. We went back to those shoes because they make us look slower. We can lull opponents to sleep.
1989 — Bob DeDoncker, Rock Island Alleman coach, whose team was known for its fast-break-oriented, run-and-gun style.

I don't wear dresses or anything. But I still love the man.
1997 — Adam Curran, Hall junior, explaining his nickname "Worm" and his feelings for Dennis Rodman.

I don't know. I just said, "Stay the hell away from us."
1988 — Bob Hembrough, Beardstown coach, when asked where parents and girlfriends of his players were staying while in Champaign.

It was me keeping my mouth shut on the bench and not yelling at the kids.
1978 — Bob Bogle, Nashville coach, on the turning point in his team's championship season.

I've seen him cheerlead. He's not an all-state cheerleader.
1991 — Doug Evans, Seneca coach, discussing all-state guard Mark Aubry's efforts cheering for the Seneca girls team in the state tournament.

It's hard to shoot with your fingers around your throat.
1987 — Roger Beals, Chrisman coach, of his team's tightness and poor shooting in the first half of a 69-56 win over Elgin St. Edward.

I feel that if my boy has the guts to take a charge from a 300-pounder the officials ought to have enough guts to call it.
1975 — Gerald "Chips" Giovanine, Buda Western coach, after a loss to Watseka in which Ed Dene flattened Buda player Rob Horton.

Chips and I went to school at Western Illinois University together, played a lot of poker and graduated at the same time.
1976 — Butkovich, on his relationship with Giovanine.

Bob Hembrough of Beardstown sets up a play during a break in the action in 1987.

Celebrating 100 years of IHSA Boys Basketball Tournaments

PINCKNEYVILLE
Class A State Champions of 2001

FRONT ROW (left to right):
Shane Hoffman, Josh Fisher,
Haven Hicks, Tim Bauersachs,
Cody Majewski, Kyle Smith.
SECOND ROW: Asst. Coach
Ryan Bruns, Asst. Coach
Mike Cheek, Zach Campbell,
Michael McConachie, Wesley
Epplin, Darren McCombs,
Jon Hicks, Jason Houghland,
Nolan Kellerman, Asst. Coach
Wes Choate, Coach Dick Corn.

CLASS A

2001 A

The south rose again in 2001.

After dominating the first decades of Class A play, southern Illinois teams had found the going rough in recent years. No team from the state's two southernmost super-sectionals had won a title since Pinckneyville in 1994.

But from the moment they stepped onto Carver Arena for a 71-44 quarterfinal win against Fairbury Prairie Central, this group of Panthers looked like champs. Even in a tournament that saw Westmont's Pierre Pierce pass Lawrenceville legend Jay Shidler in the record book, the most lasting impression was Pinckneyville's precise passing, tough defense and inspiring team play.

And after Pinckneyville (31-4) drubbed its Elite Eight opponents by an average of 24 points, southern Illinois was once again singing.

"We carried the banner not just for Pinckneyville, but for the entire south," Panthers coach Dick Corn said after a 77-50 win over Pana in the title game. "And I take great pride in that."

The title game also provided Corn and 11th-ranked Pinckneyville a measure of revenge against 16th-ranked Pana (29-5). In 1988, a lightly regarded Pana squad had shocked top-ranked Pinckneyville in the championship. Not so this time, as Pinckneyville shot 58 percent in the first half to take a commanding 42-18 lead.

"We felt like we couldn't do anything to stop them," Pana coach Gary Bowker said. "They were hitting inside, hitting outside. They just do everything well."

Added motivation for Pinckneyville came from the tragic loss suffered by senior all-stater Tim Bauersachs. His mother, Debbie, died on Feb. 3 after a two-year battle with breast cancer. From that point on, the team wore arm bands in her memory.

The other main story of the tournament was Iowa recruit Pierce, who finished with 159 points to top the record of 157 set by Shidler in 1976. After scoring 28 in the super-sectional, the 6-foot-4 Pierce went for 41 in a quarterfinal win against Columbia, added 42 in a semifinal loss to Pinckneyville, and then racked up 48 in a losing effort against Bureau Valley — his 13th game of the season over 40 points.

"[An assistant coach] told me I needed 47 before the game and I felt like I couldn't do it because I was tired," Pierce said. "With three minutes left they told me I needed seven and I said, 'I'd better take it to the hole.'"

Pierce got his final two points on free throws with 22 seconds left in the consolation game to give him a record 33 in the second half. Pierce also broke Westmont season and career scoring records held by Joe Morganfield, son of blues legend Muddy Waters.

Worth noting is that Shidler had set his mark in a consolation game against Buda Western, one of the schools that merged into Bureau Valley.

While Pierce got his records, Bureau Valley earned its second straight third-place finish. Along the way, Bureau Valley had stormed past Macomb, which had knocked out defending champ and top-ranked Pleasant Plains in the super-sectionals.

State Final Tournament Scores

Super-Sectionals
At Normal [ISU]—Fairbury (Prairie Central) 58, Mason City (Illini Central) 55
At Carbondale [SIU]—Pinckneyville 59, Harrisburg 44
At Kankakee [Olivet]—Westmont 48, Momence 45
At Charleston [EIU]—Columbia 68, Effingham (St. Anthony) 59 (OT)
At Decatur [Millikin]—Pana 81, Macon (Meridian) 59
At East Moline (United)—Farmington 70, Rock Falls 56
At Macomb [WIU]—Macomb 48, Pleasant Plains 46
At DeKalb [NIU]—Manlius (Bureau Valley) 60, Huntley 43

Quarterfinals
Pinckneyville 71, Fairbury (Prairie Central) 44
Westmont 67, Columbia 65 (OT)
Pana 66, Farmington 62
Manlius (Bureau Valley) 65, Macomb 51

Semifinals
Pinckneyville 77, Westmont 61
Pana 66, Manlius (Bureau Valley) 59

Finals
Manlius (Bureau Valley) 70, Westmont 61 (third place)
Pinckneyville 77, Pana 50 (title)

Scoring Leaders

Player, School	G	FG	3P	FT	Pts
Pierre Pierce, Westmont	4	58	13	30	159
Justin Shrake, Pana	4	37	22	12	108
Tim Bauersachs, Pinckneyville	4	33	0	9	75
Jake Sinclair, Pana	4	27	4	14	72
Reuben Slock, Manlius (Bureau Valley)	4	25	12	5	67

All-Tournament First Team

Player, School	Ht.	Yr.
Tim Bauersachs, Pinckneyville	6-5	Sr.
Pierre Pierce, Westmont	6-4	Sr.
Justin Shrake, Pana	6-1	Jr.
Jake Sinclair, Pana	6-0	Sr.
Reuben Slock, Manlius (Bureau Valley)	6-6	Sr.

Championship Game Box Score
Carver Arena, Peoria, March 10, 2001

PINCKNEYVILLE (77)
Coach Dick Corn

Player	FG-A	3P-A	FT-A	Pts	PF	Rb	As	St	Bl
Tim Bauersachs	7-9	0-0	0-2	14	3	4	1	2	1
Zach Campbell	0-1	0-1	0-2	0	0	0	0	0	0
Wesley Epplin	1-1	0-0	0-0	2	0	1	0	0	0
Josh Fisher	4-7	0-0	4-6	12	1	2	4	0	0
Haven Hicks	6-10	4-8	4-6	20	2	6	6	1	0
Jon Hicks	0-1	0-0	0-0	0	0	2	0	0	0
Shane Hoffman	0-0	0-0	0-0	0	0	0	0	0	0
Jason Houghland	1-1	0-0	2-2	4	0	1	0	0	0
Nolan Kellerman	0-0	0-0	0-0	0	0	0	1	0	0
Cody Majewski	6-9	2-2	3-4	17	3	6	2	1	0
Darren McCombs	0-0	0-0	0-0	0	0	1	0	0	0
Michael McConachie	0-0	0-0	0-0	0	0	1	1	0	0
Danny Siefert	0-0	0-0	0-0	0	0	0	0	0	0
Kyle Smith	3-7	0-1	2-2	8	3	2	6	4	0
Jordan Sutton	0-0	0-0	0-0	0	0	1	0	0	0
TEAM						3			
TOTAL	28-46	6-12	15-24	77	13	29	21	8	1

PANA (50)
Coach Gary Bowker

Player	FG-A	3P-A	FT-A	Pts	PF	Rb	As	St	Bl
Aaron Beyers	1-2	1-1	0-0	3	0	0	0	0	0
Todd Beyers	0-3	0-0	0-0	0	1	4	0	0	0
Steve Carroll	0-2	0-0	0-0	0	1	1	1	0	0
David Chernisky	0-0	0-0	0-0	0	0	0	0	1	0
Jared Cook	0-0	0-0	0-2	0	1	0	0	0	0
Josh Evans	8-11	0-0	0-0	16	2	4	0	2	0
Joe Fitzpatrick	0-0	0-0	0-0	0	0	1	0	0	0
Andy Lebon	0-0	0-0	0-0	0	0	0	0	0	0
J. I. McDowell	1-4	0-3	0-0	2	4	1	0	0	0
Brian McMillen	0-4	0-3	0-0	0	3	4	4	0	0
Ryan McVickers	0-0	0-0	0-0	0	0	0	0	0	0
Troy Pinkston	0-2	0-2	1-2	1	0	2	1	0	0
Justin Shrake	4-11	3-8	2-2	13	1	4	2	0	1
Jake Sinclair	6-15	1-1	2-3	15	3	3	2	1	0
TEAM						1			
TOTAL	20-54	5-18	5-9	50	16	23	11	5	1

Pinckneyville	16	26	19	16	—	77
Pana	11	7	22	10	—	50

Officials: Edwin Gardner, Kevin Schnitker, Terrence Andrews.

Haven Hicks of Pinckneyville sets up the offense while Jake Sinclair of Pana maintains a defensive stance.

TOSS-UP

Pana's Jake Sinclair sends a shot skyward over the grasp of Pinckneyville's Tim Bauersachs. Pinckneyville won the title contest 77-50.

Westmont's Pierre Pierce tears down a rebound in the third-place contest against Bureau Valley. Pierce's 48-point effort gave him a tournament scoring record of 159 in four games.

2001A

Pana's Troy Pinkston reaches for a steal in the championship game against Pinckneyville.

PLEASANT PLAINS
Class A State Champions of 2002

FRONT ROW (left to right): Mgr. Alex Humphrey, Curtis Nelson, Aaron Rapaport, Jamie Kleimenhagen, Joe Albsmeyer, Matt Bryant, Michael Lucchesi, Ryan Needham. Ballboy Michael Cameron, Ballboy Chris Barnes. SECOND ROW: Cliff Cameron, Thomas Suchy, Brett Oswald, Joe Miles, Jordan Roth, John Edmison, Ryan Sunley, Steven Brown, Andy Crompton, Coach Danny Watson.

2002A

One year later than some expected, Pleasant Plains claimed a second state championship.

With two major contributors back from its 2000 champs (all-stater Dusty Bensko had left for the University of Illinois), Pleasant Plains joined an elite group. The Cardinals became one of only five teams with multiple Class A titles, joining Lawrenceville (1972, 1973, 1982, 1983), Venice (1975, 1987), Madison (1977, 1981), and Pinckneyville (1994, 2001).

Unlike any of those teams — or any other Class A champion — Plains (32-3) survived two overtime games at state and a third in sectional play to earn its crown.

"We've been in these tight situations in the past couple of weeks and they're nerve-wracking," Plains coach Cliff Cameron said. "It can't be good for my heart."

Better than the heartburn of one year earlier, though, when top-ranked Pleasant Plains was upset in the super-sectional by Macomb. That game was not far from the minds of Plains following its overtime victory against Herrin in the title game — the third Class A title decided in an extra period.

"I actually thought we'd win two more," said Ryan Sunley, who started for Pleasant Plains as a sophomore in 2000. "After the heartbreak last year, this one is even sweeter."

Plains' success this time was built on full-court pressure defense, balanced scoring and good fortune. In a 60-53 quarterfinal win over surprising Bloomington Central Catholic (which started the season 1-9 and finished 15-16), Pleasant Plains rallied from a 10-point third-quarter deficit and then survived a driving, last-second shot by BCC's Ryan Scheets that could have won the game in regulation.

In the title game, Herrin (26-8) missed two lay-ups in the last 47 seconds of regulation. Once in overtime, Plains' top scorer, Jordan Roth, made 4 of 6 free throws to help seal the victory. Pleasant Plains also held Herrin's 6-9 center Brian Algee to nine points — seven below his average.

Overall, this was not a tournament for highly touted players. Third-ranked Robinson had two Division I starters in 6-5 all-stater Nick Brooks (Butler) and Tyson Schnitker (Indiana State) but was shocked by unranked Tolono Unity.

In quarterfinal action, Bureau Valley got the best of Providence-St. Mel, whose top guns included Minnesota recruit Stanley Gaines and eventual Seton Hall signee Justin Cerasoli. From there, Bureau Valley made history by claiming its third straight third-place trophy, the first team in Class A to win a trophy in three consecutive tournaments. Pinckneyville also placed third three straight years in single-class play from 1953 to 1955.

State Final Tournament Scores

Super-Sectionals

At Carbondale [SIU]—Herrin 49, Pinckneyville 39
At Moline [The Mark]—Farmington 57, Rock Falls 53
At Decatur [Millikin]—Tolono (Unity) 70, Warrensburg (W.-Latham) 54
At Charleston [EIU]—Robinson 47, Trenton (Wesclin) 31
At Normal [ISU]—Bloomington (Central Catholic) 59, Cissna Park 55
At Macomb [WIU]—Pleasant Plains 75, Macomb 59
At Kankakee [Olivet]—Chicago (Providence-St. Mel) 46, Chicago (Hales Franciscan) 34
At DeKalb [NIU]—Manlius (Bureau Valley) 48, Yorkville 47

Quarterfinals

Herrin 60, Farmington 52
Tolono (Unity) 64, Robinson 57 (OT)
Pleasant Plains 60, Bloomington (Central Catholic) 53 (OT)
Manlius (Bureau Valley) 60, Chicago (Providence-St. Mel) 53

Semifinals

Herrin 52, Tolono (Unity) 45
Pleasant Plains 65, Manlius (Bureau Valley) 36

Finals

Manlius (Bureau Valley) 64, Tolono (Unity) 55 (third place)
Pleasant Plains 50, Herrin 47 (OT) (title)

Scoring Leaders

Player, School	G	FG	3P	FT	Pts
Tyler Smith, Tolono (Unity)	4	27	8	18	80
Mike Gavic, Herrin	4	26	0	13	65
Phil Endress, Manlius (Bureau Valley)	4	21	8	14	64
Joey Albsmeyer, Pleasant Plains	4	17	11	10	55
Adam Gutshall, Manlius (Bureau Valley)	4	18	0	17	53

All-Tournament First Team

Player, School	Ht.	Yr.
Joey Albsmeyer, Pleasant Plains	5-10	Sr.
Brian Algee, Herrin	6-9	Sr.
Phil Endress, Manlius (Bureau Valley)	6-3	Sr.
Mike Gavic, Herrin	6-3	Jr.
Jordan Roth, Pleasant Plains	6-7	Sr.

Championship Game Box Score

Carver Arena, Peoria, March 9, 2002

PLEASANT PLAINS (50)
Coach Cliff Cameron

Player	FG-A	3P-A	FT-A	Pts	PF	Rb	As	St	Bl
Joey Albsmeyer	3-7	3-7	2-2	11	2	4	2	1	0
Matt Bryant	0-1	0-1	0-0	0	0	0	0	0	0
John Edmison	3-8	0-0	4-4	10	4	1	2	1	0
Joe Miles	2-2	0-0	0-0	4	3	2	2	0	0
Heather Roth	3-9	0-3	7-11	13	3	9	1	1	0
Adam Suchy	0-0	0-0	0-0	0	3	1	0	0	0
Ryan Sunley	3-9	1-2	5-7	12	2	7	3	2	4
TEAM						4			
TOTAL	14-36	4-13	18-24	50	17	28	10	5	4

HERRIN (47)
Coach Mike Mooneyham

Player	FG-A	3P-A	FT-A	Pts	PF	Rb	As	St	Bl
Brian Algee	4-8	0-3	1-2	9	5	4	0	0	1
Mike Gavic	5-14	0-0	3-5	13	4	9	1	2	1
Joe Maeser	1-1	0-0	2-2	4	2	5	0	1	0
Greg Murphy	0-0	0-0	0-0	0	0	1	0	0	0
Mike Oldani	0-3	0-3	0-0	0	0	2	2	1	0
Brad Walker	3-13	0-3	2-2	8	1	4	1	0	0
Eddie Wills	5-14	1-3	2-2	13	2	1	1	6	1
TEAM						5			
TOTAL	18-53	1-12	10-13	47	14	31	5	10	3

Pleasant Plains	13	12	11	7	7	—	50
Herrin	7	7	17	12	4	—	47

Officials: Brian Schaumburg, Kevin Coughenour, Richard Hornickel.

Bureau Valley's Gregg Cooley gets all ball in the third-place contest against Tolono Unity.

John Edmison of Pleasant Plains finds the going touch against Herrin's Brian Algee in the title match.

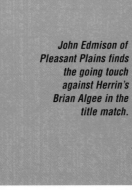

Mike Gavic of Herrin soars toward the backboard while Ryan Sunley can only play catch-up. Pleasant Plains won the 2002 championship 50-47 in overtime.

Sunley gets revenge on Gavic, blocking a shot at the same end of the Carver Arena court.

TURNING THE TABLES

Herrin's Joe Maeser plays keep-away with Sunley in the early going.

2002A

2003

Hales Franciscan did more than win a state championship against Mt. Carroll. On its way to victory, the South Side Chicago school ended 17 years of excuses from previous Windy City contenders.

For all that is good about Chicago basketball, much of what was not good had showed up in previous Class A tournaments. Despite a steady procession of teams deemed ready by the Chicago

London also regularly used up to nine players, including Robinson and 6-foot-3 Nate Minnoy. The pair of sophomores proved particularly effective down the stretch against Mt. Carroll (32-2), combining for 11 of the Spartans' final 15 points.

That was enough to outlast Mt. Carroll (enrollment 149), which fell behind 19-2 after one quarter but rallied behind 26 points from 6-5 all-stater

sparked talk of late Mt. Pulaski coach Ed Butkovich, who had passed away the previous November while riding a bus to a junior college game. Butkovich's daughter Cindi Butkovich-Harris was athletic director at Warrensburg and coach Vic Binkley was an assistant to the Mt. Pulaski legend.

CHICAGO (HALES FRANCISCAN)
Class A State Champions of 2003

FRONT ROW (left to right): Blake Craft, Brandon Kendall, Jerod Haynes, Michael Robinson, Junies Heyward. SECOND ROW: Coach Gary London, Nate Minnoy, Earry Hall, Andre Johnson, Lavell Richardson, Nate Hood, Asst. Coach Marlo Finner. Not pictured: Ivano Clay, Adam Taylor, Norman Shropshear, Austin Chapital, Jeffery Wilson, Jerome Randle.

media, no team since Providence-St. Mel in 1985 had enjoyed small-school glory.

But sixth-ranked Hales (27-6) ended the drought by downing second-ranked Mt. Carroll 58-53.

"We couldn't come back to Chicago without this trophy," Hales sophomore Mike Robinson said. "We were second in 1993 and we didn't want to be second again."

Unlike that Hales squad, which had several players admit they took unranked Staunton too lightly, Coach Gary London's team was focused and disciplined on both ends of the court.

After dropping a quarterfinal to Hales, Breese Central coach Stan Eagleson said, "They played very intelligent and showed great patience in the last few minutes."

The comment summed up Hales perfectly. The Spartans were particularly effective on defense, using pressure to take a toll on all three opponents at state.

Jeremy Haas and some hot three-point shooting. The Hawks, whose only loss was to East Chicago (Ind.) Central, were bidding to become the third-smallest Class A champ.

The only negative for Hales was the fallout from comments London made during the state finals about the possible recruitment of Minnoy, who transferred to Hales after one season at Chicago's Mt. Carmel. After a lengthy investigation, the IHSA barred Hales from defending its title in 2004. Here's what London said that set off the inquiry:

"When [Minnoy] was in the eighth grade, he was probably one of the most highly recruited players. We recruited him coming out of eighth grade, but he chose at that time to go to Mt. Carmel. We were on his short list, and that's why we got consideration when they made the coaching change at Mt. Carmel."

Finally, on its way to third place, ninth-ranked Warrensburg-Latham

State Final Tournament Scores

Super-Sectionals

At Normal [ISU]—Cissna Park 42, Tremont 41
At Decatur [Millikin]—Warrensburg (W.-Latham) 50, Monticello 49 (OT)
At Charleston [EIU]—Breese (Central) 53, Paris 51
At Kankakee [Olivet]—Chicago (Hales Franciscan) 66, Addison (Driscoll) 57
At Macomb [WIU]—Auburn 63, Mt. Sterling (Brown County) 54
At Moline [The Mark]—Mt. Carroll 59, Abingdon 48
At DeKalb [NIU]—Lisle 52, Princeton 51
At Carbondale [SIU]—Cairo 73, Benton 69

Quarterfinals

Warrensburg (W.-Latham) 63, Cissna Park 50
Chicago (Hales Franciscan) 65, Breese (Central) 47
Mt. Carroll 69, Auburn 62
Cairo 73, Lisle 52

Semifinals

Chicago (Hales Franciscan) 62, Warrensburg (W.-Latham) 45
Mt. Carroll 73, Cairo 64

Finals

Warrensburg (W.-Latham) 58, Cairo 56 (third place)
Chicago (Hales Franciscan) 58, Mt. Carroll 53 (title)

Scoring Leaders

Player, School	G	FG	3P	FT	Pts
Jeremy Haas, Mt. Carroll	4	41	1	15	98
Andy Calmes, Warrensburg (W.-Latham)	4	27	1	23	78
Jordan Delp, Mt. Carroll	4	21	12	14	68
Anthony Mackins, Cairo	4	28	3	6	65
Nate Minnoy, Chicago (Hales Franciscan)	4	19	0	18	56

All-Tournament First Team

Player, School	Ht.	Yr.
Andy Calmes, Warrensburg (W.-Latham)	6-6	Sr.
Jordan Delp, Mt. Carroll	6-1	Jr.
Jeremy Haas, Mt. Carroll	6-5	Sr.
Jerod Haynes, Chicago (Hales Franciscan)	6-1	Jr.
Nate Minnoy, Chicago (Hales Franciscan)	6-4	So.

Championship Game Box Score

Carver Arena, Peoria, March 15, 2003

CHICAGO (HALES FRANCISCAN) (58)
Coach Gary London

Player	FG-A	3P-A	FT-A	Pts	PF	Rb	As	St	Bl
Ivano Clay	0-1	0-0	0-0	0	1	0	0	0	0
Blake Craft	2-5	1-3	0-0	5	2	2	2	4	0
Jerod Haynes	4-10	0-1	0-2	8	2	1	1	2	0
Nathan Hood	4-5	1-1	0-0	9	2	0	1	0	0
Andre Johnson	0-0	0-0	0-0	0	1	0	0	0	0
Nate Minnoy	4-14	0-0	3-6	11	3	7	1	2	0
Jerome Randle	1-2	0-0	0-0	2	1	1	1	1	0
Lavell Richardson	5-11	0-0	1-2	11	1	11	1	2	0
Michael Robinson	4-7	0-0	4-5	12	2	5	1	2	0
TOTAL	24-55	2-5	8-15	58	15	30	8	13	0

MT. CARROLL (53)
Coach Chris Payne

Player	FG-A	3P-A	FT-A	Pts	PF	Rb	As	St	Bl
Colin Bausman	0-1	0-1	0-0	0	0	0	0	0	0
Jordan Delp	4-14	2-9	0-0	10	0	5	3	1	0
Marcus Foltz	1-2	0-1	2-2	4	3	2	0	1	0
Jeremy Haas	11-18	1-1	3-6	26	3	15	2	3	0
Matt Kreuder	0-0	0-0	0-0	0	0	0	0	0	0
Justin Moshure	0-1	0-1	0-0	0	1	0	0	0	0
Devon Schneider	4-7	3-5	0-0	11	0	1	2	0	0
Brett Yochem	1-3	0-0	0-0	2	4	7	1	1	0
TOTAL	21-46	6-18	5-8	53	10	33	8	6	1

Chicago (Hales Franciscan)	19	10	14	15	—	58
Mt. Carroll	2	18	18	15	—	53

Officials: Bruce Jokisch, Ronald Kuhlmann, Timothy Laesch.

Cairo's Seville Bell denies Korte Long of Warrensburg-Latham in the third-place contest.

Jordan Delp of Mt. Carroll drives upcourt in the title game with Hales Franciscan.

Jerome Randle of Hales scoops a lay-up in the championship game against Mt. Carroll.

2003A

FLIGHT PATTERN

Nate Minnoy of Hales Franciscan puts up a short jumper in the title contest against Mt. Carroll. Hales won its first state title with a 58-53 decision.

CHICAGO (LEO)
Class A State Champions of 2004

FRONT ROW (left to right):
Jalil Harvey, Kevin Brown.
SECOND ROW: James Jackson,
Michael Stipe, Keelan Donald,
Stephen Benjamin, Terrance
Robinson, Henry Peters.
THIRD ROW: Marvin Ezell,
Tracy Robinson, Donald Lawson,
Dionte Gaskew, Kijuane Leach.
Not pictured: Alan Downing,
Frank Clair.

Noah Cannon didn't coach like a rookie.

And Chicago Leo didn't play like so many Windy City entrants in previous Class A tournaments.

Instead, Leo claimed a second straight small-school championship for Chicago in what was becoming familiar style. Like fellow Catholic League member Hales Franciscan the year before, Leo relied on depth, defense and discipline.

That defending champ Hales was ruled ineligible for postseason play by the Illinois High School Association only served as added motivation for third-ranked Leo (28-5).

"In a way we were kind of defending it for them," Leo senior Frank Clair said after a 65-57 victory over Winnebago for the championship.

Leo was also busy making history. The 26-year-old Cannon was the youngest coach to win a state title in the two-class system. A Leo graduate, Cannon spent three years as an assistant before becoming the first rookie coach to win a boys' championship since Wayne McClain of Peoria Manual in 1995.

The Lions' toughest test came in a title game pitting programs previously best known for runners: Leo for track and Winnebago for cross country. In a role reversal — from a running standpoint — Leo pulled away down the stretch of the title game.

Credit for that went to Cannon switching to a full-court press in the second half and to the 6-foot-6 Clair, who had 25 points and two thunderous dunks.

But Leo was no one-man show. When Clair had foul trouble in the quarterfinals, the Lions roared past Breese Central thanks to seniors Alan Downing and Keelan Donald (14 points apiece) and Tracy Robinson (13 points).

Despite coming off the bench, the 6-7 Robinson scored 40 points in the Elite Eight — fifth best overall. Throughout the tournament, Cannon relied on a rotation of eight to 10 players.

"I don't know if many Class A teams have played a team with that speed and height," Winnebago coach Joe Murphy said.

Eighth-ranked Winnebago (31-2) reached the Elite Eight by upsetting No. 2 Rock Falls in the super-sectionals, 57-56, on a late free throw by sophomore Devan Bawinkel. One week earlier, Massac County had shocked top-ranked and unbeaten Cairo in the regional finals.

While Massac lost in the quarters, Winnebago stayed alive when Bawinkel nailed two free throws for a 62-60 win over St. Anne. Bawinkel then added 14 in a semifinal win over Peoria Christian, a team in just its sixth year as an IHSA member.

Like his teammates, Bawinkel was off in the title game. Winnebago shot 31 percent and was 6-of-32 on 3-pointers.

Even so, three days after the title game Winnebago voters approved a 95-cent education tax fund referendum. One year earlier a 65-cent increase had failed, and there was concern extracurriculars — including basketball — would be cut.

State Final Tournament Scores

Super-Sectionals

At Decatur [Millikin]—Peoria (P. Christian) 47, Pleasant Plains 42
At Carbondale [SIU]—Metropolis (Massac County) 47, Pinckneyville 46
At Kankakee [Olivet]—St. Anne 51, Downs (Tri-Valley) 43
At DeKalb [NIU]—Winnebago 57, Rock Falls 56
At Wheaton [Wheaton College]—Chicago (Leo) 67, Niles (Northridge Prep) 36
At Edwardsville [SIU-E]—Breese (Central) 61, Carrollton 44
At Moline [The Mark]—Quincy (Notre Dame) 62, Rock Island (Alleman) 50
At Charleston [EIU]—Pana 62, Olney (East Richland) 58

Quarterfinals

Peoria (P. Christian) 79, Metropolis (Massac County) 65
Winnebago 62, St. Anne 60
Chicago (Leo) 59, Breese (Central) 43
Quincy (Notre Dame) 87, Pana 66

Semifinals

Winnebago 68, Peoria (P. Christian) 55
Chicago (Leo) 70, Quincy (Notre Dame) 55

Finals

Quincy (Notre Dame) 87, Peoria (P. Christian) 73 (third place)
Chicago (Leo) 65, Winnebago 57 (title)

Scoring Leaders

Player, School	G	FG	3P	FT	Pts
Joe Terwelp, Quincy (Notre Dame)	4	28	1	19	76
Frank Clair, Chicago (Leo)	4	25	1	15	66
Micah Lavender, Peoria (P. Christian)	4	25	4	10	64
Devan Bawinkel, Winnebago	4	20	0	14	54
Johnny Bocke, Quincy (Notre Dame)	4	17	3	14	51

All-Tournament First Team

Player, School	Ht.	Yr.
Devan Bawinkel, Winnebago	6-5	So.
Frank Clair, Chicago (Leo)	6-6	Sr.
Micah Lavender, Peoria (P. Christian)	6-0	Sr.
Tracy Robinson, Chicago (Leo)	6-7	Sr.
Joe Terwelp, Quincy (Notre Dame)	6-5	Sr.

Championship Game Box Score

Carver Arena, Peoria, March 13, 2004

CHICAGO (LEO) (65)
Coach Noah Cannon

Player	FG-A	3P-A	FT-A	Pts	PF	Rb	As	St	Bl
Stephen Benjamin	2-2	0-0	0-0	4	4	2	0	0	0
Frank Clair	10-13	1-2	4-5	25	3	6	0	2	2
Keelan Donald	2-4	0-0	2-4	6	4	5	3	0	0
Alan Downing	4-12	0-4	4-4	12	1	2	1	0	0
Dionte Gaskew	0-0	0-0	0-0	0	2	1	0	0	1
Jalil Harvey	0-0	0-0	0-0	0	0	0	0	0	0
Kijuane Leach	0-1	0-0	0-0	0	0	1	0	0	0
Henry Peters	0-0	0-0	0-0	0	0	0	0	0	0
Terrance Robinson	3-9	0-0	0-1	6	0	7	3	0	0
Tracy Robinson	4-9	0-2	0-0	8	0	3	2	1	1
Michael Stipe	2-2	0-0	0-0	4	5	2	0	1	0
TOTAL	27-52	1-8	10-15	65	19	35	9	4	4

WINNEBAGO (57)
Coach Joe Murphy

Player	FG-A	3P-A	FT-A	Pts	PF	Rb	As	St	Bl
Devan Bawinkel	4-14	0-5	3-4	11	3	8	3	1	0
Robert Brooks	0-1	0-1	0-0	0	0	0	0	0	0
Brennan Crull	0-0	0-0	0-0	0	0	0	0	0	0
Chase Jensen	0-0	0-0	0-0	0	0	2	0	0	0
Brandon Johnson	0-3	0-0	2-2	2	2	4	0	0	0
Ryan Kaufman	1-3	0-2	0-0	2	0	0	0	0	0
Adam Meacham	0-0	0-0	0-0	0	0	0	0	0	0
David Merchant	6-12	2-7	0-0	14	3	7	1	0	0
Chad Nelson	1-6	0-3	2-2	4	2	2	1	0	0
Ben Powers	2-5	0-1	1-3	5	0	6	2	1	0
Caleb Snyder	1-1	0-0	0-0	2	0	1	0	0	0
Kevin Terviel	2-5	2-4	2-2	8	2	0	0	0	0
Bobby Tisdale	2-12	2-9	3-4	9	4	2	2	1	0
Curt Zoet	0-0	0-0	0-0	0	0	0	0	0	0
TOTAL	19-62	6-32	13-17	57	16	34	9	3	0

	1	2	3	4		
Chicago (Leo)	14	15	20	16	—	65
Winnebago	14	12	16	15	—	57

Officials: Mark Moberly, Martin Flaherty, Robin Roberts.

Winnebago's Devan Bawinkel blocks a shot by
Alan Downing of Leo in the 2004 Class A championship.

Frank Clair of Leo slams home two points as Winnebago's
Kevin Terviel gets out of the way.

HEADED TO THE HOLE

Leo's Tracy Robinson puts the
move on Ryan Kaufman of
Winnebago in the title game.

Joe Terwelp of
Quincy Notre Dame
slides past Tyler
Griggs of Peoria
Christian in the
2004 third-place
game, won 87-73
by Notre Dame.

2004A

Hales Franciscan of Chicago and Winnebago square off in the 2005 Class A title game.

No team in Class A history created more drama off court than Chicago's Hales Franciscan.

Champion in 2003, Hales was forced to sit out the 2004 postseason for violating Illinois High School Association recruiting by-laws. By the time 2005 rolled around, Hales was hungry for a return to Peoria.

"From the beginning of the season, that's all we've talked about is getting down to the championship game and getting our redemption," Hales senior Mike Robinson said. "I really felt bad for the seniors last year who didn't get a chance to play for it. They'll know we did this for them."

What Hales did was hold the No. 1 ranking all year, finish unbeaten against Class A competition and hand the Windy City a third straight small-school title.

At least Chicago held the title for a few months.

In November, the IHSA learned Hales had failed to maintain its accreditation from the Illinois State Board of Education. Since state accreditation is a prerequisite for IHSA membership, Hales was forced to forfeit every sports contest it won from June 10, 2003 to Dec. 1, 2005, including every victory of its 30-4 basketball season.

On paper, at least, that left the 2005 title vacant. But anyone who saw the tournament would have a hard time forgetting Hales' dominance.

"The kids who played (in 2005) can say that was an adult problem, we won the title," Hales Principal John Young said. "We as adults dropped the ball."

The Spartans' toughest test at state came in the quarterfinals against ninth-ranked Nashville (28-6). By slowing the tempo and keeping the ball in the hands of 6-foot-6 sophomore Lucas O'Rear (game-

high 29 points), Nashville led 44-39 after three quarters. But Hales stormed back in the fourth, outscoring Nashville 17-2 behind eight points from Robinson.

From there Hales seldom lost momentum in the ensuing eight quarters, even though all-state forward Nate Minnoy was bothered by the flu. Depth was the key as teammates helped pick up the slack for the ailing Purdue recruit.

First was speedy junior point guard Jerome Randle, who led Hales with 17 points in a semifinal win over fifth-ranked Seneca. Then in the title game, Robinson took center stage despite playing with a stress fracture in his right hand. The injury had forced Robinson to miss Hales' first two postseason games. But the senior could not stand missing March Madness again. So without his doctor's consent, he used pliers to remove his cast.

"Some people can look at it as selfish, but I think I needed to be there for my team," Robinson said.

Nobody argued that point after Hales downed No. 7 Winnebago 78-62. Robinson scored 30 points, shot 13-of-19 from the floor and had 15 points in the third quarter to outduel Winnebago's junior all-stater Devan Bawinkel. Bawinkel scored 13 of his 24 points in the third and had a game-high 11 rebounds.

For the second time in as many years, Winnebago faltered down the stretch against a deeper Chicago team.

"If we finish second every year for the next 20 years I don't care who we lost to," Coach Joe Murphy said. "It's just nice to be in the championship game."

For Hales it was just nice to be in the tournament, though it had lost the chance to win back-to-back titles as Lawrenceville had done in 1982 and 1983.

The implications of Hales' one-year absence was not lost on Minnoy. "In my mind there will always be an asterisk next to Leo in 2004," he said.

Ironically, the same thing will always be true of Hales in 2005.

State Final Tournament Scores

Super-Sectionals
At Charleston [EIU]—Flora 69, Tuscola 58
At Kankakee [Olivet]—Seneca 55, Colfax (Ridgeview) 44 (OT)
At Wheaton [Wheaton College]—Chicago (Hales Franciscan) 82, Lisle 61 (forfeited)
At Carbondale [SIU]—Nashville 55, Bluford (Webber) 45
At Normal [ISU]—Eureka 53, Manito (Midwest Central) 50
At Macomb [WIU]—Liberty 52, Farmington 51
At Edwardsville [SIU-E]—Breese (Central) 42, Rochester 24
At DeKalb [NIU]—Winnebago 60, Rock Falls 56

Quarterfinals
Seneca 45, Flora 39
Chicago (Hales Franciscan) 65, Nashville 57 (forfeited)
Liberty 49, Eureka 47
Winnebago 71, Breese (Central) 66

Semifinals
Chicago (Hales Franciscan) 54, Seneca 36 (forfeited)
Winnebago 73, Liberty 60

Finals
Seneca 55, Liberty 33 (third place)
Chicago (Hales Franciscan) 78, Winnebago 62 (forfeited) (title)

Scoring Leaders

Player, School	G	FG	3P	FT	Pts
Devan Bawinkel, Winnebago	4	31	9	13	84
Michael Robinson, Chicago (Hales Fran.)	4	26	9	11	72
Garrett Callahan, Seneca	4	23	10	16	72
Nate Minnoy, Chicago (Hales Franciscan)	4	28	3	13	72
Joe Starnes, Liberty	4	22	8	15	67

All-Tournament First Team

Player, School	Ht.	Yr.
Devan Bawinkel, Winnebago	6-5	Jr.
Justin Brock, Liberty	6-8	Jr.
Nate Minnoy, Chicago (Hales Franciscan)	6-4	Sr.
Lucas O'Rear, Nashville	6-6	So.
Michael Robinson, Chicago (Hales Franciscan)	5-10	Sr.

Championship Game Box Score

Carver Arena, Peoria, March 12, 2005

CHICAGO (HALES FRANCISCAN) (78)
Coach Gary London

Player	FG-A	3P-A	FT-A	Pts	PF	Rb	As	St	Bl
Ryan Bass	1-1	1-1	0-0	3	0	0	0	0	0
Austin Chapital	3-4	1-1	1-2	8	4	1	1	2	3
Courtney Coleman	0-0	0-0	0-0	0	0	0	0	0	0
Matthew Humphrey	0-0	0-0	0-0	0	0	0	1	0	0
Evin McCrimon	0-0	0-0	2-4	2	2	2	1	2	0
Darius Melchor	2-6	1-3	0-1	5	1	0	0	1	0
Nate Minnoy	6-10	0-0	6-7	18	2	6	3	2	1
Jerome Randle	3-8	1-1	3-4	10	2	1	2	0	0
Michael Robinson	13-19	2-6	2-3	30	3	6	7	3	1
Rashod Vaval	0-0	0-0	0-0	0	0	0	0	0	0
Jeff Wilson	1-3	0-0	0-2	2	2	5	0	1	1
Shannon Yerger	0-1	0-0	0-0	0	0	1	0	0	0
TOTAL	29-52	6-12	14-23	78	16	23	15	11	6

WINNEBAGO (62)
Coach Joe Murphy

Player	FG-A	3P-A	FT-A	Pts	PF	Rb	As	St	Bl
Devan Bawinkel	7-17	5-9	5-6	24	3	11	4	0	0
Jacob Bronkema	0-0	0-0	0-0	0	0	0	0	0	0
Robert Brooks	1-4	0-1	0-1	2	2	4	0	0	0
Brennan Crull	6-11	3-5	2-3	17	3	2	0	1	0
Linghao Dong	0-0	0-0	0-0	0	0	0	0	0	0
Brandon Droy	0-0	0-0	0-0	0	0	0	0	0	0
Dale Falconer	0-0	0-0	0-0	0	0	0	0	0	0
Shaun Griseta	3-7	0-0	0-0	6	3	4	1	0	1
Chase Jensen	0-0	0-0	0-0	0	0	0	0	0	0
Adam Meacham	0-0	0-0	0-0	0	0	0	0	0	0
Craig Nelson	2-2	1-1	0-0	5	0	1	1	0	1
Wes Reinke	2-5	0-2	2-4	6	4	3	2	1	0
Ryan Sanden	0-0	0-0	0-0	0	0	0	0	0	0
Caleb Snyder	1-2	0-0	0-0	2	4	5	2	0	0
Jake Spencer	0-0	0-0	0-0	0	0	0	0	0	0
TOTAL	22-48	9-18	9-14	62	19	34	10	2	2

Chicago (Hales Franciscan)	17	18	23	20	—	78
Winnebago	14	16	25	7	—	62

Officials: Eric Brannock, Robert Smith, Roger Grumley.

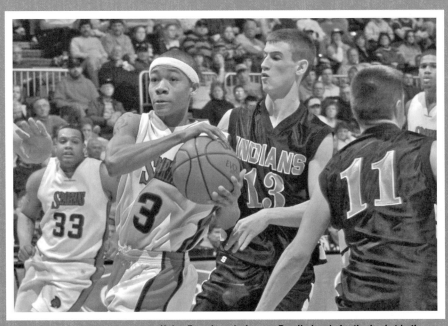

Hales Franciscan's Jerome Randle heads for the basket in the title contest with Wes Reinke of Winnebago in hot pursuit.

Jeff Wilson of Hales Franciscan reaches to block a shot by Winnebago Devan Bawinkle. Hales won 78-62, but later forfeited both the game and 2005 Class A championship.

BIG BLOCK

2005A

Seneca's Robert Rexroade works inside against Liberty's Justin Brock in the third-place game.

Gavin Huber of Liberty just misses blocking a shot by Garrett Callahan of Seneca in the consolation game. Seneca took third place with a 55-33 win.

SENECA
Class A State Champions of 2006

FRONT ROW (left to right): Seth Evans, Marty Hetelle, Seth Hobbs, Luke Underhill, Travis Misener. SECOND ROW: Coach Doug Evans, Alex Spicer, Tim Schmanske, Nick Andreatta, Steven Pearson, Ben Paulsen, Tyler Smith, Garrett Callahan, Nathan Hogue, Griffan Callahan, Robert Rexroade, Asst. Coach Jeff Stenzel.

Why have there been so few unbeaten Class A champions in recent decades? "Parity," said Seneca coach Doug Evans, moments after a title game that proved his point.

Despite holding the No. 1 ranking for much of the season, Evans' top-ranked team was pushed to the brink by a scrappy Chillicothe IVC team that was unranked in the final regular-season poll.

Illinois Valley Central (27-6) actually led by three points with 5:52 to play and had onlookers in a packed Carver Arena recalling 1998 champ Nauvoo-Colusa, another poster child for Class A parity.

"How many people actually thought we were going to be in the title game? Think about that," said IVC coach Jim Thornton, whose team called this season a dream before the Elite Eight even began.

Ultimately, destiny belonged not to Cinderella but to the first perfect Class A squad in 20 seasons. Unbeaten Seneca (35-0) held on for a 47-44 win as Chris Shindley missed a hurried three-pointer as time expired. Seconds earlier Seneca had turned the ball over after Shindley banked in a trey.

"My heart was in my throat there for a second, but our guys were all over them and all they got was another prayer," Evans said.

After that prayer went unanswered, the Fighting Irish and their fans celebrated a truly memorable campaign. Ranked first since January, Seneca featured experience (four starters from a third-place team in 2005), size (6-foot-8 Robert Rexroade and 6-4 Griffan Callahan), the intangible benefits of a coach's son (freshman Seth Evans) and most of all a smothering, trapping man-to-man defense that allowed just 35.1 points per game.

The stingy defense was reminiscent of 1986 champ Teutopolis — the last small-school winner to go unbeaten. Like T-Town, Seneca also faced the burden of lofty expectations. "Nothing else would have done," Seneca senior Garrett Callahan said. "This is what we worked so hard for all year. To win this. This was it for us."

Garrett Callahan did his part to live up to expectations. The all-tournament senior guard was third-leading scorer in the Elite Eight and had 13 points in the title game while brother Griffan Callahan added 12. That helped Seneca become the first team from the DeKalb Super-Sectional or from LaSalle County to win a hoops title.

The final marked a second straight struggle for Seneca, which shot 70 percent in the semifinals but somehow had a tough time in a 44-38 win over Pinckneyville (32-3). That odd semifinal set five record lows. Seneca attempted just 17 field goals, making 12, while Pinckneyville had only eight rebounds; together the teams combined for just 54 shots and 27 boards.

"We've relied on our defense all season to pick us up and they did it again," Evans said. Seneca also had a scare against T-Town before extending its trapping defense for a 13-6 surge down the stretch and a 47-41 win in the tightest quarterfinal.

IVC's road was not much easier, despite the hot hand of Ryan Thornton. The 6-7 guard had 30 points and made 7 of 12 three-pointers in a quarterfinal upset of Chicago North Lawndale, which had won a regular-season meeting 60-49. IVC had a tougher time in the semis against unheralded Maroa-Forsyth and a five-guard lineup that included Robert Kreps.

The Grey Ghosts trailed by five with 6:37 remaining but rallied to win 57-54 thanks largely to 6-6 Zach McAllister's dominance inside. McAllister, picked in the third round of the major league entry draft by the New York Yankees, made 9 of 11 field goals and had nine rebounds against Maroa.

For IVC, the win was part of a remarkable year at a school whose only previous postseason trophy was a fourth in girls' bowling in 1980. Along with a second-place basketball trophy, IVC's football team reached the playoffs for the first time, two of its wrestlers won state titles, and its baseball team claimed the Class A championship.

State Final Tournament Scores

Super-Sectionals
At Moline [The Mark]—Chillicothe (Illinois Valley Central) 54, Forreston 22
At Kankakee [Olivet]—Chicago (North Lawndale) 74, Chicago (CICS-Longwood) 59
At Normal [ISU]—Maroa (M.-Forsyth) 51, Cissna Park 50
At Jacksonville—Carlyle 56, Liberty 37
At DeKalb [NIU]—Seneca 64, Winnebago 29
At Charleston [EIU]—Teutopolis 53, Nokomis 44
At Macomb [WIU]—Macomb 44, Riverton 29
At Carbondale [SIU]—Pinckneyville 58, McLeansboro (Hamilton County) 39

Quarterfinals
Chillicothe (Illinois Valley Central) 58, Chicago (North Lawndale) 40
Maroa (M.-Forsyth) 70, Carlyle 55
Seneca 47, Teutopolis 41
Pinckneyville 54, Macomb 40

Semifinals
Chillicothe (Illinois Valley Central) 57, Maroa (M.-Forsyth) 54
Seneca 44, Pinckneyville 38

Finals
Maroa (M.-Forsyth) 58, Pinckneyville 49 (third place)
Seneca 47, Chillicothe (Illinois Valley Central) 44 (title)

Scoring Leaders

Player, School	G	FG	3P	FT	Pts
Robert Kreps, Maroa (M.-Forsyth)	4	31	11	17	90
Austin Peebles, Maroa (M.-Forsyth)	4	32	3	15	82
Garrett Callahan, Seneca	4	18	2	30	68
Ryan Thornton, Chillicothe (IVC)	4	20	16	9	65
Zach McAllister, Chillicothe (IVC)	4	19	0	16	54

All-Tournament First Team

Player, School	Ht.	Yr.
Garrett Callahan, Seneca	6-2	Sr.
Robert Kreps, Maroa (M.-Forsyth)	6-0	Jr.
Austin Peebles, Maroa (M.-Forsyth)	6-3	Sr.
Robert Rexroade, Seneca	6-8	Sr.
Ryan Thornton, Chillicothe (Illinois Valley Central)	6-7	Sr.

Championship Game Box Score

Carver Arena, Peoria, March 11, 2006

SENECA (47)
Coach Doug Evans

Player	FG-A	3P-A	FT-A	Pts	PF	Rb	As	St	Bl
Garrett Callahan	2-11	1-8	8-8	13	0	4	2	1	0
Griffan Callahan	4-9	1-4	3-4	12	3	6	1	2	0
Seth Evans	2-4	1-2	0-0	5	3	0	2	2	0
Marty Hetelle	2-4	1-3	3-4	8	1	3	2	1	0
Seth Hobbs	0-0	0-0	0-0	0	0	1	0	0	0
Nathan Hogue	0-0	0-0	0-0	0	0	0	0	0	0
Robert Rexroade	4-7	0-2	1-2	9	4	4	1	0	2
Tyler Smith	0-0	0-0	0-0	0	0	1	1	2	0
Alex Spicer	0-0	0-0	0-0	0	2	0	0	0	0
TEAM						2			
TOTAL	14-35	4-19	15-18	47	14	21	9	8	2

CHILLICOTHE (ILLINOIS VALLEY CENTRAL) (44)
Coach Jim Thornton

Player	FG-A	3P-A	FT-A	Pts	PF	Rb	As	St	Bl
Tyler Anderson	2-5	1-2	0-0	5	4	7	2	1	0
Zach McAllister	3-9	0-0	4-6	10	1	6	1	0	0
Joel Perez	0-0	0-0	0-0	0	2	1	0	2	0
Billy Seiler	1-2	0-0	2-2	4	1	2	1	2	0
Chris Shindley	3-7	2-4	2-3	10	4	3	5	1	0
Ryan Thornton	5-14	3-10	2-2	15	2	5	2	0	0
TEAM						3			
TOTAL	14-37	6-16	10-13	44	14	27	11	6	0

Seneca	10	4	14	19	— 47
Chillicothe (IVC)	5	11	9	19	— 44

Officials: Chris Bergschneider, Dan Snodgrass, Stephen Smith.

OVER THE TOP

Seneca's Garrett Callahan intimidates
Zach McAllister of IVC in the 2006 Class A championship game.

IVC's Ryan Thornton
runs into interference
from Seneca's Griffin
Callahan in the
championship game at
Carver Arena.

IVC's Chris Shindley launches a shot over the reach of Derrick
White of North Lawndale. IVC won the quarterfinal game 58-40.

2006A

Robert Kreps of Maroa-Forsyth works his dribble against
Darrell Johnson of Carlyle in quarterfinal action at Carver Arena.

TEAMS

Selected by Jeff Lampe

Providence, 1979

The first Chicago-area team to win in Class A, Providence (32-1) meshed 6-foot-8 Walter Downing's inside presence with Barney Mines' outside shooting and won every tournament game by double figures. Lone loss for Frank Palmasani's team was to Class AA Lincoln-Way.

Lawrenceville, 1982

This 34-0 team had both Marty Simmons (25 ppg) and Doug Novsek (24.5 ppg) and battled through an Elite Eight whose .906 win percentage is still best in Class A. And what a great encore: the unbeaten 1983 Indians, who had the pressure of an unbeaten streak to deal with.

Providence-St. Mel, 1985

Cruised through the tournament with an average 25-point margin of victory and set 17 team records, many still standing. A 31-3 season finally delivered on the promise of a group featuring 6-foot-7 Lowell Hamilton, Fernando Bunch, and 6-4 Joe Jackson.

Teutopolis, 1986

Defense and rebounding can win championships. Easily. The 33-0, top-ranked Wooden Shoes' stomped Assembly Hall foes by an average 28 points and allowed just 33 percent shooting. Four starters scored in double figures led by 6-6 Bob Zerrusen's 17.4 ppg and all could rebound and defend.

Hales Franciscan, 2005

Though the team lost its title and forfeited its wins because of an administrative foul-up, players on this 30-4 finisher went unbeaten against Class A competition and held their No. 1 ranking all year. In Nate Minnoy, Jerome Randle, and Mike Robinson, Hales had as good a trio as Class A has seen in years plus a coach in Gary London who used depth and control.

COACHES

Ron Felling
Lawrenceville

Four state titles, a 68-game win streak, a 388-77 record, and the state's second-best win percentage of .834 (behind only Landon Cox) put Felling ahead of all other Class A coaches. Also had 12 all-staters and a knack for developing shooters. Went 19-3 in games at state and holds numerous Class A coaching records.

Larry Graham
Madison

Won titles in 1977 and 1981, when his team upended top-ranked New Lenox Providence. Graham went 223-41 at Madison, where he also finished fourth in 1980 and won a Class A record nine straight regionals from 1976-84. Overall was 354-143 at Madison, Mt. Auburn, and St. Elmo.

Ed Butkovich
Mt. Pulaski

Seems his teams were always upsetting a favored foe. Though he surprised many by winning state in 1976, the gravel-voiced Butkovich is probably best known for upsetting Providence-St. Mel en route to second in 1984. The man in the green leisure suit also had three other Sweet 16 appearances and 628 career wins.

Ken Crawford
Teutopolis

Career winning percentage of .794 (624-200) with only losing season his first. Took four teams to state, winning with an unbeaten squad in 1986, placing second in 2000, and losing in the 1994 quarterfinals to eventual champion Pinckneyville on a last-second shot. All that with home-grown players, as he is proud to mention.

Dick Corn
Pinckneyville

Won titles in 1994 and 2001 and was upset in 1988 championship. Tried to retire twice but was called back and finished 682-254 in 31 seasons with just one losing campaign. Almost always calm and collected on the bench, he holds a record for most regional titles with 23.

PLAYERS

Jack Sikma, *St. Anne, 1973*

Though he got better as his career went on, the 6-foot-8 Sikma still put on a show at state. His quarterfinal line of 36 points, 24 rebounds, and 12 blocked shots against Cerro Gordo in 1973 is one of the most complete in Class A. Overall he averaged 25 ppg and 18 rpg as St. Anne placed fourth.

Jay Shidler, *Lawrenceville, 1974-76*

Even 30 years later the 6-1 Blond Bomber is still a household name in Class A for his 157 points in the 1976 tournament. That included Elite Eight games of 37, 45, and 48 points — the last two on a super Saturday. Blessed with a quick release, he averaged 32.7 ppg in 1976 to finish with 2,183 in his career. With a three-point line would still own the scoring records.

Mike Duff, *Eldorado, 1975-76-77*

One of the smoother Class A big men offensively, the 6-7 Duff averaged 31.3 ppg in the 1977 tourney. Also finished fourth in 1975 and reached state in 1976. Averaged 25.2 points and 12.1 rebounds in his 10 games at state

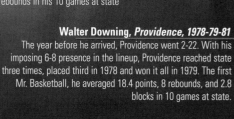

Walter Downing, *Providence, 1978-79-81*

The year before he arrived, Providence went 2-22. With his imposing 6-8 presence in the lineup, Providence reached state three times, placed third in 1978 and won it all in 1979. The first Mr. Basketball, he averaged 18.4 points, 8 rebounds, and 2.8 blocks in 10 games at state.

Marty Simmons, *Lawrenceville, 1982-83*

The "Mule" carried his team to back-to-back 34-0 seasons and scored 2,986 career points. The second Class A Mr. Basketball, Simmons was at his best in the 1983 semifinal against St. Mel when he scored 43 points — including all 23 his team scored in the second half.

Lowell Hamilton, *Providence-St Mel, 1982-83-84-85*

St. Mel reached at least the Sweet Sixteen in all four of Hamilton's seasons, placing third in 1984 and first in 1985. The smooth 6-7 center holds tournament records for finals appearances, blocked shots in a tournament (19), blocked shots in a career (30), and fouls in a tournament.

Gary Tidwell, *Pana 1988; Prairie Central, 1989-90*

The only Class A player to start for a champion (1988 at Pana), runner-up (1990 at Prairie Central), and third-place finisher (1989 at Prairie Central). A true Class A guard at 5-11, he averaged 17.3 ppg at state, had 16 steals, and holds eight tournament records.

Tom Michael, *Carlyle, 1989*

Amazingly accurate from the field, the 6-8 forward carried Carlyle to its title by averaging 30.3 ppg and 8.3 rpg in the Sweet 16 and shooting 72 percent. That included 45 points against Prairie Central in the semifinals. Shot 10-for-12 in the title game to set a record at 83.3 percent.

Shawn Jeppson, *Spring Valley Hall, 1997-98*

The 6-2 shooting guard led Hall to two tough-luck runner-up finishes. Averaged 22.8 ppg in eight tourney games, including a record 51 in the 1997 finale in which he set title-game records for field goals made (16), free throws made (15), and free-throw percentage (.937).

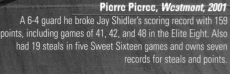

Pierre Pierce, *Westmont, 2001*

A 6-4 guard he broke Jay Shidler's scoring record with 159 points, including games of 41, 42, and 48 in the Elite Eight. Also had 19 steals in five Sweet Sixteen games and owns seven records for steals and points.

Playing Above the Rim   1972–2006

The Class AA tournament has lived in two worlds.

During its 24 years in Assembly Hall, the tournament gave birth to its greatest champions, including 1981 Quincy and the first-born, 1972 Thornridge, still considered by many to be the most amazing of them all.

But the Class AA tournament did not reach its apex until it moved to the cozy confines of Carver Arena in 1996.

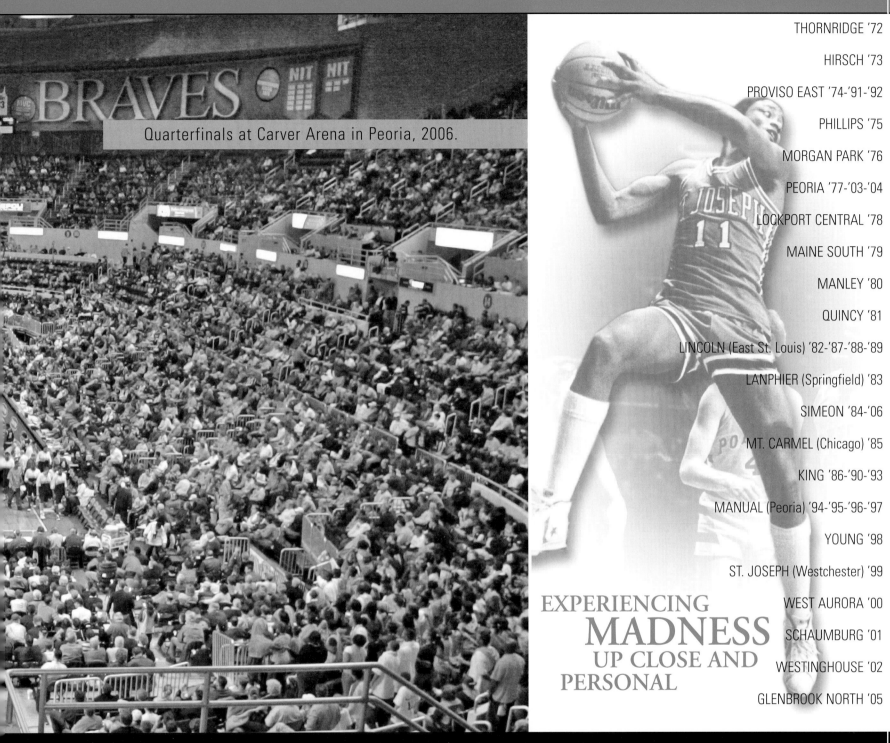

Quarterfinals at Carver Arena in Peoria, 2006.

THORNRIDGE '72

HIRSCH '73

PROVISO EAST '74-'91-'92

PHILLIPS '75

MORGAN PARK '76

PEORIA '77-'03-'04

LOCKPORT CENTRAL '78

MAINE SOUTH '79

MANLEY '80

QUINCY '81

LINCOLN (East St. Louis) '82-'87-'88-'89

LANPHIER (Springfield) '83

SIMEON '84-'06

MT. CARMEL (Chicago) '85

KING '86-'90-'93

MANUAL (Peoria) '94-'95-'96-'97

YOUNG '98

ST. JOSEPH (Westchester) '99

WEST AURORA '00

SCHAUMBURG '01

WESTINGHOUSE '02

GLENBROOK NORTH '05

EXPERIENCING
MADNESS
UP CLOSE AND
PERSONAL

CLASS AA

With seats right up to the sidelines, Carver brought the hard-charging, fast-breaking action right into your face, as more than one front-row patron could attest.

Four future pros moved directly from the finals on the Carver floor to careers in the NBA.

The arena sold out for virtually every session.

And the March Madness Experience was just that.

Bob Leavitt reports on 35 years of the Class AA tournament, where big schools and big players made it to the big time.

THORNRIDGE FALCONS STATE BASKETBALL CHAMPS "71"

DOLTON (THORNRIDGE)
Class AA State Champions of 1972

FRONT ROW (left to right): Ernie Dunn, Quinn Buckner, Boyd Batts, Greg Rose, Mike Bonczyk. SECOND ROW: Coach Ron Ferguson, Ken Rose, Fred Knutsen, Joe King, Sidney Lewis, Keith Hutchinson, Nee Gatlin, Bill Redman, Dave Anderson, Asst. Coach Dave Lezeau.

The transition into Class AA state finals was a smooth one — for every team that didn't have to play defending one-class champion Thornridge.

The first Class AA boys state basketball championship turned out exactly the same as the last one-class tournament. Thornridge picked up right where it left off. The stars and the style were largely the same; only the spreads were changed to reflect the outclassed.

Arguably the best team in state schoolboy history, Thornridge led Quincy by 31 points at halftime of the title game and cruised to a 104-69 victory.

It was stop No. 54 on a then-state-record journey of 58 consecutive victories. And it gave Thornridge a 33-0 season with an average point spread of 27 in its three Elite Eight games. No opponent came closer than 14 points all year.

Thornridge forward-guard Quinn Buckner would further his image as one of the finest all-around athletes in state history by starting as a defensive back on Indiana University's football team before adding NCAA (Indiana), Olympic (USA) and NBA (Boston Celtics) basketball championships to his résumé.

One opposing coach said it was almost impossible for a player to get through Thornridge's press — even if he didn't have the ball. Another suggested the only

way to stop the Falcons was to roll a hand grenade into their huddle.

A record three Thornridge players were accorded all-state honors: seniors Buckner, 6-foot-7 center Boyd Batts (the only starter over 6-3) and point guard Mike Bonczyk.

Bonczyk's toughest job was spreading the wealth among a trio that totaled 91 title points, including a championship-

game record 37 by Batts, 28 by Buckner and 26 by junior forward Greg Rose.

"The two biggest changes in the first 24 years of AA ball," Thornridge coach Ron Ferguson would say, "were the dunk coming back and the three-point shot. And I'm glad we didn't have them, because Batts would have wanted to do both at once."

Some folks said all the pressure was on the bus driver to get the Falcons safely to Champaign. Others said he'd already fouled up by not taking them where they belonged — the NCAA finals.

The banner headline in the *Champaign-Urbana News-Gazette* dubbed the tourney "Thornridge and the Seven Dwarves."

Despite the ton of talent, Ferguson may have had the toughest task facing any coach. "Of course, all I hear is the only way we can lose is if I screw it up," he said.

Overshadowed by Thornridge's dominance was the tournament's overall firepower in what was by far the highest-scoring meet of all time. Quincy, East Aurora, and Hinsdale Central all brought run-and-gun teams to Champaign.

Several tourney points records fell in Quincy's 107-96 semifinal win over East Aurora: the 44 by Aurora center Greg Smith and the scores by a winning team, a losing team, and both teams combined.

OFFICIAL 25¢ PROGRAM

CLASS AA 65TH ANNUAL ILLINOIS STATE HIGH SCHOOL CHAMPIONSHIP

BASKETBALL TOURNAMENT

PRESENTED BY ILLINOIS HIGH SCHOOL ASSOCIATION

ASSEMBLY HALL MAR. 17-18 1972

State Final Tournament Scores

Super-Sectionals

At Crete (C.-Monee)—Dolton (Thornridge) 74, Lockport (Central) 46
At Carbondale [SIU]—Collinsville 78, Mascoutah 69
At Evanston [NU]—Evanston (Twp.) 62, North Chicago 60
At Peoria [Bradley]—Peoria (Manual) 61, Rock Island (Alleman) 51
At Aurora (East)—Hinsdale (Central) 66, LaGrange (Lyons) 59
At DeKalb [NIU]—Aurora (East) 93, Hoffman Estates (Conant) 53
At Chicago [Amphitheatre]—Chicago (Crane) 75, Chicago (Marshall) 63
At Normal [ISU]—Quincy 76, Kankakee (Eastridge) 70

Quarterfinals

Dolton (Thornridge) 95, Collinsville 66
Peoria (Manual) 82, Evanston (Twp.) 53
Aurora (East) 83, Hinsdale (Central) 81
Quincy 87, Chicago (Crane) 71

Semifinals

Dolton (Thornridge) 71, Peoria (Manual) 52
Quincy 107, Aurora (East) 96

Finals

Aurora (East) 74, Peoria (Manual) 66 (third place)
Dolton (Thornridge) 104, Quincy 69 (title)

Scoring Leaders

Player, School	G	FG	FT	Pts
Greg Smith, Aurora (East)	4	47	18	112
Larry Moore, Quincy	4	44	22	110
Boyd Batts, Dolton (Thornridge)	4	41	21	103
Mike Davis, Peoria (Manual)	4	39	12	90
Greg Rose, Dolton (Thornridge)	4	43	1	87

All-Tournament First Team

Player, School	Ht.	Yr.
Boyd Batts, Dolton (Thornridge)	6-7	Sr.
Quinn Buckner, Dolton (Thornridge)	6-3	Sr.
Jim Flynn, Hinsdale (Central)	6-2	Sr.
Paul Maras, Peoria (Manual)	6-5	Sr.
Larry Moore, Quincy	5-11	Sr.
Greg Smith, Aurora (East)	6-6	Sr.

Championship Game Box Score

Assembly Hall, Champaign, March 18, 1972

DOLTON (THORNRIDGE) (104)
Coach Ron Ferguson

Player	FG-A	FT-A	Pts	PF	Rb	As	St	Bl
Dave Anderson	0-1	0-0	0	0	0	0		
Boyd Batts	14-18	9-10	37	3	15	0		
Mike Bonczyk	1-4	2-2	4	4	0	5		
Quinn Buckner	11-17	6-6	28	4	11	7		
Ernie Dunn	2-5	1-2	5	2	6	1		
Bill "Nee" Gatlin	1-2	0-0	2	2	1	0		
Keith Hutchinson	0-0	0-0	0	0	1	0		
Joe King	0-0	0-0	0	0	0	0		
Fred Knutsen	0-0	0-0	0	0	0	0		
Ken Kremer	0-0	0-1	0	1	2	0		
Bill Redman	1-1	0-0	2	2	1	1		
Greg Rose	13-21	0-2	26	4	8	3		
TEAM					4			
TOTAL	43-69	18-23	104	22	49	17		

QUINCY (69)
Coach Sherrill Hanks

Player	FG-A	FT-A	Pts	PF	Rb	As	St	Bl
Bart Bergman	1-1	0-0	2	0	0	0		
Rick Ely	2-4	1-4	5	3	3	0		
Mark Frageman	0-1	0-0	0	0	0	0		
Kelvin Gott	2-5	1-2	5	5	6	1		
Dan Long	0-0	0-0	0	0	0	0		
Larry Moore	5-22	5-5	15	3	1	2		
Mike Sellers	0-1	0-0	0	0	2	0		
Don Sorenson	3-8	10-10	16	3	4	0		
Bob Spear	4-5	4-6	12	1	5	0		
Jim Wisman	6-16	2-2	14	1	3	0		
TEAM					4			
TOTAL	23-63	23-29	69	16	28	3		

Dolton (Thornridge)	25	32	21	26	—	104
Quincy	15	11	26	17	—	69

Officials: Robert Burson, Otho Kortz Jr..

Quinn Buckner holds the championship trophy while Greg Rose dons the net after Thornridge won the inaugural Class AA championship at Assembly Hall.

MIGHTY QUINN

Greg Rose rises above the crowd to sink a shot in a Thornridge's 104-69 win over Quincy. Boyd Batts (31) and Quinn Buckner (25) observe.

Greg Smith of East Aurora battles a Hinsdale Central player in quarterfinal action.

Boyd Batts of Thornridge stretches for a rebound in the second quarter of the championship game.

Only four of the first 29 Class AA state champions were ranked lower than No. 12 Chicago Hirsch, which propagated a pattern of all-or-nothing, also known as: "Send 'em back to Chicago while you have the chance."

This was the second of nine years in a row where the Chicago Public League survivor was either eliminated in the quarterfinals (five times) or went all the way (four times).

Some of the tourney's biggest upsets have come when Chicago's automatic Elite Eight entry hit March Madness still groggy from Chicago Craziness.

felled a team featuring half a dozen future Division I college recruits (including future NBA player Jeff Wilkins) 54-49.

In the last quarterfinal, unranked New Trier East and John Castino, who went on to play baseball for the Minnesota Twins, stunned Collinsville despite Bob Bone's 27 points.

The surprises continued in the semifinals when Hirsch derailed Lockport 83-67, with Green scoring 25 and snatching eight rebounds.

Finally, the wheels fell off West Aurora's bandwagon when New Trier East held the Blackhawks scoreless in the

CHICAGO (HIRSCH)
Class AA State Champions of 1973

LEFT TO RIGHT: Alfred Bowens, Reece Morgan, Robert Brooks, Gordon Smith, Morris Ross, Joshua Smith, John Robinson, Michael Mathews, Gregory Jones, Michael Turner, Frank Byrd, Rickey Green, Carl Henderson, Gregory Allen, Roderick Cook.

Hirsch's only close call at state was a seven-point quarterfinal, after which the Huskies pressed on to the title, winning 65-51 over New Trier East.

Hirsch featured a pair to draw to in guard Rickey Green and forward John Robinson, who split 142 state-finals points. But the Huskies' ease in winning was surprising because the tournament field included five of the six top-rated teams: Lincoln, Lockport, Elgin, West Aurora, and Collinsville.

After Hirsch held underdog Moline at bay in the first quarterfinal, the remainder of the field commenced bumping off the big dogs.

First Lockport, led by Al Green and Ellis Files, sidelined top-ranked Lincoln and all-stater Norman Cook, who was held to 14 points and six rebounds.

Then West Aurora and Elgin, co-champions of the Upstate Eight Conference, squared off in a double-overtime battle. West, led by John Bryant,

third quarter, the only such shutout in Class AA state-finals history. New Trier East went on to a 39-33 upset.

While talent bounded on the court, it abounded on the benches of an Elite Eight loaded with lore.

Coaches who were or would become legend with their final career win totals: Collinsville's Vergil Fletcher (792); Lincoln's Duncan Reid (643); New Trier East's John Schneiter (641 — 387 boys, 254 girls); Elgin's Bill Chesbrough (573); West Aurora's John McDougal (556) and Lockport's Bob Basarich (496).

Schneiter had the strangest coaching career in the bunch, if not the state. It began when the late, great Gay Kintner (649-299) died at halftime of a Stephen Decatur game and Schneiter had to step in as co-head coach.

Schneiter's career included a 1962 title at Decatur and second-place finishes in 1973 with the New Trier East boys and 1989 with the New Trier girls.

State Final Tournament Scores

Super-Sectionals
At Peoria [Bradley]—Moline 67, Pekin 46
At Chicago [Amphitheatre]—Chicago (Hirsch) 55, Chicago (Parker) 53
At Normal [ISU]—Lincoln 61, Bradley (B.-Bourbonnais) 49
At Crete (C.-Monee)—Lockport (Central) 62, Chicago Heights (Bloom Twp.) 47
At Aurora (East)—Elgin 67, Maywood (Proviso East) 66
At DeKalb [NIU]—Aurora (West) 60, Rockford (West) 52
At Carbondale [SIU]—Collinsville 77, Murphysboro 68
At Evanston [NU]—Winnetka (New Trier East) 54, Skokie (Niles West) 50

Quarterfinals
Chicago (Hirsch) 57, Moline 50
Lockport (Central) 62, Lincoln 54
Aurora (West) 54, Elgin 49 (2 OT)
Winnetka (New Trier East) 61, Collinsville 59

Semifinals
Chicago (Hirsch) 83, Lockport (Central) 67
Winnetka (New Trier East) 39, Aurora (West) 33

Finals
Aurora (West) 67, Lockport (Central) 45 (third place)
Chicago (Hirsch) 65, Winnetka (New Trier East) 51 (title)

Scoring Leaders

Player, School	G	FG	FT	Pts
Matt Hicks, Aurora (West)	4	36	13	85
John Robinson, Chicago (Hirsch)	4	25	22	72
Rickey Green, Chicago (Hirsch)	4	29	12	70
Al Green, Lockport (Central)	4	23	15	61
John Bryant, Aurora (West)	4	22	15	59

All-Tournament First Team

Player, School	Ht.	Yr.
Bob Bone, Collinsville	5-11	Sr.
John Castino, Winnetka (New Trier East)	5-11	Sr.
Al Green, Lockport (Central)	6-2	Sr.
Rickey Green, Chicago (Hirsch)	6-0	Sr.
Matt Hicks, Aurora (West)	6-4	Sr.
Frank Moran, Winnetka (New Trier East)	6-5	Jr.

Championship Game Box Score

Assembly Hall, Champaign, March 24, 1973

CHICAGO (HIRSCH) (65)
Coach Charles Stimpson

Player	FG-A	FT-A	Pts	PF	Rb	As	St	Bl
Gregory Allen	1-2	2-2	4	2	4	2		
Alfred Bowen	0-1	0-0	0	0	0	0		
Robert Brooks	2-8	0-0	4	0	1	4		
Frank Byrd	0-0	0-0	0	0	0	0		
Rodrick Cook	0-0	0-0	0	0	1	0		
Rickey Green	7-10	2-2	16	2	1	3		
Carl Henderson	0-0	0-0	0	0	0	0		
Gregory Jones	1-1	0-0	2	0	0	0		
Mike Matthews	4-6	0-0	8	3	3	1		
John Robinson	6-14	5-7	17	2	8	0		
Gordon Smith	0-0	0-0	0	0	0	0		
Joshua Smith	7-14	0-0	14	0	4	1		
TOTAL	28-56	9-11	65	9	22	11		

WINNETKA (NEW TRIER EAST) (51)
Coach John Schneiter

Player	FG-A	FT-A	Pts	PF	Rb	As	St	Bl
Mike Allen	1-3	0-0	2	2	1	0		
Jim Cassady	6-16	0-2	12	2	7	3		
John Castino	4-8	1-4	9	1	2	4		
Jim Fuhrman	0-0	0-0	0	0	0	0		
David Harvey	0-1	0-0	0	0	0	0		
David Holton	0-1	0-0	0	0	1	0		
Derek Kilimnik	3-11	0-0	6	3	12	1		
Frank Moran	1-5	0-0	2	1	2	2		
Stu Ordman	1-2	0-0	2	1	0	3		
Tom Ureill	0-0	0-0	0	1	0	0		
Chris Wall	9-17	0-0	18	0	13	1		
Jeff Welch	0-0	0-0	0	0	0	0		
TOTAL	25-64	1-6	51	10	38	14		

Chicago (Hirsch)	14	20	12	19	—	65
Winnetka (New Trier East)	16	18	2	15	—	51

Officials: Raymond Brooks, Dan Davey.

Stu Ordman of New Trier East takes aim at the basket in the title game while teammate Chris Wall (53) and Mike Mathews of Hirsch await the result.

DRIVING LESSON

New Trier East's John Castino finds a open path to the basket in the championship game as he drives past Hirsch's Rickey Green (12) and Joshua Smith.

All-staters duel in a tense quarterfinal game as Lincoln's Norman Cook flies past Ellis Files of Lockport.

Elgin's Jeff Wilkins loses control of the ball in a double-overtime quarterfinal shootout won by West Aurora.

1973AA

MAYWOOD (PROVISO EAST)
Class AA State Champions of 1974

FRONT ROW (left to right): Rich Westbrook, Dan Williams, Gene Davis, Dave Ekstrom.
SECOND ROW: Jerry Montgomery, Michael Stockdale, Joe Ponsetto, Roderick Floyd, Doron Dobbins.
Third row: Coach John Blomquist, Briant Johnson, Marlon Thomas, Terry Williams, Ron Hodges, Jack Karstens, Coach Glenn Whittenberg.

The late Glenn Whittenberg (301-68) may have been a tad too conservative to appreciate the unholy humor of the late Sam Kinison.

But the Proviso East coach would have had to at least crack a knowing smile when the politically incorrect comedian advised starving desert dwellers to "go where the food is."

Whittenberg left the south to roam 'round the poles of power — the industrialized areas of the state that produced all but one of the first nine large-school state champs.

He left Herrin to follow fellow southern Illinois native Tom Millikin to where the talent was — in this case Proviso East, which had won state in 1969.

Whittenberg's drill-instructor style was best evidenced by the way his Pirates played and the way his hair was cut — a flat-top in an era when some teams looked like a bunch of rock stars.

Proviso East (29-4) methodically banged away with such leaders as 6-5 all-state center Joe Ponsetto to win the title 61-56 over Bloom and Audie Matthews.

Bloom had sidelined Hersey and 6-11 future Chicago Bulls player Dave Corzine by 20 points in the quarterfinals. No thanks to Corzine, who scored 18 points despite having to help deal with Bloom's press.

Bloom had to work even harder in its semifinal to survive Peoria Central, 67-66. Matthews, Bloom's 6-4 all-state senior, led the way to the title fray with 25 points and 12 rebounds.

Meanwhile, No. 10 Proviso East cruised into the final by eliminating Breese Mater Dei 64-42, with 29 points from Ponsetto.

Matthews, rated the nation's No. 2 prep player behind Moses Malone, had a nightmare of a final, missing 17 of 23 shots for the third-ranked Trojans. Bloom led at the start of the last quarter but was outscored 21-13 in the final eight minutes.

Fourth-place Breese Mater Dei became one of the smallest schools (enrollment 754) ever to win a Class AA trophy thanks to a quarterfinal win over Oswego, which had one of the shortest starting lineups (average height 5-11) in AA Elite Eight history. Twenty-two years later, Mater Dei would be down one class but up two notches with a second-place finish in the 1996 Class A tourney.

State Final Tournament Scores
Super-Sectionals
At Joliet (Central)—Chicago Heights (Bloom) 83, Olympia Fields (Rich Central) 69
At Evanston [NU]—Arlington Heights (Hersey) 39, Waukegan 31
At Normal [ISU]—Danville 66, Quincy 60
At Peoria [Bradley]—Peoria 54, Freeport 51
At Aurora (East)—Maywood (Proviso East) 67, Elgin 57
At Chicago [Amphitheatre]—Chicago (Morgan Park) 84, Chicago (Phillips) 73
At DeKalb [NIU]—Oswego 64, Crystal Lake 47
At Carbondale [SIU]—Breese (Mater Dei) 66, Belleville (West) 60

Quarterfinals
Chicago Heights (Bloom) 56, Arlington Heights (Hersey) 51
Peoria 68, Danville 67
Maywood (Proviso East) 75, Chicago (Morgan Park) 55
Breese (Mater Dei) 63, Oswego 49

Semifinals
Chicago Heights (Bloom) 67, Peoria 66
Maywood (Proviso East) 64, Breese (Mater Dei) 42

Finals
Peoria 80, Breese (Mater Dei) 55 (third place)
Maywood (Proviso East) 61, Chicago Heights (Bloom) 56 (title)

Scoring Leaders

Player, School	G	FG	FT	Pts
Joe Ponsetto, Maywood (Proviso East)	4	37	14	88
Audie Matthews, Chicago Heights (Bloom)	4	35	16	86
Lance Reilmann, Breese (Mater Dei)	4	34	8	76
Al Hightower, Peoria	4	26	6	58
Mike White, Peoria	4	23	11	57
Steve Harper, Peoria	4	25	7	57

All-Tournament First Team

Player, School	Ht.	Yr.
Dave Corzine, Arlington Heights (Hersey)	6-11	Sr.
Audie Matthews, Chicago Heights (Bloom)	6-5	Sr.
Joe Ponsetto, Maywood (Proviso East)	6-5	Sr.
Ray Watson, Danville	6-7	Sr.
Mike White, Peoria	6-7	Sr.

Championship Game Box Score
Assembly Hall, Champaign, March 23, 1974

MAYWOOD (PROVISO EAST) (61)
Coach Glenn Whittenberg

Player	FG-A	FT-A	Pts	PF	Rb	As	St	Bl
Eugene Davis	1-3	0-2	2	2	2	2		
Doron Dobbins	4-8	3-8	11	2	5	2		
Roderick Floyd	4-6	0-1	8	4	10	0		
Briant Johnson	0-0	0-0	0	0	0	0		
Jack Kartsens	0-0	0-0	0	1	0	1		
Jerry Montgomery	8-12	0-0	16	4	1	4		
Joe Ponsetto	9-17	2-2	20	3	14	2		
Michael Stockdale	1-5	2-2	4	5	7	0		
TEAM					8			
TOTAL	27-51	7-15	61	21	47	11		

CHICAGO HEIGHTS (BLOOM) (56)
Coach Wes Mason

Player	FG-A	FT-A	Pts	PF	Rb	As	St	Bl
Emir Hardy	5-13	2-6	12	3	15	0		
Alvin Higgins	2-7	1-3	5	2	2	4		
Alan Lee	0-0	0-0	0	0	0	0		
Audie Matthews	6-23	7-10	19	4	11	2		
Robert McCoy	5-23	2-2	12	1	5	1		
Kelvin Small	0-1	0-0	0	2	2	0		
Derrick Smith	3-6	0-0	6	3	5	3		
Larry Thomas	1-1	0-0	2	1	1	0		
TEAM					5			
TOTAL	22-74	12-21	56	16	46	10		

Maywood (Proviso East)	19	11	10	21	—	61
Chicago Heights (Bloom)	16	17	10	13	—	56

Officials: Richard Dietz, James Meyer.

Doron Dobbins of Proviso East launches a quarterfinal-game shot over James Robinson of Morgan Park. Proviso East beat Bloom in the championship contest 61-56.

Brian Young of Peoria Central rips the ball away from Danville's David Caslow in a quarterfinal game won by Peoria.

Bloom cheerleaders raise the noise level in Assembly Hall.

FULL OF CHEER

James Robinson of Morgan Park and Michael Stockdale of Proviso East battle for a rebound in quarterfinal action.

1974AA

219

Pumping up the theory there is no stopping Chicago Public League champions once they break through the quarterfinals, Chicago Phillips escaped its first state-finals outing by six points over Waukegan before romping to the title.

Second-ranked Phillips pressed into Champaign as one of the tournament favorites, along with No. 3 Peoria Richwoods and No. 4 Proviso East. The defending champions had started the season slowly but easily handled top-ranked and unbeaten East Leyden in super-sectional play. (At least this Leyden team produced a sectional title, something three subsequent years of regular-season unbeatens did not.)

The remaining favorites ran into some serious obstacles in their quarterfinal encounters.

Waukegan outrebounded Phillips 46-40, and only balanced scoring from Robert Byrd, Norman Perry, Marty Murray, and Larry Williams — all of whom notched 14 points or more — kept Phillips afloat en route to a 67-61 win.

Proviso East opened against Bloom in a rematch of the 1974 title game. Bloom, with nine losses and a fifth-place conference finish, was lightly regarded. But Kelvin Small disregarded the experts and poured in 31 points, including the game winner, as Bloom pulled off a 57-56 upset.

A third quarterfinal featured all-American guard Bob Bender, the first player to toil in both Class A and AA state finals. Bender had competed for Quincy Catholic Boys in the 1972 quarterfinals and returned in 1975 with Bloomington in a loss to East St. Louis Senior. Bender also became the only player on NCAA championship teams from two schools (Indiana and Duke).

In the semifinals, second-rated Phillips and its vaunted press pasted third-rated Peoria Richwoods by 17. And in one of only five semifinal meetings between unranked teams in Class AA history, Bloom dumped East St. Louis Senior by 13.

But Bloom's unlikely bid for the state title ran out of the gas in the final, where

the Trojans were no match for Phillips in a 76-48 blowout. Larry Williams, who would star for Louisville, led the state champs with 28 points and 14 boards.

Bloom's 10 losses were a Class AA record for a top-two finisher and the most by a one-class or AA school since Centralia's 1946 runner-up ended 29-10.

Balance was the key for Herb Brown's champions, four of whom averaged double digits in Assembly Hall.

It was the first trip for Richwoods coach Wayne Hammerton (571-229), who like so many found the state finals a humbling experience.

"We came in here with a total of three losses in two years and lost twice in one day," Hammerton said after falling to East St. Louis Senior in the consolation contest, which annually guarantees that one of the state's elite will lose its last two games.

CHICAGO (PHILLIPS)
Class AA State Champions of 1975

KNEELING (left to right): Herman Hoskins, Louis Reymond, Marty Murray, Mgr. G. Wilkes. STANDING: Ike Deal, Norman Perry, Teddy James, Vincent Robinson, Levon Richmond (front), Larry Williams, Darius Cleamons, Robert Byrd, Mgr. C. Martin, Coach Herb Brown.

Class AA
Boys State Final
Basketball Tournament

Assembly Hall

Official
$1.00
Program

March 21-22, 1975

State Final Tournament Scores
Super-Sectionals
At Chicago [Amphitheatre]—Chicago (Phillips) 65, Chicago (Morgan Park) 60
At Evanston [NU]—Waukegan 50, Park Ridge (Maine South) 41
At DeKalb [NIU]—Rockford (Auburn) 58, Aurora (West) 45
At Peoria [Bradley]—Peoria (Richwoods) 94, Sterling 63
At Carbondale [SIU]—East St. Louis 89, Olney (East Richland) 77
At Normal [ISU]—Bloomington 71, Decatur (Eisenhower) 63
At Aurora (East)—Maywood (Proviso East) 72, Franklin Park (East Leyden) 60
At Joliet (Central)—Chicago Heights (Bloom) 57, New Lenox (Lincoln-Way) 30
Quarterfinals
Chicago (Phillips) 67, Waukegan 61
Peoria (Richwoods) 65, Rockford (Auburn) 52
East St. Louis 73, Bloomington 66
Chicago Heights (Bloom) 57, Maywood (Proviso East) 56
Semifinals
Chicago (Phillips) 86, Peoria (Richwoods) 69
Chicago Heights (Bloom) 68, East St. Louis 55
Finals
East St. Louis 83, Peoria (Richwoods) 75 (third place)
Chicago (Phillips) 76, Chicago Heights (Bloom) 48 (title)

Scoring Leaders

Player, School	G	FG	FT	Pts
Herbert Hoosman, East St. Louis	4	37	13	87
Kelvin Small, Chicago Heights (Bloom)	4	34	11	79
Anthony Williams, East St. Louis	4	32	13	77
Larry Williams, Chicago (Phillips)	4	35	6	76
Charles Anthony, East St. Louis	4	33	6	72

All-Tournament First Team

Player, School	Ht.	Yr.
Bob Bender, Bloomington	6-3	Sr.
Herbert Hoosman, East St. Louis	6-5	Sr.
Robert McCoy, Chicago Heights (Bloom)	6-5	Jr.
Marty Murray, Chicago (Phillips)	5-11	Sr.
Kelvin Small, Chicago Heights (Bloom)	6-7	Sr.
Michael Stockdale, Maywood (Proviso East)	6-5	Sr.
Larry Williams, Chicago (Phillips)	6-8	Sr.

Championship Game Box Score
Assembly Hall, Champaign, March 22, 1975

CHICAGO (PHILLIPS) (76)
Coach Herb Brown

Player	FG-A	FT-A	Pts	PF	Rb	As	St	Bl
Robert Byrd	5-13	2-3	12	1	8	5		
Darius Clemons	0-1	0-0	0	0	1	0		
Ike Deal	1-2	0-0	2	1	2	0		
Herman Hoskins	0-2	0-0	0	2	0	2		
Teddy James	2-4	1-1	5	1	3	0		
Marty Murray	1-3	0-0	2	5	0	0		
Norman Perry	5-10	3-5	13	1	7	2		
Louis Reymond	2-7	0-3	4	3	1	0		
Levon Richmond	1-1	1-2	3	2	0	0		
Vincent Robinson	2-10	3-6	7	1	4	5		
Larry Williams	12-20	4-6	28	0	14	0		
TEAM					12			
TOTAL	31-73	14-26	76	17	52	14		

CHICAGO HEIGHTS (BLOOM) (48)
Coach Wes Mason

Player	FG-A	FT-A	Pts	PF	Rb	As	St	Bl
Dave Barba	0-1	2-3	2	2	4	3		
Kevin Carrabine	0-1	0-0	0	0	1	0		
Joe Hagemaster	1-2	3-5	5	2	2	5		
Ernest Harper	1-2	0-0	2	3	0	1		
Tony Kennedy	0-2	0-0	0	1	4	1		
Alan Lee	5-13	0-0	10	2	2	2		
Larry Lowe	4-9	0-0	8	1	10	1		
Robert McCoy	1-13	5-6	7	2	15	1		
Jeff Segert	3-5	0-0	6	2	0	0		
Kelvin Small	4-11	0-0	8	4	4	0		
Columbus Terrell	0-0	0-0	0	0	0	0		
TEAM					4			
TOTAL	19-59	10-14	48	19	46	14		

Chicago (Phillips)	19	9	18	30	—	76
Chicago Heights (Bloom)	10	10	12	16	—	48

Officials: Wilton Crotz, Wayne Meece.

Waukegan's Chris Calhoun can't keep the ball inbounds in quarterfinal action. Phillips defenders are Levon Richmond (12) and Robert Byrd (33), while Ernest Gurley (31) and Angelo Kyle (23) wait for Waukegan.

OVER THE LINE

Bloom's Alan Lee puts it in second gear to race past Dan Williams of Proviso East in the quarterfinals.

Waukegan's Eric Garrett wins the rebound against Robert Byrd of Phillips in a quarterfinal game.

East St. Louis players can only observe as Chris Williams of Peoria Richwoods lays in an easy two in the consolation game.

Phillips team members proudly raise the 1975 Class AA championship trophy.

1975AA

221

CHICAGO (MORGAN PARK)
Class AA State Champions of 1976

FRONT ROW (left to right): Morris Griffin, Cornell Smith, Jeff Berry. SECOND ROW: Kevin Glover, Greg Harris, David Johnson, Warren Morgan. THIRD ROW: Coach Bill Warden, Laird Smith, Eric Bowman, Levi Cobb, Everett Bell, Tony Ferguson.

There were two kinds of sportswriters covering the title game in our country's bicentennial year: those who came up with "The shot heard 'round the state" for a lead sentence, and those who wished they had.

In keeping with their underdog status, No. 14 Chicago Morgan Park became the second-lowest-ranked team to win a Class AA title with the greatest title shot since sophomore sub Anthony Smedley's steal and 18-footer gave Chicago Carver the 1963 crown.

Laird Smith did the honors this time, nailing a 20-footer with no time remaining after all-stater Levi Cobb had controlled a jump ball at the free-throw circle.

Smith was far from the deep-reserve status of Smedley, but this shot made him a statewide name and Morgan Park the most efficient AA titlist until 1989.

Smith's jumper gave Morgan Park (28-5) a 45-44 win over West Aurora and a total victory margin of only seven points for its three Elite Eight outings, including a one-point semifinal win over Oak Park-River Forest.

It was anybody's state final in a year when quarterfinalists came to Champaign loaded down with 37 losses. Three of the state's four top-rated teams lost on the same day of regional play. Regional host Galesburg upset unbeaten poll-topper Peoria Richwoods in overtime. Chicago Weber ended the career of East Leyden great Glen Grunwald. And Chicago Vocational halted Phillips' bid to repeat as state champ.

That "Friday Night Massacre" left few favorites for the finals. The first quarterfinal, however, between No. 3 West Aurora and No. 5 Dolton Thornridge, was supposed to be the barnburner that branded a title favorite.

It turned out the only fire came from West, which roasted the Falcons 82-52. Five Aurora starters scored in double digits, while Thornridge all-stater Bill Cunningham was held to six points. Meanwhile, Morgan Park sneaked past Galesburg and Oak Park-River Forest into the title game.

West Aurora, attempting to become the first state champion from that basketball-crazy community, fell victim to 33 percent shooting in the final. Even so, West led 38-30 with 5:25 left.

Morgan Park rallied, and Cobb's 30-footer pulled the Mustangs to within 44-42. After Smith had made one free throw and missed the next, Cobb forced a jump ball, setting up one of the most famous shots in tourney history.

State Final Tournament Scores

Super-Sectionals
At Joliet (Central)—Dolton (Thornridge) 66, Flossmoor (Homewood-F.) 64 (OT)
At DeKalb [NIU]—Aurora (West) 53, McHenry 40
At Carbondale [SIU]—Marion 76, Edwardsville 74
At Normal [ISU]—Decatur (Eisenhower) 75, Normal (Community) 65 (OT)
At Chicago [Amphitheatre]—Chicago (Morgan Park) 75, Chicago (C. Vocational) 60
At Peoria [Bradley]—Galesburg 52, Moline 47
At Evanston [NU]—Wilmette (Loyola Academy) 50, Skokie (Niles West) 44
At Aurora (East)—Oak Park (O.P.-River Forest) 71, Elgin 55

Quarterfinals
Aurora (West) 82, Dolton (Thornridge) 52
Decatur (Eisenhower) 81, Marion 66
Chicago (Morgan Park) 53, Galesburg 48
Oak Park (O.P.-River Forest) 56, Wilmette (Loyola Academy) 53 (OT)

Semifinals
Aurora (West) 63, Decatur (Eisenhower) 51
Chicago (Morgan Park) 59, Oak Park (O.P.-River Forest) 58

Finals
Oak Park (O.P.-River Forest) 73, Decatur (Eisenhower) 61 (third place)
Chicago (Morgan Park) 45, Aurora (West) 44 (title)

Scoring Leaders

Player, School	G	FG	FT	Pts
Levi Cobb, Chicago (Morgan Park)	4	37	10	84
Jeff Roth, Decatur (Eisenhower)	4	34	11	79
Chuck Dahms, Oak Pk. (O.P.-River Forest)	4	27	11	65
Hubert Carter, Decatur (Eisenhower)	4	27	10	64
Tom Norris, Oak Park (O.P.-River Forest)	4	24	12	60

All-Tournament First Team

Player, School	Ht.	Yr.
Hubert Carter, Decatur (Eisenhower)	6-3	Sr.
Levi Cobb, Chicago (Morgan Park)	6-5	Sr.
Chuck Dahms, Oak Park (O.P.-River Forest)	6-9	Sr.
Ron Hicks, Aurora (West)	6-5	Sr.
Bill Roth, Decatur (Eisenhower)	6-3	Jr.

Championship Game Box Score

Assembly Hall, Champaign, March 20, 1976

CHICAGO (MORGAN PARK) (45)
Coach Bill Warden

Player	FG-A	FT-A	Pts	PF	Rb	As	St	Bl
Jeff Berry	0-6	0-0	0	4	1	4		
Eric Bowman	5-12	0-0	10	2	7	2		
Levi Cobb	8-15	3-4	19	4	7	0		
Anthony Ferguson	0-2	0-0	0	2	1	1		
David Johnson	1-5	0-0	2	3	2	3		
Laird Smith	5-10	4-7	14	1	5	2		
TEAM					8			
TOTAL	19-50	7-11	45	16	31	12		

AURORA (WEST) (44)
Coach John McDougal

Player	FG-A	FT-A	Pts	PF	Rb	As	St	Bl
Jay Bryant	3-16	8-9	14	5	8	3		
Jerry Harris	3-5	0-0	6	1	4	1		
Larry Hatchett	1-9	2-3	4	2	6	2		
Ron Hicks	4-5	5-8	13	4	8	1		
Bruce Johnson	2-3	1-2	5	2	7	0		
Joe Michels	1-4	0-0	2	0	1	0		
Randy Schulz	0-0	0-0	0	1	0	0		
TEAM					4			
TOTAL	14-42	16-22	44	15	38	7		

Chicago (Morgan Park)	12	6	8	19	—	45
Aurora (West)	12	9	12	11	—	44

Officials: Ron Fahnestock, Larry Leitner.

Celebrating 100 years of IHSA Boys Basketball

Jay Bryant of West Aurora drives the lane against the Thornridge defense in quarterfinal action. West Aurora earned a 82-52 decision.

Jubilant Morgan Park players celebrate with the IHSA first-place trophy. Laird Smith, who made the last-second shot to win the game, is at right.

IN THE NICK OF TIME

Scott Kelley of Galesburg struggles to retain possession under pressure from Morgan Park's Laird Smith.

West Aurora's Bruce Johnson stretches for a loose ball as Eric Bowman of Morgan Park watches. Morgan Park won the title 45-44.

1976AA

From the IHSA to the NBA
Tourney stars graduate to the big time

On March 20, 2004, Shaun *Livingston* walked to center court at *Peoria's* Carver Arena in front of a cheering, hometown crowd and hoisted a Class AA first-place *trophy*.

by Jeff Lampe

Isiah Thomas of Westchester St. Joseph grabs a rebound during the 1978 Class AA championship game against Lockport.

On June 24, 2004, Livingston walked to the front of a crowded room at New York's Madison Square Garden theater, smiled for television cameras, and hoisted a Los Angeles Clippers hat.

Drafted fourth by the Clippers just three months after he helped Peoria Central defend its Class AA state basketball title, Livingston is the most recent and most dramatic example of players who have reached the lofty summit of both the Illinois state finals and the NBA.

While Livingston's journey to the pros was meteoric, it was not unique. Since the 1940s, 80 players who appeared in the Illinois High School Association's Elite Eight have gone on to play at least one game in the NBA, ABA, or BAA according to a review of records kept by www.basketballreference.com.

The list of pros who made the Illinois state tournament includes such luminaries as NBA Hall of Famers Isiah Thomas (St. Joseph 1979) and Andy Phillip (Granite City 1940) and such little-known pros as Dave Scholz (Stephen Decatur 1965), who made one field goal in the only game he played as a Philadelphia 76er.

There has even been a small Class A contingent in the pro ranks, led by Jack Sikma (St. Anne 1973). Though he never won a title at St. Anne, Sikma enjoyed a championship as a Seattle Supersonic and finished his 14-year pro career averaging 15.6 points and 9.8 rebounds per game.

No question, though, the pros are the domain of former Class AA tournament players. And no question the overwhelming majority of those players hail from Chicago and vicinity.

In fact, Chicago schoolboy stars provided one of the undisputed highlights for Illinois preps in the pros. The year was 1981 and prospects for the draft were very deep, thanks in part to Thomas's decision to leave Indiana University after winning a national championship

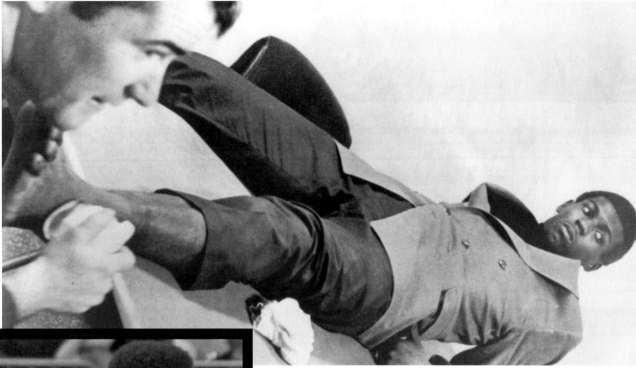

Shaun Livingston of Peoria Central decides on his next move during the 2004 title game against Homewood-Flossmoor. Livingston was one of a handful of Illinois preps to move directly to the pros.

East to a championship, Collins never enjoyed a trip to state as a prep.

Cazzie Russell (Chicago Carver 1962) is the only other Illinois prep picked first in an NBA draft. That came in 1966 when Russell was selected by the New York Knicks after helping the University of Michigan to three straight Big Ten titles and two Final Four appearances. Prior to college, Russell led Carver to second in the 1962 state tournament and almost single-handedly won a championship, scoring 24 points in a 49-48 loss to Stephen Decatur in the title game. Russell also enjoyed a long and successful NBA career, playing for the Knicks' famous 1970 champions and averaging 15.1 points per game over 12 seasons.

That only Brewer won a state title from that quintet of elite NBA draft picks says something about the caliber of play in the Illinois postseason. But the list of former preps in the pros does include numerous other state champions. In fact, you could field a pretty fair pro team just from former winners. The starting line-up for our imaginary Illinois Elite would have to include Granite City great Phillip along with Michael Finley (Proviso East 1991), LaPhonso Ellis (East St. Louis Lincoln 1988), Quentin Richardson (Chicago Young 1998), and then a fifth position rotating between veterans Rickey Green (Chicago Hirsch 1973), Quinn Buckner (Thornridge 1972), and Kevin Gamble (Springfield Lanphier 1983).

Most of those pros who didn't enjoy championships in Illinois at least got to help hoist a second-, third-, or fourth-place trophy. Rare is the future NBA player who did not get to handle some hardware. Most decorated of all was Frank Williams (Peoria Manual 1998) who played on three state champs. Alas, he did not enjoy the same success in his pro career.

Just the opposite was true of Kevin Garnett (Farragut 1985), whose disappointment at state was followed by meteoric pro success. Three months after losing in the state quarterfinals, Garnett was picked fifth by the Minnesota Timberwolves. In the process, he became the first high school senior since

as a sophomore. Thomas didn't have to wait long to hear his name called.

The Dallas Mavericks used the first pick to take Mark Aguirre (Chicago Westinghouse 1978), who had just finished his career as DePaul's all-time leading scorer. Then the Detroit Pistons tabbed Thomas with the second pick, making it an impressive one-two punch for Illinois preps. Both Thomas and Aguirre went on to play 13 pro seasons, win two NBA titles together, and make multiple all-star teams.

Prior to that, the only other time Illinois preps went 1-2 in the NBA draft was 1973. That year the Philadelphia 76ers picked Doug Collins, a standout at Benton and Illinois State University, while Jim Brewer of Proviso East and University of Minnesota fame went to the Cleveland Cavaliers with the next selection. Of course, while Brewer was all-tournament in 1969 and led Proviso

continued on next page

Eric Anderson of St. Francis de Sales in Chicago was a star at Indiana University before embarking on a pro career.

Granite City's Andy Phillip (47, in background) in action against Moline in the 1940 state meet. Phillip had an 11-year pro career and was later inducted into the Naismith Memorial Hall of Fame.

Bill Willoughby in 1976 to declare himself eligible for the draft. Needless to say, Garnett also became the first player to go straight from the IHSA to the NBA.

In recent years, though, that's become a trend. Livingston is the most recent of five players who have gone from the state tournament to the pros, joining Eddy Curry (Thornwood 2001), Darius Miles (East St. Louis 2000), Leon Smith (Chicago King 1999), and Garnett.

History has not always treated Garnett fairly regarding his state showing. Some recollections even paint him as a goat in the 46-43 loss top-ranked Farragut suffered against fifth-ranked Harvey Thornton. That's not accurate. Despite 6-for-17 shooting, Garnett finished with 17 points, 16 rebounds, six blocks and three steals.

Afterwards, slumped over in the bowels of the Assembly Hall, he kept telling reporters, "You got what you wanted. We lost." Actually, for most reporters and fans that was not true. Part of the joy of watching a state tournament is seeing a player like Garnett in action. It's seeing Livingston deliver a game-winning shot and then still hear comments that he's not ready for the pros. It's seeing Ellis battle Eric Anderson (St. Francis de Sales 1988) in the title game, then watching both players again

in the NBA. Or watching Marcus Liberty (Chicago King 1987) get the upper hand in a championship against Kendall Gill (Rich Central 1986), and then seeing those roles reversed in the pros.

Contrary to what Garnett said back in 1995, not getting to see top players compete on the ultimate prep stage in Illinois is disappointing. Unfortunately, it happens fairly often. Just as winning a state title doesn't mean a player will reach the NBA, reaching the heights of professional basketball is not always foreshadowed by prep success. In fact, you can field what is probably a stronger NBA team of Illinois non-Elite players — those pro standouts who never reached state.

Consider that NBA Hall of Famers Dan Issel (Batavia 1966), George Mikan (Chicago Quigley Prep 1941), and Harry Gallatin (Roxana 1944) never made the Elite Eight.

Though Issel starred in high school and was an all-American, the best his team fared was a regional title in 1965. That's one round better than Roxana great Gallatin ever enjoyed. "The Horse" helped his team to a district title as a junior but never enjoyed the laurels in the preps that he would find in the pros, where he was a seven-time all-star and Coach of the Year in 1963 with the St. Louis Hawks.

Thornwood's Eddy Curry swats away a shot during the 2000 Class AA meet.

Even so, Gallatin's one district title is one more than Mikan enjoyed while in high school. Actually, the man voted greatest player in the first half-century of pro basketball by the Associated Press never played an organized game as a freshman at Joliet Catholic or in his next three years of high school at Chicago's Quigley Prep. Only after he went to DePaul University and coach Ray Meyer began working with him did the 6-10 Mikan blossom into a dominant big man. From there he won six NBA scoring titles and six league championships and was so dominant that the league made changes to reduce his dominance, widening the foul lane and outlawing goaltending. All that only makes it harder to believe Mikan never got a chance to flash his stuff in high school.

But it's just as hard to imagine the long list of other top pros who fell just short. Players on that list include Eddie Johnson (Chicago Westinghouse 1977), who shot 10-for-11 from the floor in a 1977 super-sectional, but still lost to Chicago Phillips. The next year, Westinghouse made state with Aguirre leading the way. Ditto Jeff Hornacek (LaGrange Lyons 1981), who lost to fourth-place finisher Wheaton Central in the supers. And ditto Brian Cardinal (Tolono Unity 1996) whose prep career ended in a Class A super-sectional loss to Shelbyville despite 35 points and 15 rebounds. Then there's Tim Hardaway (Chicago Carver 1985), who, despite scoring 21 points in the game, suffered a Sweet Sixteen loss to Simeon and fellow pro Nick Anderson.

Many others who made a name in the NBA never even got to the Illinois Sweet Sixteen, players such as Doc Rivers (Proviso East 1979), Terry Cummings (Chicago Carver 1982), Hersey Hawkins (Chicago Westinghouse 1984), Juwan Howard (Chicago Vocational 1990), and Dwyane Wade (Richards 2000).

Reading the names of all those successful pros does hammer home one point, though: There's no debating the high level of basketball played in Illinois.

Kevin Garnett's state-finals appearance was a short one — a single game in 1995 — but he more than made up for that with a stellar pro career.

From the IHSA to the NBA

A list of players who competed in the quarterfinal round of the IHSA basketball tournament and went on to play in the NBA or ABA. Seasons played refers to NBA, unless otherwise noted. Statistics for professional basketball from www.basketballreference.com through the 2005-06 season.

1940s

Andy Phillip, Granite City, 1940
Picked in 1947 BAA draft, NBA Hall of Fame (1961), five-time all-star, nine NBA seasons, two BAA seasons (9.1 ppg, 4.4 rpg, 5.4 apg)

Dwight "Dike" Eddleman, Centralia, 1942
Picked 3rd round in 1949 BAA draft, two-time all-star, four seasons (12.1 ppg, 4.5 rpg, 2.1 apg)

Earl Dodd, Wood River, 1942
Picked in 1949 BAA draft, 9 games in one season for Denver Nuggets (1.7 ppg)

Max Morris, West Frankfort, 1943
Played one season for Sheboygan Redskins (12.6 ppg, 3.1 apg)

Jack Burmaster, Elgin, 1944
Picked in 1948 BAA draft, one season for Sheboygan Redskins (9.8 ppg, 2.9 apg)

Johnny Orr, Taylorville, 1944
Picked in 1948, 1949 BAA drafts, one season (2.7 ppg)

Jake Fendley, Chicago South Shore, 1947
Picked 3rd round in 1951 by Fort Wayne Pistons, two seasons (2.8 ppg, 1.2 rpg)

Irv Bemoras, Chicago Marshall, 1948
Picked in 1953 by Milwaukee Hawks, two seasons (6.3 ppg, 2.6 rpg)

Johnny "Red" Kerr, Chicago Tilden, 1949
Picked 6th in 1954 by Syracuse Nationals, three-time all-star, 12 seasons (13.8 ppg, 11.2 rpg)

Ken McBride, Centralia, 1949
Picked in 1952 draft by Syracuse Nationals, 12 games in one season (9.8 ppg, 2.6 rpg)

1950s

Bob Carney, West Aurora, 1950
Picked 6th round in 1954 by Milwaukee Hawks, 19 games in one season (3.6 ppg, 2.4 rpg)

Don Ohl, Edwardsville, 1954
Picked 5th round in 1958 by Philadelphia Warriors, five-time all-star, 10 seasons (15.9 ppg, 3 rpg, 3.1 apg)

Joe Ruklick, Princeton, 1955
Picked 2nd round in 1959 by Philadelphia Warriors, three seasons (3.5 ppg, 2.5 rpg)

Shellie McMillon, Chicago DuSable, 1954
Picked 6th round in 1958 by Detroit Pistons, four seasons (9.1 ppg, 6 rpg)

Gary Phillips, Quincy, 1957
Picked 9th in 1961 by Boston Celtics, five seasons (6.7 ppg, 2.6 rpg)

1960s

George Wilson, Chicago Marshall, 1960
Picked 8th in 1964 by Cincinnati Royals, seven seasons (5.4 ppg, 5.2 rpg)

Duane "Skip" Thoren, East Rockford, 1961
Picked 4th round in 1965 by Baltimore Bullets, one-time all-star, three ABA seasons (13.2 ppg, 11 rpg)

Marlbert Pradd, Chicago Carver, 1962
Picked 9th round in 1965 by Los Angeles Lakers, 6th round in 1967 by Chicago Bulls, two ABA seasons (4.2 ppg)

Cazzie Russell, Chicago Carver, 1962
Picked 1st in 1966 by New York Knicks, one-time all-star, 12 seasons (15.1 ppg, 3.8 rpg)

Jim Dawson, York, 1963
Picked 16th round by Chicago Bulls in 1967, 21 games in one ABA season (5.6 ppg)

Jim Burns, McLeansboro, 1963
Picked 4th round in 1967 by Chicago Bulls, 36 games in one season (4.4 ppg, 1.7 rpg)

Steve Kuberski, Moline, 1965
Picked 4th round in 1969 by Boston Celtics, nine seasons (5.5 ppg, 3.8 rpg)

Dave Scholz, Stephen Decatur, 1965
Picked 4th round in 1969 by Philadelphia 76ers, one game, made only field goal

Dick "Eldo" Garrett, Centralia, 1966
Picked 2nd round in 1969 by Los Angeles Lakers, five seasons (10.3 ppg, 3 rpg)

Jim Ard, Thornton, 1966
Picked 6th in 1970 by Seattle Supersonics, four NBA seasons, four ABA seasons (4.4 ppg, 4.3 rpg)

Dave Robisch, Springfield, 1967
Picked 3rd round in 1971 by Boston Celtics, eight NBA seasons, five ABA seasons (11.4 ppg, 6.6 rpg)

Bob Lackey, Evanston, 1968
Picked 5th round in 1972 by Atlanta Hawks, 71 games in two seasons (5.8 ppg, 2.3 rpg)

Mark Sibley, West Rockford, 1968
Picked 4th round in 1973 by Chicago Bills, 28 games in one season (1.6 ppg)

Jim Brewer, Proviso East, 1969
Picked 2nd in 1973 by Cleveland Cavaliers, nine seasons (5.8 ppg, 6.3 rpg)

Nate Hawthorne, Mt. Vernon, 1969
Picked 7th round in 1973 by Los Angeles Lakers, three seasons (5.4 ppg, 2.1 rpg)

1970s

C.J. Kupec, Oak Lawn, 1971
Picked 4th round in 1975 by Los Angeles Lakers, three seasons (4.1 ppg, 2.1 rpg)

Quinn Buckner, Thornridge, 1972
Picked 7th in 1976 by Milwaukee Bucks, 10 seasons (8.2 ppg)

Norm Cook, Lincoln, 1973
Picked 16th in 1976 by Boston Celtics, 27 games in two seasons (2.4 ppg)

Rickey Green, Chicago Hirsch, 1973
Picked 16th in 1977 by Golden State Warriors, 14 seasons (9.4 ppg, 5.5 apg)

Jack Sikma, St. Anne, 1973

Picked 8th in 1977 by Seattle Supersonics, seven-time all-star, 14 seasons (15.6 ppg, 9.8 rpg)

Jeff Wilkins, Elgin, 1973

Picked 2nd round in 1977 by San Antonio Spurs, six seasons (7.9 ppg)

Dave Corzine, Hersey, 1974

Picked 18th in 1978 by Washington Bullets, 13 seasons (8.5 ppg, 5.9 rpg)

Mark Aguirre, Chicago Westinghouse, 1978

Picked 1st in 1981 by Dallas Mavericks, 13 seasons, three-time all-star, (20 ppg, 5 rpg)

Isiah Thomas, St. Joseph, 1979

Picked 2nd in 1981 by Detroit Pistons, NBA Hall of Fame (2000), 11-time all-star, 13 seasons (19.2 ppg, 9.3 apg)

1980s

Russell Cross, Chicago Manley, 1980

Picked 6th in 1983 by Golden State Warriors, 45 games in one season (3.7 ppg, 1.8 rpg)

Mike Williams, Chicago De La Salle, 1980

Picked 3rd round in 1986 by Golden State Warriors, 21 games in one season (0.7 ppg)

Uwe Blab, Effingham, 1981

Picked 17th in 1985 by Dallas Mavericks, five seasons (2.1 ppg, 1.8 rpg)

Bruce Douglas, Quincy, 1982

Picked 3rd round in 1986 by Sacramento Kings, 8 games in one season (1.8 ppg, 1.8 rpg)

Scott Meents, Herscher, 1982

Picked 4th round in 1986 by Chicago Bulls, 39 games in two seasons (1.8 ppg)

Kevin Gamble, Springfield Lanphier, 1983

Picked 3rd round in 1987 by Portland Trail Blazers, 10 seasons (9.5 ppg, 2.2 rpg)

Kenny Battle, West Aurora, 1984

Picked 27th in 1989 by Detroit Pistons, four seasons (4.7 ppg, 2.8 rpg)

Everette Stephens, Evanston, 1984

Picked 2nd round in 1988 by Philadelphia 76ers, 38 games in two seasons (1.9 ppg)

Ed Horton, Springfield Lanphier, 1985

Picked 2nd round in 1989 by Washington Bullets, one season (4.5 ppg, 2.4 rpg)

Melvin McCants, Chicago Mt. Carmel, 1985

Played 13 games in one season for Los Angeles Lakers (1.7 ppg)

Nelison "Nick" Anderson, Chicago Simeon, 1986

Picked 11th in 1989 by Orlando Magic, 13 seasons (14.4 ppg, 5.1 rpg)

Steve Bardo, Carbondale, 1986

Picked 2nd round in 1990 by Atlanta Hawks, 33 games in three seasons (2.2 ppg, 1.8 rpg)

Kendall Gill, Rich Central, 1986

Picked 5th in 1990 by Charlotte Hornets, 15 seasons (13.4 ppg, 4.1 rpg)

Chad Gallagher, Rockford Boylan, 1987

Picked 2nd round in 1991 by Phoenix Suns, made all three FGs in one season

Marcus Liberty, Chicago King, 1987

Picked 2nd round in 1990 by Denver Nuggets, four seasons (7.3 ppg, 3.5 rpg)

Eric Anderson, St. Francis de Sales, 1988

Played 27 games in two seasons for New York Knicks (1.6 ppg)

Andrew (Ashraf) Amaya, Walther Lutheran, 1988

Played two seasons (4.5 ppg, 4.2 rpg)

LaPhonso Ellis, East St. Louis Lincoln, 1988

Picked 5th in 1992 by Denver Nuggets, 11 seasons (11.9 ppg, 6.5 rpg)

1990s

Cuonzo Martin, East St. Louis Lincoln, 1990

Picked 2nd round 1995 draft by Atlanta Hawks, 7 games in two seasons (1.3 ppg)

Donnie Boyce, Proviso East, 1991

Picked 2nd round in 1995 by Atlanta Hawks, 30 games in two seasons (2.6 ppg)

Michael Finley, Proviso East, 1991

Picked 21st in 1995 by Phoenix Suns, two-time all-star, active in 2006 (19 ppg, 5.1 rpg, 3.7 apg)

Sherrell Ford, Proviso East, 1991

Picked 26th in 1995 by Seattle Supersonics, 28 games in one season (3.2 ppg)

Howard Nathan, Peoria Manual, 1991

Played 5 games in one season for Atlanta Hawks, 5-for-9 FGs

Kiwane Garris, Chicago Westinghouse, 1993

Played 31 games in two seasons (2.3 ppg)

Thomas Hamilton, Chicago King, 1993

Played 33 games in two seasons (3.2 ppg, 3.4 rpg)

Keon Clark, Danville, 1994

Picked 13th in 1998 by Orlando Magic, six seasons (8.2 ppg, 5.9 rpg)

Troy Hudson, Carbondale, 1994

Free-agent signee by Utah in 1998, active in 2006 (9.3 ppg, 3.6 apg)

Tyrone Nesby, Cairo, 1994

Played four seasons (1999-2002), averaged 9.4 ppg

Kevin Garnett, Chicago Farragut, 1995

Picked 5th in 1995 by Minnesota Timberwolves, eight-time all-star, active in 2006 (20.2 ppg, 11.1 rpg)

Sean Lampley, St. Francis de Sales, 1997

Picked 2nd round in 2001 by Chicago Bulls, two seasons (4.5 ppg, 2.1 rpg)

Maurice Baker, Madison, 1998

Played five games in one season

Quentin Richardson, Chicago Young, 1998

Picked 18th in 2000 by Los Angeles Clippers, active in 2006 (12.6 ppg, 4.9 rpg)

Frank Williams, Peoria Manual, 1998

Picked 25th in 2002 by Denver Nuggets, three seasons (2.9 ppg, 1.9 apg)

Corey Maggette, Fenwick, 1998

Picked 13th in 1999 by Seattle Supersonics, active in 2006 (14.8 ppg, 4.8 rpg)

Melvin Ely, Thornton, 1998

Picked 12th in 2002 by Los Angeles Clippers, active in 2006 (5.6 ppg, 3.5 rpg)

Brian Cook, Lincoln, 1999

Picked 24th in 2003 by Los Angeles Lakers, active in 2006 (5.7 ppg, 3 rpg)

Leon Smith, Chicago King, 1999

Picked 29th in 1999 by Dallas Mavericks, two seasons (2.2 ppg, 1.5 rpg)

2000s

Darius Miles, East St. Louis, 2000

Picked 3rd in 2000 by Los Angeles Clippers, active in 2006 (10.3 ppg, 5.2 rpg)

Eddy Curry, Thornwood, 2001

Picked 4th in 2001 by Chicago Bulls, active in 2006 (11.8 ppg, 4.9 rpg)

Andre Iguodala, Springfield Lanphier, 2002

Picked 9th in 2004 by Philadelphia 76ers, active in 2006 (9 ppg, 5.7 rpg)

Shaun Livingston, Peoria Central, 2004

Picked 4th in 2004 by Los Angeles Clippers, active in 2006 (7.4 ppg, 5 apg)

PEORIA, *Class AA State Champions of 1977*

FRONT ROW (left to right): Mgr. Ken Smith, Mgr. Don Lewis. SECOND ROW: Mgr. Bill Robertson, Bil Winkler, Tony Gower, Dwayne Banks, Marc Utley, Michael Martin, Mike Potts, Eddie Ruffin. THIRD ROW: Asst. Coach Ken Meischner, Asst. Coach John Venturi, Tim McGarney, Kelvin Jordan, Ernie Banks, Kevin Jordan, Percy Neal, Kevin Young, Coach Bruce Boyle.

State Final Tournament Scores

Super-Sectionals

At Chicago [Amphitheatre]—Chicago (Phillips) 77, Chicago (Westinghouse) 65
At Joliet (Central)—Burbank (St. Laurence) 57, Flossmoor (Homewood-F.) 53
At DeKalb [NIU]—Barrington 58, Lisle (Benet Academy) 56
At Peoria [Bradley]—Peoria 58, Ottawa (Twp.) 44
At Normal [ISU]—Springfield (Lanphier) 64, Kankakee (Eastridge) 47
At Evanston [NU]—Northfield (New Trier West) 69, Chicago (Gordon Tech) 55
At Aurora (East)—Chicago (De La Salle) 83, Chicago (Weber) 71
At Carbondale [SIU]—Collinsville 64, Carbondale 56

Quarterfinals

Burbank (St. Laurence) 56, Chicago (Phillips) 50
Peoria 67, Barrington 40
Springfield (Lanphier) 62, Northfield (New Trier West) 59
Chicago (De La Salle) 67, Collinsville 66

Semifinals

Peoria 69, Burbank (St. Laurence) 48
Springfield (Lanphier) 60, Chicago (De La Salle) 56

Finals

Chicago (De La Salle) 65, Burbank (St. Laurence) 47 (third place)
Peoria 72, Springfield (Lanphier) 62 (title)

Scoring Leaders

Player, School	G	FG	FT	Pts
Kevin Boyle, Burbank (St. Laurence)	4	26	24	76
Darryl Allen, Chicago (De La Salle)	4	28	13	69
Shelly Tunson, Springfield (Lanphier)	4	26	14	66
Ray Rhone, Chicago (De La Salle)	4	25	15	65
Gordon Smith, Springfield (Lanphier)	4	23	12	58
Percy Neal, Peoria	4	27	4	58

All-Tournament First Team

Player, School	Ht.	Yr.
Darryl Allen, Chicago (De La Salle)	6-6	So.
Dwayne Banks, Peoria	6-3	Sr.
Kevin Boyle, Burbank (St. Laurence)	6-6	Jr.
Tony Gower, Peoria	6-0	Sr.
Joel May, Northfield (New Trier West)	6-5	Jr.
Ray Rhone, Chicago (De La Salle)	6-2	Sr.
Shelly Tunson, Springfield (Lanphier)	6-3	Sr.

Championship Game Box Score

Assembly Hall, Champaign, March 19, 1977

PEORIA (72)
Coach Bruce Boyle

Player	FG-A	FT-A	Pts	PF	Rb	As	St	Bl
Dwayne Banks	8-13	2-2	18	2	2	4		
Ernie Banks	4-12	1-2	9	3	11	4		0
Tony Gower	3-10	0-0	6	2	2	9		
Mike Martin	0-0	0-0	0	0	0	0		
Percy Neal	8-13	0-2	16	3	12	1		
Eddie Ruffin	4-7	2-2	10	5	1	2		
Marc Utley	5-7	3-5	13	2	7	2		
TEAM					5			
TOTAL	32-62	8-13	72	17	40	18		

SPRINGFIELD (LANPHIER) (62)
Coach Bob Nika

Player	FG-A	FT-A	Pts	PF	Rb	As	St	Bl
Tim Barbian	0-3	0-2	0	0	3	0		
Tim Hulett	4-9	4-5	12	2	1	5		
Kevin Jones	2-6	1-3	5	4	7	0		
Gordon Smith	5-13	4-4	14	4	2	2		
Shelly Tunson	5-8	3-4	13	3	10	0		
Mike Watson	6-18	6-6	18	1	7	3		
TEAM					6			
TOTAL	22-57	18-24	62	14	36	10		

Peoria	16	17	17	22	—	72
Springfield (Lanphier)	18	14	10	20	—	62

Officials: Stan Decker, Ed Norfleet.

This state final acted as a tiebreaker when Peoria Central (29-3) emerged with a 2-1 season record against Springfield Lanphier by winning the title game 72-62.

It was also a game where superstition could have cost coach Bruce Boyle the first crown for a Peoria school since Manual won in 1930, not to mention Central's first title since the inaugural state championship in 1908.

Peoria had lost by 15 at Lanphier in the season opener with Marc Utley starting but then won the third-place meeting at the Pekin Christmas tourney by 17 when the 6-foot-3 senior forward was sidelined by the flu.

Accordingly, Boyle didn't start a hale-and-healthy Utley in the title game ... and promptly fell behind 9-0.

Not that fortune hadn't already smiled on two title-game teams nicknamed Lions. Two unbeaten teams (Collinsville and Chicago Phillips) came into the Elite Eight, but neither Peoria nor Lanphier had to face either.

In the Chicago Public League final, top-ranked Phillips, led by Darius Clemons, had turned back second-rated Westinghouse, with future University of Illinois stars Mark Aguirre and Eddie Johnson, in a classic battle of unbeatens. Aguirre and Johnson would go on to total 37,648 NBA points.

But the Windy City hangover from a game that drew some 12,000 fans left Phillips flat in Champaign, losing its quarterfinal to eventual fourth-place finisher St. Laurence. The only trouble for St. Laurence was that standout Jim Stack suffered an ankle injury in the final minutes, sidelining him for a 21-point loss to Peoria in the semifinals.

Collinsville, with future college coach Kevin Stallings an all-state junior, lost in the quarterfinals by a point to unranked third-place finisher Chicago De La Salle when light-scoring Dave Bonko banked in a shot with three seconds left.

That gave the Chicago Catholic League, which had just entered the IHSA and thus the state tournament in 1975, two of the semifinalists. But it would be eight more years before a private school prevailed in the Class AA tournament.

Peoria's Boyle not only bested his high school alma mater in the title match that assured the first downstate AA champion, he also beat coach Bob Nika, his former high school teammate and college buddy at Illinois State.

Only once before had a championship game matched two schools with the same nickname (1925, Elgin vs. Champaign).

HEAT LIGHTNING

A thunder slam? Not until 1978. But Percy Neal's lay-up was still worth two points as Peoria Central ran to a 72-62 win over Springfield Lanphier. Teammates Dwayne Banks (32) and Marc Utley (44) watch.

Peoria's championship in 1977 was its first since winning the inaugural tournament in 1908.

Jim Cesario of St. Laurence finds little room to maneuver against Peoria's Tony Gower in a Saturday semifinal.

Jim Stack of St. Laurence contemplates his fate after spraining his ankle in a quarterfinal game against Phillips.

1977AA

231

LOCKPORT (CENTRAL), Class AA State Champions of 1978

FRONT ROW (left to right): Asst. Coach Rollie Bolattino, Coach Bob Basarich. SECOND ROW: Brian Davis, Jeff Young, Terry Brehn, Jeff Robinson, Mike Murray, Gerry Barbeauld, Scott Parzych, Terry Green, Ernie Banks, Tony Johnson, Chuck Travis, Elgie Young.

It was the year the dunk returned to high school basketball. But getting that close to any basket defended by Lockport was another story.

The stingy Porters (33-0) outdistanced a flashy field that featured lifelong friends and future NBA standouts Isiah Thomas of St. Joseph and Mark Aguirre of Chicago Westinghouse.

Lockport averaged only 56 points in its three Elite Eight games, beating St. Joseph 64-47 for the title behind 26 points by center Scott Parzych.

That left some wondering if the championship had really been decided in the sectional, where top-ranked Lockport survived second-rated St. Laurence 42-41 when Jim Stack missed a 30-footer at the buzzer.

Extending the season was just fine with Lockport's Terry Green, who had missed much of it with an injury. His 13 points led Lockport to a 49-43 win over Ottawa in the quarterfinals.

Then came the showdown quarterfinal battle between junior Thomas and senior Aguirre.

Thomas, arguably the most creative guard in state-final history, was outscored 28-26 by Aguirre. But St. Joseph (31-1) survived Westinghouse by a 63-60 count, with Ray Clark making game-winning free throws after Thomas fouled out.

The finals' two most unlikely entries were paired in the quarterfinals, where East Rockford, from a school district that sponsored no sports the previous year because of a budget crunch, won 61-48 over Danville, which brought a mere 14-14 record to Champaign.

Collinsville and Lockport hooked up in an electrifying semifinal, with the Porters finally prevailing 55-53. Parzych, a future star at North Carolina State, led the way with 17 points and 12 rebounds.

In the second semifinal, Thomas and his St. Joseph teammates ended East Rockford's Cinderella season 60-56.

Collinsville, in the last finals for coaching legend Vergil Fletcher, got 27 points from future college coach Kevin Stallings to beat East Rockford 96-65 for third place.

Stallings set the Class AA Elite Eight assist record of 30, with a record half of those coming in a quarterfinal win over New Trier West.

In the championship game, Lockport held Thomas to 14 points and two assists.

Thus did Dike Eddleman of Centralia '42 remain the only NBA all-star player (Tri-Cities Blackhawks; inaugural all-star game in 1951) with an Illinois state championship on his résumé.

The dunk returned to high school basketball at the start of the 1977-78 season.

State Final Tournament Scores

Super-Sectionals

At Carbondale [SIU]—Collinsville 79, Olney (East Richland) 58
At Evanston [NU]—Northfield (New Trier West) 77, Chicago (Gordon Tech) 63
At Peoria [Bradley]—Ottawa (Twp.) 52, Peoria 45
At Joliet (Central)—Lockport (Central) 59, Chicago Heights (Bloom Twp.) 48
At Aurora (East)—Westchester (St. Joseph) 71, Barrington 59
At Chicago [Amphitheatre]—Chicago (Westinghouse) 71, Chicago (Manley) 68
At Normal [ISU]—Danville 65, Lincoln 59 (OT)
At DeKalb [NIU]—Rockford (East) 70, Lisle (Benet Academy) 55

Quarterfinals

Collinsville 71, Northfield (New Trier West) 56
Lockport (Central) 49, Ottawa (Twp.) 43
Westchester (St. Joseph) 63, Chicago (Westinghouse) 60
Rockford (East) 61, Danville 48

Semifinals

Lockport (Central) 55, Collinsville 53
Westchester (St. Joseph) 60, Rockford (East) 56

Finals

Collinsville 96, Rockford (East) 65 (third place)
Lockport (Central) 64, Westchester (St. Joseph) 47 (title)

Scoring Leaders

Player, School	G	FG	FT	Pts
Isiah Thomas, Westchester (St. Joseph)	4	38	17	93
John Griffin, Rockford (East)	4	32	27	91
Kevin Stallings, Collinsville	4	35	17	87
John Belobraydic, Collinsville	4	35	15	85
Scott Parzych, Lockport (Central)	4	31	15	77

All-Tournament First Team

Player, School	Ht.	Yr.
Mark Aguirre, Chicago (Westinghouse)	6-7	Sr.
Ray Clark, Westchester (St. Joseph)	5-10	Sr.
Scott Parzych, Lockport (Central)	6-7	Sr.
Kevin Stallings, Collinsville	6-5	Sr.
Isiah Thomas, Westchester (St. Joseph)	6-0	Jr.

Championship Game Box Score

Assembly Hall, Champaign, March 18, 1978

LOCKPORT (CENTRAL) (64)
Coach Bob Basarich

Player	FG-A	FT-A	Pts	PF	Rb	As	St	Bl
Bob Autman	0-2	0-0	0	0	0	0		
Gerry Barbeauld	6-12	0-1	12	1	8	4		
Terry Brehn	0-0	0-0	0	0	1	0		
Brian Davis	0-0	0-0	0	0	0	0		
Terry Green	2-5	1-2	5	1	2	0		
Tony Johnson	0-0	0-0	0	0	0	0		
Mike Murray	0-0	0-0	0	0	0	0		
Scott Parzych	10-16	6-8	26	3	11	3		
Jeff Robinson	4-7	1-1	9	4	6	1		
Chuck Travis	6-12	0-1	12	1	6	4		
TEAM					4			
TOTAL	28-54	8-13	64	10	38	12		

WESTCHESTER (ST. JOSEPH) (47)
Coach Gene Pingatore

Player	FG-A	FT-A	Pts	PF	Rb	As	St	Bl
Greg Austin	0-0	0-0	0	0	0	0		
Chuck Behrendt	0-1	0-0	0	0	1	0		
Tyrone Brewer	4-6	1-2	9	3	4	1		
Pat Callahan	0-0	0-0	0	0	1	0		
Ray Clark	5-14	3-4	13	0	5	4		
Hector Gonzalez	1-2	0-0	2	1	3	2		
George Johnson	3-10	3-4	9	2	1	0		
Jim Lenc	0-0	0-0	0	0	1	3		
Isiah Thomas	6-21	2-3	14	4	6	2		
Bob Weigel	0-0	0-0	0	0	0	0		
TEAM					8			
TOTAL	19-54	9-13	47	11	32	10		

Lockport (Central)	18	11	17	18	—	64
Westchester (St. Joseph)	12	8	14	13	—	47

Officials: Ed Norfleet, Jim Harmison.

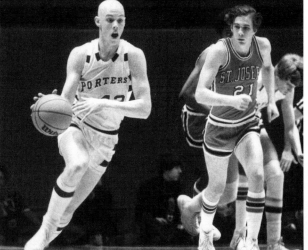

Lockport's Gerry Barbeauld outraces Jim Lenc of St. Joseph in the 1978 title-game match-up. Lockport completed an undefeated season with a 64-47 victory.

Kevin Stallings of Collinsville fakes before putting up a jump shot against East Rockford in the consolation contest.

Future NBA star Isiah Thomas of St. Joseph passes away from the defense of East Rockford's Jamie Pendelton.

Collinsville's John Belobraydic prepares to dunk against New Trier West. Collinsville won the quarterfinal game 71-56.

DYNAMIC DUO

Coach Gene Pingatore gives instruction to his backcourt — Ray Clark (center) and Isiah Thomas — in an early-round game.

1978AA

1979 AA

PARK RIDGE (MAINE SOUTH)
Class AA State Champions of 1979

FRONT ROW (left to right):
Mgr. Joe Stornello, Trainer Bob Loll,
Dave Hoelscher, John Crowl,
Jay Huyler, Jim Walewander,
John Jensen, Mgr. Tony Seng.
SECOND ROW: Mike McCarthy,
Dan Fiddler, Todd Vukovich, Tim
Loeffler, Chris Theodore,
Jeff Baker, Brian Sir.

With only one loss, Maine South couldn't exactly be called a Cinderella team. But the eighth-ranked Hawks' gaudy title win over top-rated Quincy certainly seemed the stuff of fantasy.

Maine South, coached by Quitman Sullins, shot a tournament-record 66 percent from the field and 85 percent from the foul line in a 83-67 victory over the Blue Devils. Maine South's Jeff Baker, a 6-foot-4 senior forward, led the barrage with 26 points.

Despite its rich state-tourney history and an unbeaten season record, Quincy might well have been considered the fairy-tale team, not starting a player taller than 6-2.

Keith Douglas, the first of three Quincy brothers who would perform state-finals heroics, was the all-stater this year. Brother Bruce, a freshman, was already a starter.

The smallish Blue Devils showed no fear in their quarterfinal match against Manley and 6-9 junior all-stater Russell Cross, outrebounding the Chicagoans 37-24 en route to a 75-63 victory.

On the other end of the quarterfinal spectrum, Maine South survived De La Salle's physical squad 37-27 thanks to a slowdown style for which the crowd did not thank the Hawks. It was the lowest scoring game in Class AA finals history until the 2006 title game.

De La Salle had already done the field a favor by denying second-ranked Proviso East a Sweet Sixteen berth. And Maine South had survived a one-point super-sectional scare from unranked New Trier West.

Overtime thrillers were the rule in the semifinals.

In the first contest, Maine South beat East Moline United Township 77-76 in overtime. East Moline's Brent Carmichael notched a record 11 steals to go with nine assists, but his effort wasn't enough to overcome 30 points by Baker.

And the second semi went one overtime better, with Quincy surviving Benet Academy 53-51 in two extra periods.

Bruce Douglas, just 14 years old, put the Blue Devils into the title game with a lay-up off a Mike Rudd steal and backhanded pass with only six seconds left in the second overtime against Benet.

Quincy was 5-0 against top-16 teams before getting burned by the No. 8 Hawks.

Perhaps the best guard in state history, future NBA all-star Isiah Thomas, failed to reach the Sweet Sixteen in his senior year when St. Joseph was upset by De La Salle in sectional play.

State Final Tournament Scores

Super-Sectionals
At Peoria [Bradley]—East Moline (United) 69, Peoria 61
At Carbondale [SIU]—East St. Louis 71, Effingham 59
At Evanston [NU]—Park Ridge (Maine South) 65, Northfield (New Trier West) 64
At Aurora (East)—Chicago (De La Salle) 65, Barrington 62
At DeKalb [NIU]—Lisle (Benet Academy) 60, Rockford (Auburn) 51
At Joliet (Central)—Lockport (Central) 43, Chicago Heights (Bloom Twp.) 20
At Normal [ISU]—Quincy 47, Joliet (Catholic Academy) 46
At Chicago [Amphitheatre]—Chicago (Manley) 88, Chicago (Westinghouse) 83 (2 OT)

Quarterfinals
East Moline (United) 64, East St. Louis 56
Park Ridge (Maine South) 37, Chicago (De La Salle) 27
Lisle (Benet Academy) 43, Lockport (Central) 39
Quincy 75, Chicago (Manley) 63

Semifinals
Park Ridge (Maine South) 77, East Moline (United) 76 (OT)
Quincy 53, Lisle (Benet Academy) 51 (2 OT)

Finals
Lisle (Benet Academy) 69, East Moline (United) 60 (third place)
Park Ridge (Maine South) 83, Quincy 67 (title)

Scoring Leaders

Player, School	G	FG	FT	Pts
Keith Douglas, Quincy	4	36	23	95
Jeff Baker, Park Ridge (Maine South)	4	36	17	89
Mike Lang, Lisle (Benet Academy)	4	26	15	67
Troy Mayfield, East Moline (United)	4	22	21	65
Kevin Conrad, Lisle (Benet Academy)	4	24	15	63

All-Tournament First Team

Player, School	Ht.	Yr.
Jeff Baker, Park Ridge (Maine South)	6-4	Sr.
Kevin Conrad, Lisle (Benet Academy)	6-0	Sr.
Keith Douglas, Quincy	6-2	Sr.
Luther Hughes, East Moline (United)	6-4	Sr.
Mike Lang, Lisle (Benet Academy)	6-8	Sr.
Mike Rudd, Quincy	5-8	Sr.

Championship Game Box Score
Assembly Hall, Champaign, March 24, 1979

PARK RIDGE (MAINE SOUTH) (83)
Coach Quitman Sullins

Player	FG-A	FT-A	Pts	PF	Rb	As	St	Bl
Jeff Baker	10-15	6-6	26	2	10	4		
John Crowl	0-0	4-4	4	2	2	7		
Dan Fiddler	9-12	5-6	23	3	9	2		
Dave Hoelscher	0-1	0-0	0	0	0	0		
Jay Huyler	5-8	2-2	12	4	1	12		
John Jensen	0-0	0-0	0	0	0	0		
Tim Loeffler	0-0	0-0	0	1	1	0		
Mike McCarthy	0-0	0-0	0	0	0	0		
Brian Sir	1-1	0-0	2	0	0	0		
Chris Theodore	8-12	0-2	16	4	3	0		
Todd Vukovich	0-0	0-0	0	0	0	0		
Jim Walewander	0-1	0-0	0	0	0	0		
TEAM					4			
TOTAL	33-50	17-20	83	16	30	25		

QUINCY (67)
Coach Jerry Leggett

Player	FG-A	FT-A	Pts	PF	Rb	As	St	Bl
Steve Ball	8-23	3-4	19	2	9	1		
John Bloom	0-0	0-0	0	1	0	2		
Tim Cissna	1-2	0-0	2	0	0	0		
Bruce Douglas	1-3	0-0	2	3	3	1		
Keith Douglas	11-22	3-4	25	4	13	2		
John Lepper	0-0	0-0	0	0	0	0		
Scott McGaughey	0-0	0-0	0	0	0	0		
Michael Payne	0-1	0-0	0	1	0	0		
Doug Reed	1-5	0-0	2	4	3	5		
Chuck Robinson	1-2	0-0	2	0	1	0		
Mike Rudd	5-14	3-4	13	1	2	5		
Steve Sandercock	1-1	0-0	2	0	0	0		
TEAM					6			
TOTAL	29-73	9-12	67	16	37	16		

Park Ridge (Maine South)	21	22	12	28	— 83
Quincy	22	13	12	20	— 67

Officials: Stan Heth, Jack Razor.

Maine South shot 66 percent from the field and 85 percent from the free throw line — a recipe for success.

OUT OF REACH

Bruce Douglas of Quincy (left) and Chris Theodore of Maine South consider their options during the 1979 title game.

Brian Officer of East Moline puts an exclamation point on his basket as radio announcers on media row call the action.

Kevin Conrad of Benet Academy and Keith Douglas of Quincy scramble near the baseline near the start of a semifinal battle. Quincy won 53-51 in double overtime.

Dan Fiddler of Maine South uses a left-handed dribble to swing past Quincy's Steve Ball in the championship game.

1979AA

235

HEARTS 45

For the second straight season, two private schools reached the Elite Eight. But this time both were one-and-done, with Effingham beating De La Salle 68-56 and Lincoln routing Gordon Tech 66-47.

Willie Little's patient Manley crew made short work of Maine South's record for title-game accuracy with a .675 field-goal percentage (27 of 40).

I n a battle of future Big Ten college rivals, Chicago Manley's 6-foot-10 Russell Cross (Purdue) got 17 points and held Effingham's 7-2 Uwe Blab (Indiana) to eight points and four rebounds to win the title 69-61.

Another future Big Ten Conference player, 6-5 Effingham all-American Mitch Arnold (Illinois), scored 26 in the title game after almost single-handedly dispatching De La Salle in the quarterfinals with 39 points.

For the second straight season, De La Salle kept Proviso East and Glenn "Doc" Rivers out of the Sweet Sixteen. Rivers, one of the most talented and respected players in state history, never got out of a sectional.

The Elite Eight field's gain was the state-final fans' loss of a team ranked No. 1 in the country and a player who still holds an NBA playoff record of 15 assists in one half.

Blab, a foreign-exchange student from West Germany, would be the tallest Elite Eight player by at least two inches until Chicago King put its twin giants on the Assembly Hall court in 1993.

Blab would take Effingham to the quarterfinals the next year, prompting the IHSA to make a rule change restricting foreign-exchange students to one year of athletic eligibility. The towering redhead later made two appearances in the Olympics for his native country.

Manley senior Roy Spearman scored a title-game total of six points, which his son, Ronnie Fields, would be capable of scoring in a matter of seconds for Chicago Farragut's 1994-95 squads.

In quarterfinal action, Manley survived a 55-54 scare from Downers Grove South and future University of Michigan standout Dan Pelekoudas.

Downers South had dispatched the last Class AA unbeaten, No. 2 Rich Central, 54-52 in super-sectional play.

West Aurora, back for another shot at this elusive state title, edged Peoria Richwoods and future University of Illinois standout Doug Altenberger 44-43 in a quarterfinal duel.

State Final Tournament Scores

Super-Sectionals
At DeKalb [NIU]—Aurora (West) 68, Rockford (Jefferson) 48
At Peoria [Bradley]—Peoria (Richwoods) 64, Moline 51
At Aurora (East)—Chicago (De La Salle) 58, Hoffman Estates (Conant) 36
At Carbondale [SIU]—Effingham 74, East St. Louis (Lincoln) 58
At Evanston [NU]—Chicago (Gordon Tech) 58, Northfield (New Trier West) 51
At Normal [ISU]—Lincoln 67, Springfield (Southeast) 57
At Crete (C.-Monee)—Downers Grove (South) 54, Olympia Fields (Rich Central) 52
At Chicago [Amphitheatre]—Chicago (Manley) 67, Chicago (Collins) 55

Quarterfinals
Aurora (West) 44, Peoria (Richwoods) 43
Effingham 68, Chicago (De La Salle) 56
Lincoln 66, Chicago (Gordon Tech) 47
Chicago (Manley) 55, Downers Grove (South) 54

Semifinals
Effingham 55, Aurora (West) 43
Chicago (Manley) 59, Lincoln 45

Finals
Aurora (West) 68, Lincoln 63 (third place)
Chicago (Manley) 69, Effingham 61 (title)

Scoring Leaders

Player, School	G	FG	FT	Pts
Mitch Arnold, Effingham	4	48	19	115
Russell Cross, Chicago (Manley)	4	28	17	73
James Malone, Aurora (West)	4	31	4	66
Tim Anderson, Chicago (Manley)	4	26	13	65
Uwe Blab, Effingham	4	25	9	59

All-Tournament First Team

Player, School	Ht.	Yr.
Tim Anderson, Chicago (Manley)	6-4	Sr.
Mitch Arnold, Effingham	6-5	Sr.
Uwe Blab, Effingham	7-2	Jr.
Russell Cross, Chicago (Manley)	6-10	Sr.
Jeff Fichtel, Aurora (West)	6-6	Sr.
Dan Pelekoudas, Downers Grove (South)	6-1	Sr.

Championship Game Box Score

Assembly Hall, Champaign, March 22, 1980

CHICAGO (MANLEY) (69)
Coach Willie Little

Player	FG-A	FT-A	Pts	PF	Rb	As	St	Bl
Tim Anderson	4-7	4-5	12	4	4	1		
Michael Buchanan	0-0	1-2	1	1	1	0		
Russell Cross	7-10	3-3	17	1	5	0		
Vincent Johnson	6-9	2-2	14	3	5	0		
Leonard Jones	4-7	5-11	13	3	1	2		
Craig Pickett	0-0	0-0	0	0	0	0		
Roy Spearman	3-3	0-0	6	2	1	9		
Ronald Washington	3-4	0-1	6	4	1	3		
TEAM					5			
TOTAL	27-40	15-24	69	18	23	15		

EFFINGHAM (61)
Coach Jim Maxedon

Player	FG-A	FT-A	Pts	PF	Rb	As	St	Bl
Mitch Arnold	9-17	8-9	26	3	11	3		
Uwe Blab	4-6	0-1	8	5	4	0		
Steve Bushue	0-0	2-3	2	1	2	6		
Don Dueker	0-0	0-0	0	0	0	0		
Dale Grupe	8-13	1-2	17	3	1	1		
Gehl Higgs	0-0	0-0	0	0	1	0		
Chuck Keller	0-0	0-0	0	0	0	0		
Brad Neet	3-6	0-0	6	3	1	6		
Dallas Orsborn	1-3	0-0	2	3	1	2		
Jim Shadowens	0-0	0-0	0	0	0	0		
Jeff Woelfer	0-0	0-0	0	0	0	0		
TEAM					3			
TOTAL	25-45	11-15	61	18	24	18		

Chicago (Manley)	16	17	14	22	—	69
Effingham	14	15	14	18	—	61

Officials: Dennis Freund, Larry Nemmers.

CLASS AA

1980 AA

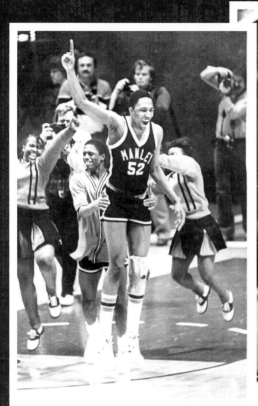

Russell Cross jumps for joy as Manley wins the Class AA state championship by a 69-61 decision over Effingham.

Effingham's 7-foot-2 center Uwe Blab garners a rebound in semifinal action against West Aurora. Behind Blab, ready to react, are David Heiss (32) and Mitch Arnold (43).

ACE OF HEARTS

Uwe Blab of Effingham scores an easy basket against Manley in the title game.

Russell Cross shields the ball from Effingham's Dallas Orsborn in the first quarter of the Class AA championship contest at Assembly Hall.

1980AA

1981 AA

QUINCY
Class AA State Champions of 1981

FRONT ROW (left to right):
Scott Allen, Dave Sandercock,
Joel Myers, Phil Hoffman,
Mgr. Jim Powell. SECOND ROW:
Bruce Douglas, Shane Barnes,
Mark Kaufman, Brad Schrader,
Mark Sparrow, Trainer Steve Brace.
THIRD ROW: Mgr. Kyle Cookson,
Dennis Douglas, John Leeper,
Mike Payne, Tim Huseman,
Richard Hawkins, Trinell Hickman.

Leave it to colorful coach Jerry Leggett to stir controversy with a 33-0 Quincy team that won its Sweet Sixteen games by 28, 25, 31, and 29 points.

With underclass Douglas brothers Bruce (junior) and Dennis (sophomore) dividing 40 points, and 6-foot-11 senior center Michael Payne claiming 16 rebounds, Quincy beat Proviso East 68-39 for the title.

The Blue Devils' lopsided Sweet Sixteen victory margins gave Quincy an easy state title but also gave Leggett grounds to argue his 1981 squad was the best-ever Illinois prep team. His closing statement was Quincy being named No. 1 in the nation.

However, the other seven state finals entries had combined to lug a Class AA-record 43 losses into this Elite Eight.

Geography was partly responsible for the sub-par finals field, what with Quincy dispatching second-ranked Lincoln by 16 points in a sectional showdown matching the state's only AA unbeatens. Lincoln would suffer a similar fate in 1987, when its second-rated squad was sidelined in the sectional by top-ranked and unbeaten Peoria Manual.

Wheaton Central opened the tournament by felling defending runner-up Effingham and 7-foot-2 senior Uwe Blab 38-33.

Then, although no one needed much convincing, Quincy made believers of everyone. The Blue Devils were ahead of Antioch 24-2 before some fans in C Section had finished the climb to their Assembly Hall seats.

Chicago Public League upset winner Westinghouse, led by Wayne Montgomery and Melvin Bradley, rallied from a 12-point halftime deficit to defeat a New Trier East team that included future White Sox outfielder Mike Huff.

Quincy's semifinal victim, Wheaton Central, didn't offer much more resistance than Antioch as the Blue Devils ran to a 19-2 advantage.

Proviso East won the second semifinal over Westinghouse 72-66. But after a quarter of the title game, Proviso East found itself on the short end of a 19-8 score.

Just as 1972 Thornridge was noted for defense, 1981 Quincy held state-finals foes to a Class AA record-low average of 41 points per game.

If there are hoops in heaven, a match-up between 1981 Quincy and 1972 Dolton Thornridge might be the second-hottest ticket for Illinois basketball fans — right behind a pass through the pearly gates.

State Final Tournament Scores

Super-Sectionals
At Aurora (East)—Wheaton (Central) 65, LaGrange (Lyons) 61
At Carbondale [SIU]—Effingham 77, East St. Louis 61
At Normal [ISU]—Quincy 72, Kankakee (Westview) 44
At DeKalb [NIU]—Antioch 35, Palatine 34
At Evanston [NU]—Winnetka (New Trier East) 61, Evanston (Twp.) 58
At Chicago [UIC]—Chicago (Westinghouse) 79, Chicago (Marshall) 66
At Hinsdale (Central)—Maywood (Proviso East) 69, Chicago (Marist) 67
At Peoria [Bradley]—Moline 70, Chillicothe (Illinois Valley Central) 68

Quarterfinals
Wheaton (Central) 38, Effingham 33
Quincy 75, Antioch 50
Chicago (Westinghouse) 62, Winnetka (New Trier East) 60
Maywood (Proviso East) 74, Moline 62

Semifinals
Quincy 65, Wheaton (Central) 34
Maywood (Proviso East) 72, Chicago (Westinghouse) 66

Finals
Chicago (Westinghouse) 53, Wheaton (Central) 47 (third place)
Quincy 68, Maywood (Proviso East) 39 (title)

Scoring Leaders

Player, School	G	FG	FT	Pts
Wayne Montgomery, Chi. (Westinghouse)	4	33	22	88
Earnest Hubbard, Maywood (Proviso East)	4	35	16	86
Bruce Douglas, Quincy	4	35	9	79
Melvin Bradley, Chicago (Westinghouse)	4	31	17	79
Dennis Douglas, Quincy	4	21	14	56

All-Tournament First Team

Player, School	Ht.	Yr.
Melvin Bradley, Chicago (Westinghouse)	6-1	Sr.
Bruce Douglas, Quincy	6-3	Jr.
Earnest Hubbard, Maywood (Proviso East)	5-10	Sr.
Justyne Monegain, Maywood (Proviso East)	6-5	Sr.
Michael Payne, Quincy	6-10	Sr.

Championship Game Box Score

Assembly Hall, Champaign, March 21, 1981

QUINCY (68)
Coach Jerry Leggett

Player	FG-A	FT-A	Pts	PF	Rb	As	St	Bl
Scott Allen	3-9	0-1	6	0	7	0	0	0
Bruce Douglas	9-14	1-4	19	2	7	7	1	0
Dennis Douglas	7-9	7-8	21	3	13	1	1	0
Mark Foley	0-0	0-0	0	0	1	0	0	0
Richie Hawkins	4-9	0-2	8	2	6	2	0	0
Tim Huseman	0-1	0-0	0	1	1	0	0	0
Mark Kaufman	0-0	0-0	0	1	0	0	0	0
John Lepper	1-2	1-3	3	0	1	0	0	0
Joel Myers	0-0	0-0	0	0	0	0	0	0
Michael Payne	4-11	1-2	9	2	16	4	0	3
Dave Sandercock	0-0	0-0	0	0	1	0	0	0
Mark Sparrow	1-1	0-0	2	1	2	0	0	0
TEAM					4			
TOTAL	29-56	10-20	68	12	58	15	2	3

MAYWOOD (PROVISO EAST) (39)
Coach Glenn Whittenberg

Player	FG-A	FT-A	Pts	PF	Rb	As	St	Bl
Ronald Armstrong	0-0	1-3	1	0	0	0	0	1
Earnest Ashford	0-0	1-2	1	0	1	0	0	0
Danny Austin	0-2	0-0	0	2	0	1	0	0
Donald Conrad	0-1	0-0	0	2	1	0	0	0
Corey Cooper	3-13	2-4	8	4	3	1	0	0
Maurice Frison	1-1	0-0	2	1	0	0	0	0
Tracy Henderson	2-7	2-4	6	4	3	1	1	0
Earnest Hubbard	6-17	1-2	13	0	0	2	1	0
Lawrence Mack	0-2	0-0	0	0	0	0	0	0
Darryl McDonald	0-1	0-0	0	2	1	1	0	0
Justyne Monegain	4-12	0-0	8	4	7	0	1	0
Eric Sims	0-1	0-2	0	1	2	0	0	0
TEAM					6			
TOTAL	16-57	7-17	39	20	24	6	4	1

Quincy	19	13	18	18	—	68
Maywood (Proviso East)	8	12	11	8	—	39

Officials: John Bittner, Robert Conte.

BROTHERS-IN-ARMS

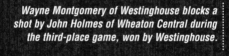

Wayne Montgomery of Westinghouse blocks a shot by John Holmes of Wheaton Central during the third-place game, won by Westinghouse.

Dennis (left) and Bruce Douglas signal Quincy's supremacy after closing a perfect season with a win over Proviso East.

Eric Sims of Proviso East sizes up the bucket while Quincy's Michael Payne closes in during Quincy's 68-39 championship-game conquest.

Michael Payne of Quincy uses his knee to great effect against Antioch's Tim Koesser during Quincy's 75-50 quarterfinal victory.

Coach Jerry Leggett gets the ride of his life after his Blue Devils captured Quincy's second state title.

1981 AA

EAST ST. LOUIS (LINCOLN), *Class AA State Champions of 1982*

FRONT ROW (left to right): Edmund Jones, Earl Jones, Carlton Cannon, Derrick Moses, Napolian Sanders. *SECOND ROW:* Darryl Morgan, Baron Wilson, Calvin Phiffer. *THIRD ROW:* Tommy Reed, Todd Porter, Tyrone Jackson, Roderick Horne, Dwayne Chatman, Mark Dale.

The loud end of Quincy's Class AA state-record streak of 64 wins overshadowed the quiet beginning of a decade of dominance by East St. Louis Lincoln and coach Bennie Lewis.

The first of four championships in an eight-year span came with a 56-50 win over Chicago Mendel Catholic, after an exhausting semifinal round and a third-place finish that had the crowd buzzing well into the main event.

Elite Eight scoring leader Michael Hampton got seventh-ranked Mendel into the title game 53-52 with a 22-footer as the clock went to 0:00 on top-rated Quincy.

But Quincy coach Jerry Leggett got the football equivalent of an untimed down when he claimed the buzzer had yet to sound as Quincy was given a timeout. In the bedlam, nobody could have heard the horn even if it had gone off.

The scoreboard did eventually sound, but not before all-American Bruce Douglas narrowly missed laying in a floor-length inbound lob from brother Dennis. It was only the fifth loss in a four-year span that saw the Blue Devils win 122 games.

As if Chicago Marshall wasn't disappointed enough after a three-point semifinal loss to East St. Louis Lincoln, the

Commandos were one-point victims of a similar Quincy strategy in the last seconds of the third-place game.

Only this time, the all-state brothers put a new twist on the play. Bruce Douglas had to leap five feet over the end line to bat his brother's 70-foot inbounds pass into the hands of Tim Huseman for a buzzer-beating lay-up.

"That's the second option on that play," said Leggett, who claimed to have more than 100 inbounding plays. A Quincy star later explained, "We've got 'em all right . . . but we only ever use three or four of them."

By comparison, the title game was tame as Todd Porter paced East St. Louis Lincoln (29-1) with 22 points.

Lincoln's semifinal squeaker over Marshall finally quelled a Commando raid that included a surprise title in the Chicago Public League championships and a 20-point upending of second-ranked St. Joseph in the quarterfinals.

The 1982 season produced the first of 15 Sweet Sixteen entries in 22 years for Rockford Boylan under coach Steve Goers. Before Goers took over for the legendary Dolph Stanley in 1981, Boylan had only one sectional title to its credit. The last state crown won by a Rockford school was West's second title in 1956.

State Final Tournament Scores

Super-Sectionals
At Carbondale [SIU]—East St. Louis (Lincoln) 64, Murphysboro 50
At Evanston [NU]—Arlington Heights (Arlington) 68, Highland Park 59
At Aurora (East)—Westchester (St. Joseph) 52, Palatine 50 (OT)
At Chicago [UIC]—Chicago (Marshall) 58, Chicago (Crane) 48
At DeKalb [NIU]—Lisle (Benet Academy) 56, Rockford (Boylan) 43
At Normal [ISU]—Quincy 80, Danville 63
At Peoria [Bradley]—Peoria (Manual) 71, Rock Island 66
At Hinsdale (Central)—Chicago (Mendel) 59, Elmhurst (York) 47

Quarterfinals
East St. Louis (Lincoln) 60, Arlington Heights (Arlington) 46
Chicago (Marshall) 79, Westchester (St. Joseph) 59
Quincy 65, Lisle (Benet Academy) 45
Chicago (Mendel) 53, Peoria (Manual) 51

Semifinals
East St. Louis (Lincoln) 57, Chicago (Marshall) 54
Chicago (Mendel) 53, Quincy 52

Finals
Quincy 62, Chicago (Marshall) 61 (third place)
East St. Louis (Lincoln) 56, Chicago (Mendel) 50 (title)

Scoring Leaders

Player, School	G	FG	FT	Pts
Bruce Douglas, Quincy	4	32	25	89
Mike Hampton, Chicago (Mendel)	4	36	11	83
Andre Banks, Chicago (Mendel)	4	30	19	79
Todd Porter, East St. Louis (Lincoln)	4	30	16	76
Dennis Douglas, Quincy	4	32	9	73
Fred Marshall, Chicago (Marshall)	4	28	17	73

All-Tournament First Team

Player, School	Ht.	Yr.
Andre Banks, Chicago (Mendel)	6-3	Sr.
Bruce Douglas, Quincy	6-3	Sr.
Dennis Douglas, Quincy	6-5	Jr.
Mike Hampton, Chicago (Mendel)	6-4	Sr.
Todd Porter, East St. Louis (Lincoln)	6-5	Sr.
Joe Stiffend, Chicago (Marshall)	6-3	Jr.

Championship Game Box Score

Assembly Hall, Champaign, March 20, 1982

EAST ST. LOUIS (LINCOLN) (56)
Coach Bennie Lewis

Player	FG-A	FT-A	Pts	PF	Rb	As	St	Bl
Mark Dale	5-8	2-4	12	3	12	1		
Rod Horne	0-0	0-0	0	0	0	0		
Tyrone Jackson	3-6	2-2	8	4	8	1		
Darryl Morgan	3-8	1-2	7	4	6	2		
Calvin Phiffer	2-7	1-2	5	1	1	6		
Todd Porter	8-18	6-7	22	3	10	1		
Baron Wilson	1-3	0-0	2	1	0	2		
TEAM					1			
TOTAL	22-50	12-17	56	16	38	13	7	3

CHICAGO (MENDEL) (50)
Coach Michael Flaherty

Player	FG-A	FT-A	Pts	PF	Rb	As	St	Bl
Andre Banks	6-14	7-9	19	3	11	1		
Mark Dunn	2-7	2-2	6	1	2	4		
Mike Hampton	9-22	2-2	20	4	10	2		
Saterial Harris	0-2	0-0	0	1	4	0		
Donald Johnson	1-3	0-0	2	1	2	1		
Byron Wallace	0-1	0-0	0	0	0	0		
Jim Williams	1-6	1-2	3	5	1	2		
TEAM					3			
TOTAL	19-55	12-15	50	15	33	10	5	1

East St. Louis (Lincoln)	12	19	16	9	—	56
Chicago (Mendel)	14	14	9	13	—	50

Officials: James Jones, Dave Carnaghi.

Tyrone Jackson of East St. Louis Lincoln tips in a rebound in the
Tiger's 56-50 win over Mendel Catholic.

Mendel assistant coach Mike Manderino cannot contain his glee
after his team upset Quincy in the semifinals on a last-second shot.

BEST. THIRD-PLACE GAME. EVER.

Most replayed shot in tournament history: Down by a point in the consolation game,
Quincy's Dennis Douglas launches a towering pass downcourt...

... to Bruce Douglas, who leaps beyond the end line to catch and throw the ball in a single
motion (ball is at 10 o'clock in white circle) ...

... to Tim Huseman, who lays in the game-winning basket as the buzzer sounds.

Quincy's Dennis Douglas sneaks a shot
past Andre Banks of Mendel. Mendel's win in the semifinal
match ended Quincy's 64-game winning streak.

1982AA

Who's your AA starting five?
A dream team to reign supreme

Every year it gets harder — and more absurd — to pick all-time *all-stars* from the boys' state **basketball** finals. Too many tourneys. Too much *talent*.

by Bob Leavitt

So, let's narrow it down from a century of state play to the Class AA state finals (1972-2006). We'll still make five friends . . . but hundreds fewer enemies.

The ground rules: Five AA guys to play as a team based only on how they looked in Elite Eights.

You pick first. No, go ahead. Be my guest.

Take Isiah Thomas at point guard, Jon Scheyer for your designated bomber, Quinn Buckner as your small forward (and team captain), Quentin Richardson at power forward, Marcus Liberty anywhere.

My turn.

I'll make Thomas deal with 6-foot-7 Shaun Livingston's long arms on both ends of the court, match Scheyer point-for-point with Jamie Brandon, let Michael Finley keep Buckner from doing his thing (winning), assign Darius Miles to Liberty's mobility and finesse, and stick a body like LaPhonso Ellis on muscleman Richardson.

Hey, I'll be looking pretty good for a guy who lost the coin flip. At least until somebody comes along and starts rummaging through our leftovers.

That could make us both wish we'd chosen Bruce Douglas to run the show, Brandon Cole to park outside the arc, Joey Range to score from everywhere, Cuonzo Martin as our designated banger, and Rashard Griffith or Eddy Curry to pound the paint.

Wait a minute. What about all those future pros who didn't shine so brightly in state-finals play? Anybody want to try to hold Kevin Garnett, Mark Aguirre, Nick Anderson?

King's 7-foot Rashard Griffith soars above Danville's Keon Clark, also a 7-footer, in a 1993 semifinal.

Forgot Nick? Look for "Nelison Anderson" in the IHSA box scores, averaging 11 points in two Sweet Sixteen games. Did somewhat better (14 ppg) for somewhat longer (800 games) in the NBA.

This is odd — nobody's taken a Peoria Manual point guard yet.

Howard Nathan was so slick that until Dee Brown, he was the shortest Mr. Basketball honoree by a full five inches. Or Frank Williams, the guy who swiped Mr. Basketball from Richardson. When Frankie was in seventh grade, future high school coach Wayne McClain called him "already something Nathan will never be . . . 5-foot-10."

And let's thank our lucky stars our stars don't have to face a team of guys who never set foot on a state-finals court.

Anybody want to defend A.J. Guyton taking that last-second shot? Certainly not anybody in his Big Ten MVP season.

Tim Hardaway? Five trips to NBA all-star games, but nary a visit to Champaign. Juwan Howard? Zero Elite Eight experience, NBA points 14,517, rebounds 6,289, blocks 281 through the 2005-06 season — and counting.

Who would take Hersey Hawkins as a 6-2 prep center? Who wouldn't want him as a pro shooting guard who fell just shy of 1,000 NBA games.

Quinn Buckner is all smiles as Thornridge returns home from the 1972 tournament with its second state championship trophy in as many years.

Frank Williams of Peoria Manual looks for an opening in a 1997 semifinal battle with Thornton.

Future pro sensation Kevin Garnett lays in an easy bucket against Thornton in the 1995 quarterfinals.

Whoops, almost forgot possibly the best all-around player and most polished prep in state history, Glenn "Doc" Rivers. The name does not appear in a state finals box score. But plug it into an Internet search along with NBA and your computer might smoke.

Maybe we should just pick an all-winner team.

Sure, Buckner (state, NCAA, Olympic, and NBA championships) is taken. But what about Sergio McClain? All he did was go 32-0 as a postseason starter. For crying out loud, Manual's jaded Class of '97 graduated without ever shedding a tear over a state-tourney loss.

Maybe us French-pastry fans should turn purest and craft all-defensive all-star teams. Won't take long. Finley's gone, so let's just take Dolton Thornridge '72 intact.

While we're specializing, how about an all-gunner team? (Jamie) Brandon and Brandon (Cole) are spoken for, but Mike Lipnisky is still available.

Come on, think back: 1990, 29-for-54 in two Sweet Sixteen outings. Maybe if he'd had a neat nickname, say "The Polish Popgun." Maybe if Rolling Meadows wasn't 0-1 lifetime in Elite Eight action?

OK, a sharpshooter from a more memorable program. How's about Brandun Hughes going 6-for-6 on threes in the second half to begin Manual's four-feat?

Let's pick a coach. I'll take Rivers. Call it a consolation prize. Got to get him on the state-finals court somehow. Hope he's not too busy bossing the Celtics.

What about the bane of all all-time all-star pickers — the what-have-you-thrilled-us-with-lately syndrome?

Guess we could take 2006 title hero Derrick Rose. But he might not be done yet.

And we can always do this again next year.

Joey Range of Galesburg puts an exclamation point on his score against Centralia in 1998 quarterfinal action.

1983AA

SPRINGFIELD (LANPHIER)
Class AA State Champions of 1983

FRONT ROW (left to right): Clark Douglas, Darrin Kelly, Clarence Briggity, Leslie Lee. SECOND ROW: Mark Alstott, Rick Poggi, Mike Wolosick, Kevin Gamble. STANDING: Michael Craig, Tyrone Petitt, Ed Horton, Moose Nika, Jerome Taylor, Ralph Matthews

CLASS AA

Springfield Lanphier and Peoria Central reprised and reversed their 1977 state title roles.

The two met in the final game of a wide-open tournament, as all five of the state's top-ranked teams failed to make it to Champaign. In their place came four of the teams that delivered those early knock-out blows.

Lanphier was one of the underdogs, unranked in the final state poll despite ending the regular season 22-3 and boasting 6-foot-6 all-state senior Kevin Gamble as well as 6-8 sophomore Ed Horton, Mr. Basketball 1985.

Future NBA players Gamble and Horton combined to make 15 of 19 shots in the title game, including a crucial three-point play by Gamble, for a 57-53 win over Central.

That allowed Lanphier and coach Bob Nika to avenge their 1977 title loss to Peoria. His only regret was that former Lanphier teammate and college buddy Bruce Boyle had by then escaped into retirement.

Tony Wysinger, a future assist record-setter at the University of Illinois, led Peoria with 21 points in the title contest. Wysinger, a 5-10 guard, made 31 of 53 Sweet Sixteen shots. Shot charts showed he would have had at least a dozen more points had he not predated the three-point arc by five years.

This was the fourth championship in Springfield history but the first for Lanphier. Springfield High won in 1917, 1935, and 1959.

Eighth-ranked Central started strong, controlling a No. 10 St. Joseph squad that had been atop the national poll at one point during the season. Then came another set of semifinals that left players and fans equally drained by last-second decisions.

Peoria beat Chicago Marshall 58-57 on a 12-footer at the buzzer by 5-10 forward Timmy Williams, who averaged only five points per game. The Lions trailed 34-26 at halftime, but Wysinger and Ivan Stone each scored 18 in the comeback win.

"I didn't want a timeout after we drew the charge in the last seconds because I didn't want Marshall to set up its defense," Peoria coach Chuck Buescher said. But he sure wanted one after Marshall seamlessly slipped into box-and-one defense on gunslinger Wysinger.

"Tiny Tim did his job — which was to look for anybody else to pass it to — right up until the last second, when he had to let it fly," Buescher said.

And Gamble did his job in the title game, twice returning entry passes before making the third time charming with the game-deciding three-point play.

In yet another season of sensational semifinals, Lanphier needed a put-back by Gamble (19 points, 16 rebounds) to outlast No. 9 Harvey Thornton, 54-52.

State Final Tournament Scores

Super-Sectionals

At Rockford [Metro Centre]—Elgin 71, Crystal Lake (South) 64
At Chicago [UIC]—Chicago (Marshall) 67, Chicago (Collins) 62 (2 OT)
At Aurora (East)—Westchester (St. Joseph) 49, Arlington Heights (Arlington) 38
At Peoria [Carver Arena]—Peoria 55, Ottawa (Twp.) 48
At DeKalb [NIU]—Lisle (Benet Academy) 45, Winnetka (New Trier) 35
At Hinsdale (Central)—Harvey (Thornton) 53, Chicago (De La Salle) 37
At Normal [ISU]—Springfield (Lanphier) 46, Lockport (Twp.) 45
At Carbondale [SIU]—East St. Louis (Lincoln) 53, Benton 49

Quarterfinals

Chicago (Marshall) 59, Elgin 46
Peoria 71, Westchester (St. Joseph) 60
Harvey (Thornton) 56, Lisle (Benet Academy) 43
Springfield (Lanphier) 55, East St. Louis (Lincoln) 47

Semifinals

Peoria 58, Chicago (Marshall) 57
Springfield (Lanphier) 54, Harvey (Thornton) 52

Finals

Harvey (Thornton) 65, Chicago (Marshall) 60 (third place)
Springfield (Lanphier) 57, Peoria 53 (title)

Scoring Leaders

Player, School	G	FG	FT	Pts
Ivan Stone, Peoria	4	26	22	74
Ken Mixon, Chicago (Marshall)	4	29	10	68
Tony Wysinger, Peoria	4	31	6	68
Kevin Gamble, Springfield (Lanphier)	4	31	5	67
Tyrone Thigpen, Harvey (Thornton)	4	25	11	61

All-Tournament First Team

Player, School	Ht.	Yr.
Kevin Gamble, Springfield (Lanphier)	6-7	Sr.
Tony Reeder, Westchester (St. Joseph)	6-7	Sr.
Joe Stiffend, Chicago (Marshall)	6-3	Sr.
Ivan Stone, Peoria	6-5	Sr.
Tyrone Thigpen, Harvey (Thornton)	6-5	Sr.
Tony Wysinger, Peoria	5-10	Sr.

Championship Game Box Score

Assembly Hall, Champaign, March 19, 1983

SPRINGFIELD (LANPHIER) (57)
Coach Bob Nika

Player	FG-A	FT-A	Pts	PF	Rb	As	St	Bl
Clarence Briggity	0-5	0-2	0	2	1	5	1	0
Clark Douglas	1-2	0-0	2	0	0	1	0	0
Kevin Gamble	8-9	3-4	19	4	6	1	0	0
Ed Horton	7-10	4-5	18	3	9	1	1	1
Leslie Lee	4-8	2-3	10	1	6	5	2	0
Moose Nika	4-10	0-0	8	1	3	4	1	0
TEAM					1			
TOTAL	24-44	9-14	57	11	26	17	5	1

PEORIA (53)
Coach Chuck Buescher

Player	FG-A	FT-A	Pts	PF	Rb	As	St	Bl
Dennis Broadnax	0-0	0-0	0	0	1	1	0	0
Tony Foote	0-0	0-0	0	1	0	0	0	0
Lamont Hanson	6-10	2-2	14	3	9	0	0	0
Steve Harvey	0-1	2-2	2	1	0	8	2	0
Ivan Stone	5-11	4-4	14	2	6	2	0	0
Tim Williams	0-3	2-3	2	3	0	1	1	0
Tony Wysinger	10-17	1-1	21	5	1	4	1	0
TEAM					0			
TOTAL	21-42	11-12	53	15	17	16	4	0

Springfield (Lanphier)	12	16	10	19	—	57
Peoria	10	10	19	14	—	53

Officials: Don Hakes, David Tosh.

Celebrating 100 years of IHSA Boys Basketball

Peoria players reach for a rebound in the title game against Springfield Lanphier. Visible is Tim Williams (24).

Kevin Gamble of Springfield Lanphier gets a boost from teammate Ed Horton after the Lions captured the state title with a 57-53 win over Peoria Central.

UNDER COVER

Ivan Stone of Peoria is surrounded by Kevin Gamble and Moose Nika of Springfield Lanphier in the 1983 title game.

Coach Bob Nika of Springfield Lanphier rallies his troops in a quarterfinal match-up with East St. Louis Lincoln.

1983AA

245

CHICAGO (SIMEON)
Class AA State Champions of 1984

FRONT ROW (left to right): Aurelia Davidson, Terrell Binlon, Pamela Shannon. SECOND ROW: Timothy Bankston, Rodney Hull, Edgar Chapman, Thomas Price. THIRD ROW: Asst. Coach George Stanton, Bobby Tribble, Daniel Patton, David Knight, Ronnie Doss, Coach Bob Hambric. FOURTH ROW: Asst. Coach Bill Alderson, Terry Sampson, Kenneth Allen, Ben Wilson, Tony Rice.

I f ever there was a case of a team living on borrowed time, it was this edition of the Evanston Wildkits.

Evanston came into the state finals with a 30-0 record, but this was possibly the shakiest undefeated record in state history.

The Wildkits survived five regular-season games by one or two points. And the close calls kept right on coming. In sectional play, Evanston won by two and three. In the super, the 'Kits advanced by four.

So when unranked Benton, the Cinderella entry with only 725 students, took Evanston (enrollment 3,550) to overtime in the quarterfinals, Wildkits fans were wondering if their bandwagon was finally going to turn into a pumpkin. But Evanston escaped again, tipping Benton 65-63.

It was the same story in the semifinals, this time with unranked St. Joseph playing the potential spoiler. And again Evanston emerged by a pair, 58-56.

But coming out of the other bracket was Chicago Simeon, the all-tall Public League champion. Ranked only No. 5, Simeon had to complete a 4-0 season against Chicago Carver and future NBA all-star Tim Hardaway and go 3-0 against No. 7 Chicago Robeson to win the Public League playoffs. That title was won 44-42 thanks to a steal by Tim Bankston and a three-point play by Bob Tribble in the closing seconds.

Simeon didn't have any giants. But neither did the Wolverines have any small starters. Despite not having a starter over 6-7, Simeon's regulars averaged 6-5 1/4, the fourth-highest figure among Class AA champs.

Simeon stopped perennial contender and third-rated West Aurora and Sweet Sixteen scoring leader Kenny Battle 67-58 in the second semifinal to set up the title confrontation.

There, the well of Evanston squeakers finally ran dry.

Bankston outscored Evanston all-stater Everette Stephens 25-15 in the finale to deny Evanston's bid for an unbeaten state title. The final count was 53-47.

West Aurora battled back from a 23-point deficit to overcome St. Joseph 55-54 in the third-place game.

Sadly, surviving play in the Chicago Public League would take on a new and sobering meaning not only for champion Simeon but schoolboy athletics everywhere.

On the day before the next season's opening game, junior center Ben Wilson, the only non-senior starter for the 30-1 defending state champs, was shot to death near the school during lunch hour.

Wilson would live on in the memory of his friends at Simeon, including Nick Anderson, who wore Wilson's number (25) throughout his high school and NBA career.

State Final Tournament Scores

Super-Sectionals
At Carbondale [SIU]—Benton 60, Collinsville 52
At Evanston [NU]—Evanston (Twp.) 71, Buffalo Grove 67
At Aurora (East)—Westchester (St. Joseph) 60, St. Charles 50
At Hinsdale (Central)—Harvey (Thornton) 63, Chicago (Weber) 42
At Normal [ISU]—Champaign (Centennial) 66, Joliet (West) 59
At DeKalb [NIU]—Aurora (West) 69, Rockford (East) 56
At Peoria [Carver Arena]—Rock Island 51, Peoria (Manual) 49
At Chicago [UIC]—Chicago (Simeon) 44, Chicago (Robeson) 42

Quarterfinals
Evanston (Twp.) 65, Benton 63 (OT)
Westchester (St. Joseph) 52, Harvey (Thornton) 50
Aurora (West) 73, Champaign (Centennial) 44
Chicago (Simeon) 48, Rock Island 44

Semifinals
Evanston (Twp.) 58, Westchester (St. Joseph) 56
Chicago (Simeon) 67, Aurora (West) 58

Finals
Aurora (West) 55, Westchester (St. Joseph) 54 (third place)
Chicago (Simeon) 53, Evanston (Twp.) 47 (title)

Scoring Leaders

Player, School	G	FG	FT	Pts
Kenny Battle, Aurora (West)	4	32	22	86
Everette Stephens, Evanston (Twp.)	4	33	13	79
Chris Funchess, Westchester (St. Joseph)	4	29	18	76
Tony Freeman, Westchester (St. Joseph)	4	27	16	70
Bobby Tribble, Chicago (Simeon)	4	24	16	64

All-Tournament First Team

Player, School	Ht.	Yr.
Bruce Baker, Benton	6-7	Sr.
Kenny Battle, Aurora (West)	6-6	Sr.
Chris Funchess, Westchester (St. Joseph)	6-5	Sr.
Everette Stephens, Evanston (Twp.)	6-2	Sr.
Ben Wilson, Chicago (Simeon)	6-7	Jr.

Championship Game Box Score

Assembly Hall, Champaign, March 24, 1984

CHICAGO (SIMEON) (53)
Coach Robert Hambric

Player	FG-A	FT-A	Pts	PF	Rb	As	St	Bl
Kenneth Allen	0-2	1-2	1	2	5	4	0	0
Tim Bankston	12-21	1-2	25	3	12	3	4	0
Ronnie Doss	1-2	0-0	2	0	3	1	1	0
Rodney Hull	3-8	0-7	6	3	9	1	0	5
Teri Sampson	0-2	0-0	0	0	0	0	0	0
Bobby Tribble	5-13	5-8	15	1	3	7	1	0
Ben Wilson	2-8	0-2	4	4	5	1	0	2
TEAM					7			
TOTAL	23-56	7-21	53	13	44	17	6	7

EVANSTON (TWP.) (47)
Coach Herb Williams

Player	FG-A	FT-A	Pts	PF	Rb	As	St	Bl
Kevin Ackles	1-2	0-0	2	0	1	0	0	0
Brian Brown	0-2	0-0	0	0	1	0	0	0
Derrick Brown	1-4	0-0	2	2	2	4	2	0
Mike Cobb	5-10	2-4	12	3	3	1	0	0
Eric Dortch	0-0	0-0	0	0	0	0	0	0
Jim Finucane	0-0	0-0	0	0	0	0	0	0
Francois Jean-Paul	0-1	0-0	0	2	0	0	0	0
Steve Kling	0-0	2-2	2	3	3	1	0	0
Tony Mason	4-13	0-0	8	4	9	1	1	0
Everette Stephens	6-16	3-3	15	4	8	1	0	1
Louis Wool	2-9	2-4	6	2	8	1	0	0
Steve Wool	0-0	0-0	0	0	0	0	0	0
TEAM					6			
TOTAL	19-57	9-13	47	20	41	9	3	1

Chicago (Simeon)	10	17	11	15	—	53
Evanston (Twp.)	12	13	6	16	—	47

Officials: Harry Bohn, Matt Laurich.

Simeon's Tim Bankston finishes off a flying dunk in the second quarter of the championship game against Evanston.

Simeon players hoist their coach, Bob Hambric, to the sky after winning the state crown with a 53-47 win over Evanston.

JUST JAMMIN'

Kenny Battle of West Aurora rattles the rim with one of several dunks he made during the 1984 tournament.

Evanston's Everette Stephens looks for an outlet while Simeon's Tim Bankston keeps up the pressure in the Class AA championship game.

Ben Wilson made his only Assembly Hall appearance in 1984.

1984AA

CHICAGO (MT. CARMEL), *Class AA State Champions of 1985*

FRONT ROW (left to right): T.J. Civik, Rich Zoller, Nick Miketinac. SECOND ROW: Ed McQuillan, Ed Murray, Melvin McCants, Melvin Johnson, Michael Roland, Derek Boyd. THIRD ROW: Coach Ed McQuillan, Marc Dobbins, Chris Calloway, Jim Cleland, James Farr, Kevin Maloney, Asst. Coach Mike McCord, Asst. Coach Paul Rybarczyk.

The second overtime game in 78 years of championship contests produced two firsts: a private-school champion in the tournament's largest class and a double-overtime game.

Chicago Mt. Carmel sophomore Derek Boyd got wide open for half his points on an eight-footer at the buzzer off a baseline inbounds pass for the only points of either overtime and a 46-44 win over Springfield Lanphier.

All-state Mt. Carmel center Melvin McCants (a future Purdue standout) was plagued by fouls and limited to four points versus 21 by Lanphier counterpart Ed Horton (Iowa), who was named Mr. Basketball.

But senior guard James Farr (Creighton) accounted for almost two-thirds of Mt. Carmel's scoring with 30 points, including 14-for-15 foul shooting.

Lanphier played for the last shot in regulation and each of the two overtimes. All three missed. Worse, the last one came a tad too early. Mt. Carmel had enough time to make a floor-length pass that went over the baseline off a Lanphier player with two seconds left.

Boyd was an unlikely hero, having missed 9 of 10 previous shots. And Mt. Carmel was an unlikely champ, coming in ranked only 14th in the state.

But the Caravan got some help along the way.

No. 1-ranked Proviso West bowed to Leyden in the sectional, leaving second-rated Chicago Simeon as the state favorite despite not having a starter left from its 1984 championship.

But the Wolverines and future University of Illinois and NBA stalwart Nick Anderson fell 52-48 in the quarterfinals to Lanphier, which had finished second in the Mid-State 9 Conference, a third of which was ranked among the state's top 11 teams.

Mt. Carmel nipped Leyden by three in super-sectional play, then cruised past Hersey in the quarterfinals and Cahokia in the semis. It was a bad bracket break for a Leyden team some consider the best-ever from a school district boasting four (1975-78) regular-season unbeatens (all of which fell short of Champaign).

Lanphier reached the title match with a costly victory over Homewood-Flossmoor, which was wearing what were generally regarded as the ugliest shorts (wide vertical red and white stripes) in Class AA history.

The Lions won 65-54, but playmaking guard Paul Piphus was injured in the final minutes and was unable to answer the bell for the title bout.

After 14 years of Class AA state finals, no school had more than one first-place trophy. But that was about to change.

State Final Tournament Scores

Super-Sectionals

At Normal [ISU]—Springfield (Lanphier) 82, Bolingbrook 74
At Chicago [UIC]—Chicago (Simeon) 65, Chicago (Carver) 54
At Aurora (East)—Flossmoor (Homewood-F.) 58, Elgin 42
At DeKalb [NIU]—Rockford (Boylan) 67, Aurora (East) 65
At Hinsdale (Central)—Chicago (Mt. Carmel) 37, Northlake (Leyden) 34
At Evanston [NU]—Arlington Heights (Hersey) 71, Mundelein (Carmel) 48
At Peoria [Carver Arena]—Ottawa (Twp.) 67, Peoria (Richwoods) 65
At Carbondale [SIU]—Cahokia 66, Carbondale 59

Quarterfinals

Springfield (Lanphier) 52, Chicago (Simeon) 48
Flossmoor (Homewood-F.) 39, Rockford (Boylan) 36
Chicago (Mt. Carmel) 56, Arlington Heights (Hersey) 43
Cahokia 81, Ottawa (Twp.) 66

Semifinals

Springfield (Lanphier) 65, Flossmoor (Homewood-F.) 54
Chicago (Mt. Carmel) 60, Cahokia 51

Finals

Flossmoor (Homewood-F.) 56, Cahokia 46 (third place)
Chicago (Mt. Carmel) 46, Springfield (Lanphier) 44 (2 OT) (title)

Scoring Leaders

Player, School	G	FG	FT	Pts
Ed Horton, Springfield (Lanphier)	4	39	26	104
James Farr, Chicago (Mt. Carmel)	4	25	21	71
Stan Sillas, Cahokia	4	28	15	71
Melvin McCants, Chicago (Mt. Carmel)	4	29	12	70
Wali Abdul-Rahim, Springfield (Lanphier)	4	26	10	62

All-Tournament First Team

Player, School	Ht.	Yr.
Wali Abdul-Rahim, Springfield (Lanphier)	6-2	Sr.
James Farr, Chicago (Mt. Carmel)	5-9	Sr.
Ed Horton, Springfield (Lanphier)	6-8	Sr.
Melvin McCants, Chicago (Mt. Carmel)	6-8	Sr.
Dick Seidel, Flossmoor (Homewood-F.)	6-5	Jr.
Stan Sillas, Cahokia	6-1	Sr.

Championship Game Box Score

Assembly Hall, Champaign, March 23, 1985

CHICAGO (MT. CARMEL) (46)
Coach Ed McQuillan

Player	FG-A	FT-A	Pts	PF	Rb	As	St	Bl
Derrick Boyd	2-11	0-1	4	4	7	1	1	0
Chris Calloway	1-1	0-0	2	1	3	0	0	
James Farr	8-14	14-15	30	2	1	3	5	0
Melvin McCants	2-4	0-0	4	4	9	0	0	1
Ed McQuillan	0-0	0-0	0	0	0	0	0	0
Ed Murray	2-3	0-0	4	0	1	0	0	0
Sam Smallwood	1-5	0-0	2	0	8	2	2	0
TEAM					2			
TOTAL	16-38	14-16	46	12	29	9	8	1

SPRINGFIELD (LANPHIER) (44)
Coach Bob Nika

Player	FG-A	FT-A	Pts	PF	Rb	As	St	Bl
Wali Abdul-Rahim	3-8	2-2	8	0	7	0	2	0
Willie Grier	0-3	1-2	1	4	0	0	0	0
Ed Horton	7-18	7-10	21	3	8	1	2	1
William Horton	3-9	2-2	8	3	1	5	0	0
Bryan Johnson	0-0	0-0	0	1	0	0	0	0
Pat McGuire	2-5	0-0	4	0	1	4	2	0
Kevyn Samuels	0-0	0-0	0	1	4	1	0	1
Mike Tapley	1-1	0-0	2	1	0	0	0	0
TEAM					2			
TOTAL	16-44	12-16	44	13	23	11	8	2

Chicago (Mt. Carmel)	8	12	18	6	0	2 —	46
Springfield (Lanphier)	8	12	10	14	0	0 —	44

Officials: John Duncan, Edward Schmidt.

1985AA

Derek Boyd, who scored the winning basket in double overtime, waves to fans after Mt. Carmel's 46-44 win over Springfield Lanphier.

A Springfield Lanphier player buries his head in a towel after suffering a last-second loss in the championship game.

Cahokia's Marvin Wallace fights off a teammate to control a loose ball.

BOARDINGHOUSE REACH

Ed Horton of Lanphier and Mt. Carmel's Melvin McCants do battle in the tournament's first double-overtime championship game. Mt. Carmel won 46-44.

Tracy Wilson of Homewood-Flossmoor struggles for control of a loose ball while Steve Langley of Rockford Boylan stands guard.

1985AA

1986 AA

They may have already knocked off state and national rankings leader Simeon — the last unbeaten Class AA team in the state, complete with Mr. Basketball winner Nick Anderson — but that didn't keep once-beaten King from having to battle for its state title.

King boasted 6-foot-8 all-state junior Marcus Liberty. But it was 6-6 senior Levertis Robinson who led the Jaguars past Evanston in the quarterfinals with 25 points and No. 2 Manual in the semifinals with 27.

It took a 10-footer with five seconds left by David Weatherall to beat unranked Evanston. And he came back for 18 points in a 47-40 title win as King limited Olympia Fields Rich Central all-stater Kendall Gill to five points on 2-of-14 shooting.

The Olympians led 34-30 at halftime, but King held them to just six points in the second half.

Rich Central had eliminated Carbondale and all-stater Steve Bardo 54-43.

Gill, Liberty, Bardo, Anderson, Kenny Battle (of 1984 third-place West Aurora) and Lowell Hamilton (of 1985 Class A champ Chicago Providence-St. Mel) would all return to Assembly Hall and in 1989 spark the University of Illinois to its first NCAA Final Four in 37 years.

King's championship kicked off an incredible period of Class AA dynasties that would last a dozen years. From 1986 to 1997, four schools — Peoria Manual (4), East St. Louis Lincoln (3), King (3) and Proviso East (2) — hogged all the first-place hardware.

In the championship game, King countered Rich Central's ball-control tactics with offensive patience of its own.

The Jaguars hit the boards for such short shots they ended up 57 percent from the field but only 41 percent from the foul line in the title game. For its four Sweet Sixteen games, King was more accurate on field goals (.592) than free throws (.590).

The state's final four would soon be known as the Terminal Three when Romeoville went from 27-6 to 0-33 and had to return its fourth-place trophy for the season-long use of an over-age Chicago transfer. Romeoville had eliminated fourth-ranked St. Joseph in the quarterfinals on a free throw with no time remaining.

State Final Tournament Scores

Super-Sectionals
At DeKalb [NIU]—Rockford (Boylan) 60, Wheaton (North) 56
At Peoria [Carver Arena]—Peoria (Manual) 70, Rock Island 58
At Elgin—Evanston (Twp.) 71, Mundelein (Carmel) 65
At Chicago [UIC]—Chicago (King) 49, Chicago (Simeon) 46
At Carbondale [SIU]—Carbondale 58, East St. Louis (Lincoln) 55
At Aurora (East)—Olympia Fields (Rich Central) 77, Palatine (Fremd) 47
At Normal [ISU]—Romeoville 65, Decatur (Stephen Decatur) 46 (forfeited)
At Hinsdale (Central)—Westchester (St. Joseph) 61, Chicago (Leo) 49

Quarterfinals
Peoria (Manual) 49, Rockford (Boylan) 41
Chicago (King) 64, Evanston (Twp.) 62
Olympia Fields (Rich Central) 54, Carbondale 43
Romeoville 51, Westchester (St. Joseph) 50 (forfeited)

Semifinals
Chicago (King) 79, Peoria (Manual) 62
Olympia Fields (Rich Central) 73, Romeoville 56

Finals
Peoria (Manual) 75, Romeoville 57 (third place) (fourth place trophy forfeited)
Chicago (King) 47, Olympia Fields (Rich Central) 40 (title)

Scoring Leaders

Player, School	G	FG	FT	Pts
Jamere Jackson, Peoria (Manual)	4	28	16	72
Shaun Vandiver, Romeoville	4	29	6	64
Marcus Liberty, Chicago (King)	4	25	14	64
Levertis Robinson, Chicago (King)	4	26	12	64
Curtis Stuckey, Peoria (Manual)	4	21	13	55

All-Tournament First Team

Player, School	Ht.	Yr.
Kendall Gill, Olympia Fields (Rich Central)	6-3	Sr.
Jamere Jackson, Peoria (Manual)	6-3	Sr.
Reggie King, Chicago (King)	5-10	Sr.
Marcus Liberty, Chicago (King)	6-8	Jr.
Levertis Robinson, Chicago (King)	6-7	Sr.
Shaun Vandiver, Romeoville	6-8	Sr.

Championship Game Box Score

Assembly Hall, Champaign, March 15, 1986

CHICAGO (KING) (47)
Coach Landon "Sonny" Cox

Player	FG-A	FT-A	Pts	PF	Rb	As	St	Bl
Reggie King	2-4	4-5	8	1	3	6	1	0
Marcus Liberty	6-12	2-7	14	2	13	0	1	0
Emmett Lynch	1-1	1-2	3	2	2	2	0	0
Levertis Robinson	1-5	0-3	2	1	5	0	0	6
David Weatherall	9-12	0-0	18	3	3	1	0	0
Kevin Williams	1-1	0-0	2	0	2	0	1	1
TEAM					0			
TOTAL	20-35	7-17	47	9	28	9	3	7

OLYMPIA FIELDS (RICH CENTRAL) (40)
Coach Ron Brauer

Player	FG-A	FT-A	Pts	PF	Rb	As	St	Bl
Keith Gill	3-8	2-2	8	1	1	3	0	0
Kendall Gill	2-14	1-2	5	1	5	4	3	1
Ronnie Jamison	0-0	0-0	0	0	1	0	0	0
Maurice Rayford	4-6	1-4	9	4	8	0	1	0
Robert Respress	0-0	0-0	0	0	0	0	0	0
Bobby Smith	5-13	2-2	12	5	1	1	1	0
Charles Warnell	3-6	0-0	6	3	4	0	1	0
TEAM					1			
TOTAL	17-47	6-10	40	14	21	8	6	1

Chicago (King)	9	21	7	10	—	47
Olympia Fields (Rich Central)	18	16	2	4	—	40

Officials: Kurtis Anderson, James Czocher.

PAIR OF KINGS

Reginald King of Chicago King twists to get off a shot over Jamere Jackson of Peoria Manual. King won the semifinal contest 79-62 to advance to the championship game.

Marcus Liberty of King nearly peeks above the rim as he completes a dunk during the 1986 Class AA tournament.

Kendall Gill of Rich Central sets up a play in a quarterfinal match-up with Carbondale.

Levertis Robinson of King takes to the air against Lynn Collins of Manual in a semifinal match.

Billy Stanback of St. Joseph fakes Romeoville's Artie Preston out of position during a quarterfinal game.

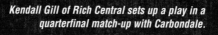

1986AA

Long journeys begin with a single step. Sometimes even with an opponent's misstep.

East St. Louis Lincoln was not the state-finals focus as it zeroed in on the first of what would be a record three straight championships.

Unranked Quincy stunned unbeaten and top-ranked Peoria Manual in the quarterfinals by making its last 13 shots from the field, including a pull-up 26-footer by 5-foot-6 guard James Bailey with two ticks left in overtime for a 61-59 victory.

That Manual team included future Missouri Valley Conference offensive player of the year Curtis Stuckey (Drake and Bradley), future DePaul career scoring leader David Booth, and future Arizona State point guard Lynn Collins.

With Manual out of the hunt, third-ranked East St. Louis Lincoln took over.

The Tigers, led by 6-9 junior LaPhonso Ellis, pounded King 79-62 in the title game for the first jewel in their triple crown. Ellis turned in a thunderous performance with 27 points and 10 rebounds, and 6-8 James Harris added 23 to the count. But those numbers didn't dominate.

That honor went instead to 6-8 Mr. Basketball Marcus Liberty, who registered a Class AA-record 41 title-game points and 15 rebounds for King. Freshman teammate Jamie Brandon, a future Mr. Basketball, added 12 points.

Both No. 10 King (coached by Landon "Sonny" Cox) and No. 3 East St. Louis Lincoln (under Bennie Lewis)

had to beat back upset bids to get to the title game.

Lincoln had to escape early and often, getting a late score to beat Collinsville in sectional play and digging out of an 18-point, first-quarter hole to overtake Oak Forest in the quarterfinals.

Fourth-ranked St. Joseph of Westchester was back in the semis again. And the Chargers held all but one of King's players to six or fewer points. That one, however, was Liberty, who accounted for 38 of King's 60 in a two-point win.

Lincoln stood its ground in the semis with a 55-49 decision over Quincy. Chris Rodgers put up 25 points, and Ellis pulled down 15 rebounds.

Liberty, who would be named national prep player of the year, ended with a Class AA Sweet Sixteen record of 143 points — a 34.0 average.

Brandon would end his prep career in 1990 with 3,157 points, the most by any player to reach the Class AA Elite Eight. And 269 of those points came in Sweet Sixteen play, also a record for any tournament.

Quincy wound up fourth, making Jerry Leggett the first coach with a complete set of Class AA final-four trophies. Manual's Dick Van Scyoc would join that exclusive club with a win in 1994 title, as would St. Joseph's Gene Pingatore with his 1999 championship.

State Final Tournament Scores

Super-Sectionals
At Rockford [Metro Centre]—Rockford (Boylan) 64, Winnetka (New Trier) 52
At Hinsdale (Central)—Westchester (St. Joseph) 77, Chicago (Leo) 65
At DeKalb [NIU]—Elgin 71, Aurora (East) 66 (OT)
At Chicago [UIC]—Chicago (King) 93, Chicago (Crane) 66
At Aurora (East)—Oak Forest 62, Evanston (Twp.) 60
At Carbondale [SIU]—East St. Louis (Lincoln) 35, Mt. Vernon 26
At Peoria [Carver Arena]—Peoria (Manual) 67, Rock Island 63
At Normal [ISU]—Quincy 43, Lockport (Twp.) 42

Quarterfinals
Westchester (St. Joseph) 85, Rockford (Boylan) 67
Chicago (King) 70, Elgin 58
East St. Louis (Lincoln) 64, Oak Forest 58
Quincy 61, Peoria (Manual) 59 (OT)

Semifinals
Chicago (King) 60, Westchester (St. Joseph) 58
East St. Louis (Lincoln) 55, Quincy 49

Finals
Westchester (St. Joseph) 72, Quincy 65 (third place)
East St. Louis (Lincoln) 79, Chicago (King) 62 (title)

Scoring Leaders

Player, School	G	FG	FT	Pts
Marcus Liberty, Chicago (King)	4	54	35	143
Cliff Scales, Westchester (St. Joseph)	4	38	14	90
Brian Molis, Westchester (St. Joseph)	4	36	12	84
Chris Rodgers, East St. Louis (Lincoln)	4	27	13	67
Larry Loethen, Quincy	4	25	12	62

All-Tournament First Team

Player, School	Ht.	Yr.
Mark Baugh, Elgin	6-5	Sr.
Marcus Liberty, Chicago (King)	6-8	Sr.
Larry Loethen, Quincy	6-5	Sr.
Brian Molis, Westchester (St. Joseph)	6-4	Sr.
Chris Rodgers, East St. Louis (Lincoln)	6-7	Sr.
Cliff Scales, Westchester (St. Joseph)	6-2	Sr.

Championship Game Box Score

Assembly Hall, Champaign, March 21, 1987

EAST ST. LOUIS (LINCOLN) (79)
Coach Bennie Lewis

Player	FG-A	FT-A	Pts	PF	Rb	As	St	Bl
Lawrence Bradford	4-7	0-0	8	1	2	2	1	0
Mark Chambers	2-3	0-0	4	3	2	2	1	0
Rodney Chavis	1-9	2-2	4	1	5	11	1	0
LaPhonso Ellis	12-18	3-4	27	4	10	1	2	4
James Harris	11-13	1-2	23	2	4	2	3	2
Chris Rodgers	6-9	1-4	13	3	13	13	2	3
TEAM					1			
TOTAL	36-59	7-12	79	14	37	21	10	9

CHICAGO (KING) (62)
Coach Landon "Sonny" Cox

Player	FG-A	FT-A	Pts	PF	Rb	As	St	Bl
Karl Anderson	0-3	3-4	3	1	9	2	2	1
Jamie Brandon	6-13	0-3	12	1	3	3	2	0
Anthony Burwell	0-0	0-0	0	0	0	0	0	0
Keith Calbert	0-0	0-0	0	0	0	0	0	0
Terrance Cheeks	0-0	0-0	0	0	1	0	0	0
Michael King	0-0	0-0	0	0	0	0	0	0
Marcus Liberty	16-33	9-13	41	4	15	0	1	0
Emmett Lynch	1-5	0-0	2	2	1	0	0	0
Johnny Selvie	0-7	0-0	0	2	3	1	3	0
Richard Smith	0-3	0-0	0	3	2	0	0	2
Carl Stanley	2-2	0-0	4	0	1	1	2	0
TEAM					1			
TOTAL	25-66	12-20	62	13	36	7	10	3

East St. Louis (Lincoln)	15	26	18	20	— 79
Chicago (King)	11	13	24	14	— 62

Officials: Rich Firebaugh, Kirby Hamm.

BATTLE ON THE GLASS

There's nothing LaPhonso Ellis can do as King's Marcus Liberty hits the glass for two. Ellis had the last laugh as East St. Louis Lincoln won the championship 79-62.

Coach Bennie Lewis of East St. Louis Lincoln celebrates his second state title with Mark Chambers.

Larry Loethen of Quincy sneaks a shot past the long arms of LaPhonso Ellis in a semifinal battle. Lincoln won 55-49 to set the stage for the first of three straight state titles.

King's Johnny Selvie can't make it through the defense of St. Joseph's Brian Molis (20) and John Dragas (34). King took the semifinal showdown 60-58.

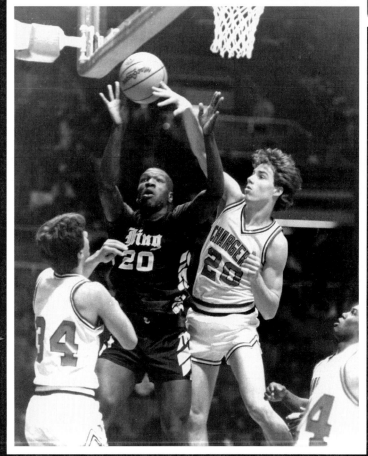

Marcus Liberty is surrounded by reporters. King lost the championship to East St. Louis Lincoln but Liberty set a tournament scoring record.

1987AA

What was billed as the title-game Battle of the Behemoths ended in a virtual standoff. East St. Louis Lincoln's 6-foot-10 LaPhonso Ellis got 26 points and 15 rebounds, while 6-9 Chicago St. Francis de Sales counterpart Eric Anderson got 23 points and 17 rebounds.

But Lincoln won the war 60-52 with the help of 20 points and 10 boards by 6-6 junior Cuonzo Martin.

Anderson and Ellis would wind up one-two, respectively, in Mr. Basketball voting.

The dandy duo of Ellis and Martin made the middle season the strongest chapter in a splendid saga spanning three years, with senior Ellis averaging 25 points in this Elite Eight and Martin scoring at a 17-point pace.

Ellis set the Class AA Sweet Sixteen career rebounding record with 82 caroms in six games. A year later, Martin would up that to 87 in a total of nine outings. Peoria Manual's Sergio McClain would jump that standard to 101 by 1997, but it would take the 6-3 forward the maximum 16 career games to do it.

The big-guy battle actually started in the quarterfinals, where Anderson and company outlasted Chicago Simeon and 6-9 future Mr. Basketball winner Deon Thomas 60-57 in overtime. Anderson also claimed the personal battle, outscoring Thomas 26-18 and outrebounding him 11-7.

East St. Louis Lincoln started its trip to the title with a 24-point quarterfinal conquest of Evanston as Ellis and Martin combined for 40 points.

In the semis, St. Francis de Sales had to work overtime to outlast Rock Island 60-58, as Anderson again piled up the stats with 25 points and 15 rebounds.

East St. Louis Lincoln warmed up on the final day with Peoria Manual, which had reversed two regular-season losses to bump off top-ranked Peoria Central in sectional play. The Tigers advanced 67-50 over No. 9 Manual, with Ellis overcoming 6-7 David Booth in shooting (10-for-19 vs. 9-for-27), scoring (27 vs. 20) and rebounding (17 vs. 12).

Ironically, all these paint-pounders hogged the limelight in the first Class AA tournament with the three-point shot. Only 29 treys were tallied in this state finals, an all-time low.

The long ball would gain importance in postseason play as old-school coaches realized shooting 33 percent outside the arc netted the same number of points as being 50 percent accurate inside of 19 feet, 9 inches. Not surprisingly, players adapted to long-range bombing strategy faster than coaches.

EAST ST. LOUIS (LINCOLN)
Class AA State Champions of 1988

FRONT ROW (left to right): Ricky Lewis, Chris McKinney, Jason Rogers, Stanford Riley, Lawrence Bradford, Marco Harris, Trainer Byron Jackson. SECOND ROW: Principal John Bailey, Jr., Coach Bennie Lewis, Mgr. Vince Staten, Darian Nash, Vincent Jackson, Bryant Stevenson, LaPhonso Ellis, Cuonzo Martin, James Lewis, Sharif Ford, Asst. Coach Jethro Brown, Asst. Coach Lealand Seaberry.

State Final Tournament Scores

Super-Sectionals
At Chicago [UIC]—Chicago (Simeon) 66, Chicago (King) 59
At Hinsdale (Central)—Chicago (St. Francis de Sales) 67, Westchester (St. Joseph) 58
At Aurora (East)—Chicago Heights (Bloom Trail) 58, Joliet (Catholic Academy) 56
At Rockford [Metro Centre]—Rock Island 60, Rockford (Boylan) 56
At Elgin—Evanston (Twp.) 66, Gurnee (Warren) 61
At Carbondale [SIU]—East St. Louis (Lincoln) 69, Centralia 41
At Peoria [Carver Arena]—Peoria (Manual) 86, Jacksonville 66
At DeKalb [NIU]—Aurora (East) 72, Palatine (Fremd) 68 (OT)

Quarterfinals
Chicago (St. Francis de Sales) 60, Chicago (Simeon) 57 (OT)
Rock Island 69, Chicago Heights (Bloom Trail) 52
East St. Louis (Lincoln) 80, Evanston (Twp.) 56
Peoria (Manual) 75, Aurora (East) 62

Semifinals
Chicago (St. Francis de Sales) 58, Rock Island 56 (OT)
East St. Louis (Lincoln) 67, Peoria (Manual) 50

Finals
Peoria (Manual) 59, Rock Island 42 (third place)
East St. Louis (Lincoln) 60, Chicago (St. Francis de Sales) 52 (title)

Scoring Leaders

Player, School	G	FG	3P	FT	Pts
Eric Anderson, Chi. (St. Francis de Sales)	4	41	1	24	107
LaPhonso Ellis, East St. Louis (Lincoln)	4	34	1	25	94
David Booth, Peoria (Manual)	4	43	0	3	89
Ken Sydnor, Peoria (Manual)	4	34	1	3	72
Cuonzo Martin, East St. Louis (Lincoln)	4	32	0	4	68

All-Tournament First Team

Player, School	Ht.	Yr.
Eric Anderson, Chicago (St. Francis de Sales)	6-9	Sr.
John Barnes, Rock Island	5-10	Sr.
David Booth, Peoria (Manual)	6-5	Sr.
LaPhonso Ellis, East St. Louis (Lincoln)	6-10	Sr.
Cuonzo Martin, East St. Louis (Lincoln)	6-5	So.
Deon Thomas, Chicago (Simeon)	6-9	Jr.
Thomas Wyatt, Aurora (East)	6-5	So.

Championship Game Box Score

Assembly Hall, Champaign, March 19, 1988

EAST ST. LOUIS (LINCOLN) (60)
Coach Bennie Lewis

Player	FG-A	3P-A	FT-A	Pts	PF	Rb	As	St	Bl
Lawrence Bradford	2-7	1-4	0-0	5	2	2	5	1	0
LaPhonso Ellis	9-17	1-1	7-12	26	3	15	2	0	9
Vincent Jackson	1-9	0-2	2-2	4	3	3	3	0	0
Cuonzo Martin	9-16	0-0	2-2	20	3	10	1	3	0
Chris McKinney	0-0	0-0	1-2	1	0	0	0	0	0
Bryant Stevenson	2-2	0-0	0-0	4	1	5	0	0	0
TEAM						0			
TOTAL	23-51	2-7	12-18	60	12	35	11	4	9

CHICAGO (ST. FRANCIS DE SALES) (52)
Coach Mike Kaczmarz

Player	FG-A	3P-A	FT-A	Pts	PF	Rb	As	St	Bl
Don Akins	4-17	0-8	0-1	8	0	1	4	2	0
Rod Amison	0-0	0-0	0-0	0	0	0	0	0	0
Eric Anderson	7-18	1-2	8-8	23	3	17	0	0	2
Bob Clay	0-0	0-0	0-0	0	0	0	0	0	0
Trent Lowery	0-0	0-0	0-0	0	0	0	0	0	0
Sean McNabb	0-5	0-0	0-2	0	3	6	0	2	0
Tony Michalski	4-10	3-6	0-0	11	5	5	5	1	0
Timel Moore	0-0	0-0	0-0	0	0	0	0	0	0
Dale Parrish	0-0	0-0	0-0	0	0	0	0	0	0
Doug Salus	0-0	0-0	0-0	0	0	0	0	0	0
John Simmons	4-11	0-0	2-2	10	3	6	0	1	0
Jeff Thormeyer	0-0	0-0	0-0	0	2	0	0	2	0
TEAM						2			
TOTAL	19-61	4-16	10-13	52	16	37	9	8	2

East St. Louis (Lincoln)	8	21	16	15	— 60
Chi. (St. Francis de Sales)	13	10	10	19	— 52

Officials: Kurtis Anderson, Reuben Norris.

TIGERS 1988 State Champions

THE EYES HAVE IT

Five-foot-seven Don Akins of St. Francis de Sales scoots past 5-6 Jackie Crawford of Simeon during quarterfinal action. De Sales won the overtime contest 60-57.

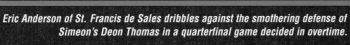

Eric Anderson of St. Francis de Sales dribbles against the smothering defense of Simeon's Deon Thomas in a quarterfinal game decided in overtime.

LaPhonso Ellis of East St. Louis Lincoln stares a hole through a pair of pesky Peoria Manual defenders, Tom Wilson (52) and Ken Sydnor (32).

THE EYES HAVE IT

Ellis eyes the basket in the Tigers' 60-52 championship-game win. Trent Lowery and Eric Anderson of St. Francis de Sales spectate.

1988AA

EAST ST. LOUIS (LINCOLN)
Class AA State Champions of 1989

FRONT ROW (left to right):
Henry Edwards, Torey McCray,
Riley Stanford, Jason Rogers,
Terry Little, Rico Sylvester.
SECOND ROW: Tori Rodgers,
Chris McKinney, Rudy Hurt,
Cuonzo Martin, Ronald Willis,
Vincent Jackson, Sharif Ford.

CLASS AA

1989 AA

Third might have been charming for East St. Louis Lincoln, what with being ranked third in the state before winning titles in each of the two previous years.

But poll voters — apparently no students of history — didn't believe the third time would be as charming for the record-seeking Tigers.

Wrong. But not wrong by much.

Not only did seventh-ranked East St. Louis Lincoln complete the triple crown, the Tigers did it in triple overtime in what many consider the most marvelously contested title contest in state basketball history.

With one second left, Vincent Jackson unlocked the state's consecutive-title record with a running 18-footer under double-team pressure in the top of the key, giving Illinois' Jewel of the Mississippi (29-4) and coach Bennie Lewis a 59-57 victory over unbeaten and second-rated Peoria Central.

Cuonzo Martin led Lincoln with 20 points. Mike Hughes (21) and Charles White (20) paced Central.

Third-ranked Chicago King, which handed top-rated Chicago Simeon and Mr. Basketball winner Deon Thomas its only loss in the Chicago Public League finals, finished third after a 60-57 semifinal loss to East St. Louis Lincoln.

The irony of the tourney was that Jackson's legendary shot came from a player who missed 14 of 19 in the title game of an Elite Eight that included two of the purest scorers in state history: Jamie Brandon of King and fellow junior Brandon Cole of Bloom.

Jamie Brandon scored 31 in a 60-57 semifinal loss to East St. Louis Lincoln. And Brandon Cole, who scored 35 in a one-point super-sectional win, struck for 25 to no avail as Bloom fell 62-61 to Central in the quarterfinals, despite 61 percent shooting.

Of the triple-treat title game, Central coach Chuck Buescher said: "As hard as those kids competed, you just knew it was going to take a great play like that to decide it."

Veteran Lincoln coach Bennie Lewis called it not only the best game he'd ever coached but also the best game he'd ever seen.

Lincoln's fabled title shot would never have happened but for a remarkable comeback to win its quarterfinal 72-70 over No. 5 East Aurora and 31-point scorer Thomas Wyatt.

Martin stole an Aurora throw-in with four seconds remaining and passed upcourt to Sharif Ford, who had the presence of mind to pull up 18 feet from the basket for the game-winner with only one tick left on the clock.

Never let it be said that East St. Louis Lincoln wasted anything in this Elite Eight. Not with a three-game total victory margin of a mere seven points.

And never let it be said his players proved Buescher wrong when he said "basketball has become, first-of-all, a game of guards." Indeed, all five of his regulars wound up starting at least one Division I college game as a point guard.

The game's turning point may have come in the first overtime, when Peoria's Chris Reynolds received a technical foul

for a comment he made to the one of the officials.

That call set up four-for-four foul shooting to untie the game with 78 seconds left in the first overtime. But Central worked through it to tie at the buzzer on a 10-foot put-back by Mike Hughes, who might well have pushed off to grab the rebound.

Peoria Central missed a similar shot in an identical situation as time ran out on the second extra four-minute period.

State Final Tournament Scores

Super-Sectionals
At Chicago [UIC]—Chicago (King) 67, Chicago (Simeon) 57
At Hinsdale (Central)—Dolton (Thornridge) 70, Chicago (Gordon Tech) 67
At Carbondale [SIU]—East St. Louis (Lincoln) 55, Mt. Vernon 47
At DeKalb [NIU]—Aurora (East) 84, Palatine (Fremd) 65
At Aurora (East)—Chicago Heights (Bloom Twp.) 69, Joliet (Central) 68
At Peoria (Carver Arena)—Peoria 60, Jacksonville 43
At Rockford [Metro Centre]—Rock Island 55, Rockford (Boylan) 47
At Elgin—Winnetka (New Trier) 64, Gurnee (Warren) 54

Quarterfinals
Chicago (King) 63, Dolton (Thornridge) 46
East St. Louis (Lincoln) 72, Aurora (East) 70
Peoria 62, Chicago Heights (Bloom Twp.) 61
Rock Island 52, Winnetka (New Trier) 47

Semifinals
East St. Louis (Lincoln) 60, Chicago (King) 57
Peoria 52, Rock Island 47

Finals
Chicago (King) 76, Rock Island 58 (third place)
East St. Louis (Lincoln) 59, Peoria 57 (3 OT) (title)

Scoring Leaders

Player, School	G	FG	3P	FT	Pts
Jamie Brandon, Chicago (King)	4	34	3	29	100
Mike Hughes, Peoria	4	35	3	9	82
Cuonzo Martin, East St. Louis (Lincoln)	4	32	0	16	80
Thomas Wyatt, Aurora (East)	2	21	0	21	63
Vincent Jackson, East St. Louis (Lincoln)	4	21	4	14	60
Brandon Cole, Chicago Heights (Bloom)	2	19	10	12	60

All-Tournament First Team

Player, School	Ht.	Yr.
Jamie Brandon, Chicago (King)	6-3	Jr.
Brandon Cole, Chicago Heights (Bloom Twp.)	6-1	Jr.
Mike Hughes, Peoria	6-6	Sr.
Cuonzo Martin, East St. Louis (Lincoln)	6-5	Jr.
Chris Reynolds, Peoria	6-1	Sr.
Thomas Wyatt, Aurora (East)	6-5	Jr.

Championship Game Box Score

Assembly Hall, Champaign, March 18, 1989

EAST ST. LOUIS (LINCOLN) (59)
Coach Bennie Lewis

Player	FG-A	3P-A	FT-A	Pts	PF	Rb	As	St	Bl
Sharif Ford	2-4	0-0	0-1	4	0	7	0	0	1
Vincent Jackson	5-19	1-4	5-6	16	2	8	3	1	0
Cuonzo Martin	10-16	0-0	1-2	21	0	9	0	2	0
Chris McKinney	5-9	0-0	0-0	10	4	3	6	0	0
Rico Sylvester	2-5	2-2	2-3	8	2	1	5	0	0
Ronald Willis	0-0	0-0	0-0	0	1	2	0	0	1
TEAM						3			
TOTAL	24-53	3-6	8-12	59	9	33	14	3	2

PEORIA (57)
Coach Chuck Buescher

Player	FG-A	3P-A	FT-A	Pts	PF	Rb	As	St	Bl
Tyrone Howard	2-7	0-0	0-0	4	0	5	5	1	0
Mike Hughes	10-25	0-6	1-1	21	2	9	2	1	0
Mike Kirksey	0-0	0-0	0-0	0	0	0	0	0	0
Chris Reynolds	2-12	0-3	6-6	10	4	6	6	2	0
Cartney Sazone	1-5	0-0	0-0	2	2	6	0	0	1
Charles White	8-13	2-3	2-2	20	3	6	1	1	1
TEAM						2			
TOTAL	23-62	2-12	9-9	57	11	34	14	5	2

East St. Louis (Lincoln)	13	10	14	9	4	2	7	— 59
Peoria	12	14	6	14	4	2	5	— 57

Officials: Scott Jones, Bill Vangel.

The race is on as Ronald Willis of East St. Louis Lincoln and Chris Reynolds of Peoria Central go after a loose ball.

Ronald Willis of East St. Louis Lincoln swipes at a title-game shot by Reynolds.

With an unprecedented triple-overtime victory, Lincoln becomes the first team to win three consecutive state titles.

THREE TIMES A WINNER

Chris McKinney of East St. Louis Lincoln launches a shot against the Peoria defense in the championship contest.

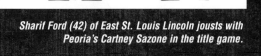

Sharif Ford (42) of East St. Louis Lincoln jousts with Peoria's Cartney Sazone in the title game.

1989AA

Class AA dynasties
Four of a kind tough to beat

The first 15 *Class AA* state-title trophies went to as many different schools. Beginning with the 1986 championship, a mere four schools would dominate AA state *finals* for a dozen years, a period like none other in IHSA lore.

by Bob Leavitt

Peoria Manual guard Sergio McClain and his father and coach, Wayne, reached the pinnacle of success with four straight titles from 1994 to 1997. Wayne McClain coached the last three after veteran mentor Dick Van Scyoc retired.

So much for spreading the wealth.

During that 1986-97 stretch, East St. Louis Lincoln claimed three of its four firsts, Chicago King donned three crowns, Proviso East picked up a pair of its three Class AA titles, and Peoria Manual set the gold standard with four consecutive championships.

It was the golden age of dynasties for the large-school state finals.

The five titles following Manual's four-peat in 1997 went to first-time state champions. But then Peoria Central strung the 2003 and 2004 crowns to tie Manual's state record of five trips to Class AA title games.

A look at the top four programs in the Class AA era:

PEORIA MANUAL
The Hits:

To appreciate how hard it is for a school to dominate, consider that Manual's five first-place trophies are tops after 99 years of state tourneys.

It took nearly a quarter-century to get the first one (1930), then 64 more years to add another. But the latter opened the floodgates for the Rams, and the hits just kept on coming.

In 1994, the only hint of hoggery in the making was post-sectional speculation in the *Peoria*

Journal Star that "a title this year could be the start of something grand."

Notice the newspaper waited until after the Rams had won what was historically the toughest of the then-14 Class AA sectionals.

From 1994-97, the Peoria Sectional boasted 11 top-16 teams. When told of the pile of letters the IHSA had from Quincy fans pleading not be routed through this sectional, one Peoria coach said: "Hey, we don't want to be here either."

The newspaper's speculation was based on a freshman (Sergio McClain) starting, a classmate (Marcus Griffin) budding, a pair of junior guards (Willie Coleman, Ivan Watson) ripening, and a wonderfully athletic senior (Brandun Hughes) surging.

"To win a championship in this state, it's not enough to be good; you also have to be lucky," warned Manual coach Dick Van Scyoc. He ought to know. In his 45th season as a head high school coach, "The Godfather" was within sight of the all-time record for prep victories — yet still searching for his first title.

The first jewel in Manual's unprecedented quadruple crown proved the hardest to swipe, at least spread-wise. But Hughes, regarded as one of the

258

two best all-around athletes in Peoria's storied schoolboy history, simply would not let the Rams lose.

He went a title-game-record 6-for-6 on threes the second half and made one-and-one foul shots with 3.6 seconds left for a one-point win over Carbondale.

Manual's Brandun Hughes drives to the hoop in a 1994 quarterfinal game against Chicago Westinghouse.

How athletic was Hughes? With a minute left and Manual leading by a point, the 6-footer, despite four fouls, skied to block a seemingly sure lay-up by Carbondale's 6-7 Rashad Tucker, who as a collegian would record the first triple-double in Missouri Valley Conference Tournament history.

Hughes graduated and Van Scyoc retired with a then state-record 826 wins.

But the beat went on for the South Side in Peoria's unit district of four high schools.

Assistant Coach Wayne McClain, a starter on Manual's fourth-place team in the first Class AA finals, took over. He was buoyed by fellow Rams aide Chuck Westendorf, who in 2003 and 2004 would run his gold-medal collection to six by assisting Peoria Central's state champs.

Only Carbondale would finish within a point of Manual while it was running its four-year post-season record to 32-0. But there were plenty of potential pitfalls on the road to dynasty.

There was the missed three-pointer by Joliet Township at the end of Manual's two-point state semifinal win in 1995. There was the made 24-footer by sophomore Frank Williams at the final buzzer to break a sectional tie in 1996 and avenge an overtime shootout loss to East Peoria. Then came Springfield Lanphier and its five Division I college prospects in the 1996 super-sectional.

And finally, the 18-4 deficit in the legendary 1997 semifinal battle with Harvey Thornton, to be followed in a matter of hours by the four-point fourth-quarter deficit to West Aurora in the title game.

If a program's greatness is measured by the ferocity of its foes, the Rams can credit Harvey Thornton, the mother of all state-tourney roadblocks, for three-quarters of the icing on their four-layer cake.

It started for Thornton in the 1995 quarterfinals when it brought down Chicago Farragut, which boasted Kevin Garnett (1995 Mr. Basketball and national prep player of the year) and Ronnie Fields (1996 Mr. Basketball). Maybe that was an omen, since Manual was the only other team to beat Farragut that season.

The three years of epic Manual-Thornton battles are detailed elsewhere in this book. Suffice it to say that but for Manual and McClain, Thornton and Rocky Hill would have been what this dynasty article was about.

The nuance is in the numbers for 1997 national prep coach of the year McClain, who lost only five of his first 99 games and won his first 28 state-tourney contests.

The frustration is in the figures for Hill, who lost only four games his first three seasons — three of them to Manual on the final day of three straight seasons.

The lone consolation for Thornton's would-be dynasty was finishing second to Manual in the final 1997 national rankings by *USA Today*.

The Misses:

What might have been Manual's best-ever team did not take a trophy. That's because what Manual was to Thornton, Quincy was to Manual. Despite winning two-thirds of 1,226 games, the conservative Van Scyoc went 0-6 against Quincy under the flamboyant Jerry Leggett.

The most hurtful wound was inflicted by the most unlikely assassin, an unranked Quincy squad with starters averaging only six feet tall. And the death blow for those unbeaten and top-rated (in the state and nation) Rams in that 1987 quarterfinal might just as well have been delivered by the proverbial David, as 5-foot-6 guard James Bailey, who slung in a 26-footer at the overtime buzzer for a 61-59 stunner.

continued on next page

The next year, Manual reversed a pair of conference losses in bumping off top-ranked Central in the Peoria Sectional before losing to state champ East St. Louis Lincoln in the semis and settling for the third-place trophy.

Quincy played the roll of spoiler again in 1990 when the No. 7 Blue Devils upended the No. 3 Rams by one point in super-sectional play at Carver Arena after Manual missed two free throws with no time left.

Manual bounced back to finish second in 1991. And the rest of the 1990s is legend.

EAST ST. LOUIS LINCOLN
The Hits:

On the theory it takes one to know one, consider what Peoria Central coach Chuck Buescher said in 1989 just moments after suffering perhaps the most heart-breaking title loss ever.

"Believe me, I know how hard it is to win a championship in this state, and that man just won his third in a row. My hat's off to him."

That man was Bennie Lewis, the coach of East St. Louis Lincoln's four 1980s title teams and boss of that bygone school's entire 20-5 mark in Sweet Sixteen play.

And after Lincoln folded into East St. Louis Senior for the 1998-99 school year, Lewis added a 4-2 Sweet Sixteen record and a third-place trophy.

That's 24-7 doing battle against the cream of the crop in a state famous for growing corn and basketball stars.

There is even something special about three of those seven losses — they came at the hands of eventual state champions.

It not only took an eventual state champ to deny Lincoln a fourth straight title in 1990, it took unbeaten, No. 1-in-the-nation Chicago King.

Lewis never met a championship game he didn't win.

There was something special about the 1989 Lincoln-Peoria Central showdown. And not necessarily that it was the first triple-overtime title game or that it made the Tigers the first program to three-peat.

Arguably it was the hardest-fought title contest in a tournament now on the eve of its centennial. Certainly it was the longest. And it took one of the Class AA tourney's two most-famous title shots to keep it from going into a fourth overtime.

Emotionally and physically drained spectators who called it "a game-and-a-half" were not far from the technical truth.

The Misses:

About all the Tigers missed in the '80s was a shot at Quincy.

The 1982 squad, which Lewis has called his best ever, not getting a chance to break Quincy's state-record winning string of 64 games. Chicago Mendel Catholic beat Lincoln to the punch in a one-point semifinal that ended with Quincy just missing a miracle tip-in at the buzzer.

Even so, Quincy continued to bedevil Lincoln, making the Tigers' workmanlike title win seem anticlimactic after the Douglas brothers' last-second heroics in the third-place game.

PROVISO EAST
The Hits:

Although this article is restricted to Class AA dynasties in general and the so-called golden age of domination in particular, Proviso's part began with its one-class crown in 1969 under Tom Millikin with standout Jim Brewer.

They laid the groundwork for a trio of titles: 1974 under Glenn Whittenberg and 1991 and 1992 under alumnus Bill Hitt to go with Whittenberg's 1981 runner-up finish to unbeatable Quincy.

And perhaps those 1969 Pirates have an even more significant claim to social fame, having risen above the chaos of rapid racial change in the district to unite a school by replacing prejudice with pride.

In 1974, Joe Ponsetto, the straight-talking, blue-collar banger who led the championship charge, was the perfect player for Whittenberg's disciplined, conservative style.

In 1991, "The Three Amigos" — a major-college trio of Sherrell Ford (Illinois-Chicago), Donnie Boyce (Colorado) and Michael Finley (Wisconsin) — were the perfect match for any coach.

Despite that squad ending up 32-1 and state champion, Hitt felt his team, one of only a handful to boast three consensus all-staters, didn't play up to its potential down the stretch. "There was so much hype and pressure we started playing not to lose," Hitt said.

He doubtless enjoyed the next season more. With the Three Amigos graduated and only one starter (6-4 Jamal

Robinson) standing over 6-3, the Pirates parlayed teamwork into a 33-0 record.

Hitt reached the quarterfinals in 1993 but fell victim to Chicago King's unbeaten champs. He left coaching after that season with a 235-55 record (.810).

The Misses:

Proviso East fans might be forgiven for feeling that getting to state is the hardest part. After all, the school has survived its nasty sectional grouping only 10 times the last 38 seasons — but half of those Sweet Sixteen entries netted four championships and a runner-up trophy.

The Pirates' sectional route has taken a heavy toll, denying Sweet Sixteen fans so much as a glimpse of Glenn "Doc" Rivers (1978-80), one of the finest all-around players ever produced in Illinois. In fact, the 1980 Pirates carried a No. 1 national ranking.

And that wasn't the only time talent did not pace the Pirates to state booty.

Proviso East's 2001 and 2002 teams never reached the Elite Eight despite a pair of players (Dee Brown and Shannon Brown) who in 2005 would be instrumental in getting Illinois and Michigan State to the NCAA Final Four.

CHICAGO KING

The Hits:

Many would argue an article about Chicago King and colorful coach Landon "Sonny" Cox belongs in this book's all-star section rather than its dynasty department.

In theory, King was then a school with open enrollment for Chicago students looking to work in television. In practice,

Cox made it a school for basketball players looking to be *on* television.

But there is no denying Cox's two decades at King (1982-2002) were stunningly successful with an average of 25 wins per season. And one nine-season span during the era of state dynasties was particularly prolific.

By the numbers — 1986 (1st place at 32-1); 1987 (2nd at 28-5); 1988 (lost Chicago Public League final, 25-5); 1989 (3rd at 31-2); 1990 (1st at 32-0); 1991 (lost CPL semifinal, 26-2), 1992 (lost CPL final, 27-2); 1993 (1st, 32-0); 1994 (lost CPL final, 29-1).

By the totals — 9 years, 262 wins, 18 losses, 3 firsts, 1 second, 1 third. (Not to mention Sonny's state-finals swan song — third in 1999 at 28-7.)

King's 1990 edition was named national champion. But its 1993 squad looked even better after the Jaguars beat their four Sweet Sixteen foes by an average of more than 30 points a game.

It took the state finals 72 years to come up with a seven-footer — and even then, Effingham's 7-2 Uwe Blab had to be imported from Germany. Ten years later in 1990, Cox didn't go nearly so far to fetch two seven-footers in freshmen Rashard Griffith and Thomas Hamilton III.

Under Cox, King came up with three Mr. Basketballs — Liberty in 1987 (also named the nation's top prep player), Jamie Brandon in 1990 and Griffith in 1993. King players came in second in three Mr. Basketball elections.

The Misses:

The once-beaten, second-ranked team was zapped in the 1992 Public League final when Kiwane Garris (27 points) and David Greer (19) went off for No. 8 Westinghouse, which held Griffith to 11.

The third-ranked, once-beaten 1989 team handed state and national ratings leader Simeon and Mr. Basketball Deon Thomas their only loss in the CPL final, only to come up short against state champ East St. Louis Lincoln in the semis.

The unbeaten, top-rated 1994 squad was nipped by a point in the CPL final by sixth-rated Westinghouse.

King's Levertis Robinson signals the Jaguars' first state title in 1986.

LEFT:
Proviso East's Ray Gay jumps to block a shot against King in the 1993 quarterfinals.

Coach Landon "Sonny" Cox led King to three state championships and two other trophies in eight seasons from 1986 to 1993.

1990 AA

CHICAGO (KING)
Class AA State Champions of 1990

FRONT ROW (left to right):
Fred Sculfield, Jerard Billingsley,
Michael Irvin, Anthony King,
Keith Johnson. SECOND ROW:
Noah Miller, Anton Little,
Jamie Brandon, Rashard Griffith,
Johnny Selvie, Damian Porter,
Ahmad Shareef, Chayim
Cunningham, Sylvester Ware.

East St. Louis Lincoln's bid to extend its run of state championships to four was improbable. Even so, it took eventual state and mythical national champion Chicago King to end it with an 11-point decision in the semifinals.

But at least the pollsters were learning. The final regular-season poll had East St. Louis Lincoln ranked No. 16 at 15-7, the most losses from 1972 to 1999 for a Class AA top-16 team. If not a scientific pick, at least it was a smartly sentimental one.

In the only all-Windy City title game in state history, top-ranked King (32-0) won 65-55 over fourth-rated Gordon Tech (30-2). It was the second Chicago title in four years for King and Coach Landon "Sonny" Cox.

Gordon Tech junior Tom Kleinschmidt won the battles, scoring 27 in the title game and averaging 30.3 for the state finals.

But King won the war with senior guard-forward Jamie Brandon getting 25 points and a dozen rebounds, teammate Rashard Griffith making his title debut as a 6-11 freshman with 12 points on 6-for-6 shooting, and Johnny Selvie adding 17 points and 11 boards.

Mr. Basketball winner Brandon ended four years of Sweet Sixteen play with a 10-3 record, trophies for first, second, and third, a 20.7 scoring average, and an all-time tournament career record of

269 points. His all-games career total of 3,157 ranks third on the state's all-time scoring list.

After winning 30 consecutive games in the state tournament series, East St. Louis Lincoln and coach Bennie Lewis settled for third with a one-point win over Quincy in the last Sweet Sixteen for coach Jerry Leggett (528-233).

The Tigers' chances had been boosted by the addition of two starters from East St. Louis Assumption's 1989 Class A quarterfinal team. Maurice Horton and Artagus Williams joined up after the private school was shut down.

Gordon Tech, a school of 1,946 boys whose doubled enrollment of 3,892 made it the third-largest school to reach a Class AA title game, had to survive a 72-70 quarterfinal scare from Rolling Meadows and 43-point scorer Mike Lipnisky.

King's coach also wound up on top when *USA Today* named Cox prep coach of the year.

State Final Tournament Scores

Super-Sectionals

At Rockford [Metro Centre]—Elgin 71, Sterling 64
At Carbondale [SIU]—East St. Louis (Lincoln) 51, Marion 47 (OT)
At DeKalb [NIU]—Aurora (West) 45, Hoffman Estates (Conant) 44
At Chicago [Amphitheatre]—Chicago (King) 83, Chicago (Westinghouse) 48
At Hinsdale (Central)—Chicago (Gordon Tech) 82, Blue Island (Eisenhower) 80
At Evanston [NU]—Rolling Meadows 68, Arlington Heights (Hersey) 64
At Aurora (East)—Chicago Heights (Bloom Twp.) 65, Joliet (West) 49
At Peoria [Carver Arena]—Quincy 58, Peoria (Manual) 57

Quarterfinals

East St. Louis (Lincoln) 64, Elgin 54
Chicago (King) 66, Aurora (West) 58
Chicago (Gordon Tech) 72, Rolling Meadows 70
Quincy 54, Chicago Heights (Bloom Twp.) 51

Semifinals

Chicago (King) 60, East St. Louis (Lincoln) 49
Chicago (Gordon Tech) 71, Quincy 62

Finals

East St. Louis (Lincoln) 61, Quincy 60 (third place)
Chicago (King) 65, Chicago (Gordon Tech) 55 (title)

Scoring Leaders

Player, School	G	FG	3P	FT	Pts
Tom Kleinschmidt, Chi. (Gordon Tech)	4	47	7	24	125
Jamie Brandon, Chicago (King)	4	39	2	26	106
Mike Lipnisky, Rolling Meadows	2	29	5	17	80
Chris McKinney, East St. Louis (Lincoln)	4	26	1	20	73
Antoine Gillespie, Chicago (Gordon Tech)	4	26	0	8	60

All-Tournament First Team

Player, School	Ht.	Yr.
Jamie Brandon, Chicago (King)	6-3	Sr.
Brandon Cole, Chicago Heights (Bloom Twp.)	6-1	Sr.
Tom Kleinschmidt, Chicago (Gordon Tech)	6-4	Jr.
Mike Lipnisky, Rolling Meadows	6-2	Sr.
Chris McKinney, East St. Louis (Lincoln)	6-2	Sr.
Todd Wemhoener, Quincy	6-2	Sr.

Championship Game Box Score

Assembly Hall, Champaign, March 17, 1990

CHICAGO (KING) (65)
Coach Landon "Sonny" Cox

Player	FG-A	3P-A	FT-A	Pts	PF	Rb	As	St	Bl
Jamie Brandon	11-20	0-1	3-7	25	4	12	4	2	0
Rashard Griffith	6-6	0-0	0-2	12	4	4	1	0	0
Damian Porter	0-3	0-0	1-2	1	0	3	1	0	0
Fred Sculfield	0-3	0-0	2-2	2	2	2	2	1	0
Johnny Selvie	8-13	0-0	1-1	17	1	11	1	0	1
Ahmad Shareef	1-5	0-0	6-7	8	2	1	4	3	1
Sylvester Ware	0-0	0-0	0-0	0	0	1	0	0	0
TEAM						1			
TOTAL	26-50	0-1	13-21	65	13	35	13	6	2

CHICAGO (GORDON TECH) (55)
Coach Steve Pappas

Player	FG-A	3P-A	FT-A	Pts	PF	Rb	As	St	Bl
Brian Allen	1-4	1-3	0-0	3	3	0	4	0	0
Jerrem Anderson	1-3	0-0	0-0	2	0	1	1	1	1
Jason Bey	1-2	0-0	0-0	2	1	3	1	0	0
Antoine Gillespie	5-13	0-1	2-4	12	3	13	0	0	0
Bernard Hopson	1-3	0-1	0-0	2	0	0	0	0	0
Tom Kleinschmidt	10-19	2-7	5-6	27	4	6	2	2	1
Anthony McGowan	0-1	0-0	0-0	0	0	0	0	0	0
Keith Starr	3-9	0-2	1-2	7	4	2	0	0	0
Arthur Stewart	0-1	0-0	0-0	0	0	0	0	0	0
TEAM						3			
TOTAL	22-55	3-14	8-12	55	15	28	8	3	2

Chicago (King)	16	14	19	16	—	65
Chicago (Gordon Tech)	14	14	14	13	—	55

Officials: Jim Lapetina, Bo Paprocki.

Cuonzo Martin looks upcourt on the fast break. Martin and his East St. Louis Lincoln teammates fell short of their goal of four consecutive state championships, losing to King in the semifinals.

Tom Kleinschmidt of Gordon Tech secures the ball while Brian McIntyre of Rolling Meadows reaches in. Steve Thompson watches in the background.

King's Jamie Brandon rebuffs a challenge from Brian Allen of Gordon Tech in the title contest. Brandon scored a record 269 points in 13 games in the state finals.

King's Johnny Selvie has that helpless feeling as West Aurora's Billy Taylor (44) passes to Michael Simmons (14) in a quarterfinal game. Morris Gray is ready to step in.

THE CITY GAME King's Ahmad Shareef flies past Anthony McGowan and Jason Bey of Gordon Tech. King won the first title game to pair two Chicago schools, 65-55.

1990AA

Those who insist high school basketball has become a game of guards didn't have to face Proviso East's terrific trio of tall talent.

Peoria Manual had 5-foot-10 point guard Howard Nathan, by five inches the shortest honoree in the first 22 years of Mr. Basketball (until 5-11 Dee Brown in 2002).

But top-ranked Proviso East had three future NBA players as its front line: 6-7 Sherrell Ford (23 points), 6-5 Donnie Boyce (15) and 6-6 Michael Finley (14).

Then again, Finley played like a guard in the title game, hounding Nathan into 33 percent shooting for his 19 points.

Both title-game teams could and would pass the ball. Proviso East simply did it at a higher level with a three-to-one advantage in future NBA players.

Fifth-rated Manual led 28-23 at intermission before Proviso East doubled its halftime count in a 23-9 third quarter. The final total was 68-61 as the Maywood school won its third championship.

The award-winning film *Hoop Dreams* documented the life and times of two Chicago-area high school basketball players: William Gates and Arthur Agee.

Gates, who played for St. Joseph, seemed destined for success but never made it to the state finals. Agee, who began at St. Joseph but ended up at Marshall, unexpectedly lived out the schoolboy fantasy of playing in the state finals after the Commandos upset King in the Chicago Public League semifinals.

However, Hollywood couldn't provide a storybook ending for Agee, who had to settle for third place.

The toughest pressure Proviso faced might have come from within, what with such great expectations for a team packed with three all-staters.

Pirates coach Bill Hitt did not see his team's state tourney struggles as a chemistry problem of too many scorers and only one ball.

"I think that with all the hype, we just started playing not to lose," Hitt said.

MAYWOOD (PROVISO EAST)
Class AA State Champions of 1991

FRONT ROW (left to right): Willie Colvin, Lonzell Yancy, James Jenkins, Robert Hopkins, Corey Chandler, Chris House. SECOND ROW: Johnny Perryman, Asst. Coach Jim Pecilunas, Asst. Coach Andrew Johnson, Asst. Coach Lawrence McCall, Asst. Coach David Holmes, Asst. Coach, Gene Mobley. STANDING: Jamal Robinson, Terence Horton, Donnie Boyce, Anthony Barthelemy, Sherell Ford, Walter Flowers, Coach Bill Hitt, Danny Jefferson, Michael Finley, Thaddeus Smith, Rodney Woodruff, Kenny Davis, Ray Gay.

State Final Tournament Scores
Super-Sectionals
At Evanston [NU]—Libertyville 61, Winnetka (New Trier) 39
At Aurora (East)—Country Club Hills (Hillcrest) 82, Aurora (Waubonsie Valley) 71
At Carbondale [SIU]—Carbondale 81, Collinsville 71
At Hinsdale (Central)—Maywood (Proviso East) 75, South Holland (Thornwood) 66
At DeKalb [NIU]—Batavia 61, Mt. Prospect (Prospect) 48
At Chicago [Amphitheatre]—Chicago (Marshall) 58, Chicago (Westinghouse) 38
At Peoria [Carver Arena]—Peoria (Manual) 77, Danville 50
At Rockford [Metro Centre]—Rock Island 69, Elgin (Larkin) 57

Quarterfinals
Libertyville 68, Country Club Hills (Hillcrest) 57
Maywood (Proviso East) 77, Carbondale 66
Chicago (Marshall) 56, Batavia 46
Peoria (Manual) 89, Rock Island 60

Semifinals
Maywood (Proviso East) 47, Libertyville 44
Peoria (Manual) 68, Chicago (Marshall) 55

Finals
Chicago (Marshall) 67, Libertyville 65 (third place)
Maywood (Proviso East) 68, Peoria (Manual) 61 (title)

Scoring Leaders

Player, School	G	FG	3P	FT	Pts
Howard Nathan, Peoria (Manual)	4	32	7	20	91
Sherrell Ford, Maywood (Proviso East)	4	30	5	18	83
Matt Williams, Libertyville	4	27	7	21	82
Andy Bauer, Libertyville	4	23	11	11	68
Cesare Christian, Chicago (Marshall)	4	24	7	6	61

All-Tournament First Team

Player, School	Ht.	Yr.
Dan Cross, Carbondale	6-2	Sr.
Michael Finley, Maywood (Proviso East)	6-4	Sr.
Sherrell Ford, Maywood (Proviso East)	6-6	Sr.
Howard Nathan, Peoria (Manual)	5-11	Sr.
Matt Williams, Libertyville	6-4	Sr.

Championship Game Box Score
Assembly Hall, Champaign, March 16, 1991
MAYWOOD (PROVISO EAST) (68)
Coach Bill Hitt

Player	FG-A	3P-A	FT-A	Pts	PF	Rb	As	St	Bl
Donnie Boyce	6-9	0-0	3-5	15	3	11	5	3	2
Kenny Davis	1-1	0-0	2-2	4	0	0	2	0	0
Michael Finley	6-10	0-0	2-5	14	2	4	2	0	1
Sherrell Ford	8-17	0-2	7-8	23	1	12	0	0	3
Ray Gay	0-2	0-1	0-0	0	2	3	1	0	0
Jamal Robinson	5-8	0-0	0-3	10	1	5	0	0	0
Thaddeus Smith	1-2	0-0	0-0	2	1	3	8	0	0
TEAM						0			
TOTAL	27-49	0-3	14-23	68	10	38	18	3	6

PEORIA (MANUAL) (61)
Coach Dick Van Scyoc

Player	FG-A	3P-A	FT-A	Pts	PF	Rb	As	St	Bl
Derek Booth	0-3	0-1	0-1	0	2	2	2	2	0
Sam Davis	0-4	0-0	0-0	0	2	3	0	0	0
Clint Ford	10-17	0-0	3-5	23	3	5	0	1	0
Tony Freeman	4-11	2-7	0-0	10	3	1	1	0	0
Mike Grayer	2-5	1-1	0-0	5	1	2	8	0	0
Jerry Hester	2-2	0-0	0-0	4	0	1	0	2	0
Howard Nathan	6-18	3-13	4-6	19	4	7	6	2	0
Lee Reddick	0-0	0-0	0-0	0	2	2	0	0	0
TEAM						3			
TOTAL	24-60	6-22	7-12	61	17	26	17	5	2

Maywood (Proviso East)	14	9	23	22	—	68
Peoria (Manual)	12	16	9	24	—	61

Officials: John Hornacek, Dan Korvas.

The closest state-finals call for the Pirates (32-1) was a three-point semifinal win over plucky Libertyville, which lost by two to Chicago Marshall in the third-place game but still took home what was then only the second boys basketball trophy in Lake County history (Waukegan was fourth in 1959).

Marshall, Manual's 68-55 victim in the semifinals, became a belated favorite on the big screen four years after the tournament was played.

And in the end, Proviso East was right where it was supposed to be, while No. 2 West Aurora and No. 3 Chicago King failed to reach the Sweet Sixteen.

Finley would become only the second IHSA product in nearly a century of state tourneys with both a prep championship and NBA all-star recognition on his résumé, having played in the 2001 and 2001 all-star games while with Dallas.

The other champ and all-star is Dike Eddleman (Centralia '42).

Sherrell Ford of Proviso East jokes with an unidentified victim after winning the state title.

Coach Bill Hitt of Proviso East looks pensive as his team works its way toward a state championship.

CONCENTRATED EFFORT

Clint Ford of Peoria Manual gets on the scoreboard in the championship game.

Jamal Robinson of Proviso East prepares to score while Mike Grayer of Peoria Manual looks on. Proviso East took the championship 68-61.

1991 AA

MAYWOOD (PROVISO EAST)
Class AA State Champions of 1992

FRONT ROW (left to right): Terrence Horton, Cedric Meredith, Shaheed Hadee, David Hart, Robert Hopkins. SECOND ROW: Asst. Coach Corey Cooper, Asst. Coach Johnny Perryman, Asst. Coach Gene Mobley, Asst. Coach Jim Pecilunas, Asst. Coach Andrew Johnson, Asst. Coach Tom Jeske, Asst. Coach Dave Holmes, Asst. Coach Frank Montgomery. STANDING: Asst. Coach Lawrence McCall, James Jenkins, Walter Flowers, Corey Chandler, Jamal Robinson, Tony Barthelemy, Kenneth Jones, Kenny Davis, Kevin Jones, Stefen Fisher, Ray Gay, Dymphna Gibson, Coach Bill Hitt.

1992 AA

When "The Three Amigos" graduated to major-college careers, defending champ Proviso East was left with players responsible for only 14 of its 68 title-game points and only 5 of its 38 rebounds.

But returnees who had honed their skills by going against state champs five days a week could hardly be called inexperienced. And all the dues they paid in practice banked a fourth set of gold medals for the Pirates.

The only unbeaten team coming into the state tournament left that way when top-ranked Proviso East beat seventh-rated Peoria Richwoods 42-31 to go the previous Pirates champion one better at 33-0. Six teams carried one-loss records into the postseason, where they all doubled their displeasure.

Enjoying his second consecutive state championship, Bill Hitt called it a victory for the program, as three Proviso East head coaches had a hand in four titles over 22 years.

This one came under the still-watchful eye of retired Tom Millikin, the only person to be a player (Pinckneyville '48), coach (Proviso East '69), and principal (Proviso East '74) at state-title schools.

Returning regulars Jamal Robinson (at 6-foot-4 the only Proviso East starter over 6-2) and junior Kenny Davis led the balanced Pirates with Elite Eight averages of 14 and 13 points.

Richwoods got into trouble in the title game when star Troy Taylor picked up his second and third fouls in a 30-second span in the second quarter. Still boasting three players capable of taking the ball to the basket, Richwoods went to a four-corners offense to protect a 14-12 first-quarter lead. But the only team that strategy slowed was Richwoods, which scored only two points each in the second and third quarters to trail 29-18.

It was the lowest scoring championship game since Dike Eddleman suited up for Centralia half a century earlier.

But it was a laugher compared to previous Proviso East struggles, which included trailing three times (once by 16) before reaching Champaign, there to survive Collinsville by two in the quarterfinals.

Future Fighting Illini Richard Keene led Collinsville in that 53-51 loss with 29 points and six treys.

Proviso East had to put down another celebrated Illini, guard Kiwane Garris of third-place Chicago Westinghouse, in a 64-47 semifinal.

State Final Tournament Scores

Super-Sectionals
At Carbondale [SIU]—Collinsville 49, Mt. Vernon 46
At Hinsdale (Central)—Maywood (Proviso East) 63, Dolton (Thornridge) 55
At Chicago [UIC]—Chicago (Westinghouse) 76, Chicago (King) 68
At DeKalb [NIU]—Aurora (East) 62, Palatine (Fremd) 50
At Rockford [Metro Centre]—Rockford (Boylan) 70, Elgin (Larkin) 54
At Aurora (East)—Bradley (B.-Bourbonnais) 75, Country Club Hills (Hillcrest) 50
At Peoria [Carver Arena]—Peoria (Richwoods) 67, Danville 53
At Evanston [NU]—Lincolnshire (Stevenson) 75, Northbrook (Glenbrook North) 73 (3 OT)

Quarterfinals
Maywood (Proviso East) 53, Collinsville 51
Chicago (Westinghouse) 63, Aurora (East) 42
Rockford (Boylan) 49, Bradley (B.-Bourbonnais) 47
Peoria (Richwoods) 86, Lincolnshire (Stevenson) 75

Semifinals
Maywood (Proviso East) 64, Chicago (Westinghouse) 47
Peoria (Richwoods) 47, Rockford (Boylan) 46

Finals
Chicago (Westinghouse) 96, Rockford (Boylan) 69 (third place)
Maywood (Proviso East) 42, Peoria (Richwoods) 31 (title)

Scoring Leaders

Player, School	G	FG	3P	FT	Pts
David Greer, Chicago (Westinghouse)	4	35	1	5	95
Sean Kimble, Peoria (Richwoods)	4	28	0	16	72
Kiwane Garris, Chicago (Westinghouse)	4	14	0	10	65
Michael Slaughter, Rockford (Boylan)	4	29	0	5	63
Kenny Davis, Maywood (Proviso East)	4	20	9	12	61

All-Tournament First Team

Player, School	Ht.	Yr.
Kenny Davis, Maywood (Proviso East)	5-11	Jr.
David Greer, Chicago (Westinghouse)	6-6	Sr.
Richard Keene, Collinsville	6-4	Sr.
Jamal Robinson, Maywood (Proviso East)	6-5	Sr.
Troy Taylor, Peoria (Richwoods)	6-4	Sr.

Championship Game Box Score
Assembly Hall, Champaign, March 21, 1992

MAYWOOD (PROVISO EAST) (42)
Coach Bill Hitt

Player	FG-A	3P-A	FT-A	Pts	PF	Rb	As	St	Bl
Tony Barthelemy	2-7	0-0	0-3	4	1	6	2	0	0
Corey Chandler	0-0	0-0	0-0	0	0	0	0	0	0
Kenny Davis	4-8	1-3	1-3	10	2	0	0	1	0
Stefan Fisher	0-0	0-0	0-0	0	0	0	0	0	0
Walter Flowers	0-1	0-0	0-0	0	0	1	0	0	0
Ray Gay	4-5	0-1	0-0	8	1	3	1	0	0
Terence Horton	0-0	0-0	0-0	0	0	0	0	0	0
James Jenkins	1-4	0-0	0-0	2	0	5	1	1	0
Kevin Jones	2-3	0-0	2-2	6	3	4	0	0	1
Jamal Robinson	3-6	0-0	6-11	12	1	12	1	1	3
TEAM						0			
TOTAL	16-34	1-4	9-19	42	8	31	5	3	4

PEORIA (RICHWOODS) (31)
Coach Wayne Hammerton

Player	FG-A	3P-A	FT-A	Pts	PF	Rb	As	St	Bl
Greg Clore	0-7	0-0	1-2	1	2	2	0	0	0
Brian Franklin	0-1	0-1	0-0	0	1	0	1	0	0
Neil Hess	0-0	0-0	0-0	0	0	0	0	0	0
Sean Kimble	5-15	0-1	1-2	11	2	6	0	0	0
Frank McIntosh	5-8	2-5	3-3	15	3	4	0	2	0
Earnest Rodgers	0-0	0-0	0-0	0	0	0	0	0	0
Nick Rutherford	0-0	0-0	0-0	0	0	0	0	2	0
Troy Taylor	1-4	0-1	2-4	4	4	2	1	1	1
Jarvis Williams	0-0	0-0	0-0	0	2	0	0	1	1
TEAM						3			
TOTAL	11-35	2-8	7-11	31	14	17	2	6	2

Maywood (Proviso East)	12	8	9	13	—	42
Peoria (Richwoods)	14	2	2	13		31

Officials: Tom Abramowicz, Lionell Yates.

Terrance Nicholas of Westinghouse blocks a shot by Boylan's Johnny Hernandez in the third-place game. Durell Banks (23) and Kiwane Garris (22) await the rebound.

BLOCK PARTY

Jim Flynn of the IHSA presents Batavia's Corey Williams with a plaque for winning the inaugural slam-dunk competition.

Tom Barthelemy of Proviso East and Tim Reynolds of Collinsville battle for a rebound in a quarterfinal game.

Sean Kimble of Peoria Richwoods plays keep away with Jonas Jocson of Stevenson in a quarterfinal battle.

1992AA

Flying high for the rebound, Jamal Robinson of Proviso East towers over the Peoria Richwoods defenders. Proviso won its second straight title 42-31.

CHICAGO (KING)
Class AA State Champions of 1993

FRONT ROW (left to right): Coach Landon "Sonny" Cox, Ronald Minter, Alexander Morris, Leonard Myles. SECOND ROW: Dewarren Stewart, Jermaine Williams, Michael Hermon, Toporis Nash, Eddie Washington, Thomas Hamilton, Rashard Griffith, Antone Simmons, Lamont Adams, Jerard Billingsley, Harold Mapp, Larry Allaway.

Not only did this year feature the sec-second, third, and fourth seven-footers to play in the state tournament, two of them played for the same team — unbeaten and top-ranked Chicago King — with predictable results.

Mr. Basketball winner Rashard Griffith (7-0) wasn't even the tallest player on his team. That honor went to 7-2 senior classmate Thomas Hamilton III.

The only question was how — without chainsaws — Rockford Guilford lasted so long in a championship game that King won 79-42 thanks to a 32-2 fourth quarter.

When the carnage had cleared, the Jaguars (32-0) had Sweet Sixteen point spreads of 25, 28, 31 and 37 to win going away.

The latter was the widest margin of victory in any Class AA Elite Eight game, overtaking the 35-point spread in Dolton Thornridge's 1972 title win. And King's average Sweet Sixteen victory margin of 30.25 points per game broke the record of Quincy '81 — albeit by only a quarter-point.

King's lineup was so powerful that neither of its all-state 7-footers was the title-game scoring leader. That honor went to DeWarren Stewart, with 19 points.

By the tourament's conclusion, King coach Landon "Sonny" Cox owned a state-record winning percentage of .900 for his first 13 seasons (he would end up with a record mark of .850) and King ('90 and '93) and LaGrange Lyons ('53 and '70) were the only Class AA schools to post a pair of perfect seasons.

Giants abounded in the second quarterfinal session at Assembly Hall. The opener matched 7-1 Jamar Holcomb of Glenbrook North against 6-11 Keon Clark of Danville, with the latter team prevailing in a 60-40 split.

King then took the floor against two-time defending champion Proviso East. That 82-54 laugher pretty much ended serious talk of final-day upsets.

It was the second time in four years King had to hurdle a defending champ at state en route to a title.

Cox, who was fond of touting the Chicago Public League playoffs as a harder place to win than Champaign, made his own point. King would win 6 of 10 CPL finals, and in all six of those seasons the Jaguars netted at worst a third-place finish at state.

State Final Tournament Scores
Super-Sectionals
At DeKalb [NIU]—Palatine (Fremd) 66, Naperville (Central) 59
At Aurora (East)—Bradley (B.-Bourbonnais) 68, Lockport (Twp.) 58
At Rockford [Metro Centre]—Rockford (Guilford) 55, LaSalle (L.-Peru) 48
At Carbondale [SIU]—Edwardsville 58, Centralia 45
At Normal [ISU]—Danville 59, Springfield 40
At Evanston [NU]—Northbrook (Glenbrook North) 70, Libertyville 68 (2 OT)
At Chicago [UIC]—Chicago (King) 77, Chicago (Westinghouse) 52
At Hinsdale (Central)—Maywood (Proviso East) 76, Harvey (Thornton) 66

Quarterfinals
Palatine (Fremd) 50, Bradley (B.-Bourbonnais) 48
Rockford (Guilford) 48, Edwardsville 40
Danville 60, Northbrook (Glenbrook North) 40
Chicago (King) 82, Maywood (Proviso East) 54

Semifinals
Rockford (Guilford) 60, Palatine (Fremd) 58
Chicago (King) 69, Danville 38

Finals
Danville 42, Palatine (Fremd) 36 (third place)
Chicago (King) 79, Rockford (Guilford) 42 (title)

Scoring Leaders

Player, School	G	FG	3P	FT	Pts
Rashard Griffith, Chicago (King)	4	27	0	16	70
Thomas Hamilton, Chicago (King)	4	28	0	7	63
DeWarren Stewart, Chicago (King)	4	22	7	10	61
Ben Holmstrom, Rockford (Guilford)	4	24	0	12	60
Mike Mangan, Palatine (Fremd)	4	23	0	10	56

All-Tournament First Team

Player, School	Ht.	Yr.
Keon Clark, Danville	6-11	Sr.
Rashard Griffith, Chicago (King)	7-0	Sr.
Thomas Hamilton, Chicago (King)	7-2	Sr.
Ben Holmstrom, Rockford (Guilford)	6-8	Jr.
DeWarren Stewart, Chicago (King)	6-0	Sr.

Championship Game Box Score
Assembly Hall, Champaign, March 20, 1993

CHICAGO (KING) (79)
Coach Landon "Sonny" Cox

Player	FG-A	3P-A	FT-A	Pts	PF	Rb	As	St	Bl
Lamont Adams	0-0	0-0	0-0	0	0	0	0	0	0
Larry Allaway	1-2	0-0	0-0	2	2	0	1	2	0
Jerrad Billingsley	6-11	0-0	2-4	14	1	4	1	3	1
Rashard Griffith	3-5	0-0	5-5	11	3	10	3	0	2
Thomas Hamilton	7-14	0-0	2-3	16	1	10	3	0	2
Michael Hermon	1-7	0-0	0-0	2	3	3	1	2	0
Harold Mapp	0-1	0-1	0-0	0	0	0	0	0	0
Ronald Minter	2-6	1-4	0-0	5	1	5	3	2	0
Alexander Morris	1-1	0-0	0-0	2	0	0	0	0	0
Leonard Myles	1-1	0-0	0-0	2	1	0	0	1	0
Toporis Nash	0-0	0-0	0-0	0	0	2	0	0	0
Antone Simmons	0-1	0-0	0-0	0	0	0	0	0	0
DeWarren Stewart	7-15	2-6	3-4	19	0	4	0	2	0
Eddie Washington	2-6	0-0	0-0	4	2	5	1	2	0
Jermaine Williams	0-1	0-0	2-2	2	0	1	0	0	0
TEAM						1			
TOTAL	31-71	3-11	14-18	79	14	45	13	14	5

ROCKFORD (GUILFORD) (42)
Coach Mike Miller

Player	FG-A	3P-A	FT-A	Pts	PF	Rb	As	St	Bl
Wayne Bailey	0-1	0-0	0-0	0	0	1	0	0	0
Rob Buss	0-1	0-0	0-0	0	0	0	0	0	0
Tony Fletcher	4-9	0-0	6-8	14	4	3	1	0	0
Hank Haime	0-0	0-0	0-0	0	0	0	0	0	0
Chuck Hanserd	0-0	0-0	0-0	0	1	3	2	0	0
Ben Holmstrom	3-8	0-2	0-0	6	3	4	0	0	1
Dan Kroger	2-5	2-5	1-2	7	0	3	1	0	0
Ernie McConnell	0-2	0-0	0-0	0	0	1	0	0	0
Eric Porchia	0-0	0-0	0-0	0	0	0	0	0	0
Dan Rahn	0-1	0-0	0-0	0	1	0	0	0	0
Kevin Rennert	0-5	0-1	0-0	0	1	5	0	1	0
Johnny Rucker	6-19	0-4	0-0	12	2	7	4	2	1
Andy Saunders	0-1	0-1	0-0	0	0	1	0	0	0
Jeremy Sherman	0-1	0-0	0-0	0	0	0	0	0	0
Brian Thiede	1-3	1-2	0-0	3	1	1	1	0	0
TEAM						5			
TOTAL	16-56	3-15	7-10	42	13	34	9	3	2

Chicago (King)		15	18	14	32	— 79
Rockford (Guilford)		13	13	14	2	— 42

Officials: Michael Devening, Ken Thaxton.

Celebrating 100 years of IHSA Boys Basketball Tournaments

Guilford's Johnny Rucker is too late to stop the shot in the title game against King. King used a 32-2 margin in the final quarter to capture its third title in eight years.

King's Rashard Griffith elevates to score over the defense of Guilford's Brian Thiede in the championship match-up.

King's Thomas Hamilton unloads with a monster dunk. Hamilton was one of two seven-footers on the Chicago squad.

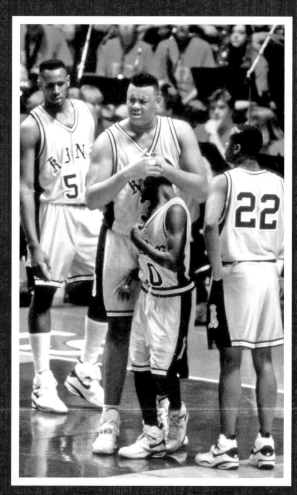

THE LONG AND SHORT OF IT

Hamilton (7-foot-2) puts the squeeze on teammate Ronald Minter, a mere 6-footer. Rashard Griffith, King's other tower, looms in the background.

DeWarren Steward of King eludes Proviso East's Donte Parker in a quarterfinal contest.

1993AA

Like so many Illinois schoolboys, Brandun Hughes had been in this situation before. But only in his dreams.

Down one. Only a couple of ticks left on the clock. One-and-one free throws. State title on the line.

And just as he had so often dreamed it on so many driveways, playgrounds and

and pulled down 17 rebounds in the loss to Manual. And it took 37 points by tourney scoring champ Troy Hudson of Carbondale to overcome Joliet's Ty Calderwood (28) and Gary Bell (27), who combined for 55 points.

But while the title game was a storybook ending to the prep career of

prep coaching victories, surpassing the legendary Arthur Trout, who went 809-344 at Centralia from 1914 to 1951.

Van Scyoc downplayed his accomplishments by saying, "If you coach long enough, you see everything happen." Then he walked the walk, stepping down from coaching and away from what

PEORIA (MANUAL)
Class AA State Champions of 1994

FRONT ROW (left to right):
Brandon Allen, Courtland Tubbs, Ivan Watson, Willie Coleman, Jimmie Cross, Jeff Walraven.
SECOND ROW: Coach Dick Van Scyoc, Tony Byrd, Sergio McClain, Kahlil Gayton, Marcus Griffin, Willie Simmons, Brandun Hughes, Darrell Ivory, Mgr. Sidney South.

gym floors, the senior guard swished the shots that set the championship score at Peoria Manual 61, Carbondale 60.

And why not? Hughes had hit all six of his second-half three-point shots for 13th-ranked Manual (27-6) against eighth-rated Carbondale (28-4).

Both title-game teams were improbable trophy winners, what with drawing the two top-ranked Elite Eight entries in the quarterfinals. The third-place game was even more surprising, matching a pair of unrated teams, LaGrange Lyons and Rockford Boylan.

In the quarterfinals, Manual ousted sixth-ranked Chicago Westinghouse, which had stunned top-rated and undefeated defending state champ Chicago King in the Chicago Public League title game. Meanwhile, Carbondale sidelined unbeaten and second-ranked Joliet Township.

LaGrange, in a game that marked the end of Ron Nikcevich's 33-year coaching career at 562-288, beat Boylan 56-42 for third.

It was the Sweet Sixteen of shooting stars, with several gunners going down in a blaze of baskets.

Collinsville's Cory Garcia (39) and John Curry (26) combined for 65 points only to fall a step short of Champaign in an 86-78 super-sectional loss to Carbondale. Westinghouse center Damion Dantzler poured in 35 points

Hughes, the season proved to be the final chapter in the legendary saga of Manual coach Dick Van Scyoc.

The season left the 45-year head coach (28 at Manual) with his first state championship and an 826-400 mark that includes the all-time state record for boys'

would become the longest title streak in state basketball history.

Call it tradition. Telfer Mead, the rookie boss of Manual's only previous state title in 1930, promptly left prep coaching. Now, 64 years later, Manual was beginning another tradition.

State Final Tournament Scores

Super-Sectionals

At Normal [ISU]—Peoria (Manual) 65, Danville 56
At Chicago [UIC]—Chicago (Westinghouse) 59, Chicago (King) 58
At Rockford [Metro Centre]—Rockford (Boylan) 63, Geneseo (Darnall) 59
At Evanston [NU]—Libertyville 61, Chicago (Weber) 52
At Aurora (East)—Joliet (Twp.) 72, Downers Grove (South) 59
At Carbondale [SIU]—Carbondale 86, Collinsville 78
At Hinsdale (Central)—LaGrange (Lyons) 48, Chicago (Brother Rice) 40
At DeKalb [NIU]—Hoffman Estates (Conant) 69, Naperville (North) 56

Quarterfinals

Peoria (Manual) 81, Chicago (Westinghouse) 76
Rockford (Boylan) 79, Libertyville 70
Carbondale 92, Joliet (Twp.) 80
LaGrange (Lyons) 59, Hoffman Estates (Conant) 51

Semifinals

Peoria (Manual) 80, Rockford (Boylan) 67
Carbondale 70, LaGrange (Lyons) 54

Finals

LaGrange (Lyons) 56, Rockford (Boylan) 42 (third place)
Peoria (Manual) 61, Carbondale 60 (title)

Scoring Leaders

Player, School	G	FG	3P	FT	Pts
Troy Hudson, Carbondale	4	31	14	33	109
Brandun Hughes, Peoria (Manual)	4	39	10	9	97
Lee Lampley, Rockford (Boylan)	4	27	10	15	79
Rashad Tucker, Carbondale	4	27	0	21	75
Steve Davis, LaGrange (Lyons)	4	25	0	4	54

All-Tournament First Team

Player, School	Ht.	Yr.
Damion Dantzler, Chicago (Westinghouse)	6-8	Sr.
Troy Hudson, Carbondale	6-1	Sr.
Brandun Hughes, Peoria (Manual)	6-0	Sr.
Lee Lampley, Rockford (Boylan)	6-0	Sr.
Rashad Tucker, Carbondale	6-7	Sr.

Championship Game Box Score

Assembly Hall, Champaign, March 19, 1994

PEORIA (MANUAL) (61)
Coach Dick Van Scyoc

Player	FG-A	3P-A	FT-A	Pts	PF	Rb	As	St	Bl
Brandon Allen	0-1	0-0	0-0	0	1	0	0	1	0
Willie Coleman	3-5	0-0	0-0	6	3	0	5	2	0
Jimmie Cross	1-3	1-3	0-0	3	0	0	0	0	0
Marcus Griffin	0-0	0-0	0-0	0	0	0	0	0	0
Brandun Hughes	9-20	6-10	3-4	27	4	5	2	0	1
Darrell Ivory	2-3	0-0	0-0	4	3	6	1	1	0
Sergio McClain	4-7	0-0	1-1	9	3	5	1	0	0
Courtland Tubbs	0-0	0-0	0-0	0	1	0	0	0	0
Ivan Watson	5-12	2-5	0-0	12	3	3	4	2	0
TEAM						2			
TOTAL	24-51	9-18	4-5	61	18	21	13	6	1

CARBONDALE (60)
Coach Tim Bleyer

Player	FG-A	3P-A	FT-A	Pts	PF	Rb	As	St	Bl
Dylan Bates	3-5	1-3	2-2	9	2	1	5	0	0
Leinad Cross	1-1	0-0	2-4	4	4	4	0	0	1
Donald Green	5-8	0-0	1-1	11	1	5	0	0	0
Troy Hudson	6-20	2-11	6-6	20	1	2	2	1	0
Tony Penn	0-0	0-0	2-2	2	3	1	1	1	0
Rashad Tucker	5-8	0-0	4-6	14	2	14	3	1	1
TEAM						1			
TOTAL	20-42	3-14	17-21	60	13	28	11	3	2

Peoria (Manual)	15	10	19	17	—	61
Carbondale	12	16	17	15	—	60

Officials: Charles Brown, Jessie Knighten.

1994 AA

Troy Hudson, Carbondale guard, dribbles between his legs to get past the pressure of Manual's Jimmie Cross in the championship game.

Carbondale's Rashad Tucker pushes past Steve Davis of Lyons Township in a semifinal game won by Carbondale.

Brandun Hughes seems to change directions in mid-air to avoid contact with Westinghouse's Ty Juan Finley in quarterfinal action.

UNSCHEDULED FLIGHT

Joyous Manual players hug at center court after notching the school's first state title since 1930.

Dick Van Scyoc closed out his historic career with a state record for games won and his first state title after 45 years of coaching.

1994AA

271

a team with more athletes, McClain said: "Yes, but we have more *basketball players*."

Sure enough, Manual got 20-point games from senior all-state guards Willie Coleman (title-game record seven steals) and Ivan Watson in a 65-53 title win. All-around Thornton athlete Tai Streets moved on to a football career in the Big Ten and NFL, a path that would be followed by sophomore teammate Antwaan Randle El.

Seconds after the final buzzer, Manual players were sporting "Back2Back" caps, courtesy of a semi-superstitious follower who had not told a soul of his preparation. "We lose, they'd say I jinxed us," he said.

The first modern state-title meeting of first-year head coaches produced some wonderful basketball (not to mention wardrobe wonders with Hill's school-color purple suits). But the state's most colorful trophy rivalry was just beginning to bloom.

PEORIA (MANUAL)
Class AA State Champions of 1995

FRONT ROW (left to right): Sergio McClain, Sean Walls, Ivan Watson, Jeff Walraven, Charles Russell, Willie Williams, Tim Caldwell. SECOND ROW: Marcus Griffin, Frank Williams, Kahlil Gayton, Willie Simmons, Willie Coleman, Darrell Ivory, DeWayne Johnson, manager. THIRD ROW: Scorekeeper Jim Watson, Asst. Coach Tim Kenny, Coach Wayne McClain, Asst. Coach Chuck Westendorf, Business Mgr. Dana Davis, Mgr. Sidney South.

Peoria Manual coach Dick Van Scyoc left his successor nifty players but nasty pressure.

If the Rams won another state title, it would be Van Scyoc who'd built the juggernaut. If they didn't, it would be Wayne McClain who'd broken it.

Van Scyoc's legacy also included the prototype schedule for a team preparing to face an Illinois Sweet Sixteen.

Yet Wayne McClain, who had played for the state's all-time boys' win leader when Van Scyoc led the Rams to fourth in 1972, never whined and never blinked.

In the regular season, McClain and Manual went 10-1 against teams ranked in the top 16 at least sometime during the season, knocking off the No. 1s of Illinois (Chicago Farragut) and Missouri (St. Louis Vashon).

Second-ranked Manual was but one of four top-16 entries in the Peoria Sectional Complex, including Peoria Central and all-stater A.J. Guyton, who would be a Big Ten MVP at Indiana.

Then Manual needed to beat its historical nemesis, No. 14 Quincy, to reach Champaign for an Elite Eight also packed with the Nos. 1, 3, 5, 7 and 8 state squads.

"We actually wanted to play Farragut, because we had better guards," McClain said of the Chicago team ranked No. 1 despite its only loss coming against Manual at Thanksgiving.

But Harvey Thornton and coach Rocky Hill tore up that script and submitted one for a series of heavyweight bouts with Manual. Thornton felled Farragut and its two Mr. Basketballs (6-foot-11 Kevin Garnett this season, high-flyer

Ronnie Fields the next) 42-39 in the quarterfinals.

After a 28-point quarterfinal romp, McClain had to face his worst fear — third-ranked Joliet Township and its strong guard play. Manual had beaten Joliet by 16 at Pontiac. But in the state semifinals, the Steelmen had a three-pointer in the air at the buzzer that could have overcome Manual's 62-60 lead. Neither did Thornton romp in the semis, surviving No. 8 Rock Island by the smallest of margins.

Facing a title game where it was suggested Manual finally might have run into

State Final Tournament Scores

Super-Sectionals

At Evanston [NU]—Northbrook (Glenbrook North) 47, Gurnee (Warren) 44
At Aurora (East)—Joliet (Twp.) 76, Downers Grove (South) 64
At DeKalb [NIU]—Arlington Heights (Hersey) 73, St. Charles 58
At Normal [ISU]—Peoria (Manual) 74, Quincy 63
At Carbondale [SIU]—Edwardsville 53, Centralia 52
At Rockford [Metro Centre]—Rock Island 72, Rockford (Boylan) 67
At Chicago [UIC]—Chicago (Farragut) 71, Chicago (Carver) 62
At Hinsdale (Central)—Harvey (Thornton) 66, Westchester (St. Joseph) 41

Quarterfinals

Joliet (Twp.) 42, Northbrook (Glenbrook North) 39
Peoria (Manual) 64, Arlington Heights (Hersey) 36
Rock Island 75, Edwardsville 56
Harvey (Thornton) 46, Chicago (Farragut) 43

Semifinals

Peoria (Manual) 62, Joliet (Twp.) 60
Harvey (Thornton) 56, Rock Island 55

Finals

Rock Island 69, Joliet (Twp.) 59 (third place)
Peoria (Manual) 65, Harvey (Thornton) 53 (title)

Scoring Leaders

Player, School	G	FG	3P	FT	Pts
Pete Mickeal, Rock Island	4	29	0	23	81
Ivan Watson, Peoria (Manual)	4	25	8	9	67
Gary Bell, Joliet (Twp.)	4	23	1	18	65
Monte Jenkins, Rock Island	4	21	9	8	59
Joel House, Joliet (Twp.)	4	22	4	8	56

All-Tournament First Team

Player, School	Ht.	Yr.
Gary Bell, Joliet (Twp.)	6-5	Sr.
Willie Coleman, Peoria (Manual)	6-1	Sr.
Pete Mickeal, Rock Island	6-6	Jr.
Tai Streets, Harvey (Thornton)	6-4	Sr.
Ivan Watson, Peoria (Manual)	6-0	Sr.

Championship Game Box Score

Assembly Hall, Champaign, March 18, 1995

PEORIA (MANUAL) (65)
Coach Wayne McClain

Player	FG-A	3P-A	FT-A	Pts	PF	Rb	As	St	Bl
Tim Caldwell	0-0	0-0	1-3	1	0	0	0	0	0
Willie Coleman	9-19	2-4	2-4	22	2	4	0	7	0
Kahlil "Cleo" Gayton	0-0	0-0	0-0	0	0	0	0	0	0
Marcus Griffin	1-1	0-0	0-0	2	4	4	0	0	1
Darrell Ivory	4-7	0-0	1-2	9	2	4	1	2	1
Dewayne Johnson	1-2	0-0	2-2	4	2	3	0	2	0
Sergio McClain	1-6	0-2	2-2	4	3	4	5	2	1
Willie Simmons	0-0	0-0	0-0	0	0	0	0	0	0
Jeff Walraven	0-0	0-0	0-0	0	0	1	1	0	0
Ivan Watson	7-16	1-5	6-6	21	3	0	4	0	0
Willie Williams	1-1	0-0	0-0	2	0	0	0	0	0
TEAM						1			
TOTAL	24-52	3-11	14-19	65	16	21	11	13	3

HARVEY (THORNTON) (53)
Coach Rocky Hill

Player	FG-A	3P-A	FT-A	Pts	PF	Rb	As	St	Bl
Carlton DeBose	4-5	0-0	0-0	8	2	1	0	0	0
Denard Eaves	1-1	0-0	0-0	2	0	0	0	0	0
Melvin Ely	6-7	0-0	3-4	15	4	5	1	2	4
Corey Harris	0-0	0-0	0-0	0	0	0	0	0	0
Erik Herring	1-5	0-2	0-0	2	2	3	1	0	1
James Johnson	5-7	0-0	2-3	12	0	3	0	0	0
Chauncey Jones	1-7	0-2	5-6	7	4	4	4	0	0
Richard King	0-1	0-0	0-0	0	0	0	0	0	0
Nick Love	0-0	0-0	0-0	0	0	0	0	0	0
Antwaan Randle El	0-1	0-0	0-0	0	0	0	0	0	0
Curtis Randle El	0-0	0-0	0-0	0	0	0	0	0	0
Maurice Scott	0-1	0-1	0-0	0	0	0	0	0	0
Tai Streets	2-5	0-0	3-4	7	4	15	5	0	0
TEAM						2			
TOTAL	20-40	0-5	13-18	53	16	33	11	2	5

Peoria (Manual)	13	12	11	29 — 65
Harvey (Thornton)	11	10	12	20 — 53

Officials: E. C. "Connie" Pier, Ken Maziarka.

The 1995 Class AA tournament was the last to be played in Champaign-Urbana after a run of 77 years.

Farragut's Kevin Garnett gets off a shot over Thornton's Melvin Ely in their 1995 quarterfinal face-off. Thornton upset the top-ranked Admirals 46-43.

BEFORE THEY WERE STARS

Willie Coleman of Peoria Manual finishes off a fast break in the final tournament played at Assembly Hall in Champaign.

Thornton's Erik Herring lays in two points in a early-round contest.

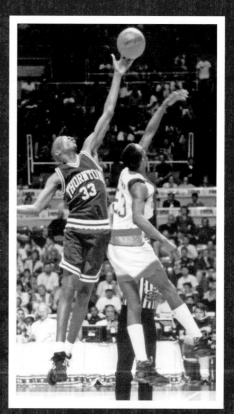

Melvin Ely of Thornton and Monte Jenkins of Rock Island tip off a semifinal barnburner. Thornton won 56-55 to move into the championship contest.

Joliet's Gary Bell beats the press by dribbling against Sergio McClain of Peoria Manual in semifinal action.

1995AA

"No problem"
Peoria's can-do spirit made move possible

Purists say a treasured *tradition* was trashed by the 1996 move from Assembly Hall on the University of Illinois campus in Champaign to *Carver Arena* in the Peoria Civic Center.

by Bob Leavitt

Cynics say the Illinois boys state high school basketball championships were going to play in Peoria from the moment IHSA officials laid eyes on the financial incentives offered the association.

In a chart listing pros and cons of potential tourney sites, the *Peoria Journal Star* gave its hometown a tongue-in-cheek nod among the top three bidders because it had more Avanti's restaurants than Normal or Champaign.

But Loren Tate, former sports editor of the *Champaign-Urbana News-Gazette*, said it best: "If we lose this tournament, shame on us.

"Granted, at that time I didn't know the large extent of Peoria's financial proposal," said the selector for decades of all-state prep teams and as big a U of I fan as ever was. "But I certainly felt we should have worked harder to keep the tournaments."

continued on page 276

Post-tournament fireworks cap off a weekend of excitement at Carver Arena. Fireworks were part of the celebration the first few years in Peoria.

The inaugural Peoria tournaments in 1996 featured a banner (left of scoreboard) with the names and locations of the participating schools, reminiscent of the map that hung on the wall in Huff Gym.

Celebrating 100 years of
IHSA Boys Basketball Tournaments

continued on next page

For years, fans complained about an indifferent attitude in Champaign-Urbana, where the tournaments had been held since 1919. When the IHSA decided to explore its options, it got serious about looking for a place folks would feel more welcome.

Notwithstanding making it worth the IHSA's while, the Peoria area tailored its proposal toward taking the hassle out of this business and making a game played by kids in short pants fun again for all involved.

And the River City, despite a less-than-awesome basketball arena and a potential parking nightmare, had just the roll-up-your-sleeves folks to make good on that promise.

The Peoria area has long enjoyed a legion of volunteers going great lengths to promote activities for youth. And the area being in the midst of a 20-year run of outstanding prep basketball players, teams, and coaches added fuel to their fire. After all, Peoria Manual was smack in the middle of what turned into a record four-year title run.

It takes 2,000 volunteers to set up and run the March Madness Experience, a virtually free carnival right across the hall from the basketball court.

"No problem," said Dick Greene, the former Peoria principal who first marshaled that effort largely from area high school personnel. "In fact, I had volunteers angry because I couldn't find them a job."

> "There are up to 2,500 volunteers involved with the two tourney weekends here. But when you look at the events around our area, we've always been blessed with a lot of people who love doing things for kids."

"All told," said Bill Roeder of the Peoria Park District and tourney steering committee, "there are up to 2,500 volunteers involved with the two tourney weekends here. But when you look at the events around our area, we've always been blessed with a lot of people who love doing things for kids."

Not exactly the type of folks who see state finals in terms of dollar signs.

Truth be known, the grandiose figures promoters often throw out about how much money sporting events net a host area's civic coffers seldom subtract the cost to taxpayers of such as police and sanitation overtime.

But a community putting its best feet forward for you, well, that's priceless.

Kids try their skill at Bankshot Basketball. The March Madness Experience, in the Exhibition Hall adjacent to Carver Arena, provides games and entertainment for spectators through both tournament weekends.

The IHSA tournament received a warm welcome from Peoria citizens when it moved to Carver Arena in 1996.

A CENTURY OF MEMORIES
20 07
100
IHSA
Celebrating 100 years of IHSA Boys Basketball Tournaments

Young fans wait in line to have their programs autographed by participants in the slam-dunk and three-point shooting contests.

1996AA

CLASS AA

I f two-time defending state champ Peoria Manual caught a break when the state finals moved into its own back yard, one sure couldn't prove it by the Rams' record of 6-5 in games played on the Carver Arena court in the Peoria Civic Center.

Over that 13-year period, Manual had gone 350-52 overall, 102-3 in its home gym, 29-9 in Bradley University's Field House and 43-5 at the Pontiac Holiday Tournament.

In fact, Manual had survived the Peoria Sectional by beating a fourth-ranked East Peoria team that had beaten Manual at Carver a month earlier in the River City Shootout — and it took a last-second 24-footer by sophomore Frank Williams to do it.

And then second-ranked Manual needed double-digit scoring from all five starters to stop a talent-laced, sixth-rated Springfield Lanphier squad in the Normal Super- Sectional just to get a shot at ending a three-game Carver Arena losing streak.

On the other side of the bracket, top-ranked and unbeaten Thornton squelched a third-rated Rock Island crew in the quarterfinals en route to the title game.

The final scene in this Sweet Sixteen followed the same script as the previous one as Manual bested Harvey Thornton 57-51 for the title, the Class AA tournament's first title-game rematch. It was also the first AA title clash in to match teams ranked No. 1 and 2 in the final regular-season poll.

With the victory, Manual (31-2) tied East St. Louis Lincoln's 1987-89 record run of three Class AA titles. And the battle of four junior front-liners (Manual's Marcus Griffin and Sergio McClain vs. Thornton's Melvin Ely and Napoleon Harris) plus a pair of underclass guards (Manual's Williams vs. Thornton's Antwaan Randle El) set the stage for a three-match of the title game in 1997.

While the big guys muscled, Williams finessed, leading all scorers with 17 points on 7-for-10 shooting.

For two straight years, Thornton had everything it took to be a state champion — except a win over Manual. All the Wildcats could hope for was that a third meeting might be a charm.

Despite all the underclass talent on the court in the title tilt, a reserve senior might well have made the difference. Manual 6-footer Marshall Dunnigan had a half-dozen points and rebounds by seeming to always be in the right place at the right time.

Six weeks later, the well-regarded student-athlete and son of a veteran Peoria policeman was murdered, the random shooting victim of a gang member on Peoria's South Side.

1996 CLASS AA BOYS MARCH MADNESS

State Final Tournament Scores

Super-Sectionals
At Normal [ISU]—Peoria (Manual) 72, Springfield (Lanphier) 59
At Aurora (East)—Hinsdale (Central) 60, Flossmoor (Homewood-F.) 45
At Carbondale [SIU]—Belleville (East) 57, Highland 50
At Evanston [NU]—Winnetka (New Trier) 65, Deerfield 56
At Hinsdale (Central)—Harvey (Thornton) 47, Hillside (Proviso West) 38
At Rockford [Metro Centre]—Rock Island 73, Rockford (Boylan) 66
At DeKalb [NIU]—Hoffman Estates 52, Aurora (West) 42
At Chicago—Chicago (Westinghouse) 55, Chicago (Farragut) 46

Quarterfinals
Peoria (Manual) 60, Hinsdale (Central) 53
Winnetka (New Trier) 70, Belleville (East) 58
Harvey (Thornton) 51, Rock Island 34
Chicago (Westinghouse) 42, Hoffman Estates 41

Semifinals
Peoria (Manual) 53, Winnetka (New Trier) 41
Harvey (Thornton) 69, Chicago (Westinghouse) 54

Finals
Chicago (Westinghouse) 60, Winnetka (New Trier) 58 (third place)
Peoria (Manual) 57, Harvey (Thornton) 51 (title)

Scoring Leaders

Player, School	G	FG	3P	FT	Pts
Melvin Ely, Harvey (Thornton)	4	30	0	9	69
Sergio McClain, Peoria (Manual)	4	16	4	31	67
Jimmy Sanders, Chicago (Westinghouse)	4	22	8	11	63
Jerry Happ, Winnetka (New Trier)	4	19	6	15	59
Jack Kidd, Winnetka (New Trier)	4	18	0	19	55

All-Tournament First Team

Player, School	Ht.	Yr.
Melvin Ely, Harvey (Thornton)	6-10	Jr.
Napoleon Harris, Harvey (Thornton)	6-5	Jr.
Sergio McClain, Peoria (Manual)	6-5	Jr.
Jimmy Sanders, Chicago (Westinghouse)	5-6	Sr.
Frank Williams, Peoria (Manual)	6-4	So.

Championship Game Box Score
Carver Arena, Peoria, March 16, 1996

PEORIA (MANUAL) (57)
Coach Wayne McClain

Player	FG-A	3P-A	FT-A	Pts	PF	Rb	As	St	Bl
Tim Caldwell	1-6	1-4	3-4	6	1	2	2	2	0
Marshall Dunnigan	3-5	0-1	0-0	6	0	6	0	0	0
Kahlil "Cleo" Gayton	2-4	0-0	0-0	4	1	0	0	1	0
Marcus Griffin	5-10	0-0	0-1	10	4	11	0	0	3
Sergio McClain	4-8	2-3	5-8	15	2	2	3	4	1
Jerral Page	0-0	0-0	0-0	0	0	1	0	0	0
Charles Russell	0-0	0-0	0-0	0	0	0	0	0	0
Frank Williams	7-10	0-0	2-6	16	0	5	6	2	0
TEAM						1			
TOTAL	22-43	3-8	10-19	57	8	28	11	9	4

HARVEY (THORNTON) (51)
Coach Rocky Hill

Player	FG-A	3P-A	FT-A	Pts	PF	Rb	As	St	Bl
Melvin Ely	6-9	0-0	2-6	14	3	5	0	1	2
Corey Harris	0-0	0-0	0-0	0	1	0	0	0	0
Napoleon Harris	7-12	0-0	0-3	14	3	5	1	2	0
Erik Herring	5-8	1-2	0-0	11	5	4	5	1	0
Tamon Holloway	2-4	1-3	0-0	5	0	3	1	0	0
Antwaan Randle El	2-6	1-2	0-0	5	4	4	4	1	0
Maurice Scott	1-8	0-5	0-0	2	0	1	0	2	0
TEAM						3			
TOTAL	23-47	3-12	2-9	51	15	26	11	7	2

Peoria (Manual)	15	10	19	13	—	57
Harvey (Thornton)	10	14	15	12	—	51

Officials: Richard Dietz, Donald Cobb.

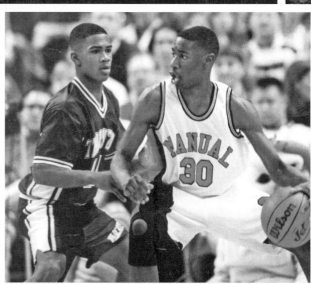

Frank Williams of Peoria Manual looks inside as Thornton's Antwaan Randle El applies pressure. Manual won the title-game rematch by a 57-51 tally.

Peoria Manual's Marcus Griffin scores over New Trier's Alex Klein in semifinal action at Carver Arena.

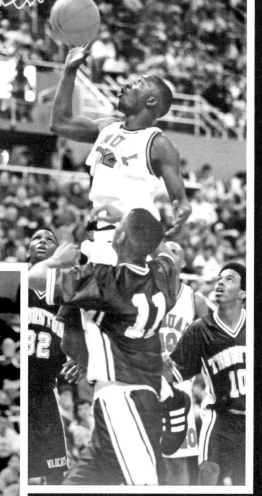

Marshall Dunnigan of Peoria Manual brings the ball to the hoop through heavy traffic in the title game. Thornton's Napoleon Harris (32) and Tamon Holoway (10) watch.

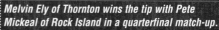

Melvin Ely of Thornton wins the tip with Pete Mickeal of Rock Island in a quarterfinal match-up.

PATH OF LEAST RESISTANCE

Sergio McClain completes a baseline move against Hinsdale Central in a quarterfinal game.

1996AA

It coulda, shoulda, woulda been the most anticipated title game in state history. But three-time defending champ Peoria Manual and two-time runner-up Harvey Thornton wound up on the same side of the tournament bracket.

Still, it made for such a spirited semifinal the title game was pretty much an afterthought. That is, until scrappy 13th-ranked West Aurora and seasoned coach Gordon Kerkman darn near screwed up a final scene that was four years in the staging.

Manual coach's son Sergio McClain led all title-game scorers with 22 points in a 47-43 win over West Aurora, which had led by four in the last quarter before Frank Williams nailed back-to-back threes.

Serg ended his high school career having started every post-season game for four years and going 32-0 as Manual became the first Illinois school to accomplish a state-title four-feat.

That alone would have made this Elite Eight special. But even before a semifinal for the ages, Manual had to send once-beaten, third-ranked Chicago Whitney Young and future NBA star Quentin Richardson home to plot their future state championship.

It took three years, but the Associated Press state pollsters had learned their

"With wounded warrior Sergio McClain on the bench and Manual down by 14, junior Frank Williams hoisted the Rams on his slim shoulders and scored 16 to forge a 29-26 lead they never . . ."

"Down six points, spiritual leader Sergio McClain shrugged off a pulled muscle and rose from the Manual bench like the legendary Phoenix to personally run 11 points for a 40-37 lead that was the beginning of the end for . . . "

"Down by 15 with 2:24 left and seemingly resigned to perennially playing second-fiddle to its arch-nemesis, Thornton orchestrated 23 points and . . ."

In an epic bout that should have ended with a ringside bell clanging, Manual was so convinced this heavyweight fight was headed for overtime that McClain strongly challenged the desperation 35-footer that fell short at the buzzer, leaving the Rams a 65-62 survivor.

McClain and teammate Marcus Griffin would end up one-two in Mr. Basketball voting and move on to Big Ten titles at Illinois. Ditto for future Big Ten MVP Williams, named Mr. Basketball the next season.

Thornton didn't catch its breath until it had oustscored Rockford Boylan by 21

string four Big Ten titles under two coaches and reach the 2005 NCAA title game.

On the Peoria parade route when Manual was only halfway to history in 1995, McClain had shrugged off a yard sign reading "Three-peat?" by saying: "We created this monster, and we're the only ones who can slay it."

And by George, from the doorstep of dynasty, Manual stepped over the threshold into history.

PEORIA (MANUAL)
Class AA State Champions of 1997

FRONT ROW (left to right): Jerron Hobson, Marlon Brooks, Robert Johnson, Seneca Davis, Greg Andrews, Drake Ford. SECOND ROW: Alphonso Pollard, Frank Williams, Marcus Griffin, Alex Stephens, Sergio McClain, Jerral Page.

lesson, ranking once-beaten Manual on top, with unbeaten Thornton second in the final regular-season poll. The unluck of the draw kept the Rams and Wildcats from going one-two a third straight season. But nothing could keep them from ending one-two in the national *USA Today* rankings.

Momentum in this splendid semifinal swung so wildly reporters were writing then rewriting lead sentences in their heads from start to finish.

"Thornton raced to an 18-4 lead against traditional tormentor Manual and was never . . ."

points in the second half to win the third-place game. But some Wildcats just kept right on going: center Melvin Ely to Fresno State and the No. 12 NBA draft pick, forward Napoleon Harris to Northwestern and the NFL, and guard Antwaan Randle El to Big Ten football MVP at Indiana and a Super Bowl ring.

Thornton had only four losses in three years — all but one of them to Manual on the last day of three straight seasons.

Four years later, with a coaching mark of 177-35, Wayne McClain became an assistant coach at Illinois, where he helped

State Final Tournament Scores

Super-Sectionals

At Evanston [NU]—Niles (Notre Dame) 40, Deerfield 33
At Moline [The Mark]—Rockford (Boylan) 56, Moline 54
At Carbondale [SIU]—Mt. Vernon 60, Alton 53
At DeKalb [NIU]—Aurora (West) 45, Hoffman Estates (Conant) 32
At Aurora (East)—Hinsdale (Central) 48, Richton Park (Rich South) 37
At Hinsdale (Central)—Harvey (Thornton) 40, Oak Park (Fenwick) 33
At Chicago—Chicago (Young) 72, Chicago (Manley) 50
At Normal [ISU]—Peoria (Manual) 57, Springfield 49

Quarterfinals

Rockford (Boylan) 58, Niles (Notre Dame) 40
Aurora (West) 71, Mt. Vernon 53
Harvey (Thornton) 77, Hinsdale (Central) 61
Peoria (Manual) 51, Chicago (Young) 46

Semifinals

Aurora (West) 60, Rockford (Boylan) 55
Peoria (Manual) 65, Harvey (Thornton) 62

Finals

Harvey (Thornton) 76, Rockford (Boylan) 51 (third place)
Peoria (Manual) 47, Aurora (West) 43 (title)

Scoring Leaders

Player, School	G	FG	3P	FT	Pts
Erik Herring, Harvey (Thornton)	4	31	11	4	77
Sergio McClain, Peoria (Manual)	4	21	5	18	65
Nicholas Zachery, Rockford (Boylan)	4	22	6	12	62
Frank Williams, Peoria (Manual)	4	19	7	12	57
Melvin Ely, Harvey (Thornton)	4	22	0	13	57

All-Tournament First Team

Player, School	Ht.	Yr.
Melvin Ely, Harvey (Thornton)	6-10	Sr.
Erik Herring, Harvey (Thornton)	6-5	Sr.
Sergio McClain, Peoria (Manual)	6-5	Sr.
Brian Wardle, Hinsdale (Central)	6-5	Sr.
Frank Williams, Peoria (Manual)	6-4	Jr.

Championship Game Box Score

Carver Arena, Peoria, March 22, 1997

PEORIA (MANUAL) (47)
Coach Wayne McClain

Player	FG-A	3P-A	FT-A	Pts	PF	Rb	As	St	Bl
Marlon Brooks	0-0	0-0	0-0	0	1	3	2	1	0
Drake Ford	0-1	0-1	0-0	0	1	0	0	0	0
Marcus Griffin	1-9	0-0	0-0	2	3	7	3	2	0
Robert Johnson	2-3	2-3	1-2	7	1	6	1	2	0
Sergio McClain	10-18	1-3	1-4	22	3	5	0	2	0
Jerral Page	3-6	0-0	0-0	6	1	5	0	0	0
Frank Williams	3-12	2-7	2-3	10	0	1	2	3	0
TEAM						2			
TOTAL	19-49	5-14	4-9	47	10	29	8	10	0

AURORA (WEST) (43)
Coach Gordon Kerkman

Player	FG-A	3P-A	FT-A	Pts	PF	Rb	As	St	Bl
Dustin Burrell	0-1	0-1	0-0	0	0	0	0	0	0
Vincent Green	6-11	0-0	3-5	15	3	4	1	2	0
Greg Miller	7-9	0-0	1-2	15	3	12	1	0	0
Andre Newson	3-8	0-0	0-0	6	3	5	1	1	0
Jason Passley	2-7	1-3	0-2	5	1	5	4	2	0
Jason Paul	0-0	0-0	0-0	0	0	0	0	0	0
Jeff Ruffin	0-0	0-0	0-0	0	0	0	0	0	0
Byron Thompson	0-0	0-0	0-0	0	1	0	0	0	1
Trevis Williams	0-4	0-3	2-2	2	2	2	6	1	0
TEAM						1			
TOTAL	18-40	1-7	6-11	43	13	29	13	6	1

Peoria (Manual)	11	7	10	19	— 47
Aurora (West)	12	6	15	10	— 43

Officials: John Dacey, Rick Bieterman.

Jerral Page of Manual pivots toward the basket while Napoleon Harris of Thornton moves in for a steal. Manual won the semifinal game, knocking Thornton out of contention for the third straight year.

Marcus Griffin of Peoria Manual dunks in a quarterfinal match with Chicago Young as Lonnie Holland arrives a step too late.

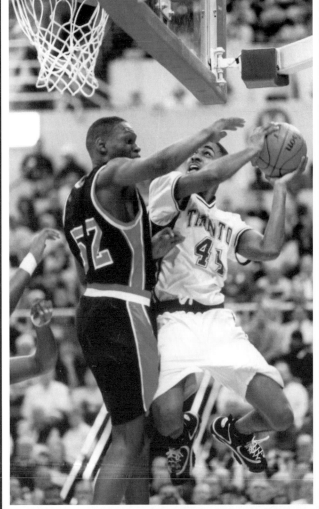

Jason Passley of West Aurora pulls up outside the lane in the Blackhawks' 47-43 title-game loss to Manual.

Manual players, led by Sergio McClain, marvel at their record performance — four consecutive state titles.

GOOD THINGS COME IN FOURS

Thronton's Eric Herring goes behind the basket to avoid Marcus Griffin of Peoria Manual in a critical semifinal battle.

1997AA

CHICAGO (YOUNG)
Class AA State Champions of 1998

FRONT ROW (left to right):
Coach George Stanton,
Asst. Coach Cyrus McGinnis,
Lavelle Walson, Cordell Henry,
Christopher Yates, Marcus
Sankey, Jasand Parker,
Scorekeeper Monique Spence,
Trainer Sheldon Lo,
Statistician Mike Naditch.
SECOND ROW:
Asst. Coach Anthony Spivey,
Reginald Jones, Najeeb Echols,
Quentin Richardson, Corey Harris,
Marquis Wright, Kristopher
Clemmons, Dennis Gates,
Asst. Coach Billy Brown.

CLASS AA
1998 AA

Talk about being forged in fire.

The year before, Chicago Whitney Young would have had to hurdle the top two high school teams in the nation just to reach the state title game. Young finished that season 30-2, with both losses inflicted by Manual, named the country's No. 1 team by *USA Today*.

A year later, battle-tested Young ended as one of the two top teams in those national rankings.

Not that the state's top-ranked team had an easy route this time around, what with having to beat No. 9 Chicago King, No. 8 Elgin and No. 14 Quincy to earn a title shot against No. 3 Galesburg.

But Young, no longer the team that had appeared tight against Manual's uncharacteristic zone defense in the 1997 quarterfinals, was ready for everything.

Young hit 22 of 28 free throws and held King to 30 percent shooting for a 21-point romp in the high-pressure Chicago Public League title game. Young then powered into Carver Arena and dominated Elgin 68-50 in the quarterfinals thanks to 32 points and 16 rebounds from 6-6 future NBA star Quentin Richardson.

But as powerful a force as Richardson was on offense, he led a defense that was equally impressive.

The Dolphins held King's vaunted guard Imari Sawyer to eight points on 4-for-20 shooting — twice the number of shots Richardson needed to score 23 points in that one.

Young's defense put the same straitjacket on Elgin, limiting gunning guard Sean Harrington to a mere seven shots and nine points.

Perhaps peeved at not having an opportunity to avenge its 1997 quarterfinal loss to Manual, Young jumped to a 26-8 semifinal lead over the Quincy team

that had drilled second-ranked Manual and Mr. Basketball winner Frank Williams by 20 points in super-sectional play. In the process, Young limited all-state Quincy center Luis Rivas to three shots and as few points.

Galesburg's all-state pair of Joey Range and 6-foot-8 Chicago Carver transfer Rod Thompson presented Young's defense with double trouble. But while they combined for 31 points, Young's Dennis Gates (20) and Richardson (18) totaled 38.

Meanwhile, Richardson's one-man boarding party turned the tide in a 61-56 title win the Dolphins never led by more than eight. Richardson's 20 boards tied all of the Silver Streaks put together.

George Stanton's Dolphins finished 30-1, the lone loss 60-58 in overtime to a Lexington (Ky.) Catholic team that ended No. 17 in the country.

State Final Tournament Scores
Super-Sectionals
At DeKalb [NIU]—Elgin 69, Naperville (North) 58
At Chicago [UIC]—Chicago (Young) 67, Chicago (King) 46
At Aurora (East)—Joliet (Twp.) 64, Oak Lawn (Richards) 63
At Normal [ISU]—Quincy 72, Peoria (Manual) 52
At Rockford [Metro Centre]—Galesburg 68, Rockford (Boylan) 63
At Carbondale [SIU]—Centralia 51, East St. Louis (Lincoln) 41
At Evanston [NU]—Des Plaines (Maine West) 74, Zion (Z.-Benton) 44
At Hinsdale (Central)—Oak Park (Fenwick) 75, Olympia Fields (Rich Central) 56

Quarterfinals
Chicago (Young) 68, Elgin 50
Quincy 66, Joliet (Twp.) 53
Galesburg 71, Centralia 56
Des Plaines (Maine West) 76, Oak Park (Fenwick) 64

Semifinals
Chicago (Young) 62, Quincy 34
Galesburg 73, Des Plaines (Maine West) 70

Finals
Quincy 66, Des Plaines (Maine West) 63 (third place)
Chicago (Young) 61, Galesburg 56 (title)

Scoring Leaders

Player, School	G	FG	3P	FT	Pts
Quentin Richardson, Chicago (Young)	4	34	3	15	86
Joey Range, Galesburg	4	32	3	14	81
Kevin Frey, Des Plaines (Maine West)	4	26	1	19	72
Luis Rivas, Quincy	4	30	0	12	72
Rod Thompson, Galesburg	4	28	8	7	71

All-Tournament First Team

Player, School	Ht.	Yr.
Kevin Frey, Des Plaines (Maine West)	6-7	Sr.
Cordell Henry, Chicago (Young)	5-10	Sr.
Joey Range, Galesburg	6-5	Sr.
Quentin Richardson, Chicago (Young)	6-6	Sr.
Rod Thompson, Galesburg	6-6	Sr.

Championship Game Box Score
Carver Arena, Peoria, March 21, 1998

CHICAGO (YOUNG) (61)
Coach George Stanton

Player	FG-A	3P-A	FT-A	Pts	PF	Rb	As	St	Bl
Kristopher Clemmons	1-2	0-0	0-0	2	3	1	0	0	0
Najeeb Echols	0-0	0-0	0-0	0	1	0	0	0	0
Dennis Gates	8-15	2-5	2-3	20	0	4	1	1	1
Corey Harris	2-8	0-0	1-2	5	1	7	2	1	0
Cordell Henry	4-15	1-6	1-1	10	0	2	4	0	0
Reginald Jones	0-0	0-0	0-0	0	0	0	0	0	0
Jasand Parker	0-0	0-0	0-0	0	0	0	0	0	0
Quentin Richardson	7-16	0-4	4-5	18	3	20	1	3	1
Marcus Sankey	0-0	0-0	0-0	0	0	0	0	0	0
Lavelle Walson	0-0	0-0	0-0	0	0	0	0	0	0
Marquis Wright	2-5	1-1	1-2	6	3	3	0	1	0
Christopher Yates	0-0	0-0	0-0	0	0	0	0	0	0
TEAM						3			
TOTAL	24-61	4-16	9-13	61	11	40	8	6	2

GALESBURG (56)
Coach Mike Miller

Player	FG-A	3P-A	FT-A	Pts	PF	Rb	As	St	Bl
Steve Glasgow	0-5	0-2	0-0	0	2	3	9	0	0
Patrick Hanlon	0-0	0-0	0-0	0	1	1	1	0	0
Kevin Heimann	0-0	0-0	0-0	0	0	0	0	0	0
Travis Howe	0-0	0-0	0-0	0	0	0	0	0	0
Toby Lannholm	0-0	0-0	0-0	0	0	0	0	0	0
Alfonso Pugh	0-0	0-0	0-0	0	0	0	0	0	0
Lorenzo Pugh	0-0	0-0	0-0	0	0	0	0	0	0
Joey Range	7-12	0-2	1-2	15	2	7	1	0	2
Beau Shay	0-0	0-0	0-0	0	0	0	0	0	0
Mike Tapper	4-8	2-6	3-6	13	4	2	0	0	0
Taylor Thiel	4-6	4-6	0-0	12	1	1	3	0	0
John Thompson	0-0	0-0	0-0	0	0	0	0	0	0
Rod Thompson	5-10	3-4	3-3	16	3	6	2	1	0
Ryan Wood	0-0	0-0	0-0	0	0	0	0	0	0
Nick Young	0-0	0-0	0-0	0	0	0	0	0	0
TEAM						3			
TOTAL	20-41	9-20	7-11	56	13	23	16	1	2

Chicago (Young)	15	16	19	11	—	61
Galesburg	17	9	16	14	—	56

Officials: Joe Tomlinson, Mike Bromley, Paul Norfleet.

During a quarterfinal game with Centralia, Galesburg's Joey Range unleashes one of the many dunks he registered during the weekend.

Dennis Gates launches a three-pointer in Young's 62-34 win over Quincy in the semifinals.

BASKET ON THE SIDE

Galesburg's Rod Thompson works hard to find a baseline shot against Young in the title contest. Young's Najeeb Echols (33) sets up for the rebound.

Quentin Richardson of Young sets up for a three-point attempt in the championship game. Richardson led all scorers with 86 points.

1998AA

WESTCHESTER (ST. JOSEPH)
Class AA State Champions of 1999

FRONT ROW (left to right): Mgr. Henry Hargrove, Mgr. Dan Lawless, Mgr. Doug Pabst. SECOND ROW: Michael Coleman, John Stamas, Damien McIntosh, Brandon Watkins, Leonard Houseworth. THIRD ROW: Coach Gene Pingatore, Asst. Coach Bill Riley, Mgr. Peter Cromey, Mark Thomas, Chad Tancil, James Stewart, Ivan Jackson, Nick Murphy, Jon Brown, Steve Morgan, Keith Perry, Ken Gadomski, Steve Davis, Jabari Mattox, Mgr. Eugene Poulin, Asst. Coach Terry Kusnierz.

What Westchester St. Joseph couldn't accomplish with superstars such as Isiah Thomas, it did with an unheralded player whose spiffy state tournament title run vaulted him into the Big Ten.

Although he came into the Elite Eight without a Division I college scholarship offer, point guard Brandon Watkins was everything St. Joe needed to become the second private school to win a one-class or Class AA boys state basketball championship.

Timing also proved to be everything for Gene Pingatore, In 30 years of coaching, Pingatore had produced a 621-203 record, 41 major-college scholarship players, and state trophies in 1978 (second), 1984 (fourth) and 1987 (third) — but no state title.

Ranked only fourth despite a 24-1 regular-season record, St. Joe figured to face No. 2 Mt. Vernon and No. 1 Chicago Westinghouse just to reach the title game.

But that North-South showdown of the state's only two unbeatens unraveled when Westinghouse (called the quickest team in the country by *USA Today*) and Mt. Vernon both were undone a game short of playing in Peoria.

In fact, the only state-rated team St. Joe wound up facing in the Sweet Sixteen was No. 11 Chicago King. But the Chargers dispatched King 59-40 in the quarterfinals, thanks to 23 points by

Watkins and a 24-7 fourth-quarter scoring spree.

If St. Joe reaching the title game was a surprise, Gurnee Warren getting there was a shock.

Warren won its super-sectional by 30 points but hadn't faced a ranked team all season before running into No. 7 Lincoln and all-American Brian Cook in the quarterfinals. The Blue Devils answered the challenge in the last quarter, padding a one-point lead to beat Lincoln by 15.

Next up for an upset was No. 8 Schaumburg in the semis, where Jourdain Milot and reserve Rickey Higgins scored 15 apiece in a 16-point win.

Sweet Sixteen scoring leader Watkins, who averaged 20.5 points in the four games, opened the door for Warren to become the first unranked champ since 1983 by missing 14 of 18 shots in the title game. But then the future Penn State player nailed it shut by making 10 of 14 foul shots for a 61-51 victory.

Pingatore called St. Joseph's championship a dream come true and a prize worthy of the wait. "I just wish my mother and aunt had lived to be part of it," he said.

St. Joe ended No. 7 in the national rankings at 32-1, with only a four-point loss to the state's 14th-rated team, Chicago Dunbar, denying the Chargers a perfect season. The loss came in the Proviso West Holiday Tournament, where two other eventual Elite Eight entries (Schaumburg and Hillcrest) also lost first-round games.

King took third place in the state-finals swan song for coach Landon "Sonny" Cox, who wound up 15-3 in Elite Eight games.

State Final Tournament Scores

Super-Sectionals

At Evanston [NU]—Gurnee (Warren) 61, Park Ridge (Maine South) 31
At Normal [ISU]—Lincoln 54, Peoria (Manual) 50
At DeKalb [NIU]—Schaumburg 60, Aurora (East) 54 (OT)
At Moline [The Mark]—Rock Island 75, Rockford (Boylan) 65
At Carbondale [SIU]—East St. Louis 72, Mt. Vernon 58
At Hinsdale (Central)—Westchester (St. Joseph) 49, Dolton (Thornridge) 39
At Chicago—Chicago (King) 59, Chicago (Westinghouse) 39
At Aurora (East)—Country Club Hills (Hillcrest) 70, Downers Grove (North) 65

Quarterfinals

Gurnee (Warren) 59, Lincoln 43
Schaumburg 55, Rock Island 51
Westchester (St. Joseph) 66, East St. Louis 61
Chicago (King) 49, Country Club Hills (Hillcrest) 46 (OT)

Semifinals

Gurnee (Warren) 69, Schaumburg 53
Westchester (St. Joseph) 59, Chicago (King) 40

Finals

Chicago (King) 67, Schaumburg 58 (third place)
Westchester (St. Joseph) 61, Gurnee (Warren) 51 (title)

Scoring Leaders

Player, School	G	FG	3P	FT	Pts
Brandon Watkins, Westch. (St. Joseph)	4	24	5	29	82
Leon Smith, Chicago (King)	4	33	1	8	75
Antoine McDaniel, Schaumburg	4	20	6	16	62
Steve Morgan, Westchester (St. Joseph)	4	22	0	11	55
Jourdain Milot, Gurnee (Warren)	4	19	2	14	54

All-Tournament First Team

Player, School	Ht.	Yr.
Darius Miles, East St. Louis	6-8	Jr.
Jourdain Milot, Gurnee (Warren)	6-2	Jr.
Steve Morgan, Westchester (St. Joseph)	6-5	Sr.
Leon Smith, Chicago (King)	6-10	Sr.
Brandon Watkins, Westchester (St. Joseph)	6-0	Sr.

Championship Game Box Score

Carver Arena, Peoria, March 20, 1999

WESTCHESTER (ST. JOSEPH) (61)
Coach Gene Pingatore

Player	FG-A	3P-A	FT-A	Pts	PF	Rb	As	St	Bl
Jon Brown	2-6	0-0	1-2	5	2	5	2	0	1
Michael Coleman	0-0	0-0	0-0	0	0	0	0	0	0
Ken Gadomski	0-0	0-0	0-0	0	0	0	0	0	0
Ivan Jackson	0-0	0-0	0-0	0	0	0	0	0	0
Jabari Mattox	3-5	0-0	4-6	10	1	6	2	0	0
Damien McIntosh	1-2	1-2	4-6	7	3	4	1	0	0
Steve Morgan	6-6	0-0	2-5	14	4	8	0	1	0
Nick Murphy	0-0	0-0	0-0	0	0	1	0	0	0
Keith Perry	2-3	0-0	0-0	4	0	6	2	2	0
Chad Tancil	1-4	0-0	0-0	2	2	0	1	0	0
Mark Thomas	0-0	0-0	0-0	0	0	0	0	0	0
Brandon Watkins	4-18	1-5	10-14	19	1	4	0	0	0
TEAM						2			
TOTAL	19-44	2-7	21-33	61	14	36	8	3	1

GURNEE (WARREN) (51)
Coach Chuck Ramsey

Player	FG-A	3P-A	FT-A	Pts	PF	Rb	As	St	Bl
Nate Alden	0-0	0-0	0-0	0	0	0	0	0	0
Mike Brandow	7-14	0-0	0-1	14	4	5	2	0	2
C.J. Cusker	0-0	0-0	0-0	0	0	0	0	0	0
Steve Davis	0-0	0-0	0-0	0	0	0	0	1	0
Chris Foreman	0-0	0-0	0-0	0	0	1	0	0	0
Rickey Higgins	0-2	0-1	0-0	0	1	5	0	0	0
Langston Hughes	2-11	1-7	5-7	10	4	6	2	1	0
Mike Kolar	1-4	0-1	3-3	5	4	3	5	1	0
Matt Lewis	0-0	0-0	0-0	0	0	0	0	0	0
Jourdain Milot	6-16	1-6	1-3	14	3	9	1	1	0
Dave Piepenbrink	0-0	0-0	0-0	0	0	0	0	0	0
Ryan Ramsey	1-2	1-2	0-0	3	4	0	1	0	0
Joel Walker	1-4	1-4	2-2	5	1	1	0	0	0
TEAM						4			
TOTAL	18-53	4-21	11-16	51	21	34	11	4	2

Westchester (St. Joseph)	9	17	17	18	—	61
Gurnee (Warren)	11	10	6	24	—	51

Officials: Mau Cason, Paul Moseley, William Jones Jr..

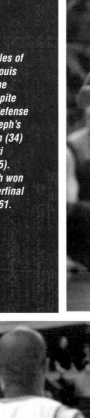

Darius Miles of East St. Louis crashes the hoop, despite the best defense of St. Joseph's Jon Brown (34) and Jabari Mattox (15). St. Joseph won the quarterfinal game 66-61.

Mattox looks for options as Warren's Joel Walker readies for the steal in the 1999 Class AA championship game at Carver Arena.

St. Joseph's Brandon Watkins is all concentration in the title game against Warren while Mike Brandow calls for the pass from Jourdain Milot.

SPECIAL DELIVERY

Watkins sets and shoots a long-distance bomb against King in the semifinals.

Darius Miles of East St. Louis finishes off a crowd-pleasing slam in the quarterfinal against St. Joseph.

1999AA

2000AA

AURORA (WEST)
Class AA State Champions of 2000

FRONT ROW (left to right): Mike Wolf, Nathan Keyes, Otis Payne, Bryan Wredling. SECOND ROW: Branndon Foster, Asst. Coach Curtis Shaw, Coach Gordon Kerkman, Asst. Coach Skip Ulrich, Mike Fowler. THIRD ROW: Nathan Eimer, Jordan Lonzano, Louis Smith, Austin Real, Jamaal Thompson, Pat Drews, Derik Hollyfield, Kevin Jenkins. FOURTH ROW: John Slocum, Mark Watson, Adam Garcia, Jarod Tobler, Kris Jenkins, Josh Huberty.

As if the law of averages was finally getting around to righting wrongs, the second veteran coach in as many years claimed his first state championship. And this was the first for a city teeming with basketball tradition.

West Aurora was 0-4 in one-class (1928 and 1959) and Class AA (1976 and 1997) title games. In its latest two heartbreakers, the Blackhawks had been victimized by one the most spectacular last-second shots in tourney history and then by a team that finished atop the national ratings.

Add East Aurora going 0-2 in semifinals (1969 and 1972) to the city's frustration file. Neither was there any pity shown for Aurora's private schools, with both Central Catholic and Aurora Christian coming up short in Class A title games.

Obviously this jinx would not end easily. Not until West Aurora and coach Gordon Kerkman found a way — on the same day — to defeat one opponent boasting a future NBA all-star and another carrying the state's No. 1 ranking.

Some argue the IHSA's final-day doubleheader format diminishes coaching strategy and rewards players able to save themselves for the nightcap.

But fourth-ranked West Aurora had to go all out in the semifinals to outlast No. 3 East St. Louis and 6-foot-8 Mr. Basketball Darius Miles. West Aurora hung on for a 43-39 victory and earned the right to match 31-1 records with No. 1 Chicago Westinghouse in the title game.

Down eight late in the third quarter, the Blackhawks finally wore out Miles.

Despite playing the point on the Flyers press and bringing the ball up against West Aurora's pressure, Miles never left the court, scoring 18, blocking nine shots, grabbing eight rebounds, making four steals, and handing out three assists. But by crunch time, the smooth stringbean was drained.

The title game proved just as harrowing for West Aurora. Leading by nine with only 62 seconds left between the city of Aurora and that elusive championship, West missed four straight foul shots. Westinghouse's Cedrick Banks closed the gap to two with a three-point play at 0:28. But two pairs of free throws by junior Jamaal Thompson gave the Blackhawks a 60-57 victory.

Balance was the key for West Aurora, with Thompson, Derik Hollyfield and Austin Real all ending Sweet Sixteen play with from 53 to 56 points.

Those three, plus Louis Smith, each had a least one 20-point outing.

The trio of Martell Bailey, Banks and Dennis Trammell accounted for all but two of Westinghouse's 57 points.

East St. Louis's consolation win over Peoria Richwoods marked the farewell appearance of Bennie Lewis, who'd coached four 1980s title teams at East St. Louis Lincoln.

State Final Tournament Scores

Super-Sectionals

At Carbondale [SIU]—East St. Louis 48, Mt. Vernon 35
At Evanston [NU]—Winnetka (New Trier) 51, Gurnee (Warren) 43
At Hinsdale (Central)—Chicago (Gordon Tech) 55, Chicago (St. Ignatius) 46
At DeKalb [NIU]—Aurora (West) 67, Glen Ellyn (Glenbard South) 46
At Rockford [Metro Centre]—Rock Island 50, Rockford (Boylan) 41
At Normal [ISU]—Peoria (Richwoods) 46, Quincy 43
At Chicago [United Center]—Chicago (Westinghouse) 82, Chicago (Young) 60
At Aurora (East)—Chicago Heights (Bloom Twp.) 42, Chicago (Brother Rice) 40

Quarterfinals

East St. Louis 68, Winnetka (New Trier) 48
Aurora (West) 74, Chicago (Gordon Tech) 64
Peoria (Richwoods) 48, Rock Island 44
Chicago (Westinghouse) 74, Chicago Heights (Bloom Twp.) 48

Semifinals

Aurora (West) 43, East St. Louis 39
Chicago (Westinghouse) 43, Peoria (Richwoods) 35

Finals

East St. Louis 70, Peoria (Richwoods) 47 (third place)
Aurora (West) 60, Chicago (Westinghouse) 57 (title)

Scoring Leaders

Player, School	G	FG	3P	FT	Pts
Phillip Gilbert, East St. Louis	4	21	9	21	72
Cedrick Banks, Chicago (Westinghouse)	4	28	5	9	70
Darius Miles, East St. Louis	4	28	0	11	67
Austin Real, Aurora (West)	4	22	0	12	56
Jamaal Thompson, Aurora (West)	4	22	0	11	55

All-Tournament First Team

Player, School	Ht.	Yr.
Martell Bailey, Chicago (Westinghouse)	5-10	Sr.
Cedrick Banks, Chicago (Westinghouse)	6-3	Sr.
Phillip Gilbert, East St. Louis	6-3	Sr.
Derik Hollyfield, Aurora (West)	6-3	Jr.
Darius Miles, East St. Louis	6-8	Sr.

Championship Game Box Score

Carver Arena, Peoria, March 18, 2000

AURORA (WEST) (60)
Coach Gordon Kerkman

Player	FG-A	3P-A	FT-A	Pts	PF	Rb	As	St	Bl
Nate Eimer	0-0	0-0	0-0	0	0	0	0	0	0
Mike Fowler	1-3	1-2	0-0	3	3	0	2	0	0
Derik Hollyfield	4-7	4-6	0-2	12	1	3	2	0	0
Kevin Jenkins	1-3	0-0	0-0	2	1	2	0	1	0
Austin Real	5-12	0-0	7-12	17	0	9	2	0	1
Louis Smith	2-9	2-8	2-4	8	2	8	3	1	1
Jamaal Thompson	4-6	0-0	7-8	15	3	2	1	0	1
Jarod Tobler	1-1	0-0	1-2	3	1	3	1	0	0
TEAM						5			
TOTAL	18-41	7-16	17-28	60	11	32	11	2	3

CHICAGO (WESTINGHOUSE) (57)
Coach Chris Head

Player	FG-A	3P-A	FT-A	Pts	PF	Rb	As	St	Bl
Martell Bailey	7-14	1-4	4-4	19	3	3	3	0	0
Cedrick Banks	9-23	2-10	2-2	22	5	6	1	2	0
Craig Franklin	1-4	0-2	0-0	2	4	6	3	1	1
Berron Hill	0-0	0-0	0-0	0	0	0	0	0	0
Johnny Tate	0-1	0-0	0-0	0	3	6	1	0	0
Dennis Trammell	5-8	4-6	0-0	14	4	2	1	2	1
Jamal Washington	0-1	0-0	0-0	0	3	1	0	0	0
Tavaris Wiggins	0-4	0-2	0-0	0	0	1	0	0	0
TEAM						5			
TOTAL	22-55	7-24	6-6	57	22	30	9	5	2

Aurora (West)	17	11	17	15	—	60
Chicago (Westinghouse)	15	10	9	23	—	57

Officials: Mark Newquist, Rich Grube, Stan Donegan.

Westinghouse's Dennis Trammell drives the free throw lane as West Aurora's Derik Hollyfield moves to block the attack.

Jamal Washington of Westinghouse has little room to maneuver as Austin Real and Kevin Jenkins of West Aurora surround him under the basket.

West Aurora's Louis Smith passes out of trouble in the championship contest against Westinghouse.

ALL TIED UP

West Aurora's Derik Hollyfield battles for a loose ball with Cedrick Banks (34) and Martell Bailey (33) of Westinghouse.

Louis Smith and Derik Hollyfield of West Aurora stretch for a rebound in the 2000 Class AA title game against Westinghouse.

2000AA

Pearls of postgame wisdom
Class AA edition

Landon "Sonny" Cox was *anything* but *predictable* while coaching *Chicago King.*

Coach Landon Cox of Chicago King explains his tournament strategy to reporter Hank Sundeen at a 1986 press buffet.

by Jeff Lampe

At times Cox could be confrontational. He could be obstinate. He could be obscure. But he was almost always quotable. In fact, no Class AA coach provided the media with more fodder than Cox.

Consider this gem quoted in the *Peoria Journal Star* prior to King's Elite Eight appearance in 1999. "They know if I'm coming downstate, I'm coming with something. We're not tiptoeing through the tulips, you understand," Cox said. "We're going down there to win it."

But Landon is not alone atop Mount Mouth. The large-school tournament has had its share of larger-than-life characters willing to speak their minds. Bob Basarich, Jerry Leggett, Duncan Reid and John Schneiter were all coaches who kept reporters and readers chuckling.

In the 1973 quarterfinals, following a 62-54 win over previously unbeaten and top-ranked Lincoln, Lockport Central coach Basarich needed only a few minutes to cue up a season's worth of one-liners for most. As he concluded Basarich said, "You can say these kinds of things when you win."

Winning is not a prerequisite for spouting off, though, as you can see in this collection of comments from Class AA Elite Eight history.

Classic Cox

At times, Sonny Cox's postgame show was as entertaining as the play of his Chicago King team on the floor. And that's saying plenty since King won 87 percent of its games and three state titles under Cox.

Why should I feel for him? He had Isiah Thomas and a whole lot of other dudes.
1999 — Cox on St. Joseph coach Gene Pingatore, who had played for a title only once before 1999.

There are kids here who couldn't score 27 points if you stood 'em on the shore and let them roll the ball into Lake Michigan.
1990 — Cox, arguing with the claim his all-stater Jamie Brandon started slow after scoring 27 points in a win over East St. Louis Lincoln.

He can run all day and all night. But you can be sure that I'm getting him to bed. You can't fly with the buzzards all night and make it with the eagles all day.
1987 — Cox, commenting on Marcus Liberty.

This ain't football. There ain't but five players out there. Marcus is a horse. You know what a horse is? You've got to ride a horse.
1987 — Cox, answering critics who said he relied too much on Marcus Liberty.

My coaches say I've mellowed. They say I take more back talk from the fellas than I used to. They say I don't crack 'em like I used to. But see, that's the new rule now. You can't put your hands on kids these days. With Johnny [Selvie], I could pop him upside the head and keep on smokin'.
1999 — Cox.

We have a saying at King that you check your ego at the door.
1986 — Cox.

Even the University of Illinois doesn't have anybody who can stop Jamie Brandon one-on-one.
1990 — Cox.

Leggett's legacy

Colorful definitely describes the late Jerry Leggett, who established a new rule for Quincy coaches: In addition to winning games you must also provide juicy quotes.

I wore this blue-and-white outfit because if I lost I'd sell ice cream next week. They wouldn't let me coach again.
1981 — Leggett, after capping a 33-0 season by winning a state championship.

That's only because he picks his hair up that high. He's really about 5-4 1/2 or 5-5, but he's got a 6-4 heart.
1979 — Leggett, on Quincy guard Mike Rudd, who claimed to be 5-7.

By the time they catch on to me I'm on the move again.
1981 — Leggett, discussing how at that point he had coached six teams in 20 years.

Third-place reactions

Love it or hate it, the third-place game sure generates comments.

Our welcome-home plans depend on our place. For third the kids get to ride on the fire engine. For fourth they have to trot along behind it.
1990 — Leggett, Quincy coach.

I'm going to enjoy that third-place trophy all the way home ... maybe even hug it.
1981 — Frank Lollino, Westinghouse coach after defeating Wheaton Central.

Any game worth playing is worth winning.
1993 — Gene Gourley, Danville coach, after defeating Palatine Fremd for third.

We didn't come here to play for third place. I just hope I can get them all to show up for tonight's game.
1989 — Cox, after a semifinal loss to East St. Louis Lincoln

Lockport legend

Though his time in the tournament spotlight was more than two decades ago, Lockport coach Bob Basarich's comments still resonate.

I let the players set their own schedules. Of course, if they want a 2 a.m. bedtime, we negotiate.
1973 — Basarich.

I have had great talent. And they play like I coach. When we get excited we punch each other and wrestle in the huddle and then everything's all right.
1978 — Basarich, after winning the state title.

That's just Gerry. He's like me. He gets upset if a fly lands on his head.
1978 — Basarich, discussing the technical foul Gerry Barbeauld was whistled for during the title game.

I probably speak louder prayers than anybody in the state of Illinois.
1978 — Basarich.

Teams play like their coaches and my name isn't Father Bob
1978 — Basarich.

On winning

There have been at least a thousand players and coaches who said winning a game at state is "like a dream come true." Now and then someone follows a big victory with a unique response.

After a state championship what's ahead for me? First-period gym class Monday morning.
1980 — Willie Little, Chicago Manley coach, after title win over Effingham.

It's everything I hoped it would be. Actually, it's a little more.
2003 — Daniel Ruffin, Peoria Central point guard, after winning a state championship.

The horn went off at the right time. That game could have been played until tomorrow afternoon and there would be 84 guys fouled out and it would still be a one-point game.
2004 — Chuck Buescher, Peoria Central coach, after a 42-40 quarterfinal win over Chicago Farragut.

I'm a Christian man and I have to think there was something more going on out there other than the coach.
1976 — Bill Warden, Chicago Morgan Park coach, after Laird Smith's 18-foot shot with no time left sealed a 45-44 win over West Aurora in the title game.

We were joking before the game that we'd have the trophy in the case at home and they'd still be calling us the underdog.
1979 — Jay Huyler, Park Ridge Maine South guard, after his team upset Quincy in the title game.

Like I told Bob. If I beat you, I'll never be able to go home again.
1977 — Bruce Boyle, Peoria Central coach, a Lanphier graduate and Springfield native while talking to Lanphier coach Bob Nika prior to the title game Peoria won 72-62.

This should end the myth that Public League basketball is inferior.
1975 — Herb Brown, Chicago Phillips coach, after beating Chicago Heights Bloom for the championship.

Lockport coach Bob Basarich, shown here during his team's 1978 championship run, never held back on or off the court.

continued on next page

On losing

Everyone responds to losing basketball games in a different way. Nowhere are responses to defeat scrutinized by as many media members as at the state tournament.

Quincy's Jerry Leggett regales the crowd in the IHSA interview room after a 1981 victory.

That was a good old-fashioned, out-behind-the-barn whipping.
1991 — Duncan Reid, Rock Island coach, after an 89-60 loss to Peoria Manual in the quarterfinals.

I felt kind of funny going down there with [Kevin] Garnett and [Ronnie] Fields and those guys and not bringing back any hardware.
2004 — William "Wolf" Nelson, Chicago Farragut coach, on losing a 1995 quarterfinal to Harvey Thornton.

At least they let us have our uniforms when we left the floor.
1973 — Bob Basarich, Lockport Central coach, after an 83-67 semifinal loss to eventual champ Chicago Hirsch.

We tried to pull the "We're N.C. State and they're Houston" or "We're Villanova and they're Georgetown." Then we went out and got beat, bad. Hocus-pocus tricks aren't going to work.
1993 — Mike Miller, Rockford Guilford coach, discussing his team's 79-42 loss to Chicago King in the title game.

We were drunk with fatigue out there.
1975 — Howard "Whitey" Long, Rockford Auburn coach, after a quarterfinal loss to Peoria Richwoods.

Rich Central's quickness broke our glass slipper.
1986 — Jack Hermanski, Romeoville coach.

Officiating

The men in stripes are a frequent target for barbs by Class AA coaches.

I'll tell the kids they play touch-and-foul down there — you touch 'em, you get a foul.
1973 — Charles Stimpson, Chicago Hirsch coach.

I was frustrated with the officials. We had kids with footprints on their shoulders.
1987 — Jerry Leggett, Quincy coach, after quarterfinal win over Peoria Manual.

It's unfortunate that a technical has to decide the game.
1989 — Chuck Buescher, Peoria Central coach, after a technical was called on Chris Reynolds with the title game tied 48-48 and 1:18 remaining in the first overtime. East St. Louis Lincoln won in triple overtime.

Coach Steve Goers of Rockford Boylan talks with broadcaster Jim Feather before one of Boylan's many state tournament appearances.

Remembering Thornridge

A few Quincy fans and perhaps Landon Cox will argue the point, but many believe Thornridge's 33-0 state champions in 1972 are the finest in Illinois history.

This should probably be a three-class tournament — with Thornridge alone in Class AAA.
1972 — Jack Burmaster, Evanston coach.

Of course, the only thing I hear is that the only way we can lose is if I screw it up.
1972 — Ron Ferguson, Thornridge coach.

I'm not sure that Thornridge couldn't compete in the Big Ten. That was probably the best basketball team to ever play high school ball.
1972 — Sherrill Hanks, Quincy coach.

He said what?

Some comments defy classification but deserve repeating.

Everywhere we go, though not as much lately, we hear the cheer from the other student body of "Overrated." I just sit there on the bench and go, "Just wait. Just wait 'til the end of the game and you won't be cheering that." And they never are.
2005 — Dave Weber, Northbrook Glenbrook North coach, on guard Jon Scheyer.

They must have meant downstate.
1973 — Schneiter responding to preseason press clippings that predicted a "down" year.

He's figured out a state tournament medal lasts longer than a Whopper.
1991 — Wayne McClain, then Peoria Manual assistant coach, on 6-4, 250-pound Clint Ford's efforts to keep in shape.

I just found out a couple of years ago, I had a couple of great uncles who were 7-foot-4 and 7-foot-2 back in the day. I'm Norwegian. I think they were Vikings and lived before basketball was invented.
2003 — John Smith, 6-foot-8 Johnsburg center.

He took off from 25 feet away and thought he was gonna land at O'Hare. Instead he came down in Assembly Hall.
1986 — Steve Goers, Rockford Boylan coach, discussing a failed dunk by all-stater Danny Jones that also netted him a technical foul in a quarterfinal loss to Peoria Manual.

In deinen Gesicht. *We don't say that in Germany.*
1980 — Uwe Blab, Effingham center,
providing the German translation for the phrase "in your face."

They decided playing basketball was easier than ducking shoes and being stuffed in lockers at halftime.
1975 — Wes Mason, Bloom coach, whose team was second at state after placing fourth in its conference and struggling through the first half of its super-sectional.

I call our attack "organized disorder."
1975 — Herb Brown, Chicago Phillips coach.

Long hair? Get with it. It's 1972. What the hell's long hair got to do with playing basketball?
1972 — Sherril Hanks, Quincy coach, responding to a question about his "long-haired" guards Larry Moore and Jim Wisman.

It just seemed Satan was tugging at us the whole season.
1996 — Rocky Hill, Thornton coach.

It's nice not to see Darius Miles when you walk off the bus.
2002 — Rick Malnati, New Trier coach, whose team was trounced in the 2001 quarterfinals by East St. Louis and future NBA player Miles.

Not unless the whole King team falls dead.
1990 — Bennie Lewis, East St. Louis Lincoln coach, when asked if King could be beaten.

Chemistry is the key. Nobody can bake a cake without baking soda.
1997 — Wayne McClain, Peoria Manual coach.

There's nothing in life you can't do if you can set up bingo tables the way Gene Pingatore wants them set up.
1999 — Brandon Aldridge, St. Joseph assistant coach.

Bobby's had games they could have put the whole team and the cheerleaders on him and they still weren't going to stop him.
1975 — Joel Galvin, Bloomington center, discussing teammate Bob Bender.

I thought all along we were the Rodney Dangerfield of basketball.
1986 — Jack Hermanski, Romeoville coach.

I really don't know what to do with Roth. He's the first player I've coached in five years that listens to what I tell him.
1976 — Bob Witt, Decatur Eisenhower coach, on Jeff Roth.

I think I got killed a little on that rebound.
1974 — Brian Young, Peoria Central forward, whose rebound in the closing second sealed a quarterfinal win over Danville but left him with three deep scratches in his cheek.

The only time I consider it is when we do room assignments.
2001 — Bob Williams, Schaumburg coach, discussing the gender of assistant Kelly O'Connor, believed to be the first woman to coach in a boys' title game.

I grew up in Jerseyville. I love that southern Illinois basketball. We love taking it to Chicago.
1980 — Loren Wallace, Lincoln coach, discussing the possibility of an all-downstate final pitting Effingham against Lincoln.

As far as AA is concerned, the south is probably dead. They don't have the talent we have up north.
1974 — Glenn Whittenberg, Maywood Proviso East coach, who started his coaching career in the southern Illinois town of Zeigler and whose team defeated Breese Mater Dei in the semifinals.

Dolph always used to say, "You meet a lot of strangers on the Assembly Hall floor. You might not recognize some of the kids on your own team."
1975 — Howard "Whitey" Long, Rockford Auburn coach, quoting former Auburn coach Dolph Stanley.

We do a lot of things that aren't considered fundamentally sound. All I can say is that's the way we play. If you play run-and-gun you got to play it all the way.
1977 — Bob Nika, Springfield Lanphier coach.

I don't like newspapers. The newspapers didn't rate us until the end of the year. Either you became smarter or we became better awfully quick.
1983 — Sam Cameli, Thornton.

We don't want to be the best basketball team of all time. Just the best team in 1991.
1991 — Bill Hitt, Proviso East coach.

If that's what got us here, hell, I'd retire every year.
1996 — Mel Sheets, New Trier coach, who announced his retirement before reaching the Elite Eight.

One of the old guys around here told me Tuesday I had to win one more ... so he could die.
1998 — Rick Moss, Centralia coach, discussing the importance of his team winning its super-sectional game and reaching the Elite Eight for the first time in 34 years.

I think Isiah [Thomas] was and is unique to the game of basketball here or anywhere else.
1987 — Gene Pingatore, St. Joseph coach

I forgot, I'll be able to charge for autographs next year.
2001 — Eddy Curry, South Holland Thornwood center, who skipped to the NBA the next year.

A CENTURY OF MEMORIES
20 100 07
IHSA
Celebrating 100 years of IHSA Boys Basketball Tournaments

Coach Bennie Lewis of East St. Louis Lincoln speaks with television reporter Frank Bussone during the 1990 Class AA meet.

Only once — in 1983 — had an unranked team won a Class AA state championship.

Not that Schaumburg didn't have the record. It just didn't have the respect.

Coming to Peoria at 23-3 two years after its first Elite Eight appearance, Schaumburg packed its bus with depth. Meanwhile, Eddy Curry was probably taking up three seats for top-ranked Thornwood.

The 6-foot-11, 290-pound Curry led the Sweet Sixteen in scoring. But three of

There was another lasting impression made on young minds that day when Thornwood coach Kevin Hayhurst benched a season-long starter for violating team rules after the quarterfinal round. It was the kind of hard-earned lesson that can benefit a program in the long run.

And sure enough, Thornwood (albeit under a new coach) was back in the title game two years later with a balanced bunch of disciplined overachievers.

Schaumburg's 56-44 semifinal win over LaGrange Lyons marked only the fourth time in Class AA history that two unranked teams had squared off a step from the title game. On six occasions, the Class AA third-place game has matched teams not among the top 16 in the final regular-season poll.

SCHAUMBURG
Class AA State Champions of 2001

FRONT ROW (left to right): Kevin Pearson, James Han, Tom Huber, Garrett Bruni, Roger Hendrickson. SECOND ROW: Tony Young, Greg Dorgan, David Gibson, Scott Zoellick, Zach Pancratz, Tim Foecking. THIRD ROW: Coach Bob Williams, Mark Pancratz, Craig Reichel, Tom Burke, Ryan Walter, Brandon Reichel, Asst. Coach Mark Stilling.

the next five players on that list were Schaumburg's Scott Zoellick, Mark Pancratz, and Tony Young.

Curry had 32 points, making 12 of 14 from the field and 8 of 9 from the foul line. He also pulled down a dozen rebounds in the title game. But Schaumburg's offensive trio proved that three is greater than one, totaling 54 points in a 66-54 championship win.

And when it came to defensive hustle, it appeared as if Coach Bob Williams' bench extended out into the Carver Arena parking lot.

With Curry coming into the title game 62 percent accurate in Sweet Sixteen play, Williams chose to concentrate his defensive forces where he thought they could do the most good — on everybody not named Curry.

Not many soon-to-be millionaires cry in heartbreak and frustration. But that's what Curry did only a couple months before the Chicago Bulls made him the No. 4 pick in the NBA draft. It was a disappointment the likes of which Curry doubted he would ever suffer again, no matter the path of his pro career.

State Final Tournament Scores

Super-Sectionals
At Chicago [United Center]—Chicago (Morgan Park) 67, Chicago (Crane) 60
At Carbondale [SIU]—Alton 62, Belleville (West) 59
At Normal [ISU]—Peoria (Richwoods) 48, Mt. Zion 44
At Chicago [St. Xavier U.]—South Holland (Thornwood) 60, New Lenox (Lincoln-Way) 44
At Evanston [NU]—Schaumburg 78, Zion (Z.-Benton) 59
At DeKalb [NIU]—Aurora (West) 63, St. Charles (East) 59
At Moline [The Mark]—Moline 45, Cary (C.-Grove) 42 (OT)
At Hinsdale (Central)—LaGrange (Lyons) 52, Chicago (St. Patrick) 48 (OT)

Quarterfinals
Chicago (Morgan Park) 64, Alton 50
South Holland (Thornwood) 65, Peoria (Richwoods) 36
Schaumburg 64, Aurora (West) 51
LaGrange (Lyons) 44, Moline 40

Semifinals
South Holland (Thornwood) 49, Chicago (Morgan Park) 46
Schaumburg 58, LaGrange (Lyons) 57

Finals
Chicago (Morgan Park) 56, LaGrange (Lyons) 44 (third place)
Schaumburg 66, South Holland (Thornwood) 54 (title)

Scoring Leaders

Player, School	G	FG	3P	FT	Pts
Eddy Curry, South Holland (Thornwood)	4	36	0	25	97
Scott Zoellick, Schaumburg	4	24	16	5	69
Mark Pancratz, Schaumburg	4	21	5	22	69
Quinnel Brown, Chicago (Morgan Park)	4	23	1	19	66
Melvin Buckley, S. Holland (Thornwood)	4	19	11	13	62

All-Tournament First Team

Player, School	Ht.	Yr.
Quinnel Brown, Chicago (Morgan Park)	6-6	Sr.
Melvin Buckley, South Holland (Thornwood)	6-7	Jr.
Eddy Curry, South Holland (Thornwood)	6-11	Sr.
Mark Pancratz, Schaumburg	6-3	Sr.
Scott Zoellick, Schaumburg	6-4	Sr.

Championship Game Box Score

Carver Arena, Peoria, March 17, 2001

SCHAUMBURG (66)
Coach Bob Williams

Player	FG-A	3P-A	FT-A	Pts	PF	Rb	As	St	Bl
Garrett Bruni	0-1	0-1	0-0	0	0	0	0	1	0
Tom Burke	0-0	0-0	0-0	0	0	0	0	0	0
Greg Dorgan	0-0	0-0	0-0	0	0	0	0	0	0
Tim Foecking	0-0	0-0	0-0	0	0	0	0	0	0
David Gibson	1-3	0-1	0-0	2	1	2	0	1	0
James Han	0-0	0-0	0-0	0	2	2	2	2	0
Roger Hendrickson	0-0	0-0	0-0	0	0	0	1	0	0
Mark Pancratz	6-13	1-4	8-9	21	4	3	0	0	0
Zach Pancratz	0-2	0-2	0-0	0	2	0	0	0	0
Kevin Pearson	1-1	0-0	0-0	2	0	0	0	0	0
Brandon Reichel	1-1	0-0	0-0	2	2	1	0	2	0
Craig Reichel	0-0	0-0	0-0	0	0	0	0	0	0
Ryan Walter	3-5	0-2	0-1	6	3	2	2	2	0
Tony Young	6-12	1-3	1-2	14	2	4	4	2	0
Scott Zoellick	7-8	5-6	0-0	19	1	2	1	0	0
TEAM						4			
TOTAL	25-46	7-19	9-12	66	17	20	10	10	0

SOUTH HOLLAND (THORNWOOD) (54)
Coach Kevin Hayhurst

Player	FG-A	3P-A	FT-A	Pts	PF	Rb	As	St	Bl
Geremie Allison	0-0	0-0	0-0	0	1	0	0	0	0
Jeff Briney	0-0	0-0	0-0	0	0	0	0	0	0
Melvin Buckley	3-11	2-9	1-2	9	2	0	2	0	0
Aubrey Conerly	1-4	1-2	0-1	3	4	0	4	1	0
Eddy Curry	12-14	0-0	8-9	32	1	12	1	1	2
Sean High	0-0	0-0	0-0	0	0	0	0	0	0
Chris Jones	0-0	0-0	0-0	0	0	0	0	0	0
Cory Jones	0-0	0-0	0-0	0	0	0	0	0	0
Jeremy Jones	2-6	1-4	0-0	5	4	1	4	2	0
David Moss	1-3	0-2	0-1	2	3	4	3	1	0
Joe Pacyga	0-0	0-0	0-0	0	0	0	0	0	0
Pierre Thomas	1-2	0-0	1-2	3	2	5	0	1	0
DeWaun Wells	0-0	0-0	0-0	0	0	0	0	0	0
TEAM						2			
TOTAL	20-40	4-17	10-15	54	17	24	14	6	2

Schaumburg	11	17	20	18	—	66
South Holland (Thornwood)	13	11	9	21	—	54

Officials: Clifford Bailey, Mark Mayhood, Peter King.

Thornwood's 6-foot-11 Eddy Curry towers over Morgan Park's Jonathan Byrd in a semifinal contest.

Aubrey Conerly of Thornwood leads the charge in the championship game against Schaumburg.

A Thornwood cheerleader and junior cheerleader stand at attention for the National Anthem.

LOOK OUT BELOW

Schaumburg's defenders have limited options as Curry goes up for a dunk in the title game.

Derik Hollyfield of West Aurora scoots around Schaumburg's Scott Zoellick in quarterfinal play.

2001 AA

293

Number 13 certainly wasn't unlucky for "The House."

This was the 13th Sweet Sixteen appearance for Chicago Westinghouse, a school that didn't make its first until 1977. But while respect for Westinghouse basketball was already so universal the program had been given a nickname, it had yet to win a state championship.

Not in 1977, when its unbeaten No. 2 team ran afoul of unbeaten No. 1 Phillips in the Chicago Public League final. Not in 1999, when its unbeaten No. 1 was pounded by 20 points in the CPL final. Not in 2000, when a No. 1 House came up short in the championship game under first-year boss Chris Head.

Not with Mark Aguirre and Eddie Johnson or Hersey Hawkins or Kiwane Garris — all future major-college stars who combined to play in 3,177 NBA games.

Not under respected coaches Frank Lollino and Roy Condotti. Nor under Frank Griseto, who claimed a third-place trophy.

Meanwhile, Springfield Lanphier was busy shedding its Rodney Dangerfield image. This would be Lanphier's fourth championship game in 25 years. In the first two, the Lions were not ranked among the top 16 in the final regular-season prep poll. And they were rated only eighth the third time around.

This time was different. Lanphier would finish in the same poll and state-finals position: No. 2.

Fifth-ranked Westinghouse, led by Darius Glover, overcame Lanphier's one-two punch of Andre Iguodala and Richard McBride, 76-72 for the title. The

House finally got the big trophy to go with three for third (1981, 1992 and 1996) and one for second (2000).

A put-back by light-scoring Randon Williams with 55 seconds left got Westinghouse up 73-72 and proved to be the winning score.

Glover hit 12 of his 16 title shots, scored 28 and pulled down 10 rebounds. Three teammates added from 11 to 15

points each, and Westinghouse needed it all to overcome Iguodala (29 points) and McBride (22 points, 11 rebounds, 6-for-12 on threes).

Lanphier fell short despite scoring 34 points in the fourth quarter against a defense that had limited its two other Elite Eight foes to game totals of 48 and 46.

Westinghouse, which wound up avenging all three of its in-state losses, had fallen to Lanphier 77-71 in the title game of the Pekin Christmas tournament. This was the third time in Class AA history that the state title game was a rematch of final-four Pekin tourney foes.

State Final Tournament Scores

Super-Sectionals
At Chicago [United Center]—Chicago (Westinghouse) 62, Chicago (Farragut) 58
At DeKalb [NIU]—Carol Stream (Glenbard North) 68, Aurora (West) 65
At Chicago [Loyola U.]—Highland Park 41, Barrington 38
At Chicago [United Center]—Winnetka (New Trier) 60, Maywood (Proviso East) 51
At Normal [ISU]—Springfield (Lanphier) 58, Pekin 53
At Chicago [United Center]—South Holland (Thornwood) 46, Joliet (Twp.) 45
At Carbondale [SIU]—Centralia 79, East St. Louis 49
At Rockford [Metro Centre]—Moline 51, Rockford (Boylan) 49 (OT)

Quarterfinals
Chicago (Westinghouse) 71, Carol Stream (Glenbard North) 48
Winnetka (New Trier) 59, Highland Park 48
Springfield (Lanphier) 66, South Holland (Thornwood) 50
Centralia 51, Moline 37

Semifinals
Chicago (Westinghouse) 63, Winnetka (New Trier) 46
Springfield (Lanphier) 56, Centralia 52

Finals
Centralia 75, Winnetka (New Trier) 64 (third place)
Chicago (Westinghouse) 76, Springfield (Lanphier) 72 (title)

Scoring Leaders

Player, School	G	FG	3P	FT	Pts
Andre Iguodala, Springfield (Lanphier)	4	28	3	27	86
Darius Glover, Chicago (Westinghouse)	4	31	0	21	83
Richard McBride, Springfield (Lanphier)	4	23	10	20	76
Lance Marcum, Centralia	4	22	16	10	70
Ted Rosinski, Winnetka (New Trier)	4	23	11	4	61

All-Tournament First Team

Player, School	Ht.	Yr.
Jamaal Brown, Chicago (Westinghouse)	5-11	Sr.
Darius Glover, Chicago (Westinghouse)	6-4	Sr.
Andre Iguodala, Springfield (Lanphier)	6-6	Sr.
Richard McBride, Springfield (Lanphier)	6-3	Jr.
Matt Shaw, Centralia	6-6	So.

Championship Game Box Score

Carver Arena, Peoria, March 16, 2002

CHICAGO (WESTINGHOUSE) (76)
Coach Chris Head

Player	FG-A	3P-A	FT-A	Pts	PF	Rb	As	St	Bl
Anthony Bennett	5-7	0-0	1-2	11	5	3	2	1	1
Byron Booker	0-0	0-0	0-0	0	0	2	0	0	0
Jamaal Brown	3-7	2-3	4-4	12	2	0	4	2	0
Clide Crosby	0-2	0-0	0-2	0	4	3	3	0	0
Jamarcus Ellis	1-7	0-1	4-4	6	3	5	1	2	0
Darren Gafford	0-0	0-0	0-0	0	0	0	0	0	0
Darius Glover	12-16	0-0	4-9	28	4	10	2	0	2
Richard Russell	5-9	0-0	5-7	15	5	5	1	0	0
Randon Williams	2-4	0-0	0-1	4	2	3	0	2	0
TOTAL	28-52	2-4	18-29	76	25	33	13	7	3

SPRINGFIELD (LANPHIER) (72)
Coach Craig Patton

Player	FG-A	3P-A	FT-A	Pts	PF	Rb	As	St	Bl
Ademola Adeniji	0-3	0-1	2-2	2	4	5	1	1	0
Andre Iguodala	8-18	1-6	12-16	29	4	6	4	0	0
Tyler Klunick	0-0	0-0	0-0	0	0	0	0	0	0
Richard McBride	6-17	6-12	4-6	22	4	11	4	0	2
Terell Pearson	3-6	2-5	0-0	8	4	0	0	3	0
Niccos Scott	1-2	0-0	2-5	4	5	2	0	2	0
Tony Smith	3-10	1-3	0-0	7	2	5	3	0	0
TOTAL	21-56	10-27	20-29	72	23	30	12	6	2

Chicago (Westinghouse)	19	13	18	26	—	76
Springfield (Lanphier)	11	7	20	34	—	72

Officials: Kevin Cates, Kevin Wiggs, Ray Piagentini.

> *Westinghouse won the state in its 13th Sweet Sixteen appearance.*

CHICAGO (WESTINGHOUSE)
Class AA State Champions of 2002

FRONT ROW (left to right): Darren Gafford, Anthony Bennett, Clide Crosby Jr., Stephen Collum, Cortney Thornton, Parief Smith, Johnny Collier, Jamaal Brown, DeAndre Billingsley. SECOND ROW: Randon Williams, Richard Russell, Byron Booker, Jamarcus Ellis, Darius Glover, Aaron Moore, Edward Whitaker.

Andre Iguodala of Springfield Lanphier stops on a dime in the 2002 championship game against Westinghouse.

Anthony Bennett of Westinghouse storms the lane to get off a short jumper against two Lanphier defenders.

THREADING THE NEEDLE

Darius Glover of Westinghouse launches a baseline jumper against New Trier in the semifinals. Westinghouse won by a 63-46 count.

Jamaal Brown of Westinghouse puts a short runner over Lanphier's Tony Smith in the title game.

Westinghouse's Darius Glover tries a short left-handed hook in the title game against Lanphier as Niccos Scott (50) puts up resistance.

2002AA

295

2003 AA

S haun Livingston found himself going one-on-one for a state title. Turns out there was a reason this Peoria Central junior would become the first high school point guard ever drafted in the NBA's first round.

He was so slight of body some folks questioned his chances of withstanding the pounding of the pros. But despite banging from two defenders, Livingston's drive to and then along the baseline produced a 45-43 championship win over Thornwood.

The potential for another series of state showdowns between a Peoria survivor and northern power (à la Manual vs. Thornton) had fizzled when top-ranked West Aurora lost in the sectional semifinals.

But second-rated Peoria still found plenty of competition in the Elite Eight, especially from a Thornwood squad that sophomore coach Bob Curran had unexpectedly inherited in October. Curran then had to nurse his new team back from a four-game mid-season losing streak to make a third straight state trip.

Central avenged its only loss by pounding once-beaten No. 5 Bartonville

Limestone 62-29 in sectional play. Then the Lions used a 23-2 scoring spree to sideline No. 5 Lincoln by 26 in the Normal Super-Sectional.

In a quarterfinal against an equally young Chicago Von Steuben squad, Peoria got 16 of the last 18 points in 2:45 to survive one of the two Chicago Public League teams making the Windy City's first non-guaranteed Class AA Elite Eight appearances.

In the semifinals, Peoria needed 23 points and eight steals from its only senior starter, Daniel Ruffin, for a 58-48 win

over unranked Evanston. Meanwhile, Thornwood needed a monster trey from Eric Gray at 0:09 to upstage fellow upstart Glenbrook North 40-39.

Glenbrook North finished third as 6-foot-6 freshman Jon Scheyer emerged on the state stage with a 13-rebound quarterfinal and 20 points plus seven assists in the consolation contest.

Other than the point totals in the championship box score, only turnovers gave a clue to the outcome. Peoria won the turnover tally 6-14.

After 13 lead changes and nine ties, it came down to a single big play — just like Central coach Chuck Buescher's 1983 and 1988 title tries. But this time, Buescher had the perfect playmaker. And Livingston, who sprained an ankle in the quarterfinals and had only a so-so state finals, made the driving basket to leave Central 31-1.

Central, the oldest existing high school west of the Allegheny Mountains (1856) and winner of the state's first tourney (1908), had waited 69 years for its second basketball championship in 1977, then 26 more for its third crown. With Livingston only a junior, the Lions threatened to cut title-wait time to zero.

PEORIA
Class AA State Champions of 2003

FRONT ROW (left to right): Jacob Metteler, Orlando Edwards, Jermaine Dunigan, O'Bryan Jackson, Payton Wadley, Brandon Lee, Daniel Ruffin, Tyson Langhorn. SECOND ROW: Asst. Coach Dan Ruffin, Asst. Coach Chuck Westendorf, Asst. Coach Meechie Edwards, Reggie Russell, DeAndre Miranda, Shaun Livingston, Brandon Foster, Lesley Weatherspoon, John Ruffin, Asst. Coach Eric Heath, Coach Chuck Buescher.

State Final Tournament Scores

Super-Sectionals
At Chicago [United Center]—Evanston (Twp.) 65, Chicago (Hubbard) 61
At Carbondale [SIU]—Belleville (West) 39, Troy (Triad) 34
At Chicago [United Center]—Chicago (Von Steuben) 65, Chicago (Brother Rice) 56
At Normal [ISU]—Peoria 67, Lincoln 41
At DeKalb [NIU]—Downers Grove (South) 67, Batavia 49
At Aurora (East)—South Holland (Thornwood) 76, Burbank (St. Laurence) 70
At Moline [The Mark]—Johnsburg 51, East Moline (United) 22
At Chicago [Loyola U.]—Northbrook (Glenbrook North) 71, Zion (Z.-Benton) 55

Quarterfinals
Evanston (Twp.) 58, Belleville (West) 50
Peoria 63, Chicago (Von Steuben) 43
South Holland (Thornwood) 46, Downers Grove (South) 44
Northbrook (Glenbrook North) 47, Johnsburg 24

Semifinals
Peoria 58, Evanston (Twp.) 48
South Holland (Thornwood) 40, Northbrook (Glenbrook North) 39

Finals
Northbrook (Glenbrook North) 73, Evanston (Twp.) 65 (third place)
Peoria 45, South Holland (Thornwood) 43 (title)

Scoring Leaders

Player, School	G	FG	3P	FT	Pts
Eytan Azaria, Northbrook (Glenbrook N.)	4	34	11	6	85
Mike McKinney, Evanston (Twp.)	4	25	2	12	64
Jon Scheyer, Northbrook (Glenbrook N.)	4	15	6	21	57
Brandon Lee, Peoria	4	20	3	13	56
Shaun Livingston, Peoria	4	13	0	25	51

All-Tournament First Team

Player, School	Ht.	Yr.
Eytan Azaria, Northbrook (Glenbrook North)	6-6	Sr.
Shaun Livingston, Peoria	6-6	Jr.
Mike McKinney, Evanston (Twp.)	6-3	Sr.
Brendan Mullins, Downers Grove (South)	6-01	Sr.
Daniel Ruffin, Peoria	5-10	Sr.

Championship Game Box Score

Carver Arena, Peoria, March 22, 2003

PEORIA (45)
Coach Chuck Buescher

Player	FG-A	3P-A	FT-A	Pts	PF	Rb	As	St	Bl
Tyson Langhorn	0-2	0-2	0-0	0	1	1	1	1	1
Brandon Lee	5-11	1-2	1-3	12	2	1	1	1	0
Shaun Livingston	5-9	0-0	4-4	14	2	6	2	0	0
DeAndre Miranda	0-2	0-0	0-0	0	1	2	0	1	0
Jacob Motteler	1-2	1-2	0-0	3	0	1	0	0	0
Daniel Ruffin	3-8	0-1	1-2	7	0	1	4	3	0
John Ruffin	3-4	0-0	0-0	6	2	4	0	0	0
Payton Wadley	1-2	1-2	0-0	3	0	0	0	0	0
TOTAL	18-40	3-9	6-9	45	8	18	8	6	1

SOUTH HOLLAND (THORNWOOD) (43)
Coach Bob Curran

Player	FG-A	3P-A	FT-A	Pts	PF	Rb	As	St	Bl
Geremie Allison	4-7	4-7	0-0	12	3	1	1	1	0
Eric Gray	1-8	0-4	0-0	2	2	2	1	0	0
Cordell Liggins	1-3	0-0	0-0	2	0	1	0	1	0
Maurice Montgomery	5-7	1-2	2-3	13	1	5	3	1	0
Andre Muse	3-3	2-2	0-0	8	4	5	2	0	0
Martell Nelson	3-3	0-0	0-1	6	2	8	0	1	1
Lante Ward	0-3	0-0	0-0	0	0	1	1	0	0
Darnell Westbrook	0-0	0-0	0-0	0	0	1	0	0	0
Lorenzo Williams	0-1	0-1	0-0	0	1	0	0	0	0
TOTAL	17-35	7-16	2-4	43	13	26	8	4	1

Peoria	9	12	15	9	—	45
South Holland (Thornwood)	11	11	13	8	—	43

Officials: Carlos Burton, Ken Schell, Terry Murphy.

Eytan Azaria of Glenbrook North looks for an opening against Johnsburg's George Salminen. Azaria topped the tournament scoring charts with 85 points in four games.

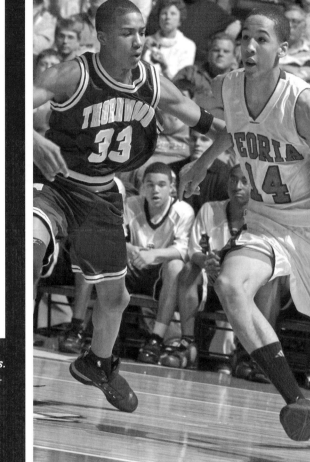

Shaun Livingston of Peoria Central makes a baseline move against Thornwood's Andre Muse in the championship game at Carver Arena.

Peoria's DeAndre Miranda beats the defense of Thornwood's Martell Nelson in the title game.

WATCHFUL EYES   Eric Gray of Thornwood zeroes in on his target in championship-game action.

2003AA

CLASS AA

PEORIA
Class AA State Champions of 2004

FRONT ROW (left to right): Jeff Wires, Michael Perkins, Asst. Coach Chuck Westendorf, Asst. Coach Meechie Edwards, Coach Chuck Buescher, Asst. Coach Dan Ruffin, Asst. Coach Eric Heath, Jacob Motteler, Zachary Davis. SECOND ROW: Orlando Edwards, Brandon Lee, Terrence Smith, Reggie Russell, Dustin Warfield, Deandre Miranda, Shaun Livingston, Brandon Foster, Lesley Weatherspoon, Jeremy Rawls, Kennedy Green, Mgr. Toemi Haughn.

This year, not only was West Aurora expected to get to the state finals, it was assumed they'd beat fellow national top-10 team Peoria Central for the title. And why not: The Blackhawks had dominated Peoria in a January shootout at Northwestern University to snatch the No. 1 state poll position from the Lions.

But third-rated Homewood-Flossmoor spoiled the rematch, relegating West Aurora to third place with a 58-46 semifinal victory, thanks to 22 points by guard Exell Hardy on 7-for-10 shooting.

The title game again came down to all-American Peoria point guard Shaun Livingston making a play. Actually, to Livingston making play after play after play.

The skinny 6-foot-7 hero of the 2003 title game had 20 points and 11 rebounds all-stater Brandon Lee. Livingston and the 6-foot Lee shared title-game rebounding honors with nine apiece.

Central shot 4-for-7 on threes despite Livingston not attempting one. Homewood-Flossmoor was 1-for-12 from outside the arc.

"Our two extra hours rest helped," Central coach Chuck Buescher said of being in the upper bracket on double-header day. "I don't want to be chasing us 10 points down on tired legs."

Homewood-Flossmoor boasted all-stater Julian Wright, but balance was its strong point. All five starters led the Vikings in scoring at least once in their eight post-season games, while three players garnered game rebounding honors.

It was a tourney that went as predicted — sort of. Nine of the teams ranked in

in a 58-47 semifinal win over 10th-ranked Carbondale. Then he poured in 27 points on a vast variety of moves and shots for a 53-47 title win over H-F.

With Peoria leading 46-35 after three quarters, defense and deliberation did the rest. Livingston did all of Central's fourth-quarter scoring — on a jumper with 6:02 remaining and 5-for-6 foul shooting over the last 3:18.

The Vikings got only 1-for-9 shooting from Hardy, who was hounded by Peoria

the final regular-season Associated Press poll reached the Sweet Sixteen. Four of the other seven lost to rated squads.

The top three poll picks took home the top three trophies — just not the ones predicted: No. 1 West Aurora got third, No. 2 Central first and No. 3 Homewood-Flossmoor second.

Buescher promptly retired from prep coaching with an overall record of 530-168 and a stunning Sweet Sixteen mark of 14-2, moving to Bradley University as an

aide for its 2006 Sweet Sixteen entry. Mr. Basketball-lock Livingston was the No. 4 pick in the NBA draft by the Los Angeles Clippers.

The title repeat by Central (with an enrollment of 883, the smallest one-class or AA champ since Carver in 1963) gave Peoria, a city of four public high schools, 6 of 11 Class AA state championships from 1994 to 2004.

State Final Tournament Scores

Super-Sectionals

At Edwardsville [SIU-E]—Carbondale 58, East St. Louis 56
At Chicago [UIC]—Chicago (Simeon) 60, Westchester (St. Joseph) 56
At Chicago [United Center]—Chicago (Farragut) 53, Chicago (Von Steuben) 44
At Normal [ISU]—Peoria 69, Mt. Zion 54
At Rockford [Metro Centre]—Moline 58, Crystal Lake (Prairie Ridge) 45
At Chicago [United Center]—Flossmoor (Homewood-F.) 41, Harvey (Thornton) 36
At DeKalb [NIU]—Aurora (West) 40, Downers Grove (South) 36
At Chicago [Loyola U.]—Hoffman Estates 54, Waukegan 45

Quarterfinals

Carbondale 65, Chicago (Simeon) 46
Peoria 42, Chicago (Farragut) 40
Flossmoor (Homewood-F.) 41, Moline 34
Aurora (West) 47, Hoffman Estates 42

Semifinals

Peoria 58, Carbondale 47
Flossmoor (Homewood-F.) 58, Aurora (West) 46

Finals

Aurora (West) 68, Carbondale 50 (third place)
Peoria 53, Flossmoor (Homewood-F.) 47 (title)

Scoring Leaders

Player, School	G	FG	3P	FT	Pts
Justin Dentmon, Carbondale	4	31	14	23	99
Shaun Livingston, Peoria	4	26	0	19	71
Shaun Pruitt, Aurora (West)	4	23	0	13	59
Brandon Lee, Peoria	4	21	6	9	57
Julian Wright, Flossmoor (Homewood-F.)	4	19	3	8	49

All-Tournament First Team

Player, School	Ht.	Yr.
Justin Dentmon, Carbondale	6-1	Sr.
Brandon Lee, Peoria	6-0	Sr.
Shaun Livingston, Peoria	6-6	Sr.
Shaun Pruitt, Aurora (West)	6-9	Sr.
Julian Wright, Flossmoor (Homewood-F.)	6-8	Jr.

Championship Game Box Score

Carver Arena, Peoria, March 20, 2004

PEORIA (53)
Coach Chuck Buescher

Player	FG-A	3P-A	FT-A	Pts	PF	Rb	As	St	Bl
Orlando Edwards	0-0	0-0	0-0	0	0	0	1	0	0
Brandon Foster	0-0	0-0	0-0	0	0	0	0	0	0
Brandon Lee	4-13	1-3	3-6	12	5	9	1	1	0
Shaun Livingston	9-16	0-0	9-13	27	2	9	1	0	1
DeAndre Miranda	1-4	0-0	0-0	2	2	2	0	0	0
Jacob Motteler	2-3	2-3	0-0	6	2	0	3	1	0
Dustin Warfield	1-1	1-1	0-0	3	2	1	0	0	1
Lesley Weatherspoon	1-2	0-0	1-4	3	0	3	1	0	0
Jeff Wires	0-0	0-0	0-0	0	0	0	0	0	0
TOTAL	18-39	4-7	13-23	53	13	26	7	2	2

FLOSSMOOR (HOMEWOOD-F.) (47)
Coach Roy Condotti

Player	FG-A	3P-A	FT-A	Pts	PF	Rb	As	St	Bl
Freddie Barnes	2-7	1-1	0-0	5	4	6	3	1	0
Excell Hardy	1-9	0-5	5-6	7	3	3	1	2	0
Mitchell Hayes	1-3	0-0	0-0	2	0	0	0	0	0
Tim Johnson	0-1	0-0	0-0	0	0	1	0	0	0
Brian Nussbaum	0-7	0-5	3-4	3	4	3	1	2	0
Cyrus Tate	6-7	0-0	5-7	17	4	3	0	0	0
Neil Trainor	0-1	0-0	0-0	0	0	1	0	0	0
Julian Wright	6-9	0-1	1-1	13	4	7	2	0	4
TOTAL	16-44	1-12	14-18	47	19	25	7	5	4

Peoria	14	16	16	7 — 53
Flossmoor (Homewood-F.)	10	13	12	12 — 47

Officials: Dan Manning, Fred Allman, Keith McClellan.

Peoria Central's Shaun Livingston flirts with the sideline as he drives upcourt against Brian Nussbaum of Homewood-Flossmoor.

NOWHERE TO TURN

Homewood-Flossmoor's Cyrus Tate finds himself in a pickle as four Peoria players encircle him in the 2004 championship game.

Carbondale's Justin Dentmon makes a move on Simeon's Timonthy Green in a quarterfinal match-up.

Peoria fans rejoice after defeating Carbondale for the school's second consecutive state championship.

Shaun Livingston flies high for the dunk as Farragut's Jeffrey Herred watches from below.

2004AA

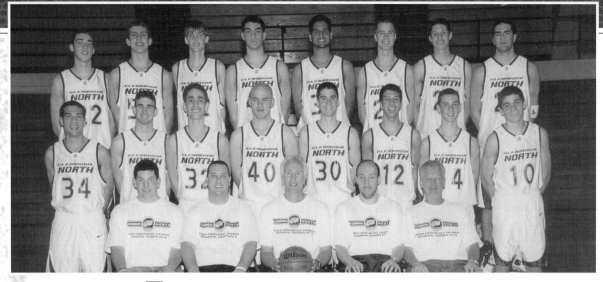

**NORTHBROOK
(GLENBROOK NORTH)**
Class AA State Champions of 2005

*FRONT ROW (left to right):
Mgr. Jordan Gaffen, Asst. Coach
Scott Lidskin, Coach David Weber,
Asst. Coach Bryan Halpern,
Admin. Asst. Frank Kiningham.
SECOND ROW: Michael Rosen,
Michael Rubo, Alex Prosperi,
Scott Inns, Jeff Nathan, Sean
Wallis, Matt Shamis, John Karis.
THIRD ROW: Tyler Cullitan,
Jonathan Radke, Ryan Richardson,
Zachary Kelly, Malick
Valliani, Jonathan Scheyer, Matt
Gold, Phil Weisberg.*

Even before the curtain rose on this postseason, critics predicted classical Greek theater.

Each of the most celebrated casts had some kind of flaw that portended tragedy. But in the end, No. 7 Glenbrook North's hustle and heady play saved the day.

And unlike so many Sweet Sixteen dramas where the leading man did not wind up the hero, this time he walked away with a gold medal.

Many of the main characters in this drama didn't make the state-finals scene. Top-billed St. Joseph and second-banana Chicago Westinghouse folded their shows short of playing in Peoria. No. 4 Thornton, once rated tops in the nation, flopped in the first act at state.

No. 3 Carbondale reached the title game without having to face a top-16 team. But what a team and what a player the Terriers tangled with in the climax.

Although the tourney brackets benefited both finalists, fate favored Glenbrook North and junior Jon Scheyer, a 6-foot-6 scoring machine with flawless flow and a smooth stroke.

Both finalists made the most of good fortune along the way. Carbondale's quarterfinal victim, upstart Chicago Crane, had lost a top player to an appendectomy two days earlier. Then unranked Downers Grove South cleared No. 4 Thornton from Carbondale's semifinal path.

Meanwhile, Glenbrook North was guaranteed a non-ranked semifinal foe if it could get past No. 10 Chicago Brother Rice in the quarters. There, Scheyer wound up doubling up on the tourney's other shooting star, Rice guard Bobby Frasor, a McDonald's All-American headed to North Carolina and potential rematches with Scheyer at Duke.

With the aid of Class AA-record 16-for-16 foul shooting, Scheyer tallied 35 points to Frasor's 16. The law of averages

seemed to catch up with Brother Rice, which had sidelined No. 6 Chicago Simeon by a point in double overtime and followed with a one-point win over No. 9 Proviso East.

With major credits on their résumés, the characters in the final act were no strangers to finals followers. Neither Glenbrook North's quality (32-2 record) nor Scheyer's quantity (34-point Sweet Sixteen average) surprised anybody who had seen an unranked Spartans squad and its fresh-faced freshman finish third two years before. Meanwhile, Carbondale was making a second straight semifinal appearance with the added motivation of having finished 0-2 the final day of the previous season.

But questions remained: Could Carbondale win the first Class AA title for the deep south? Could Glenbrook North capture the first AA crown for the suburbs north of Chicago?

The Spartans and Scheyer had all the answers to ace this final exam. Glenbrook North roared to a 35-18 lead that Carbondale could never cut under five. The final score was 63-51, with Scheyer getting 27 points while finishing off a Sweet Sixteen record of 31 consecutive free-throw makes.

Glenbrook's path to the finals was a rocky one. The Spartans survived a sectional scare by beating Hoffman Estates Conant 37-36 when a pair of point-blank shots failed to fall in the last two seconds.

The next week, Scheyer rang up 48 points in a super-sectional win that came the day after Spartans coach Dave Weber and his brother, University of Illinois coach Bruce Weber, buried their 81-year-old mother. She died in emergency surgery the night of Dave's sectional title and Bruce's quarterfinal win in the Big Ten tourney.

State Final Tournament Scores
Super-Sectionals
At Edwardsville [SIU-E]—Carbondale 64, Alton 60
At Chicago [United Center]—Chicago (Crane) 58, Winnetka (New Trier) 40
At Chicago [United Center]—Harvey (Thornton) 46, Flossmoor (Homewood-F.) 40
At DeKalb [NIU]—Downers Grove (South) 85, Naperville (Central) 61
At Chicago [Loyola U.]—Northbrook (Glenbrook North) 70, Waukegan 58
At Chicago [UIC]—Chicago (Brother Rice) 59, Maywood (Proviso East) 58
At Moline [The Mark]—Rockford (Jefferson) 73, Elgin (Larkin) 60
At Normal [ISU]—Lincoln 47, Washington 46
Quarterfinals
Carbondale 78, Chicago (Crane) 55
Downers Grove (South) 39, Harvey (Thornton) 37
Northbrook (Glenbrook North) 68, Chicago (Brother Rice) 47
Rockford (Jefferson) 51, Lincoln 40
Semifinals
Carbondale 53, Downers Grove (South) 42
Northbrook (Glenbrook North) 51, Rockford (Jefferson) 33
Finals
Downers Grove (South) 57, Rockford (Jefferson) 44 (third place)
Northbrook (Glenbrook North) 63, Carbondale 51 (title)

Scoring Leaders

Player, School	G	FG	3P	FT	Pts
Jon Scheyer, Northbrook (Glenbrook N.)	4	42	13	37	134
Ray Nelson, Carbondale	4	22	3	17	64
Robert Eppinger, Rockford (Jefferson)	4	19	0	24	62
Elliot Engelmann, Downers Grove (So.)	4	23	2	11	59
Manual Cass, Carbondale	4	21	0	16	58

All-Tournament First Team

Player, School	Ht.	Yr.
Manual Cass, Carbondale	6-6	Jr.
Sherron Collins, Chicago (Crane)	5-10	Jr.
Bryan Mullins, Downers Grove (South)	6-1	Sr.
Ray Nelson, Carbondale	6-1	Sr.
Jon Scheyer, Northbrook (Glenbrook North)	6-6	Jr.

Championship Game Box Score
Carver Arena, Peoria, March 19, 2005

NORTHBROOK (GLENBROOK NORTH) (63)
Coach David Weber

Player	FG-A	3P-A	FT-A	Pts	PF	Rb	As	St	Bl
Matt Gold	2-3	1-2	3-5	8	3	7	3	1	0
Zach Kelly	2-3	1-2	4-5	9	4	7	2	1	0
Jonathan Radke	0-1	0-0	1-2	1	3	2	1	1	1
Mike Rubo	0-0	0-0	0-0	0	0	0	0	0	0
Jon Scheyer	9-17	1-4	8-9	27	3	3	3	0	2
Matt Shamis	0-0	0-0	0-0	0	0	0	1	0	0
Malick Valliani	0-0	0-0	3-4	3	0	3	2	0	0
Sean Wallis	5-8	2-5	3-4	15	1	1	2	0	0
TOTAL	18-32	5-13	22-29	63	14	26	15	5	3

CARBONDALE (51)
Coach Jim Miller

Player	FG-A	3P-A	FT-A	Pts	PF	Rb	As	St	Bl
Bryce Basler	0-0	0-0	0-0	0	0	0	0	0	0
Davon Bell	0-0	0-0	0-0	0	0	0	0	0	0
Manual Cass	3-7	0-0	3-7	9	5	3	0	1	0
Michael DeWalt	4-7	0-3	0-0	8	4	6	1	3	0
Phillip Fayne	4-6	1-1	0-0	9	5	2	1	1	0
Sharron Greer	0-0	0-0	0-0	0	1	0	0	0	0
Chris Harper	0-0	0-0	0-0	0	2	1	0	0	0
Steven Haynes	1-6	0-2	4-4	6	0	2	0	0	0
Ray Nelson	4-10	0-1	3-6	11	3	5	3	0	0
Josh Tabb	3-7	0-3	2-5	8	3	4	2	3	0
TOTAL	19-43	1-10	12-22	51	23	21	9	8	0

Northbrook (Glenbrook N.)	19	19	14	11	—	63
Carbondale	11	13	12	15	—	51

Officials: Craig Jeffreys, Kevin White, Scott Massie.

Ray Nelson of Carbondale drives the lane against Jon Scheyer of Glenbrook North in the 2005 Class AA championship game.

NOTHING BUT NORTH

Fans of Glenbrook North show their spirit after the title-game victory.

Scheyer delivers a three-pointer over two Carbondale defenders. Glenbrook North defeated Carbondale 63-51 to win the state title.

Glenbrook North players leap into each other's arms after winning the state championship at Carver Arena.

Carbondale's Manual Cass pops a short jumper over Glenbrook North's Zach Kelly in the title contest.

Glenbrook North's Jon Scheyer passes out of trouble in the lane. Scheyer led all tournament scorers with 134 points in four games.

2005AA

On paper, teams ranked Nos. 1, 2, 4 and 5 in the final regular-season poll stood between No. 3 Chicago Simeon and its first championship in over two decades. But in the end, the Wolverines got their toughest test from a most unlikely source.

The Wolverines dispatched both, starting with a box-and-one defense on 30-point averager Scheyer. Then, in the first state-finals meeting of Chicago Public League schools, Simeon reversed a 22-point loss to No. 4 Marshall with a 13-point semifinal win. Marshall had raced into his own hands with his late-game heroics.

The combined total of 60 points made this the lowest-scoring title game in Class AA history, shoving Proviso East's 42-31 win over Richwoods in 1992 from the record books.

CHICAGO (SIMEON)
Class AA State Champions of 2006

FRONT ROW (left to right): Brandon Hall, Randall Hampton, Dexter Williams, Demarco Sams, David McKinnie, Deon Butler. SECOND ROW: Bryant Orange, Joshua Davis, Jelani Poston, Timothy Flowers, Kevin Johnson, Derrick Rose, Arnold Coleman.

2006AA

CLASS AA

Peoria Richwoods, which started 2-4 and was not among the top 20 going into the postseason, was poised for its fourth upset of this Sweet Sixteen with the ball and 15 seconds left in overtime.

But Simeon all-stater Derrick Rose did what great players do — make great plays. And he did it at both ends of the court.

The junior guard's steal and eight-footer with one second left gave Simeon a 31-29 victory and Chicago its third championship in a 13-year span.

Simeon (33-4) rode athleticism tempered by discipline to overcome the teamwork and mental toughness of Richwoods (27-7).

Thanks to unranked Proviso East bumping off No. 1 St. Joseph in sectional play, Simeon's toughest tests figured to come downstate against second-ranked defending champion Glenbrook North and Jon Scheyer in the quarterfinals and Chicago Marshall in the semis.

into the semis by dispatching No. 6 Edwardsville, the last Class AA unbeaten.

Enter Richwoods, which reached the Elite Eight by avenging a 15-point loss to Bloomington. Down seven with three minutes left, the Knights came up with 20 straight points to secure the win.

Feeding on the Peoria mystique, the River City's least-acclaimed Elite Eight entry in some three decades refused to go away, sending home No. 5 West Aurora in the quarterfinals and smothering Thornwood in the semis.

After junior Justin Dehm split a double-team to make a miracle three at the regulation buzzer, anything seemed possible for the Knights.

But in overtime, reason returned when Rose, a huge talent normally content to let the game come to him, took matters

State Final Tournament Scores

Super-Sectionals
At Rosemont [Allstate Arena]—Aurora (West) 67, Lockport (Twp.) 61
At Normal [ISU]—Peoria (Richwoods) 70, Bloomington 55
At Chicago [UIC]—South Holland (Thornwood) 40, Flossmoor (Homewood-F.) 38 (3 OT)
At DeKalb [NIU]—Schaumburg 67, Rock Falls 52
At Chicago [UIC]—Chicago (Simeon) 67, Maywood (Proviso East) 57
At Rosemont [Allstate Arena]—Northbrook (Glenbrook North) 48, Gurnee (Warren) 41
At Chicago [DePaul U.]—Chicago (Marshall) 83, Wilmette (Loyola Academy) 61
At Carbondale [SIU]—Edwardsville 53, East St. Louis 41

Quarterfinals
Peoria (Richwoods) 70, Aurora (West) 59
South Holland (Thornwood) 40, Schaumburg 35
Chicago (Simeon) 61, Northbrook (Glenbrook North) 44
Chicago (Marshall) 65, Edwardsville 54

Semifinals
Peoria (Richwoods) 39, South Holland (Thornwood) 26
Chicago (Simeon) 69, Chicago (Marshall) 56

Finals
Chicago (Marshall) 85, South Holland (Thornwood) 60 (third place)
Chicago (Simeon) 31, Peoria (Richwoods) 29 (OT) (title)

Scoring Leaders

Player, School	G	FG	3P	FT	Pts
Patrick Beverley, Chicago (Marshall)	4	34	10	16	94
Derrick Rose, Chicago (Simeon)	4	26	1	20	73
Justin Dehm, Peoria (Richwoods)	4	18	11	18	65
Tim Flowers, Chicago (Simeon)	4	19	0	12	50
Mike Stovall, Chicago (Marshall)	4	21	1	5	48

All-Tournament First Team

Player, School	Ht.	Yr.
Patrick Beverley, Chicago (Marshall)	6-2	Sr.
Bill Cole, Peoria (Richwoods)	6-9	Jr.
Justin Dehm, Peoria (Richwoods)	6-1	Jr.
Tim Flowers, Chicago (Simeon)	6-5	Jr.
Derrick Rose, Chicago (Simeon)	6-4	Jr.

Championship Game Box Score

Carver Arena, Peoria, March 18, 2006

CHICAGO (SIMEON) (31)
Coach Robert Smith

Player	FG-A	3P-A	FT-A	Pts	PF	Rb	As	St	Bl
Joshua Davis	5-10	1-2	0-0	11	3	5	0	1	1
Tim Flowers	4-11	0-0	1-2	9	1	9	0	0	1
Randall Hampton	0-3	0-3	0-1	0	0	0	1	1	1
David McKinnie	0-2	0-2	0-0	0	1	0	0	0	0
Bryant Orange	0-2	0-0	0-0	0	2	0	0	1	0
Derrick Rose	3-8	0-2	3-5	9	1	4	2	1	0
Dexter Williams	1-2	0-0	0-0	2	2	3	1	1	0
TEAM						1			
TOTAL	13-38	1-9	4-8	31	10	22	4	5	3

PEORIA (RICHWOODS) (29)
Coach Mike Ellis

Player	FG-A	3P-A	FT-A	Pts	PF	Rb	As	St	Bl
Bill Cole	0-6	0-3	1-2	1	4	8	2	1	5
Justin Dehm	5-8	4-5	0-0	14	2	2	0	1	0
Patrick Hogan	1-4	0-2	0-0	2	1	5	5	0	0
Dan Mathis	1-1	0-0	0-0	2	3	3	1	0	0
Nick Morgan	1-3	0-2	0-0	2	1	2	0	1	0
Ryan Phillips	3-8	0-2	2-3	8	3	6	2	1	2
James Robertson	0-1	0-1	0-0	0	0	0	0	0	0
Cortney Smith	0-0	0-0	0-0	0	0	0	0	0	0
TEAM						1			
TOTAL	11-31	4-15	3-5	29	14	27	10	4	7

Chicago (Simeon)	7	10	8	4	2	— 31
Peoria (Richwoods)	7	6	10	6	0	— 29

Officials: Gary Gustafson, Ron Leitner, Stephen Ficker.

Ryan Phillips of Peoria Richwoods puts up a short jumper in the title game against Simeon.

Richwoods guard Justin Dehm lets fly with a desperation three-point shot to tie the championship game at 29 at the end of regulation.

LAST CHANCE TO TIE

Simeon coach Robert Smith sets up a play during action at Carver Arena.

Simeon's Derrick Rose goes to the glass to score over Richwoods' Bill Cole in the title game. Rose scored the game-winning basket in the closing seconds of overtime.

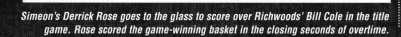

Rose holds the ball and waits during the championship game against Peoria Richwoods, the lowest-scoring title contest since 1940.

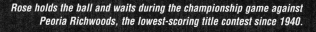

2006AA

TEAMS

Selected by Bob Leavitt

Thornridge, 1972
Size, strength, and quickness in scorers, playmakers, and defenders solidified by great team leader (Quinn Buckner) and wrapped up in outstanding coaching (Ron Ferguson).

Quincy, 1981
Players who could make plays dressed up by wonderful playmaker (Bruce Douglas) and packaged by coach who designed hundreds of clever ones (Jerry Leggett).

Proviso East, 1991
Three consensus all-staters (Michael Finley, Sherrell Ford, and Donnie Boyce) handled by a coach (Bill Hitt) who the next year proved strong enough to win without such.

Chicago King, 1993
Two 7-footers (Rashard Griffith and Thomas Hamilton) plus two other physical scorers and the good sense to let the big dogs hunt netted Elite Eight shooting percentage of .511 and average victory margin of 30 points.

Peoria Manual, 1997
The 1-2 Mr. Basketball vote-getters (Sergio McClain and Marcus Griffin) plus the next season's award winner (Frank Williams) with the top-notch leadership from a father-son/coach-player combination was enough to handle the pressure of a four-peat.

A CLOSER LOOK AT SOME OF THE OUTSTANDING TEAMS, COACHES,
AND PLAYERS WHO PARTICIPATED IN STATE FINAL TOURNAMENTS FROM **Class AA**

(listed in chronological order)

COACHES

Jerry Leggett
Quincy

Micromanaged to win without talent, pounded square pegs into his well-rounded system to win with talent, earning complete set of final-four trophies from 1979 to 1987.

Bennie Lewis
East St. Louis Lincoln

You can't argue with success: Lewis ended 23-7 in Sweet Sixteen play with four titles.

Bill Hitt
Proviso East

Marshaled talent to win 1991 title with trio of major-college recruits, then without them the next year crafted overachievers into an unbeaten title team.

Chuck Buescher
Peoria Central

Forged in the crucible of a nasty sectional in the midst of two-decade run of Peoria-area talent, took four teams to Sweet Sixteen and ended 14-2 with two titles, losing one final to pair of future NBA players, the other to a three-peater in triple overtime.

Wayne McClain
Peoria Manual

Won first 28 post-season games and wound up 12-2 in Sweet Sixteen play despite having to follow the act of the state's all-time leader in boys' prep coaching victories (Dick Van Scyoc).

PLAYERS

Quinn Buckner, *Thornridge, 1971-72*
Not great in any statistical aspect of the game, but put him with some talent and he would lead them to prep, NCAA, Olympic, and NBA championships.

Isiah Thomas, *St. Joseph, 1978*
Only player on list not to win at least one title, state runner-up's inventive playmaker averaged 23 points, 8 boards, 49 percent shooting in only Elite Eight.

Bruce Douglas, *Quincy, 1979-81-82*
Few folks can average 21 points in their last eight Sweet Sixteen games. Fewer still find time to average five assists, including most athletic, game-saving one ever in last second of prep career to turn a consolation into a classic.

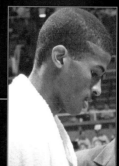

Marcus Liberty, *Chicago King, 1986-87*
Arguably most versatile player in state history could play any position, averaging 26 points in eight Sweet Sixteen outings and going 1-1 in title games.

LaPhonso Ellis, *East St. Louis Lincoln, 1986-87-88*
Nobody ever owned Class AA paint like in his senior Elite Eight, scoring 75 (25.0), rebounding 44 (14.7), blocking 25 (8.3), shooting 28-for-48 (.583) from the floor, 18-for-25 (.720) from the line. Even stepped outside to go 1-for-2 on threes. Got school two-thirds of way to first-ever three-peat.

Jamie Brandon, *Chicago King, 1987-88-89-90*
Six-foot-four forward-guard played in four Sweet Sixteens (where he averaged 20.7 points in 13 games for teams that finished first, second, and third) and totaled 3,157 for coach who insisted he wasn't a great shooter.

Sergio McClain, *Peoria Manual, 1994-95-96-97*
Just win, baby. Started four years for teams that never lost (32-0) a post-season game, mostly because he wouldn't let them.

Quentin Richardson, *Chicago Young, 1997-98*
Some can score, some can rebound, some can guard. He could dominate all three categories. Led two Elite Eight entries, losing to national rankings leader in 1997 and getting as many boards (20) as runner-up Galesburg totaled in 1998 title game.

Jon Scheyer, *Glenbrook North, 2003-05-06*
Slick-shooting guard rolled up sleeves and won gold with perfect portions of skill and will. Led three teams of otherwise unremarkable talent to Elite Eights, averaging 33.5 points as junior in 2005 title run with 31 straight free-throw makes.

Shaun Livingston, *Peoria Central, 2003-04*
Made title-winning play as junior then dominated championship game as senior while helping hold eight Sweet Sixteen foes to average of 45 points per game.

Afterword

Lewis Omer's vision was simple: Bring the *best* basketball high school teams in Illinois together, roll the ball out on the floor, and see what *happens.*

The Oak Park athletic director was a superb salesman, persuading hesitant high school administrators to buy into his state championship scheme, but it's doubtful his foresight extended much past 1908.

Could he have imagined, for instance, that his tournament would one day play at the University of Illinois, in a gymnasium full of 3,000 — no, 7,000 — no, 16,000 spectators?

Could he have anticipated, before he departed Oak Park for Carthage College, that his tournament would one day involve 917 schools and over 10,000 boys?

Could he have conceived that his basketball tournament alone, conducted on an annual basis, would provide all the income necessary to run the state high school athletic association for the next 50 years?

Could he have imagined it growing into March Madness? Would he have guessed it would still be going strong 100 years later?

Decade after decade, Omer's brainchild proved remarkably resilient.

It outlived the Depression, which fed the fervor for escapist entertainment that high school basketball provided, and it overcame wartime gas and rubber rationing, which threatened to derail the tournament completely.

It knocked down the color barrier in southern Illinois, integrating the basketball court a decade before the U.S. Supreme Court did the same for the classroom. And when the tournament itself stood before the Supreme Court, it won there, too, in a 1963 ruling that held the IHSA had the right to set its own eligibility standards.

Those were tough struggles, but nothing compared to 1970.

The war that flared up that year was internal — but not always civil — as schools fought among themselves over whether two classes were really better than one.

The rhetoric was harsh and the consequences often characterized as dire, but in the end, the issue was resolved democratically. When classification won by a 312-293 vote, traditionalists watched carefully to see whether a tournament divided could still stand.

It stood.

And in the land of March Madness, peace and tranquility reigned for 30 years.

No doubt something was lost when the tournament split in two. Gone forever were once-in-a-lifetime Little Davids, who fascinated so many fans and inspired so many sportswriters in the tournament's first 64 years. But something was gained, too:

a yearly parade of equally fascinating, never-before-heard-from schools and communities that now enjoyed legitimate chances of reaching state and winning it all.

As the centennial approaches, Omer's tournament stands at a similar crossroads. Illinois held out for a traditional one-class system longer than almost every other state, but now that the pie has been cut, the question is simple: How many more times can you cut it before you are no longer left with slices, but crumbs?

The answer depends on whom you ask. Many coaches are reluctant to give up the two-class tournament, with its own tradition that now spans well over a generation. But the voting members of the IHSA, the principals, often see things differently from coaches. When the four-class movement finally bubbled to the surface, principals twice indicated their support: once in a 2004 survey (318-245, 56% in favor) and once in a 2005 advisory referendum (273-153, 64% in favor), after which the IHSA Board of Directors voted to approve the format for 2008.

For those who worry, understandably, that four classes leads to six, and six leads to eight, history argues otherwise. The state's movement away from the traditional system has been slow, cautious, almost glacial.

Illinois is not Nebraska, which in 1926 invited every team in the state to its finals and set up 22 classes — Class A through Class V — for a tournament that took a week to complete. And Illinois is not South Dakota, with a large-school class made up of just 16 teams.

The IHSA's proposed Class 1A tournament, with about 225 schools, will still be one of the largest high school tournaments in the country. The other three tournaments will not be far behind. Despite the tradition that argues strongly against the change, it's difficult to make the case that crowning four state champions out of a pool of over 700 schools is overkill.

And so Omer's tournament continues its incredible odyssey, tossed by tempests, rocked by high seas, but sailing ever forward.

We cannot go back to the one-class days, but it seems we no longer want to.

We will soon sail away from two classes as well, perhaps never to return.

When the principals who make up the IHSA voted for four classes, they knew that something would be lost, but hoped something would be gained.

Whether they pointed Lewis Omer's tournament in the right direction is left for the next generation to decide.

Scott Johnson
December, 2006

State champions and runners-up

YEAR	CHAMPION	COACH	RUNNER-UP	COACH	SCORE
			AT OAK PARK YMCA		
1908	Peoria (H.S.) (17-1)	Les Straeser	Rock Island (H.S.) (10-5)	W.E. Brown	48-29
			AT BLOOMINGTON YMCA		
1909	Hinsdale (20-3)	Arthur Collins	Washington (20-3)	Charles Wright	18-13
1910	Bloomington (H.S.) (14-2)	Tom O'Neill	Rock Island (H.S.) (14-2)	F.W. Gray	32-25
			AT BRADLEY GYM, PEORIA		
1911	Rockford (H.S.) (19-1)	Ralph Vennum	Mt. Carroll (13-6)	*unknown*	60-15
			AT DECATUR YMCA		
1912	Batavia (27-2)	K.C. Merrick	Galesburg (14-5)	T.W. Callihan	28-25
			AT BRADLEY GYM, PEORIA		
1913	Galesburg (17-1)	Harry Hayes	Peoria (Manual) (17-2)	Charles Mason	37-36
			AT DECATUR YMCA		
1914	Hillsboro (14-5)	D.O. Kime	Freeport (H.S.) (17-1)	Dan Daugherty	42-19
			AT MILLIKIN GYM, DECATUR		
1915	Freeport (H.S.) (18-2)	Dan Daugherty	Springfield (H.S.) (12-8)	Arthur Nevins	27-11
1916	Bloomington (H.S.) (13-6)	E.W. McClure	Robinson (21-4)	William Livingston	25-17
1917	Springfield (H.S.) (10-3)	Roy Wentz	Belvidere (10-4)	Joseph Swanson	32-11
			AT SPRINGFIELD HIGH SCHOOL		
1918	Centralia (23-4)	Arthur Trout	Normal (University) (14-6)	Francis James	35-29
			AT MEN'S GYM ANNEX, URBANA		
1919	Rockford (H.S.) (23-1)	Frank Winters	Springfield (H.S.) (14-10)	Martin Shale	39-20
1920	Mt. Vernon (16-8)	Floyd Stables	Canton (23-4)	R.A. Deffenbaugh	18-14
1921	Marion (H.S.) (26-4)	E.H. Schreiber	Rockford (H.S.) (18-2)	E.U. McDonald	24-23
1922	Centralia (26-4)	Arthur Trout	Atwood (21-1)	Lawrence Hamilton	24-16
1923	Villa Grove (23-2)	Curtis Pulliam	Rockford (H.S.) (19-1)	E.U. McDonald	32-29
1924	Elgin (H.S.) (25-3)	Mark Wilson	Athens (35-2)	H.V. Porter	28-17
1925	Elgin (H.S.) (24-2)	Cliff Adams	Champaign (21-5)	Les Moyer	25-17
			AT HUFF GYMNASIUM, CHAMPAIGN		
1926	Freeport (H.S.) (19-2)	Glenn "Pat" Holmes	Canton (23-12)	Mark Peterman	24-13
1927	Mt. Carmel (31-2)	Cliff Garrett	Peoria (H.S.) (30-3)	Salen Herke	24-18
1928	Canton (37-7)	Mark Peterman	Aurora (West) (24-5)	Ralph Fletcher	18-9
1929	Johnston City (29-3)	LaRue Van Meter	Champaign (28-4)	Les Moyer	30-21
1930	Peoria (Manual) (25-5)	Telfer Mead	Bloomington (H.S.) (20-4)	Eugene Harrison	38-25
1931	Decatur (H.S.) (29-5)	Gay Kintner	Galesburg (24-4)	Gerald Phillips	30-26
1932	Cicero (Morton) (25-4)	Norm Ziebell	Canton (24-4)	Archie Chadd	30-16
1933	Harvey (Thornton) (24-3)	Jack Lipe	Springfield (H.S.) (22-9)	Mark Peterman	14-13
1934	Quincy (Sr.) (31-2)	Selmer "Sam" Storby	Harvey (Thornton) (35-2)	Jack Lipe	39-27
1935	Springfield (H.S.) (34-3)	Mark Peterman	Harvey (Thornton) (28-5)	Jack Lipe	24-19
1936	Decatur (H.S.) (24-11)	Gay Kintner	Danville (H.S.) (23-1)	Ned Whitesell	26-22
1937	Joliet (Twp.) (27-4)	Herman Walser	Decatur (H.S.) (23-12)	Gay Kintner	40-20
1938	Dundee (34-1)	Eugene DeLacey	Braidwood (Reed-Custer) (33-3)	Louis Bottino	36-29
1939	Rockford (H.S.) (23-2)	James Laude	Paris (37-3)	Ernie Eveland	53-44
1940	Granite City (29-5)	Byron Bozarth	Herrin (23-8)	Russell Emery	24-22
1941	Cicero (Morton) (23-4)	Norm Ziebell	Urbana (H.S.) (22-11)	Lew Stephens	32-31
1942	Centralia (34-6)	Arthur Trout	Paris (39-1)	Ernie Eveland	35-33
1943	Paris (36-2)	Ernie Eveland	Moline (24-4)	Roger Potter	46-37
1944	Taylorville (45-0)	Dolph Stanley	Elgin (H.S.) (21-4)	John Krafft	56-33
1945	Decatur (H.S.) (37-2)	Gay Kintner	Champaign (34-2)	Harry Combes	62-54
1946	Champaign (38-1)	Harry Combes	Centralia (29-10)	Arthur Trout	54-48

State champions and runners-up

YEAR	CHAMPION	COACH	RUNNER-UP	COACH	SCORE
		AT HUFF GYMNASIUM, CHAMPAIGN			
1947	Paris (40-2)	Ernie Eveland	Champaign (33-4)	Harry Combes	58-37
1948	Pinckneyville (33-1)	Merrill "Duster" Thomas	Rockford (East) (26-4)	James Laude	65-39
1949	Mt. Vernon (30-3)	Stanley Changnon	Hillsboro (25-7)	Fred Ewald	45-39
1950	Mt. Vernon (33-0)	Stanley Changnon	Danville (H.S.) (29-2)	Lawrence Newtson	85-61
1951	Freeport (H.S.) (31-2)	Harry Kinert	Moline (22-9)	Norm Ziebell	71-51
1952	Hebron (Alden-H.) (35-1)	Russ Ahearn	Quincy (Sr.) (28-5)	George Latham	64-59 (OT)
1953	LaGrange (Lyons) (29-0)	Greg Sloan	Peoria (H.S.) (29-4)	Dawson "Dawdy" Hawkins	72-60
1954	Mt. Vernon (29-3)	Harold Hutchins	Chicago (DuSable) (31-2)	Jim Brown	76-70
1955	Rockford (West) (27-1)	Alex Saudargas	Elgin (H.S.) (26-4)	Bill Chesbrough	61-59
1956	Rockford (West) (28-1)	Alex Saudargas	Edwardsville (Sr.) (28-6)	Joe Lucco	67-65
1957	Herrin (31-2)	Earl Lee	Collinsville (34-1)	Vergil Fletcher	45-42
1958	Chicago (Marshall) (31-0)	Isadore "Spin" Salario	Rock Falls (33-2)	Dick Haselton	70-64
1959	Springfield (H.S.) (33-1)	Ray Page	Aurora (West) (22-7)	Dick Dorsey	60-52
1960	Chicago (Marshall) (31-2)	Isadore "Spin" Salario	Bridgeport (33-2)	Ray Estes	79-55
1961	Collinsville (32-0)	Vergil Fletcher	Harvey (Thornton) (27-3)	Bill Purden	84-50
1962	Decatur (Stephen Decatur) (31-4)	John Schneiter	Chicago (Carver) (28-5)	Larry Hawkins	49-48
		AT ASSEMBLY HALL, CHAMPAIGN			
1963	Chicago (Carver) (28-5)	Larry Hawkins	Centralia (32-2)	Bob Jones	53-52
1964	Pekin (30-3)	Dawson "Dawdy" Hawkins	Cobden (32-3)	Dick Ruggles	50-45
1965	Collinsville (30-2)	Vergil Fletcher	Quincy (Sr.) (26-6)	Sherrill Hanks	55-52
1966	Harvey (Thornton) (30-2)	Bob Anderson	Galesburg (27-3)	John Thiel	74-60
1967	Pekin (31-2)	Dawson "Dawdy" Hawkins	Carbondale (29-3)	John Cherry	75-59
1968	Evanston (Twp.) (30-1)	Jack Burmaster	Galesburg (27-3)	John Thiel	70-51
1969	Maywood (Proviso East) (30-1)	Tom Millikin	Peoria (Spalding) (28-4)	Ron Patterson	58-51
1970	LaGrange (Lyons) (31-0)	Ron Nikcevich	East Moline (United) (30-3)	Cliff Talley	71-52
1971	Dolton (Thornridge) (31-1)	Ron Ferguson	Oak Lawn (Community) (30-3)	Len Scaduto	52-50
1972A	Lawrenceville (25-8)	Ron Felling	Mounds (Meridian) (30-2)	Jim Byassee	63-57
1972AA	Dolton (Thornridge) (33-0)	Ron Ferguson	Quincy (Sr.) (28-5)	Sherrill Hanks	104-69
1973A	Ridgway (32-1)	Bob Dallas	Maple Park (Kaneland) (20-12)	George Birkett	54-51
1973AA	Chicago (Hirsch) (29-2)	Charles Stimpson	Winnetka (New Trier East) (21-5)	John Schneiter	65-51
1974A	Lawrenceville (30-3)	Ron Felling	Ottawa (Marquette) (29-4)	Bob Strickland	54-53
1974AA	Maywood (Proviso East) (29-4)	Glenn Whittenberg	Chicago Heights (Bloom) (30-3)	Wes Mason	61-56
1975A	Venice (32-2)	Rich Essington	Elmhurst (Timothy Christian) (27-6)	Don Greenfield	65-46
1975AA	Chicago (Phillips) (32-1)	Herb Brown	Chicago Heights (Bloom) (23-10)	Wes Mason	76-48
1976A	Mt. Pulaski (29-2)	Ed Butkovich	Oneida (ROVA) (28-3)	Bob Meredith	59-58
1976AA	Chicago (Morgan Park) (28-5)	Bill Warden	Aurora (West) (30-3)	John McDougal	45-44
1977A	Madison (29-3)	Larry Graham	Aurora (Central Catholic) (23-10)	Richard Fick	71-55
1977AA	Peoria (H.S.) (29-2)	Bruce Boyle	Springfield (Lanphier) (28-5)	Bob Nika	72-62
1978A	Nashville (30-3)	Bob Bogle	Havana (29-4)	Bob Gregurich	54-38
1978AA	Lockport (Central) (33-0)	Bob Basarich	Westchester (St. Joseph) (31-2)	Gene Pingatore	64-47
1979A	New Lenox (Providence) (32-1)	Frank Palmasani	Havana (31-1)	Bob Gregurich	46-33
1979AA	Park Ridge (Maine South) (31-1)	Quitman Sullins	Quincy (Sr.) (32-1)	Jerry Leggett	83-67
1980A	Chicago (Luther South) (27-5)	Cliff Doll	Peoria (Bergan) (23-8)	Rudy Keeling	56-51
1980AA	Chicago (Manley) (31-1)	Willie Little	Effingham (H.S.) (30-2)	Jim Maxedon	69-61
1981A	Madison (30-2)	Larry Graham	Dunlap (28-5)	John Kimble	58-47
1981AA	Quincy (Sr.) (33-0)	Jerry Leggett	Maywood (Proviso East) (28-5)	Glenn Whittenberg	68-39
1982A	Lawrenceville (34-0)	Ron Felling	Monmouth (H.S.) (31-2)	Mike Mueller	67-53
1982AA	East St. Louis (Lincoln) (29-1)	Bennie Lewis	Chicago (Mendel) (29-3)	Michael Flaherty	56-50

State champions and runners-up

YEAR	CHAMPION	COACH	RUNNER-UP	COACH	SCORE
			AT ASSEMBLY HALL, CHAMPAIGN		
1983A	Lawrenceville (34-0)	Ron Felling	Flanagan (30-1)	Jerry Pohl	44-39
1983AA	Springfield (Lanphier) (30-3)	Bob Nika	Peoria (H.S.) (28-4)	Chuck Buescher	57-53
1984A	McLeansboro (35-0)	David Lee	Mt. Pulaski (29-3)	Ed Butkovich	57-50
1984AA	Chicago (Simeon) (30-1)	Robert Hambric	Evanston (Twp.) (32-1)	Herb Williams	53-47
1985A	Chicago (Providence-St. Mel) (31-3)	Tom Shields	Chrisman (28-5)	Roger Beals	95-63
1985AA	Chicago (Mt. Carmel) (28-4)	Ed McQuillan	Springfield (Lanphier) (29-4)	Bob Nika	46-44 (2 OT)
1986A	Teutopolis (33-0)	Ken Crawford	Ohio (29-3)	Lloyd Johnson	82-45
1986AA	Chicago (King) (32-1)	Landon "Sonny" Cox	Olympia Fields (Rich Central) (31-2)	Ron Brauer	47-40
1987A	Venice (29-3)	Clinton Harris	Okawville (29-7)	Dave Luechtefeld	56-54
1987AA	East St. Louis (Lincoln) (28-1)	Bennie Lewis	Chicago (King) (28-5)	Landon "Sonny" Cox	79-62
1988A	Pana (28-3)	Charlie Strasburger	Pinckneyville (32-3)	Dick Corn	62-58
1988AA	East St. Louis (Lincoln) (28-4)	Bennie Lewis	Chicago (St. Francis de Sales) (29-2)	Mike Kaczmarz	60-52
1989A	Carlyle (32-3)	Brad Weathers	Rock Island (Alleman) (24-8)	Bob DeDoncker	65-56
1989AA	East St. Louis (Lincoln) (29-4)	Bennie Lewis	Peoria (H.S.) (32-1)	Chuck Buescher	59-57 (3 OT)
1990A	Trenton (Wesclin) (30-3)	Paul Lusk	Fairbury (Prairie Central) (31-1)	Charlie Strasburger	83-78 (2 OT)
1990AA	Chicago (King) (32-0)	Landon "Sonny" Cox	Chicago (Gordon Tech) (30-2)	Steve Pappas	65-55
1991A	Pittsfield (28-6)	Dave Bennett	Seneca (27-5)	Doug Evans	45-35
1991AA	Maywood (Proviso East) (32-1)	Bill Hitt	Peoria (Manual) (31-3)	Dick Van Scyoc	68-61
1992A	Findlay (31-2)	Michael Reynolds	Normal (University) (29-4)	Cal Hubbard	61-45
1992AA	Maywood (Proviso East) (33-0)	Bill Hitt	Peoria (Richwoods) (30-3)	Wayne Hammerton	42-31
1993A	Staunton (27-4)	Randy Legendre	Chicago (Hales Franciscan) (23-11)	Tom Shields	66-62
1993AA	Chicago (King) (32-0)	Landon "Sonny" Cox	Rockford (Guilford) (27-7)	Mike Miller	79-42
1994A	Pinckneyville (33-2)	Dick Corn	Eureka (30-2)	Tim Meiss	67-65
1994AA	Peoria (Manual) (27-6)	Dick Van Scyoc	Carbondale (28-4)	Tim Bleyer	61-60
1995A	Normal (University) (29-3)	Cal Hubbard	Aurora (Christian) (32-2)	Don Davidson	56-54
1995AA	Peoria (Manual) (32-2)	Wayne McClain	Harvey (Thornton) (30-2)	Rocky Hill	65-53
			AT CARVER ARENA, PEORIA		
1996A	Shelbyville (34-1)	Sean Taylor	Breese (Mater Dei) (29-5)	Dennis Trame	58-45
1996AA	Peoria (Manual) (31-2)	Wayne McClain	Harvey (Thornton) (31-1)	Rocky Hill	57-51
1997A	Warsaw (29-3)	Jeff Dahl	Spring Valley (Hall) (27-6)	Eric Bryant	92-85 (OT)
1997AA	Peoria (Manual) (31-1)	Wayne McClain	Aurora (West) (29-4)	Gordon Kerkman	47-43
1998A	Nauvoo (N.-Colusa) (32-3)	Reno Pinkston	Spring Valley (Hall) (32-1)	Eric Bryant	45-39
1998AA	Chicago (Young) (30-1)	George Stanton	Galesburg (30-3)	Mike Miller	61-56
1999A	Rock Falls (31-3)	Thom Sigel	Waterloo (Gibault) (28-7)	Dennis Rueter	45-43
1999AA	Westchester (St. Joseph) (32-1)	Gene Pingatore	Gurnee (Warren) (28-5)	Chuck Ramsey	61-51
2000A	Pleasant Plains (34-2)	Cliff Cameron	Teutopolis (33-2)	Ken Crawford	56-43
2000AA	Aurora (West) (32-1)	Gordon Kerkman	Chicago (Westinghouse) (31-2)	Chris Head	60-57
2001A	Pinckneyville (31-4)	Dick Corn	Pana (29-5)	Gary Bowker	77-50
2001AA	Schaumburg (29-3)	Bob Williams	South Holland (Thornwood) (32-2)	Kevin Hayhurst	66-54
2002A	Pleasant Plains (32-3)	Cliff Cameron	Herrin (26-8)	Mike Mooneyham	50-47 (OT)
2002AA	Chicago (Westinghouse) (30-5)	Chris Head	Springfield (Lanphier) (32-2)	Craig Patton	76-72
2003A	Chicago (Hales Franciscan) (27-6)	Gary London	Mt. Carroll (32-2)	Chris Payne	58-53
2003AA	Peoria (H.S.) (31-1)	Chuck Buescher	South Holland (Thornwood) (27-6)	Bob Curran	45-43
2004A	Chicago (Leo) (28-5)	Noah Cannon	Winnebago (31-2)	Joe Murphy	65-57
2004AA	Peoria (H.S.) (31-2)	Chuck Buescher	Flossmoor (Homewood-F.) (31-3)	Roy Condotti	53-47
2005A	*title vacated*		Winnebago (30-3)	Joe Murphy	78-62
2005AA	Northbrook (Glenbrook North) (32-2)	David Weber	Carbondale (31-3)	Jim Miller	63-51
2006A	Seneca (35-0)	Doug Evans	Chillicothe (Illinois Valley Central) (27-6)	Jim Thornton	47-44
2006AA	Chicago (Simeon) (33-4)	Robert Smith	Peoria (Richwoods) (26-7)	Mike Ellis	31-29 (OT)

Tournament firsts and lasts

1908 — First player to score 20 points in a state-finals game: Either Godwin Clark of Hinsdale (26 vs. Riverside-Brookfield) or Grossberg of Mt. Carroll (24 vs. Geneva) (games were played simultaneously)

1908 — First team to score 60 points in a state-finals game: Hinsdale (60 vs. Riverside-Brookfield)

1908 — First school to win a state tournament game: Either Hinsdale or Mt. Carroll (games were played simultaneously)

1908 — First school to win a state championship: Peoria

1916 — First school to win two state championships: Bloomington

1921 — First player to score 30 points in a state-finals game: Leland Stillwell, Olney (34 vs. Champaign)

1922 — First coach to win two state championships: Arthur Trout, Centralia

1925 — First school to win two consecutive state championships: Elgin

1926 — First team to win a game in state finals at Huff Gymnasium: Canton

1931 — First Chicago school to qualify for a state-final tournament: Harrison Tech

1935 — First coach to win a state championship at two schools: Mark Peterman, Springfield (won at Canton in 1928)

1938 — First "district schools" to qualify for the Sweet Sixteen: Braidwood Reed-Custer and Milton

1939 — First school to win three state championships: Rockford

1940 — First team to score 70 points in a state-finals game: Dundee (72 vs. Rushville)

1940 — First school to win a state championship despite losing a game in the tournament series: Granite City

1942 — First coach to win three state championships: Arthur Trout, Centralia

1949 — First team to score 80 points in a state-finals game: Decatur (82 vs. Pittsfield)

1952 — First "district school" to win a state championship: Hebron

1954 — First school to win four state championships: Mt. Vernon

1958 — First player to score 40 points in a state-finals game: Jerry Kuemmerle, Danville Schlarman (49 vs. Rock Falls)

1958 — First team to score 100 points in a state-finals game: Rock Falls (101 vs. Danville Schlarman)

1958 — First Chicago school to win a state championship: Marshall

1962 — Last player to score in state finals at Huff Gymnasium: Ken Barnes, Decatur

1963 — First team to win game in state finals at Assembly Hall: Centralia

1971 — Last player to score in a single-class game: Jim Bocinsky, Thornridge

1971 — Last school to win a single-class state championship: Thornridge

1972 — First player to score in a Class A Elite Eight game: Carroll Alters, Elgin St. Edward

1972 — First player to score in a Class AA Elite Eight game: Greg Rose, Thornridge

1972 — First school to win a Class A Elite Eight game: Mounds Meridian

1972 — First school to win a Class A state championship: Lawrenceville

1972 — First school to win a Class AA Elite Eight game: Thornridge

1972 — First school to win a Class AA state championship: Thornridge

1983 — First coach to win four state championships: Ron Felling, Lawrenceville

1989 — First player to make a three-point field goal in an Elite Eight game: Tom Funneman, Pana

1989 — First school to win three consecutive state championships: East St. Louis Lincoln

1995 — Last player to score in state finals at Assembly Hall: Denard Eaves, Thornton

1996 — First player to score in state finals at Carver Arena: Roger Jones, Shelbyville

1996 — First team to win game in state finals at Carver Arena: Shelbyville

1997 — First player to score 50 points in an Elite Eight game: Shawn Jeppson, Spring Valley Hall (51 vs. Warsaw)

1997 — First school to win four consecutive state championships: Peoria Manual

1997 — First school to win five state championships: Peoria Manual

Hundreds of pages of additional records, including box scores of every game played at the state finals and super-sectionals, Associated Press polls, and names and statistics of every coach and player who ever participated in the state finals, are available in the records sections of **www.ihsa.org** and **www.marchmadness.org**.

Acknowledgments

A collaborative work by five authors cannot come to fruition without the support of many others.

The authors would like to extend their sincere thanks to Connie Heston and Monica Lampe for their unflagging encouragement and support. Thanks also to Nick Vlahos, Jim Gordillo, and Bob Pruter for their critical appraisals of our work, and to Chuck Herron for years of help on the trail of research.

We owe Larry Clore and Brandon Burwell of MultiAd a huge debt of gratitude for making sure this book saw the light of day.

In the IHSA Office, several colleagues assisted in preparing copy and assembling photographs: Tina Brown, Kelly Rutledge, Carol Carr, and intern Brian James. Thanks also go to Anthony Holman and Kurt Gibson for their work in overseeing the 100 Legends program, and Marty Hickman and the IHSA Board of Directors for greenlighting this project.

Jim Flynn is a legend for many reasons, but with regard to this book, his foresight in preserving documents and photographs from previous state tournaments was a prerequisite for success.

During the lonesome copyediting phase, things might have ground to a complete halt without the loyal support, both moral and editorial, of Julie Kistler, who proofread the manuscript multiple times and suggested many important improvements.

When the time came to turn words in print, Jackie Iverson and Kathy Casper worked around the clock to put this project to bed. Kathy's wonderful graphic design had a magical effect on the words we wrote.

*Celebrating 100 years of
IHSA Boys Basketball Tournaments*

About the authors

SCOTT JOHNSON probably would have found a job if high school sports did not exist, but it wouldn't have been nearly as fulfilling as his position at the Illinois High School Association. Hired in 1994, Johnson has served as an assistant executive director since 2001. The same year, he and his wife, Julie Kistler, researched and wrote *Once There Were Giants*, the story of the 1952 Hebron Green Giants. Someday he may try his hand at a topic other than basketball.

CURT HERRON caught March Madness fever the year before he started high school, when Lockport's Porters wrapped up a perfect 33-0 season. His love for the sport grew during his four years in at the University of Illinois, when he began researching the history of the sport, tracking down all the regional champions and sectional qualifiers in tournament history. After his college days, he and his brother, Chuck, traveled the state doing more research. For the past 20 years he has reported on boys' basketball, as well as almost every other sport, for several papers in the south suburbs of Chicago, with most of that time spent at his current stop, *The Star Newspapers* in Tinley Park.

PAT HESTON caught the high school basketball bug as a child when his hometown team went to state in a one-class system. To this day, he remains hopelessly but happily infected. Having researched Illinois basketball and, in particular, the state tournament for 45 years, he has written on the topic since 1969. In 1999, he published "The Millennium Picks," a look back at the greatest teams, games, coaches, and players in IHSA boys' state tournament history.

A native of Buffalo, N.Y., **JEFF LAMPE** moved to Illinois in 1989 too late to see Carlyle win it all. But he has attended every Class A basketball tournament since 1990, has covered small-school hoops for three newspapers and from 1996-98 published the *Illinois Class A Weekly* newsletter. Since 1998 he has worked as outdoors columnist at the *Peoria Journal Star*. Lampe lives in Elmwood with wife Monica, sons Henry and Victor, and a Llewellin setter named Hawkeye.

BOB LEAVITT began a 40-year sports-writing career as a high school sophomore and never felt the urge to "move up" from covering preps, which he considers the last level at which athletics is still mostly pure. A University of Illinois grad, he worked for the *Champaign-Urbana Courier* under the legendary Bert Bertine before moving in 1969 to the *Peoria Journal Star*, where he founded the popular JS Honor Roll Meet, a track and field competition for high schools in the newspaper's 23-county circulation area.

About the photographs

The photographs in the book were gathered from a wide variety of sources.

Through the years several newspapers and news organizations have donated photographs to the Illinois High School Association for use in its publications. Thanks for the use of their work go to the Associated Press, United Press International, the *Champaign News-Gazette*, the *Urbana Courier,* and Sportron Sports.

Many of the photographs do not bear the name of the photographer. Among those that do, we recognize the special talents of Curt Beamer, Phil Greer, John C. Dixon, Brian K. Johnson, Robert K. O'Daniell, Lou McClellan, Rick Myers, David Boe, James Appel, and Art Sievers.

More recently the IHSA has employed its own photographers to take action and feature shots. The professionals who did this work were Jim Reiter, Jeff Soucek, Tom Roberts, and from VIP Photography, Brian Hurley, Matt Tonn, and Joe Dick.

Many of the oldest photos came from libraries. Special thanks go to the University of Illinois Archives, which house several years of historic photos from the *Champaign News-Gazette,* and the Millikin University Archives.

Some of the action photos of the 1952 Hebron team were taken by Don Peasley of Woodstock and by Larry Burrows for *LIFE* magazine.

Group photos of the championship teams were, for the most part, supplied by the schools. A few action shots were culled from school yearbooks. Several other photos were provided by the Illinois Basketball Coaches Association, which maintains a large collection of photographs of its inductees and honorees.

To all the photographers, named and unnamed, whose work is featured in this book, we give our sincere appreciation for helping preserve the history of the IHSA boys' basketball state tournament.

Celebrating 100 years of
IHSA Boys Basketball Tournaments

Further reading

Several books — though not nearly enough — have been written about the Illinois High School Association boys' basketball tournament or persons and teams associated with it. Following is a fairly thorough list of those titles:

Bates, Paul E. *Vicarious Thrills: A Championship Season of High School Basketball* (Carbondale: Southern Illinois University Press, 1995).

Bell, Taylor. *Sweet Charlie, Dike, Cazzie, and Bobby Joe* (Champaign: University of Illinois Press, 2004).

Bell, Taylor. *Glory Days: Legends of Illinois High School Basketball* (Champaign: Sports Publishing, 2006).

Berkow, Ira. *The DuSable Panthers: The Greatest, Blackest, Saddest Team from the Meanest Street in Chicago* (New York: Atheneum, 1978).

Campbell, Nelson, ed. *Grass Roots and Schoolyards: A High School Basketball Anthology* (Lexington, Mass.: Viking Penguin, 1988).

Campbell, Nelson, ed. *Illinky: High School Basketball in Illinois, Indiana, and Kentucky* (Lexington, Mass.: The Stephen Green Press/Pelham Books, 1990).

Enright, Jim. *March Madness: The Story of High School Basketball in Illinois* (Bloomington: Illinois High School Association, 1977).

Johnson, Scott, ed. *March Madness Encyclopedia: Boys Basketball* (Bloomington: Illinois High School Association, 1995).

Johnson, Scott, and Julie Kistler. *Once There Were Giants: How Tiny Hebron Won the Illinois High School Basketball Championship and the Hearts of Fans Forever* (Bloomington: Illinois High School Association, 2002).

Joravsky, Ben. *Hoop Dreams: A True Story of Hardship and Triumph* (New York: HarperCollins, 1995).

Lenzi, Diana Eddleman. *Dike Eddleman: Illinois' Greatest Athlete* (Champaign: Sagamore Publishing, 1997).

McGivern, Gene. *Here's Johnny Orr* (Ames: Iowa State University Press, 1992).

Porter, H.V. *H.V.'s Athletic Anthology: Highlights of Gridiron, Track, and Court in Verse and Prose* (n.p.: 1939).

Powell, Shawn, with Jeff Lampe and Bob Leavitt. *Classical Madness: A Celebration of Class A and AA Boys Basketball in Illinois* (Bloomington: Illinois High School Association, 1996).

Rodgers, Randall Rene, "A History of the Illinois State High School Basketball Tournament (1908-1971)," Master's Thesis, University of Illinois at Urbana-Champaign, 1971.

Roustio, Mel, compiler. *Courtside Memories: A History of Remembrances* (Jacksonville: Creative Ideas, 1998).

Schnake, Don. *Trout: The Old Man and the Orphans* (Elk Grove Village: Richview Press, 1992).

Whitten, Charles W. *Interscholastics: A Discussion of Interscholastic Contests* (Chicago: Illinois High School Association, 1950).